European Product Liability

European Product Liability

Edited by:

Patrick Kelly

Partner, Solicitor, Laytons

Rebecca Attree

Solicitor, Laytons

Butterworths
London, Dublin, Edinburgh, Munich
1992

United Kingdom	Butterworth & Co (Publishers) Ltd, 88 Kingsway, LONDON WC2B 6AB and 4 Hill Street, EDINBURGH EH2 3JZ
Australia	Butterworths Pty Ltd, SYDNEY, MELBOURNE, BRISBANE, ADELAIDE, PERTH, CANBERRA and HOBART
Canada	Butterworths Canada Ltd, TORONTO and VANCOUVER
Ireland	Butterworth (Ireland) Ltd, DUBLIN
Malaysia	Malayan Law Journal Sdn Bhd, KUALA LUMPUR
New Zealand	Butterworths of New Zealand Ltd, WELLINGTON and AUCKLAND
Puerto Rico	Equity de Puerto Rico, Inc, HATO REY
Singapore	Malayan Law Journal Pte Ltd, SINGAPORE
USA	Butterworth Legal Publishers, AUSTIN, Texas; BOSTON, Massachusetts; CLEARWATER, Florida (D & S Publishers); ORFORD, New Hampshire (Equity Publishing); ST PAUL, Minnesota; and SEATTLE, Washington

A CIP Catalogue record for this book is available from the British Library.

ISBN 0 406 17944 1

Typeset by Phoenix Photosetting, Chatham, Kent
Printed and bound in Great Britain by
Mackays of Chatham plc, Chatham, Kent

Preface

Liability for defective products is a key concern to manufacturers, wholesalers and retailers throughout Europe, particularly since the issue of the EC Product Liability Directive. The need to know and understand the laws of each country through which goods are to pass is becoming ever more important. This book seeks to offer a practical guide to those laws. To achieve this aim, we have brought together contributions from leading practitioners in the field of product liability in their respective jurisdictions. We have included a chapter relating to product liability insurance and a comparative table summarising liability for defective products in the countries covered. The law is stated as at September 1991.

We would like to thank Kathryn Albert, Beryl Blackburn, Elaine Gardiner, Phaedra Hesse, Stephen Hobbs, Antonia Kennett, Jane Landy, Lynn Richards, Lorna Roberts and everyone else at Laytons for all their help and support in producing this book. We would also like to thank each of the contributors without whom this book would not, of course, have been possible.

Patrick Kelly
Rebecca Attree
Laytons

December 1991

Contributors

Rebecca Attree
Laytons
16 Lincoln's Inn Fields
London WC2A 3ED
England

Tel ++ 44 71 404 5177
Fax ++ 44 71 405 1883

Sonia Cortes
Bufete Mullerat & Rosell
Paseo de Gracia 81
08008 Barcelona
Spain

Tel ++ 34 3 215 0233
Fax ++ 34 3 215 8602

Muriel de Courrèges
43 rue du Faubourg Saint-Honoré
75008 Paris
France

Tel ++ 33 1 42 66 50 31
Fax ++ 33 1 42 66 58 95

Gabriele Dara
Studio Consulerte Associati
AD & M
Via Noto 12
90141 Palermo
Italy

Tel ++ 39 91 625 2628
Fax ++ 39 91 349600

René Diederich
Loesch & Wolter
Avocats—Avoués
8 Rue Zithe
Boîte postale 1107
L-1011 Luxembourg

Tel ++ 352 494 015
Fax ++ 352 494 944

Tom Ellis
Laytons
Sunlight House
Quay Street
Manchester M3 3LD
England

Tel ++ 44 61 834 2100
Fax ++ 44 61 834 6862

Peter Honegger
Niederer Kraft & Frey
Bahnhofstrasse 13
8001 Zürich
Switzerland

Tel ++ 41 1 217 1000
Fax ++ 41 1 217 1400

Manuela von Kuegelgen
Stibbe & Simont
Rue Henri Wafelaerts 47–51 (box 1)
1060 Brussels
Belgium

Tel: ++ 32 2 533 5211
Fax: ++ 32 2 533 5212

Georg Lett
Lett, Lett, Steglich-Petersen & Petersen
Østergade 3–5
PO Box 2231
1019 Copenhagen K
Denmark

Tel ++ 45 3 312 0066
Fax ++ 45 3 312 1266

Klaus-Ulrich Link
Lichtenstein, Körner & Partners
Heidehofstrasse 9
7000 Stuttgart 1
Federal Republic of Germany

Tel ++ 49 711 48 9790
Fax ++ 49 711 48 1577

Peter Madl
Schönherr Barfuss Torggler & Partner
Tuchlauben 13
(Eingang Kleeblattgasse 4)
Postfach (POB) 41
A-1014 Vienna
Austria

Tel ++ 43 1 534 370
Fax ++ 43 1 533 2521

Wilhelm Matheson
Wiersholm, Mellbye & Bech
PO Box 400 Sentrum
0103 Oslo 1
Norway

Tel ++ 47 2 410 600
Fax ++ 47 2 400 600

Ramon Mullerat
Bufete Mullerat & Rosell
Paseo de Gracia 81
08008 Barcelona
Spain

Tel ++ 34 3 215 0233
Fax ++ 34 3 215 8602

Jorge Santiago Neves
Menezes Falcao e Associados
Assessores em Direito
Av Da Republica 48-B, 5-D
1000 Lisbon
Portugal

Tel ++ 351 1 793 8524
Fax ++ 351 1 793 8541

Thomas Sambuc
Lichtenstein, Körner & Partners
Heidehofstrasse 9
7000 Stuttgart 1
Federal Republic of Germany

Tel ++ 49 711 48 9790
Fax ++ 49 711 48 1577

LK Shields & Partners
31 Merrion Square
Dublin 2
Ireland

Tel ++ 353 1 610866
Fax ++ 353 1 610883

Lucien Simont
Stibbe & Simont
Rue Henri Wafelaerts 47–51 (box 1)
1060 Brussels
Belgium

Tel ++ 32 2 533 5211
Fax ++ 32 2 533 5212

D A Thomas
Willis Corroon Limited
Willis Wrightson House
Wood Street
Kingston-upon-Thames
Surrey KT1 1UG
England

Tel ++ 44 81 787 6290
Fax ++ 44 81 943 4297

Michael Thornton
Laytons
Sunlight House
Quay Street
Manchester M3 3LD
England

Tel ++ 44 61 834 2100
Fax ++ 44 61 834 6862

Andrew Turner
Laytons
16 Lincoln's Inn Fields
London WC2A 3ED
England

Tel ++ 44 71 404 5177
Fax ++ 44 71 405 1883

Christer Wagenius
Brenner & Wagenius HB
Kullagatan 8–10
252 20 Helsingborg
Sweden

Tel ++ 46 42 18 01 30
Fax ++ 46 42 12 21 54

S S H Wibbens
Van der Kroft cs
Keizersgracht 561–563
1017 DR Amsterdam
Netherlands

Tel ++ 31 20 626 48 47
Fax ++ 31 20 620 36 58

Contents

CHAPTER I

The EC Product Liability Directive

Andrew Turner Esq

Laytons
16 Lincoln's Inn Fields
London WC2A 3ED
England

Tel ++ 44 71 404 5177
Fax ++ 44 71 405 1883

CHAPTER I

The EC Product Liability Directive of 25 July 1985

1. BACKGROUND

Council Directive 85/374/EC on the approximation of the laws, regulations and administrative provisions of the Member States concerning liability for defective products was issued on 25 July 1985. It was notified to the Member States on 30 July 1985. This chapter summarises and explains the principal provisions and implications of the Directive.

This chapter is arranged in the following sections:

2. Introduction;
3. Objectives;
4. The system;
5. Structure;
6. Liability;
   - 6.1 The producer;
   - 6.2 Damage;
   - 6.3 Product;
   - 6.4 Defects;
7. Burden of proof;
8. Defences;
9. Compensation;
10. Limitations;
11. Implementation;
12. Enforceability;
13. Conclusion.

2. INTRODUCTION

The Directive was introduced within the framework of the continuing drive towards European harmonisation, to unify throughout the Common Market the law relating to defective products.

Historically, national legal systems have imposed a variety of obligations on producers and afforded different levels of protection to consumers.

By introducing the Directive the Community recognised that these different levels of protection could distort the movement of goods within the Common Market and sought to remove this obstruction to free trade.

3. OBJECTIVES

The Directive was issued to implement throughout the Common Market a strict liability system to compensate consumers for death, personal injury or damage to personal property due to defects in industrially produced, movable products.

Essential to the Commission's consumer protection policy, it aims to harmonise the laws of the Member States in readiness for completion of the single market in 1992.

4. THE SYSTEM

The system to be implemented introduces a fundamental change to product liability law in more than half of the Member States. Before the introduction of the Directive, in Denmark, Germany, Italy, the Netherlands and the United Kingdom, strict product liability was not available under national law to the consumer as a cause of action against the producer of a product.

The new system does not replace but instead supplements, the prevailing systems of consumer protection. It is designed to afford additional protection, co-existing with other consumer rights, whether based upon contract, negligence or breach of statutory duty. Consumer rights which go beyond its scope are not precluded. Hence, national law may provide consumer rights whereby the producer of a product will be strictly liable for defects without limit.

The Directive, therefore, seeks to introduce a system under which there are prescribed minimum consumer rights, upon which consumers throughout the Common Market can rely and according to which producers will be held responsible.

5. STRUCTURE

The Directive broadly divides into the following areas:

- (a) Liability;
- (b) Burden of proof;
- (c) Defences;
- (d) Compensation;
- (e) Limitations;
- (f) Implementation;

6. LIABILITY

Article 1 provides that *the producer* shall be liable for *damage* caused by a *defect* in his *product*. This article sets out the basis upon which the Directive is formulated. It introduces the concept of liability without the need to prove fault. The obligation on a producer under article 1 arises from the fact of the supply of defective goods and there is no need for the consumer to prove that the producer is 'at fault' nor that a contractual relationship exists between them.

The *fault basis of liability* does *not* provide a consumer with a right of action against the manufacturer or supplier of defective products where:

(a) there is no contractual link;
(b) he is unable to show that the manufacturer (or supplier) owed him a duty of care and failed to take reasonable care towards him in supplying the defective product; or
(c) he is unable to prove that the manufacturer (or supplier) failed to comply with a particular consumer safety, or health and safety at work, law relating to the product.

The *strict liability* approach extends the liability of manufacturers (and suppliers) to members of the public injured or who suffer loss through defective products, *without* the need to prove a contractual link, a duty of care and failure to take reasonable care, or a failure to comply with relevant legislation.

6.1 The producer

Under article 3, the producer means not only the manufacturer of a finished product, but also the producer of any raw material or the manufacturer of a component part; and includes any person who, by putting his name, trademark or other distinguishing feature on the product, presents himself as the producer. This seems to preclude a person who is stated on the product packaging as being responsible for packaging the product only, for example, where wine is stated to be 'bottled by . . . .'.

Unless the person responsible for selling the product to the consumer is also its producer he will not be liable except in those limited circumstances discussed below or under some other general principle of national law, for example, contract law.

Any person who imports into the Common Market a product for sale, hire, lease or any form of distribution in the course of his business shall be responsible as if he was its producer. This rule is fundamentally important: it ensures the consumer will have a right of action where the actual producer is not within the Common Market. However, on its true construction, the rule may enable an importer to avoid liability provided the products brought into the Common Market are imported for use, as opposed to distribution.

If the producer cannot be identified then each and every supplier is to be treated as if he was in fact the producer, except where he informs the claimant, within a reasonable time, of the producer's true identity or of the person who supplied the product to him. This rule is also to apply where an imported product does not indicate the importer's identity, even though the name of the producer is indicated.

The definition of 'producer' gives rise to a number of uncertainties.

Firstly, the liability of co-producers will be joint and several. The ability of a co-producer to obtain contribution or indemnity from another co-producer will depend upon national laws allowing a right to contribution or recourse.

Secondly, as to what constitutes 'a reasonable time' is unclear. This should not in any event be more than ten years from the date on which the producer put into circulation the product which caused the damage and after which the injured person's rights are extinguished (article 11). A three-year limitation period applies to recovery of damages (article 10) – this could be the relevant period for the purposes of determining whether a claim can be brought by an injured person against a supplier. Limitation periods are discussed in more detail below.

Finally, the Directive is unclear as to those details which must be given on a product (or its packaging) to identify the supplier, importer or producer: this will presumably fall to be determined by national law.

6.2 Damage

For there to be a cause of action against a producer damage must be caused by his product (article 1). Under article 9 'damage' means:

(a) damage caused by death or by personal injuries;
(b) damage to or destruction of any item of property other than the defective product itself, with a minimum threshold of ECU 500, provided that the item of property:
   (i) is of a type ordinarily intended for private use or consumption; and
   (ii) was used by the injured person mainly for his own private use or consumption.

Consequently, in an action for damage to property, the loss sustained must not be less than ECU 500 and the property damaged must be consumer (private) as opposed to business property. As the Directive recites, its scope is limited to damage to goods for private use or consumption; for example, damage caused to a company car would be excluded.

Article 9 states that the definition of 'damage' is without prejudice to national law relating to non-material damage. According to the Directive's recitals, 'non-material damage' includes pain and suffering, and such other non-material loss, arising under the applicable national law.

This may preclude actions for 'non-material damage' arising through the Directive by restricting them to claims brought under national law.

An alternative interpretation would be that claims for 'non-material damage' are permitted only where they may be brought under the relevant national law. On this basis the Directive might provide a convenient route for victims of defective products, such as the drug Thalidomide, to claim compensation for pain and suffering. Since article 16.1 links the limits on maximum liability to damage resulting from death or personal injury, Member States have no authority to limit the maximum compensation payable for pain and suffering. Limitations on liability are discussed in section 10 of this chapter, below.

Whether claims for pain and suffering are included within those for death and physical injury is unclear from the Directive.

6.3 Product

Under article 2 'product' means physical property and goods (viz movables), as opposed to land or rights in or to real property (eg a house) and could include a whole product, part of another product or part of a fixture attached to real property (eg a light switch). Electricity is expressly included. Exclusions include primary agricultural products and game, even where they are incorporated into another product. (Article 15.1(a) allows Member States to provide for 'products' to include primary agricultural products and game, which would otherwise be excluded.)

Primary agricultural products are products grown in the soil, of stock farming or fisheries: but those products which have undergone *initial processing* are *not* excluded. Claims for compensation for damage caused by hormone-treated meat and contaminated or rotten foodstuffs or drink will therefore be excluded unless the meat or foodstuffs causing the damage have been processed.

It is unclear what constitutes 'initial processing'. This should probably be construed in its widest possible sense. A victim might argue it includes even packaging and labelling of the merchandise giving rise to his cause of action.

Determining at what point an agricultural product is produced may cause difficulty. For instance, a potato would arguably have not been subjected to processing if the seed from which it is grown were subjected to a chemical application, since, at that stage, the seed would not constitute a 'primary agricultural product'. However, if the potato is cooked and mashed to be used for the top of a meat pie (viz subject to an industrial process) this would constitute the initial processing thereby rendering the potato a product.

6.4 Defects

A product is defective when it does not provide the safety which a person is entitled to expect, taking all the circumstances into account, including:

(a) the presentation of the product;
(b) the use to which it could reasonably be expected that the product would be put; and
(c) the time when the product was put into circulation (article 6.1).

The Directive does not therefore provide for liability without any fault at all on the producer's behalf, since the victim still has to prove the existence of a defect. The use to which the product could reasonably be expected to be put is likely to depend on its presentation and, for example, any instructions on the packaging would be taken into account. The producer's responsibility may be further limited, or even removed when, having regard to all the circumstances, it is concluded that the damage caused to the victim is both due to the defect in the product and also the fault of the injured person or any person for whom the injured person is responsible (article 8.2). The effect is similar to contributory negligence.

The Directive is unclear as to the point in time at which the product enters circulation. It does not specify whether this relates to the first sale of the product by the manufacturer, the date of sale by the actual supplier to the victim, or to any other of its potential producers (for the purposes of the Directive). It is not even clear that the product concerned relates to the specific product itself, rather than the class of products to which it belongs, although article 11 appears to suggest it may be the product class.

Article 6.2 provides that a product will not be defective solely because a better product is subsequently put into circulation: a product must simply conform to the state of the art of products of that type available on the market at the time the product was first put into circulation. Consequently, provided a dangerous product is believed to be safe on first circulation, it may be offered for sale to unknowing purchasers even if the producer subsequently becomes aware of the risk. Whether under article 6.2 'circulation' occurs on sale from manufacturer to supplier or supplier to end-user is unclear.

7. BURDEN OF PROOF

Article 4 provides that 'the injured person shall be required to prove the damage, the defect and the causal relationship between defect and damage'.

Article 4 is difficult to reconcile with article 7(b) (see section 7, para (b), below) under which a producer is not to be liable if he proves that, 'having regard to the circumstances, it is probable that the defect which caused the damage did not exist at the time when the product was put into circulation by him or that this defect came into being afterwards'. Article 7(b) implies that to avoid liability the producer has only to prove that he complied with the general duty of care to which he might have been expected to conform in manufacturing and supplying a product.

The producer might, therefore, be able to rely on this article if he shows that he took reasonable steps to ensure that a defect in the product did not exist when the product was put into circulation by him. He could thereby show that the defect probably did not exist at that time.

Likewise, it is hard to reconcile article 4 with article 8.2 under which liability may be limited or removed altogether because the injured person was in some way jointly responsible with a defect for the damage caused (see section 6.4, above).

By qualifying article 4 in this way, articles 7(b) and 8.2 prevent the Directive from following the strict liability approach: this should extend liability for defective products without the need to prove a failure by the producer to take reasonable care.

8. DEFENCES

Article 7 provides the producer with six defences. In this context it seems that the producer includes the real producer, not suppliers or other persons deemed to be the producer, but the Directive is unclear.

The burden of providing the defences lies with the producer. The defences are as follows:

(a) *The producer did not put the product into circulation*: there seems no logic to this provision except where it applies to equipment constructed for a producer's own use.

(b) *Having regard to the circumstances, it is probable that the defect which caused the damage did not exist at the time when the product was put into circulation by the producer or that this defect came into being afterwards*: this contradicts the fundamental principle of strict liability that there is no need to prove fault. It appears that the defence may be satisfied merely by the producer proving that he complied with the general standard of care (see section 7, above).

(c) *The product was neither manufactured by the producer for sale or any form of distribution for economic purpose nor manufactured or distributed by him in the course of his business.*

(d) *The defect is caused by compliance of the product with mandatory regulations issued by public authorities*: hence, compliance with voluntary standards would not provide a defence.

(e) *The state of scientific and technical knowledge at the time when the producer put the product into circulation was not such as to enable the existence of the defect to be discovered*: the 'state of the art' defence. The producer must not only be ignorant of prevailing scientific and technical knowledge but there must be a universal lack of knowledge of the defect at that time. It is unclear whether by virtue of the real producer succeeding with this defence, importers or other re-sellers would then be excused in the event that a defect becomes known subsequent to circulation but prior to importation or resale.

The 'state of the art' defence does not require that upon subsequent discovery of a defect the product concerned should be recalled or that the public be notified.

Member States have a general discretion whether or not to incorporate this defence within their national legislation. A Member State may provide that the producer shall be liable even if he proves that the state of scientific and technical knowledge at the time when he put the product into circulation was not such as to enable the existence of a defect to be discovered (article 15.1(b)). Here, the Directive fails to address the conflict of laws which will arise where the sale of products occurs from a country excluding this defence to another country in which it is included: it does not indicate which law will apply. The ordinary international rules for determining the applicable law which are discussed in Chapter 17 will therefore have to be applied by the national court in which an action is commenced.

(f) *In the case of a manufacturer of a component, it will be a defence that a defect is attributable to a design of the product in which the component has been fitted or to the instructions given by the manufacturer of the product*: sub-contractors may therefore rely on product specifications as a defence – and it appears that knowledge of the defect would not prevent the defence applying.

9. COMPENSATION

Rules for quantification of loss sustained by a victim of a defective product are not set out in the Directive. It simply sets out parameters within which national law must operate.

As discussed in section 6.2, above, in an action for damage to property the loss sustained must be not less than ECU 500, so the first ECU 500 of loss sustained will not be recoverable and co-existing routes to compensation would have to be followed, for example, insurance, contract or by fault-based proceedings, for the balance (article 9). No upper parameter is provided.

Non-material damages, which include pain and suffering, and may also include loss of enjoyment or loss of earning capacity, are subject to no such limits.

In their implementing legislation, Member States have the option to limit compensation for damage caused by death or personal injuries arising from a defect to not less than ECU 70m, whether affecting a single product or a class of products (article 16.1).

Where claims are brought to compensate for death and personal injury, Member States' limits will vary because of divergent national laws.

As mentioned, the Directive fails to set out rules for dealing with the conflict of laws, therefore the ordinary rules of international law governing the applicable national law will need to be followed. It is unfortunate that the point was not taken up since quite clearly, where a discrepancy between national laws exists, the victim will wish to assert his rights in the court of the country of the least limitation. For the producer, this adds uncertainty as to his liability from one Member State to another. The potential for discrepancy means insurance policies have either to be geared to an unlimited basis of liability or carefully checked to ensure an appropriate level of cover representing the maximum limit for each Member State in which the product may be circulated. The opportunity for Member States to incorporate this limit within their legislation was presumably intended to give producers certainty as to their maximum liability: where products are imported from one Member State to another this object is not achieved – there is no certainty as to which national law will apply.

10. LIMITATIONS

These broadly divide into three categories: time, liability and compensation. Compensation is dealt with in section 9, above.

There are two principal rules governing the time of actions. Under article 10, the time period within which actions may be commenced is limited to the period of *three years* from the earlier of the following two days:

(a) the day on which the plaintiff *became aware* of the damage, the defect and the identity of the producer;
(b) the day on which the plaintiff *should reasonably have become aware* of the damage, the defect and the identity of the producer.

This limitation period is, however, subject to national law regulating suspension or interruption of limitation periods generally.

Once again the uniformity of application which was a primary objective of the Directive has not been obtained: both victim and producer will be affected where the cause of action relates to products imported from one Member State to another, firstly, due to lack of certainty as to the applicable national law and, secondly, in ascertaining the relevant limitation provisions. The need for the victim to obtain advice under the appropriate law will add complexity and increase costs. It will be in each party's interest to try to assert the application of the national law most beneficial to his cause.

Other uncertainties exist. For example, does the victim need to be aware of the identity of the manufacturer alone, or also of all the other persons deemed to be the producer? The Directive remains silent as to what constitutes an awareness of damage or defect.

National law regulating suspension of the limitation period remains intact. This means, for example, that in the UK, where the victim is a minor, the three-year time limit may be suspended until the victim is no longer a minor.

An overall time limit is also imposed (article 11). *Ten years* after the date on which the producer put into circulation the *actual* product causing the damage, the right to institute proceedings against the producer is extinguished. This rule is mandatory and cannot be overridden by laws of Member States regulating suspension. Hence, although the three-year period can be suspended, that suspension will not be allowed to take effect where the ten-year rule would be breached.

However, the Directive fails to define at what point circulation of the product occurs. If circulation occurs when the manufacturer first sells the product to the supplier, then that could have problems for the end-user. The interval between sale by the manufacturer to the supplier and the sale from the supplier to the end-user may exceed ten years. If that period was taken into account then the time limit could run out before the end-user had even purchased the product! Arguably, the widest possible interpretation will apply so that the time limit runs from circulation by the supplier on the basis that he is deemed also to be the producer (see section 6.1, above). In turn, the supplier would then have a right of action under national law against the person from whom he purchased the product, and likewise up the chain.

In addition to time constraints, the producer's liability to an injured person may not be contractually limited or excluded. The Directive is silent as to sale of secondhand products or products sold at a discount due to condition.

11. IMPLEMENTATION

The Directive should have been implemented in every Member State on or before 30 July 1988, applying to products put into circulation after the date on which the implementing legislation was effective.

The Directive was, however, introduced on time in less than one third of the Member States.

As at 1 March 1991 Belgium, France, the Republic of Ireland and Spain had still not passed implementing legislation. Even where legislation has been passed a number of Member States, including the UK, have failed to implement the Directive correctly. Discrepancies in national law are discussed in subsequent chapters.

It is therefore important to consider the extent to which individuals are able to enforce rights the Directive intended them to have, but which because of defective implementing legislation are not protected.

12. ENFORCEABILITY

The issue of whether and to what extent Community law can create rights for and impose obligations upon individuals which are enforceable within national courts is unclear.

The leading case on the application and operation of Community law is *Van Gend En Loos* (Case 26/62 ECJ). In that case the European Court held that:

> the Community constitutes a new legal order of international law for the benefit of which the States have limited their sovereign rights, albeit within limited fields, and the subjects of which comprise not only Member States but also their nationals. Independently of the legislation of Member States, Community law therefore not only imposes obligations on individuals but is also intended to confer upon them rights which become part of their legal heritage. These rights arise not only where they are expressly granted by the Treaty [of Rome], but also by reason of obligations which the Treaty [of Rome] imposes in a clearly defined way upon individuals as well as upon the Member States and upon the institutions of the Community.

The principal sources of Community law are found in the Treaty of Rome, Regulations, Directives and Decisions, each of which are legally binding acts of the Community.

A Directive is binding, as to the result to be achieved, upon each Member State to which it is addressed, but leaves to the national authorities the choice of form and method. In contrast, a Regulation has general application, is binding in its entirety and directly applicable in all Member States.

Directives mandate a given policy but leave it to the Member States' discretion as to their implementation. They often provide a transitional period for this to be accomplished. The European Court has rejected the view that obligations imposed by directives can be invoked and enforced only by Community institutions or Member States. If an obligation is 'by its legal nature, layout and wording capable of creating direct effects on the legal relations between the addressee of the measure and third parties' then the provision can be pleaded in national courts to enforce the right which flows from it. Hence, the measure must be clear and precise, expressed in unconditional terms, and any transitional period ended.

For legal certainty and clarity, Member States are expected to legislate for national procedures to ensure compliance with the legal rules mandated. It is not sufficient for Member States to implement a Directive only in part or even substantially. A Directive must be implemented in *full* despite the fact it may already be *directly effective*. In *Commission v Italy* (Cases 91 and 92/79 [1980] ECR 1099, para 6 and [1980] ECR 1115, para 6) the European Court stated that the 'full and exact application of the provisions of a Directive' in the national legal system is required. There are no legal or political excuses which the European Court will accept for failure to implement a Directive correctly.

An individual affected by a failure to implement the Directive correctly or in total may have legal rights to enforce it in the national courts.

The *effects doctrine* may give affected individuals rights against the national state at fault. To rely on the Directive against the national state it would be necessary to show the provision relied on is clear and precise, unconditional, and capable of operating without further action by the Community or the Member State.

Whether or not a Directive has 'vertical' direct effect as between the Community and the Member States *and* 'horizontal' direct effect imposing rights as between one individual (or company) and another is not entirely clear.

The concept of 'vertical' direct effect is well established: Directives are addressed to Member States. 'Horizontal' direct effect is not, and has been subject to considerable debate.

In *Marshall v Southampton and South West Hampshire Area Health Authority (Teaching)* (Case 152/84 [1986] 1 CMLR 688) the European Court ruled that whilst Directives bind Member States they cannot be invoked against private individuals. In *Johnston v Chief Constable of the Royal Ulster Constabulary* (Case 222/84 [1986] 3 CMLR 240) the European Court confirmed the position, stating that Directives only create 'vertical' direct effect.

Although this doctrine will not enable individuals to claim against each other, the Principle of Interpretation, otherwise known as the 'indirect' direct effects doctrine, may be relied upon instead.

In *Von Colson* (Case 14/83 [1984] ECR 1891) having concluded that under the direct effects doctrine a Directive could not create obligations upon which one individual could rely against another, the European Court considered whether national courts were bound to interpret national law in accordance with a Directive. The Court stated:

> The Member States' obligation arising under a Directive to achieve the result envisaged by the Directive, and their duty under Article 5 of the Treaty [of Rome] to take all necessary measures, whether general or particular, to ensure the fulfilment of that obligation, is binding on all the authorities of Member States, including for matters within their jurisdiction, the [national] courts. It follows that, in applying the national law and in particular the provisions of a national law specifically introduced in order to implement [the Directive] national courts are required to interpret their national law in the light of the wording and the purpose of the Directive in order to achieve the result referred to in the third paragraph of Article 189 [of the Treaty of Rome].

This principle was followed in *Marleasing SA v La Commercial Internacional de Alimentacion SA* (Case C106/89, 13 November 1990). There the European Court found that insofar as Community law has not been implemented, national courts are bound to disapply national law or ignore its application insofar as this may be necessary to comply with European law.

In *Factortame Ltd v Secretary of State for Transport* (*No 3*) (25 July 1991), the European Court reconfirmed this approach and consolidated its position finding that various provisions of the Merchant Shipping Act 1988 were in breach of Article 52 of the Treaty of Rome because they discriminate on the basis of nationality. The Court decided yet again that national law, in this case UK law, must be interpreted in accordance with European Community law.

It follows that national courts must interpret national law according to the wording and purpose of the Directive. Where it has not been fully and accurately implemented national courts nevertheless have a duty to interpret relevant national legislation (not just implementing legislation) in accordance with the Directive.

13. CONCLUSION

It will become evident from subsequent chapters that the harmonisation of product liability law has been impeded by the Member States' failure to implement the Directive on time, consistently or in accordance with its terms. However, where incorrectly or not fully implemented that is not to say that individuals will not derive the rights discussed in this chapter from the Directive. European case law confirms that individuals may enforce those rights by relying on them in the national courts on the basis that national law (eg implementing legislation, statute or common law) must be interpreted to give effect to the words and aims of the Directive.

To the extent that accurate implementing legislation is passed by Member States or national laws are interpreted according to its wording and purpose, the Directive will therefore succeed in achieving its aim of a common strict liability system throughout the European Community in readiness for completion of the single market in 1992.

CHAPTER II

Austria

Dr Peter Madl

Schönherr Barfuss Torggler & Partner
Tuchlauben 13
(Eingang Kleeblattgasse 4)
Postfach (POB) 41
A-1014 Vienna
Austria

Tel ++ 43 1 534 370
Fax ++ 43 1 533 2521

CHAPTER II

Austria*

1. INTRODUCTION

1.1 Overview of the law relating to defective products in Austria

(1) The law relating to damages for defective products as contained in the Austrian General Civil Code (ABGB) sections 1293 ff is based on the principle of liability for fault. The ABGB distinguishes between liability in tort and liability for breach of contract. In the latter case it is for the defending party to prove that he did not act culpably (ABGB section 1298). Further, he will be liable for any fault – as if it were his own fault – on the part of a person who participated in the performance of the duties of the defending party with the knowledge and intention of the defending party (ABGB section 1313a). In addition, the person who has caused the damage may be liable for pure financial loss.

If liability cannot be based on breach of contract, the plaintiff has to furnish proof of all the facts on which his claim is based, which includes proof of fault of the defending party. In tort, the defending party is only liable for a third party insofar as the third party is unfit or known to be dangerous (ABGB section 1315).

As there is usually no contract between the producer and the consumer, the stricter form of liability for breach of contract is – in principle – not applicable.

Contractual relations usually exist only between a consumer and a retailer. However, it will in most cases be possible for the retailer to prove that he carefully performed his duties (ie he properly controlled the product) and consequently cannot be charged with negligence. In response to this dilemma, legal theory and practice searched – before the adoption of the Product Liability Directive – for new solutions beyond the statutory basis.

The approach in Austria is based on the extension of contractual liability. The legal concept was that a contract may have protective effects for third parties. The end-user of a product is linked with the producer by a chain of contracts and, therefore, the producer owes duties of protection and care to him. A violation of these duties, therefore, constitutes a breach of contract to the end-user.[1]

(2) The Directive was implemented in Austria by way of the Federal Act of 21 January 1988 on liability for a defective product (*Bundesgesetz vom*

* The translation of this article has been reviewed by Dr Alan Key and Dr Christian Herbst.

1 Compare Welser 'Das neue Produkthaftungsgesetz' WB1 1988, 165, 166 with further reference; Bydlinski in Klang *Kommentar zum Allgemeinen bürgerlichen Gesetzbuch* (2nd edn) vol IV/2, pp 180 ff.

21.1.1988 über die Haftung für ein fehlerhaftes Produkt—Produkthaftungsgesetz, BGB1 99/1988 [PHG]) took effect on 1 July 1988. The main reason for the enactment of the PHG was the realisation that the prior system of liability could not keep pace with the development of technical products.[2] The wish to keep up with the changes in EC law has – at least, pursuant to the printed materials of the PHG – been of minor importance.

Liability based on the PHG is in addition to liability based on other Austrian legislation. The provisions of the Austrian Civil Code concerning warranty and damages as well as, for example, the provisions of Acts on pharmaceutical products and food are still valid and have to be observed.

2. LIABILITY IN CONTRACT

2.1 Liability for pre-contractual statements or representations

As soon as two persons come into contact to conclude a contract they have to comply with obligations to give information and to take care of the person and the other objects of legal protection of the other party. These obligations exist independently of the conclusion of a contract. In a contract for sale of goods, the parties are especially obliged to give information on the condition of the product in question. For example, it is necessary to tell a prospective customer if the product being sold does not fulfil the requirements of which he has informed the seller (eg the compatibility of a computer with a particular type of software) or if certain prerequisites are necessary (eg high voltage supply). The seller is also obliged to see to it that a prospective customer is not injured on retail premises (eg because of a banana peel or a slippery floor).

Any failure to comply with these obligations results in a liability which is based on the principles of liability in contract.[3] The seller could be held liable for the costs of a newly hired computer operator, the adaptation of a room for the computer and loss of income if the computer sold is not able to fulfil the requirements of the customer which were known to the seller.

2.2 Outline of contract law relevant to defective products in Austria

Many contracts in Austria are concluded on the basis of general terms and conditions. As with the other provisions of a contract, general terms and conditions are only valid upon mutual agreement of both parties. This agreement can be reached either expressly or impliedly. Therefore, it is enough if one party states before the conclusion of the contract that he is only willing to conclude the contract under his general terms and conditions and the other party nevertheless concludes the contract. For an implied agreement, it is necessary to make it clear to the customer that the producer is only willing to

2 Regierungsvorlage, 272 der Beilagen zu den Stenographischen Protokollen des Nationalrates XVII. GP (suggestion of the government, 272 of the enclosures to the shorthand protocols of the national assembly XVII legislation period).

3 Compare Koziol and Welser *Grundriß des bürgerlichen Rechts* (8th edn) vol I, p 435 with further reference.

conclude under his general terms and conditions. In addition, the customer must at least have the possibility to see the contents of the general terms and conditions.[4]

Provisions in the general terms and conditions which are disadvantageous for the customer and which the customer would not normally expect are not deemed to be part of the contract (ABGB section 864a).

Even if general terms and conditions are incorporated into an agreement, it is still possible that certain provisions contrary to public policy will be void. These include the complete exclusion of a seller's warranty for new goods[5] and the exclusion of liability for stringent gross negligence.[6] Stringent gross negligence is defined as a fault which comes very near to intention and would never happen to an average attentive person in a similar situation.

The Austrian Act for Protection of Consumers (KSchG) which applies to contracts concluded between a businessman (any person who enters into a contract in the course of his business) and a non-businessman, provides that certain provisions of the ABGB (especially warranty of quality and liability for damages) are mandatory.

2.3 Contractual warranties relating to the quality and safety of products

The seller must warrant that the product has the stipulated or customarily required characteristics (ABGB section 922). Depending on the defect, the buyer has the right either to have the defect corrected, the price reduced or the contract cancelled. In this respect it is irrelevant whether there is any fault on the part of the seller.

However, the right based on warranty does not constitute a claim for damages. Damage other than that to the product sold itself (eg personal injury or damage to other products) can only be recovered under the prerequisites of ABGB sections 1293 ff.

2.4 Breach of contract for the supply of defective products

2.4.1 Types of defect

Constructural defects are defined as those where the construction, the design or the composition of the product are inadequate. In this case not only the individual item, but all products of the same series, are considered defective.

Instructional defects are those where the product itself is free from defects, but damage is caused by missing or faulty directions on use or installation, or insufficient warning against dangerous qualities of the product.

A manufacturing defect is a defect of one or more products of a correctly constructed series of products which is caused by the failure of a machine or a worker.

The producer must check his product to see whether it has any – so far unknown – dangerous qualities. This is especially true for newly developed,

4 Compare *Koziol and Welser* vol I, p 106 with further reference.
5 Austrian Sup Ct in JB1 1970, 271.
6 Austrian Sup Ct in SZ 57/184; JB1 1986, 144.

mass-produced articles. In addition, the producer has – still as a contractual obligation – to follow the development of the state of the art and if a safer product is developed, he must adapt his product. The producer and, to a certain extent, the distributor, are obliged to warn either the users or the general public if they find a defect in the product. According to the prevailing opinion the producer is also obliged to recall defective products.[7]

2.4.2 Causation

A condition for the liability of the producer is that his act or omission has caused the damage. In the former case, the question to be determined is whether the damage would have occurred if the act had not happened. Where damage as the result of an omission is the issue, the question is whether the damage would equally have occurred as a result of reasonable behaviour ('conditio sine qua non').[8]

2.4.3 Remoteness of loss and damage

Further, the producer is only liable for damages if the cause of the damage is, according to its general nature, not completely inappropriate to bring about such a result and if this cause has not been just part of an extremely extraordinary chain of circumstances.[9]

A further restriction of liability is that a person is only liable for damage caused by the unlawful act or omission that should have been prevented by the infringed standards of conduct. This 'purpose of protection' is important for determining which heads of damages and whom is to be compensated.[10]

Basically, only those persons whose absolute rights have been injured, who are protected by a specific rule of conduct or with whom contractual obligations existed which have not been complied with have the right to be compensated. The standard example given for these cases is the following: somebody destroys a power station and due to the lack of electrical power a third party suffers damage, eg frozen food is destroyed. According to the prevailing opinion the third party cannot claim damages from the person who destroyed the power station.[11]

2.5 Quantum of damage

Liability for damages includes medical expenses, loss of earnings and damages for pain and suffering. The highest amount of damages for pain and suffering ever awarded by an Austrian court amounted to AS 1m. (In the case at hand, medical malpractice had resulted in the victim vegetating below the level of an intelligent animal for the rest of his life.)

7 Welser *Produkthaftungsgesetz* (1988), annotation 33 to § 5 with further reference.
8 *Koziol and Welser* vol I, p 412 with further reference.
9 *Koziol and Welser* vol I, p 413 with further reference.
10 *Koziol and Welser* vol I, pp 417 f.
11 Austrian Sup Ct in SZ 49/96; SZ 50/34 and others.

Any claim for medical expenses is generally transferred by virtue of a legal provision (ASVG section 332) to the social security institutions so that it can no longer be claimed by the injured party. The claimants are then the social security institutions.

Loss of profit can in principle only be recovered in cases of gross negligence. According to commercial law loss of profit can also be recovered in case of minor negligence if one party to the contract is a businessman.[12]

Punitive or exemplary damages are not awarded under Austrian law.

2.6 Burden of proof

The plaintiff is required to prove the defectiveness of the product, the damage and the causal relationship between the two. The producer can avoid liability by proving that he took all necessary measures and therefore neither he nor any of the persons for whom he is responsible can be charged with negligence. The burden of proof for gross negligence lies with the injured person.[13]

2.7 Exclusion or limitation of liability

Under Austrian law liability may be excluded for damages which are caused by negligence provided that the negligent act or omission is not intentional.[14] Under the Austrian Act for Protection of Consumers liability can only be excluded for minor negligence.

In Austria, however, it is recognised that – consistent with the attempt to base liability of the producer on a chain of contracts (see section 1.1, above) – a release from liability is permissible for product liability too.[15] If the producer has excluded liability for damage in his contract with the first dealer, it may commonly be expected that he has also no intention to assume any duties of protection and care to the consumer. Consequently, it is possible largely to exclude liability for damages to the consumer by means of a simple clause in the first contract.

2.8 Limitation

Claims for damages in contract are subject to a limitation period of three years. The limitation runs from the moment when the injured person had knowledge or ought reasonably to have had knowledge of the damage and the person liable for the damage.[16] Irrespective of this knowledge claims for damages become statute-barred after 30 years. The limitation period of 30 years also

12 *Koziol and Welser* vol I, pp 422 f.

13 Austrian Sup Ct in SZ 43/80; JBl 1977, 648 and others; for other opinion see *Koziol and Welser* vol I, p 421 with further reference.

14 *Koziol and Welser* vol I, p 108 with further reference.

15 Austrian Sup Ct in SZ 51/169.

16 Schubert in Rummel *Kommentar zum Allgemeinen bürgerlichen Gesetzbuch* (1984), annotation 3 ff to §1489 with further reference.

applies if the damage has been caused by an intentional criminal offence with a possible imprisonment of more than one year (ABGB section 1489).

Negotiations to reach a settlement cause a suspension of the statute of limitation. At the end of the suspension the remaining time begins to run.[17]

The limitation period is interrupted if the debtor acknowledges the claim or the injured person files a law suit. If the limitation period is interrupted, the time that ran before the interruption is disregarded. The whole time begins to run afresh after the interruption.[18]

2.9 Liability for third parties

The defendant is liable for any fault on the part of the person who participated in the performance of the duties of the defendant with the knowledge and intention of the defendant (ABGB section 1313a). However, the defendant is only liable for damage which has been caused by the performance of his duties. There is no liability of the defendant for damage which has been caused by the third person which happens to coincide with the performance of the contract (eg if the third person hits the plaintiff upon delivery of the product for personal reasons).[19]

3. LIABILITY IN TORT

3.1 Outline of the relevant tort law giving rise to liability for personal and property damage in Austria

The prerequisite for liability in tort is the violation of either an absolute right which is enforceable against everyone or a protective law,[20] such as, for example, the Austrian Road Traffic Regulations (StVO), the Act on Pharmaceutical Products (AMG) or the Food Act (LMG).

Liability in tort may be concurrent with liability for breach of contract. The differences are that in tort the plaintiff must prove the fault of the defending party (ABGB section 1296 applies instead of section 1298), the defendant is only to a lesser extent liable for third persons (ABGB section 1315 applies instead of section 1313a) and that there is, as a rule, no liability for pure financial loss.

3.2 Causation and remoteness of loss and damage

The same principles as for liability for breach of contract apply. In addition, the relevant protective law must have intended to prevent damages such as the ones which occurred. For example, an employer is not liable if one of his

17 *Koziol and Welser* vol I, p 179 with further reference.
18 *Koziol and Welser* vol I, pp 179 f with further reference.
19 *Koziol and Welser* vol I, p 449.
20 *Koziol and Welser* vol I, pp 414 f with further reference.

employees is injured by a customer outside normal working hours. However, the employer would be liable if his employee suffers damage because he works too long hours.[1]

3.3 Quantum of damage

Pure financial loss can only be recovered if there is a protective law which intends to prevent those damages.[2]

Medical expenses, loss of income and damages for pain and suffering can be recovered on the same basis in tort as in contract.

3.4 Burden of proof

The plaintiff has to prove all the facts on which his claim is based. Unlike in a claim for breach of contract, in tort the plaintiff has also to prove that the defending party acted culpably.[3]

3.5 Exclusion of limitation of liability

Although the exclusion of liability in tort is not very practical, it is nevertheless possible with the same prerequisites as the exclusion of liability for breach of contract.

3.6 Limitation

Pursuant to ABGB section 1489 the same provisions regarding the limitation period, the suspension and the interruption of limitation apply for claims in tort and contract.

3.7 Liability for third parties

A principal may be liable for the fault of a person he engages for the performance of any obligation whatsoever if the person is unfit or the principal knows that the person is dangerous (ABGB section 1315). A special duty of care owed by the principal to the injured person is no condition for the liability based on ABGB section 1315.[4]

A person is unfit in the sense of ABGB section 1315 if he is not fit for the activity he is engaged to do. In order for a person to be qualified as unfit, it is not enough that he makes a mistake. One can infer unfitness only from the commission of several mistakes or a single serious mistake.

1 *Koziol and Welser* vol I, p 418.
2 *Koziol and Welser* vol I, pp 415 f.
3 *Koziol and Welser* vol I, p 421 with further reference.
4 *Koziol and Welser* vol I, p 449.

The term 'dangerous' refers to the general human characteristic (eg the plumber who steals or the painter who starts a fire at the work place). The principal is liable for these persons only if the dangerous characteristic is known to him and the damage is caused by this dangerous characteristic.

The limited liability of the principal pursuant to ABGB section 1315 is expanded by certain specific provisions relating to dangerous items (eg section 10 of the Law on Pipelines and section 35 of the Law on Liability in the Field of Nuclear Energy). Based on these provisions, legal theory and practice generally impose a liability on the owners of dangerous items for the gross negligence of their personnel.[5]

4. LIABILITY FOR DEFECTIVE PRODUCTS BROUGHT ABOUT BY BREACH OF STATUTORY REGULATION DESIGNED TO PROTECT CONSUMERS AND/OR TO PROMOTE SAFETY

4.1 Outline of the nature of protective regulations

In Austria, the Federal Act of 3 March 1983 on Protection against Dangerous Products (Product Safety Act) requires public authorities to take appropriate measures if a product (any movable tangible property which is produced to serve profit-making purposes) cannot be used with the safety for life and health which can be expected. Public authorities can oblige the manufacturer or seller (section 5):

(a) to change the directions for use or the presentation (especially the packaging) of the product;
(b) to change its advertising activities;
(c) to divulge or alter certain features of the product;
(d) to accept restrictions on the sale of the product (eg limitation of the persons to whom the product may be sold or of distribution channels);
(e) to give a warning notice to customers and users of the product.

The violation of such measures is treated like the violation of a protective law (ABGB section 1311) and has, therefore, the consequences outlined in section 3, above.

4.2 Burden of proof

The plaintiff has to prove all the facts on which his claim is based, including the negligence of the defending party. It is, however, enough that he proves the defending party acted culpably when violating the protective law. He need not prove that the defending party had or could have foreseen that the damage would have occurred.[6]

5 *Koziol and Welser* vol I, p 451 with further reference.
6 *Koziol and Welser* vol I, p 436 with further reference.

4.3 Nature of liability, damages or criminal sanctions

Besides the obligation to compensate the damage according to the principles of liability in tort, the violation of a measure made pursuant to the Product Safety Act is subject to an administrative fine of up to AS 100,000.

In addition, there are several provisions in the Criminal Code on the (intentional or negligent) endangering of the life or health of human beings or of the environment.

5. SPECIAL LIABILITIES ARISING IN RESPECT OF PARTICULAR PRODUCTS

Pursuant to the Austrian Act on Liability in the Field of Nuclear Energy the owner of a nuclear installation is liable for all damage caused by this nuclear installation or by nuclear material in this installation regardless of whether he or his personnel acted culpably. The maximum liability is AS 500m.

The processor of a radioactive product is liable for all damage caused by the radioactive product unless he can prove that neither he nor his personnel acted culpably. In this case, the liability is limited according to the level of radioactivity to between AS 1.2m and AS 18m.

6. LIABILITY FOR DEFECTIVE PRODUCTS ARISING FROM NATIONAL LAW IN AUSTRIA: IMPLEMENTATION OF THE DIRECTIVE

6.1 Introduction

The PHG, which is based on the Directive, came into force on 1 July 1988. At the time of writing, the Austrian Supreme Court has not yet decided a case based on the PHG and, therefore, the following is based only on legal theory.

6.2 Outline of provisions in Austria

6.2.1 Extent of liability

(1) Pursuant to section 1 of the PHG, liability for damages arises if a defect of a product causes the death of a person, physical injury, harm to a person's health or damage to an item of material property (other than the product itself).

Therefore, liability occurs in cases of personal injury and property damage other than to the product itself. Whether the buyer of a product has a remedy for a defect of the product itself depends on the provisions on warranty in the General Civil Code (ABGB sections 922 ff). According to the explanatory notes,[7] pure economic damages cannot be recovered under the PHG. For

7 Erläuterungen zur Regierungsvorlage, 272 der Beilagen zu den Stenographischen Protokollen des Nationalrates XVII. GP, p 8.

example, profits which are lost due to a defective product must be recovered pursuant to the general rules of liability in contract and tort. However, since this restriction is not expressly stated in the text of the PHG, some[8] are of the opinion that – besides the repair cost – even pure economic damages can be recovered. In accordance with the intention of the PHG, this provision should be restrictively interpreted pursuant to the Directive, and damages only in respect of property damage, medical costs, loss of earnings and pain and suffering are recoverable.[9]

(2) Only property damage exceeding AS 5,000[10] can be recovered (section 2). According to the text of the PHG this minimum shall be applied to each individual damaged item. This means, for example, that liability under the PHG will not arise if the damage to one item amounts to AS 4,000 and the damage to another amounts to AS 3,000.[11] However, the intention of the PHG demands that the PHG is applicable if the sum of the damages exceeds AS 5,000.[12] Action for damages not exceeding AS 5,000 can still be brought under the general rules of contract and tort.

6.2.2 *Persons subject to liability*

The producer, the importer and the dealer are all potentially liable under the PHG.

i. Producer. (1) The producer is the person who has manufactured and distributed the finished product, or a primary component, or a raw material thereof. If a component (eg the tyre of a car) is defective, the injured person may choose whether to sue the producer of the tyres or the producer of the car. A car with defective tyres is considered a defective car and as such the producer is not liable for the destruction of the car itself, but is liable for the injuries suffered by the driver (and bystanders). The producer of the defective tyre has distributed it as an individual product distinct from the car itself, thus, he is liable for the damage to the car itself as well as all damage for which the car producer is liable.[13]

(2) According to the explanatory notes of the PHG the assembler may also be liable. This is incongruous with the Directive (which corresponds very closely to the Austrian PHG on this point).[14] In any event the definition of a producer does not cover the supplier of services. But the supplier of goods and services can be held liable under the PHG as a producer, importer, or dealer of the goods supplied.

(3) Considerable problems of definition – whether a person is a producer or a dealer – arise in connection with the packing, transferring and mixing-up of products.

8 Fitz, Purtscheller and Reindl *Produkthaftung* (1988), annotation 21 to §1.
9 Compare Welser *Produkthaftungsgesetz*, annotation 7 to §1; Welser in WB1 1988, 168; Andréewitch 'Anmerkungen zum Produkthaftungsgesetz' ÖJZ 1988, 225, 227 ff.
10 Approximately US $400.
11 Welser in WB1 1988, 170.
12 Welser *Produkthaftungsgesetz*, annotation 2 to §2; Barchetti and Formanek *Das Österreichische Produkthaftungsgesetz* (1988) p 49.
13 Compare Fitz, Purtscheller and Reindl *Produkthaftung*, annotation 16 to §1; Schmidt-Salzer and Hollmann *Kommentar EG-Richtlinie Produkthaftung* (1986), annnotation 28 to art 9; other opinion Welser *Produkthaftungsgesetz*, annotation 5 to §1.
14 Welser in WB1 1988, 171; Welser, *Produkthaftungsgesetz*, annotation 5 to §3.

There is presumably no disagreement that a person transferring liquids from big to small containers or putting tea from a large into a small bag is not a producer under the PHG.[15] Indeed, the person who repacks has to be careful to avoid being liable as a quasi-producer. The dilution and refilling of liquid extracts is held to be the act of a producer, because the diluted, refilled liquid is essentially a new product.[16]

Is the physician who adds distilled water to a powdered medicine before giving it to the patient a producer under the PHG? It is thought not.[17] The theoretical difference between this act and the dilution of liquid extracts by a distributor is difficult to make.

ii. Importer. (1) The national business entity that imports the product and distributes it on the domestic market is referred to as an importer (section 3).

(2) Induced by the word 'national', the doctrine of the 'foreign importer' has been established.[18] This is the person transferring the products from a foreign country into Austria and distributing them on the home market. The 'foreign importer' is not liable as an importer under the PHG since the law specifically mentions the 'national businessman' (section 1(1)(2)). Therefore there must be a 'foreign businessman' who is not liable even though he has imported the product. A business entity that has its single domicile in a foreign country and which imports products without an order or mandate from an Austrian business entity, pays import duty, and sells them – possibly after some months of storage – is not liable as an importer under the PHG. In such cases the injured person can hold only the foreign producer liable, even though the foreign importer may have property in Austria and may be subject to the jurisdiction of Austrian courts.

Two solutions have been offered to avoid this inconvenient lack of liability. However, both are contrary to the wording of the law. The first business entity in the distribution chain with its domicile in Austria could be called the importer.[19] The problem is that it did not import the products, instead it bought products already duty-paid in Austria. Alternatively, the word 'national' could be interpreted as a mere repetition without special meaning which only serves to point out the difference from the foreign producer.[20]

(3) The PHG also specifically addresses the liability of 're-importers'. Re-importers are business entities which re-import a product that has been manufactured in Austria and exported afterwards. Although this liability corresponds to the clear wording of the law, it is – according to some authors – nevertheless superfluous. The reason for the introduction of the liability of the importer was to provide the injured person with an Austrian entity which can be held liable. In case of a re-import the national producer can be held liable

15 Welser *Produkthaftungsgesetz*, annotation 8 to §3.

16 Schmidt-Salzer and Hollman *Kommentar*, annotation 44 to art 3; other opinion Welser *Produkthaftungsgesetz*, annotation 8 to §3.

17 Welser *Produkthaftungsgesetz*, annotation 8 to §3; Welser in WB1 1988, 171.

18 Welser in WB1 1988, 169 ff; Welser *Produkthaftungsgesetz*, annotation 12 to §1; Fitz, Purtscheller and Reindl *Produkthaftung*, annotation 37 to §1; Fitz 'Wer ist Importeur im Sinne des Produkthaftungsgesetzes?' Handel – Wirtschaft – Recht, vol 6, October 1988, 3 ff.

19 Compare Fitz, Purtscheller and Reindl *Produkthaftung*, annotation 37 ff to §1; Fitz in Handel – Wirtschaft – Recht, 4 ff.

20 Welser *Produkthaftungsgesetz*, annotation 12 to §1; Welser in WB1 1988, 283.

anyway and, therefore, it is not necessary to have a second liable person in Austria. However, it is an advantage for the injured person if the producer is insolvent and damages can, therefore, not be recovered from him, to have another liable person in Austria. Therefore, the courts will most probably not follow this opinion.[1]

iii. Dealer. Every business entity which distributes a product is a dealer.

Pursuant to section 6 of the PHG, distribution is defined as the transfer of a product for the disposal or use of a third person based on whatever title.

6.2.3 Defective products

A party can be held liable only for defective products. The PHG contains more specific provisions defining product and defect.

i. Product. Pursuant to section 4 of the PHG, a product is any movable, tangible good. It also includes energy. Agricultural and forest products and game are exempted, as long as they have not initially been processed.

ii. Defect. (1) A product is defective if it is not as safe as can be expected considering all the circumstances. The PHG does not focus on the subjective expectations of the injured person, but considers only the general opinion of the average prospective user.[2]

(2) Relevant circumstances under the PHG are: the presentation of a product, the use to which it can reasonably be expected to be put, and the time of distribution.

(a) According to the explanatory notes of the PHG[3] the presentation of the product includes advertising, labelling, packaging, enclosed written information and additional oral information given by a salesman. Insufficient information may render a product defective under special circumstances. On the other hand, adequate information may avoid the product being held to be defective.

A warning is sufficient only if it is clear, explicit and emphasised according to its degree of importance. If too many instructions are given, the average user may feel overwhelmed and thus the effect of each instruction may decrease.[4]

In this context, an important restriction must be made. The presentation must be made either by the liable person or at least with his knowledge.[5] The reference to oral information given by a salesman, which is stated in the explanatory notes of the PHG, is misleading in two respects. First, exaggerated claims by the seller without the

1 Compare Welser in WBl 1988, 169.

2 Compare Welser *Produkthaftungsgesetz*, annotation 3 to §5i, Andréewitch in ÖJZ 1988, 228.

3 Regierungsvorlage, 272 der Beilagen zu den Stenographischen Protokollen des Nationalrates XVII. GP, to §5.

4 Compare Fitz, Purtscheller and Reindl *Produkthaftung*, annotation 10 to §5; Welser *Produkthaftungsgesetz*, annotation 12 to §5.

5 Welser *Produkthaftungsgesetz*, annotation 13 to §5; Welser in WBl 1988, 172; Andréewitch in ÖJZ 1988, 228.

knowledge of the producer will not cause liability of the producer. Second, if oral information by a salesman was considered in determining liability, then subjective expectations rather than objective expectations would be focused on. This is against the intention of the PHG.

(b) Liability arises only in respect of the use of a product which can reasonably be expected. The term 'reasonable use' has a broader meaning than that determined by the nature of the product. Therefore, to some extent a party may be liable for the incorrect use and possibly even the misuse of a product. The distinction between a use which can reasonably be expected and a use which may not be reasonably expected is one of the most difficult problems in the application of the new law and must be resolved in each individual case.[6]

(c) A very important restriction of the term 'defect' results from the third requirement, which focuses on the time of distribution. This assures that products are not considered defective for the sole reason that a newer and a more technically advanced product is subsequently put in circulation. Since a product may be distributed several times in the distribution chain, a change in the safety expectations during distribution will affect liability under the PHG. If, after the first distribution of a safe product by the producer, but during later distribution of the product through the distribution chain, the level of safety expectations justifiably rises, the producer will not be liable because he had distributed a product which was considered safe at the time he put it into circulation.[7] Eventually, however, the importer and all other dealers who have distributed a defective product based on this higher level of safety expectation may be held liable.[8] Problems of recourse will be dealt with at a later time.

(3) It is unclear whether ineffectiveness is a defect under the PHG. If, for example, a medicine is ineffective and the patient could have been cured by using another one, would this incur liability? It is assumed that such ineffectiveness is not covered by section 5 of the PHG.[9]

The effectiveness of a medicine can usually only be hoped for, not expected; even in the case of a correct prescription by a doctor and perfect quality of the product, the medicine may not help. The presentation of the product is important, especially the information enclosed with it by which an unrealistic expectation of effectiveness may be created or eliminated.

The same applies to other cases of product ineffectiveness. Generally, the question is whether the product is altogether inappropriate or whether the damage was caused by an operational difficulty or a malfunction of the product itself.[10]

6 Compare Posch 'Produkthaftungsgesetz – Eine erste Analyse der Probleme' RdW 1988, 65, 69; Welser *Produkthaftungsgesetz*, annotation 14 to §5.

7 Welser *Produkthaftungsgesetz*, annotation 17 to §5.

8 Fitz, Purtscheller and Reindl *Produkthaftung*, annotation 27 to §5; for other opinion regarding dealers see Welser *Produkthaftungsgesetz*, annotation 17 to §5.

9 Also Welser *Produkthaftungsgesetz*, annotation 20 ff to §5; other opinion Fitz, Purtscheller and Reindl *Produkthaftung*, annotation 37 to §5.

10 Welser *Produkthaftungsgesetz*, annotation 23 to §5.

6.2.4 Liability independent of fault

Liability under the PHG occurs regardless of fault. The proof that all conceivable measures have been taken is no defence. Under the PHG a party is liable, even if a single product shows dangerous defects, despite all possible care and control ('Ausreißer'). Development risk, however, is a good defence. If it is objectively impossible to recognise a defect as such under the state of science and technology at the time of distribution, liability will be excluded.[11]

6.2.5 Liability of producers and importers

The importer is liable in the same way as the producer for every defect of the product. This liability was implemented in order to spare an injured person litigation and/or execution of a judgment against a producer in a foreign country.[12]

The importer is now liable for every defect of the product, even if he has not caused the defect and even if the most diligent examination could not have revealed the defect.

The producer or the importer can avoid liability by producing the following evidence:

(a) He did not distribute the product as a business person; thus, there is no liability for products stolen from the warehouse of the producer or importer respectively, or for products which cause damage while they are stored by the producer or importer.[13]

(b) The product was not defective at the time of distribution by the producer or importer. To avoid liability it is sufficient to prove that this was probable. There is no liability for the producer or importer if the defect was caused by incorrect storage by the dealer, and the producer or the importer respectively prove that this is probable.[14] In such a case the dealer is liable, as he was until the present legislation, unless he acted free of fault.

(c) By objective standards it was impossible according to the state of science and technology at the moment of distribution to discover the defect. In this case liability for the risk of development is excluded. The PHG states it is not necessary for the business person concerned to discover the defect if at the time of distribution nothing relevant was published anywhere in the world, which would have helped specialised scientists and technicians to recognise a particular characteristic of the product as defective.[15]

11 Compare Welser *Produkthaftungsgesetz*, annotation 12 to §8; Fitz, Purtscheller and Reindl *Produkthaftung*, annotation 14 to §8.

12 Regierungsvorlage, 272 der Beilagen zu den Stenographischen Protokollen des Nationalrates XVII. GP, to §1.

13 Fitz, Purtscheller and Reindl *Produkthaftung*, annotation 6 to §7; Welser *Produkthaftungsgesetz*, annotation 6 to §7.

14 Welser *Produkthaftungsgesetz*, annotation 7 to §7; Taschner *Produkthaftung* (1986), annotation 10 to art 7.

15 Welser in WBl 1988, 174; Fitz, Purtscheller and Reindl *Produkthaftung*, annotation 14 to §8. Welser *Produkthaftungsgesetz*, annotation 12 to §8, wants to take into account unpublished discoveries too.

The time of distribution by the producer or importer is very relevant because the importer is responsible for and bears the risk of any technical developments during the period in which he stores the product.[16] This may be important especially as far as medicines are concerned: for years nobody knew that the medicines vital for haemophiliacs could transmit Aids, a virus at that time undiscovered. The Aids virus and its danger in some blood substitutes were only discovered after 1985. If an importer sells such a substitute after the discovery which he bought before the discovery, he – not the producer – will be liable regardless of whether he knew of the scientific discovery or not.

(d) The criteria which constitute a defect are based on a mandatory provision of law or an official Directive. If regulations require that a bottle must have a thickness of 3 mm but safe handling requires 5 mm, there will be no liability if the bottle is 3 mm thick. However, there will be liability if the regulation requires only certain minimum standards. The producer or importer cannot avoid liability by complying with these minimum standards.

(e) Liability has been contractually excluded by direct agreement with the injured person. As opposed to liability under the ABGB (see section 2.7, above), it is no longer possible to exclude liability in the contract with the first dealer with the effect that a consumer cannot claim damages. Furthermore, an exclusion is only possible for damage to property suffered by a businessman under the Austrian Act for the Protection of Consumers (KSchG). Liability for personal injuries as well as for damage to the property of a consumer cannot be excluded (KSchG section 9).

6.2.6 *Recourse*

The person who has caused the damage shall bear the final liability.

Therefore, the importer has a claim against the producer provided that neither he nor one of his staff has caused the defect. This claim is even valid for a foreign middleman, if the producer cannot be confirmed. If the importer has partly caused the defect, the responsibility will be shared. This joint liability depends firstly on the fault and secondly on the causal relationship (section 12).

The producer of the finished product may have recourse against the producer of a defective part of the product. Also in this case joint liability will apply.

The recourse covers in any event the justified payment of compensation for loss. As a claim for payment of the costs of proceedings is not justified[17] this question should be clarified in the supply contract.

A change in the safety expectations or in the state of science and technology after the time of distribution by the producer and before the sale to the consumer means that the – currently – perfectly good product is considered

16 Compare Welser *Produkthaftungsgesetz*, annotation 13 to §8; Welser in WB1 1988, 174.

17 Fitz, Purtscheller and Reindl *Produkthaftung*, annotation 10 to §12; Welser *Produkthaftungsgesetz*, annotation 15 to §12.

defective and causes liability to the importer or dealer without giving him a right to have recourse under the PHG.[18] A possible claim could be based only on culpable violation of the duty of the producer to inspect the product or on an exemption clause covering this possibility.

Since the recourse is independent of a damage claim which has been passed by assignment by operation of law, the limitation period is 30 years.[19] According to this interpretation, the period of liability under PHG may be considerably longer than ten years, which is stated as being the absolute limitation period under the PHG.

According to the prevailing view in Austria,[20] Austrian law is applicable to a recourse against the foreign intermediary or producer, respectively.

6.2.7 *Liability of the dealer*

According to the PHG a subsidiary liability affects dealers, if for national products the producer, or for foreign products the importer, cannot be established. If the importer or the national producer is traceable, for example by an imprint on the product, then the dealer is not liable.[1]

Even if there is liability, the dealer can avoid it if he informs the injured person, within a reasonable period of time, who the producer is or – for imported products – who the importer is, or – in any case – who his supplier is. The disclosure of a foreign producer or a foreign supplier does not exempt the dealer of his liability.

A period of time of one to two weeks is considered as reasonable.[2] The naming duty, according to this provision, includes not only providing the name, but also providing details of the particular purchase so that the injured person is able to produce evidence against the supplier that the defective product originates from him.[3]

The injured person will often succeed – for example, on the basis of an invoice – in proving that he has obtained the product from the dealer, although the product itself is no longer available. If the dealer has obtained the same kind of product from several producers and he can no longer establish by means of the invoice the producer of the defective product, the naming of all producers is enough to exempt the dealer from the liability. It is the injured person who must bear the risk that he cannot prove which producer has actually marketed the defective product.[4]

18 Welser *Produkthaftungsgesetz*, annotation 17 to §5 and annotation 13 to §8.
19 Fitz, Purtscheller and Reindl *Produkthaftung*, annotation 4 to §13; Regierungsvorlage, 272 der Beilagen zu den Stenographischen Protokollen des Nationalrates XVII. GP, to §12; Welser in WBl 1988, 175; Welser *Produkthaftungsgesetz*, annotation 10 to §13.
20 Welser *Produkthaftungsgesetz*, annotation 5 to §12 with further reference.
1 Fitz, Purtscheller and Reindl *Produkthaftung*, annotation 42 to §1; Barchetti and Formanek *Produkthaftungsgesetz* 41; other opinion Welser *Produkthaftungsgesetz*, annotation 21 to §1.
2 Erläuterung, 272 der Beilagen zu den Stenographischen Protokollen des Nationalrates XVII. GP, to §1.
3 Compare Barchetti and Formanek *Produkthaftungsgesetz* p 43; Schmidt-Salzer and Hollmann *Kommentar*, annotation 330 to art 3.
4 Schmidt-Salzer and Hollmann *Kommentar*, annotation 329 to art 3.

From this principle, that the dealer only has a duty to name his supplier, it follows that the injured person must bear the risk of insolvency of the producer or importer.[5]

In case the dealer does not name his supplier and becomes thereby liable, he may raise the same objections as those pertaining to the producer or the importer (see section 6.2.5, above). If he pays damages, then he can claim recourse against his suppliers, unless they exclude their liability by naming the domestic or foreign producer of the defective goods.

6.2.8 Burden of proof

As provided by the law before the PHG, the injured person has to prove that the product was defective, that he suffered a damage and that the defective product directly caused the damage. Furthermore, the injured person must also prove that the defendant produced or imported the defective product.[6]

Therefore, the injured person must also prove that the defendant and not a competitor was the real importer of the defective product. This has far-reaching practical consequences, for example, when there are several importers and if it cannot be established – for instance by the serial number – who really imported the defective product.[7]

The PHG reverses the general rules on the burden of proof in two cases. The producer or the importer must prove that he has not put the product on the market or that he did not act in the course of business in doing so. This shift of the burden of proof is not valid for other suppliers. Therefore, if a dealer faces a claim, the injured plaintiff must also prove that the defendant put the defective product on the market and acted thereby as a businessman.

Since it is assumed in favour of the injured person that a defective product was already defective when it had been put on the market by the defendant, the burden of proof on the defendant is relatively heavy.

6.3 Description of special or anomalous provisions in respect of product liability law in Austria

6.3.1 Quasi-producer

Anyone putting his name or his trademark on a product can be liable as if he were the producer. If the actual producer can be recognised from the product, the person additionally putting his trademark on the product will not be liable. If the trademark or name of the dealer is marked on the product, he will not be liable as a producer as long as his position as dealer is indicated clearly enough on the product. Anonymous products labelled only with the name of the dealer, without an explicit reference to his position as a mere dealer, will result in the liability of the dealer as a producer.[8]

5 Schmidt-Salzer and Hollmann *Kommentar*, annotation 335 to art 3.
6 Welser *Produkthaftungsgesetz*, annotation 1 to §7; Fritz, Purtscheller and Reindl *Produkthaftung*, annotation 1 to §7.
7 Welser *Produkthaftungsgesetz*, annotation 4 to §7; Fitz, Purtscheller and Reindl *Produkthaftung*, annotation 53 to §1 and annotation 5 to §7.
8 Welser *Produkthaftungsgesetz*, annotation 9 ff to §3; Welser in WB1 1988, 170.

The dealer, in order to avoid having the liability of a producer imputed to him, should make certain that the name of the producer is written on the package which is given to the consumer. An unambiguous indication of the dealer's position as dealer should also be made: eg 'distributed by X Company'.

6.3.2 Medical prescription

Who is the producer under the PHG, when a pharmacist mixes a pharmaceutical preparation according to a physician's medical prescription? The physician has only contributed to the manufacturing process with his prescription (an immaterial contribution) and not with a movable, tangible good. Therefore he can only be held liable for a wrong prescription under the rules heretofore in force. It is the pharmacist who should incur liability pursuant to the wording of the law. This is the opinion of most Austrian authors.[9] The opposite opinion – which is partly advanced by the Council Directive – is that a pharmacist is not liable as a producer, because he is only a small part of the production process. It is the physician who determines production; thus, if the physician is not liable as a producer, then a pharmacist who contributes only a small part to the production process should not be liable either.[10]

An argument for the opinion advanced by the Council Directive is that the physician is more likely to have been assigned to the patient than to the pharmacist who has coincidently been chosen by the patient. This case is comparable to a business entity manufacturing a product according to the specifications of a customer. In such a case, the prevailing opinion of Austrian authors[11] is that a businessman is liable – independent of fault – only for his field of activity and the materials he used; whereas for mistakes in the specification (submitted to him by the customer) he is as a rule only liable in case of fault.

6.3.3 Agricultural products

Agricultural and forest products and game are exempted from the PHG as long as they have not initially been processed.

Such initial processing triggers the liability of the producer – according to the definition. This vague legal term leaves room for confusion: the verdict on the question of initial processing will depend on the circumstances of the individual case. The destruction of natural development through harvesting, as well as later storage, is certainly not considered initial processing. The examples listed in the explanatory notes to the PHG avoid problem cases: sausages, canned vegetables, flour and wine are in any case products in the sense of the PHG.[12]

The following criteria are given to help in clarifying the distinction.[13] First, it depends in what condition a product – when properly used – must be to cause

9 Welser *Produkthaftungsgesetz*, annotation 3 to §4; Welser in WB1 1988, 171.

10 Schmidt-Salzer and Hollman *Kommentar*, annotation 14 to art 2; but compare Schmidt-Salzer and Hollmann *Kommentar*, annotation 67 to art 2.

11 Fitz, Purtscheller and Reindl *Produkthaftung*, annotation 14 to §3; for just a part of the opinion see Welser *Produkthaftungsgesetz*, annotation 18 to §3.

12 Compare Posch in RdW 1988, 69; Welser *Produkthaftungsgesetz*, annotation 11 to §4.

13 Fitz, Purtscheller and Reindl *Produkthaftung*, annotation 21 to §4.

damage; this will normally be the case only after preparation. Second, it should be assessed whether preparation causes additional risks which do not already exist in nature. The production of frozen food, the sawing of trees into boards, or the production of sugar are 'processing' under the PHG. The packing for transport and debarking of trees are not 'processing' under the PHG.

Recently an analogous expansion of liability exemption for agricultural and forest products has been advanced.[14] Farmers and restaurants primarily working with such products should be liable only for risks additionally caused by their work, but not for already damaged products. An extension of this analogy for the processing of medical herbs would seen obvious, but such an extension cannot be agreed to in the case of agricultural undertakings larger than farms. The industrial processing of products must be subject to the more severe liability of the PHG.

6.3.4 *Computer software*

Problems arise especially in connection with software and hardware because 'product' is defined as 'movable tangible goods'. Whether a person is liable for software defects under the PHG depends on whether software is a tangible good or not. Software itself is a mere intellectual achievement, and therefore – unlike hardware – its tangible substrate (eg magnetic tapes, discs) is intangible.

Consequently, it is generally considered[15] that a person is liable for damages only if the damage is caused by a defect in the hardware, but not in the software. The other less widely held view[16] is that since printed works are 'products' within the Directive the producer, the importer and the dealer are liable for mistakes with regard to the contents under the provisions of the PHG. For this reason, liability for defects of software under the PHG may arise.

6.3.5 *Damage to property*

Unlike the Directive, damage to property suffered by a businessman can also be recovered under the provisions of the PHG. The liability is not limited to damage to the property of a consumer. However, liability for the property damages of a businessman can be excluded by direct agreement with the (later) injured person (section 9).

6.3.6 *Precaution for coverage*

Producers and importers – although not dealers – are obliged to take precautions for the settlement of damage claims under the PHG in a way and to an extent which is customary in fair business practice. This can be done, for example, by entering into an insurance agreement or in another suitable way,

14 Koziol 'Zur Produkthaftung für landwirtschaftliche Erzeugnisse' RdW 1988, 154.

15 Welser *Produkthaftungsgesetz*, annotation 4 to §4; Welser in WB1 1988, 171; Andréewitch in ÖJZ 1988, 228; other opinion Fitz, Purtscheller and Reindl *Produkthaftung*, annotation 12 to §3.

16 Fitz, Purtscheller and Reindl *Produkthaftung*, annotation 12 to §3; Barchetti and Formanek *Produkthaftungsgesetz*, p 56.

so that compensation claims based on the PHG can be met. According to the report of the parliamentary committee on Justice[17] this obligation can also be met by maintaining a sufficient balance sheet reserve or by obtaining cover from a sufficiently wealthy person, for instance from a foreign parent company. Since a balance sheet reserve is, however, only an asset on paper which does not constitute an actual coverage fund, this could possibly be considered as insufficient by the courts.[18] The indications concerning the sufficiently wealthy person are so imprecise (for instance, it is not clear whether the sufficient wealthiness must exist when the covering note is given or when the damage occurs) that practically the only way of fulfilling this provision would be always to enter into an insurance agreement.

The Act does not provide for direct liability of the managers and of the senior executive officers, contrary to some legal drafts. Only the firm or company is bound to provide for a coverage provision. Managers, members of the executive or the supervisory board, 'procurists' and other senior officers of a firm which have an authoritative influence are still liable within the limits set by the regulations on negligent bankruptcy. In civil law, a violation of the duty to provide a coverage provision makes the responsible person liable according to ABGB section 1311 for the losses of creditors which would not have been suffered in the case of a proper coverage provision.[19]

6.3.7 *Transitional provisions*

According to section 19 the PHG does not apply to damage caused by products which were marketed before its commencement date, namely 1 July 1988. Even this transitional provision contains several problems.

The wording of the PHG seems to focus on marketing by the liable entity.[20] Therefore, if the importer markets a product after 1 July 1988, which he has bought before this date from the producer, then the importer but not the producer is liable under the PHG. The same must be valid for a dealer. When a dealer sells a defective, anonymous product after 1 July 1988 that he already had in stock before this date, he may be liable according to the PHG. He can still exempt himself from liability by naming his supplier, the national producer or the importer. However, according to this opinion these entities are not liable, since they marketed the product before 1 July 1988.

On the other hand, another opinion[1] is that marketing for the first time by the producer should be relevant, since the potentially liable entity could not adapt the already marketed goods to the stricter requirements of the PHG.

17 2. Bericht des Justizausschusses, 438 der Beilagen zu den Stenographischen Protokollen des Nationalrates XVII. GP (2nd report of the Committee for Juridical Matters).
18 Compare Fitz, Purtscheller and Reindl *Produkthaftung*, annotation 7 to §16.
19 Compare Karollus 'Zivil- und Strafrechtliches zur "Deckungsvorsorge" (§16 ProdHG)', RdW, 1988, 186; Roth 'Produkthaftung und Haftungsdurchgriff' GesRZ 1988, 119.
20 Fitz, Purtscheller and Reindl *Produkthaftung*, to §19; Posch in RdW 1988, 75; Posch 'Nochmals: Zur Übergangsbestimmung des Produkthaftungsgesetzes', RdW 1988, 378.
1 *Andréewitch* 'Zur Übergangsbestimmung im Produkthaftungsgesetz' RdW 1988, 283; Welser *Produkthaftungsgesetz*, annotation 2 to §19.

6.4 Optional provisions

Agricultural and forest products and game are not products under the definition of the PHG as long as they have not been initially processed.

The 'state of the art' defence is possible under the Austrian PHG.

The maximum amount of Ecu 70m for which a claim may be brought and which is optional pursuant to article 16 of the Directive does not apply in Austria.

Pursuant to the PHG, a businessman who has suffered damage to property is, in principle, also entitled to recover this damage from the producer. This is a considerable extension of the scope of liability compared to the provisions of article 9 of the Council Directive. However, it is possible to exclude the liability for such damage.

7. PRACTICAL EFFECTS EC PRODUCT LIABILITY LAW WILL HAVE ON VARIOUS BUSINESSES IN THE CHAIN OF SUPPLY OF PRODUCTS

The importer has the same liability as the producer. Therefore, it is necessary that he has more information on the product. The relationship between the producer and the importer has to become closer.

The subsidiary liability of the distributor and the dealer can in most cases be avoided by various precautions.

Probably the main effect will be the widening of the range of possible plaintiffs from the purchaser to any bystander, together with the exclusion of evidence of lack of fault.

8. COMPARISON OF THE EFFECTS OF PRODUCT LIABILITY LAW WITH THE PREVIOUS POSITION IN CONTRACT AND TORT

8.1 Previous legal situation

(a) The previous liability of producers for defective products was based on a legal contract with protective effects for third parties[2] or tort. The end-user of a product, who was linked to the producer by a chain of contracts, was entitled to sue the producer for damages based on contractual principles. The producer could avoid liability by proving that he took all necessary measures and therefore could not be found guilty. In addition, only the authorised user was protected, not the bystander. In connection with foreign products, it was often necessary to litigate abroad.

2 Compare Welser in WB1 1988, 166 with further reference; Bydlinski in Klang *Kommentar zum Allgemeinen bürgerlichen Gesetzbuch* (2nd edn) vol IV/2, pp 180 ff.

(b) Before the implementation of the Directive in Austria, the importer was to some extent liable for a product imported by him. This was especially true if he was the sole importer with a close organisational contact with the foreign producer, eg same business name or company group.[3] His duty – inspection of new goods – was in this case made stricter.

According to the Austrian Supreme Court[4] an importer must demand information about the production process from the producer who supplied him with the goods in order to warn against possible dangers. In Germany, these duties have recently been intensified by a judgment of the Federal Court of Justice (BGH), where an exclusive car importer was obliged to warn of all defective parts produced by third persons. However, this liability could be excluded by the proof of lack of fault by the importer.

(c) Under current law, the duties of inspection are very restricted for dealers who are not importers or general agents. Supervision and explanation are only required by law if the safety of the product – perhaps due to several accidents – appears doubtful.[5]

8.2 Changes in the legal situation

The previous legal situation is modified by the PHG in the following ways:

(a) Not only the producer but also the importer is liable. The standard of liability regarding distributors has also become stricter.
(b) Liability is extended to bystanders: liability under the PHG does not require a contractual relationship.
(c) Liability cannot be excluded by evidence of lack of fault.
(d) The exclusion of liability by agreement between the producer and the buyer of the products, who is the first in the distribution chain, is no longer possible (according to previous jurisdiction this was possible).
(e) It is only possible to exclude liability if a businessman (according to the Austrian Act for Protection of Consumers) suffers property damage.

8.3 Economic effects

Because of the higher risk of liability and the obligation to assure the payment of damages by entering into an insurance contract, higher costs arise for the importer.

According to the insurance industry, it is expected that the rates for a third party liability insurance (which also covers the risk of liability under the PHG) will be adjusted in the areas of trade and import in line with the rates of producers. In addition, in most cases an increase in the insurance sum will be necessary.

3 Austrian Sup Ct in EvBl 1981/159 = JBl 1982, 145.
4 Austrian Sup Ct in EvBl 1981/159 = JBl 1982, 145.
5 Compare Austrian Sup Ct in JBl 1982, 534.

9. RISK MANAGEMENT IN THE NEW ERA OF PRODUCT LIABILITY

9.1 Internal risk management

9.1.1 Quality control

Quality control should be tightened up by producers. The introduction of quality control on every level of the business scale does not seem to be necessary because of the high costs connected with quality control.

9.1.2 Documentation

In particular, because the state of the art defence is available, producers and – if possible – importers should have precise information on technical and scientific developments in their field. In addition it might be helpful to have documentation on the checks and quality control procedures which have been carried out by the producer. Documentation which proves that goods that were put into circulation have been checked for absence of defects might be accepted as proof of probability that the product was not defective at the time of distribution.

9.1.3 Record-keeping

For a dealer it is most important to keep records concerning the supplier and – if possible – the producer of a product so that the duty of identification can be met in an individual case. Although the absolute statutory period of limitation for claims under the PHG is ten years after the sale of the product, these records should be kept longer in order to be able to defend a claim of recourse. As it is possible for an importer to defend a recourse claim from a dealer by naming the foreign producer or his supplier, importers too should keep such records.

9.1.4 Warning notices, operating instructions and service manuals

As insufficient information may render a product defective and adequate information, on the other hand, may avoid defectiveness, warning notices and directions for use become a very important issue.

Producers should take care that warning notices cannot easily be removed and that directions for use contain all the necessary (but not more) information. Importers should check whether the translation of these instructions is correct. There are many instances of literal translations which make no sense to the user of the product and therefore can render the product defective.

9.2 Handling of consumer claims

9.2.1 Domestic jurisdiction

The injured person has the option not only to sue the importer but also the foreign producer. In the latter case it must – as a first step – be considered whether the requirements for the international jurisdiction of Austrian courts are fulfilled. The Austrian Code of Jurisdiction (JN) provides several venues for a specific action. If a venue for an action is found, Austrian jurisdiction is usually given.

Pursuant to JN section 92a damage claims may be made at the place where the act causing the damage occurred. As this act was the production of the defective product, which took place abroad, this provision cannot usually apply.

A foreign producer can be sued in Austria if he has property in Austria. It is sufficient that the foreign producer has claims based on contracts with Austrian partners. A problem that might arise in this connection is that judgments where the international jurisdiction is just based on the venue predicated on property are usually not recognised and enforced abroad (in this context it should be mentioned that Austria is not a member of the European Enforcement Agreement of 1968).

According to a ruling of the Austrian Supreme Court[6] domestic jurisdiction is also given if the foreign producer has permanent representation in Austria. In the case at hand the foreign producer had a general representative in Austria who was organised as an independent company and not incorporated in the organisation of the foreign producer.

9.2.2 *Private international law*

According to the Austrian Supreme Court[7] the following principles apply. If there exists a direct contractual relationship between the producer and the injured person, the law which applies on the contract also applies on the damage claims. In cases where there is no such direct contractual relationship, but just a chain of contracts which exists between the plaintiff and the defending party pursuant to section 48(2) of the Act on International Private Law (IPRG), the law of the most significant relationship applies. This is the law of the market for which the product was intended and where it was bought. If an innocent bystander is injured, the law of the place of the accident applies.

An Austrian producer who is sued by a foreign injured person before an Austrian court is not liable under the PHG but under the relevant law of the marketplace or the place of the accident.

9.3 Exclusion of liability and claims on contracts for indemnities

In order to decrease the risk of liability under the PHG the following contractual precautionary measures can be recommended to someone who imports goods into Austria.

(a) A contract with a foreign producer should provide that Austrian law is the governing law. Pursuant to Austrian international private law, Austrian law is applicable to a claim of recourse resulting from a case of product liability.

6 Austrian Sup Ct of 29 October 1987, 7 Ob 623/87; also Fitz, Purtscheller and Reindl *Produkthaftung*, introduction annotation 14.

7 Austrian Sup Ct of 29 October 1987, 7 Ob 623/87; also Welser *Produkthaftungsgesetz*, introduction annotation 5.

However, foreign international private law could provide for something different and thus foreign law could be applicable. Through an agreement based on Austrian law, the importer secures for himself the possibility of recourse against the foreign producer.

(b) If the importer does not buy from the manufacturer, but instead from a foreign middleman, he should attempt contractually to impose producers' liability on the middleman for product liability claims that the importer satisfies. By this means, the importer ensures that he has another person from which he can get recourse and he avoids the risk of not being able to identify the foreign producer.

(c) In contracts with foreign suppliers, a clause should also be included that the recourse claim, in addition to compensation amounts, includes all costs (especially court fees and lawyers' costs).

(d) The importer should also contractually oblige the foreign producer to supply him with all instructions for the presentation and use of the products and to make available to him all information (eg the state of technology at the moment of putting the product into circulation) necessary for the defence of a product liability claim.

(e) The importer should attempt to shift to the producer the risk of a justified change of safety expectations or of the state of engineering and technology between the marketing by the producer and the importer.

(f) The producer and the importer should make an agreement with their customers, who are entrepreneurs according to the KSchG, that they are not liable for material damage.

(g) A dealer can try to agree with his suppliers that they are liable to him in any case and cannot exempt themselves from this liability by naming their own supplier.

9.4 Insurance

9.4.1 Special provisions

The normal third party liability insurance which has been taken out by most of the companies in Austria covers the risks of product liability too. However, the rates for such insurance have been raised for importers and dealers to the level of producers.

A special insurance which covers just the product liability risk is not on the market in Austria.

9.4.2 Outline of the nature of cover

The general terms and conditions of the insurance companies (AHVB and EHVB 1986) cover all damage claims which are based on legal provisions (liability in tort and liability for breach of contract), the costs for the assessment of the damage and measures to avert the claim and the costs for measures which are necessary to reduce the damage.

Normally only damages which occurred in Austria are covered, but it is possible to ask for worldwide coverage. In this case the insurance companies usually exclude punitive and exemplary damages and grant coverage only insofar as a judgment can be enforced against the insured person.

Risks in connection with the production of airplanes and parts thereof are not covered.

9.4.3 Limits on cover including limitation of liability paid under contractual indemnities

The insurance sum is the maximum amount the insurer has to pay for a single event insured against. Furthermore, the liability of the insurer is limited to three times the amount of the insurance sum per year. Ten per cent of the damages, at least AS 5,000, have to be borne by the insured person.

Damage claims which are based on a contractual extension of liability are not covered. Therefore, any contractual indemnity should be discussed with the insurer first.

9.4.4 Serial damages

If several cases of damage have the same cause or similar causes they are considered as one event for insurance purposes, as long as there exists a legal, economic or technical connection between these similar causes.

9.4.5 Cover for recall of defective products

The insurance also covers the cost of measures which are necessary to reduce the damage. Therefore, costs for the recall of defective products are basically covered. However, attention has to be paid to the fact that in the case of a recall usually serial damage has occurred and the insurer will bear the costs of recall only up to the insurance sum. Furthermore, the insurer has the right to give instructions which have to be followed by the insured person.

9.5 Limitation of liability through corporate structure

9.5.1 Effect on whether a business should incorporate

If a business is incorporated the liability of the owners is restricted to the amount they have paid into the company. As the coverage provision of the PHG only applies to the company itself, and not to the owners or managers of the company, an incorporation might be a useful measure.

However, managers and owners who have an authoritative influence on the management (quasi-managers) are still liable within the limits set by the regulations on negligent bankruptcy. They can be liable to the creditors for the loss which the creditors would not have suffered in the case of a proper coverage.

To avoid this risk a product liability insurance should be entered into. To date, a maximum insurance sum of approximately AS 10m is considered customary in business dealings. Only in cases of dangerous products must this sum be increased accordingly.

If this precaution is observed, the incorporation of a business can minimise the risk for the owners and managers.

9.5.2 Liabilities of companies in groups

As mentioned above, an importer or dealer who has a close relationship to the producer is expected to have a more extensive knowledge of the product and has, therefore, pursuant to the provisions of the ABGB, a greater responsibility for the product.

9.5.3 Splitting of high risk activities from valuable assets

With regard to the considerations discussed in section 9.5.1, it would be very advisable to split high risk activities from valuable assets. However, care must be taken that the company which holds the valuable assets is neither producer nor importer.

CHAPTER III

Belgium

Lucien Simont Esq
Miss Manuela von Kuegelgen

Stibbe & Simont
Rue Henri Wafelaerts 47–51 (box 1)
1060 Brussels
Belgium

Tel ++ 32 2 533 5211
Fax ++ 32 2 533 5212

CHAPTER III

Belgium

1. INTRODUCTION

(1) The Directive is in the course of being implemented into Belgian law. The Ministry of Justice prepared preliminary draft legislation which it passed on to the Council of State (Conseil d'Etat) for consideration. A Bill was submitted to the Chamber of Representatives in July 1990 (Chambre des Représentants, the equivalent of the British House of Commons) and is likely to become law in April or May 1991. It will take the form of a specific Regulation and will probably not require amendments to the Civil Code. It is unlikely Belgium will implement any of the options in the Directive.

The new Regulation will not cause a fundamental revision of the existing system, since Belgian product liability law is already comparable to the strict liability concept set out in the Directive.[1]

(2) Product liability law is multi-disciplinary, involving elements of civil, commercial, economic, criminal and administrative law. Belgium, however, has never adopted a comprehensive Regulation on consumer protection. Most civil and commercial claims are dealt with under the provisions of the Civil Code dealing with a seller's contractual liability and a producer's liability in tort.

Until now, Belgian product liability law has largely been judge-made with provisions of the Civil Code being rudely construed in the courts so as to protect the consumer.

The 1964 Hague Convention introduced a Uniform Law for international sales of movable goods and provided a special set of rules applicable to sellers' warranties and delivery. This Uniform Law came into force in Belgium on 18 August 1972.

To date, the scope of Belgian product liability legislation has been limited to a few products or industries largely, for example, in the fields of foodstuffs, drugs and cosmetics. The enforcement of such laws has been limited, although the duties imposed on producers are backed up by criminal penalties and fines. Special regulations have introduced strict liability for certain activities.

Further, the Commercial Practices Act of 1971, which 'codified' fair commercial practices, has increased consumer protection through stricter regulation of advertising and by imposing a duty on suppliers to inform the public in respect of the price, quantity and composition of products. The Act provides a specific sanction where a supplier fails to meet its obligations: a plaintiff can issue proceedings requiring the supplier to cease the unlawful activity. This action is open to consumer groups, although in general Belgian court proceedings can

1 The new law implementing the Directive has been enacted by the Belgian Parliament while the present chapter was being typeset. An addendum summarising the main provisions of this new legislation appears at the end of this chapter.

only be brought by such groups on their members' behalf where the group itself has suffered damage. The Act was revised on 14 July 1991.

(3) Professional and trade bodies have imposed their own codes of practice on members engaged in the advertising and mail order business. Also, any trader may submit his products to the Belgian Quality Control and Informative Labelling Institute. Approval by the Institute entitles the producer to display its 'quality-control' label on his product.

(4) This chapter will be divided as follows:

Section 2: Contractual liability;
Section 3: Liability in tort;
Section 4: Special Regulations;
Section 5: The effects of the new law on liability arising from defective products;
Section 6: Risk management in the new area of product liability.

2. LIABILITY IN CONTRACT

2.1 Introduction

(1) The law relating to producers' liability under contracts of sale is mainly set out in articles 1609–1624 and 1641–1649 of the Civil Code. Those provisions refer to the seller's obligation: (a) to place in the buyer's control a product which conforms to its description in the contract, *and* (b) to ensure the purchaser's 'due possession' of it.

(2) Breach of the first obligation may lead to rescission of the contract, and a claim for damages, but any action based on such a breach will be dismissed if the purchaser accepted the object knowing of the defect.

(3) With regard to the second obligation, the seller will be liable to the purchaser if he furnishes a product which suffers from hidden defects which are detrimental or prejudicial to its normal use (article 1641). The purchaser may claim rescission of the contract or a reduction of the price. In addition, he will be entitled to additional compensation if the seller acted in 'bad faith', eg if he had knowledge of the defect and did not bring it to the purchaser's attention. In this way, Belgian courts have imposed stringent duties on professional sellers and manufacturers.

(4) Finally, if the purchaser was induced to enter into the contract by reason of a substantial mistake (ie if the mistake relates to an essential point of the contract, without which the sale would not have been concluded) he may avoid the agreement. The purchaser, however, will only be entitled to damages if the seller has committed a 'culpa in contrahendo' (ie has made a negligent pre-contractual misrepresentation) or a fraudulent misrepresentation.

2.2 Warranty for hidden defects

2.2.1 Definition and characteristics of the defect

(1) Pursuant to article 1641 of the Civil Code, the seller is bound to warrant hidden defects in the object sold which render it inappropriate for its intended

use or which would restrict its application to the extent that the purchaser would not have bought it or would have paid a lesser price if he had had knowledge of the defect(s).

(2) The purchaser discovering a hidden defect and suing the seller therefore need not prove fault on the latter's part.[2] He only has to establish that the object sold is affected by a 'vice redhibitoire', a hidden and abnormal characteristic of the product which is unknown to the purchaser, exists at the time of the sale, and the existence of which is seriously detrimental to the purpose for which the product was required (article 1641 of the Civil Code).[3] It is generally accepted that the defect renders the thing sold unfit for its intended use when the thing is improperly designed or manufactured, when it is incapable of fulfilling its function, or when the product endangers life, health or property.

(3) Quite what constitutes a 'defect' is unsettled in Belgian law. For a long time it has not been clear whether a defect must be inherent in the object supplied or whether a functional defect can also give rise to a warranty under article 1641 of the Civil Code (a functional defect consists of a hidden characteristic which is not structural but which nonetheless renders the product unfit for its purpose). The Supreme Court of Belgium has decided that a hidden defect is a defect which renders the object unfit for the use to which the buyer intended to put it, even if it does not affect the object intrinsically.[4] It is still open to argument whether or not a functional defect meets the seller's obligation of delivery,[5] but nevertheless the existence of a functional defect in a product is likely to influence the nature of the remedies granted by the court[6]. In the case of an action based on a breach of the obligation of delivery, the court can require the seller to replace or repair the object sold, while in the case of an action based on a breach of warranty for hidden defects, such performance could not be imposed on the seller.

(4) The use for which the product was intended must have been known by the seller. The seller is, however, deemed to know the normal use of the object sold[7] and any use he guaranteed in any advertising or in negotiating the contract.[8]

In this respect, professional sellers must bear in mind that their advertising must comply with the Commercial Practices Act of 1971, which forbids advertising capable of inducing the public to mistake the identity, nature, composition, origin or characteristics of a product, as well as its possible advantages or uses.[9]

(5) The seller is not bound to warrant where the defect was known to the purchaser or was not hidden at the time of the sale.

2 J L Fagnart *Product Liability* Brussels 1977, p 9, no 10; Supreme Court, 4 May 1939, Pas 1939, I, 225.

3 It is sometimes stated that the defect for which it is intended must be grave. In fact, the defect will always be grave if it *seriously* affects the purpose intended.

4 Supreme Court, 18 November 1971, Pas 1972, I, 258.

5 L Simont 'La notion fonctionnelle de vice caché: un faux problème?' *Etudes en hommage à René Dekkers* (1982) pp 331–342; L Simont, J De Gavre and P A Foriers 'Chronique de jurisprudence: Les contrats spéciaux' RCJB 1985, p 149.

6 J Van Ryn and J Heenen *Principes de droit commercial*, vol III, 1st edn, no 1717.

7 If the object is sought by the purchaser for a particular purpose which is not its normal use, he should inform the seller of such purpose, otherwise he will not be entitled to warranty if the object proves unfit for the use he intended.

8 J van Ryn and J Heenen, fn 6, above, 2nd edn, in no 696.

9 J L Fagnart, note under Supreme Court, 28 February 1980, RCJB 1983, p 235.

The seller's warranty of the object sold, whether express or implied, does not extend to cover apparent defects where they could have been revealed by the purchaser's inspection on receipt of the goods.

The hidden nature of the defect will be taken into consideration by the courts as will the degree of specialist knowledge possessed by the purchaser. No particularly high level of scrutiny is to be expected from a private purchaser.[10] The defect will nevertheless be considered to be *apparent* when it should have been discovered by a summary inspection (eg if the condition or the nature of the merchandise permitted an easy examination by the purchaser), when it is inherent to the nature of the object (eg a secondhand car could not be expected to perform as well as a new one), or when the seller has declared its existence at the time of the sale.[11]

(6) Finally, the defect must be present (at least potentially) at the time the object was acquired. If there is a dispute on this point, it is normally up to the purchaser to prove that the defect existed before title to the property passed.[12] This question will often require expert evidence.

2.2.2 *Sanctions*

(1) Where the requirements of article 1641 of the Civil Code are fulfilled, the purchaser may bring an action claiming rescission of the contract (action redhibitoire) or a reduction in the sale price (action estimatoire).

He cannot claim the repair or replacement of the product as this would constitute substantially different performance from that in the original contract, and the seller for his part cannot offer such performance to escape from his liability.[13]

If the court finds that the defect is sufficiently serious, the plaintiff will succeed even though the seller acted in good faith not knowing of the defect.

The obligation of the seller to warrant due possession is a 'warranty obligation' (obligation de garantie) the breach of which entitles the purchaser to compensation, within the limits outlined above, even if the seller has not been negligent.

Proceedings based on the seller's warranty obligations can also be brought against a *remote vendor*.[14] Sub-contractors therefore have a right of action against manufacturers, as set out in article 1615 of the Civil Code (the obligation of delivery includes the object of the sale and all its accessories). Sub-purchasers will, however, be dependent on the terms of the contract entered into by their own vendor and all defences (eg limitations, periods, contractual warranties, disclosure of the defect, etc) available to their vendor will be capable of being used

10 T Bourgoignie 'La sécurité des consommateurs et l'introduction de la directive communautaire du 25 juillet 1985 sur la responsibilité du fait des produits défectueux' JT 1987, pp 357 ff.
11 P A Foriers 'Garantie et conformité dans le droit belge de la vente', *Les ventes internationales de marchandises*, Paris 1981, p 210.
12 L Fredericq *Traité de droit commercial*, vol III, p 169.
13 Supreme Court, 21 November 1976, Pas 1975, I, 322; J Limpens *La vente en droit belge*, no 400.
14 H de Page *Traité de droit civil belge*, vol IV, no 186.

against them.[15] Further, their action against the original vendor will be dismissed if the defect did not exist at the time of the first sale.[16]

(2) Besides rescission of the contract or a reduction in the price, further compensation can be sought by the purchaser if the seller was aware of the defect and did not disclose it. In order to succeed in an action for damages in these circumstances the seller has to prove, besides the defect, the harm he has sustained and a causal link between the defect and the damage.[17] He should also give evidence of the fact that the seller actually knew of the defect's existence. On this point, the Belgian authorities have developed a special set of rules for professional sellers and to manufacturers, which we will now examine.

2.3 Special duties binding professional sellers

2.3.1 Introduction

(1) As a result of well-established court decisions, professional sellers are presumed to be acting in 'bad faith' even if they have no knowledge of the defect affecting their product. This rule applies to manufacturers, suppliers and retailers alike. The main consequences of such a presumption are to oblige the seller to compensate the purchaser for all losses he has suffered (see section 4, below) and to limit the validity of exclusion and limitation clauses in contracts (see section 5, below).

(2) Despite the case law it is legally unnecessary for professional sellers to be 'presumed to be acting in bad faith',[18] since it is the duty of any professional not only to deliver goods that are defect-free, but also to be aware of the defects affecting the product sold and to advise customers of the defects and possible dangers inherent in them.

Professional sellers thus assume two specific obligations:

(a) a duty of inspection and of skill; and
(b) a duty of information.

2.3.2 Duty of skill

(3) The duty of inspection and skill is not absolute and the Belgian courts will treat the seller as discharged from this duty if he can prove his 'invincible ignorance', ie that he could not have discovered the defect in the goods sold. This means that the presumption of 'bad faith' is rebuttable, contrary to the jurisprudential rule in France.[19] This statement of the law has traditionally been upheld by the Belgian Supreme Court,[20] although in a more recent decision it held that 'the seller is bound to pay compensation for defects in the goods unless

15 L Simont, J De Gavre 'Examen de jurisprudence: Les contrats spéciaux' RCJB 1976, p 423.
16 T Bourgoignie 'Le traitement des produits défectueux en droit belge: pratique et perspectives' JT 1976, p 509.
17 J L Fagnart 'La responsabilité du fait des produits à l'approche du grand marché' DAOR 1990, 17 p 26, no 47.
18 P A Foriers 'Chronique de jurisprudence: Les contrats commerciaux' JCB 1987, pp 46 and 47.
19 P A Foriers 'Garantie et conformité en droit belge de la vente', p 213.
20 Supreme Court, 4 May 1939, Pas 1939, I, 223; Supreme Court, 13 November 1959, Pas 1960, I, 313; Supreme Court, 6 October 1961, Pas 1962, I, 152.

he establishes the absolute undiscoverability of the defect'.[1] This Supreme Court decision could be construed as a reinforcement of the evidential requirements that a seller must meet in order to escape his liability, since the undiscoverable character of the defect presumes that the seller will have to prove that the current state of technical knowledge made the defect indiscernible.

The 'development risks' defence set out in the Directive is less stringent than a defence based on 'invincible ignorance', since it is satisfied if the seller is able to demonstrate that a normally diligent professional placed in the same circumstances could not have discovered the defect whatever steps he could have taken at the time of putting the product into circulation. However, many authors consider that the 'invincible ignorance' defence has not been superseded by the Supreme Court.

The duty of inspection and of skill will however be stronger to the extent that the seller has manufactured the product or is 'specialised' in that product line.[2]

The presumption of 'bad faith' will not apply to a sale concluded by professionals outside the scope of their normal activity.

2.3.3 Duty of information

(4) The duty of information binding professional sellers does not arise from the Civil Code, but has been progressively defined in Belgian case law.[3] A private purchaser will normally rely on the skill and statements of the seller. The duty of information rests upon this legitimate confidence and is conceived as a means to compensate for the inequality of knowledge of the product existing between buyer and seller. The seller is therefore obliged to draw the attention of the buyer to all substantial conditions of the agreement, ie to all elements which could have influenced the buyer to enter into the contract.[4]

(5) Where a purchaser is not endowed with a particular skill, both the manufacturer and the seller have a special duty of information[5] imposed upon them, especially if they are in a specialised line of business. Such sellers and manufacturers are obliged to supply accurate advice on the possible uses and defects or dangers (as they are deemed to know them) of the product.[6] Inaccurate or unclear information or an over-optimistic presentation of the product will be regarded as a tort.

Accordingly, manufacturers and sellers would be well advised to include on the product itself and/or on its packaging precise and detailed instructions and warnings as to:

1 Supreme Court, 6 May 1977, Pas, I, 907.

2 H Cousy *Problemen van Produkteannsprakelijklheid*, Brussels 1978, no 168.

3 It should, however, be stressed that special Regulations require specific information to be given to the consumer (eg for foodstuffs, drugs, cosmetics). Article 498 of the Belgian Penal Code punishes false statements concerning the quality or the origin of the product sold, as a criminal offence. Besides, as noted above, the Commercial Practices Act of 1971 forbids advertising that may induce the public into error.

4 Note M Denève under Court of Appeal Brussels, 16 June 1970, Entr et Dr 1973, p 154; Le Tourneau 'Conformité et garantie dans la vente d'objets mobiliers corporels' RTDC 1980, p 231.

5 J L Fagnart, note under Supreme Court, 28 February 1980, RCJB 1983, p 235.

6 Court of Appeal Brussels, 27 November 1963, JT 1964, p 75.

(a) the possible uses of the product (at least its normal uses);
(b) possible dangers that may arise from its use; and
(c) prohibited uses.

The more precise and accurate the instructions, the less rigorous the liability.

So far as more complex materials or products are concerned, such as computers or software, the seller must also supply information as to the potential applications of the product and its fitness for the purpose intended.[7] However, the seller is not absolutely bound to do this. He will only be held liable for breach of obligation if he has guaranteed a specific application of a complex product.[8]

(6) The duty of information is, however, less stringent in practice than it initially appears. A minimal degree of skill is expected on the part of the consumer.[9] Further, the seller is not liable if the purchaser misuses the product or uses it for purposes outside its normal use and which the purchaser did not specify when he bought the product.[10] A professional purchaser is deemed to be aware of the dangers inherent in the purchased product and of its possible uses, provided the product is related to his business.[11]

(7) According to these principles, the seller's duty of information has to be evaluated 'in concreto', taking into account all relevant circumstances including among others the possible negligence of the purchaser and the content of instructions accompanying the product.[12] In addition, the Belgian courts are more flexible if the seller did not specialise in selling the kind of product that caused the harm.[13]

(8) Sanctions relating to the duty of information are of three sorts:

(a) If the lack of information produces a justifiable and substantial mistake, the purchaser can sue the seller in order to have the contract declared void.[14] Further compensation will, however, not be awarded unless the seller is guilty of a 'culpa in contrahendo', ie a negligent pre-contractual misrepresentation.[15] This will often be the case where the seller or manufacturer was a specialist, as such people have a higher duty to give accurate information about their products.
(b) If the purchaser has been induced to enter into the contract because of a fraudulent misrepresentation (ie 'an intentionally false statement')

7 Dommering – Van Rongen L 'Produkteaansprakelijklheid en software' *Computerr*, 1988, pp 227–232; *Le Droit des contrats informatiques* Centre de recherches informatique et droit des facultés universitaires de Namur, 1983 p 137.
8 Commercial Tribunal of Brussels, 18 February 1980, RGAR 1981, no 10274.
9 P A Foriers 'Garantie et conformité en droit belge de la vente' cited above in fn 19 p 51. Supreme Court, 29 March 1976, RGAR 1977, no 9772.
10 Commercial Tribunal of Verviers, 30 November 1983, Jur Liège 1984, p 228.
11 Civil Tribunal of Liège, 23 December 1955, RGAR 1956, no 5780; T Bourgoignie 'La traitement des produits défectueux en droit belge: pratiques et perspectives' JT 1976, p 511.
12 J Ghestin *Conformité et garantie dans la vente* (Paris, 1983) pp 22 ff.
13 H Cauvin 'La responsabilité aquilienne du vendeur professionnel de produits dangereux ou insatisfaisants' RGAR 1976, no 9628.
14 H De Page *Traité de droit civil belge*, vol IV, no 171.
15 P Van Ommeslaghe 'Examen de jurisprudence: Les obligations' RCJB 1986, p 147, no 60.

the contract will be void and damages will be awarded to the purchaser.[16] If the fraudulent misrepresentation had an effect only on a term of the contract (eg the price) the purchaser will only be entitled to claim damages, not the avoiding of the agreement. Silence will not of itself constitute a negligent or fraudulent misrepresentation. However, where a party has a 'duty to speak', silence will be considered at least as negligent.[17]

(c) Finally, if the product appears to be affected by hidden defects, or if the lack of information produces a product which is unfit for the purpose intended, an action can be brought under articles 1641 ff of the Civil Code. The contract will thus be void or the price reduced and the seller will be obliged to compensate for losses or injuries sustained by the plaintiff.

(9) The previous sanctions must be clearly distinguished from claims based on the seller's obligation to deliver a product that conforms with the quantity and quality specifications set out in the contract.[18] Breach of such contractual obligations entitles the purchaser to rescission of the contract and a claim for damages if required. Such actions are only available where the product has not been approved by the purchaser.[19] Moreover, a breach of an obligation of delivery gives rise in commercial sales to particular sanctions. In such cases the purchaser is entitled to compensation for the seller's default by buying other products from another seller at the full cost and expense of the first seller.[20] This 'replacement option' (faculté de remplacement) must, however, be exercised at the purchaser's own risk, as a court may decide that the breach was not sufficiently important to set the first contract aside. In such a case, the court might only permit a claim for a reduction of the price.[1]

2.4 Damages

(1) Unlike the position where liability for a tort has been established, compensation for breach of contract is only available for foreseeable damage. This principle of foreseeability has, however, been much extended.[2] The whole damage suffered by the plaintiff must be compensated if the defendant is found to have intended the damage caused. Moreover, the possibility of damage occurring must be foreseeable, but not its extent.

(2) As explained in more detail below, a plaintiff may recover either for 'patrimonial' or 'extra-patrimonial losses'. In theory, the remedy must cover the whole loss without limitation but Belgian courts usually allow very limited damages to compensate for 'moral harm', eg pain and suffering etc.

16 P Van Ommeslaghe, fn 15, above, at p 67, no 17.
17 J L Fagnart in RCJB 1983, (cited above in fn 5 p 52) p 237; Court of Appeal Mons, 18 April 1978, Pas 1978, II, 71.
18 Court of Appeal Mons, 21 June 1989, Pas 1990, vol II, p 50.
19 H De Page *Traité de droit civil belge*, vol IV, 3rd edn, no 113.
20 J Van Ryn and J Heenen *Principes de droit commercial*, vol III, no 1702.
1 J Van Ryn and J Heenen, fn 20, above.
2 J Hayoit de Termicourt 'Dol et faute lourde en matière d'inexécution des contrats' JT 1957, p 601; Supreme Court, 23 February 1928, Pas 1928, I, 85.

(3) Patrimonial losses include personal injuries, such as physical injury, loss of income and loss of earning capacity. Capacity to earn will normally be evaluated on the basis of expert evidence. Patrimonial harm relates to material damage caused to business or private assets belonging to the victim. The damage to the product itself may also be compensated under the present law. Compensation for damage to property extends to the replacement value of the object. Intangible losses including pure economic losses such as loss of profit, of trade, of clientele or business interruption are also recoverable under Belgian law.

(4) Extra-patrimonial losses relate to 'moral harm', ie non-physical loss or damage sustained by a victim or his relatives. There are numerous types of moral harm. Compensation could, for example, be claimed for 'aesthetic suffering', injury to reputation, grief suffered as a result of the death of a loved one, etc. As has already been noted, Belgian courts are usually reluctant to grant extended compensation for such losses.

(5) The damage claimed must have occurred, or be certain to occur. Hypothetical damage is not actionable. Harm occurring later is recoverable provided its future occurrence is unquestionable.[3]

(6) The measure of damages will be determined according to different criteria. The plaintiff must be restored to his former position and, to this end, the court must take into account all the circumstances of the case and evaluate the total damage suffered as at the date of judgment.[4] If the amount of damages cannot be assessed on the basis of precise and objective criteria the court will proceed to estimate them 'ex aequo et bono', ie what appear fair and reasonable.[5] As far as personal injuries are concerned, judicial expert evidence will often be required.

(7) When considering which parties may be entitled to compensation, apart from the 'victim' and the victim's relatives (if they give evidence of their indirect moral or material harm),[6] insurers and employers may, to a certain extent, recover sums paid to the victim under the employment or insurance contract.

2.5 Causal nexus

(1) According to well-established case law, the causal link between the 'primary fact' giving rise to liability and the damage is established when the plaintiff proves that but for the 'primary fact' (negligence, defect, etc) the damage would not have occurred. This principle applies in tort and in contract.

(2) This theory, called the theory of 'equivalence of conditions' (théorie de l'équivalence des conditions) implies that where the damage occurred by reason of concurrent causes,[7] eg a defect and the negligence of a third party, the manufacturer or the seller and the third party will be liable for the whole

3 Supreme Court, 8 January 1974, Pas 1974, I, 474.

4 Supreme Court, 2 May 1974, Pas 1974, I, 907; Supreme Court, 17 May 1978, Pas 1978, I, 1063.

5 However, the plaintiff shall not be entitled to compensation 'ex aequo et bono' if such objective elements existed but he failed to produce them.

6 Relatives (descendants or children, for example) may only recover damages if they can demonstrate that their claim is based on tort. They may not start court proceedings in contract since there is no privity of contract (A Weill 'La Relativité des Conventions', RCJB 1962, p 178).

7 That is to say, 'causes acting contemporaneously and together, causing injury which would not have resulted without either'.

damage[8] jointly and severally.[9] However, if the plaintiff has also been negligent, the defendant may invoke this in order to obtain an apportionment of the liability.[10]

(3) As has been noted, compensation extends to all immediate and consequential losses. However, the plaintiff will not be able to recover for damage which is too remote or beyond the defendant's control (eg the death of a fireman as a result of a fire caused by a defective product).

2.6 Exclusion of contractual warranties

(1) Generally speaking, contractual provisions restricting or excluding liability are valid unless:[11]

(a) they contravene mandatory regulations;
(b) they are so extensive in their scope that the seller's obligation is rendered ineffective; or
(c) they extend to cover intentional wrongs.

Contractual provisions contained in standard terms and conditions of sale (conditions générales de vente) are only valid if they are expressly approved by the party not seeking to impose such terms.

(2) As far as product liability is concerned, clauses limiting or excluding liability are valid unless the seller actually knew of a defect. It has been said that professional sellers by reason of their particular position are supposed to know of the defects affecting the products they sell or manufacture.

(3) The second practical consequence of this presumption of knowledge of defects is thus to avoid disclaimer of liability on the basis of contractual limitations. This system is very similar to that provided by the Directive although, under Belgian law, manufacturers and sellers are allowed to invoke such contractual provisions provided they prove their complete ignorance of the defect, having taken all steps to check for the defect.

(4) However, some provisions remain particularly useful in order to limit product liability.[12]

8 Supreme Court, 18 June 1973, Pas 1973, I, 969; Supreme Court, 15 February 1978, Pas 1978, I, 694.

9 In this respect, Belgian courts distinguish joint and several liability from the so-called 'liability in solidum'. The latter applies to concurrent acts of negligence, the former to 'common' negligence or concurrent criminal offences. The differences between these two are, however, of minor importance.

10 Unlike the provisions of the Directive, the negligence of a third party for whom the plaintiff was liable (ie an employee) does not extenuate the producer's liability.
Moreover, the plaintiff's pathological predispositions or prior illness shall not influence liability unless they would by themselves have caused the injury.

11 L Cornelis 'Les clauses d'exonération de responsabilité couvrant la faute personnelle' RCJB 1982, pp 200 ff; Brussels Court of Appeal, 4 March 1988, JT 1988, 624.

12 F Walschot 'De invloed van de E G Richtlijn produktaanprakelijkheid op de algemene contractvoorwaarden' TPR 1988, pp 763 ff and especially pp 782 ff.

(a) Provisions defining the limitation period within which claims may be brought are valid if they are reasonable – that is to say, if they are not of such a nature that they would exonerate the seller from his liability.
(b) Provisions disclosing the defects prevent further actions for damages or rescission of the contract. Such clauses have to be precise: a vague or broad reference to the 'possible' defects would be construed as a disguised restriction of liability.
(c) Clauses imposing special duties on the purchaser, such as periodic inspection and control, will also be advantageous for the producer, as a breach thereof eventually limits the seller's liability if the damage was partially due to the purchaser's negligence. Besides, provisions defining uses and dangers of the product sold will restrict the seller's liability if the purchaser failed to comply with the warnings and instructions accompanying the product.

(5) Under the new law to be introduced pursuant to the Directive, all contractual provisions aiming at restricting liability to the consumer will be void. However, such clauses remain valid, in the limits outlined above, between parties who are jointly and severally liable under the provisions of the Directive. Further, in order to reduce his liability to a certain extent, the producer may preserve provisions defining either the losses caused by the defect (since national rules relating to the causal nexus continue to apply) or the negligence of the purchaser.[13] Those clauses, however, will probably be subject to a narrow construction in Belgian courts.

2.7 Limitation period

(1) Court proceedings based on article 1641 ff of the Civil Code must be brought within a 'brief period'.

(2) The starting-point and duration of the 'brief period' is not set out in the Code and is left to the court's discretion. In practice it is likely to depend upon the nature of the defect, the type of product and local commercial customs and practices.[14]

(3) The courts generally permit the brief period to be suspended during the negotiation of an out-of-court settlement, provided those negotiations are 'serious'.

(4) The 'brief period' requirement is necessary to preserve evidence and to prevent the courts having to hear ill founded late claims.

The lack of a unified limitation period is, however, a source of judicial uncertainty, as each court will assess the 'brief period' with more or less severity. However, it is unlikely that the new law implementing the Directive will give rise to an amendment of article 1648 of the Civil Code.

13 F Walschot, fn 12 above.

14 Supreme Court, 23 March 1984, RW 1984–1985, 127; M Fallon 'L'adaptation de la responsabilité du fait des produits à la directive européenne du 25 juillet 1985' RGAR 1987, no 11245, p 7. Depending on such criteria, the limitation period will start to run from the discovery of the defect or from the date of delivery.

2.8 Vicarious liability

The seller is liable to the buyer for negligence committed by his agents in the course of manufacturing or selling his products.[15]

The Supreme Court does not regard an agent as a party to the contract of sale in his own right. The agent may be liable in tort but only if the conditions for bringing an action in contract and tort are satisfied.

The 'agent of execution' (agent d'éxécution) is not therefore contractually bound to the victim, and may not be sued in contract.[16]

2.9 General remarks concerning the burden of proof

Under Belgian law, it is normally for the plaintiff to establish the merits of his claim. The burden of proof, however, is reversed to a certain extent insofar as product liability is concerned, since case law almost presumes a producer's liability unless he proves an 'act of God'. Nevertheless, the plaintiff needs to give convincing evidence of the defect, the damage and the causal link between the defect and the damage. The proof of the causal link may also be arrived at by a process of eliminating inadequate causes of the damage.

2.10 Builder's liability

(1) Since the Directive excludes immovable goods from its scope of application, common rules of the Civil Code relating to building contracts will remain applicable to building contractors.[17]

(2) Pursuant to article 1792 of the Civil Code, 'if a building is destroyed totally or partially by reason of a defect [whether apparent or hidden] in its construction, or the geology of its site, the architect and contractor will be responsible for the same for up to ten years'.

(3) The defect referred to by this provision must significantly impair the building's strength and stability. The limitation period of ten years runs from the time approval of the building (réception définitive) was given by the owner (maître de l'ouvrage).[18]

(4) Moreover, under a well-established line of authorities confirmed by a Supreme Court decision of 1985,[19] the contractor and architect are liable for *minor hidden defects* affecting the building. That is to say, defects which would not give rise to a breach of the provisions of article 1792 of the Civil Code

15 Supreme Court, 21 June 1979, JT 1979, p 675.

16 Supreme Court, 8 April 1983, RW 1983–1984, col 163; R O Dalcq and F Glansdorff 'Chronique de jurisprudence: La responsabilité' RCJB 1980, p 357.

17 Provided liability for hidden defects will be governed by articles 1641 ff of the Civil Code if the building was sold and provided strict liability will be applicable to the building's defective movable components.

18 Supreme Court, 4 March 1977, RW 1976–77, col 2413.

19 Supreme Court, 25 October 1985, Pas 1986, I, 226; P A Foriers 'La responsabilité de l'entrepreneur après réception: réflexions à propos de l'arrêt de la Court de cassation du 25 octobre 1986', ED 1988, pp 261 ff.

discussed above. No precise limitation period has, however, emerged from the case law on this point.[20] Probably a 'brief period', as referred to under article 1648 of the Civil Code, should apply for equitable reasons. Indeed, were the ordinary limitation period to be applicable, which is 30 years, the contractor would face greater exposure to claims in respect of minor imperfections than to major defects.[1]

2.11 Guarantees concerning services

(1) Since services are excluded from the Directive, the ordinary law of contract will continue to be applied to contracts for services. However, the rules which govern the provision of services are very similar to those applying to sale of goods. The professional contractor must, therefore, not only comply with the standards applicable in his field of activity and inform and advise his customers, but also anticipate and, where necessary, warn customers against any damage.

(2) The Supreme Court appears to consider that, insofar as the supply of services is accompanied by the delivery of goods, the rules of the guarantee for hidden defects will apply. In one case, a gas system had been installed in an 'injudicious' way. The court considered that the fault in the way the delivered goods were installed constituted a hidden defect in the article, causing it to fall within the conditions of guarantee on the basis of article 1641 of the Civil Code.[2] We are, therefore, witnessing a growing convergence between legal guarantees which apply to sales, and those which apply to contracts for services.[3]

3. LIABILITY IN TORT

3.1 Introduction

(1) Belgian tort liability is governed by the notion of fault. The theory of 'created risk' or 'profit risk'[4] has, indeed, never been generally adopted, although strict liability has occasionally been provided by specific Regulations, eg in the field of nuclear exploitation.

(2) So far as a producer's liability is concerned, the general rules set out in the Civil Code apply. A 'consumer' harmed by a defective product must establish negligence on the producer's part; in other words, a failure to meet the general duty of care or the breach of a legal obligation.

(3) A consumer has no contractual recourse against a manufacturer or seller if he did not buy the product from them. Such a person stands in a weaker position than the immediate purchaser, since liability does not arise from the mere fact that the product was defective and caused harm to the plaintiff.

20 P A Foriers, fn 19, above, at p 267.
1 P A Foriers, fn 20, above.
2 Supreme Court, 6 May 1977, Pas 1977, I, p 907.
3 M Fallon 'La cour de cassation et la responsabilité liée aux bieris de consommation' RCJB 1979, p 171. The European Commission has now elaborated a draft directive on liability concerning services (see OJ 18.01.1991).
4 According to these theories, which have been developed in France, anyone who creates an activity generating risks or makes a profit out of such activity will be liable for all damages caused to third parties, even if no negligence can be proved on his part.

(4) The purchaser may, however, have an interest in bringing an action in tort, for example, if the 'brief period' provided by article 1648 has expired, or if the defect was apparent.[5] However, where a contract was entered into, conditions allowing an action in tort are very restrictive under the Belgian Supreme Court. In order for such a tort action to be successful, the breach of contract must be a failure to meet the general duty of care or constitute a criminal offence, and (provided the breach is not also a criminal offence) the damage suffered by the plaintiff must be distinct from the contractual damage thereby caused.[6] Such a requirement is, of course, very hard to establish. An action based on tort is liable to be struck out if the parties to the action were also contracting parties.

(5) The provisions relating to extra-contractual liability are contained in articles 1382–1386 bis of the Civil Code. As far as product liability is concerned, (which in this context means liability in tort for defective products causing harm to a third party with whom the producer has no contractual relationship), articles 1382 and 1383 will be the main grounds for actions brought by 'consumers'. Under articles 1382 and 1383, any act causing injury compels the wrongdoer to pay compensation for injuries incurred whether by reason of a positive act or by negligence or lack of caution. This type of action is open to private consumers as well as to professionals so that material prejudice caused to *professional* assets are recoverable.

Article 1384 al 1 relating to the liability of a bailee for a defective product under his control will rarely apply to the producer, since the product is unlikely to be under his control when it causes the harm. The custodian, however, will have recourse against the producer if he is found liable for the damage caused by the defect in the product. A producer will also be liable under article 1384 al 3 if the defective product was negligently made or the information negligently given by the producer's employees acting in the course of their duties.

3.2 Liability for fault

(1) The notion of negligence has been extended by case law to include a form of professional misconduct. As a general rule, manufacturers and suppliers owe the public a duty of care and diligence resting upon public reliance on the producer's skill.[7]

(2) Producers must avoid manufacturing and marketing products threatening to life, health or property. They should therefore be aware of technical and scientific progress within their field of activities and adapt the manufacture of their products accordingly. Failure to meet this duty will constitute negligence, even if a specific wrong is not established.[8] A producer's liability, however, is to be evaluated in the light of all the circumstances and depends upon the defendant's particular skills. The greater the degree of skill, the

5 For a general comparison between contractual and tortious liability, R O Dalcq *Traité de la responsabilité civile*, Brussels 1967, nos 32 and ff.

6 Supreme Court, 15 September 1977, RCJB 1978, p 428; R O Dalcq and F Glansdorff 'Chronique de jurisprudence: La responsabilité' RCJB 1980, p 359. Supreme Court, 21 June 1979, JT 1979, p 675. Supreme Court, 8 April 1983, RW 1983–1984, col 163; R O Dalcq 'Chronique de jurisprudence: La responsabilité extracontractuelle' RCJB 1976, p 30.

7 T Bourgoignie, JT 1976, p 511.

8 M Fallon *Les accidents de la consommation et le droit*, Bruxelles 1982, p 84.

stricter the liability and the higher the duty of care. Consequently, a manufacturer carries a heavier obligation as he is responsible for the construction and design of the product. Suppliers for their part must avoid alterations of the product and ensure, for example, proper storage, but may not under current tort law be held liable for damage caused by a negligent manufacturer.

(3) Manufacturers must comply with public safety regulations.[9] Breach of a legal obligation constitutes the most obvious case of tort. However, merely conforming to statutory regulations does not exclude a finding of fault, and will not discharge a manufacturer from his liability.[10] For example, even if a product is consistent with a standard embodied in a statute, it could be considered as defective and the manufacturer could be held liable, unless the defect is the result of having complied with a mandatory regulation or public policy.

(4) If a product is inherently or potentially dangerous, appropriate warnings must be given to the public.[11] The manufacturer must use all precautions available to reduce the risks of an accident. Moreover, he should comply with regulations applying to advertising, such as the Commercial Practice Act mentioned above and specific legislation in relation to particular products. Also, when the manufacturer discovers a defect in the product, he must take adequate steps to prevent the damage (eg he should give warnings and notices in the newspaper, recall the product, etc).

(5) It follows from the above principles that manufacturers (and, to a certain extent, suppliers) owe a special duty of care and that their negligence is presumed.[12] Such principles are similar to those applying in contract. Causation and damages will be evaluated in the same way in contract and tort. Producers, however, will never be allowed to exclude their liability to end-users as they can with contractual provisions as no privity of contract exists between plaintiffs and themselves. Nevertheless, they will be discharged, along with the seller, if they demonstrate either their diligent professional conduct, a fault of the plaintiff or the non-existence of the defect at the time the product was put onto the market.

(6) The main difference between tort and contract lies in the limitation periods. In the case of an action in tort based on articles 1382 and 1383 of the Civil Code, the limitation period is theoretically *30 years* after the plaintiff becomes aware (or should have become aware) of the occurrence of the damage.[13] It is obvious, however, that an action brought, for example, 20 years after the damage occurred, will probably be dismissed for lack of evidence. The limitation period is varied, however, if the negligence constitutes a *criminal*

9 R O Dalcq fn 5, above, in no 301.

10 R O Dalcq 'Responsabilité quasi délictuelle et normes techniques et professionnelles' in *Le Droit des normes professionnelles et techniques* (Colloque Spa 1985) p 482. W Van Geeven 'Aansprakelijkheid voor schade veroorzaakt door produkten' SEW 1970, p 271.

11 Court of Appeal Brussels, 10 December 1963, JT 1964, p 504.

12 M Faure and W Vanbuggenhout 'Produkt aansprakelijkheid: de Europese richtliin, harmonisatie en consumenten bescherming' RW 1987–1988, part 1, no 3; Court of Appeal Brussels, 13 November 1987, Rev Liège 1987, p 1460. Court of Appeal Gent, 13 May 1988, RGDC 1990, p 219.

13 The limitation period is, however, interrupted when the plaintiff serves a writ of summons to the defendant.

offence (eg manslaughter). In this case, a civil action in tort can only be brought within five years of all the elements of the offence having arisen.[14] Such an action would not be barred if the limitation period for public prosecutions had yet to expire.

3.3 Vicarious liability

(1) As we have seen above, manufacturers are liable for their employee's negligence. They may not disclaim this liability by proving they were vigilant in exercising their authority or in choosing their employees.[15] They will however be discharged of their liability if negligence was committed outside the course of the employee's duties.[15] Employers have a recourse against employees and may recover all damages paid on their behalf provided the employee is guilty of wilful misconduct, grave fault or of repetitive negligence (article 18 of the Employment Act of 3 July 1978).

(2) Article 1385 of the Civil Code relates to the liability of a guardian for damages caused by animals under his control. Animals are, however, regarded as agricultural products and are thus excluded from the scope of the Directive.[16] A producer will rarely be the animal's guardian but an owner convicted on the basis of article 1385 could in certain circumstances exercise recourse against him.

4. SPECIAL REGULATIONS

4.1 Introduction

(1) Unlike in France and England, there is no general legislation covering liability arising from defective products in Belgium. Legislative intervention has been limited to the adoption of specific legislation in the foodstuffs, cosmetics, household products and machinery sectors amongst others. These specific laws give the government extensive statutory powers for implementing the principles which these laws lay down. In practice, their application has, however, proved to be relatively ineffective.

(2) Where *standardisation* is concerned, the IBN (Institute Belge de Normalisation) and CEB (Comité Electrotechnique Belge) have considerable power regarding the drafting of technical standards. These two institutions' membership is exclusively composed of professional federations. The standards which they prescribe can be accorded quasi-legislative force by royal decree. The IBN and the CEB also possess the power to register as Belgian, standards which are defined on an international scale. Moreover, the trade marks BENOR and CEBEC, for which the IBN and CEB are holders, may be conferred to products which comply with the relevant Belgian standards.[17]

14 P Delvaux 'La prescription de l'action civile découlant d'une infraction, son point de départ et son avenir' RGAR 1982, no 10.504; Supreme Court, 28 October 1971, Pas 1972, p 201.
15 Supreme Court, 26 October 1989, Pas 1990, I, p 241.
16 J L Fagnart 'La directive européenne sur la responsabilité du fait des produits' Cahiers du droit européen 1987, p 26, no 38.
17 T Bourgoignie 'Réalité et spécificité du droit de la consommation' JT 1979, p 298.

Furthermore, it is compulsory for these trade marks to be affixed to certain products (compulsory fire extinguishers in cars, for example).[18] The compliance of products with standards is not, however, a guarantee of non-liability and would not, for example, alter the position with regard to hidden defects or exempt the manufacturer from taking any other measures which are essential for ensuring the safety of his products.[19] It can be said, therefore, that compliance is a necessary requirement in respect of quality, but that it is not always sufficient. The general duty of care, which applies to professionals in particular, supersedes the obligations with regard to technical standards fixed by the law.[20]

4.2 The law of January 1977 relating to consumer health protection

(1) The industrial development of a continually expanding consumer society called for intervention on the part of the legislator regarding the quality of products in general consumption.

(2) The law of 24 January 1977 appeared in this sector in the form of an 'outline law',[1] defining the objectives and requirements to be met, while leaving it to the government to determine the rules of application.

(3) Its field of application is relatively broad since it covers cosmetics, tobacco, detergents, foodstuffs and food additives.

(4) These provisions deal with three main areas: prevention, inspection and sanctions.

4.2.1 Prevention

(5) Intervention of the government in this field will take place at different levels:

(a) The King may lay down rules for or prohibit the manufacture, export or marketing of the foodstuffs and 'other products' referred to by the law. Legislative action in this context will mainly consist of determining the 'negative' composition of the product, that is to say, proscribing the substances (eg additives) which the product may not contain or which may only be present in limited quantities.

(b) The King may order the circulation of certain information to the consumer; thus, with regard to cosmetics, the royal decree of 10 May 1978 provides that the name of the manufacturer, the shelf life of the product and the instructions for use, must be affixed to the product, in indelible print using unambiguous and clearly visible terms.

(c) The King may also lay down regulations concerning advertising, ie any communication having the aim of promoting sales. Thus, the royal

18 T Bourgoignie, fn 17, above. H Cousy 'Les normes techniques en doctrine et en jurisprudence' in *Le droit des normes professionnelles et techniques* (Colloque Spa, 1985) p 402 and 407; T Bourgoignie, JT 1976, p 510.
19 R O Dalcq 'Responsabilité quasi délictuelle et normes techniques et professionnelles' in fn 10.
20 R O Dalcq, fn 19, above.
1 Ie a law in which broad lines are laid down limiting the steps the government will be authorised to take by executive measures.

decree of 17 April 1990 prohibits the use in advertising of certain references relating to foodstuffs or the addition of information which is likely to mislead the public with regard to the quality or the nature of the product. Also, tobacco advertising is governed by the decree of the French-speaking community of 2 December 1982. This decree aims to restrict, and to a certain extent, prohibit, advertising campaigns for tobacco.[2]

(d) Products pending import may, by virtue of a royal decree of 9 February 1981, be stopped at the border if they appear to be damaging or harmful or if a special regulation declares them to be harmful. Products will be inspected and samples taken if necessary. If permission to import is denied, the importer has two options: to agree to the destruction of the goods or to 're-export' them. If the product is 'judged' to be harmful in accordance with a special regulation, the importer may reprocess his goods in order to make them comply with the regulatory requirements.

(e) Finally, the King may set minimum hygiene conditions to be complied with in companies and at workplaces where foodstuffs are manufactured and in places where they are consumed.

4.2.2 Inspection

(6) The authorities have the right to enter the premises where certain products destined for trade are manufactured or sold, in order to monitor the application of the law and royal decrees. They may also demand examination of commercial documents relating to these products and draw up a report on the official visit regarding the breaches which they have discovered. If a request for presentation of these documents is met with refusal or access to the site is denied, the manufacturers and traders will be liable to prosecution.

4.2.3 Sanctions

(7) Breaches of the law or of these executive measures give rise to prison sentences and fines. These sentences are more severe for manufacturers and importers than for distributors.

(8) On the other hand the 'damaging' or 'harmful' products (ie mainly products which are unsuitable for consumption or harmful to health) may be removed and destroyed. Should the manufacturer or the trader contest the harmful nature of his product, the products would be seized and samples be taken for analysis.

4.3 The law of 11 July 1961 relating to compulsory safety guarantees in respect of machinery

(1) By virtue of this law, the King has the power to determine safety conditions which must be met in respect of machinery, machine parts, equipment, tools, apparatus and dangerous containers.

2 This decree has been partially amended by a royal decree of 10 April 1990.

(2) Several decrees have been adopted pursuant to the provisions of this law, in particular a royal decree of 23 May 1977 concerning machinery, apparatus and electric conduits. This decree requires products to be constructed in compliance with a 'code of practice' (règle de l'art). The product only satisfies this test where it fulfils certain European standards or provisions laid down by the countries in which it is manufactured. The product must display an adequate level of safety with regard to the user and his property. This condition is deemed to have been fulfilled provided that IBN, or other standards offering the same quality level, have been complied with.

(3) In order to monitor compliance with executive orders, officials appointed by the King may visit companies, demand the production of documents such as accounts, take samples and draw up reports on any breaches. Moreover, they may take possession of equipment in the event of the breach being established.

(4) The law provides for penal sanctions (albeit of minimal severity) in the breach of royal decrees.

4.4 Pharmaceutical products and drugs: law of 6 June 1960

(1) The manufacture, preparation, sale or import of pharmaceutical products are subject in Belgium to permission obtained in advance from the Minister for Health. This permission is only granted subject to various conditions being met.

(2) The quality of the pharmaceutical product and its compliance with the laws and regulations on pharmaceutical products must be certified within each company by an 'industrial pharmacist'.

(3) Moreover, advertising for pharmaceutical products is strictly regulated by a royal decree of 9 July 1984 which, in particular, prohibits audio-visual advertising and certain claims about the products (eg promises of cures, the descriptions of symptoms of illnesses, etc).

4.5 Liability in the nuclear field: law of 22 July 1985

(1) The law of 22 July 1985 implements the Paris Convention of 29 July 1960 in Belgian law and aims to 'achieve a coherent entity in matters of national and international legislation on civil liability in the field of nuclear energy'.[3]

(2) The operator of a nuclear facility incurs strict liability towards third parties, based on the risk inherent in the operation of reactors and the use of fissionable materials. The liability is nevertheless limited to a ceiling of 4 billion Belgian francs. In the event of there being several parties liable, liability shall be joint and several *and* cumulative, which means that each operator shall be bound to pay compensation equal to the *maximum* amount for which he is liable.

3 Exposé des motifs de la loi du 22 juillet 1985, Documents Parlementaires, Sénat, Session 1983–1984, nos 593/1 and 593/2.

(3) The operator is required to *insure* his liability. The risks of material damage sustained by the nuclear facility and the liability with regard to damage to property and bodily damage caused to the victims are insured by a group of insurers, SYBAN, each assuming a portion of the risks existing in Belgium.

(4) Actions based on the law of 22 July 1985 shall be barred at the end of ten years from the date of the accident or at the end of three years from the date on which the victim became aware or should have become aware of the damage and/or of the identity of the liable party.

4.6 Liability arising from the distribution of electricity: law of 20 March 1925

(1) In Belgium the generation and distribution of electricity is a state monopoly. The local authorities and the associations of local authorities may generate, consume and distribute electricity within their territory. They may, moreover, grant an individual or a private company a concession for the distribution of electricity.

(2) A special regime of liability follows from article 17 of the law of 20 March 1925 which provides for operating companies to compensate owners for any damage which could result from using an electric grid. The question whether this liability is really a strict liability is, however, disputed.[4]

4.7 Liability arising from toxic waste law of 22 July 1974

(1) Under articles 2 and 3 of this law, the dumping, sale or acquisition of toxic waste (ie waste dangerous to the environment and to living organisms and which is declared as such by a royal decree) in theory is forbidden unless specifically authorised.

(2) Conditions regarding the transporation, import and export of toxic waste are determined by the King. However the quantity of harmful substances which the waste (ie by-products of industrial, scientific or agricultural activity) must contain before it can be declared toxic is relatively high.[5]

(3) Article 7 of the law introduces a system of strict liability which weighs heavily on the generator of toxic waste. The generator is obliged to have the waste destroyed, neutralised or eliminated at his own expense and remains liable to third parties for any damage occurring until it is disposed of, destroyed or neutralised, even if it is not under his control (for example, during transportation) and even if a third party is performing the destruction, neutralisation or disposal operation.

4 Répertoire Pratique du droit belge, Energie Electrique, Complément T IV, nos 158 ff.
5 B Ladot, J P Hannequdret, E Orbon de Xivry, *Droit de l'environnement*, 1988, no 400.

5. THE EFFECTS OF THE NEW LAW ON LIABILITY ARISING FROM DEFECTIVE PRODUCTS

(1) The implementation of the Directive will have only a relatively limited impact on Belgian law because the manufacturer is already strictly liable in certain circumstances where his defective product causes harm, and also the traditional dichotomy between tort and contractual liability is overcome.[6]

(2) The substantial advantage of the Directive is that it allows the end consumer of the product to be compensated for damage sustained without having to prove the negligence of the manufacturer or concern himself with the liability of intermediaries already outlined. The Directive even extends to a 'non-purchasing user'.[7]

So far as manufacturers' and sellers' liability is concerned, the Directive places primary liability on the manufacturer, the seller only being secondarily liable. Under Belgian law, manufacturers and distributor-vendors are liable on practically an equal footing. The consumer is often inclined to direct his claim at the vendor, the person with whom he dealt directly. The vendor, therefore, assumes the role of intermediary between the manufacturer and the consumer in a product liability claim and it may be that proceedings will continue to be brought against the vendor in contract.[8]

(3) Another advantage of the Directive for the consumer lies in the fact that the clauses exempting and limiting liability can no longer be invoked against him. It is nevertheless true that these clauses are of limited use in current Belgian law as a result of the presumption of 'bad faith' attributable to professional vendors.

(4) The system of liability existing under the current case law will, however, continue to be useful for the consumer as a result of the limited field of application of the Directive. The purchaser will have no recourse other than that based on articles 1641 ff (or 1382 ff) of the Civil Code when the defective product has been damaged itself or when property belonging to the purchaser and affected by the defect causing harm is of professional use or is not normally destined for private consumption.[9] On the other hand, Belgian law defines the 'defect' in the product more broadly than the Directive. Article 6 of the Directive is centred on defects regarding *safety* of the product though under current law the product is considered as 'defective' if it is unsuitable for the use for which it is destined even if all requirements with respect to safety are met. It should, however, be noted that as far as tort law is concerned the defect in the product will in most cases be a safety defect.

(5) The notion of the 'product' is also more extensive under the general law since both agricultural produce and game are covered by the provisions of the Civil Code, as a result of the general terms used in these provisions. However, latent defects in a building and to a certain extent defects in services may be covered by articles 1641 ff of the Civil Code.

6 H Bocken, Van Fout naar risico, TPR, 1984, pp 386 and 387.

7 T Bouroignie 'Realité et spécificité du droit de la consummation' JT 1987 p 360.

8 J Ghestin 'La directive communautaire du 25 juillet 1985 sur la responsabilité des produits défectueux' Dalloz 1986, vol 1, p 135.

9 A Benoit-Moury 'L'enjeu d'une directive européenne récente sur la responsabilité du fait des produits défectueux' Annales de droit de Liège 1987, pp 339–342.

(6) The notion of 'damage' itself is broader in Belgian law. As we have seen, damage caused to 'professional' property or to the product itself can be compensated. In addition actions can be brought for minor injuries since Belgian law does not have a concept of threshold amounts as introduced through the Directive for material damage. This provision has been criticised by many who believe that access to the courts will be denied to many victims of 'minor' damage. This criticism appears unjustified because the threshold amount is not very high and guarantees given by manufacturers to consumers enable a large number of claims of this nature to be redressed.[10]

(7) The Directive does not detail the means of compensation which are to be found in national legislation. For example, under Belgian law, it will be for the judge to decide, in awarding damages for personal injuries, whether to make a lump-sum award or an annuity which will generally be subject to indexation.

(8) The Directive provides for a three-year period of limitation and a ten-year forfeiture of the right to bring an action under it. It is to be hoped that the Belgian courts will take this term of limitation into consideration when they appraise the 'brief period' for limitation under article 1648 of the Civil Code.

(9) With regard to exemption from liability, the Directive will impart four innovations into Belgian law:

(a) Pursuant to article 8.2, a manufacturer may discharge himself of his liability, at least in part, in the event of a fault committed by the victim *or by a person (children, employee) for whom the victim is responsible*. Under the present law the rules governing vicarious liability only protect *the victim*.[11] The contributory negligence of a person for whom the victim is liable could thus not be invoked by a defendant in order to escape from his *entire* liability to the victim. However, the liability claimed may be shared *between* the persons who are held to be liable for the damage.

(b) Following article 7a the manufacturer will also be exempted if he proves that he did not put the product into circulation. This defence is otherwise unknown under Belgian law.

(c) The manufacturer may, under the Directive, escape liability if he can show that he did not manufacture the product or put it into circulation in the course of business. Under present law, owing to extensive interpretation of the causal nexus, the manufacturer could be held liable, on the basis of article 1383 of the Civil Code, for damage caused by the defect in the product, even if it was not destined for sale or distribution so long as actual negligence can be established on his part.

(d) Belgian law does not impose liability for development risks. It is unlikely that the Belgian Parliament will implement the option given by the Directive with this respect.

10 J L Fagnart 'La directive européenne sur la responsabilité du fait des produits' Cahiers de droit Européen, 1987, p 58.

11 H De Page *Traité de droit civil*, vol II, no 971; Supreme Court, 2 September 1976, Pas 1977, I, p 2; contra: Supreme Court, 9 February 1982, I, p 716.

As has been noted above, demonstration of the producer's 'invincible ignorance' of a defect is sufficient under the present law to exonerate the producer from liability. The Directive, for its part, obliges the producer to prove that the state of scientific and technical knowledge made the defect indiscernible at the time the product was put into circulation.

(10) By way of conclusion, if the establishment of strict liability of the manufacturer is an innovation in Belgian law, it must, however, be pointed out that Belgian law has already contributed to the recognition *in practice* of the quasi-strict liability of professional manufacturers and vendors. Moreover, the consumer will have to rely on Belgian domestic law in areas not covered by the Directive. Furthermore, Belgian law will continue to be applicable in respect of the appraisal, amongst other things, of the relation of cause and effect, for recourse between parties with joint liability, for assessment of damages or for intangible damage such as moral harm.

6. RISK MANAGEMENT IN THE NEW ERA OF PRODUCT LIABILITY

6.1 Introduction

(1) Paradoxically the implementation of the Directive will probably not fundamentally change the behaviour of manufacturers in managing their risks. The demands both of consumers and insurers have led manufacturers to adopt a policy for preventing operational risks.

(2) We all know that such risks can never be completely eliminated. Companies can, however, anticipate the number and seriousness of incidents and transfer a part of the cost arising therefrom to a third party, ie the insurer.

(3) It should be noted that what is commonly known as 'risk management' is a technique which, if not unknown in Belgium, is nevertheless relatively undeveloped at the level of small and medium-sized firms. The true 'risk manager' is the insurer who analyses risks and advises companies.[12]

(4) The broker for his part holds a certain 'advisory role', and his experience of incidents over a broad range of products qualifies him to guide his client in his choice of policy and in risk prevention.

(5) Furthermore, like the insurer, the broker is often assisted by a 'prevention engineer', whose task is to identify in each case the principal risks of the company and to propose a type of insurance which will protect the client according to his particular situation.

12 Y Macquet 'La gestion des risques aujourd'hui et demain' in *Les assurances de l'entreprise* (Brussels, 1988) p 329.

6.2 Internal risk management

6.2.1 Quality control

(1) Quality control is without doubt destined to play an increasingly important role in the field of product liability. Risk prevention using this type of control enables the risk to be partially eliminated, ie both the number and the seriousness of the incidents can be limited to a certain extent.

(2) Moreover, under the terms of article 17 of the law of 11 June 1874 on insurance, the manufacturer is obliged to guard to the greatest extent possible against damage.

(3) Quality control will be present at various levels.

(a) *In the first instance*, the manufacturer of the finished product is obliged to check the quality of the products and the raw materials he intends to incorporate in his product and must not place blind faith in his own suppliers.[13]

(b) *During manufacture* and packaging of the product, quality control not only enables certain easily detectable and rectifiable defects to be eliminated, but also establishes a means of proof.

(c) *The taking of samples* will improve the position of the company in the event of incidents occurring. By comparing the sample with the product placed on the market, it may be possible to demonstrate that the product was not defectively manufactured, but that the accident was caused by the misuse of the product by the consumer.

(4) The manufacturer must also check the quality of the packaging of the product and ensure that means of transport are satisfactory.

6.2.2 Record-keeping and documentation

(1) Belgian accountancy legislation (the law of 17 July 1975 and the royal decree of 8 October 1976) requires every company registered in Belgium to keep meticulous accounts. The larger the company is, the stricter its obligations in this respect. Companies must keep the receipts of transactions for up to ten years. Of course, certain products are likely to be obsolete within this period, as a result of advances in technology.

(2) From now on, it will be important for the producer to establish a classification system which will enable him easily to identify the product sold, its immediate consignee, the date on which it was sold and the levels of performance that could be expected of it at the time of sale.

(3) Furthermore, during the course of their operations, companies must collate statistics on their products with a view to improving their production profitability. The more information they have on potential complaints and faults, the better able they will be to deal with any case that might arise.

13 J Van Ryn and J Heenan *Principes de droit commercial*, 2nd edn, vol III, p 549.

(4) Leading experts in risk management have, in this regard, stressed that the real risk lies in the 'possibility that the objectives of a system based on one definite goal may not be achieved'.[14] Based on this perception of the matter, a method of analysis has been developed using 'centres of risk'. This method consists of analysing the company's *objectives* and determining what is needed, to achieve and safeguard them. This analysis centres on the financial means, which must be protected at all costs to enable the company to handle a crisis situation.[15] This approach moves away from classic risk management, based on management of hypothetical crises, and turns towards management working out 'alternative tactics and strategies' within the company.

6.2.3 Warning notices, operations, instruction, service manuals

(1) As has been shown, the manufacturer's obligation to 'know' his product creates for him a substantial obligation in terms of information (for the consumer) regarding contractual, as well as extra-contractual matters. This obligation is confirmed by the Directive insofar as the lack of safety of a product will increase in comparison with, among other aspects, the presentation of the product.

(2) In the case of goods which are complicated to use (like computer hardware or software), we are seeing an increasing proliferation of technical manuals. The feeling of the manufacturer, which is justified to a certain extent, is that the more he informs, the less liable he is.

(3) However, this proliferation of technical manuals raises the question of whether in the future courts might regard some of them as 'excessive'. It may be fair to require the professional to assimilate hundreds of pages of information about the product, but it is scarcely reasonable to impose such a burden on the ordinary layman. Thus, once again, the degree of competence of the user will have to be taken into account in order to assess the liability of the manufacturer.

(4) On the other hand, to what extent should technical manuals be imposed upon the user who did not buy the product; in other words, could information, not printed on the product itself, be used against the user if he made improper use of the product; and, if so, to what extent should he be obliged to inform himself?

6.2.4 Handling consumer claims

(1) As has been pointed out, the 'manufacturer-consumer' relationship is in most cases *indirect*. Thus the distributor takes on an important role in the handling of consumer claims.

(2) As a result, wherever special technical knowledge is necessary in the installation or distribution of a product, the manufacturer will require technicians to be trained by the distributor for this purpose.

14 Y Macquet, fn 12, above, at p 337.
15 Y Macquet, fn 14, above.

(3) The manufacturer will normally provide training of this kind. He will also usually agree to reimburse the distributor for any costs he may incur correcting the various problems which might arise after the sale of the product.

(4) In practice, the 'follow-up' of a product after it has been placed on the market will be essential. The consumer claim, recorded by the distributor and forwarded to the manufacturer, could bring about inspections and tests of the product, its replacement, and in certain extreme cases its total withdrawal from the market. It is therefore very important for the company to set up a 'crisis unit' capable of identifying the risk very quickly, determining the probable consequences and the measures to be taken (these measures could range from the simple replacement of a defective part to the recall and destruction of a product).

(5) According to insurance law, the insured party (in this case the manufacturer) has a duty to anticipate *the damage* and to mitigate it in every way possible.[16] The cost of damage prevention is not normally the responsibility of the insurer unless the danger is imminent or, of course, unless the contract specifically allows for it. The costs of mitigation of recall are often excluded from insurance policies. The same applies to other prevention costs, such as tests and analyses of the product, search and warning costs and the cost of replacing the product. The 'Civil Product Liability' insurance policy often also provides for the exclusion of the cost of *rehabilitating* the product.

6.3 Insurance

(1) The 'Civil Product Liability' insurance policy, although in quite widespread use has not yet gained a firm foothold, particularly in small and medium-sized companies. The manufacturer often tends to base his decision on a statistical report carried out within the company and, on the assumption that risk of a claim for damages as a result of the product is minimal, to economise on premiums. This type of attitude clearly restricts the 'spreading' of risk.

(2) The Directive does not redress this problem, since it does not impose compulsory insurance for liability arising from products.[17] Belgian insurers do not seem to be of the opinion that the introduction of a system of strict liability would have the effect of significantly increasing claims. Policies will undoubtedly be adapted according to each case, with regard to the nature of the product and the seriousness of the risk. It is certain, however, that the elimination of the development risks defence would lead to a real crisis in civil product liability insurance.

6.3.1 Nature of cover

(1) Civil liability insurance for industrial and commercial enterprise comprises two distinct sections: first, there is insurance against liability during production, with the object of covering any damage caused to third parties whilst the

16 The insured party must also prevent the occurrence of *the risk*. Failure to fulfil this obligation could be regarded as a serious omission by the insurer who could terminate the contract as a result.

17 J Vanderweckene 'L'assurance RC Produits' in *Les assurances de l'entreprise*, p 157.

company is carrying out its operations (such as damage to the environment, damage caused by fire, explosion or flood) and, secondly, there is insurance against liability after delivery for damage to third parties.

(2) Within the framework of the above, it is necessary to define several concepts in order to determine the scope of the cover.

(a) At the time of conclusion of the contract and during the period of the insurance cover, the insured party has an obligation to inform the insurer correctly and completely of the nature of the risk. In principle, therefore, the insured party must warn the insurer of any increase in the risk.[18] However, in practice it is virtually impossible to fulfil this obligation to the letter, insofar as the risk could increase at any moment during the operation. Consequently, this obligation must be interpreted reasonably. In this respect, policies quite often state that the insured party must declare any fundamental alterations to the risk and any extensions of the activities of the company.

(b) The insurance covers the actions of the policyholder, his agents, as well as his partners, executive officers and directors.

(c) The policy covers both contractual and extra-contractual liability, but does not extend to moneys paid by the insured party on the grounds of a contractual guarantee offered by him to a third party.

(d) The cover applies to damage caused by a defect in the product arising from error or negligence in the design, manufacture, preparation, packaging or description of the product.

(e) The cover extends to personal injury and damage to property. The policy also covers intangible losses provided that they are the result of bodily injury or damage to property which is covered.

(f) The cover is valid for the activities of companies located in Belgium and covers damage incurred throughout the world. However, the special conditions in the policy usually exclude damage caused by products destined to be delivered to the USA and Canada which are only covered on payment of a higher premium.

6.3.2 *Starting date and duration of the cover*

(1) The cover comes into force from the date on which the product is delivered or brought onto the market, ie the date on which title to and control of the product is relinquished by the producer.

(2) One critical point to be ascertained is the time when the obligation of the insurer arises.[19] It could be the completion of the product, the moment when the damage occurs or the time when the victim makes his claim. In practice, insurers generally take the date of the occurrence of the damage, ie when it first became evident. The damage will be covered if it *occurs* when the policy is in force.

(3) Where a series of damages occurs, ie damage resulting from the same initial cause, for example, as a result of a product accident, these damages are

18 A Janssens Brigode *L'assurance de responsabilité* Brussels, 1961, p 131.
19 J Vanderweckene, fn 17 above, at p 147.

regarded as one and the same incident. In such cases the insurance often covers the damage which occurred during the validity period of the policy or within a certain number of months since its expiry date.

6.3.3 Main exclusions

(1) Damage caused to the product itself is generally excluded as is damage arising from the fact that the product cannot be used for its intended purpose (performance defect).[20]

(2) Wilful and serious misconduct on the part of the insured party or his management executives is also excluded from the cover. Acts regarded as serious misconduct include breaches of the law, failure to take elementary precautions, the failure to submit products to sufficient tests and controls or lack of elementary technical knowledge or skill on the part of the producer.[1]

(3) Prevention costs and the costs of recalling a product are not generally covered or are covered when a considerably higher premium is paid.

(4) Damage resulting from a war, a strike or lock-out, a riot or an act of terrorism is also the object of specific exclusion.

(5) Finally, the policy does not normally cover damage resulting from a nuclear accident.

6.3.4 Premium and maximal cover

(1) The insurance premium is calculated according to the turnover of the manufacturer and the size of the risk. This premium could be raised subject to any possible increase in the risk.

(2) The insurer's contribution to damages will be limited on the one hand by a threshold amount and, on the other, by a compensation ceiling which will be fixed either per incident or per year of cover.

20 K Moustie 'Verzekering van de Produktaansprakelijkheid' TPR 1988, p 704.
1 K Moustie, fn 20, above, at p 706.

ADDENDUM

Implementation of the Directive into Belgian Law

The Belgian law implementing the Directive was passed by Parliament on 25 February 1991, published in the Belgian Official Gazette of 22 March 1991, and came into force on 1 April 1991.

As predicted, the new law has not been inserted into the Civil Code.

The law does not require any compulsory insurance. Furthermore, the law did not implement any of the three options left at the discretion of Member States by the Directive.

The following comments relate to specific provisions of the new law:

(1) The new law defines a 'product' as any tangible movable which may be incorporated in another movable or in real estate or that has become 'real property by destination', ie a movable installed in real property for the purpose of being used for the latter's operation.

It was explained in the travaux préparatoires that software is also considered as a product in the meaning of the new law.

(2) Entry into circulation of the product has been defined by the law (article 6) as being:

> 'the first action by which a producer gives effect to his intentions in respect of his product either by transferring it to a third party or by using it for the benefit of the same.'

Although this definition was considered to be rather unclear by the Council of State, it has nevertheless been retained.

The authors of the draft indeed believed that the concept of entry into circulation had to be explained, in order to distinguish it from the concept of 'the placing [of the product] onto the market'. It has also been stressed that entry into circulation could be carried out several times by each of the various economic operators whose liability may be involved.

Consequently, the definition emphasises the intention of the producer to have the product put into circulation.

(3) The new law stipulates under article 7 that the burden of proof of the damage and of the causal link lies with the victim.

An amendment to the draft law aiming at allowing consumer protection associations to bring actions on behalf of consumers was proposed in the travaux préparatoires.

This amendment has, however, been dismissed and common law will therefore continue to be applicable in this respect (cf p 47, above).

(4) The liability of several parties for the same damage will under the new law be joint and several. However, this rule will not apply where several parties are judged liable for the same damage on different bases, some on the basis of the general law and others on the basis of the new law. In this case, the rules of Belgian law regarding liability explained in contract or in tort will apply.

(5) The new law confirms that within the parameters of the rules governing this matter, the victim may claim compensation for the moral harm he may have suffered.

(6) Rules regarding suspension and interruption of the limitation period under the Civil Code will be applicable to the limitation periods provided by the new law (article 12).

(7) When the victim of damage covered by the law is receiving assistance from a social security system or an industrial accident or occupational diseases compensation system, these payments will continue and take priority.

The victim may, however, claim additional compensation from the producer on the basis of the new law, to the extent that, subsequent to the application of one of the above-mentioned systems, the damage has not been fully compensated.

Furthermore, any party who has compensated a victim for the damage suffered may have a right of indemnity from a third party, in accordance with the provisions of the new law.

(8) The new law does not apply to damages obtainable pursuant to the law of 22 July 1985 relating to civil liability in the field of nuclear energy (see p 65, above).

For a general comment on the new law, see M Fallon 'La loi du 25 fevrier 1991 relative à la responsibilité du fait des produits défectueux' JT 1991, p 465 ff.

CHAPTER IV

Denmark

Georg Lett, Advocate

Lett, Lett, Steglich-Petersen & Petersen
Østergade 3–5
PO Box 2231
1019 Copenhagen K
Denmark

Tel ++ 45 3 312 0066
Fax ++ 45 3 312 1266

CHAPTER IV

Denmark

1. INTRODUCTION

1.1 Overview of the law relating to defective products in Denmark

The Sale of Goods Act of 1906 regulates the obligations between purchaser and seller in sales of movables. The committee that drafted the Act emphasised that a contract should not govern the right to compensation for damage caused by the product (*udkast til lov om kob* p 70). Since then courts have with few exceptions based product liability on the principles of the law of tort. The law of tort is not set out in any Act, but has developed over the centuries on a case by case basis. Claims for product liability were therefore until recently almost exclusively brought on the basis of jurisprudence. The implementation of the Directive on Product Liability in Act 371 of 7 June 1989 *om produktansvar* has of course modified this position.

Further, a number of Acts deal with specific problems which also have an impact on product liability. For instance, the Act on Liability in Tort (*Lov om erstatningsanvar*) deals in general with the amount of compensation to which an injured person is entitled, and compensation and indemnity from third parties if the tortfeasor is insured, and some other general questions relating to the law of tort.

There are also Acts on Liability for Nuclear Plants and Aviation, the Railway Liability Act and the Maritime Act which deal with product liability in specific areas.

Although the problems of product liability are not solved on the basis of contract law, the existence of a contract between the parties is not irrelevant. A contract between professional parties may of course regulate and limit the product liability itself and may be important when deciding whether the product is defective or not. It may, furthermore, stipulate the applicable law and jurisdiction. In addition, a possible obligation for the purchaser to check the product may be important when deciding whether there is any contributory negligence. However, it is totally immaterial whether the seller is in breach of contract or not: it is exclusively the law of tort that applies.

1.2 Definition and classification of terms

Since there is no law on product liability in general, there is no definition of product liability as such. Product liability must be defined in relation to the problem with which one is dealing. The Product Liability Act contains a definition of product liability for the purposes of that legislation. This definition is, however, not necessarily relevant for product liability outside that Act. Furthermore, a definition of product liability is given in the standard policy on general and product liability used by Danish insurance companies.

However, the definition generally used in Danish legal literature to distinguish product liability from liability falling under the contract law of the Sale of Goods Act on the one hand, and liability in general on the other hand, is the liability for damage caused by a product after it has joined the chain of distribution, no matter whether the defect originates from the producer or a service rendered.

One should, however, be careful in drawing any conclusions from the definition, since practice is scarce and borderline cases will not be dealt with reference to any clear-cut definition, but rather from a pragmatic viewpoint considering the characteristics of each case on its facts.

2. LIABILITY IN CONTRACT

As stated above, Danish product liability law is almost exclusively based on tort. To the extent that the contract has any relevance, it will be mentioned in the appropriate place in this chapter.

The realm of contract law covers only damages that are not considered product damages. Some borderline problems are:

(a) The product's self-destruction is not governed by the rules of 'product liability'.

(b) The presence of a defective component in a complex product is more likely to render that product worthless as a whole than to result in actual damage. Consequently, any claim should be in contract rather than in tort.

(c) Denmark has implemented the UN Convention on Contracts for the International Sale of Goods (CISG). According to this Convention, product liability for damage of the purchaser's goods is based on the Convention, ie concrete law. It is an open question whether the injured can choose to make his claim on the basis of the product liability rules of tort.

The main difference between contract law and tort in relation to product liability is the limitation period for bringing claims. According to the Sale of Goods Act section 54 the limitation is one year from receipt (in CISG article 39(2), two years). Furthermore, the development risk defence is not available in contract.

3. LIABILITY IN TORT

3.1 Introduction

Since the implementation of the Directive, two sets of rules have been applicable to product liability. The Product Liability Act deals with product liability involving personal injury and damage to consumer products. Insurance companies estimate that about 10% of the sums paid under product liability insurances are paid out for such damages. The remaining 90% of the sums paid out cover damages caused on non-consumer products, which we shall call 'professional products'.

3.2 Outline of relevant tort law giving rise to liability for personal and property damage in Denmark

Danish case law on product liability distinguishes between the liability of the manufacturer and the liability of the distributor.

3.2.1 Liability of the manufacturer

The liability of the manufacturer is based on the basic principles of tort according to which liability for damage requires negligence of the tortfeasor. This is, however, somewhat misleading, since the negligence in respect of product liability means a very low degree of fault which approaches the strict liability of the Directive.

The basic criterion is that the product is dangerous or defective in the sense that it has qualities that under normal use could cause damage to things or persons. It could have qualities it should not have, or it could lack qualities it should have.

The manufacturer is liable if the defect is due to negligence on his part. It could be negligence in design or manufacturing or in providing adequate instructions for use.

Two defences are available. First, the development risk defence is based on the impossibility of having knowledge of the danger because of the absence of relevant scientific and technical knowledge at the time of marketing.

The other possible defence is system damage, ie damage caused by well-known but inevitable risks of the products. For example, the harmful effect of tobacco or alcohol. Another example is drugs which generally have good qualities, but have some well-known but undesirable side effects.

3.2.2 Distributor

If the manufacturer has delivered the product without defects to the distributor, the distributor can be held liable on the basis of negligence if he causes a defect to the product, either due to bad handling or negligence in the distribution, such as insufficient or wrong instructions or delivery of the wrong product (for example, poison instead of foodstuffs). The notion of negligence in this respect is probably also close to strict liability.

If the product delivered by the manufacturer to the distributor is defective the distributor will also be liable, but of course he will have a right of indemnity from the manufacturer. The injured party will have a free choice to hold either the manufacturer or the distributor or both liable in this situation. The liability of the distributor could be described as a kind of guarantee to the injured party for any claim against the manufacturer.

3.3 Causation

Liability presupposes that the defect has caused the damage. The question is, would the damage have happened if the defect had not been there?

If several causes have contributed to the damage there are in theory many possibilities, but courts tend to take a practical approach. If several liable causes have together effected the damage (such as the product being badly designed and the distributor issuing misleading warnings with it) the courts generally divide liability between them. If, on the other hand, some of the causes of the defect are non-liable (such as a drug bearing misleading warnings but stating certain side-effects clearly on the label), it is primarily a question of individual determination to what extent the loss has been caused by the defect and not by the non-liable cause (i.e. in this example, to what extent was the damage caused by following misleading labels rather than simply being natural side effects common to most people who take the drug in question?).

3.4 Remoteness of loss and damage

Since the chain of causation is in principle endless it has been established in tort that liability will cease if the damage is too remote. Liability presupposes that the damage is a typical consequence of the act. It is, however, usually difficult to find practical examples where liability is excluded due to the remoteness of the damage. When it comes to product liability this is even more true, since a defendant may be held liable even for very remote damages. It is certainly not a condition of liability that the tortfeasor could have foreseen that the damage could occur. An example where the remoteness of the damage might exclude liability is product liability for transporters. If a raw material has been contaminated on board a ship, for instance by salt water during transportation, and later on causes damage to the final product in which it is incorporated due to this contamination, one might argue that this damage is so remote from the point of view of the transporter that he cannot be liable for product liability. As to the loss, it is generally accepted that the extraordinary size of the loss does not in any way exclude or reduce product liability (cf U82 p 1111H). This means that it is not possible to reduce the damages recoverable by maintaining that a defect in a small standard device caused damage to a very expensive and complicated plant in which the product was installed. Furthermore, the low price of the defective product does not exclude liability for far-reaching and expensive damage later in the chain of distribution.

3.5 Quantum of damage

The quantum of damage is assessed according to the general principles of tort.

3.5.1 Personal injury

The amount of compensation for personal injury is stipulated in the Act on Liability in Tort (*lovbekendtgorelse* 599 of 8 September 1986).

According to section 1 compensation for injury is paid for the following losses:

(a) loss of income;
(b) medical expenses;
(c) other losses;
(d) compensation for pain and suffering;
(e) compensation for invalidity (*varigt mén*);
(f) compensation for loss of the possibility to earn an income by working (*tab af arbejdsevne*).

i. Loss of income. Loss of income is a temporary compensation which is paid from the date of the injury until the injured person starts working again or, in the case of lasting invalidity, until his medical situation is stable. It is in principle the full income that the injured could be expected to have in the relevant period received net of taxes. Payments received duing the period, such as salary from the employer or social security benefits or insurance payments which are paid in order to compensate loss of income, are deducted from the compensation.

ii. Medical costs. The injured can claim compensation for medical costs. Due to the Danish social benefits system where hospital treatment is free of charge there are usually no substantial claims of this kind. With the introduction of private hospitals in Denmark the question could be raised whether the injured can choose to get medical care in such a hospital and recover the costs from the person liable. Considering that the injured has an obligation to mitigate his loss he will probably not in normal situations be able to do so.

iii. Other loss. This loss is thought of as a supplement to the medical costs and is primarily a compensation for future losses such as artificial limbs and other necessary equipment such as wheelchairs, future medicine, future transport costs, necessary changes in the home and the like. The estimated loss is capitalised and paid once and for all in a lump sum.

iv. Compensation for pain and suffering. This loss is usually paid out on the basis of a fixed amount per day from the date of the injury until the injured person can return to work, or his medical situation is stable. The daily payment is at present fixed to DKK 130 per day if the injured party is confined to bed and DKK 70 per day otherwise. If the claim exceeds DKK 20,000 these rates can be adjusted, in which case they are usually lessened. The absolute maximum is about DKK 50,000.

v. Compensation for invalidity. Compensation for invalidity is fixed at an amount calculated on the basis of an estimate of the degree of invalidity from a medical point of view, without regard to the consequences of the injured's business activity. The compensation for 100% invalidity is DKK 269,000 and, under special circumstances, DKK 323,000. If the injured person is only partially disabled he will get a proportion of this amount corresponding to the degree of invalidity. Invalidity under 5% is not compensated. If the injured is over 59 years old the compensation is reduced according to a special scale.

vi. Compensation for the loss of the ability to earn income. If the injured, after his medical condition has stabilised, has permanently lost the ability to earn his income by working, he is entitled to compensation. The estimation is based on the injured's capacity to provide income and is calculated in percentages of the total loss. No compensation is paid if the loss is less than 15%. The compensation is capitalised on the basis of the annual income. The capitalisation factor is 6. The maximum yearly income that can be compensated is DKK 470,500. The following example demonstrates the principles of the calculations. The annual income of the injured in the year preceding the injury was DKK 300,000. The loss of ability to provide income by his own work is estimated at 50%. The compensation is then:

$$\text{DKK } 300{,}000 \times 6 \times 50\% = \text{DKK } 900{,}000$$

In any case where the income exceeds DKK 470,500 the calculation is based on DKK 470,500. The maximum compensation for 100% injury is accordingly:

$$\text{DKK } 470{,}500 \times 6 \times 100\% = \text{DKK } 2{,}823{,}000$$

Special rules are stipulated for children and for people who have no working income.

vii. Loss of breadwinner. In case of the injured persons death it is decisive whether they are a breadwinner or not. If the injured is not a breadwinner only the funeral costs will be compensated under this head.

If the injured is a breadwinner further compensation shall be paid. A breadwinner may work at home. An unmarried couple is entitled to compensation for the loss of the breadwinner in the same way as a married couple. The compensation is 30% of the compensation that the injured person could have been expected to receive for loss of ability to earn income by working (ie head *vi*, above). The minimum is DKK 302,500 and the maximum DKK 846,900. If the deceased was over 56 years old the compensation is reduced on a sliding scale.

If the deceased was a breadwinner for children, the children are entitled to compensation amounting to what the deceased would be obliged to pay if he was divorced and did not have custody of the children. The amount is based on a monthly payment and varies according to the income and is payable until the child is 18 years old, or 24 years old if the child undertakes further education. The amount is capitalised when paid out as compensation for the loss of a breadwinner.

3.5.2 General remarks

Information concerning the degree of invalidation and the degree of loss of the ability to earn income by working is provided by a public authority (*Arbejdsskadestyrelsen*).

Another critical element in fixing compensation is the day when the medical situation of the injured became stable. Since the injured is entitled to full compensation of his actual income until this day, but only to the schematically calculated compensation for loss of possibility to earn income by working after this day, the determination of this day is of vital importance. In principle it is a medical criterion which reflects the moment when no further improvement in the recovery process can be expected and where the residual invalidity can be considered permanent. In practice the moment is determined with great difficulty. Usually the opinion of the public authority (*Arbejdsskadestyrelsen*) is considered decisive.

The amounts mentioned above are subject to modification in relation to inflation. They are fixed as at 1 April 1991. The level of compensation is fixed at the moment of the injury and accrues interest, at present at a rate of 14% per annum.

3.5.3 Damage to property

In principle compensation is assessed with reference to the individual loss of the injured. He must mitigate his loss if possible.

In the case of total damage the loss is usually equivalent to the repurchase price of the destroyed article, or if the thing cannot be repurchased the loss is the value of the article.

If the loss is partial the compensation is the repair cost.

If the product is used in a professional context the injured can in addition claim the costs of hiring a substitute until the thing is repaired or replaced.

Consequential damages can in principle be claimed for damage to property but in practice the requirements of proof limit this. For example, if the damage has a consequence that a factory has to be closed for a period it is in principle possible to claim loss of profit. Only the direct loss will be compensated, based on a comparison with the turnover in the foregoing period. Claims for the more general loss of goodwill based on more theoretical calculations of the future development have not succeeded.

3.6 Burden of proof

In general, the burden of proof falls on the injured party, who must prove that there was a defect, that the defect caused the injury, and the size of the loss.

However, if the tortfeasor wishes to raise a defence of development risk or a system defect, the burden of proof rests on him. This is also the case if he wants to claim contributory negligence on the part of the plaintiff or his failure to mitigate his loss.

These simple rules cover much more complex problems. Although the rules concerning burden of proof are fairly clear the courts are free to assess the evidence submitted. From this has evolved a tendency to base rulings on assumptions. If, for instance, a defect is proven there is a tendency to assume that the defect caused the damage unless the opposite is proven. If however, on the other hand, a product has been in use for a long time without problems and suddenly causes damage, there is a tendency to assume that the damage is caused by normal wear and tear or lack of maintenance, rather than by a defect.

The individual case must therefore be assessed on its merits and the clear-cut rules of burden of proof have their primary function in determining which of the parties has to provide the basic facts of the case. If the injured in a complex case has not obtained an expert's opinion on the product that he claims caused the damage, it is unlikely that a defect will be assumed.

3.7 Exclusion or limitation of liability

3.7.1 Warnings

Warnings are not considered as an exclusion or limitation of liability, but rather as a part of the product or instructions concerning its proper use, and when deciding whether a product is defective one must take into consideration the warnings supplied with or affixed to the product.

The necessity of warnings has to be considered from the consumer's point of view. It is not necessary to warn against unlikely types of misuse. If, however, the possibility of misuse is obvious or natural, a warning can be relevant. Warnings are not necessary if the danger is well known (for example, sharp razor blades). However, warnings are without legal relevance if the dangerous characteristic could be avoided by better design or more careful manufacturing. If the chain of a chain saw easily comes off due to bad design, it does not prevent liability that the chain saw is provided with a warning.

3.7.2 Limitations of liability in agreements

On the basis of the concept of freedom of contract it is possible under Danish law to limit product liability in a contract. Such clauses are valid except:

(a) if the clause restricts the liability unreasonably; or
(b) if the other party to the contract is not able to protect his interests.

The clauses are always interpreted in a restrictive way, so that the restriction of the liability does not go beyond the clear wording of the clause.

Clauses restricting liability phrased in general terms in a contract are not considered to encompass product liability.

Several factors are relevant when deciding whether a clause restricting product liability is valid or not.

i. The parties. It now follows from the Product Liability Act that the seller cannot restrict product liability in a contract with a consumer (section 12). This is in accordance with the Directive article 12.

A special Danish rule has been inserted, concerning distributors who have sold the product but who are not manufacturers in the sense of the Directive article 3(1). Any other link in the chain of supply from the producer to the consumer (including manufacturers as defined in Directive article 3(2) and (3)) has a right of full indemnity from the manufacturer, if they have been held liable for product liability falling under the Act, and the manufacturer cannot limit such possibility by a contract with those parties (sections 11 and 12).

With regard to product liability falling under the Act, limitation of liability by contract is only possible between parties who are considered manufacturers in the terms of the Directive article 3(1) (Product Liability Act section 11.)

With regard to product liability falling outside the Act the parties are in principle free to agree on limitations of product liability by contract.

ii. Is the clause agreed between the parties? If the limitation clause is part of a written agreement it is presumed that it is duly agreed. If the written agreement contains a reference to general terms the clause restricting product liability is considered agreed if the general terms are standard documents well known in the trade or business, or if the general terms were incorporated in the agreement.

If the clause on limitation of product liability is printed on an order confirmation, or if it is printed on the invoice it is, according to recent legal writing, not considered to be agreed.

iii. How the clause was agreed. When considering whether the party in question could protect his interest, it must be taken into consideration whether the clause was negotiated or whether it was dictated in standard terms by the other party. If it was part of the standard terms of the other party it will be relevant whether that party informed the other party about the clause or in any other way drew his attention to the clause, eg by accentuation in the text.

iv. Contents. The main area in which clauses restricting product liability are used is consequential damage (loss of income and other damage that is not damage to persons or goods). For these losses the restriction on liability is generally accepted as valid. Furthermore, Danish standard terms on product liability encourage exclusion of liability for such losses (cf 9.4.3e). When it comes to damage to goods the possibility of restricting liability depends on whether the restriction is reasonable. On this basis it must be decided whether a total exclusion of liability is possible or whether liability can be restricted to a specified maximum, and if so, what maximum is reasonable. Clauses excluding liability for wilful or gross negligence will always be void.

If the injured party has discharged the burden of proof that the other party has caused the damage by negligence it is considered doubtful whether the clause can validly restrict the liability. The main area for the clauses restricting product liability is cases where negligence is not proved, and liability will be based on strict liability or presumptions of negligence.

3.8 Limitation period

The limitation period for bringing a claim for product liability in tort used to be five years, corresponding more or less to the three-year rule in the Directive, (ie a claim must be brought within three years of the discovery of the defect) and 20 year limitation corresponding more or less to the ten year limitation rule (ie the overall limit providing that a claim must be brought within ten years of the product being put into circulation) in the Directive. When implementing the Directive in Denmark it therefore had to be decided whether to continue with a double rule or to make a uniform limitation period for product liability falling within and outside the Directive. A solution in favour of a uniform rule was decided, and the final Act therefore contains a prescription rule for all product liability.

When implementing the rules of the Directive the Danish Act has if anything made things a little more complicated.

i. The three-year prescription rule of the Directive is implemented without modification. According to Danish law the limitation period can be suspended and interrupted according to the rules in the Act of 1908 on Prescription (Act 274 of 22 December 1908 *om foraeldelse af visse fordringer*). According to the Act the limitation period is interrupted if a law suit is initiated (complaint forwarded to the court), or if the claim is admitted by the defendant.

The limitation period is suspended if the injured person is either in excusable ignorance of his right to claim or of the domicile of the defendant and for this reason has been unable to bring the claim. Excusable ignorance in this context could be that an injured person is unaware of the fact that he will not recover his full working capacity.

As mentioned above, it is the clear intention of the Act that the three-year limitation period also limits product liability falling outside the Act. Some authors[1] claim, however, that the wording of the Act is too ambiguous to be interpreted in this way. If this is true, claims for product liability falling outside the Act can be made within five years from the date of damage.

ii. Ten-year limitation period. The claim is, furthermore, limited by the ten-year limitation period of the Directive, *but only* if the claim falls within the Directive. If the claim falls outside the Directive, the ten-year limitation rule is not applicable. If a claim falling under the Directive is prescribed according to the ten-year period but not according to the three-year period, it is still possible to raise the claim on the basis of the product liability rules based on jurisprudence (the same rules that are valid outside the Directive), if it is not prescribed according to the 20-year prescription rule (see below).

iii. Twenty-year limitation rule. According to Christian V's Danish law of 1683 5–14–4 a 20-year limitation period runs from the moment when the damage occurred. It is interrupted by any claim against the tortfeasor, for instance, a letter, with the consequence that a new 20-year period runs. It was earlier assumed that the 20-year limitation period could not be suspended. Recent jurisprudence (U89 p 1108H) has modified this. It is now doubtful whether the 20-year limitation rule has any practical bearing on product liability.

iv. Convention on International Sales of Goods. Denmark has ratified the Convention on International Sales of Goods (Act 733 7 December 1988 *om international kobelov*) which contains a limitation period for some kinds of product liability in article 39(2).

According to this rule there is a limitation period of two years from the day the goods were received by the purchaser. This limitation period also relates to damage caused by the goods to the purchaser's property (ie product liability). The more detailed rules in the Convention and the law implementing the Convention, however, are not discussed here.

1 Dahl et al Juristen 90, p 168.

3.9 Liability for third parties

Third party liability is based on Christian V's Danish law of 1683 3–19–2. According to this law a person or a company will be liable for damage caused by another person on the following conditions:

(a) the acting person is in the service of the other party or specially authorised to act on his behalf;
(b) the action is done in the course of the service and is naturally connected to that service;
(c) the acting person would himself be liable;
(d) the liability presupposes a certain possibility of control of the third party which excludes third party liability for independent contractors.

The rule is only necessary to explain the liability of the employer for product liability if one is basing the theory of product liability on the assumption of negligence. If the product liability of the employer is based on strict liability it is not necessary to presuppose negligence of the workers in order to impose liability on the employer.

In the present context it can be concluded that a manufacturer can be liable also for the actions of people who are not part of his staff, if they are acting on behalf of the manufacturer. If the design of the machinery is done outside the manufacturing premises, and if the design is inadequate and the product causes damage as a result, the manufacturer will be liable.

4. LIABILITY FOR DEFECTIVE PRODUCTS BROUGHT ABOUT BY BREACH OF STATUTORY REGULATION DESIGNED TO PROTECT CONSUMERS AND/OR TO PROMOTE SAFETY

4.1 Outline of the nature of protective Regulations

The liability for marketing defective products is not only regulated by jurisprudence on product liability and the Product Liability Act. In various Acts one can find rules concerning product safety and product standards, the breach of which can entail not only product liability but also criminal sanctions.

4.1.1 General rules

In the Act on Marketing section 3 it is stipulated:

> When an offer is made, an agreement is entered into or, considering the circumstances, at the time of delivery, the seller should give an instruction that, considering the merchandise or the service, is adequate, when this instruction is of relevance to estimate the character of the merchandise or the service or its qualities, especially in respect to proper use, duration, dangerousness and possibilities to maintain.

Violation of this clause is not sanctioned as such, but the Consumers' Ombudsman can bring a case before court, and the court can ban a possible marketing medium. A violation of the ban of the court is sanctioned by fine or imprisonment.

4.1.2 Specific rules

A number of Acts, the purpose of which is to maintain public health, stipulate rules concerning the production and distribution of certain products. Infringements are sanctioned by fines. Examples are Acts on Drugs, Chemicals and Foodstuffs, laws on the Protection of Plants and Animals in Agriculture, and Acts on Explosives, Fireworks, Electrical Devices, the Installation of Devices for Gas, Water and the Installation of Sewers, and Restaurants and Hotels.

5. SPECIAL LIABILITIES ARISING IN RESPECT OF PARTICULAR PRODUCTS

Article 13 of the Directive does not affect national law since it already provides better protection of the consumer.

In several Acts there are special rules concerning liability, which might encompass product liability. For example, the Acts on Distribution of Natural Gas, Aviation, Compensation for Persons Injured by Vaccination, and Compensation for Persons Injured during Military Service. These laws contain rules that are more favourable to the injured than the Act on Product Liability. Contributory negligence can only be claimed in cases of intent and gross negligence. Furthermore, there is no damages threshold that must be overcome in respect of property damage and the injured has a longer time limit to raise his claim.

The Workmen's Compensation Act and the Act on Compensation to Persons Injured by Vaccination and the Act on Compensation to Persons Injured during Military Service contain rules to facilitate proof that there actually was an injury caused at work or by vaccination or during the execution of military service.

Liability for damages caused by nuclear products is regulated in the Act of Nuclear Damages. Denmark has implemented the Paris Convention with the changes made in two protocols on 16 November 1982. The liability for damage caused by nuclear products is strict.

Parliament has refrained from making special rules on liability for drugs in order to eliminate the development risk defence. The reason is that the drug industry in Denmark has undertaken to provide adequate insurance. The terms of this arrangement have not yet been agreed.

6. LIABILITY FOR DEFECTIVE PRODUCTS ARISING FROM NATIONAL LAW IN DENMARK: IMPLEMENTATION OF THE DIRECTIVE

6.1 Introduction

The Directive has been implemented almost word for word with only a few amendments.

6.2 Summary

In section 1 the law defines its scope of application as being liability of the manufacturer and the distributor for damage caused by a defect in a product which is manufactured or delivered by them (product damage).

In section 2 'damage' is defined according to the terms of the Directive article 9.

In section 3 'product' is defined according to the terms of article 2 of the Directive. Denmark has elected to exclude raw agricultural products from the scope of the Act.

In section 4 'manufacturer' is defined according to the terms of article 3. Furthermore, the section defines 'distributor' as one who professionally markets the product without having manufactured it.

In section 5 a 'defect' is defined according to the terms of article 6 in the Directive.

In section 6 'strict liability' is defined according to article 1 of the Directive and the burden of proof is defined according to the terms of article 4 of the Directive.

In section 7 the defences are defined according to the terms of article 7 of the Directive.

In section 8 a damages threshold of DKK 4,000 is stipulated. This deduction shall be made even if the claim exceeds DKK 4,000. However, the injured can raise the claim for the first DKK 4,000 on the basis of the product liability rules set out in jurisprudence.

In section 9 of the rule concerning the injured's contributory negligence is stipulated according to the terms of article 8 of the Directive. It is pointed out that the deduction according to section 8 shall be made in the total amount before deduction for contributory negligence.

In section 10 it is stipulated that the distributor is liable as guarantor for the product liability of the manufacturer in relation to the injured and in relation to subsequent businesses in the chain of distribution.

In section 11 it is stipulated that manufacturers may be liable jointly and severally according to the terms of article 5 in the Directive. Additionally, liability among several manufacturers, as defined in the Directive article 3(1), is shared between them if there is no agreement to that effect in relation to:

(a) the cause of the defect;
(b) the individual manufacturer's opportunity and capability of controlling the product;
(c) possible product liability insurances;
(d) other circumstances.

In section 11(3) it is stipulated that the distributor and the 'Producer', as defined in the Directive article 3(2) and (3), have the right of full indemnity against the real manufacturer. The indemnity can be reduced in cases of contributory negligence with the distributor.

In section 12 it is stipulated that liability cannot be excluded in relation to the injured according to the terms of article 12 of the Directive. Furthermore, it is stipulated that liability cannot be excluded in relation to anyone who subrogates in the injured's claim, which means that exclusion clauses between a manufacturer and a distributor are void. Manufacturers as defined in article 3(2) and (3) of the Directive are, in this context, considered as distributors.

Section 13 stipulates that the injured does not waive possible rights in other legislation as stipulated in the Directive, article 13.

Section 14 stipulates the rules on limitation of liability in time as explained in section 3.8, above.

In section 15 nuclear damage is excluded (cf article 14 of the Directive).

In section 15 the Minister of Justice is entitled to stipulate rules to implement international agreements on the choice of law in product liability cases. It is expected that the Hague Convention of 21 October 1972 on the law applicable to product liability will soon be implemented in Denmark.

In section 17 it is stipulated that the Act comes into force when published. It came into force on 10 June 1989.

It is stipulated that the law is not applicable to products marketed by the manufacturer before the Act came into force.

In section 18 it is stipulated that the law is not applicable on the Faroe Islands and in Greenland, but that it can come into force by special decree in these territories.

6.3 Optional provisions in the Directive

i. Serial damage. Denmark has not introduced any limitation on the liability for serial damage.

ii. Development risk defence. The defence of development risk is made available for the manufacturer.

iii. Unprocessed agricultural products. Unprocessed agricultural products are not governed by the Product Liability Act.

7. PRACTICAL EFFECTS EC PRODUCT LIABILITY LAW WILL HAVE ON VARIOUS BUSINESSES IN THE CHAIN OF SUPPLY OF PRODUCTS

7.1 General rules

According to the Workmen's Compensation Act the injured has no claim against the tortfeasor in as much as he has received compensation according to workmen's compensation. It will depend on the ruling of the EC Court whether the injured can claim full compensation from a tortfeasor despite his recovering some compensation from workmen's compensation insurance. Apart from this detail there will be no distinction in the liability in relation to:

(a) users at work;
(b) other employees;
(c) the general public;
(d) employees of other firms.

As to the liability of the various businesses in the chain of supply of products their liability for defective products can be described as follows.

i. Designer. If the designer of a product is a separate legal entity his liability in relation to the injured party will not be governed by the Product Liability Act. It is doubtful whether he has any liability directly in relation to the injured party. If there is liability, it is based on the ordinary notions of liability in tort, which means that liability presupposes negligence and that the action has caused the damage.

The manufacturer will in principle be able to be indemnified by the designer.

ii. Component manufacturer and supplier of materials. The component manufacturer and the supplier of materials will be liable to the injured only if their products are defective. They are not liable just because the end product is defective.

iii. Manufacturer or assembler. The manufacturer of the end product is liable according to the Act. The liability of the manufacturer is a condition that a claim can be raised on the basis of the Act. Probably any modification of a product, whether repackaging or relabelling, will make a distributor liable according to the rules for manufacturers.

iv. Importer, distributor, dealer. Importers, distributors and dealers are liable as guarantors for any liability incurred by the manufacturer. They have the right of full indemnity from the manufacturer.

If the product was not defective when leaving the manufacturer, but the defect occurred due to, for instance, bad handling by the importer, distributor or dealer, or the defect consisted in the distributor delivering a wrong product or giving inadequate instructions, the liability of the importer, distributor or dealer will not be based on the Act on Product Liability but on jurisprudence.

v. Purchaser. As to the purchaser who uses the product in his own home or business, his liability in relation to the injured party will presuppose negligence on his part. If he is using the product in his business his responsibility will be almost strict, since he will have an obligation to secure that the workplace is safe, according to the Health and Safety at Work Act. The same liability will apply for the general public and employees of other firms if he gives them access to his premises.

The installer of a product for the end-user will be liable if the defect is caused by his negligence. His liability is not covered by the Product Liability Act, which means that his liability will not be limited in time to three years but rather to five years.

vi. Repairer. The repairer who does not add any component has liability for possible defect caused by his repair, based on negligence. If he inserts components that are defective his liability will be covered by the Product Liability Act.

7.2 Particular problems in specific businesses or industries

The Danish parliament reluctantly accepted the defence of development risks. They assumed that the medical industry would establish an insurance covering damage caused by drugs, making the defence of development risk unnecessary. Such an insurance has not yet been established, but it must be expected that if such an insurance is not established within a reasonable time, Parliament will reconsider the defence of development risk.

There has been discussion as to whether computer software is a product. From the attitude of the Commission it seems clear that software is a product, and if software is in the chain of production as, for instance, a cad/cam system, the producer of the software will be liable on the basis of the Product Liability Act. If computer software is only serving as an information base possible defects in the computer software will probably not be considered to have caused the damage.

8. COMPARISON OF THE EFFECTS OF PRODUCT LIABILITY LAW WITH THE PREVIOUS POSITION IN CONTRACT AND TORT

The differences are negligible and can be summarised as follows:

(a) Grounds for liability: The liability is strict in the Act, whereas earlier it was based on the concept of negligence. This difference is only formal since the law still presupposes a defect, and the presence of a defect will also imply liability according to the existing law of torts.

(b) Distribution of liability among several liable manufacturers: The rule is perhaps a modification compared to the earlier situation, but it is unlikely that there will be any drastic changes.

(c) Limitation in time: The limitation period has been reduced from five to three years, which must be considered as the most important change that has been brought about by the implementation of the Directive.

(d) Possibility of limiting liability in the relation between the manufacturer on the one hand and the distributor, importer and dealer on the other hand: The Act has excluded limitation of liability by contract between the manufacturer and distributor, importer and dealer, which is a restriction of the freedom of contract compared to the situation before the Act.

Apart from these points it is uncertain whether the act results in any changes to the Danish law on product liability. It may be that the defences introduced by the Directive were not available to the same extent before the implementation of the Directive.

9. RISK MANAGEMENT IN THE NEW ERA OF PRODUCT LIABILITY

9.1 Internal risk management

As to the quality control documentation and record-keeping the Act does not entail any changes, but of course the general trend makes it necessary to intensify quality control, documentation and record-keeping.

The same applies to warning notices, operating instructions and service manuals. Since, however, operating instructions are explicitly mentioned in the Directive article 6, the interpretation of this article by the EEC Court might influence the requirement. In this connection the Draft Product Safety Directive from the Commission of 7 June 1989 must also be mentioned.

9.2 Handling of consumer claims

9.2.1 Inspection of defective products and analysis of causes of failure

In the Danish context inspection and analysis will most appropriately be carried out by an expert. An expert can be appointed by the court either during a law suit or even before a law suit, and presupposes that one party gives notice to the other party that he requires an expert. The court will ask the party who to appoint. The general procedure is that the parties agree on an institution, for instance the Danish Society of Engineers, to suggest an expert. If neither of the parties have any objections to the suggested expert the court will appoint him. The requesting party has to draw up a list of questions and the other party can ask additional questions. On the basis of these questions the expert will call the parties to an inspection meeting, where he will inspect the item in question and clarify possibly unclear questions. Furthermore, he has the option to request further documentation from either party if he feels that it is necessary to resolve the issues, after which he will make a written answer to the questions. He can be called upon in court to clarify his answers.

It is of the greatest importance to ensure that the chosen expert is qualified, since the possibility of changing him later on, due to lack of competence, is very small.

9.2.2 Future damages and the need to re-design, cease selling and recall products for safety checks or replacement of defective parts

If a company fails to re-design a product that has been found to be defective and to recall the products in circulation for safety checks, etc it is obvious that the manufacturer will be liable for future damage caused by the defective products. Apart from this, non-compliance with these clear obligations can imply liability on the basis of the Penal Code. Where the law gives the authorities the opportunity to order a recall (Act on Drugs and Act on Electrical Devices) a non-compliance with such an order is punishable by a fine or imprisonment.

9.2.3 Requirements of insurers

In case of a claim against the insurer for product liability the insurance company will demand to take over the defence and to appoint a lawyer to handle the defence for the insured.

The insurer requires that the insured prevents imminent danger of damage, but gives special coverage under the insurance policy for the costs of such prevention.

9.2.4 *Correspondence with consumers*

According to the Insurance Contracts Act the insured is not entitled to come to a settlement with an injured third party without the consent of the insurance company. If an unauthorised settlement is entered into cover will be forfeited unless the insured can prove that he is only fulfilling his legal obligation against the injured third party.

9.2.5 *Preservation of evidence*

No special rules cover the preservation of evidence. The party that has the burden of proof has to suffer the detrimental effect if evidence is not preserved.

Physical items and documents can be produced by the other party in a law suit.

Witnesses are in general heard at an oral hearing which may take place years after the accident occurred. This causes a problem of preservation of the testimony of the witnesses. Although there is the possibility of hearing witnesses before trial, courts are very reluctant to accept such testimonies, unless the witness is about to leave the country or is sick and is expected to die before the trial (for instance, in asbestosis cases).

The parties are free to discuss matters with their own witnesses, but it may create problems if independent witnesses are contacted in order to preserve their testimony, since a unilateral report of their testimony may not be produced during the law suit. It is an inherent problem of Danish law that testimonies are generally very old when produced during the trial.

9.2.6 *Problems of legal proceedings*

In product liability cases the reports of experts play an important role in relation to whether the product is defective or not. The expert produces a written report and is heard during the trial more or less like a witness. He is considered as a technical assistant to the court. Being independent of the parties it means that his opinion on technical matters is used almost uncritically by the court. It is not possible for the parties to hear other experts, and it is almost impossible to prove that the expert is incompetent and should be replaced by another one.

As already mentioned, it is very difficult to preserve the testimony of witnesses for the trial, which means that the testimonies are very much influenced by what the witnesses may have heard from the preparation of the law suit and very far from a 'fresh' testimony. In spite of this courts tend to rely very much on testimony, where written documents do not decide a matter.

The court procedure is fairly slow and in first instance cases, where an expert opinion is laboured, can easily last up to three years before judgment is given.

9.3 Exclusion of liability and claims on contracts for indemnities

Since the injured party is entitled to make a claim directly against any business in the chain, an exclusion clause may become useless if the claim is made by a third party. Consequently, an addition should be made to the clause that the seller is entitled to indemnity from the purchaser for any liability to a third party, which goes beyond the exclusions of the clause. The seller must co-ordinate his sales terms with the terms on which he is buying. It is therefore important that he does not undertake more liability in relation to his purchasers that he can get indemnity for in relation to his sellers.

9.4 Insurance

9.4.1 Standard product liability policy

Terms of a standard policy of general and product liability have been agreed between the Organisation of Danish Insurance Companies (*Assurandor-Societetet*) and the Organisation of Danish Industrial Companies (*Industriradet*), and thus have the status of an agreed document. The terms are now used by the majority of Danish insurance companies.

9.4.2 Outline of the nature of the cover

According to section 3 the policy covers liability for damage to persons or property caused by the insured's products or services after they have been brought into circulation.

According to section 2 the insurance moreover covers the insured's liability in tort for damage to persons or property whilst engaged in the activities covered under the policy. Furthermore, it extends to liability for real estate used for business activity. It is therefore immaterial for the purpose of the insurance to distinguish between general and product liability. One should, however, notice that the exceptions to the two kinds of liability are not quite identical. The following deals only with product liability.

The insurance is based on the principle of claims made in time, according to which a claim is covered if the claim is made against the insured within the period in which the policy is in force.

Danish insurance policies are signed on an ongoing basis, and there is no clause limiting insurance cover within the insurance period for claims made against the insured, as long as the claims are enforceable. At the termination of the policy, however, there is a three-month notification period.

The policy defines when a claim is made, and the basic concept is that a claim is considered to be made when the insured gets the first knowledge of facts concerning damage which must be expected to lead to a claim against the insured.

The policy stipulates a sum which is the maximum cover for claims made against the insured within an insurance year.

For damage caused outside Scandinavia there is a special clause on coverage importance for US risk. Here the insurance sum is the maximum, not only for the damage but also for cover of costs of lawyers and experts.

9.4.3 Limits on cover including limitation of liability paid under contractual indemnities

(a) The insurance does not cover damage to the product or service itself. Neither does the insurance cover damage on items belonging to the insured or items that are in the custody of the insured.

(b) The insurance does not cover damage on items which the insured has undertaken to install, repair, mount, make ready or subject to other treatment, no matter whether the damage occurred during the execution of the task or after it or as a consequence of it.

(c) There is no cover for damage or loss caused by products or services used in the service of an aircraft or to off-shore installations if the product is a contributory cause of damage of the said aircraft or off-shore installation.

(d) There are exclusions concerning works on real estate and use of explosives.

(e) A very important exclusion is section 3, according to which most cases of liability for consequential damages, such as loss of fortune, are not covered. In particular, there is no cover for loss of costs in connection with recall, reproduction, re-delivery, repair, destruction, disposal or the like in relation to defective products or services.

There is no cover for loss of income, loss of profit or the like. If, however, the insured has excluded such liability in his general terms of delivery and those terms are approved by the insurance company, such losses are covered if the insured is made liable, because the exclusion is deemed to be void.

There is no cover for fines, whether private or public, and especially not punitive damages as under US law.

(f) A special problem arises in the so-called 'ingredient' and 'component' cases. A problem arises when the product is an ingredient or component in another product. If the component or ingredient is defective, there are two possibilities. Either it may damage the final product or it may cause loss because it simply does not function. For example, if a foodstuff does not contain the specified vitamins, the pigs that eat the feed are not damaged, but their growth is retarded causing the farmer to suffer loss of income.

If the feed is poisonous and causes illness amongst the pigs, the effect on the farmer's income will be the same or worse.

According to the earlier policy, only the second situation was covered under the insurance policy, but not the first. The present standard policy tries to solve this problem by making the cover alternative: either both cases are covered or neither. Several insurance companies have, however, decided not to follow the standard policy and offer coverage on special terms.

(g) The insurance policy does not provide cover to the extent that the insured has accepted contractual obligations for product liability beyond the obligations that follow under the law. Likewise the cover is reduced to the extent that the insured has waived his right to claim action for compensation and indemnity with third parties.

(h) The insurance does not cover damage caused by the insured with intent or gross negligence. The term 'gross negligence' is not used, but the wording more or less covers what is usually conceived as such.

(i) The policy only covers damage occurring within the geographical territory stipulated in the policy. Only if the product is taken outside the territory for private purposes or without the manufacturer knowing, or with no duty to know, will the policy cover damage which occurred outside the territory.

9.4.4 *Serial damage*

The claims series clause has just been modified. Now the series of claims is considered as a single claim which is deemed to have been made in the year when the first claim in the series was made. Claims in the series are covered without any limitation in time even after the expiry of the policy so long as the first claim was during the cover period.

9.4.5 *Cover for recall of defective products*

The insurance policy stipulates a specific insurance sum to cover costs related to steps necessary to avoid an imminent danger of any damage of the kind that is covered by the policy. To understand the range of this cover, it has to be stressed that the risk of damage must be imminent, and necessitate immediate action. Secondly, it is only costs in connection with steps that are necessary to avoid the immediate danger that are covered. For example, if an electrical household device has caused damage in one instance, the problem arises of what to do in connection with all other similar household devices on the market. If the danger of similar damage is imminent, the danger could be avoided by disconnecting the electric current.

Consequently the costs covered under this clause are limited to the costs of communicating to customers, either by letter or by advertisement, that the device should be disconnected. The costs of tracing the defective household devices, recalling them, repairing them or destroying them are not covered, and cover for these costs cannot be obtained under a standard policy.

9.5 Limitation of liability through corporate structure

9.5.1 *Effect on whether a business should incorporate*

Danish company law offers several ways of limiting liability through corporate structure. The two most important are by public limited company (*Aktieselskab*) and private limited company (*Anpartsselskab*). In these two forms of shareholding companies, liability is limited to the amount invested in the shares. The shareholders cannot become liable for the acts of the company, whereas the management and the Board can become personally liable if they cause a loss to a third party by negligent acts. Liability for managers and Board members has until now only been seen when creditors have incurred a loss, but not yet in the field of product liability. One could imagine this possibility especially in cases of gross negligence and intentional damage.

9.5.2 *Liability of companies in groups*

Danish law acknowledges that liability for subsidiary companies is limited to the amount invested in the shares. As a basic rule a company group may limit liability for a given activity by creating a subsidiary company as a public or private limited company to the amount invested in the said company.

9.5.3 *Splitting of high risk activities from valuable assets*

There is no case law concerning the limitation of product liability through the creation of subsidiary companies with a low capital for performing high risk activity. Further, there is no formal obstacle to:

(a) using share companies for the importation of products from outside the EEC for resale within it; or
(b) splitting manufacturing from a company's asset base through using a well-endowed parent company and leasing or hiring elements of production to tightly run manufacturing companies.

One should, however, bear in mind two factors:

(a) the courts might react to possible abuses where high risk production is made in companies with minimum capital, no assets and inadequate insurance;
(b) adequate insurance for any ordinary product liability risk outside the US is at a level where the financial side of the risk management can be solved by insurance.

The problem has especially been dealt with in relation to distribution in the US market. If a company is met with a claim for product liability and the company wants to continue to trade in the US, it must seek to defend the case and, if it loses, pay compensation.

If the company has no wish to continue on the US market or the claim is ruinous, for instance, in the case of combined action, other solutions might be considered. For this purpose it might be appropriate to have a corporate structure which places the production unit in a corporate entity with low equity and few assets. Apart from that the only possibility is to stay out of an American law suit. Denmark has no agreement with the US on acknowledgment or enforcement of judgments. In case of a judgment by default in the US the plaintiff will therefore have to start litigation in Denmark, where it will be possible for the court to try the case on its merits. It is possible that the Danish court will be more reluctant to find liability, especially if the American judgment is in default and, secondly, there is a possibility that the Danish court will revise the amount of compensation. What will come out of such a case is still to be seen, since Danish courts have not yet tried one.

CHAPTER V

France

Ms Muriel de Courrèges

43 rue du Faubourg Saint-Honoré
75008 Paris
France

Tel ++ 33 1 42 66 50 31
Fax ++ 33 1 42 66 58 95

Seconded, at the time of writing, to

Wilde Sapte
Queensbridge House
60 Upper Thames St
London EC4V 3BD
England

Tel ++ 44 71 236 9624
Fax ++ 44 71 236 3050

CHAPTER V

France

1. INTRODUCTION

French product liability law has traditionally been based on the rules relating to a seller's liability for latent defects in articles 1641 ff of the Civil Code. The courts have actively sought to extend this basic consumer protection. For example, they have developed sellers' and manufacturers' obligations to supply a product to conform with contractual provisions pursuant to articles 1603 ff of the Civil Code, as well as the obligations to inform, advise and warn the purchaser of the conditions of use of the product and its potential dangers.

French law in this area has been marked by a multiplicity of grounds for product liability actions, and the complexity of the system as well as uncertainties in the rules has been the subject of criticism.

Legislation has recently been introduced which is aimed specifically at the provision of information to, and the protection of, the consumer. The legislation is also aimed at enhancing the safety of products to be introduced onto the market. Furthermore, certain products are subject to special rules.

The Directive was a welcome opportunity to harmonise and simplify the existing law in France relating to a manufacturer's liability for defective products. The French Government presented on 23 May 1990, draft legislation to Parliament for the implementation of the Directive into French law ('the Proposal').

The Proposal also amends the existing rules for protection against latent defects. The proposal was examined and adopted with few amendments by the Law Committee ('Commission des Lois') of the National Assembly during the Spring 1991 Parliamentary session. However, neither the National Assembly nor the Senate publicly debated and voted on the Proposal during that Parliamentary session. It is expected that the Proposal will finally be adopted during the 1991 Autumn session.

2. SELLER'S LIABILITY IN CONTRACT

2.1 Liability for pre-contractual statements or representations

Pursuant to article 28 of the *Ordonnance* of 1 December 1986 regarding freedom of prices and of competition, the seller of a product or the person providing the services must inform the consumer of any limitation of contractual liability and any special conditions of the sale or provision of services.

The seller who gives the potential purchaser insufficient or inaccurate information about the product during pre-contractual negotiations will be liable if the purchaser is mistaken as to the use and benefit he expects to enjoy from the product and would not have entered into the contract, or would have entered into the contract on different terms, if he had been correctly and sufficiently informed.

Although it may be difficult in practice to distinguish between the contractual and pre-contractual obligation of the seller to inform the purchaser, the courts generally consider that the seller will be liable in tort if the statement was made before the contract was entered into.[1]

The purchaser who has been given inaccurate or insufficient information may be awarded damages to compensate for any loss of profit he may have suffered.[2]

Special statutes regarding specific information which must be given in pre-contractual statements relate mainly to credit and loan transactions. However, certain products (eg cars) are subject to specific requirements.

2.2 Liability of the seller for hidden defects: Civil Code articles 1641 ff

This cause of action is central to product liability law in France. It is the one most commonly used by a purchaser dissatisfied with a defective product.

Article 1641 of the Civil Code provides that the seller is liable in respect of hidden defects which render the product sold unsuitable for its intended use.

The seller of a product who is under an obligation to deliver it is therefore placed under a further obligation to guarantee the product against hidden defects. The purchaser should not be deprived of the expected use of the product if it proves to be defective and he is thereby protected against any inherent defects.

A purchaser can bring an action founded on liability for latent defect, not only against the retailer that sold the product to him, but against any prior seller in the chain of supply, including the manufacturer.[3] This solution adopted by the courts appears to be based on the idea that the seller's obligation to guarantee against latent defect is an 'accessory' of the product and, as such, is attached to it and therefore belongs to any sub-purchaser in his capacity as owner.

To bring such a claim no intermediate purchaser should have had knowledge of the defect in the product.[4] Furthermore, the courts have decided that the sub-purchaser who is entitled to obtain damages from the manufacturer cannot seek to rescind the contract in situations where the purchase price in successive sales was significantly different.[5]

The purchaser may also bring an action against the seller who sold the goods to him and the manufacturer, who will be held jointly liable.[6] However, only the seller to whom the goods are returned will have to repay the purchase price.[7]

1 Cour de Cassation, 3rd Civil Chamber, 7 December 1988, GP 7 February 1989.
2 Cour de Cassation, 1st Civil Chamber, 4 October 1978, Bull Civ I, no 292.
3 Cour de Cassation, 1st Civil Chamber, 9 October 1979, Bull Civ I, no 241.
4 Cour de Cassation, 1st Civil Chamber, 13 May 1981, Bull Civ I, no 165.
5 Cour de Cassation, Commercial Chamber, 27 January 1973, JCP 1973, II, 17445.
6 Cour de Cassation, Commercial Chamber, 15 May 1972, Bull Civ IV, no 144.
7 Cour de Cassation, Commercial Chamber, 17 May 1982, Bull Civ IV, no 182.

2.2.1 *Defects for which the seller may be liable*

The purchaser will have to prove the existence of the defect which has caused the damage. In most product liability cases, the courts appoint an expert to determine whether the injury has been caused by the defective product.

The courts sometimes require that the plaintiff show the specific cause of the defect.[8] When the causes of the defect remain uncertain but external causes are unlikely, the courts will generally hold the manufacturer liable.[9]

i. Defects existing at the time of sale. The purchaser has to show that the defect existed prior to or, at the latest, at the time of purchase.

It is often difficult for the purchaser to prove the existence of the defect at the time of sale and it will be necessary in most cases for the purchaser to have an expert appointed by the courts, who will investigate whether the defect existed at the time of sale or whether the defect was due to the improper use or maintenance of the product by the purchaser, or to the operation of normal wear and tear upon the product. This means that where a product has been tested by the purchaser, or repaired by him, he will find it extremely difficult to prove that a defect existed prior to sale.

The courts, in deciding whether the defect existed prior to or at the time of sale, will take into account all the facts and circumstances.

The seller will be liable, notwithstanding that the defect was only latent at the time of sale.[10]

The Proposal adds a new article 1641–1 to the Civil Code which provides that any defect occurring within the period of a contractual warranty is presumed to have existed at the time of the sale unless the contrary can be established. In the absence of such a contractual warranty, the defect will be presumed to have existed at the time of delivery for a year commencing from the date of delivery. The Proposal thereby extends the reversal of the burden of proof operated by the Directive to liability for latent defects but only for one year. However, such presumption will not exist in sales between professionals *(professionnels)*.

The notion of 'professional' was developed by the courts (in contrast with the notion of 'consumer') and has subsequently been used by the legislator. The 'professional' is any person acting in his professional capacity, in the course of his business. The consumer is generally defined as a person purchasing the goods for his private and not for any professional purpose. The obligations and the rights of a seller or a purchaser will often vary according to his 'professional' or 'non-professional' or 'consumer' status.

ii. Latent defects. Once the existence of the defect (and possibly its cause) has been established, the court must be satisfied that the defect was hidden, especially where the seller claims that the defect could have been detected by the plaintiff.

The courts have set different standards depending on the professional status of the purchaser.

8 Cour de Cassation, Commercial Chamber, 27 November 1984, GP 1985 1 pan 80.
9 Cour de Cassation, Commercial Chamber, 20 May 1986, unpublished no 84–17–675.
10 Cour de Cassation, Civil Chamber, 6 November 1974, D 1975 IR 28.

In the case of a consumer purchase, the court will be satisfied that the defect was hidden where the purchaser could not have discovered the defect upon preliminary inspection.[11]

Professionals, on the other hand, are presumed to go through an in-depth check of the product and the seller will not be liable for the defect where the purchaser who shares the same area of expertise as the seller had the capability to discover the defect.[12]

2.2.2 Limitation period

Pursuant to article 1648 of the Civil Code, the purchaser of a product having a hidden defect must commence proceedings within a short period. This limitation period runs from the time of discovery of the defect in the goods.[13] The acceptable length of such a period is left to the discretion of the courts which exercise it according to the circumstances and the nature of the defect. They may, for instance, take into account the fact that negotiations with a view to an amicable settlement have taken place and failed before court proceedings were commenced.[14] The short period therefore varies from one case to another, from a few weeks to over a year. Generally, proceedings brought within a few months from discovery of the defect fall within the time limit, but a period exceeding one year is often deemed too long. The fact that the purchaser is a foreigner domiciled abroad is one of the circumstances which may be taken into account by the courts.

Article 2244 of the Civil Code provides that the limitation period can be interrupted by an interlocutory application (*action en référé*) (eg for the appointment of a judicial expert) and not necessarily an action on the merits.

The Proposal amends the limitation provisions currently set out in article 1648 of the Civil Code and provides that the purchaser's rights will expire where he has not informed the seller of the defect within a year from the time he has discovered or should have discovered the defect. However, this period of time may be modified amongst the professionals by trade usage or agreement.

The specific reference to the one-year period would have been a great improvement reducing the uncertainty linked to the application of the short period, in which proceedings must be brought. However, such impact is lessened by (a) the notion of when the defect should have been discovered, and (b) the reference to modification by trade usage in respect of sales amongst professionals.

2.2.3 Damages

Article 1644 of the Civil Code gives the purchaser a choice of two remedies. The first is for a reduction of the price proportional to the diminished value of the product (which is estimated by a court-appointed expert) and the other is the reimbursement of the price upon the return of the goods.

The Proposal adds to the Civil Code a new article 1644–1 according to which, where the sale was made by a professional seller, the purchaser may require,

11 Cour de Cassation, Commercial Chamber, 11 May 1965, Bull Civ III, no 279 and 24 January 1984, GP 1984–2-som 176.

12 Cour de Cassation, Commercial Chamber, 8 December 1980, Bull Civ IV, no 415 and 19 March 1985, unpublished no 83–16–280.

13 Cour de Cassation, Commercial Chamber, 22 November 1965, Bull Civ III, no 593.

14 Cour de Cassation, 1st Civil Chamber, 16 July 1987, D 1987, IR 182.

unless it is obviously unreasonable, (a) a reimbursement of the price on the return of the product, or (b) a reduction in the price, or (c) the repair of the product, or (d) the replacement of the product. The purchaser may not, however, seek reimbursement of the price or replacement of the product if he is unable, without legitimate reason, to return the product.

Article 1645 of the Civil Code provides that the seller who knew about the defect in the product is liable to pay damages to the purchaser and to repay the purchase price.

The courts in such cases have also set a different standard depending on the professional capacity of the seller. They have decided that professional sellers (which includes manufacturers) are presumed to know about the defects.[15]

Such presumption is irrebuttable. The seller will be held liable even if he shows that he was not aware of, and could not himself have discovered, the defect in the product, and that he had exercised due care in the manufacture and design of his product.[16] A manufacturer who is found liable for hidden defects cannot rely on the development risk defence.

The damages payable in such cases include all losses suffered by the purchaser caused by the defective product, ie the diminished value of the products themselves, the cost of repair, loss of profits and personal injury or damage to other products. The purchaser will have to prove the causal link between the defect and the damage.

The circumstances will sometimes clearly show that the damage resulted from a hidden defect (for instance, when burglars have been able to steal a large quantity of precious goods because of a defect in a security system).[17] It may, however, be difficult in the case of commercial loss of profits to establish that the loss resulted from the use of the defective product in the business where, for instance, the purchaser argues that damage arising from such use has injured his reputation and has resulted in a loss of profits.[18]

The seller will be liable when the damage is related to the defective product and would not have occurred without it, even though other factors may have contributed to the damage.[19]

The behaviour of the plaintiff is taken into account to determine whether or not the defect was hidden at the time of purchase; the liability of the manufacturer will also be reduced where the plaintiff has used the product in abnormal conditions. Where the damage results partly from the action of a third party, the producer will in most cases be held jointly liable.

2.2.4 *Exclusion or limitation of liability*

Pursuant to article 1643 of the Civil Code, the seller may stipulate in the contract that he will not be liable for hidden defects of which he had no knowledge.

However, as the courts have held that the professional seller is presumed to know of the hidden defects in his product, such clauses, whether limiting the

15 Cour de Cassation, 1st Civil Chamber, 19 January 1965, DS 1965, 389.
16 Cour de Cassation, 3rd Civil Chamber, 28 November 1966, DS 1967, 99 and Commercial Chamber, 15 November 1971, DS 1972, 211.
17 Cour de Cassation, 1st Civil Chamber, 18 March 1986, Bull Civ I, no 75.
18 Cour de Cassation, Commercial Chamber, 17 October 1977, Bull Civ IV, no 233.
19 Cour de Cassation, 2nd Civil Chamber, 30 November 1988, unpublished, no 87–15734.

duration of the liability, the types of defect or the nature of the damage for which the seller will be responsible, are invalid when a professional seller seeks to rely upon them against a consumer.[20]

In the case of contracts entered into between professionals, the seller may nevertheless produce evidence to show that the purchaser has the same field of expertise as himself and therefore the technical capability to have discovered the defect at the time of the sale.[1] In this event, a contractual exclusion clause would be effective.

Provisions limiting or excluding liability would not, in any case, be effective in limiting or excluding liability for damages for death or personal injury.

2.3 Obligation of the vendor to supply a 'conforming' product: Civil Code articles 1603 ff and 1184

The purchaser can bring an action to rescind the sale contract and claim damages based on article 1184 of the Civil Code for the non-performance by the seller of his obligation to deliver a product conforming to the purchaser's order or the contractual provisions.

The action is subject to the general rules of contractual liability and it can vest in the sub-acquirer.[2] The courts have granted to the sub-purchaser of a product the right to bring proceedings against a prior seller on the basis of the product's 'lack of conformity' to specification or the contract's provisions, just as a sub-purchaser has a right to take action against a prior seller in respect of latent defects (see above).

The juristic reason for this has not been given by the courts but it can be assumed that the seller's obligation to deliver a 'conforming' product (and consequently the right of the purchaser to receive a 'conforming' product) is also an 'accessory' of the product and, as such, is attached to it. The right of action of the previous purchaser against his seller is transmitted to the sub-purchaser. However, a sub-purchaser has no right of action against a prior seller for the product's lack of conformity when such lack of conformity arises from a breach of specific contractual provisions for which the prior seller is not liable, since he was not a party to that particular contract. The manufacturer and the seller can be held jointly liable for damages.[3]

2.3.1 *Lack of conformity*

The product's 'lack of conformity' to specification or the contract's provisions, as distinct from a latent defect, may consist of an altered quality of the product which will not necessarily affect its intended use. The obligation can also be invoked for an apparent defect in the product. However, the courts have recognised that the same defect could at the same time constitute a breach of the obligation of the seller to supply a product in accordance with the terms of the contract and make it unfit for its purpose.[4]

20 Cour de Cassation, Commercial Chamber, 20 July 1973, Bull Civ IV, no 264.
1 Cour de Cassation, Civil Chamber, 20 December 1983, Bull Civ I, no 308; Commercial Chamber, 29 November 1983, GP 1984–1 som 112 and 18 October 1988 (Resp civ et assur 88, comm 81).
2 Cour de Cassation, 1st Civil Chamber, 9 March 1983, JCP 1984, II, 20295.
3 Cour de Cassation, Commercial Chamber, 9 November 1986, BRDA 1987, 2 p 22.
4 Cour de Cassation, 1st Civil Chamber, 8 November 1988, Bull Civ I, no 314.

The courts are anxious to hold the seller liable to indemnify the purchaser where the defects are particularly serious, even though the conditions for liability for latent defects (especially the limitation period) are not met. They are now deciding that the 'lack of conformity of the product' may consist in the seller's failure to supply a product which fulfills its normal purpose (*conforme à sa destination normale*), ie a non-defective product.[5]

2.3.2 Limitation period

An action for 'lack of conformity' is not subject to the brief limitation period provided under article 1648 of the Civil Code.[6]

In accordance with the general rules of contract liability, the limitation period is either:

(a) ten years starting from the day when the damage occurred, for an action taken against a manufacturer or commercial seller; or
(b) thirty years against a private seller.

However, clauses providing for a shorter limitation period are valid when they are agreed between professionals in the same area of expertise.[7]

2.3.3 Exclusion or limitation of liability

Provisions limiting the seller's liability in respect of either his delivery obligation or the conformity of the product to his description have traditionally been deemed valid.

The solutions given by the courts for the liability for hidden defects referred to above have been confirmed by the legislator and extended to the general law of contract. Clauses excluding or limiting the liability of a professional for failing to perform his obligations are unenforceable against a non-professional or a consumer.[8]

2.4 Contractual warranties relating to the quality and safety of goods

A seller is, of course, entitled to give special warranties in respect of the products. The professional who provides a contractual warranty is under a further obligation to specify clearly that he is still liable to the purchaser for all consequences of the hidden defects of the product sold.[9]

The manufacturer may warrant the proper functioning of the product and freely undertake to replace parts in order to make the product suitable for its intended use or to replace the whole product. This free after-sales service is

5 Cour de Cassation, 1st Civil Chamber, 5 November 1985, Bull Civ I, no 287 and 14 February 1989, Bull Civ I, no 83.
6 Cour de Cassation, General Assembly, 7 February 1986, JCP 1986, II 20616; 1st Civil Chamber, 5 November 1985, Bull Civ I, no 287 and 13 December 1989, Bull Civ I, no 393.
7 Cour de Cassation, Commercial Chamber, 5 July 1988, unpublished, no 86–19342.
8 Statute 78–23 of 10 January 1978, art 35 and Decree 78–464 of 24 March 1978, art 2.
9 Decree 78–464 of 24 March 1978, art 4.

usually provided for a limited period and exceeds the seller's liability for latent defects as it also covers any imperfection in the product for which the purchaser is not responsible.

The action that a purchaser may have pursuant to this contractual warranty is not subject to the same rules as the liability for hidden defects and does not have to be initiated within the short limitation period required by article 1648 of the Civil Code.[10]

2.5 Mistake as to the substantial qualities of the product: Civil Code article 1110

A purchaser has an additional ground for action against a seller when he is dissatisfied with a defective product. The purchaser may seek to have the contract declared void for a product's mistake as to the substantive qualities and its ability to perform in the expected manner. The existence of a latent defect does not prevent the purchaser basing his action on the mistake as to the substantive qualities of the product.[11]

Where the seller has not wilfully misled the purchaser as to the substantive qualities of the product, the latter will not be allowed damages but will be entitled to repayment of the price.

Pursuant to article 1304 of the Civil Code, the purchaser can bring such an action within five years of his mistake being discovered. The courts have held that the purchaser is not subject to the short limitation period imposed by article 1648 of the Civil Code, even though the mistake was the consequence of the latent defect making the product improper for its intended use.[12] This solution is in line with the most recent case law relating to lack of conformity.

3. LIABILITY FOR TORTIOUS OR CONTRACTUAL BREACH

As a matter of principle, a breach will be determined as either tortious or contractual, but not both.

Where the loss results from the failure of a party to perform his contractual obligations the plaintiff must bring his action in contract. A purchaser of a defective product who has a contractual link with the manufacturer or with a prior seller, but who is not able to bring an action based on liability for latent defect, may invoke a breach of an express or implied contractual term pursuant to article 1147 of the Civil Code. The sub-purchaser of the product (as well as the purchaser) must base his action against the manufacturer on contractual liability.[13]

Where the plaintiff to a product liability claim neither owns nor possesses the defective goods and has not at any time entered into a contract with either the manufacturer or any of the intermediate distributors or where the loss does

10 Cour de Cassation, Commercial Chamber, 2 May 1990, JCP 1990, IV, 246.
11 Cour de Cassation, 3rd Civil Chamber, 18 May 1988, D 1988, IR 155.
12 Cour de Cassation, 1st Civil Chamber, 28 June 1988, DS 1989, p 450.
13 Cour de Cassation, 1st Civil Chamber, 31 January 1973, JCP 1975, Ed G, I, 2679.

not result from the failure of a party to perform his contractual obligations, the plaintiff must base his action on tortious liability alone. The manufacturer can be held liable pursuant to article 1382 of the Civil Code, which places liability on those who cause injury to others as a result of the tortious breach or pursuant to article 1384 paragraph 5 of the Civil Code which makes an employer liable in respect of breaches caused by his employees acting in the course of their employment.

However, the courts have been willing to provide the victims with sufficient protection regardless of the lack of a contractual link with the manufacturer or a seller. They have developed the obligations of the manufacturer, from the articles of the Civil Code, imposing on the manufacturer similar obligations vis-à-vis contracting parties and third parties. The courts have therefore unified the remedies available in contract and tort, thereby creating a general product liability for manufacturers.

3.1 Breach

The plaintiff must prove a breach by the manufacturer either in tort or in contract. The breach may relate to design or manufacturing defects and includes a situation where the manufacturer has failed to inform or warn the purchaser of the possible dangers of the product. The manufacturer will also be liable for damage in respect of breaches caused by his employees acting in the course of employment, pursuant to article 1384 paragraph 5 of the Civil Code.

3.1.1 Design or manufacturing defects

The courts have found manufacturers who have put into circulation defective products to be in breach of their tortious or contractual duties. The manufacturer, in fact, has an obligation to deliver products that are free of defects. All the plaintiff will have to show is that the product was defective.[14]

The fact that the manufacturer has carried out control procedures and necessary checking to ensure the maximum safety of his products will not necessarily exclude him from liability.[15]

3.1.2 Lack of sufficient information for the proper use of the product

The manufacturer may be held liable for damage resulting from a lack of adequate information being given on the condition of the product and precautions that must be taken as to the use of the product, where the purchaser is subsequently deprived of the use and expected benefits arising therefrom.[16] All information and warnings regarding products marketed in France must be in French.[17]

14 Cour de Cassation, Civil Chamber, 21 January 1962, Bull Civ I, no 155, 19 July 1972, Bull Civ I, no 189 and 22 November 1978, JCP 1979, II, 19139.
15 Criminal Court of Seine, 19 December 1957, S 1958, 137.
16 Cour de Cassation, 1st Civil Chamber, 23 April 1985, Bull Civ I, no 125.
17 Statute 75–1349 of 31 December 1975, Circular of 14 March 1977 amended by Circular of 20 October 1982, and Text 83–64 Administrative Directive of 13 April 1983 (E/1) (for imported goods).

Specific labelling information requirements vary from one category of product to another (foodstuffs, cosmetics, pharmaceutical products, tobacco, dangerous products, seeds, etc).

3.1.3 *Lack of sufficient warning regarding the potential dangers of the product*

Where the product is not necessarily defective but may prove to be dangerous in use, the professional purchaser, as well as the ordinary consumer, must be warned about the possible dangers of the product.

A lack of sufficient warning regarding the risks incidental to use of the product constitutes a breach on the part of the manufacturer.[18] In the case of products comprising dangerous substances, various orders *(arrêtés)* laid down by the administration govern the various specifications (colour, size, warning, symbols etc).[19] For instance, the word 'DANGEREUX' (dangerous) must be printed in very obvious black lettering on a green stripe. Non-compliance is subject to criminal sanction.

3.2 Damages

The manufacturer may be exonerated or his liability may be reduced if he proves that the injury was due to an external cause, such as an Act of God, action of a third party or fault on the part of the plaintiff, eg when the plaintiff has used the product in abnormal conditions or ignored any warnings and advice given by the manufacturer.[20]

However, the professional purchaser may be deemed to be aware of the dangers of the product or to be under an obligation to make proper enquiries.[1]

3.3 Exclusion or limitation of liability

Clauses limiting or excluding the liability of the manufacturer will be invalid in the case of an action based on tort. When the liability arises out of a contractual breach, the clauses limiting or excluding liability are in principle valid. As discussed above, these clauses are no longer enforceable against consumers. In certain circumstances, the courts have decided that a breach constitutes gross negligence and that the clause is accordingly ineffective.[2]

4. LIABILITY IN TORT BASED ON ARTICLE 1384 PARAGRAPH 1

The courts have developed from article 1384 paragraph 1 of the Civil Code a principle of strict liability in respect of injury caused by products which a person has in his custody (*garde*).[3] This person is in most cases the owner of the product.

18 Cour de Cassation, Civil Chamber, 28 March 1968, Bull Civ III, no 144 and 14 December 1982, Bull Civ I, no 361.
19 Labour Code art L 231–6.
20 Cour de Cassation, Civil Chamber, 21 June 1962, Bull Civ II, no 537.
1 Cour de Cassation, 1st Civil Chamber, 26 November 1981, Bull Civ I, no 354.
2 Cour de Cassation, 1st Civil Chamber, 22 November 1978, JCP 1979, II, 19139.
3 Cour de Cassation, United Chambers, 13 February 1930, S 1930, 1–121.

In order to indemnify a plaintiff who has no direct contractual link with the seller or the manufacturer, the courts have developed the concept of custody of the structure of the product (*garde de la structure*) by which the manufacturer's liability continues after delivery of the product.[4] The manufacturer is deemed to be able to control the internal structure of the product and check whether the product could be used without danger, even though he no longer owns or possesses the product.[5] However, this concept of custody has been applied only to products with inherent dynamic forces capable of becoming dangerous by exploding or imploding, such as bottled gas, television sets, soft drink bottles etc.[6]

The plaintiff will only have to show a causal relationship between the damage suffered and the product.

The manufacturer of the product may exonerate himself by proving that the damage was due to an external cause, such as a mistake committed by the plaintiff. His liability will be reduced if he shows that the plaintiff has contributed to the damage.[7]

Article 1386–18 of the Proposal states that, once the product is put into circulation, the manufacturer may no longer be held liable as 'custodian' of the product. This cause of action is regarded as unnecessary, especially in the light of the implementation of the Directive.

4.1 Exclusion or limitation of liability

As stated above, clauses excluding or limiting the liability of the manufacturer have no effect in an action based on tort liability.[8]

4.2 Limitation period

Pursuant to article 2270–1 of the Civil Code the limitation period for tort actions is ten years from when the damage occurred or the loss was further aggravated.[9]

5. CRIMINAL LIABILITY

In the case of accidents resulting in death or personal injury caused by a defective product, the manufacturer will be subject to criminal liability, for example, where he is guilty of gross negligence or non-compliance with regulations.

4 Cour de Cassation, Civil Chamber, 5 January 1956, D 1957, 261.
5 Cour de Cassation, Civil Chamber, 12 November 1975, JCP 1976, Ed G, II, 18479.
6 Cour de Cassation, Civil Chamber, 5 June 1971, Bull Civ II, no 204.
7 Cour de Cassation, Civil Chamber, 5 June 1971 and 6 April 1987, JCP 1987, II, 20828.
8 Cour de Cassation, Civil Chamber, 17 February 1955, D 1956, 17.
9 Statute 85–677 of 5 July 1985.

The manufacturer of a dangerous product (and the seller when he is aware of the danger) who does not warn the purchaser of the product of its dangers, or who does not withdraw the product from sale when it has caused personal injuries, will be subject to criminal sanctions.[10]

Only individuals are subject to criminal sanctions.[11]

The manager will usually be held responsible either for his personal acts and decisions or for his failure to organise production in a way to avoid breach by an employee. In the case of a *société anonyme* managed by a Board of Directors, the chairman of the Board will be held responsible; in the case of a *société anonyme* managed by an Executive Board, the members of the Board or its single executive director, as the case may be, will be held responsible.

In the case of a *Société à Responsabilité Comitée* or a *Société en Commandite par Actions*, the manager (*gérant*) will be liable.

Where several managers could be incriminated, the allocation of tasks may enable the courts to determine which person is actually responsible.

Sanctions in the case of death resulting from a defective product consist of imprisonment from three months to two years, and fines from FF 1,000 to FF 30,000.

In the case of personal injuries, sanctions consist of imprisonment from ten days to one year and/or a fine from FF 500 to FF 5,000.

6. LIABILITY FOR DEFECTIVE PRODUCTS BROUGHT ABOUT BY BREACH OF STATUTORY REGULATION DESIGNED TO PROTECT CONSUMERS AND/OR TO PROMOTE SAFETY

6.1 Statute 83–660 of 21 July 1983 relating to consumer safety

Manufacturers are under an obligation to supply products which under normal conditions of use, or under conditions of use which could be reasonably expected by the manufacturer, provide a level of safety which a person can reasonably expect and will not injure the health of the individual.

The statute gives specific powers to the administration to regulate and prohibit the manufacture and distribution of products which do not satisfy safety requirements.

The manufacturer, or the importer who is responsible for putting the product into circulation on French territory for the first time, must check that the product complies with the current mandatory regulations and when asked by inspectors from the administration must give proof of tests and controls carried out on the product. The administration may also request manufacturers, importers or distributors to ensure that products already on the market conform to the safety rules.

When a product already on the market appears to be dangerous, or when the characteristics of a new product seem to justify such precaution, the

10 Cour de Cassation, Criminal Chamber, 14 March 1974, GP 1974–1–417 and 27 May 1972, Bull Crim 444.

11 Cour de Cassation, Criminal Chamber, 8 March 1883, S 1885–1–470.

administration may prescribe that professionals have their products checked by an authorised institution.

The administration may also order the manufacturer to issue warnings to the public and make announcements as to particular precautions for use of the product.

In case of serious or immediate danger, the administration may temporarily suspend the manufacture, importation or distribution of the product or require its modification, withdrawal or destruction.

Non-compliance with the administrative request or order will be subject to fines of a criminal nature, publicity measures and confiscation of profits arising from sale of the product.

6.2 Statute 78–23 of 10 January 1978 for the protection of and information to consumers of products and services

This statute has enabled the government to pass decrees for the prohibition, limitation or regulation of provisions included in contracts imposed by professionals upon non-professionals or consumers, regarding the extent of their liability, when such provisions constitute an abuse of their market position and afford excessive benefits to the professional.

As discussed above, Decree 78–464 of 24 March 1978 has prohibited such provisions, and has imposed on professionals providing a contractual warranty a duty to inform the consumer that they remain liable to the consumer for latent defects.

7. SPECIAL LIABILITIES ARISING IN RESPECT OF PARTICULAR PRODUCTS

Certain products which may particularly affect the health or safety of consumers are subject to particular rules – the introduction of products such as pharmaceutical products, foodstuff additives, chewing gum, seeds, cars, video tapes and video discs must be authorised before they are put into circulation on the market. Chemical products, cosmetics and diet products are subject to notification before their introduction on the market.

Manufacturers, importers or distributors who do not comply with these specific rules may be subject to criminal sanctions.

7.1 Pharmaceutical products

Although the development risk defence is not currently available under French law, medical products enjoy a particular status.

The courts have decided that a manufacturer will not be held liable for the damage caused by a pharmaceutical product which was the only one to enable a certain kind of medical treatment.[12] However, when a new competing product is put on the market and is less damaging than the first product, the manufacturer of the first product must then withdraw it from the market.[13]

12 Cour de Cassation, 1st Civil Chamber, 8 October 1970, Bull Civ I, no 248.
13 Cour de Cassation, Civil Chamber, 25 May 1973, JCP 1975, II, 17955.

The courts appear reluctant to declare the manufacturer of pharmaceutical products liable pursuant to the rules for latent defects when no development risk defence is available to the manufacturer.[14]

Manufacturers of pharmaceutical products are under an obligation to appoint a pharmacist as part of the management team. Pursuant to article L596 of the Public Health Code, this pharmacist is personally responsible for the application of rules enacted in the interests of public health.

7.2 Nuclear substances

France is a party to the OECD Paris Convention of 29 July 1960, to the Brussels Complementary Convention of 31 January 1963 and to the Additional Protocol of 28 January 1964 amended on 16 November 1982.

A first Statute 90–397 of 11 May 1990 has authorised the ratification of the Protocol of 16 November 1986 and a second Statute 90–488 of 16 June 1990 has increased the maximum amount for which French operators can be liable to FF 600m per nuclear accident. However, the total liability of the operator in respect of a 'limited risk' site is limited to FF 150m per accident. The same limit is applicable in the case of accidents occurring during transport of nuclear substances by French operators in respect of claims involving nuclear substances.

The French state will be responsible for damages exceeding these amounts pursuant to the rules of the Conventions.

When nuclear substances are in transit on French territory, the carrier is under an obligation to be insured for FF 1,500m.

The Paris Court of First Instance (*Tribunal de Grande Instance*) has exclusive jurisdiction in respect of proceedings instituted against French operators.

The statute of 16 June 1990 came into effect on the publication on 10 January 1991 of the 1982 Protocol in the French Official Journal.

8. LIABILITY FOR DEFECTIVE PRODUCTS ARISING FROM NATIONAL LAW IN FRANCE: IMPLEMENTATION OF EC DIRECTIVE 85/374 ON PRODUCT LIABILITY

8.1 Introduction

The EC Commission issued a warning to the French government in March 1990, in respect of its failure to adopt the Directive into French law. As mentioned above, the Proposal for implementing the Directive in France, already amended by the Law Committee of the National Assembly on 20 June 1991, should be discussed by Parliament and thereafter adopted during the first parliamentary session to be held in Autumn 1991.

The information below is, therefore, based only on the Proposal as amended by the Law Committee, which may of course be subject to future amendment by Parliament.

The new rules are to be inserted as a new title IVbis of the third book of the Civil Code in between title IV which relates to non-contractual liability and titles V ff which regulate various types of contracts.

14 Cour de Cassation, 1st Civil Chamber, 8 April 1986, Bull Civ I, no 82.

The new rules will apply to products first put into circulation after the date of coming into force of the new statute, even where any such products were subject to prior contract.

Except for the provisions discussed below, the Proposal reproduces faithfully the provisions of the Directive.

8.2 Description of special or anomalous provisions in respect of product liability law

8.2.1 Damages: article 1386–2

(a) The new rules for product liability would apply to a wider type of damage than that stated in the Directive.

Concerning the first category of damage, article 1386–2 of the Proposal refers to damage resulting from injury to the person. This will include not only damage resulting from death and personal injuries, but also non-material damage, such as pain and suffering.

An injured person should therefore be able to recover in respect of a range of damage caused by a single product according to a single set of rules. This solution, although not prescribed by the Directive which finally left the question of recovery of non-material damages to national legislation, avoids unnecessary complication of proceedings.

(b) The new rules will apply to damage or to destruction of any item of property (other than the defective product itself) regardless of whether the type and/or use of the product is private or professional. The Proposal has extended the field of application of the new rules to damage in respect of products of a professional nature or applied for professional use or consumption again in order to simplify the rules governing producers' liability. However, existing rules for product liability would remain applicable for damage to the defective product itself.

(c) The French version of the Directive differs from the English one as it refers not to a threshold for liability, but to a 'franchise', the effect of which, where damages are of an amount exceeding Ecu 500, renders the producer liable only for the excess balance. However, the Proposal for product liability would apply whatever the amount, whether it is below or above the threshold of Ecu 500.

It was also preferred to have a single set of rules to govern producers' liability as previous rules would have otherwise been applicable to damages of a value less than Ecu 500.

8.2.2 Release of the product: article 1386–5

The Proposal specifies that a product is put into circulation when it is voluntarily released by the producer.

8.2.3 Producers: article 1386–6

The Proposal specifies that producers who are held liable under the rules are those acting in their professional capacity.

The Proposal also states that even where the producer or the importer of the product can be identified and the injured person is informed of his identity, the vendor, lessor or supplier of the product will be treated as a producer. The vendor, lessor or supplier, as the case may be, will then have a claim against the producer by the same rules as those applying to the plaintiff. He will have to commence proceedings within a year of proceedings being initiated against him.

This solution is clearly more beneficial to the plaintiff than that provided by the Directive and confirms the existing French case law which holds the seller jointly liable with a producer for hidden defects.

8.2.4 'State of the art'; administrative approval; defences not available to the producer: article 1386–9

The Proposal specifies that the producer may be held liable even though the product and its manufacturer was 'state of the art' or was the subject of an authorisation granted by an administrative body. This is consistent with existing case law.

The courts will have to distinguish the notion of 'state of the art' from the state of scientific or technical knowledge which could enable the defect's existence to come to light. This could cause some problems before the courts in the future as it might be presumed that the 'state of the art' should reflect the state of, if not scientific, at least technical, knowledge at the time when the product was put into circulation.

8.2.5 Cause exonerating the producer from his liability: article 1386–11

The Law Committee amended the Proposal which virtually stated that the use of the product in abnormal conditions which the producer could not be expected to have foreseen mitigates or extinguishes the producer's liability.

The Law Committee made the provision conform with article 8(2) of the Directive which states that the liability of the producer may be reduced or disallowed when, having regard to the circumstances, the damage is caused by both a defect in the product and the fault of the injured person or any person for whom the injured person is responsible. The use of the product in abnormal conditions which the producer could not be expected to have foreseen was, in the initial version of the Proposal, the only fault of the victim which may be taken into account to reduce the producer's liability.

The amendment made by the Law Committee to the Proposal further specifies that the use of the product in abnormal conditions reasonably foreseeable by the producer does not constitute a fault of the victim.

Again, the courts will have to apply the 'reasonable forseeability' test to apply this provision which implies that abnormal conditions of use can reasonably be expected by the producer.

8.2.6 Appropriate measures to prevent damages: article 1386–13

This article states that where the producer does not establish that he has taken all appropriate measures to prevent injurious consequences, including (a) making information available to the public or recalling the product for appraisal, or (b) withdrawing the product, he will be liable within the conditions of title IVbis for any defect in, or danger caused by, the product which appears within ten years from the date when the product was put into circulation.

This provision appears to be a ground of exoneration of the producer not expressly referred to in the Directive. Although the Directive's definition of the defective product refers to the level of safety which a person is entitled to expect and may take into account the information given by the producer to the public, it seems that the producer could be exonerated under this defence even in circumstances where a person could reasonably expect the product to be safe. It may, however, be difficult to bring evidence (and to convince a judge) that the producer has taken all appropriate measures to prevent the injurious consequences caused by the defective product.

The Law Committee takes a different view of this provision. It analyses it as an additional obligation on the producer, introducing a new regime whereby the producer is unable to invoke any of the reductions or limitations or liability set forth in the rest of the Proposal.

8.2.7 *Provisions limiting or excluding liability: article 1386–14*

Clauses which purport to exclude or limit liability for defective products are prohibited and considered void. However, in contracts between professionals, provisions limiting or excluding liability of professionals in respect of damage to goods which are not used by the plaintiff mainly for his own private use or consumption, will be valid provided that they do not constitute an abuse of market position which would confer an undue advantage.

This is not inconsistent with the Directive, which prohibits provisions limiting or exempting the producer's liability arising from the Directive, ie in respect of damage to goods used by the victim for his own private use or consumption.

8.2.8 *Contractual or tortious breach of the producer: article 1386–15*

Unless the producer has committed a contractual or tortious breach, the rights of the victim under these rules are extinguished ten years after the product was put into circulation.

This means that after this ten-year period, the existing general rules for determining the liability of the producer for contractual or tortious breach will again apply (so long as their limitation period has not already expired).

8.2.9 *Exclusive application of the new rules: articles 1386–17 and 1386–5*

The rules of title IVbis will exclude the simultaneous application of other provisions in the Civil Code which protect the plaintiff against safety defects (including in articles 1641–1649) for the ten years after which the product was put into circulation. However, the special rules of liability in construction law will still apply (articles 1792–1799 and 2270).

Provisions governing the liability of the producer for breach and that of the persons for whom he is responsible (typically employees) may also apply simultaneously.

The articles of the Code relating to liability for hidden defects are specifically excluded. These rules would nevertheless still apply for damage to the defective product itself which is not covered by these rules.

Once the product has been put into circulation, the producer may no longer be held liable pursuant to article 1384 as 'custodian' of the product.

The reasons for excluding the simultaneous application of the new rules and the other rules of the Civil Code are given in the preamble to the Proposal as follows:

(a) to avoid a multiplicity of actions brought on different grounds, which are often unnecessarily duplicated;
(b) to enable suppliers to establish precisely the extent of their liability, which would otherwise remain uncertain.

It has been argued that this exclusion is contrary to article 13 of the Directive, which provides that it 'shall not affect any rights which an injured person may have according to the rules of the law of contractual or non-contractual or special liability existing at the moment when the Directive is notified'.

However, it seems difficult to imagine that the Directive could seek to stultify the existing national laws at their various stages of development above the harmonised minimum level of protection indicated in the Directive.

The exclusion of the simultaneous application of articles governing hidden defects is in fact the only way to provide the producer with an effective development risk defence. If the rules existing prior to the notification of the Directive were to remain fully in force, the injured party would have taken an action under articles 1641–1649 which do not allow the producer to invoke the development risk defence.

8.2.10 Lessor and lender: Articles 1713–1 and 1891

The rules governing liability for the defects of the product sold also apply to the hire, leasing or temporary loan *(prêt à usage)* of the product.

8.3 Optional provisions in the EC Directive

8.3.1 Definition of product: article 1386–3

The new rules would apply to any movables including primary agricultural products (ie products of the soil, of stockfarming and of fisheries) and game.

The option to cover agricultural products is in line with traditional case law which has held producers to be liable for hidden defects of agricultural products.

8.3.2 Development risk defence: article 1386–10(4)

The French Government strongly opposed this defence when the Directive was first drafted. The Proposal has finally adopted the development risk defence and does not take advantage of the derogation provision of article 15.1(b) of the Directive to maintain the existing law.

The defence was finally inserted into the Proposal in order to avoid creating competitive disadvantage for French producers (mainly marketing their products in France) who could have been the only ones (together with Luxembourguese producers) to bear the cost of the development risk, as against the other EC producers.

Such a defence was not available under existing French law as a producer could not avoid liability for latent defects, on the ground that he was not himself aware of the defect when he put the product into circulation, even where it was impossible for him to discover the defect.

In order to provide the producers with an effective development risk defence, it was necessary to eliminate the possibility for a person to rely on his previous rights according to the rules of contractual or extra-contractual liability existing at the moment when the Directive was implemented.

However, it is likely that the French courts will be quite strict in assessing the state of scientific and technical knowledge required to enable the producer to discover any defects in products. Mere compliance with the 'state of the art' at the time at which the product was put into circulation is an insufficient reason for exonerating the producer from liability.

8.3.3 Ecu 70m limit

The Proposal does not limit the producer's total liability to Ecu 70m for damages resulting from death or personal injury and caused by identical items.

This situation is consistent with existing French rules for product liability.

9. COMPARISON OF THE EFFECTS OF PRODUCT LIABILITY LAW WITH THE PREVIOUS POSITION IN CONTRACT AND TORT

The implementation of the Directive in French law as proposed at the time of writing should simplify the current law by reducing the possible causes of action which can be brought by victims of defective products against producers and by creating a more coherent scheme. The distinction between liability deriving from a contractual or a tortious breach would be abolished.

It is not generally anticipated that it will bring a drastic change to the current French position in respect of product liability claims since French courts have in the past interpreted and applied the provisions of the Civil Code quite stringently against producers.

However, in order to appreciate the consequences of the implementation of the Directive, it will be necessary to wait and see how and at which level the courts will apply the standard of safety which can 'reasonably' be expected from a product and whether the definition of a defective product, by reference to the lack of safety which a person could reasonably expect, differs substantially from the notion of a defective product under the view currently applied by the courts.

The position of the producer will be worsened inasmuch as the Directive has reversed the burden of proof regarding the existence of the defect prior to the supply. As indicated above, such evidence was previously difficult for the plaintiff to bring in certain circumstances (eg damage occurring many years after the purchase or where the product has been repaired by the purchaser).

It is is also worth noting that the three-year limitation period contained in the Directive and applicable to proceedings for recovery of damages is much longer than the short period currently allowed by French law for claims for hidden defects and that this may have an effect on the liability of producers (although in practice, where the defects are particularly serious, French courts have held the producers liable even though the limitation period has expired under the liability for hidden defects (see above)).

In contrast, the position of manufacturers will be improved with regard to the exoneration of responsibility for development risk.

CHAPTER VI

Federal Republic of Germany

Klaus-Ulrich Link Esq
Dr Thomas Sambuc

Lichtenstein, Körner & Partners
Heidehofstrasse 9
7000 Stuttgart 1
Federal Republic of Germany

Tel ++ 49 711 48 9790
Fax ++ 49 711 48 1577

CHAPTER VI

Federal Republic of Germany

1. INTRODUCTION

On 1 January 1990 the Product Liability Act came into force in West Germany, thereby implementing the EC Directive. The Act applies only to products that have been distributed after the Act has come into force. Even though this Act changes details of the previously existing law, it does not lead to a fundamental change of the risks involved with making and/or distributing defective products. Product liability had previously been established in West Germany, particularly by a leading decision by the Federal Supreme Court of 26 November 1968.[1] The Act only provides an additional legal ground for bringing a product liability claim, and thus facilitates the successful assertion of such claims in some cases.

Product liability claims in Germany may be based either on contractual law or on the law of torts. Contractual law applies only between parties who have entered into some sort of agreement; claims based on the law of torts may be raised by anyone who has suffered injury or loss from a defective product.

The following expressions are used frequently in this chapter. The German has been added for clarification, since the more or less literal English translations sometimes have a different meaning within the Anglo-Saxon legal systems. Thus, the definitions and explanations are meant to explain only what a German lawyer would mean by the respective expressions.

(a) The *law of torts* deals with the non-contractual liability for damage based on fault.

(b) *No-fault liability* does not presuppose fault (defined under German law as intent or negligence) on the part of the liable person.

(c) *Product liability* (*Produkthaftung* or *Produzentenhaftung* – 'producer liability') is the liability of the producer, seller, supplier, or quasi-producer for consequential damage resulting from the use of a defective product.

(d) *Breach of contract* (*positive Vertragsverletzung*) is a fault-based violation of any contractual duty other than delay or inability/impossibility of performance.

(e) *Culpa in contrahendo* or *cic* is the violation of duties before or at the time of contracting.

(f) By *producer* we mean only one who has actually produced the product (the Directive and the Act use this term in a broader sense which includes, in particular, persons who import products into the Community).

1 BGH decision of 26.11.1968 – VI ZR 212/66 – NJW 1969, 384 – 'Hühnerpest'.

(g) *Seller* is anybody who has sold the product either for further processing or to the ultimate consumer.
(h) *Suppliers* are the producers of parts or components that are being used by the producer to make the finished product.
(i) *Quasi-producer* is a person who presents himself as a producer by affixing his name, trademark or other distinguishing feature.
(j) The *Product Liability Act* (or *Act*) is the German Product Liability Act (*Produkthaftungsgesetz*) of 15 November 1989 which came into force on 1 January 1990. This Act implemented the Directive.
(k) *Protective laws* (*Schutzgesetze*) are laws designed to protect individuals from any kind of harm.
(l) The *BGB* is the German *Bürgerliches Gesetzbuch* or Civil Code of 1896.
(m) The *Directive* is the Council Directive of 25 July 1985 on the approximation of the laws, regulations and administrative provisions of the Member States concerning liability for defective products.
(n) The *courts* before which product liability cases can be brought are the Local Court (*Amtsgericht – AG*), the County Court (*Landgericht – LG*), the Court of Appeals (*Oberlandesgericht – OLG*) and the Federal Supreme Court (*Bundesgerichtshof – BGH*). The Federal Supreme Court is not a trial court, but the court of last instance which only decides legal issues.
(o) *Court decisions* are cited with their date, docket number and reference. German leading cases are generally given a name which is not derived from the parties but from the particular product or damage that the case deals with.

2. LIABILITY IN CONTRACT

Just like its tort counterpart, *contractual product liability* deals with the damage or injury someone has suffered as a *consequence* of a defect in a product. Such claims must be strictly distinguished from *warranty* claims, which concern the defective *product proper*.

In order to make the separation between the neighbouring areas of warranty and contractual product liability clear, we would first like to give an outline of warranty claims under German law.

2.1 Outline of warranty claims

Warranty claims are based on the fundamental idea that the buyer, who pays good money, should receive a good product in exchange, ie a product which is free from any defects and which can be fully used for the buyer's purposes. In contrast, product liability protects the buyer's and third parties' interest not to incur injuries or losses except for diminished value of the product proper. The integrity of protected legal interests (such as health, property or assets) must not be infringed upon by the (defective) product.[2] Since a warranty concerns only the product proper, it does not cover the consequential damage that typically gives rise to product liability claims.

2 Palandt, BGB, 49. ed, ProdHaftG, § 3 annotation 1.

In the case of a *sales* contract, the BGB gives the buyer a choice either to return the defective product in exchange for the price paid, or to reduce the sales price. The parties may also agree on having the defective product replaced, or on having it made fit for use by the seller. The buyer can only claim damages if he has been wilfully deceived by the seller, or if the product is lacking specific characteristics which have been the subject of an express representation by the seller.

The customer's legal rights are different, if he does not buy an already finished product, but if he engages in a *contract for work and services*, in which the contractor undertakes to bring about a particular result, eg to build a house or to repair a car. If the result of this work does not comply with the contractual requirements, the customer can require the contractor to make the product fit for use. Only if the contractor fails to do so may the customer ask for his money back, or reduce the agreed price, or claim damages (BGB § 635). Drawing a line between this claim for damages in the context of a contract for work and services, and a product liability claim based on the same defects, is difficult. The courts have made the following distinction: damages that can be claimed based on BGB § 635 have been limited to damage directly connected with the result of the work, whereas damage done to other objects as a consequence of the defective work can only be compensated if product liability applies.

This distinction is not only of a theoretical nature, but it has extremely important practical consequences for the calculation of recoverable damages and for the scope of coverage by a product liability insurance.

For example, it is clear that insurance does not mean that the insurance company will have to perform the contract instead of the contractor. Still, both the warranty claim based on BGB § 635 and the product liability claim are rooted in the defect of the product.

If the defect in the product has not caused any consequential damage, the producer (in his capacity as *seller*) is obliged to remedy the defect, or to compensate damage done to the product proper. As long as further damage has not occurred, the customer's claims will be satisfied by the warranty.

If, however, the producer has made a car with defective brakes, and if this defect leads to an accident, in which the buyer of the car is injured and another car is written-off, we must distinguish between the following claims:

(a) The buyer has a warranty claim against the seller because of the defective brakes.
(b) The buyer will also want to be compensated for the injury he has suffered, and to be reimbursed for the payments he will have to make for writing-off the other car. These claims against the manufacturer stem from the consequences the defective brakes have had for other protected rights which can be clearly distinguished from the defective car itself. Therefore, these are *consequential damages* that can only be recovered under product liability. They do not relate to remedying the car's defects, and thus will fall under the cover of the product liability insurance.

After this digression into warranty, we will now turn to the actual subject of this chapter, namely, contractual product liability.

The most important cases in which contractual product liability can be incurred are those involving the non-compliance with the seller's express representation that the product sold is of a specific quality, and breach of contract. Of lesser importance are culpa in contrahendo and promises of specific guarantees.

Even though the contractual product liability presupposes, as a general rule, contractual privity, third parties may also rely on it in exceptional cases.

2.2 Liability for culpa in contrahendo

Pre-contractual ties oblige both parties to take more than average care of each other's interests. Even though they have not yet reached the state of contractual privity, they are already subject to a more intricate set of duties than strangers.

Violations of such pre-contractual duties are called culpa in contrahendo.[3] This legal concept cannot be found in the BGB; it has been developed by the judiciary by well-established case law.

Culpa in contrahendo does not play an important part in contractual product liability, since losses and injuries are caused by defective products generally only *after* the product has been sold (and thus contractual privity has been established), and not during the pre-contractual stage. However, it may apply during the test phase of a product, or when duties concerning proper instructions[4] have been violated.

As always, culpa in contrahendo presupposes fault.[5]

2.3 Seller's representations relating to the quality or the safety of goods

The distinction between product liability and warranty, which we have repeatedly emphasised, is subject to an important exception in connection with the seller's representations concerning specific qualities of the product. The BGB refers to such representations only in connection with warranty claims, but they have gained increased importance in connection with product liability as well. This ambiguity is a consequence of the buyer of the defective product to choose between asking for his money back, or reducing the purchase price, or claiming damages (BGB § 463). These damages serve to compensate both for the product's defect and/or for consequential damages.

The buyer may raise these claims if:

(a) he has concluded a *sales contract* with the seller;
(b) the seller has made a *representation* that the product has *specific qualities*; and
(c) the product is actually *lacking* these qualities when handed over to the buyer.

3 Münchner Kommentar BGB, 2 ed, annotation 32 before § 275.
4 Cf Ch B IV S.
5 Cf Ch B IV.

This liability is particularly dangerous for the seller, because it does not presuppose fault.

The following points should be noted.

(1) BGB § 463 applies to the usual sale of finished goods as well as to contracts for work and services, provided that the contractor does serial work to make a serial product. Thus, machines coming out of series manufacture are subject to this strict liability. In particular, the seller's representation concerning performance specifications might trigger this strict liability.

(2) The decisive prerequisite for this strict liability is the seller's representation of a specific quality.

There are three problems that require a detailed explanation. First, the seller's representation must have been agreed upon by the parties. The terms must be express, not implied (cf (a) below). However, even though the representation must be distinctly stated, it may be tacit (cf (b), below). Finally, since the parties often negotiate the product's qualities before the sale, it is necessary to single out those qualities that are the subject of the seller's representation from other qualities upon which the parties have agreed (cf (c), below).

(a) Products which are not the subject of a representation by the seller are, eg, advertisements or general product descriptions in the usual catalogues. Both serve to attract the customer's attention before the agreement has actually been concluded.

Things may look different when a catalogue contains specific assertions upon which the customer relies. In a case where a picture had been described in an auction catalogue in a detailed manner, and had been offered for sale for a very considerable price, the Court of Appeal held that this was a representation of the picture's authenticity. The Federal Supreme Court reversed this judgment and held that statements in an auction catalogue are not legally binding.[6]

(b) Under what circumstances can the representation of a specific quality be made tacitly? During the contract negotiations, the customer must make it clear that he attributes particular importance to the seller's statements, and the overall conduct of the seller – not necessarily his verbal statements – must be such that the buyer may assume that the seller is willing to guarantee the specific quality. The Federal Supreme Court established this prerequisite in a case where the buyer had submitted samples of wood to the seller in order to enable the latter to recommend an appropriate varnish. The court held that since the seller guaranteed the actual presence of the respective quality he thus declared his readiness to be responsible for all consequences that might follow from the actual lack of this quality. Of paramount importance is not the actual intention of the seller, but the impression his overall conduct, together with all the other circumstances of the case, make upon the buyer.[7]

(c) It is particularly difficult to distinguish the usual quality of a product, which is often the subject of discussions during the contract negotiations, from additional qualities being the subject of express

6 BGH in NJW 1980, 1619 – 'Gemälde'.
7 BGH in NJW 1972, 1706 – 'Kunstharzlack'.

representations. Again, the decisive criterion is the parties' consent that this quality is of particular importance for the buyer and that the seller accepts this (if only tacitly) and guarantees the quality.

Three groups of typical cases are of great practical importance:

(a) The seller's statements are considered a valid representation, if he realises that the quality in question is of particular importance for the buyer in regard to a *particular purpose or use* of the product.[8]
(b) It is *not* sufficient, if the sales contract refers to specific *industrial standards* (like DIN standards).[9]
(c) There is a tacit representation that the seller of a processed article has carried out the processing in accordance with the general custom of his trade.[10]

Examples from specific relevant areas of business are:

(a) *Construction business*: The water and acid resistance of an anhydrite mortar is considered a binding representation; the compliance of felt insulation with the pertinent DIN standard can be the subject of a binding representation, if this compliance is particularly important to the buyer; the fitness of glue for attaching plates to the ceiling can be considered guaranteed, if tests of this fitness have been made prior to the sale; the same applies to the fitness of a particular varnish to prevent the rotting of wood. On the other hand, the reference to an invitation to bid is not sufficient to assume that the absence of tensions in lighting domes has been represented; the elasticity of a specific construction material is the subject of a representation if the seller knows for what purpose the material will be used by the buyer; the usual pressure resistance of bricks normally is the subject of a tacit representation.
(b) *Computers*: So far, no court decisions have been published with respect to data processing equipment. The compliance with DIN software standards may be considered the subject of a binding representation, if the seller alleges such compliance *and* if the software is sold under an official quality or certification mark. Statements in performance specifications are per se not the subject of quality representations.
(c) *Foodstuffs*: The statement 'The goods are guaranteed for a period of 90 days after date of shipment' is a binding representation concerning the edible lifetime of the goods, also, that the foodstuffs are not contaminated; an indication of the place of origin of fruit may be a binding representation if this particular place has a reputation for the superior quality of fruit grown there; that wine has been bottled on the premises of the vineyard is a binding representation, as well as the absence of specific chemicals in wine.
(d) *Machines*: All of the following have been considered binding representations: the description of a truck as a 'long distance transporter'; the statement that a silo can be repeatedly assembled due to being screwable; the statement that a refrigerator produces clean air by

8 BGH in WM 1971, 1121/1123 – 'Zucker'.
9 BGH in NJW 1981, 1501 – 'Gleichstrom-Nebenschlußmotoren'.
10 BGH in NJW 1988, 1018 – 'Garne'.

maintaining a certain temperature; the statement that the seller guarantees for a machine providing certain heating functions; possibly also the statement that a product comes 'fresh from the factory'.

(3) With respect to some specific products, the binding representations are required either by statutes dealing particularly with the product, or by the courts. For example, the seller of seeds is always considered to represent that his seed will produce the plant as the seed for which it is being sold; the seller of animal food is considered to represent that his food is free from adulteration.

Finally, whenever a sale is made by sample or on approval, the seller represents that the products will be as approved or comply with the sample (BGB § 494).

(4) The question whether the particular quality was or was not present when the product was handed over to the buyer does not pose difficult legal problems; however, it will often be difficult to prove. The burden of proof for the absence of the represented quality is with the buyer.

2.4 Product liability based on breach of contract

Breach of contract (as defined in our introduction) is not dealt with (specifically) in the BGB. The German Civil Code deals only with two general forms of contract violations, namely with the inability of the debtor to perform at all (in the case of the seller, to hand over the object sold to the buyer), which is called *Unmöglichkeit*, and with delayed performance (*Verzug*). It became clear soon after the BGB was enacted, that these types of contract violation were not exhaustive and that the creditor (like, in the aforementioned case of a sale, the buyer) might have numerous other reasons for complaints against the other party, since a contract of any type normally entails a number of collateral duties towards the other party all of which might be violated. Such violations have traditionally been called *positive Vertragsverletzung*[11] which translates roughly as 'breach of contract'. In common with inability to perform or delay it applies to all types of contract (leases, hire of services, shipping contracts, etc) and is not limited to sales. Therefore, it falls into a category separate from, for example, warranty (which is a remedy given specifically to the buyer) and consequently claims based on warranty are not considered claims based on breach of contract in this context.

Again, the distinction between the purchaser's interest in receiving a product which is free from defects (covered by warranty), and his interest not to suffer harm or damage to his health or *other* property (as opposed to the purchased object) is essential. We are talking here only about breaches of contract that are rooted in the defect of the product, but which have led to detrimental consequences affecting legally protected interests other than the purchased product proper.

Therefore, the cases giving rise to claims for damages based on breach of contract are comparable to those based on tort. The typical contract cases and case categories that have emerged over the years from a large body of precedents are very similar to those in torts cases (cf p 140ff, below). There are

11 Münchner Kommentar, annotation 95 before § 275.

only gradual differences in determining the required quality of the product and thus the existence of the defect: in tort law, the product requirements are standardised, whereas in breach of contract cases they must be determined with regard to the terms of the contract. Also, due to the privity of contract, the seller owes to the buyer stricter duties concerning product instruction than the producer owes to somebody that he is not contractually tied to. On the other hand, the difference between contractual and tortious liability is substantial with respect to the periods of limitation, defences and the recovery of damages for pure financial loss. Such pure financial loss is recoverable under breach of contract, but not under tort (cf section 5, below).

Since sales law is of particular importance to contractual product liability, we would like to exemplify breach of contract liability with sales cases. Wherever there are significant differences between sales and contracts for work and services, we will mention them as well.

(1) Any product liability based on breach of contract presupposes that the product is defective. BGB § 459 I says that there must be no defects in the product which diminish its value or its fitness to serve either typical purposes, or purposes which have been envisaged in the sales contract.

If specifications have been agreed upon contractually and are not being fulfilled, a product which would be fit for its usual purpose might be considered defective, and vice versa: a product which would not meet usual quality requirements might be fit for the specific purposes envisaged by the parties. For example:

(a) If a computer is sold which, based on the buyer's specification, must be able to solve very specific tasks, it will be considered defective if it cannot solve that task (for example, because its capacity is insufficient), even though the average buyer of this computer would be fully satisfied.

(b) If the parties have agreed to ship foodstuffs whose 'best before' date has already expired, these foodstuffs would not meet usual quality standards, but they will be considered free from defects, since this deviation has been agreed upon.

The liability for breach of contract is (unless the parties have stipulated otherwise) based on the violation of the same duties that the courts have imposed on the producer in tort, namely the duties to construct properly and manufacture new products and monitor the products that have already been distributed. For details and for the corresponding duties of sellers and suppliers see the section on tort below.

Instructions on use and maintenance of the product must be more specific, diligent and comprehensive within a contractual relationship than with respect to strangers. The seller will often be looked at by the buyer as the expert on whose advice he can rely. If this advice is wrong, the seller may be subject to contractual product liability, if the buyer suffers harm or damage as a consequence of being wrongly advised.[12] The instructional duties become more severe with the products becoming more complicated or sophisticated, for

12 BGH in NJW 1957, 746 – 'Chloridhaltiges Wasser'.

example, with respect to their operation and maintenance.[13] The requirements for proper instruction are particularly high with respect to electronic data processing equipment.

(2) Contractual product liability is similar to tort product liability also in so far as there must be both a chain of causation between the contract violation and the damage, and fault (ie intent or negligence).[14]

(3) Since the law governing *contracts for work and services* already provides for a damages claim as part of the warranty system, there is only room for claims based on breach of contract for such consequential damages that are not covered by the warranty provision in BGB § 635. So far, the judiciary has failed to draw a clear line between damages recoverable under warranty on the one hand, and under breach of contract on the other. This failure is particularly deplorable since the periods of limitation differ widely between these two claims. If the period for bringing warranty claims (between six months and five years, depending on the kind of work and services) has elapsed, it is often hard to predict whether the plaintiff will be able to profit from the 30-year limitation that applies in the case of breach of contract.

As a rule of thumb one can say that the chances of recovering consequential damages by relying on a warranty become less with increasing remoteness of damage, so that the plaintiff becomes more and more forced to rely on breach of contract the further away from the result of the contractor's work the damage occurs. Of course, this does not mean that the chance that his claim in contract will succeed increases with the remoteness of the damage. For example, the courts have granted damage based on breach of contract where fire damages had been caused by a ruptured oil tubing[15] or insufficient insulation,[16] or where soil and dirt had to be removed because a machine was improperly assembled.[17]

The contractor's duties to instruct and advise the customer properly are of particular importance with respect to contracts for work and services. The reason is the special expertise of the contractor who constructs or erects a machine, a house or an industrial plant. These duties are extremely severe, as can be exemplified by a recent decision by the Federal Supreme Court.[18] The object of this contract was the erection of a new type of heat generating plant which, as it turned out, was not per se defective in any way, but which did not completely comply with a contractual specification, namely 'securing' the generation of a certain heat supply with a certain amount of fuel. It turned out that the heat supply was not secured if an auxiliary machine were to fail. The court said that the contractor had been under an obligation to advise the customer of this danger, in particular, since he was offering a new type of heat generating plant. This duty comprises also aspects of economic efficiency.

Consequently, the contractor's risk of incurring liability for violating the duty to provide accurate information is considerable.

13 BGH in NJW 1983, 392 – 'Verzinkungsanlage'.
14 Cf Ch C III, IV.
15 BGHZ 58, 305.
16 BGH in NJW 1982, 2244.
17 BauR 1972, 127.
18 BGH in WM 1987, 1303 – 'Blockheizkraftwerk'.

2.5 Amounts of damages to be paid

One important difference between the product liabilities based on tort and those based on contract is that the latter do not presuppose that the damage has occurred as a consequence of bodily harm or physical damage; consequently, pure financial losses are recoverable under contractual product liability, but not under tort.

With respect to the claims dealt with heretofore (in sections 2.2, 2.3 and 2.4, above), damages will be calculated as follows.

The basic principle for the calculation of damages is laid down in BGB § 249: the claimant must be put into the position he would be in, if the circumstances giving rise to his claim for damages had not occurred. What does this mean with respect to the various contractual claims?

(1) Cases of *culpa in contrahendo* occur by definition before the conclusion of a contract. Consequently, the claimant is not yet entitled to the performance by his prospective contractual partner. Therefore, damages will not comprise the claimant's interest in the performance, but only his interest in the integrity of his vested rights.

(2) In so far as damages can be claimed because *unwarranted representations* have been made with respect to the product's quality, the seller will have to put the buyer into a position he would have been in, if the product had in fact had the represented qualities. In order to find out what position that would have been, one must examine in each case for what purpose the representation has been made. If it served only to secure the buyer's uninhibited use of the purchased product, he cannot claim consequential damages. Only if the representation was made to protect the buyer's interests beyond those in using the purchased product, may he be entitled to collect compensation for consequential damage.[19]

Thus, two questions must be answered:

(a) What specific qualities of the purchased product were the subject of the seller's representations?

(b) Is the damage in question covered by the representation's purpose and range?

Representations can also make damages recoverable that could normally not be recovered, eg those flowing from development risks which could not be foreseen at the relevant time.

(3) In so far as damages for physical damage and injury are claimed based on *breach of contract*, they are calculated as in tort law (cf below).

If, however, there has been a *pure financial loss*, it can only be recovered under breach of contract, but not under tort. These are the cases where there has been no physical damage or injury, but where the claimant has been burdened, eg with losses of earnings or with claims from injured third parties. Of great practical importance are cases where defective products have been *processed*. If it turns out that the finished product cannot be properly used due to the defective component, the processor will want to be compensated for time, money, and/or other components having been wasted.[20]

A landmark case decided by the Federal Supreme Court[1] may serve as an

19 Staudinger, 12 ed, § 463 BGB, annotation 37.
20 BGH in BB 1967, 433.
1 BGH in NJW 1983, 810 – 'Hebebühne'.

illustration of the types of damages recoverable under breach of contract. Lifting gear which had been sold to an auto repair shop had broken down, because it had been defective. As a consequence of this breakdown, a car belonging to the shop owner was destroyed, and the repair shop could not be used for a lengthy period of time. Two sorts of damage must be distinguished:

(a) the destruction of the owner's car is a typical property damage, compensation for which is recoverable both under breach of contract and under tort.
(b) The impossibility of using the repair shop leads to pure financial loss, which is recoverable only under breach of contract. The same would apply if the destroyed car had not belonged to the owner but to another customer. In this case the owner would have been burdened by a compensation claim from this customer, without having himself suffered a tangible loss. Again, this pure financial loss would only be recoverable under breach of contract, not under tort.

In an economy where division of labour has greatly increased, such pure financial losses resulting from component replacements, work and investment made in vain, etc, can be considerable.

2.6 Burden of proof

The plaintiff, relying on culpa in contrahendo or breach of contract, bears the burden of proof with respect to the defect and the chain of causation between the defect and the damage (health, property, etc) on the one hand, and between the damage and the consequential financial loss on the other. He must also prove the amount of the damages he is claiming. The defendant must show and prove that he was not at fault. For details see section 3.6 below, on torts.

With respect to the liability for representations of quality there is a peculiarity which deserves attention. Until the product is handed over to the buyer, his claims are for the seller's performance. Therefore, the seller must show and prove that until this point in time the product complied with his representations. After the buyer has accepted the sales object, he will have to prove that the product did not comply with the seller's representation.[2]

2.7 Exclusion or limitation of liability

We must distinguish clearly between contracts that have been made subject to the seller's general terms and conditions of sale (*Allgemeine Geschäftsbedingungen – AGB*) and contracts where this is not the case. Depending on whether exclusions or restrictions of liability have been agreed upon in an individual agreement, or in General Conditions, such exclusions and restrictions are subject to a more or less rigid legal control.

(1) Where no general conditions have been agreed upon, this control is rather lenient. According to BGB § 276 II one party cannot waive the other

2 Baumgärtel, Handbuch der Beweislast im Privatrecht, vol 1, annotation 3, § 463.

party's liability for intentional acts. Consequently, liabilities for all other wrongs *can* be waived.

With respect to product liability, intention presupposes that the producer must be aware of his product's defects. It is not necessary that he wants the actual physical damage or injury to occur, but it is sufficient that he foresees with some certainty that harm will occur and consents to this risk.

(2) Of much greater practical importance are exclusions and limitations contained in general conditions. The concept of 'general conditions' is defined very broadly in § 1 of the Act, Concerning General Conditions (*Gesetz zur Regelung des Rechts der Allgemeinen Geschäftsbedingungen – AGB-Gesetz*). It applies to all conditions that have been worded by one contract party for a multitude of contracts. It does not matter whether the conditions have been attached to the contract document separately, or if they have become part of the contractual document proper.

Conditions are not considered 'general' if they have been negotiated individually between the parties (AGBG § 1 II). In order to discourage efforts to evade the protection granted by the AGBG, the judiciary applies severe standards when determining whether a clause has indeed been 'negotiated individually'.

A clause excluding or limiting liability will only be considered 'individually negotiated' if the seller can show a reasonable interest in such an exclusion or limitation, and if the customer had a real opportunity to exert influence upon the wording of the conditions, eg if he had been invited to make alternative proposals for the wording of the conditions.[3]

The authority of the judiciary to hold certain clauses invalid is greater when these clauses have been used in contracts with consumers than in contracts with business people. It is fair to say that with respect to consumers a limitation of liability in general conditions is in practice not admissible, even though the judiciary has not yet ruled so expressly.

It is equally clear that liability for *gross negligence* cannot be excluded in general conditions used in contracts with business people. The contrary has been assumed only in a case involving the ship-building industry, because in that industry such clauses are common.

Therefore, among business people only liability for (*ordinary*) *negligence* can be excluded; however, the following should be observed:

(a) The clause should state expressly that *only* the liability for ordinary negligence (as opposed to gross negligence) is to be excluded. Without this restriction, the courts would attribute a sweeping meaning to this clause (including gross negligence) and consequently might invalidate the entire clause.

(b) A restriction of liability even for ordinary negligence will be held invalid if this restriction concerns contractual duties which are of the essence. The following duties have been held essential by the courts: in a contract for the finishing of textiles the duty to treat the textiles carefully; in contracts with computer sellers and installers the duty to provide for sufficient air-conditioning in the room where the computer

3 Ulmer, Brandner, Hensen, AGBG, 6 ed, § 1 annotation 51.

is installed;[4] in a storage contract the duty to provide for a sufficiently low cooling temperature.[5]

(c) If representations have been made concerning certain qualities of a product, such representations can practically not be revoked in general conditions.

All this shows that the seller cannot trust that the liability limitations in his general conditions will eventually be enforced by the courts.

2.8 Notification of defects; limitation periods

(a) Business people must examine the merchandise which they have received from the seller and must notify the seller of any defects without undue delay. Notice of hidden defects must be given after they have been discovered. If a business person does not comply with this obligation, he loses his claims for damages (HGB § 377). This applies also to claims based on breach of contract.[6]

(b) The limitation periods differ widely depending on their legal ground:
 (i) claims based on culpa in contrahendo are subject to a limitation period of 30 years;
 (ii) claims based on the absence of represented qualities or on breach of contract are subject to a limitation period of six months after delivery, provided that they are raised within a sales relationship;
 (iii) if breach of contract is relied upon within a contract for work and services, claims based on breach of contract become statute-barred only after 30 years.

2.9 Liability for third parties and claims by third parties

Since we are dealing with contractual liability, the rights and liabilities are normally those of the contracting parties. However, it is not uncommon that third parties are involved as well, either on the side of the seller or on the side of the buyer.

(1) Like all parties to any contract, the seller or contractor held liable for product liability is responsible for any fault of a person employed by him in the performance of his obligation (cf BGB § 278). 'Employment' is construed very broadly in this context, since it comprises not only employees, but also freelancers and independent contractors of whom the producer avails himself, eg of an advertising agency with respect to the proper wording of advertisements; of an architect with respect to planning and supervising construction; of a repair shop for the repair of a product.

The seller or contractor is liable for the acts of the person he employs to the same extent that he himself would be liable, if he were at fault himself.

A limitation of the liability for grossly negligent acts of the employed person

4 BGH in WM 1985, 522 – 'Klimaanlage'.
5 BGH in WM 1984, 477 – 'Kaltlagerung'.
6 BGH in NJW 1988, 52.

is not permissible in General Conditions of Sale. This rule applies without exceptions to consumers; with respect to business people, the courts have held that such a limitation is permissible unless the limitation does not comply with the customs in the respective industry and concerns duties that are of the essence.[7]

(2) A person who is not party to the contract may nevertheless claim damages from the seller or contractor based on contractual product liability, if the contract has been concluded for his benefit. This presupposes that it was clear to the seller/contractor that the third party deserved protection under the agreement and that the third party's interests might be infringed upon by a defect in the product. Contracts for the supply of goods are generally not considered to benefit third parties. Thus, the ultimate consumer does not benefit from the contractual duties the producer owes to the dealer.[8]

On the other hand, the purchaser's or the buyer's employees and the family of the customer in a contract for works and services have been considered protected as third parties. Not only the damage following from injury or property destruction is recoverable by the third party, but also pure financial losses. Therefore, the contractual protection granted to third parties is more effective than the protection arising in tort upon which third parties would normally have to rely.

3. LIABILITY IN TORT

3.1 Introduction

Unlike contractual product liability, which presupposes contractual privity between the parties, liability in tort can be relied upon by anyone. Most people who suffer injuries or damage from defective products are not contractually tied to the producer. Thus, in seeking redress for their losses they will normally rely on tortious liability.

Tort remains the most important ground for product liability, even after the no-fault Product Liability Act has come into force.

The central provision of the statutory tort law is BGB § 823, which reads:

> I. Anyone who wilfully or negligently and without justification infringes upon the life, body, health, liberty, property or other right of another person is obliged to compensate the other person for the damage resulting from such infringement.
> II. The same obligation is incurred by somebody who disregards a law that serves to protect another person. . . .

One paramount principle of the German tort product liability law becomes clear from the words of this provision: any liability presupposes that some specific right of the claimant has been infringed upon. Where this is not the case, no damages can be claimed. In particular, pure financial losses are not recoverable as a consequence of this principle.

7 Ulmer, Brandner, Hensen, op cit, § 11 Nr 7 annotation 33.
8 BGH in BB 1989, 20.

3.2 Outline of the relevant tort law giving rise to product liability

(1) Of the rights mentioned in BGB § 823 the following may become relevant with regard to product liability: life, body, health, property and, as examples of the 'other rights', possession and business operation.

(a) *Life* has been violated if a human being has been killed. Life, as defined by the BGB, starts with birth.
(b) Violations of *body* and *health* will mostly be the same, except in cases where mental health is impaired.

With regard to (b), if the health of an unborn child is damaged (eg by pharmaceuticals which the mother has taken during her pregnancy), the child may claim damages after birth.[9]

An unwanted pregnancy is considered an impairment of the mother's health.[10] Therefore, the producer of an ineffective contraceptive violates the health of a woman who becomes pregnant involuntarily.

(c) Of greatest importance are *property* violations. A considerable body of precedents deals with issues connected therewith.

The following have been considered *violations* of property: every damage, deformation, destruction or deprivation, every functional disturbance or interruption, pollution or contamination, even changes of the physical condition or physical danger which prevents use (eg risk of explosion).[11] Property violation presupposes that the defective product has had an effect upon the claimant's property. In other words, the defective product itself does not qualify as protected property. Consequently, the courts have held until 1976 that the sale of a defective product does not constitute a violation of the property of that product, because that product was defective to begin with and the seller did not inflict damage upon it. This follows from the aforementioned principle that tort liability presupposes the infringement of some right. It also makes the drawing of a line between liability in tort and under warranty easier. Product liability in tort (like the one based on contract) does not serve to remedy the product's defects, but to remedy the damages that have flowed from such defects.

This distinction has been found clear, but unsatisfactory. Since a decision issued in 1976 and called *Floating Switch*,[12] the Federal Supreme Court has adopted a more discriminating view. The seller had supplied a cleaning installation. The entire installation caught fire and was destroyed because a small floating switch was defective. This switch had been part of the sales object, and if the sales object had been taken as a whole, there would have been no room for a product liability claim, since the sales object (taken as an entity) had been defective to begin with. However, since the function of the floating switch had been clearly defined within the entire installation, the court saw fit to distinguish between this small element and the remaining installation and held that the property in the latter had been damaged by the defective switch.

9 BGH in NJW 1972, 1126.
10 BGH in NJW 1980, 1452.
11 Kullmann/Pfister KZA 1520, p 9/10.
12 BGH in NJW 1977, 379 – 'Schwimmschalter'.

Since this landmark decision, the courts have continued to distinguish between the sales object in its entirety and defective parts thereof. In a case where a motor vehicle has been destroyed due to a defective tyre, the producer of the car was held liable for damaging that car. The same was held in a case where a defective accelerator had led to the destruction of the car it was part of. Defective parts are considered as leading to a property violation of the entire product, if that defect can be clearly limited to that part, and if that defect has led to significant additional damage to the entire product.[13]

These rules are of particular importance in the *construction industry*. Whenever a defective part becomes indistinguishable within the entire product as a consequence of its being united, welded, glued, riveted, etc, into the new product, its function cannot be distinguished any more from that of the entire product, and consequently there is no room for the defective part inflicting property damage on the entire product. For example, when sand, which was unfit to be mixed with cement and chalk, was used to make rough-cast, that sand was not considered as having caused a property violation in the rough-cast. On the other hand, defective roofing was considered to have led to a violation of the property in the roof structure, after it had caused the latter to split.[14]

(d) Other rights protected by BGB § 823 I are the rights of *possession* and of *business operation*, but *not* financial assets per se. In other words, pure financial losses are not covered by BGB § 823 I.

(2) In order to be held liable for the damage caused by his defective product, the producer's conduct must have been unlawful. He must have violated one (or several) of his duties, ie he must either have done something unlawful, or he must have failed or omitted to do something that he was expected to do under the law. Generally speaking, the producer is under an obligation to distribute only safe products. The distribution of defective and thus unsafe products is unlawful. Unlawful conduct is one of several presuppositions of a tort product liability claim which must be distinguished from the violation of a right (cf section 3.1, above) and from fault (cf section 3.4, below).

The duties of the producer have been specified with respect to construction, fabrication, inspection, and follow-up product observation.

(1) A product has a *construction* or *design defect* if its concept (as opposed to the tangible product itself) cannot result in the manufacture of a product which complies with the required safety standard.

Since there is not one single safety standard for every sort of product, proper construction must take into account usual use by an average owner. However, construction must also take into consideration that use of the product will often be made in unreasonable ways or for unreasonable purposes. Designers of a machine must safeguard against blunders or mistakes by the future machine operator; a handle must be designed to allow energetic transport of the object concerned. On the other hand, the producer need not take into consideration utterly unreasonable acts of the consumer, eg the use of glue, cleansing agents, or petrol for intoxicating or narcotic purposes.

13 BGH in NJW 1978, 2241 – 'Hinterreifen'; BGH in NJW 1983, 810 – 'Gaszug'; BGH in NJW 1985, 2420 – 'Kompressor'.

14 BGH in NJW 1978, 1051 – 'Lotsand'; BGH in NJW 1985, 194 – 'Dachabdeckfolie'.

It goes without saying that all products that have to be officially approved must comply with the required approval standards. However, these official requirements will often constitute only minimum standards. In many cases the courts have held that products were wrongly designed even though they met the minimum standards. Compliance with official minimum standards does not relieve the producer of researching possible dangers himself and avoiding them in efficient, reasonable ways.[15] For example:

(a) If *asbestos* is used for making a product, its construction must ensure that the dangerous asbestos fibres are not set free in the form of cancer-generating dust.[16]

(b) *Baby toys* must be made without soluble poisonous substances, without sharp edges, and must avoid the possibility of body parts being squeezed in.

(c) *Computer programs* that are part of larger equipment (eg a processor or CNC controlled machines) are always subject to product liability.[17] The integrated software must comply with the requirements for an effective control of the equipment or the machines.

(d) The safety standards for *motor vehicles* are a classic example for the legal requirements being only minimum standards. Compliance with them will often not be sufficient. For example, steering wheels are required to have a cushioned ring, a large rebounding surface, a rebound crasher behind the wheel and a steering column must be able to divert impact from an accident sideways.[18]

(e) Likewise, the Act Concerning Appliance Safety contains only minimum safety requirements for machines and technical installations. In addition, machines must be designed in a way which allows proper handling by the user without overstraining him with an over-sophisticated construction.[19]

(f) Medico-technical apparatus must be safeguarded against power failure (eg by installing a stand-by unit) and must have a specific warning device in case of improper functioning.

(2) *Manufacturing defects* are those which occur during the manufacturing process.

The manufacturing process must be organised in a way which allows products to be made to a consistent, flawless quality.

Raw materials and partially finished goods have to be selected carefully and must be checked for defects before using them in one's own manufacturing process.

Since manufacturing defects can often not be completely avoided, there must be a verifiable quality control. Depending on the risk involved in the event of a possible undetected flaw, quality control may be limited to random samples, or may include every single product. The latter applies in cases where undetected flaws involve health or even life risks, as in brakes, airplanes or

15 BGH in NJW 1987, 1009 – 'Lenkerverkleidung'; BGH in NJW 1987, 372 – 'Verzinkungsspray'.
16 Kullmann/Pfister KZA 1520 p 32.
17 Bauer in PHI pp 39 ff, 98.
18 Kullmann/Pfister KZA 1520 p 35.
19 BGH in VersR 1952, 357 – 'Rungenverschluß'.

medicinal-technical apparatus. When conducting random tests, the legally prescribed testing methods and the relevant DIN norms (like VDE, RAL, DIN 66051 and DIN 40080) must be observed.

Moreover, typical sources of defects in the production process must be identified and eliminated. If this is not possible, quality control must focus on these critical points.

(3) Both the producer and the seller of a product must give the user proper *instructions*, if dangers cannot be ruled out even in a reasonable and foreseeable use of the product, or if harmful side effects may occur. This is so irrespective of whether or not the product has been constructed and made properly. Whether there are risks involved with the use of the product depends on the typical use by a typical user of average intelligence and proficiency.

If, however, the risk is such that it can easily be recognised and foreseen by the user, it is part of the risk generally involved with life. For such risks, the producer will not be held liable. For example, the producer of a blank cartridge pistol did not have to pay damages to a user of his product whose hearing capacity had been impaired by the noise usually connected with the operation of such a pistol.[20]

In a recent decision, the Federal Supreme Court has tightened the producer's *warning duties* further. In the past, he had only to warn of dangers that might originate from his own product. Since the so-called *Honda* decision[1] this warning duty applies also to accessories which have not been attached to the product by the producer but which might foreseeably be attached by the user. This decision deals with a motorcycle windshield spoiler, which had not been a standard feature of the motorcycle. Instead, it had been made by a company which was not related to Honda and which sold its products independently. At a certain speed, this windshield spoiler led to an instability of the motorcycle, which caused a serious accident. The defendant in this lawsuit was not the producer of the spoiler, but Honda. The court held Honda liable, because they had not appropriately warned the buyer of the motorcycle of the consequences that an additional windshield spoiler might have for the stability of motorcycle riding. The court stated that the producer of a motorcycle must not only safeguard the proper functioning of parts and accessories that are necessary to operate the motorcycle to begin with. The same applies to accessories the use and the attaching of which the motorcycle producer has made possible by providing drill holes, lugs, fixing devices, mountings, or the like.

If the producer must give a warning, the question is, how must this be done? The following basic rules apply:

(a) The warning must be easily understood. If the product is typically being used by a large number of people, the warning must take into account the intelligence and the capability of an average user. Normally it cannot be assumed that the product will only be used by experts.
(b) The warning must be clearly visible.
(c) The warning must not be limited to the usual instructions in an owner's manual, but must be emphasised.

20 OLG Köln in VersR 1987, 573.
1 BGH in WM 1987, 176.

(d) Warnings affixed to long-lived and durable goods must last as long as the product, and must remain visible and readable at any time.

(4) Finally, the producer must *follow up* on his product's performance in daily use by consumers and *observe* its performance. He must keep himself continuously informed about what consequences his product's use actually has. In particular, he must think of instances where:

(a) an originally harmless product becomes dangerous by simultaneous use together with other products;
(b) new scientific research shows dangers that emanate from the product;
(c) practical experience during the daily use of the product shows flaws;
(d) it becomes apparent that buyers do not know how to use the product properly;
(e) new technology allows the elimination of product weaknesses.

In a case where between 0.5 and 1.0% of all products showed the same defect after they had been used, the producer was held liable because he had not bothered to eliminate the defect.[2]

The performance of mass products must be followed up and observed throughout the world.[3]

As the *Honda* decision shows, the producer must also observe dangers that arise from the combination of his products with those of other manufacturers.

If the product observation leads to the conclusion that the product is dangerous, the users must be notified of these dangers in an appropriate manner. Often, a *subsequent warning* will suffice, but in particularly grave instances a *recall* must be organised. Everyone who watches television or listens to the radio knows that such recalls take place quite often, particularly with respect to motor vehicles.

Since the costs of a recall are considerable and can be insured only in the automotive and aviation industry, it is of particular interest under what circumstances a recall will be required (and a subsequent warning will be considered insufficient). If the dangers connected with the use of the product cannot be averted by warning alone, *and* if there is considerable danger for the health or the lives of users, a recall will be necessary (but not necessarily if 'only' material goods are at stake).

Another criterion for the necessity of a recall is the possibility or impossibility of safeguarding the interests of third parties (as opposed to the user) by a mere warning. The car owner who has been notified of a brake problem may choose to ignore the problem, because he is willing to take the risk himself, but he endangers not only himself, but also innocent by-standers. Their interests must be taken into consideration by the producer as well.

3.3 Causation

Product liability presupposes two subsequent links of causation. First, a product defect must have led to the violation of one of the claimant's rights (section

2 LG Freiburg in Kullmann/Pfister KZA 7508/1.
3 BGH in NJW 1981, 1606 – 'Apfelschorf II'.

3.2, para 1), and this violation must have been the cause of the eventual financial loss for which compensation is sought.

(1) If the violation of the claimant's right(s) would have occurred even if the product had not been defective, the defect was no cause of the violation. Also, the producer cannot be made responsible if the chain of causes that has led to the violation of the claimant's right is so extraordinary and unusual that it could not have been foreseen, even by a particularly experienced and careful person.[4]

(2) Of greater practical importance is the question whether the eventual financial loss can be traced back to the violation of the claimant's right.

Again, the decisive criterion is whether an experienced and careful person could have foreseen that the particular infringement of the particular right of the claimant was apt to lead to the particular financial loss for which redress is sought.

This is considered *not* to be the case when:

(a) a car runs into a truck that has broken down due to brake failure, even though the truck has been properly guarded against the traffic;
(b) a defective product makes treatment by a doctor necessary, and the doctor commits grave malpractice;[5]
(c) a person contracts a flu infection in a hospital where he stays for the treatment of another disease, and dies from the flu.

3.4 Who is liable for what sort of fault?

(1) Liability based on BGB § 823 I presupposes fault (intent or negligence). Negligence is disregard of due care. What care is due for a producer of goods has been described above (cf section 3.2, para (2)(a)–(d), above).

There are two degrees of negligence, namely, ordinary negligence and gross negligence. Whether the defendant is guilty of one or of the other, or even of intent, will affect the coverage of his liability by insurance.

(2) An important question is, *who* must exercise what care at what point in time of the production or distribution process? Details are dealt with at p 140ff above. Here we will deal only with the particulars connected with fault liability, as opposed to non-fault liability.

(a) The ground rule is that only the *producer* is responsible for the production, and that consequently he must have been at fault with respect to the presence of a defect.

This means for *suppliers* that only the supplier is responsible for the defective part he has made, unless the producer had an obvious opportunity to check the part upon receipt. For example, a motorcycle accident occurred because a steering part had minuscule cracks. This defect could have been detected only by a very sophisticated method, a so-called magnetic flooding. The magnetic flooding should have been carried out by the supplier of the steering part, since he was the expert

4 Produkthaftungshandbuch § 22, annotation 6.
5 BGH in NJW 1968, 247 – 'Schubstrebe'.

in this field. Consequently, a claim against the motorcycle manufacturer was dismissed.[6]

(b) The *seller* is not responsible for defects caused during the production. He is, however, responsible for his own selling organisation and the functions connected therewith. For example, he must advise the buyer that a product is not fit to serve the buyer's needs or purposes, and he must warn the buyer of incorrect and possibly dangerous applications of the product. The seller must be aware of the qualities of the goods he sells and the applicability of those qualities to his customers' requirements. Thus a pharmacist should not supply headache pills to a customer who needs pills for an upset stomach. The seller must not distribute goods that have perished or spoilt (particularly foodstuffs); nor may he sell dangerous substances to people who can obviously not handle them.

(c) *Distribution organisations*, which are directly connected to the producer, owe their customers a higher degree of instruction and information, since they are more expert with respect to the products' quality and specifications. Still, as long as such organisations are not identical to the producer company, they are not responsible for defects stemming from the production process.

However, *exclusive representatives* of a foreign producer must follow up on and observe their products' performance in the domestic territory.[7]

(d) Under *fault-based* product liability the *quasi-producer*, who presents himself as a producer by affixing his name or trademark to the product, is not considered as producer, but only as seller.[8]

(e) Nor is the *importer* treated like a producer. This applies particularly in cases where products from other EC countries have been imported, since the importer may rely that quality standards are applied in these countries that are comparable with domestic ones.[9] Imports from less developed countries need not be checked for construction or production defects unless the importer has reason to believe that the foreign producer may not have been capable properly to construct or make the product (for example, if it is a sophisticated one, or requires special technology or skills which may not be present in the particular country of origin).

3.5 Amounts of damages to be paid

The general rule of compensation is that the claimant must be put into a (financial) situation that would have existed if the damaging event had not happened.

One must always bear in mind that the particular financial loss for which compensation is claimed must flow from the infringement of a *protected right* of the claimant. With respect to these particular rights, the following should be noted.

6 OLG Frankfurt in BB 1986, 1117 – 'Motorrad'.
7 Kullmann/Pfister KZA 1524 pp 8 ff.
8 BGH in NJW 1980, 1219 – 'Klappfahrrad'.
9 Münchner Kommentar, BGB § 823 annotation 304.

(a) *Property*: Either the damaged property must be fully repaired, or the loss of property value must be compensated financially. Furthermore, lost profits which would probably have been made if the damaged property could have been used, are to be compensated. But if *other* property, which is not physically affected by the damage, cannot be employed as a consequence of the damage done to one object, such losses would be considered purely financial, and consequently not recoverable under tort law. If an entire shop has to go out of business for some time because one machine was destroyed, the losses from this interruption are not totally recoverable, but only in so far as they are connected with the particular damaged machine.[10]

(b) *Violations of life, body and health*: the statutory tort law provides for special regulations:
   (i) BGB § 842 says that if a person is injured the recoverable damages comprise also disadvantages flowing from the diminished capacity to make a living. If this capacity is permanently diminished or even destroyed, the injured person is entitled to a lump sum indemnification and/or periodical payments (cf BGB § 843).
   (ii) If a person is killed, a subsistance allowance must be paid to those who are entitled to maintenance.

   An injured person is entitled to receive damages for *pain and suffering*. What amounts are fair and reasonable will be determined by the courts. The amounts that are awarded differ widely. Where no permanent disability is involved, the amounts will normally be below DM 10,000. If an eye or a limb is lost, damages up to DM 100,000 will be awarded. The maximum amount so far has been DM 350,000 in a case of paraplegia.

3.6 Burden of proof

The general rule in German law is that the plaintiff must prove all facts and circumstances on which his claim is based, including causation and fault. *This rule does not apply to product liability*. The courts have partially reversed this burden of proof in favour of the plaintiff. The burden of proof differs depending on which of the following facts is disputed:

(a) whether there has been a defect;
(b) whether the defect is rooted in the fabrication process;
(c) whether there has been a negligent or intentional disregard of due care, and whether this disregard has caused the defect;
(d) whether the defect has caused a violation of the claimant's right(s);
(e) whether the plaintiff's damage or injury has led to the financial loss for which compensation is being sought.[11]

(1) The plaintiff must prove that the product was defective.

10 Produkthaftungshandbuch vol 1, § 30 annotation 9.
11 BGH in NJW 1988, 2611 ff – 'Mehrwegflasche II'.

(2) Generally, the plaintiff must also prove that the defective product was made by the defendant, and that the product was already defective when it left the producer's premises.

Practically speaking, the burden of proof with respect to the latter has been reversed by the Federal Supreme Court.[12] A bottle containing a carbonated beverage had exploded due to a crack in the bottle. It was unclear whether this crack had already been present when the bottle was filled, or whether it had been caused during the subsequent distribution of the bottle from the beverage factory to the consumer. Since the bottle had been a reusable one, it seemed at least possible that the crack had been caused during previous use. The court imposed upon the maker of the beverage the burden of showing that the bottle had left his factory intact. This duty could in practice only be fulfilled by the quality control of every bottle, and the documentation and repetition of this check. Since this duty had not been met by the producer of the beverage, he was held liable even though it was impossible to establish that the bottle in question was already defective when it was shipped from his premises.

(3) The burden of proof with respect to *fault* on the producer's side must be met by the plaintiff *or* by the defendant, depending on whether due care was (allegedly) disregarded, *within* or *without* the factory.

Everything concerning internal operations, ie whether the producer has exercised due care in the areas of construction and fabrication, must be proven by the producer. This means that he must *exonerate* himself from fault.

In practice, this exoneration almost never succeeds.

On the other hand, the plaintiff must prove lack of care on the producer's side in the areas of instructions and follow-up product observation.[13]

(4) The plaintiff also bears the burden of proof regarding both steps of causation, ie between the defendant's conduct and the infringement of the plaintiff's right(s), and between this infringement and the financial loss (cf section 3.3, above).

(5) It is often difficult to determine exactly what financial loss has occurred. The amount must be proven by the plaintiff, but the Code of Civil Procedure in § 287 enables the court to award damages based on estimation.

3.7 Exclusion or limitation of liability

Liability can only be excluded or limited within the framework of a contract. Therefore, it plays no significant part where product liability is based on torts.

However, where the producer (or another person responsible for the defect) is at the same time the seller of the defective product, the rules governing contractual product liability apply (cf section 2.7, above).

Recently, so-called 'quality protection agreements' have gained practical and legal importance. In such an agreement, the supplier not only undertakes to furnish the producer with goods which are free from any defects, but also to take upon himself all duties concerning quality control. The producer of the finished product (eg a car manufacturer) is indemnified from product liability regarding that particular part through a contractual right against his supplier. Especially in the automotive industry such agreements are of considerable

12 BGH in NJW 1981, 104 – 'Derosal I'.
13 Kullmann/Pfister KZA 3250, pp 11 ff.

importance for just-in-time deliveries (ie where the manufacturing process is run on the basis that minimum stock levels are held at all times).

Of course, such quality protection agreements shift the responsibility only internally between the supplier and the producer, and do not diminish the consumer's or user's rights vis-à-vis the producer.

Quality protection agreements are admissible when the supplier is able to ensure the safe and reliable performance of his duties. The range of these duties has to be stipulated specifically in the agreement.[14]

3.8 Limitation period

According to BGB § 852 claims for damages become statute-barred after three years counting from the day when the plaintiff became aware of the damage and of the liable person. The period does not run as long as negotiations take place between the parties. It continues to run if one of the parties refuses to continue the negotiations.

Irrespective of the plaintiff's awareness of the damage and of the responsible person, the period of limitation is 30 years.

3.9 Liability for third parties

The law distinguishes between executive bodies of a company, and its employees, who in tort law terminology are called 'vicarious agents'.

(1) BGB § 31 determines that culpable conduct of an executive body is considered conduct of the company. Therefore, whatever the management does is attributed directly to the company.

(2) According to BGB § 831, the company is also liable for the conduct of the persons it employs in the pursuit of the company's activities. This concerns mainly workers and employees. However, the company can exonerate itself from the liability for these persons if it shows that it has carefully selected and supervised them.

This possibility of exoneration comes into play particularly with respect to manufacturing and fabrication defects. The defendant company may raise the defence that it has carefully selected and supervised the entire production staff. However, the courts require the defendant to name the particular person who has been responsible for the product defect. This is extraordinarily difficult in the area of mass production. Even if the company could exonerate itself in this way, it might still be found guilty of a so-called 'organisational fault' if production has not been organised in a manner by which the occurrence of production defects could be avoided. In particular, quality control must be properly organised.

4. LIABILITY BASED ON THE DISREGARD OF PROTECTIVE LAWS

BGB § 823 II says that anyone who disregards a law which serves to protect someone else must make compensation to the other person for the damage he

14 RG, decision of 23.10.1915 cited at Kullmann/Pfister KZA 7653/1.

has suffered as a consequence of such disregard. Thus, the plaintiff is spared one difficulty he faces if he relies on the first paragraph of § 823, namely, to show the infringement of a particular right. Instead, he faces another difficulty: he must show that the particular law which the defendant has disregarded indeed served his (the plaintiff's) protection.

(1) What is a *law* in this context, and when does it serve the *protection* of the claimant?

(a) 'Laws' are all Acts of Parliament (state or federal), statutory instruments (*Rechtsverordnungen*), EC law and sometimes even Acts of administrative authorities.[15]

(b) In order to serve the *protection* of individuals, the law must order a certain conduct (to do something or to refrain from doing something) which is meant to avert disadvantages for other individuals. This may also be the case if the law is for the protection of the public at large. However, if the law's requirements of conduct are too general, the individual may not fall into its protective scope. Laws which themselves provide for the payment of damages do not qualify as 'protective laws' in the sense of § 823 II.

Classic protective laws are the criminal laws.

(2) It may be difficult to determine the exact reach of the protective scope of a particular law. Sometimes it will reach further than the protection provided for individual rights in BGB § 823 I, sometimes it will fall short of this protection. For example, when certain requirements for the quality of animal food had been disregarded, the Animal Food Act was assumed to protect animal owners from the destruction of their livestock.[16] On the other hand, the Act Concerning Appliance Safety was not even considered to protect property.[17]

(3) Some of the most important protective laws will be dealt with in section 5, below.

A number of provisions in the Penal Code serve to protect life, health and property. These are protective laws in the sense of § 823 II. Consequently, offences against criminal laws lead to *double sanctions*, namely penalties and damages. The responsible members of the management might be criminally convicted, particularly in cases of offences against bodily integrity and human life.

(4) The *burden of proof* is not shifted when it comes to the disregard of protective laws; instead, it remains entirely with the plaintiff.

5. SPECIAL LIABILITIES ARISING IN RESPECT OF PARTICULAR PRODUCTS

A number of laws contain special provisions related to product liability.

15 BGH in VersR 1989, 91.
16 BGH in NJW 1983, 812 – 'Hebebühne'.
17 Act of 24 August 1976 (Bundesgesetzblatt I S. 2445, last amended by Act of 20 July 1988 (Bundesgesetzblatt I S. 1050).

i. Injuries caused by medicines.[18] A special product liability for defective medicines was introduced as a consequence of the infamous *Contagan* case, where unborn babies had been severely deformed by a soporific drug which their mothers had taken. This liability – like the EC product liability – is based on no-fault. However, a number of restrictions apply; cf § 84 of the Medicine Act (*Arzneimittelgesetz – AMG*):

(a) The damaging effect of the medicine must occur as a consequence of *reasonable use* of the drug. Liability is already excluded when larger quantities of the drug have been taken than was recommended. Therefore, the producer should always indicate the maximum dosage and the maximum treatment period.
(b) The adverse effect of medicine must exceed what is acceptable according to the state of the art in medicine. Consequently, insignificant side effects cannot give raise to damage claims. A benefit/risk balance must be struck with respect to each particular drug. Serious side effects may be accepted in a medicine which is apt to treat life-threatening conditions.[19] On the other hand, the benefit/risk balance does not allow the distribution of a drug against headache that causes defects of vision.
(c) The Medicine Act does not give a ground for action, if a medicine has no effects at all.
(d) Liability may also be based on defects or mistakes in the legally required instructions for use. This applies also to the information on or within the packaging. The wording of instructions for use need not take into account the average user's medicinal knowledge, but may use scientific terminology. However, there must be clear warnings of the possibly adverse effects of an overdose. The producer of an asthma spray was held liable, after a patient had suffered from an overdose of this spray, because there was no pertinent warning. The court said that there is a considerable danger of excessive use of drugs that are taken in situations where the patient may panic, like in the case of an asthma attack.[20]
(e) The person or company who offers and distributes the drug under their name in West Germany is liable for product defects. Under the Medicine Act § 9 I, the importer is obliged to affix his name to the drugs he distributes. Consequently, the importer will generally be held liable instead of the foreign producer.
(f) The Medicine Act § 88 provides for maximum amounts of liability. If a person is killed, the maximum amount is DM 500,000 and an annual pension of DM 30,000. If several people are killed, the maximum amount (irrespective of the number of people) is DM 200m and a total of annual pensions in the amount of DM 12m.

ii. Food Act.[1] The Food Act (*Lebensmittel- und Bedarfsgegenständegesetz – LMBG*) is a protective law in the sense of BGB § 823 II. The Food Act

18 BGH in NJW 1977, 2120; Kullmann/Pfister KZA 3800, p 22.
19 BGH decision of 24.01.1989, Az.: VI ZR 112/88.
20 Act of 15 August 1974 (Bundesgesetzblatt I S. 1945), last amended by the ordinance of 26.11.1986 (Bundesgesetzblatt I S. 2089).
1 Kullmann/Pfister KZA 2014 p 9.

prohibits the production and distribution of foodstuffs for humans which contain certain dangerous additives, pesticides, artificial hormones and other pharmacological substances, etc, as well as the distribution of foodstuffs that are spoilt or otherwise unfit for consumption, or labelled in a misleading manner.

These provisions serve to protect human health.

Only illnesses that qualify as such under medicinal categories are considered as health damage, but the illness need not be severe. Eg, nausea is not considered a health impairment. The producer of the foodstuffs, as well as one who treats or processes them, and the seller to the ultimate consumer, may be liable, depending on at what point in the production and distribution chain the defect has occurred. In particular, retailers are under an obligation to examine foodstuffs about to be sold to check whether they comply with the various food laws.[2]

iii. The Act Concerning Technical Tools and Appliances.[3] This Act is a protective law in the sense of BGB § 823 II. It protects the life and the health of the users of certain tools and appliances, both in the private and in the business spheres.

The Act concerns technical tools, protective equipment, lighting, heating, cooling and air-conditioning appliances, household appliances, toys and sporting goods. Both the producer and the importer may be liable. The objective of the Act is to prevent defects that are contrary to industrial safety regulations and it requires warning instructions concerning dangers that can be prevented by proper installation of the tools or appliances. It also deals with the omission of furnishing the user with instructions for use. The *Bundesanstalt für Arbeitsschutz* (Federal Industrial Safety Agency) has issued a helpful guide for the wording of instructions for use.[4]

6. LIABILITY FOR DEFECTIVE PRODUCTS ARISING FROM THE PRODUCT LIABILITY ACT (IMPLEMENTATION OF THE DIRECTIVE ON PRODUCT LIABILITY)

6.1 Introduction

The Directive has been implemented in West Germany with the Product Liability Act ('Act') of 15 December 1989. The Act came into force on 1 January 1990 (cf § 19). According to § 16, the Act will not be applied to products which have been distributed prior to 1 January 1990.

The German Parliament has availed itself of the discretional scope provided for in the Directive in favour of industry and agriculture:

(a) Primary agricultural products and game are not covered by the Act (cf Directive article 15(1)(a); Product Liability Act § 2 second sentence).
 The liability for development risks has been excluded (Directive article 15(1)(b); Product Liability Act § 1(2)(5)).

2 Gesetz über technische Arbeitsmittel of 24.06.1968, Bundesgesetzblatt I S. 717, last amended by the Act of 13.08.1980 Bundesgesetzblatt I S. 1310, 1357.
3 Amtliche Mitteilung der Bundesanstalt für Arbeitsschutz Nr 2/1988, pp 3ff.
4 Cf Ch C II 1 lit c.

(b) A limitation of a producer's total liability has been provided for (Directive article 16(1) Product Liability Act § 10).
(c) The Product Liability Act does not apply to medicinal drugs (§ 15).

In order to make the practical consequences of the Act clear, we will explain where its provisions are in conformity with the existing tort law, and where they are not. In short, the important modifications may be listed as follows:

(a) no-fault liability;
(b) a broader notion of 'producer'; and
(c) limitation of property infringements to objects of private use and consumption.

6.2 Outline of the provisions of the Act

The full wording of the Act can be found in Bundesgesetzblatt I 1989 S 2198. The most important concepts and provisions are the following.

(1) Similar to the traditional product liability based on contract and torts, the new law is based on the principle of *protected rights*. These are life, body and health, and things (and therefore property and possession); cf § 1(1).

Under the Act, the defective product itself does not qualify as 'property' that can be infringed upon by the defect. As we explained earlier,[5] it is possible under fault-based product liability to recover compensation for damage caused to a complex product by a single, clearly distinguishable defective part. The Act requires expressly that *an object other* than the defective product itself must be damaged.

However, this does not affect cases where a *supplier* has provided a defective part, if this part damages the product into which it has been built.

The emphasis the Act gives to consumer protection has led to a restriction of liability for property infringement. Liability under the Act arises only if the damaged property is usually used privately and has also been used by the plaintiff mainly for private purposes (cf § 1(1) second sentence). It is obvious that it will often be difficult to draw a line between private and business or professional use.

Property that is objectively normally used for business purposes is not protected by the Act. For example, it does not provide for compensation for damage done to an excavator, even if the owner of a construction business should have used its excavator for a private purpose during the weekend. If the damaged property does not typically belong in the private or the business sphere, it depends on whether its owner (*subjectively*) has used it predominantly for private or for business/professional purposes. The plaintiff who used his car for pleasure most of the time, and only makes occasional business trips, does not lose the protection provided by the Act. On the other hand, an attorney who uses his personal computer to work on his briefs will not be able to recover compensation under the Act for damage done to this computer.

(2) The notion of 'product' is defined in § 2 of the Act as a movable thing, including parts of other movable or immovable things. Electricity is expressly

5 Cf Ch C II 2 lit a, b.

included among the products. Exempted, however, are primary agricultural products of the soil, of stock-farming, bee-keeping and fishery, unless they have been processed at least once.

By including parts of movable or immovable things in the 'products', the Act makes the liability of the supplier of parts possible.

The extension of product liability to movable things that are integrated into immovable things makes sure that the producer of defective construction material and the supplier of complete industrial plants are subject to product liability based on the Act. On the other hand, the no-fault liability does not concern immovable things that have been made from movable ones, eg the complete building as opposed to the bricks it was made from.

(3) According to § 3(1) of the Act, a product is *defective* if it does not provide the safety that can reasonably be expected considering all the circumstances. The producer must account for all uses of his product by the consumer that are not completely unusual or unreasonable. The required safety standard is the one that can be expected at the time when the product is being distributed.

As to the required product safety, we may refer to the treatment of general tortious liability, as far as *construction/design defects* and *manufacturing defects* are concerned.[6] The factual and the legal treatment are the same. Section 3(1)(b) of the Act makes it clear that the producer must not only foresee that his product will be used for the purposes it is meant for, but also for purposes that can *reasonably be expected*. This coincides with judgments of Federal Supreme Court with respect to general tort law. For example, we have said that the inhalation of soluble substances contained in glue for the purpose of intoxication is too unreasonable to be taken into account by the producer.[7]

The following is a rule of thumb:

> The more remote the plaintiff's use of the product was from the usual purposes of the product, the more it is for him to explain why in his opinion the producer should have accounted for the way in which he, the plaintiff, has actually made use of the product.[8]

The duties concerning proper *instructions* are referred to in § 3(1)(a) of the Act by the notion of 'presentation of the product.' This notion extends the instructional duties that we have known heretofore. Until now, only cases of missing or insufficient warnings of dangers or harmful side effects were covered. In addition, 'presentation' means also descriptions of the product (for example, in advertising), of its qualities and its possible purposes.

Further, under the aspect of 'presentation' there can be liability for products having no effect at all. If a product is advertised as having certain beneficial effects (like avoiding dangers normally connected with the use of such a product), it is being 'presented' as effective.

Product observation is not dealt with in the Act. Therefore, it provides no ground for action if the producer has not properly observed and followed up his product's performance in the marketplace.

When determining whether a product is defective, the time when the product

6 Cf Ch C II 2 lit b.
7 Kullmann/Pfister, KZA, 3604, p 11.
8 Cf Ch C III.

was distributed is the relevant one (§ 3(1)(b)). It is clear from § 3(2) that a product shall not be considered defective for the sole reason that subsequently an improved product was distributed. This applies only to design/constructional changes. The words 'for the sole reason' mean that improvements do not necessarily serve to eliminate defects. If improvements are made, this may or may not mean that the product had previously been defective.

(4) The wording of § 1(1), first sentence, 'if the defect of a product *leads to* the death of a person', means that there must be causal relationship between defect and damage. The general rules explained above in the context of tortious liability[9] apply. The number of relevant causes is restricted by the Act's requirement that the damage must be attributable to specific product risks. Thus, compensation cannot be claimed (in spite of a causal relationship between defect and damage) if risks other than those emanating from the product have materialised, eg if a product defect causes an injury that would not have been deadly, but the injured person dies in a traffic accident on his way to the hospital.

(5) The liability based on the Act requires only an infringement of a protected right, and a causal relationship between the defect and this damage. Fault is not necessary. Unlike the classic tortious liability, the one based on the Act is *no-fault*.

This principle is modified in § 6(1) of the Act in so far as the plaintiff is *contributorily negligent*. Thus, it is immaterial for the liability whether the producer was at fault, but contributory negligence on the part of the person who has suffered loss or injury is taken into consideration when it comes to determining the amount of damages to be paid.

Contributory negligence is dealt with generally in BGB § 254. According to this provision, the amount of damages payable to a contributorily negligent plaintiff is reciprocal to the degree to which he has contributed to causing the damage. Thus, operational mistakes or plain product abuse on the part of the user/consumer can be accounted for.

(6) Section 1(2) and (3) of the Act deal with *exemptions from liability*.

(a) The producer is not liable if he has *not distributed* the product (§ 1(2)(1) of the Act). Distribution has taken place when the product has been put into the distribution channel in order to have it sold.

(b) Further, there is no liability if the product was *free from defects* at the time of distribution (§ 1(2)(2) of the Act). Consequently, the producer is not liable for damages caused by changes in the product that have been brought about by, eg, improper storage, contamination, or sabotage.

(c) Nor is the producer liable if the product was neither manufactured by him for sale or another form of distribution for economic purpose, nor manufactured or distributed by him in the course of his business (§ 1(2)(3) of the Act).

(d) According to § 1(2)(4), the producer is also exempted from liability, if the *defect* is due to compliance of the product *with mandatory regulations* issued by the public authorities. Contrary to what the wording of this exemption suggests, its scope of applicability will be very narrow. It

9 Cf Ch G I.

is a prerequisite that the regulation forces the producer to make or present his product in the specific way he has done, and in no other way. He is not exempted from liability if he has merely complied with certain standards prescribed by law (eg DIN norms, accident prevention regulations, etc).

(e) The exemption from liability in cases where *the defect could not be discovered based on the scientific and technical knowledge* at the time when the product was distributed (§ 1(2)(5) of the Act) will be construed narrowly. It does not matter whether the producer himself or someone else in the industry could have discovered the defect. This exemption can only be relied upon if the defect could not have been avoided even if the responsible person had been in possession of the entire available human knowledge.

(f) A parts supplier is not responsible for defects following from the design or construction of the finished product that his part goes into; nor is he responsible for damages caused by the producer's instructions.[10]

(7) Section 4 of the Act introduces a significantly broadened concept of who is to be considered as a *producer*.[11]

Consumer protection is further enhanced by § 5, which allows the plaintiff to hold several injurers liable jointly and severally.

(8) The kind and the amount of damages that can be awarded are largely the same under the Act (cf §§ 5–11) and in tort).[12] An important difference is that under the Act *no compensation for pain and suffering* can be claimed. Further, § 10 provides for a maximum liability of DM 160m, and § 11 for a threshold in the amount of DM 1,125 *in cases of property damage*. Producers may significantly profit from such retentions if they add up in cases of mass defects.

(9) Section 1(4) expressly states that the *burden of proof* with respect to the defect, the damage and the chain of causation between the two is with the plaintiff. On the other hand, the producer must show and, if necessary, prove the presuppositions for an exclusion or a restriction of his liability. Since it is extremely difficult to prove that the product was free from defects at the time of its first distribution, circumstantial evidence will be admitted. Thus, the court will only ask whether, given all the circumstances of the case, the product could normally be expected to be free from defects. It need not fully convince itself that this was the case.

(10) Section 14 outlaws any contractual exemptions from liability.

(11) The *period of limitation* provided for in § 12 of the Act is the same as the one in tort (three years), cf BGB § 852.[13]

However, the injured parties' rights will be extinguished upon expiry of a ten-year period after the distribution of the product by the producer. Since there may be several 'producers' due to the broad definition in § 4, their respective ten-year periods may not coincide. For example, the supplier will normally distribute his part earlier than the producer of the finished product.

(12) Finally, § 15(2) of the Act expressly states that the previously existing

10 Cf Ch G I.
11 Cf Ch C V.
12 Cf Ch C VIII.
13 Cf Ch E, 1.

law of product liability continues to be in force. However, this does *not* apply to *drug manufacturers*, cf § 15(1). Thus, drug manufacturers are *privileged* under the Act. Under § 84 of the Drug Act, the producer is only liable for damages caused by consumption of his product which is in accordance with its purpose (and not, as provided for in § 3(1)(b) of the Act, for damages caused by any means of consumption that could reasonably be expected). Also, the Drug Act § 84 limits the liability to *medicinal information* printed on the leaflet included inside the package[14] (cf § 3(1)(a) of the Act).

6.3 Particularities concerning selected industrial areas

6.3.1 Primary agricultural products

According to § 2, second sentence, of the Act such products are not considered 'products' in the sense of the Act, unless they have been subject to an initial *processing*.

The purpose of this rule is not to submit farmers, whose products have been affected by adverse environmental factors for which others were responsible, to product liability. Consequently, this exemption is limited to unprocessed products. 'Initial processing' is to be construed broadly and includes, eg, the boiling of shrimps, the slaughtering of animals, or the grinding of grain.

6.3.2 Electricity

Since electricity is not a 'thing' in the sense of the Civil Code, § 2, first sentence of the Act makes express mention of it. It should be observed that an interruption of electricity supply does not trigger product liability, since in such a case *no defective product* has been supplied.

6.3.3 Waste

§ 3(1)(b) requires that the defective product be *used*. Therefore, the liability for risks emanating from waste is limited under the Act. The legislative history shows that waste is only to be considered a product in the sense of the Act if it has, eg, been collected as raw material and subsequently been distributed again as a recycled product.

6.3.4 Drugs

According to § 15(1) of the Act, drugs are not covered by it. 'Drugs' in the sense of the Act are only those dealt with in the Drug Act. The Drug Act § 2 contains a *final enumeration*.[15]

14 Act of 24.08.1976 (BGB1, I S. 2445), last amended on 20.07.1988 (BGBI, I S. 1050).
15 Kullmann/Pfister, KZA, 3603 p 4.

6.3.5 Leased objects

A producer, and liable as such under the Act, is any person who imports products into the territory of the European Community for the purposes of hiring them out or of leasing them (cf § 4(2) of the Act). Therefore, the lessor who imports products from countries outside the EC is liable for ensuring they are free from defects. On the other hand, mere use cannot lead to being or becoming a producer. If, eg, an airline imports an airplane from the United States and uses this airplane within the EC, it will not be considered the airplane's producer if it should be defective. If, however, a leasing company is employed for financial or tax reasons, that company will be held responsible for the defects of the airplane.

6.3.6 Books and printed matter

A 'product' is only the physical book or other printed paper, but not the contents that are printed in or on it.[16] Therefore, faults or erroneous contents of a book do not lead to product liability. If, however, the book's cover has been dyed with a toxic substance, its producer will be subject to the Act.

6.3.7 Computer software

Generally, computer programs are divided into standard programs and individually designed programs. Since standard programs have been considered subject to sales-like contracts, it is argued that they should be looked upon as 'products' in the sense of the Act. This would mean a different treatment than in the case of books, but there is justification for this difference in that defective software can cause damage directly by controlling machines, whereas wrongly printed information can lead to damage only indirectly, namely after influencing human conduct.[17] In the case of individually designed software, it is generally held that it should be treated like printed matter, ie its contents are not a 'product'.

In our opinion, this distinction between standard and individually designed software is not convincing. In both cases, information is stored and, if it is wrong, possible damage is caused directly. Therefore, the distinction between standard and individually designed software should not be the decisive factor, but rather the way in which the software is used. If it is integrated into comprehensive processing equipment and fulfils certain functions within that equipment, it must be looked at as a part of this equipment and program defects make its supplier subject to product liability.

7. PRACTICAL EFFECTS EC PRODUCT LIABILITY LAW WILL HAVE ON VARIOUS BUSINESSES IN THE CHAIN OF SUPPLY OF PRODUCTS

7.1 Liability of the various producers

Section 4 of the Act has led to a considerable increase in the number of people and businesses involved in the production and distribution process which may be held liable for product defects. The following points deserve attention.

16 Kullmann/Pfister, KZA, 3603 p 5.
17 Kullmann/Pfister, KZA, 3605 p 5/6.

(1) The *designer* is not subject to liability under the Act, since he has not been listed as producer or similar responsible person in § 4. Other than the producer's responsibility for the individual product, the designer's contribution is an intellectual one. It does not make a difference whether his ideas have materialised in drawings, descriptions, or the like.

Likewise, licensors or franchisors are not considered producers in the sense of the Act.

(2) The supplier of component parts is also considered a producer in the sense of § 4(1), first sentence of the Act. However, according to § 1(3), the producer of a component part is not liable if his product has been free from defects, but was damaged when being built into the finished product, or if the component part was made according to the instructions of the producer. If, however, the supplier of the component part has recommended his product to be used in the finished product, or if he has recognised that his component part is not fit to function properly within the finished product the defect is not only caused when the component part is being built into the finished product, but where the component part was defective to begin with.

(3) According to § 4(1), first sentence of the Act, the maker of *basic raw materials* is also responsible as a producer, but at the same time he is – like the supplier of component parts – privileged under § 1(3).

(4) The *producer of the finished product* is always liable. It is completely immaterial whether he makes the component parts himself, or buys them elsewhere. Therefore, the *assembler* is also considered as a producer of the finished product.

In the light of the very restricted liability of the seller, the distinction between a simple sales activity and assembling (which will lead to full liability) is of particular practical importance.

One does not become an assembler by simply adding protective devices or accessory parts to a finished product. On the other hand, someone who is putting the finished product together based on construction plans or other instructions, will be considered as an assembler. The same goes, eg, for those who do complete re-designs of motor vehicles (and not only improve their outer appearance). A producer is also a person who makes a new product by following instructions or prescriptions on how to combine the components or ingredients.[18]

(5) The liability of the so-called *quasi-producer* is of eminent practical importance. A quasi-producer is somebody who presents himself as a producer by affixing his name, trademark, or other distinguishing feature to the product. Thus, companies who avail themselves of cheap labour in less developed countries by having their products made there become liable. This applies particularly to mail order businesses, chain stores, etc.

By including all distinguishing features, more companies or individuals will fall under this provision than would be justified by the purpose of product liability. Therefore, it is of crucial importance to bear in mind that the trademark etc must lead to a *presentation as producer*. Many names or trademarks do not identify producers, but trade or sales organisations, or simply the

18 Cf Ch F II 1.

owners of prestigious trademarks who have merchandised their trademark in a product field different from the one where the trademark has obtained its initial recognition. It is doubtful whether the consumer will be able to distinguish between traders', manufacturers', and merchandised trademarks.

(6) According to § 4(2) of the Act, the *importer* will be considered as a producer if he imports the merchandise into the European Community from an outside country. It is immaterial whether this merchandise consists of finished products, or of product parts.

(7) *Sellers* (*dealers*) are considered as producers if the actual producer cannot be identified (cf § 4(3) of the Act). The same applies to products imported into the EC from non-EC countries, if their importer cannot be established.

(8) Individuals or companies who merely *install*, *purchase*, or *repair* products, are *not* considered producers, unless they fulfil the prerequisites of § 4. Thus, a purchaser may be liable as producer if he buys products in a non-EC country and leases them within the EC; fitters or repairers may do work that qualifies them as assemblers.

(9) *Workers and employees* are not subject to product liability under the Act.

7.2 Contribution and recourse

A plaintiff in a product liability case may hold each company or individual liable that qualifies as producer or quasi-producer under § 4. They are liable jointly and severally. However, recourse may take place among them. For example, if one of the liable producers has completely indemnified the victim, he may be reimbursed for part or even all of his payment by one or several of the other liable producers. By attributing the share of responsibility, the law requires that the degree to which each one has contributed to the damage be taken into consideration.

The relations among jointly and severally liable debtors on the one hand, and the relations between them and the creditor on the other hand, are dealt with in detail in the Civil Code §§ 421 ff.

8. COMPARISON OF THE EFFECTS OF PRODUCT LIABILITY LAW WITH THE PREVIOUS POSITION IN CONTRACT AND TORT

8.1 Comparison between the Act and torts law

Our treatment of product liability under the new Act in section 6, above, and of product liability law as it existed before the Act (and continues to exist) has shown that the new Act does not cover all the areas that are covered by tort law. In the following areas, the traditional *fault-based tort law* will continue to play an important part:

(a) According to § 1(1), second sentence of the Act, it gives rise to claims for property infringement only if the property was for private use or consumption and had in fact mainly been used privately. Thus, whenever the destruction or damage to property used for commercial or professional purposes is at stake, only tort law will apply.[19]

Likewise, property damage caused to a compound machine or structure by an integrated part fulfilling a limited function, can only give rise to compensation claims under tort law, since § 1(1), second sentence of the Act is applicable only to damage done to 'another object'.

(b) Defective agricultural products that have not yet undergone any processing can only give rise to a product liability claim under tort law,[20] since they are exempted from strict liability in § 2 of the Act.

(c) Since the Act does not deal with claims based on missing or insufficient product observation, such claims must also be based on tort law.[1]

(d) By requiring a direct causation of damage or injury by risks emanating from the product, the Act excludes the compensation of damages that have been caused by the interference of other factors. Again, the plaintiff must in such cases rely on tort law.[2]

(e) The same goes for cases in which product defects could not be discovered based on the state of scientific and technical knowledge at the time of distribution.[3]

(f) Compensation for pain and suffering can only be claimed under tort law, since the Act does not deal with immaterial damages.[4] *Immaterial damages* means damages for pain and suffering (for non-pecuniary losses).

(g) Where the financial loss exceeds the maximum amount stated in § 10 of the Act, the excess amount may be recoverable under tort law. Also, if the plaintiff wants to avoid the retention provided for in § 11 of the Act, he must rely on tort law. Therefore, whenever more than DM 1,125 is claimed as property damage, the courts must examine whether this claim is justified under the Act or under tort law.

(h) If the product in question has been distributed more than ten years before the accident, tort law must be relied upon exclusively due to the time limit in § 13.

(i) Where strict liability for defective drugs is excluded either under § 15 of the Act or under the Drug Act § 84 (cf section 5.1, above), the plaintiff must again rely on tort law.

(j) All persons or companies involved in the production or distribution who cannot be held liable under the Act (designers, dealers, workers and employees) can only be held liable, if at all, under tort law.

8.2 Comparison between the Act and contractual product liability

(a) Pure financial losses can only be recovered under contractual product liability.[5]

19 Cf Ch F II 2.
20 Cf Ch F II 3 und C II 2 lit d.
1 Cf Ch F II 6 und C III Ziff.
2 Cf Ch F II 6 lit e und § 1 Abs. 2 Ziff. 5 ProdHaftG.
3 Cf Ch C V 2.
4 Cf Ch A V 3.
5 Cf Ch A IV.

(b) Where the Act does not apply (cf section 1.1, above), and where no fault can be found (thus excluding tort liability), the plaintiff may still rely on contractual liability in relation to missing qualities the existence of which have been represented by the seller.

(c) Also, where the producer has contractually agreed to furnish a product of a special quality which is supposed to meet more than the usual requirements, claims for not having met the superior standards can be based only on contractual product liability.[6]

9. RISK MANAGEMENT IN THE NEW ERA OF PRODUCT LIABILITY

In the previous sections the risks involved with tort, contract and statutory liability were described. These risks are considerable. Particularly mass damages, but also the destruction of valuable property and severe bodily injuries can, even if reasonable diligence has been applied, lead to the ruin of an enterprise. Therefore, we would like to deal with the benefits, but also with the limits, of reasonable risk management in this section.

9.1 Internal risk management

The quality of its products are decisive for the market success of an enterprise. Risk management therefore is not only necessary to avoid product liability, but also to maintain the esteem of, and favourable recognition by, the public.

(a) In order to avoid design and fabrication defects, quality must be reliably secured. The following principles should be observed.

(i) The premises must be organised in a way which allows the complete recognition and registration of defects. Therefore, the final quality control must take place before the product leaves the premises. Sophisticated product components that are hard to examine must be submitted to quality control before they are fitted into a more complex structure.

(ii) Before construction and design are finally determined, prototypes must be submitted to extensive, long-term testing.

(iii) Suppliers of component parts must be selected based on their suitability and reliability. Exact specifications and requirements must be given for the parts that are to be supplied. Their prototypes must be scrutinised and the production process of the supplier must be permanently controlled.

(iv) Special sophisticated parts must be made subject to express quality-securing agreements,[7] by which the supplier will be obliged to carry out an independent quality control for his parts.

(v) Quality control measures must take into consideration the specific nature of the products. The latest technical and scientific

6 Cf Ch C VII.
7 BGH in NJW 1988, 2611 ff – 'Mehrwegflasche II'.

knowledge must be observed when selecting methods of quality control.

(vi) To what extent quality control must take place depends on the risks involved with the use of the product. If these risks can lead to bodily injury or even death, every single item should be controlled. If not, random sample tests are sufficient.

(b) Closely connected to securing quality is the *documentation* of the data established during the quality control processes. The enterprise should at any time be in a position to show that its products were free from defects when leaving the premises. Since § 1(2)(2) of the Act precludes compensation claims if the product has initially been distributed without defects, and since the producer bears the burden of proof in that respect (cf § 1(4), second sentence), the necessity of an appropriate, complete documentation has become even more evident than under the case law preceding the Act.[8]

(c) The documentation should be kept available for ten years, because that is the time period during which product liability claims may be brought (cf § 13).

(d) The following measures are advisable in order to comply with *instruction duties* and those relating to *product observation and follow-up*:

(i) The product's *presentation* (§ 32(1)(a) of the Act) must be accurate and true. Exaggerated advertising of the product's potential and benefits should be avoided. If the product is said to have certain effects, they should be limited to those that can actually be proven.

(ii) *Warnings* concerning risks or hazardous side effects should not only relate to the product proper, but also to accessories often used in connection with the product. If such accessories can be obtained from third parties, the producer should refrain from passing negative judgments upon such products offered by third parties.

Warnings must be given in a way which is understandable for the average consumer or user. They must be clearly visible, even after years of use.

(iii) Manuals and other instructions for use are required by law (*Gerätesicherungsgesetz*)[9] to contain, in particular, the following:

- clear identification of dangers; however, dangers that are so obvious that every reasonable person is aware of them, need not be mentioned expressly;
- handling instructions that also extend to combinations with accessories and other equipment that is commonly known to be used together with the product;
- instructions concerning installation, assembly and fitting of spare parts. If such work should only be performed by trained personnel or experts, there must be notice to that effect;
- instructions concerning care and maintenance, and safety measures to be observed in connection therewith.[10]

8 Cf Ch E Ziff. 3.

9 Amtliche Mitteilungen der Bundesanstalt für Arbeitsschutz No 2/1988, pp 3 ff.

10 Cf Ch C II 2 lit d.

(iv) *Product observation* requires a system which allows user information and experience to make its way to the producer. This presupposes sufficient contacts between the producer and the users, either directly, or indirectly via the distribution system. Defects that occur often must be reported by the distribution organisation to the producer. The same goes of the product is frequently used or applied in a wrong way. Warnings and recalls must be adequately organised. If possible, the distribution organisation should maintain a list of customers, including their addresses.

Recalls[11] must be organised at short notice if there is a clear and immediate danger to users. They must be announced in the mass media. Dangers that may only materialise in the long run must be eliminated in the course of regular service or maintenance, like in the automotive industry.

9.2 Exclusion of liability

Many people think that product liability may be excluded by contractual stipulations, particularly general conditions of sale. However, even though contractual stipulations are a necessary part of risk management, they can by no means provide sufficient protection against product liability claims.

i. Liability limitation by general conditions of sale. The following should be observed when wording and using general conditions:

(a) They will become effective only between the contractual partners. They cannot exclude claims by third parties, particularly by the consumer against the producer.
(b) The Product Liability Act § 14 does not permit the limitation or exclusion by general conditions of claims based on that Act.
(c) General conditions must be worded in the negotiation language, or the language of the customer.
(d) General conditions must be agreed upon, and must be made accessible to the partner, before or during the conclusion of the agreement.
(e) Exclusions or limitations of liability for personal injury are not admissible.
(f) Liability for property damage cannot be excluded or limited in cases of grossly negligent or wilful conduct.
(g) General conditions should provide for the applicable law and for venue in order to provide for uniform treatment where parts are being bought from different suppliers.
(h) The choice of venue clauses must be entered into in writing within the EC. Therefore, general conditions should be either added to a written agreement, or should be signed by the contract partner.

11 Cf Ch A VII 2.

ii. Individual agreements. Whenever there are high risks at stake, individual agreements (as opposed to general conditions) should be stipulated.

Individual agreements permit the exclusion of liability for gross negligence as well.

However, they will again not affect liability based on the Act, or claims raised by third parties.

9.3 Insurance

(1) Companies generally buy a general insurance against liabilities to third parties. This insurance covers personal injury and property damage (normally including harm done to third parties by the company's workers and employees).

However, product liability may be incurred not only for health or property infringement (torts), but also for lack of product qualities that have been represented, and for purely financial losses (contractual product liability).

If a product does not have the represented qualities, the respective product liability claims are not covered by the general liability insurance, nor are pure financial losses. A company that might be subject to such claims therefore should buy *product liability insurance* that covers these two types of claims as well. Still, the general as well as the product liability insurance, cover only liabilities incurred by the producer under the law. Obligations which have been contractually agreed in order to broaden the purchaser's rights are not normally covered by liability insurance. The two most frequent instances in which the purchaser's rights are extended are:

(a) contractual extension of the statutory (cf BGB § 477) six-month limitation period for making a complaint in respect of a product defect; and
(b) the waiver of the requirement that a merchant must examine goods upon receipt and must make complaints in respect of defects immediately (cf HGB § 377; Commercial Code).

Such extensions of the statutory liability can be brought under the umbrella of insurance protection by particular agreements with the insurer. The extended insurance coverage must be agreed upon *expressly*.

(2) What is and what is not covered by product liability insurance.

(a) A normal type of product liability insurance covers the following risks:
    (i) property damage caused by lack of represented qualities;
    (ii) liability arising from the combination or mixture of defective products with other goods, eg if a defective component leads to the destruction of the more complex product the component has gone into;
    (iii) damage attributable to improper treatment or processing by the producer.
(b) Even though product liability insurance seems absolutely necessary in the light of the limited possibilities of excluding liability contractually,

it will by not any means cover all the sorts of damage the producer might be held liable for, in particular:

(i) claims based on contractual agreements extending the purchaser's statutory rights;
(ii) defects caused by *assembly* or *fitting* by the producer, including cases where the assembly or the fitting takes place on the user's premises;
(iii) costs for mounting and dismounting parts of vehicles;
(iv) reimbursement for expenses incurred by the user which turned out to be useless due to failing or improper performance;
(v) consequential damages following from interruptions in the operation of, and production on manufacturing or shop premises (a special insurance against interruption of shop operations is possible);
(vi) warranty commitments that go beyond the representation of certain product qualities;
(vii) risks connected with product testing;
(viii) wilful infringements;
(ix) liability for sub-contractors. It should be ensured that the *sub-contractor buys a product liability insurance policy of his own.*

(3) Every insurance policy is limited by *maximum liability amounts*. These maximum liability amounts become relevant particularly in cases of *mass defects*. If a defect in several like products can be traced back to the same flaw, mistake or defect in construction/design, production or instructions, we may assume a mass defect. All instances of damage caused by a mass defect are considered as having occurred at the same point in time and cannot be spread over several years. Therefore, the insurer may invoke the maximum liability amount for one year. Since that maximum amount may have to suffice, it should be sufficiently high.

(4) It is particularly disadvantageous that recall costs are not insurable (except in the automotive industry).

9.4 Limitation of liability through corporate legal structure

Since we have come to the conclusion that product liability risk cannot be fully controlled by contractual limitations nor by insurance, we will now have to examine whether the risk can be additionally minimised by choosing an appropriate corporate legal structure.

(1) Limiting the overall liability involved with business activity in Germany is possible by conducting business either as a company limited by shares (*Aktiengesellschaft – AG* or *Gesellschaft mit beschränkter Haftung – GmbH*), or as a limited partnership (*Kommanditgesellschaft – KG*) whose partner with full personal liability for the liabilities of the partnership (*Komplementär*) is a GmbH (GmbH & Co KG).

The GmbH and the GmbH & Co KG are generally preferable to an AG, because they are easier to found and to operate, and because their share capital may be lower.

(2) In order not to have private assets jeopardised by product liability, nor to expose a company to product liability risks it would not normally incur, some companies have started to establish subsidiaries for the purpose of producing possibly dangerous products and to concentrate the product liability risk there.

In order to accomplish this most efficiently, and at relatively small expense, the shareholders and/or managers of the related companies are often identical. In order to cut costs further, the administrative and clerical work may be carried out by the original company for the new subsidiary. All of this leads to very close interrelations between the respective companies.

In a company law landmark decision,[12] the Federal Supreme Court has allowed a plaintiff to 'pierce through the corporate veil' in a case where the two companies were too closely related. One shareholder had dominated both companies and had been sued personally, even though the plaintiff had had contractual ties with only one of the companies. The court permitted the plaintiff to hold the shareholder personally liable, and he had to satisfy the plaintiff's claim from his private assets.

Therefore, if it should be found necessary to establish a separate subsidiary in order to avoid product liability claims against the parent company, it should be ensured that the management is not identical, that the managers have a capacity to act which is largely independent from the shareholders, and that there are separate administrations.

If such a strict division is not possible, there should at least be a holding company with limited liability for the shares of the related companies. Thus, there will be no personal liability of the shareholders.

An alternative to establishing a subsidiary for the production of potentially dangerous products is so-called *company splitting*. This concept was originally developed purely for tax purposes. A so-called 'active' company (normally a GmbH) operates the production facilities which, however, have been leased (along with the premises and the real property) from another company. If the active company should go bankrupt, the valuable assets remain with the other company which may then terminate the lease at any time and take over the production facilities, so that a new company may continue with the production.

However, the courts are already trying to impose limitations on this concept as well.[13] For example, the rent owed by the bankrupt company to the lessor cannot be claimed by the lessor (the surviving 'inactive' company) from the receiver. It is to be expected that the courts may in the future permit the receiver not only to withhold outstanding claims from the inactive company, but also to realise the objects that had been leased to the active company. In a recent decision, the Federal Supreme Court has raised this issue, but saw no need to decide it yet.

A further alternative in order to maintain the tax advantages of *leasing* without incurring an increased liability risk when importing from outside the Community (Product Liability Act § 4(2)) might be to use as a leasing company a company whose liability is limited and that does not own substantial assets.

12 BGHZ 95, 330.
13 BGH in WM 1989, 1844.

9.5 Product identification

In the light of the quasi-producer liability established by § 4(1), second sentence of the Act, it is most advisable not to affix trademarks, names or other means of identification to a product wherever this may result in product liability not otherwise incurred. At least, dealers who put their own name on the product should make sure that the producer is identified simultaneously.

9.6 The handling of consumer claims

(1) Whenever a producer is confronted with product liability claims by consumers, he will have to notify his product liability insurance company of a potential insurance contingency. The insurance conditions further require the producer not to make any promises to the third party without the insurance company's consent.

(2) In order to possibly take advantage of the liability exemptions in the Act, anyone facing consumer claims should ask himself whether he is indeed a producer in the sense of the Act, and whether the product was defective when it was first distributed.

(3) The consumer should be asked as early as possible to come up with any evidence he may have with respect to the defect, its causation of the damage and, where necessary, fault on the producer's side.

Promises concerning compensation should not be made since under German law they could be construed as binding acknowledgments of the producer's obligation. If the producer's liability has been determined beyond doubt, an out-of-court settlement concerning the amount of damages to be paid is often advisable.

(4) If litigation cannot be avoided, the following additional aspects should be observed:

(a) The producer must tie his insurance company into the litigation.

(b) Where the producer may be indemnified by taking recourse against a supplier, he must make sure that the facts found by the court in the initial lawsuit (where the producer is a defendant) will also be held valid in a possible second lawsuit brought by the producer against the supplier. This can be achieved by making the supplier a third party defendant. However, the producer will benefit from the results found in the first lawsuit in his own litigation against the supplier only if he will be able to sue the supplier in a German court as well. This is one reason why it is essential to agree with the supplier on German law as governing the relationship between the parties, and on the claim being brought before a German court.

(c) One should always bear in mind that most judges in product liability cases tend to sympathise with the victims rather than with the producers. When conducting product liability litigation, this psychological effect must be taken into consideration and must be overcome, if possible, by close reasoning and stringent giving of evidence.

(d) What we have said about risk management should have made clear that producers need not face product liability risks in a helpless and hopeless manner.

CHAPTER VII

Ireland

L K Shields & Partners

31 Merrion Square
Dublin 2
Ireland

Tel ++ 353 1 610866
Fax ++ 353 1 610883

CHAPTER VII

Ireland

1. THE IRISH LEGAL SYSTEM: AN INTRODUCTION

There are four main sources of law. The primary source is the 1937 Constitution, Bunreacht na hEireann. The second source is legislation, statute law, passed by those Parliaments which had jurisdiction over Ireland before 1922 as well as the Oireachtas (Parliament) which existed during the Irish Free State (1922–1936) and, finally, the Oireachtas which operates under the 1937 Constitution. The third source is common law, the rules developed by judges in decided cases both prior to and also since 1922. These rules are constantly being refined and further explained in cases which proceed through the courts. Judges play an important role in the manner in which existing laws, including common law rules, are applied in practice. Irish judges pay great attention to what has been decided in similar cases in the past including cases decided outside the jurisdiction. The deference to previous decisions is a central feature of a common law legal system and is known as the Doctrine of Precedent. This doctrine provides a guideline for a judge deciding a case today while not being strictly binding upon him. The fourth source of Irish law has been the law which the European Communities have generated which has become part of Irish law since Ireland joined the European Communities in 1972.

When deciding cases, Irish judges are obliged to have regard to the provisions of the Irish Constitution to ensure that they are being adhered to. If a statutory provision is in conflict with any provision of the Constitution, the Constitution will prevail and the statutory provision shall be declared unconstitutional. Irish statute law takes precedence over decided cases and if there is a conflict between a statute and a decided case, the statute will prevail. If a provision of Irish statute law has resulted from Ireland's membership of the European Communities, however, there is an express provision in the Constitution that if the enactment was necessary for Ireland to fulfil its obligations as a member of the Community then it will not be declared invalid because it is inconsistent with a provision of the Constitution. The Constitution expressly provides in Article 19.4.3 that 'no provision of the Constitution invalidates laws enacted, acts done or measures adopted by the State necessitated by the obligation of membership of the Communities or prevents laws enacted, acts done or measures adopted by the Communities, or institutions thereof, from having the force of law in the State'. Therefore, the Treaty of Rome and Directives, Regulations and other legislative enactments made thereunder take precedence over the provisions of the Constitution.

2. PRODUCT LIABILITY: INTRODUCTION

2.1 Overview of the law relating to defective products in Ireland

Under Irish law there are three principal ways by which liability may be imposed on manufacturers of defective goods. Liability may arise by virtue of tort, contract or statute law and each will be considered in greater detail below. The following is a brief summary of the main principles involved.

2.1.1 Tort

Liability in tort for negligence in the manufacture of goods depends principally on the establishment of the following factors:

(a) that the manufacturer owed the injured party a duty of care when producing the goods;
(b) that the manufacturer failed in this duty of care; and
(c) that as a result of this failure the injured party suffered the injury of which he complains.

Perhaps the greatest difficulty for the injured party suing in negligence is to establish the existence of a duty of care in the particular circumstances. Further, in tort the question whether economic loss is recoverable or not frequently arises. Tort also affords the manufacturer, in certain circumstances, the ability to exclude or reduce his liability to injured parties. The topic of exclusion of liability is dealt with in greater detail later in this chapter.

2.1.2 Contract

In addition to the terms which a manufacturer or retailer of goods and the consumer of such goods may agree in their contract, legislation also imposes certain conditions, such as merchantability and fitness for purpose. However, the manufacturer/retailer is restricted by statute in his ability to exclude many such terms. The establishment of liability under contract may be difficult because of the doctrine of privity of contract which means that for a party to have obligations or rights under a contract it is necessary for him to be a party to the contract. Thus, if the person injured by defective goods has no contractual relationship with the manufacturer or the retailer, contract law may not afford him a remedy.

2.1.3 Statute

Manufacturers may be liable in respect of defective products by virtue of statute law and statutory instruments. However the statutes or regulations concerned frequently cover a restricted range of products and the liability imposed by such statutes or statutory instruments is frequently criminal as opposed to civil. The issue of whether one can obtain civil compensation for breach of a statute or statutory instrument is discussed later in the chapter.

2.2 Definition and classification of terms

The following abbreviations are used throughout this chapter.

1980 Act	Sale of Goods and Supply of Services Act 1980
1893 Act	Sale of Goods Act 1893
1957 Act	Statute of Limitations 1957
1961 Act	Civil Liability Act 1961 (as amended)
1963 Act	Companies Act 1963 (as amended)
Cheshire, Fifoot and Furmston	Cheshire, Fifoot and Furmston *Law of Contract* (11th edn)
WLR	Weekly Law Reports
AC	Appeal Cases
ILRM	Irish Law Reports Monthly
ILTR	Irish Law Times Reports
SC	Supreme Court
unrep	Unreported judgment
IR	Irish Reports
Ir LR	Irish Law Reports
HC	High Court
DC	District Court
QB	Queen's Bench
Exch	Exchequer Division
All ER	All England Reports
KB	King's Bench
McMahon and Binchy	McMahon & Binchy *Irish Law of Torts* (2nd edn)
Salmond and Heuston	Salmond & Heuston *Law of Torts* (19th edn)
NICA	Northern Ireland Court of Appeal
QBD	Queen's Bench Division
Lloyds Rep	Lloyd's Reports
Brady and Kerr	Brady and Kerr *The Limitation of Actions in the Republic of Ireland* (1st edn)
TLR	Times Law Reports
JISLL	The Journal of the Irish Society for Labour Law
NI	Northern Ireland
IIF	Irish Insurance Federation
M & W	Meeson & Wellsby's English Exchequer Reports
Ball & B	Ball & Beatty, IR
CBNS	English Common Bench Reports, New Series by John Scott
Doug	Douglas English King's Bench Reports
HL Cas	House of Lords Cases, English
the Constitution	*Bunreacht na hEireann* 1937.

3. LIABILITY IN CONTRACT

3.1 Introduction

The law of contract in Ireland on the sale of goods is broadly covered by the terms of the 1980 Act. Prior to the 1980 Act this area was covered by the 1893

Act. The 1980 Act amends and updates the 1893 Act. As we shall see later in this section the 1980 Act implies certain terms into contracts falling within its ambit. Important points to note about the 1980 Act are as follows:

(a) Many of the terms deemed to be incorporated into contracts by the 1980 Act are deemed to be contractual conditions. Section 11 of the 1980 Act would appear to confirm the view that breach of such conditions may give the purchaser the right to repudiate the contract.
(b) Not all contracts are covered by the 1980 Act. The Act deals with contracts for the sale of goods and contracts for the supply of services. The terms which are deemed to be incorporated into contracts covered by the 1980 Act may be expressly excluded by the vendor of goods or the provider of services but as we shall see later the circumstances in which this can be done are limited and uncertain.

Contractual terms are not determined solely by the 1980 Act. The conduct of the parties and to a lesser extent their bargaining position will also be relevant in determining the terms of any contract. We shall see later that pre-contractual statements or representations by a vendor of goods may, in certain circumstances, be held to be part of a contract.

3.2 Liability for pre-contractual statements or representations

3.2.1 Liability for pre-contractual representations or misrepresentations

i. Representations. As stated by *Cheshire, Fifoot and Furmston*[1]

> a representation is a statement of fact made by one party to the contract (the representor) to the other (the representee) which, while not forming a term of the contract, is yet one of the reasons that induces the representee to enter into the contract. A misrepresentation is simply a representation that is untrue.

A representation must be a statement of fact and not of intention, opinion or law. However, a statement of opinion can be a misrepresentation if it is an opinion not truly held or even if the representor had an opportunity to check its validity and the representee did not have such opportunity.[2] An example of an opinion which was held not to be a representation is found in *Bisset v Wilkinson*[3] where the defendant said that in his opinion land he was selling to the plaintiff would hold 2,000 sheep. The land had not previously been a sheep farm and the opinion, though wrong, was found to be honestly held and not a representation.

For there to be a representation there must be a statement. However silence, it has been held, may be a misrepresentation in the following circumstances:

(a) where silence distorts a positive representation; or
(b) where the contract requires the utmost good faith (*uberrimae fides*), eg insurance contracts.

1 At p 257.
2 *Esso Petroleum v Mardon* [1976] 2 WLR 583.
3 [1927] AC 177.

Where the representation alleged is a case of silence or non-disclosure as opposed to a positive false disclosure, the question as to whether the contract is void depends on whether the representation related to a material fact of the contract. In the *Chariot Inns* case[4] the test was stated by Kenny J in the Supreme Court to be:

> It is not what the person seeking insurance regards as material, nor is it what the insurance company regards as material. It is a matter or circumstance which would reasonably influence the judgment of a prudent insurer in deciding whether he would take the risk and, if so, in determining the premium which he would demand.

A general duty of disclosure also exists in cases where a fiduciary relationship exists between the parties.[5]

ii. The need for inducement. A false statement alone does not give rise to a cause of action. The statement must have been one of the reasons why the plaintiff entered into the contract. It follows that if the plaintiff did not let the representation influence his decision to enter into the contract, no cause of action arises for the representation.[6]

Similarly, if the plaintiff was aware of the untruth of the representation at the time it was made he cannot subsequently seek to rely on it to found a cause of action.

These are three classes of representation and misrepresentation. These claims are relevant in determining what remedy attaches to the particular representation or misrepresentation in issue.

A summary of these classes or misrepresentations are as follows:

i. Fraudulent mispresentation. This is where the representor makes a false statement which at the time he makes the representation he did not honestly believe to be true.[7]

ii. Negligent misrepresentation. In *Derry v Peek*[8] the house of Lords ruled that an action would lie in the tort of deceit for a fraudulent misrepresentation but there is no liability in deceit for a false statement made carelessly and without reasonable grounds for believing it to be true. For liability to attach to a false statement there needs to be a contractual or fiduciary relationship between the parties. In *Hedley Byrne v Heller & Partners*[9] the House of Lords held that liability for negligent misstatements could arise in tort. In *Stafford v Keane Mahony Smith*[10] the requirements for liability to attach to a negligent statement were stated to be that:

4 *Chariot Inns Ltd v Assicurazioni Generali SPA and Coyle Hamilton* [1981] 1 ILRM 173, SC.
5 *Dunbar v Tredennick* (1813) 2 Ball & B 304, Ch.
6 *Smith v Chadwick* (1884) 9 App Cas 187 and *Smith v Lynn* (1954) 85 ILTR 57). In the latter case the court held that the plaintiff had not relied on the representation of the defendant but had relied on his own inspection of the premises.
7 *Carbin v Somerville* [1933] IR 227. SC and *Pearson v Dublin Corpn* [1907] 2 IR 27.
8 [1889] 14 App Cas 337.
9 [1964] AC 465.
10 [1980] ILRM 53, HC.

> there must first of all be a person conveying the information or the representation relied upon; secondly, there must be a person to whom that information is intended to be conveyed or to whom it might reasonably be expected that the information will be conveyed; thirdly, the person must act upon such information or representation to his detriment so as to show that he is entitled to damages.

iii. Innocent misrepresentation. An innocent misrepresentation is a misrepresentation which is neither fraudulent nor negligent and gives the plaintiff limited redress. Section 45(1) of the 1980 Act has created a statutory right of damages for a misrepresentation not made fraudulently, ie negligently or innocently. However section 45(1) of the 1980 Act enables the representor to avoid liability if the representor believed and had reasonable grounds for believing the truth of the statement.

3.2.2 Incorporation of pre-contractual statements

Not every statement which precedes a contract will be held to form part of such contract. A pre-contractual statement having no contractual effect may be called a 'mere puff' or a mere representation'. Such statements are treated as mere representations or puffs if the representation was not seriously meant and the other party, ie the representee, should have realised this.

A pre-contractual statement will be held to be part of the ensuing contract if it falls under the category of 'warranty' although the formal use of the expression 'warrant' does not have to have been used.[11]

The view of the Irish courts on whether a pre-contractual statement is a mere representation, which is not incorporated into the contract, or a warranty, which is, was expressed by Kenny J in *Bank of Ireland v Smith*[12] where he stated that the modern cases show a welcome tendency to 'regard a representation made in connection with the sale as being a warranty unless the person who made it can show that he was innocent of fault in connection with it'. The meaning of 'innocent of fault' in this connection is unclear but it is submitted that it should be taken as an expression of no more than an honestly held opinion.

Therefore it is a matter of construction whether a pre-contractual statement is incorporated into a contract.

3.2.3 Statements and representations and the Product Liability Directive

The manner in which pre-contractual statements or representations may be relevant under the impending product liability legislation arises perhaps most directly from article 6 of the Directive. This article details the factors to be taken into acount when a party is considering whether a product is defective and provides that:

> A product is defective when it does not provide the safety which a person is entitled to expect, taking all circumstances into account including:
> (a) the presentation of the product;

11 *Scales v Scanlan* (1843) 6 IrLR 367, Exch.
12 [1966] IR 646.

(b) the use to which it could reasonably be expected that the product would be put; and
(c) the time when the product was put into circulation.

The relevance of a pre-contractual statement or representation is clear when consideration is given to article 6.1(b). The use to which one could reasonably expect that a product could be put may be dependent upon pre-contractual statements or representations. For example, where a purchaser is unsure whether a product will meet his needs and the vendor represents that the product will in fact meet his needs, such a representation will be likely to be treated as a pre-contractual statement. In circumstances such as these it would seem that the product could be held to be defective by virtue of article 6 if damage was caused while the product was being utilised in the manner in which the vendor represented that it could be used.[13]

In summary, a representation will be incorporated in the contract if it:

(a) is a statement of fact made by one party to the contract;
(b) is made to the other party to the contract;
(c) is one of the reasons that induces the party to whom it is made to enter into the contract.

Section 46 of the 1980 Act is relevant where the vendor of goods attempts to restrict his liability to the purchaser in respect of a pre-contractual statement or misrepresentation. This section provides that where an agreement contains a provision attempting to exclude or restrict the liability of one party (usually the vendor of goods), for a misrepresentation made by him before the contract was made, or where the contract contains a provision limiting a remedy available to another party to the contract by reason of such a misrepresentation, then the provision restricting the vendor's liability shall not be enforceable unless it is shown that it is fair and reasonable. The term 'fair and reasonable' is defined in the Schedule to the 1980 Act by reference to the circumstances which were or ought reasonably to have been known or in the contemplation of the parties when the contract was made including the relative bargaining position of the parties, whether the purchaser had the chance of entering into a similar contract with another vendor but without the offending term, whether the purchaser knew or ought to have known of the existence of the term and whether the goods involved were manufactured, processed or adapted to the special order to the purchaser.

Therefore it is, at least in theory, possible to limit any liability which a party may have in respect of a misrepresentation. However, it should be noted that the 1980 Act restricts the ability to exclude liability for a misrepresentation which offends the conditions implied by section 10.[14]

3.3 Outline of contract law relevant to defective products in Ireland

The basic statute governing this in Ireland is the 1980 Act which updated the 1893 Act. The 1893 Act in sections 12–15 contained provisions covering such

13 See pp 208–9.
14 See pp 178–184.

areas as implied undertakings as to title, sales by description, implied undertakings as to quality or fitness and sale by sample. Section 10 of the 1980 Act has brought together sections 11–15 of the 1893 Act. Section 11 of the 1980 Act limits the effect of statements which endeavour to restrict the rights of the buyer. Sections 12 and 13 respectively of the 1980 Act deal specifically with warranties as to spare parts and servicing and implied conditions governing the sale of motor vehicles. The 1980 Act also implies certain conditions into guarantees.[15]

3.4 Contractual warranties relating to quality of goods and safety of goods

In relation to the quality of goods the relevant provision is contained in section 10 of the 1980 Act, whereas in relation to safety of goods there are provisions contained in numerous pieces of legislation including the Health, Safety and Welfare at Work Act 1989.

3.4.1 Quality of goods

Section 10 of the 1980 Act, which incorporates section 14 of the 1893 Act, states that there is no implied condition or warranty as to the quality or fitness for any particular purpose of goods supplied under a contract of sale. However, the section goes on to state that where the seller sells goods in the course of a business there is an implied condition that the goods supplied are of merchantable quality. This implied condition will not apply:

(a) to defects specifically drawn to the buyer's attention before the contract is made; or
(b) (if the buyer examines the goods before the contract is made), to defects which that examination ought to have revealed.

The section goes on to state that goods are of merchantable quality:

> if they are as fit for the purpose or purposes for which goods of that kind are commonly bought and as durable as it is reasonable to expect having regard to any description applied to them, the price (if relevant) and all other relevant circumstances.

Where the seller sells goods in the course of a business and the buyer makes known (either expressly or impliedly) to the seller any particular purpose for which the goods are being brought then there is an implied condition that the goods supplied under the contract are reasonably fit for that purpose, whether or not that is a purpose for which such goods are commonly supplied. This implied term may be negatived where it can be shown that the buyer did not rely on or it was unreasonable for him to rely on the seller's skill or judgment in relation to the particular purpose. Furthermore, an implied condition or warranty as to quality or fitness for a particular purpose may be annexed to a contract of sale by usage.

15 Ss 15–19.

Section 12 of the 1980 Act implies into contracts for the sale of goods a warranty that spare parts and an adequate after-sales service will be made available by the seller in such circumstances as are stated in an offer, description or advertisement by the seller on behalf of the manufacturer or on his own behalf and for such a period as is so stated or if no period is so stated for a reasonable period. The section allows the Minister for Industry and Commerce, by order, to state what constitutes a reasonable period. Any term of a contract exempting the seller from all or any of the provisions of section 12 is void.

Section 13 of the 1980 Act sets out conditions implied in every contract for the sale of motor vehicles. The section implies (except where the buyer is a person whose business it is to deal in motor vehicles) a condition that at the time of delivery of the vehicle it is free from any defect which would render it a danger to the public, including persons travelling in the vehicle. However, this condition is not to be implied if the seller and buyer have agreed that the vehicle is not intended for use in the condition in which it is to delivered and a statement to that effect is signed by or on behalf of the seller and the buyer and given to the buyer before or on delivery and that the agreement between the buyer and the seller that the vehicle is not to be used in its condition when delivered is fair and reasonable.

Other provisions relating to the quality of goods in section 13 of the 1893 Act are incorporated in the 1980 Act and provide that where goods are sold by description there is an implied condition that the goods shall correspond with the description and if the goods are sold by example as well as by description it is not sufficient that the bulk of the goods correspond with the sample if they do not also correspond with the description. The section further states that there can be a sale by description notwithstanding the fact that the goods so sold, being exposed for sale, are selected by the buyer.

In relation to sales by sample section 15 of the 1893 Act (incorporated in the 1980 Act) states that in contracts for sale by sample three terms are implied:

(a) a condition that the bulk corresponds with the sample in quality; and
(b) a condition that the buyer shall have a reasonable opportunity of comparing the bulk with the sample, and
(c) a condition that the goods shall be free from any defect rendering them unmerchantable which would not be apparent on reasonable examination of the sample.

The ability to exclude some of these terms is discussed later in the chapter.[16]

i. Advantages of contractual liability. Although contractual liability may arise from negligence,[17] where a representor does not use reasonable care, it may also be strict, such as where there is a breach of a warranty as to quality or fitness of goods for a particular purpose. It was held in *Henry Kendall & Son Ltd v William Lillico & Sons*[18] that liability for breach of such a warranty would be imposed even where the defect was such that 'the utmost skill and judgment on the part of the seller' would not have detected it.

16 See pp 183–4.
17 See section 4, p 185 ff.
18 [1969] 2 AC 31.

An advantage of contractual liability is that in certain circumstances not only may the contracting party reject the defective goods, he may also recover compensation for any damage flowing from their use. In addition, in contract the limitation period is greater than for some actions in tort. A further advantage is that the contracting party is also able to claim compensation in contract for purely financial loss. While this may also be recoverable in tort under the *Hedley Byrne* principle, there are, in tort, certain requirements to be overcome such as the existence of a 'special relationship' between the parties.

The major disadvantage of contractual liability arises from the doctrine of privity of contract which allows only those who are parties to the contract to sustain an action in contract. While the purchaser may claim against his immediate vendor, any person who used the goods without any contractual relationship with the vendor may have no remedy in contract for any defect which may cause him loss.

ii. Implied terms in hire purchase contracts. The implied statutory terms in a contract for the sale of goods apply to the vendor. In hire purchase contracts on the other hand the implied statutory terms apply to the owner. Sections 25–38 of the 1980 Act govern the terms implied in hire purchase contracts. These sections contain similar provisions in relation to title, letting by description, sample, etc as are implied in contracts for the sale of goods.

iii. Conditions and warranties. With regard to breach, not all terms of a contract are of the same importance. At common law all terms of a contract were independent. If two parties had entered into a contract with one another and one was in breach of a terms of the contract, the other had to fulfil his side of the contract and sue for the loss which he suffered as a result of the breach by the other party. Later (Lord Mansfield in *Kingston v Preston*)[19] it was stated that there were three types of contractual covenants:

(a) dependent covenants, ie there was a condition precedent to the particular covenant arising at all;[20] and
(b) concurrent conditions, ie where the conditions applicable to the plaintiff and those applicable to the defendant had to be performed together and one party could not sue in respect of non-performance by the other unless he himself had or was willing to peform his conditions; and
(c) independent covenants, ie where the plaintiff could sue in respect of the non-performance of the defendant without reference to his own covenant.

The difficulty in the interpretation of conditions in contracts and the importance of these conditions is recognised by section 11(2) of the 1893 Act (now part of section 10 of the 1980 Act) which states:

> whether a stipulation in a contract of sale is a condition, the breach of which may give rise to a right to treat the contract as repudiated, or a warranty, the breach of which may give rise to a claim for damages but not to a right to reject the goods and treat the contract as repudiated, depends in each case on the construction of the contract. A stipulation may be a condition, though called a warranty in the contract.

19 (1773) 2 Doug 689.
20 *Re Application of Butler* [1970] IR 45, HC.

In deciding whether a term is a condition or a warranty Irish courts tend to look at the contract in the light of all the surrounding circumstances of the case and then to decide what the parties had intended the term of the contract to be.[1] It should be noted that many of the terms implied into contracts for the sale of goods under the 1980 Act (section 10) are deemed to be conditions. Therefore if the seller is in breach of any of these conditions the buyer may be entitled to repudiate the contract pursuant to the 1980 Act. It should also be noted that under section 11(1) of the 1893 Act (now incorporated in section 10 of the 1980 Act) the buyer is given the option of treating a breach of any condition imposed upon the seller as if it were a breach of warranty and seeking damages and not repudiation of the contract.

3.4.2 Safety of goods

The 1980 Act regulates, inter alia, the quality or fitness of goods. However, it may be argued that the effect in practice of section 10 of the 1980 Act, and specifically the implied condition therein as to the merchantable quality of goods supplied under contract, is to lay down a minimum safety standard which has to be met by all goods supplied under contracts covered by the 1980 Act. It could also be argued that the definition of merchantable quality which requires the goods to be as fit for the purpose or purposes for which goods of that kind are commonly bought and as durable as it is reasonable to expect, in effect means that manufacturers should produce goods of a reasonable standard of safety as it is difficult to see how goods could comply with the definition of merchantable quality and yet be unsafe.

Where a party is injured by defective goods supplied under contract the normal course is to bring an action in negligence.[2] The safety of goods itself is not dealt with in any comprehensive manner in any legislation. This is perhaps due to the fact that there is such a wide variety of goods that the drafting of any legislation attempting to lay down minimum safety standards for each product would indeed be difficult.

Consumers expect that products which they purchase will live up to certain standards of safety. In most transactions the consumer will enter into a contractual relationship with the retailer of the product and not the manufacturer. Since the contract is normally with the retailer, it is the retailer who will normally bear the consequences of an action for breach of contract if the goods fail to meet the required standard of safety. In such circumstances the purchaser has the option of bringing an action in contract against the retailer or an action in tort against the manufacturer.

While the law of negligence in general terms imposes certain safety standards upon manufacturers, the legislature has not enacted a great deal of legislation dealing with safety standards required for specific products. The areas where the legislature has provided for minimum standards are areas where the products concerned affect public health. For example, legislation covers the sale of

1 *Bentsen & Son v Taylor* [1893] 2 QB 274.
2 See sections 4.1 and 4.2, p 185 ff.

food and drugs,[3] the production of pharmaceuticals[4] and medical and health preparations.[5]

3.5 Breach of contract for the supply of defective products

3.5.1 Types of defect

The types of defect which will be held to infringe section 14(2) of the 1893 Act (as incorporated by section 10 of the 1980 Act) are those which render the goods supplied of unmerchantable quality. This is so save where the defect has been specifically drawn to the attention of the purchaser before the contract is made or where the purchaser examines the goods before the contract is made in which case the vendor will not be liable for any defects which the examination ought to have revealed. Section 14(3) of the 1893 Act (as incorporated by section 10 of the 1980 Act) states that goods are of merchantable quality:

> if they are as fit for the purpose or purposes for which goods of that kind are commonly bought and as durable as it is reasonable to expect having regard to any descriptions applied to them, the price (if relevant) and all other relevant circumstances.

The definition of merchantable quality would appear to exclude products unmerchantable due purely to an aesthetic defect. This of course might not be the case where the article bought was an aesthetic article and was sold as such.

3.5.2 Causation

Liability under the 1980 Act flows from a finding that the product does not comply with the requirements of the Act. Once this is established the purchaser becomes entitled to redress.

However, where the plaintiff is alleging loss arising from breach of contract he must, as in tort, prove that there is a causal connection between the defendant's breach of contract and his loss.[6] Much of what will be stated on causation in the section dealing with tort[7] is equally relevant. The courts have avoided laying down any formal test for causation preferring to ascertain whether a particular breach of contract is a sufficiently substantial cause of a particular plaintiff's loss. As in tort the intervening acts of third parties and the plaintiff himself are important in establishing if there is a causal connection.

3.5.3 Remoteness of loss and damages

The area of damages and breach of contract was fully considered in *Hadley v Baxendale*.[8]

The loss which the plaintiff may recover for breach of contract is the loss which was, at the time contract, a reasonably foreseeable consequence of the breach. The knowledge of the parties at the time of the contract is therefore important.

3 Sale of Food and Drugs Act 1875–1936 and Regulations thereunder.
4 Misuse of Drugs Act 1977.
5 Health Acts 1947 to 1970.
6 *Sykes v Midland Bank Executor and Trustee Co Ltd* [1971] 1 QB 113.
7 See section 4.3, p 188 ff.
8 (1854) 9 Exch 341.

In *Heron II*[9] the House of Lords potentially widened the defendant's liability by holding that the question was not whether the defendant should have foreseen the damage but rather whether the probability of its occurrence should have been within the reasonable contemplation of the parties at the time the contract was made, having regard to their knowledge at that time.

In *Lee and Donoghue v Rowan*[10] a farmer had to destroy his crops when a drying shed which he was having erected was not completed in accordance with the contract. Though this damage was held not recoverable as it was not within the reasonable contemplation of the defendant, the plaintiff was allowed the estimated costs of putting his crops into storage, including transport costs. It should also be noted that as in tort the plaintiff is under an obligation to mitigate his damages.[11]

3.6 Quantum of damage

Under section 51(3) of the 1893 Act, where the seller fails to deliver goods which are readily available in the market-place the buyer can go to the market, purchase the goods and the measure of damages is the difference between the price he paid for the goods in the market and that which he contracted to pay upon delivery.

Where there has been late delivery of goods the loss is measured as the fall in the value of the goods from the date of delivery in the contract to the date of actual delivery.[12]

3.7 The burden of proof

The degree of proof required in civil proceedings, including contract and tort, is the balance of probabilities.[13]

3.8 Exclusion and limitation of liability

There is an inherent conflict contained in sections 11 and 22 of the 1980 Act which deal with the exclusion of terms. Section 11(4) states that:

> it shall be an offence for a person in the course of a business to furnish to a buyer goods bearing, or goods in a container bearing, or any document including any statement, irrespective of its legal effect, which sets out, limits or describes rights conferred on a buyer or liabilities to the buyer in relation to goods acquired by him or

9 [1969] 1 AC 350.
10 17 November 1981, HC, unrep, Costello J.
11 *Board Iascaigh Mhara v Scallan* (8 May 1973 unrep), HC, Pringle J).
12 *Heron II* [1969] 1 AC 350.
13 *Millar v Minister of Pensions* [1947] 2 All ER 372 at 373–374 per Denning J: 'If the evidence is such that the tribunal can say: "We think it more probable than not", the burden is discharged but if the probabilities are equal it is not'; and *Cooper v Slade* (1858) 6 HL Cas 746 at 772.

any statement likely to be taken as such a statement, unless that statement is accompanied by a clear and conspicuous declaration that the contractual rights which the buyer enjoys by virtue of sections 12, 13, 14 and 15 of the Act of 1893 are in no way prejudiced by the relevant statement.

On the other hand, section 22 of the 1980 Act states that whereas a party cannot contract out of or exclude section 12 of the 1893 Act, which relates to the seller's title to sell the goods in question, under any circumstances, a party may in certain circumstances exclude the provisions of sections 13 to 15 of the 1893 Act (now incorporated in section 10 of the 1980 Act) relating to sales by description, sample and implied terms as to quality of goods.

These terms may be contracted out of where the buyer of the goods does not deal as a consumer[14] and where the exclusion is fair and reasonable.[15]

Thus, the inconsistency is apparent. While a party may contract out of terms implied under sections 13 to 15 of the 1893 Act (now incorporated in section 10 of the 1980 Act) so long as the exclusion is fair and reasonable and the buyer does not deal as a consumer, if a party makes any statement to the effect that it is contracting out of sections 13 to 15 a criminal offence is committed under section 11(4).

Further, according to section 22 of the 1980 Act (incorporating section 55(1) of the 1893 Act):

subject to the subsequent provisions of this section, where any right, duty or liability would arise under a contract of sale of goods by implication of law, it may be negatived or varied by express agreement, or by the course of dealing between the parties, or by usage if the usage is such as to bind both parties to the contract.

Thus, it is difficult to envisage a case where a party could in accordance with the above section exclude the implied conditions contained in sections 13 to 15 in accordance with section 22 of the 1980 Act without the use of a statement as defined in section 11 and the subsequent criminal liability attaching thereto.

The same inconsistency is apparent in sections 30 and 31 in relation to the hire purchase of goods and the exclusion of implied conditions broadly similar to those contained in sections 12 to 15.

3.9 Limitation period

An action based on a simple contract,[16] must be brought within six years from the date on which the cause of action accrued, which normally is the date of the breach. The contract terms may determine the date on which the cause of action accrued. However, as in tort,[17] where there is an action for damages for breach of a duty and the damages claimed include damages in respect of personal injuries, a party has three years to bring the action from the date the cause of action accrued.[18]

14 Dealing as a consumer is defined in s 3 of the 1980 Act.
15 See p 177.
16 S 11(1)(a) of the 1957 Act.
17 S 11(2)(b) of the 1957 Act.
18 In the case of a deceased defendant a two-year limitation period applies: Civil Liability Act 1961 s 9. A period of three years after attaining majority may apply in certain circumstances to an infant.

Where a person using a motor vehicle with the consent of the buyer suffers loss as a result of a breach by the seller of the implied condition inserted by the 1980 Act[19] he may bring an action against the seller in respect of the breach as if he were the buyer. In such cases a two-year limitation period applies.[20]

An action brought upon an instrument under seal upon the expiration of 12 years from the date on which the cause of action accrued will be statute-barred.[1]

The case of action accrues on the date on which the breach occurred and not on the date when damage is suffered. Accordingly it will be necessary to consider the terms of the contract to establish the date of its breach.[2]

In an action for breach of condition or warranty against a vendor of goods the date of accrual of the cause of action is the time the goods are delivered and not the date on which the breach is discovered.[3]

3.10 Liability for third parties: vicarious liability

Liability is most frequently sought to be excluded in respect of employees or agents. The conditions and warranties implied by the 1980 Act cannot be excluded, save as indicated earlier.

Another obstacle to excluding liability in respect of third parties is the doctrine of privity of contract.[4] In *Scruttons Ltd v Midland Silicones Ltd*[5] the court was of the opinion that notwithstanding lack of privity the liability in respect of third parties may be excluded in certain circumstances, namely:

(a) if the contract makes it clear that the stevedores are to be protected by the provisions in it which limit liability; and
(b) if the contract clearly provides that as well as contracting on his own behalf the carrier also contracts as agent for the stevedores in relation to these provisions; and
(c) that the carrier has the stevedores' authority to contract on his behalf as agent; and
(d) that difficulties about consideration moving from the stevedores are overcome.

4. LIABILITY IN TORT

4.1 Introduction

The Courts formerly were reluctant to impose liability in tort on a manufacturer of goods in respect of persons injured by those goods unless privity of contract between the parties was shown to exist. To this general reluctance,

19 1980 Act s 13.
20 S 13(8) amends s 11(2) of the 1951 Act.
1 1957 Act s 11(5)(a).
2 *Morgan v Park Developments Ltd* [1983] ILRM 156.
3 *Lynn v Bamber* [1930] 2 KB 72.
4 See p 180.
5 [1962] AC 446.

there were some exceptions, such as a supplier of goods was under a duty to refrain from deceit.[6] There was also a recognised duty to give a warning when there was an awareness of a defect or danger.[7] Liability was also recognised in respect of goods which were inherently dangerous.[8]

4.2 Outline of relevant tort law giving rise to liability for personal and property damage in Ireland

Liability for the negligent manufacture and supply of defective goods in Ireland was developed in broadly the same manner as English law following the decision of *Donoghue v Stevenson*[9] and the 'neighbour' formula enunciated by Lord Atkin therein, namely:

> the rule that you are to love your neighbour becomes in law you must not injure your neighbour; and the lawyer's question, who is my neighbour? receives a restricted reply. You must take reasonable care to avoid acts or omissions which you can reasonably foresee would be liable to injure your neighbour. Who, then in law, is my neighbour? The answer seems to be – persons who are so closely and directly affected by my act that I ought reasonably to have them in contemplation as being so affected when I am directing my mind to the acts or omissions which are called in question.

This principle was applied in England by cases such as *Home Office v Dorset Yacht Co Ltd*[10] and *Anns v Merton London Borough Council.*[11] In the latter case Lord Wilberforce restated the 'neighbour' formula previously enunciated by Lord Atkin stating that in order to determine whether a duty of care exists in any particular situation, two questions fall to be determined:

> First one has to ask whether, as between the alleged wrongdoer and the person who has suffered damage, there is a sufficient relationship of proximity or neighbourhood such that, in the reasonable contemplation of the former, carelessness on his part may be likely to cause damage to the latter, in which case a prima facie duty of care arises. Secondly, if the first question is answered affirmatively, it is necessary to consider whether there are any considerations which ought to negative, or to reduce or limit the scope of, the duty or the class of person to whom it is owed or the damages to which a breach of it may give rise.

Lord Wilberforce's position was criticised. In *Governors of the Peabody Donation Fund v Sir Lindsay Parkinson & Co Ltd*[12] Lord Keith favoured the position that a court in determining whether or not a particular defendant was under a duty of care should consider whether it was 'just and reasonable' to impose such a duty. In *Leigh and Sillivan Ltd v Aliakmon Shipping Co Ltd*[13]

6 *Langridge v Levy* (1837) 2 M & W 519.
7 *Heaven v Pender* (1883) 11 QBD 503 at 517 and *Farrant v Barnes* (1862) 11 CB (NS) 553.
8 *Longmeid v Holliday* (1851) 6 Ex 761 at 767, *O'Gorman v O'Gorman* (1903) 21 IR 573; see also the unreported judgment of Walsh J in *O'Sullivan v Noonan* (28 July 1972) SC (89/103/109–1970).
9 [1932] AC 562.
10 [1970] AC 1004.
11 [1978] AC 728.
12 [1985] AC 210.
13 [1986] AC 785 at 815.

Lord Brandon also criticised Lord Wilberforce's approach and considered that Lord Wilberforce could not have intended to provide a universally applicable test of the existence and scope of a duty of care in the law of negligence. Lord Wilberforce was dealing with a novel type of factual situation which was not analogous to any factual situations in which such a duty had already been held to exist.

The Supreme Court in *Ward v McMaster*[14] followed Lord Wilberforce's restatement in *Anns v Merton London Borough Council*. In Ireland, since its exposition by Lord Atkin in *Donoghue v Stevenson* and its subsequent restatement by Lord Wilberforce in *Anns v Merton London Borough Council*, the 'neighbour' formula or proximity principle continues to be the cornerstone of the law of negligence,[15] despite its recent apparent demise in England. Previously, landlords could not be made liable in negligence in respect of defects existing in premises which they let.[16] The court in *Siney v Dublin Corpn* stated that in the light of recent developments this could no longer be so. O'Higgins CJ made strong obiter dicta statements that 'in these circusmstances I can see no basis for suggesting that the principle of *Donoghue v Stevenson* should not apply'. The circumstances referred to by the Chief Justice were that the defendants were providing statutory housing, remained privy to the design of the dwellings, supervised the construction and inspected the completed flat before accepting it from the builders. The Chief Justice appeared to be of the view that as the defendant should have had the plaintiff in its contemplation when making its inspection of the premises and made the inspection accordingly, it could be liable in negligence for having failed to do so. A further case in this line of authority is *Purtill v Athlone UDC*.[17] The defendants owned and controlled an abattoir in which the method of slaughter was a humane killer. A pistol-like instrument and detonators were kept on the premises to facilitate its use. Some children had been allowed on to the abattoir on previous occasions and had taken detonators which they exploded off the premises. On one of these occasions a young boy was severely injured when a detonator exploded in his hand. The plaintiff argued that the defendants had been negligent and should have foreseen that the detonators were a cause of allurement to the boys. The defendants argued that the boys were trespassers and therefore the only duty of care they owed was a duty not to set traps for them. However, Walsh J stated that 'the liability, if established, is therefore one which arose by virtue of the proximity of the parties and it would be the same wherever the parties might find themselves, provided their proximity to each other was the same'.

Walsh J considered that the first question to be considered was that of the proximity of the parties. The duty, he stated 'is based upon the duty that one man has to those in proximity to him to take reasonable care they are not injured by his acts. What amounts to sufficient care must vary necessarily with circumstances, the nature of the danger and the age and knowledge of the person likely to be injured'.

14 10 May 1988, SC.
15 *Siney v Dublin Corpn* [1980] IR 400.
16 *Robbins v Jones* 15 CB (NS) 240.
17 [1968] IR 205.

Further cases which accepted and relied on the 'neighbour principle' are *McNamara v ESB*,[18] *McMahon v Ireland*[19] and *Ward v McMaster*.[20] The 'neighbour' formula would appear to apply also to cases of damage to property.[1]

4.3 Causation

4.3.1 Factual causation

Factual causation means that if the defendant did not in fact cause the plaintiff's injury, other than on grounds of vicarious liability, then he cannot be liable for such injury. If he did in fact cause the plaintiff's injury then he may be liable. Various qualifying adjectives have been attached to the word 'cause' to determine whether the consequence is too remote. Adjectives such as effective, real or substantial have been used by the courts at various stages. Therefore if the defendant's action was not the substantive or the real or effective causes of the plaintiff's injury then the defendant will not be made liable.

The 'but for' test is frequently relied on by the courts in determining factual causation. The courts look at the possible causes of the plaintiff's injury and ask the question: '"but for" the act of the defendant, would the plaintiff have suffered the injury?.[2] This test rules out events which were not factual causes of the plaintiff's injury and leaves the remaining causes to be scrutinised to establish whether they were ther legal causes of the plaintiff's injury.

4.3.2 Legal causation

Once it is established that the act was factually the cause of the plaintiff's injury it must then be established that the act was legally the cause of the plaintiff's injury.[3] An important question in determining whether the defendant will be made liable for the plaintiff's injury is whether there was a '*novus actus interveniens*', an act which occurs between the defendant's act and the plaintiff's injury caused by the plaintiff himself or by some third party. For the *novus actus interveniens* to absolve the defendant or liability for his action it must be of such substance as to break the causal connection between the defendant's act and the plaintiff's injury.[4]

Since *Crowley v AIB*[5] it appears that for the intervening act to break the causal connection it must be a reckless or intentional act on behalf of the plaintiff or a third party and not an act which is merely foreseeable by the

18 [1975] IR 1.
19 [1988] ILRM 610.
20 10 May 1988 SC.
1 *Frank Lynch v Liam Hetherton* [1990] ILRM 857.
2 *Kenny v O'Rourke* [1972] IR 339, *Meehan v Reid and Murphy* (5 March 1985, unrep), HC, Murphy J, *Hanrahan v Merck Sharpe and Dohme (Irl) Ltd* [1989] ILRM 629.
3 *Burke v John Paul & Co Ltd* [1967] IR 277, *Connolly v South of Ireland Asphalt Co* [1977] IR 99.
4 *Power v Bedford Motor* [1959] IR 391.
5 [1988] ILRM 225.

defendant. This principle is illustrated in *Conole v Redbank Oyster Co*[6] where the defendant's captain had put to sea in a boat which he knew to be unseaworthy and was sued for causing loss of life following the capsizing of the boat. The defendant sought to join the manufacturers as co-defendants but was held not entitled to do so as the manufacturers' negligence was not the cause of the accident. The court held that the defendant's decision to put to sea in a boat which it knew to be unseaworthy was a reckless act and as such was sufficient to act as a *novus actus interveniens* and thus discharge the manufacturers' liability. Recklessness in this regard is equated with gross carelessness and does not require the perpetrator of the act to appreciate the risk he is taking.[7]

4.4 Remoteness of loss and damage

Re Polemis and Furness Withy & Co Ltd[8] laid down the strict test that if any reasonable person would foresee that an act such as that in issue would cause damage then the actor would be liable for all damage which was directly traceable to the act in question. However, the fairness of the test of reasonable foreseeability to establish liability and then to use a different test of direct consequences to establish the parameters of such liability was questioned in the case of *Overseas Tank Ship (UK) Ltd v Morts Dock & Engineering Co Ltd (The Wagon Mound, No 1)*[9] which held that the question of liability and the extent of liability were not two questions but one and that the test of reasonable foreseeability should be the only test to be used when deciding the question of liability. The test of reasonable foreseeability, as expounded in *The Wagon Mound, No 1,* in relation to remoteness of damage, has been followed in Ireland.[10]

4.5 Quantum of damage

Damages in Irish Law fall under five separate headings;[11]

i. Nominal damages. Where the plaintiff's legal right has been infringed but the plaintiff has suffered no real damage, the award which he is given will be of a nominal amount only.

ii. Contemptuous damages. Where the plaintiff's right to damages is based on a mere technicality but for which he would not be entitled to damages, the court may go against the general rule and may award the plaintiff damages but may award costs against him.

6 [1976] IR 191.
7 *Donovan v Landys Ltd* [1963] IR 441 at 461–462.
8 [1921] 3 KB 560, CA.
9 [1961] AC 388, PC.
10 *Condon v CIE* (16 November 1984), HC, Barrington J, and *Egan v Sisk* [1986] ILRM 283.
11 *McMahon and Binchy* p 769.

iii. Special and general damages. General damages are those which it is is said are assumed to flow from the act complained of whereas special damages are those (beyond the general damage) which result from the particular circumstances of the case and ought to be set out by the plaintiff in his pleadings.

iv. Restitutio in integrum and compensation. Where possible the plaintiff should be placed in the same position as if the tort had not occurred but this is not always possible and where this is so damages are awarded according to what is deemed to be 'fair'.

v. Exemplary damages. There has always existed a controversy as to whether a court should award exemplary or punitive damages over and above normal damages where there was a 'wanton' interferences with the plaintiff's rights.[12]

In *Rookes v Barnard*[13] the court's ability, in limited circumstances, to award such exemplary damages was accepted. In that case the court held that exemplary damages could be awarded in three categories:

(a) where there was 'oppressive, arbitrary or unconstitutional action by the servants of the government';
(b) where 'the defendant's conduct has been calculated by him to make a profit for himself which may well exceed the compensation payable to the plaintiff'; and
(c) where such damages were 'expressly authorised by statute'.

However, even if the plaintiff's claim fell within one of these three classes the court's power to award exemplary damages was to be used with restraint and the party's means, normally irrelevant in calculating damages, would be relevant in calculating exemplary damages.

The classes set forth in *Rookes v Barnard* have received much criticism as being arbitrary and ambiguous. The decisions of the High Court in this jurisdiction show two schools of thought in relation to the award of exemplary damages, some judgments favouring *Rookes v Barnard* and its consequent limitations and other judgements disapproving of it.[14]

Some judges have used, as a basis for an award of exemplary damages, sections 7(2) and 14(4) of the 1961 Act. An example in this regard is the judgement of Hamilton P in *Kennedy v Ireland*[15] where he stated that it was 'quite clear from a consideration of the Civil Liability Act 1961 and in particular sections 7(2) and 14(4) thereof that Irish law recognises a distinction as between "punitive damages" and "exemplary damages"'.

However, a judgment taken from the other school of thought is Barron J in *Conway v Ireland*[16] where he stated that 'The exemplary damages should be measured in an amount to meet the wrongdoing rather than to benefit the wronged'.

12 *Loudon v Ryder* [1953] 2 QB 202.
13 [1964] AC 1129.
14 Judgments against *Rookes v Barnard: Dillon v Dunnes Stores* (20 December 1968, unrep), (SC), *McDonald v Galvin*, (23 February 1976, unrep), HC, McWilliams J. Decisions for *Rookes v Barnard: Whelan v Madigan* [1978] ILRM 136, *Kearney v Minister for Justice* [1986] IR 116.
15 [1988] ILRM 472.
16 2 November 1988, HC, Barron J.

4.5.1 Damages for personal injury

In contrast to other EC jurisdictions, Irish courts may only make lump sum awards in respect of personal injury as distinct from instalment awards. Since 1988 juries have been abolished in personal injury actions but the quantum of damages would not appear to have fallen.

The factors to be taken into consideration when calculating damages for personal injury were set out by Walsh J in *Long v O'Brien & Cronin Ltd*:[17]

> It is the duty of the plaintiff to adduce evidence sufficient to go to the jury when he sets out to establish that the result of his injuries will be to cause him pecuniary loss in the future . . . Not merely is the former earning capacity of the plaintiff relevant but so also is the present physical condition, his prospective physical condition, the state of the labour market, the particular trade or skill which he has and the prospects for exercising it in the future having regard to the diminution of his capacity to do so resulting from the injuries he has sustained.

The plaintiff may also be awarded damages for pain and suffering and loss of expectation of life, though in regard to damages for pain and suffering the Supreme Court in *Sinnott v Quinnsworth Ltd*[18] has stated that there should, in most cases, effectively be a ceiling of IR £150,000 for general damages and this guideline has been adopted in subsequent cases.[19] With in regard to damages for loss of expectation of life, section 7(2) of the 1961 Act provides that where a cause of action for personal injury passes to the estate of a deceased plaintiff, damages are not to be awarded under this heading to his estate. It was recognised by the House of Lords that damages may be awarded under the heading of loss of expectation of life,[20] and it was stated:

> A man has a legal right that his life should not be shortened by the tortious act of another. His normal expectancy of life is a thing of temporal value, so that its impairment is something for which damages should be given. However, the courts have been inclined to award moderate amounts in respect of damages under this heading.[1]

4.5.2 Damages for injury to property

Henchy J[2] has stated that relevant factors in deciding on damages for injury to property are:

> the nature of the property, the plaintiff's relation to it, the nature of the wrongful act causing the damage, the conduct of the parties subsequent to the wrongful act, and the pecuniary, economic or other relevant implications or consequences of reinstatement damages as compared with diminished-value damages.

17 24 March 1972, unrep, SC.
18 [1984] ILRM 523.
19 *Griffiths v Van Raaj* [1985] ILRM 582.
20 In *Rose v Ford* [1937] AC 826.
1 See judgment of O'Dalaigh J in *McMorrow v Knott* (21 December 1959, unrep), SC.
2 *Munnelly v Falcon Ltd* [1978] IR 387 at 400.

4.6 Burden of proof

The general rule is that the person alleging negligence must prove it on the balance of probabilities. This general rule is subject to the principle of *res ipsa loquitur*, discussed below. The plaintiff's evidence must 'pass beyond the region of pure conjecture into that of legal interference'.[3] Where the negligence alleged consists of an omission rather than a commission it has been held that it is sufficient for the plaintiff to prove, not that the omitted act, had it been committed, would have prevented his injury, but that the omission materially increased the risk of the harm occurring'.[4] O'Dalaigh CJ stated:

> all that is required for a plaintiff to succeed is to establish facts from which an inference of negligence on the part of the defendant may reasonably be inferred . . . it is a mistake to think that because an event is unseen its cause cannot be reasonably inferred.[5]

4.6.1 Res ipsa loquitur

It would be an impossible task in some cases for the plaintiff to prove negligence as frequently the defendant is the only person with knowledge of how the act or omission occurred. In such cases the doctrine of *res ipsa loquitur* may assist the plaintiff:

> Where the thing is shown to be under the management of the defendant or his servants, and the accident is such as in the ordinary course of things does not happen if those who have the management use proper care, it affords reasonable evidence, in the absence of explanation by the defendant, that the accident arose from want of care.[6]

From this statement the conditions required to invoke the doctrine are:

(a) that the thing was under the management of the defendant or his servants; *and*
(b) that the accident would not occur in the normal course of events if proper care had been used.

Some courts have held that for a thing to be under the required degree of management the thing must be under the actual management of the defendant while others have held this to include former possession.

The procedural effect of this doctrine is uncertain. One view is that once the doctrine applies the plaintiff has established a case. Another view is that the defendant has the burden of proving that the accident was not in fact due to his negligence. In cases where the courts are willing to draw an inference of negligence the burden of proof shifts to the manufacturer who is then obliged to prove that he is not at fault. The manufacturer may frequently be faced with a difficulty in discharging this onus of proof. In *Mills v Coca-Cola Bottling Co (Dublin) Ltd*,[7] it was held that evidence of a specific nature must be produced if the producers of mass manufactured products are to succeed in rebutting

3 *Salmond and Heuston*.
4 *McGhee v National Coal Board* [1973] 1 WLR 1.
5 *Gahan v Engineering Products Ltd* [1971] IR 30 at 32.
6 *Scott v London & St Katherine Docks Co* (1865) 3 H & C 596 at 601.
7 8 May 1984, unrep, DC.

inferences of negligence. Evidence of general care is not enough. Even if a manufacturer demonstrates that he has a high standard of quality control in his factory the courts may then say to him that an employee must have been guilty of negligence, in which case vicarious liability will attach to the manufacturer.[8]

4.7 Exclusion on limitation of liability

Section 22 of the 1980 Act provides that any attempt to exclude the conditions implied in consumer contracts by section 10 of the 1980 Act is void and where the contract is not a consumer contract the exclusion must be shown to be fair and reasonable (other than the implied condition in section 12 of the 1893 Act) in accordance with the Schedule to the 1980 Act.

An exclusion clause has to be incorporated into the contract.[9] Generally, an exclusion clause will only be binding if notice of it is given before the contract is concluded. Once it is established that an exclusion clause has in fact been incorporated into the contract the clause must then be construed and this can give rise to certain difficulties. There is the difficulty of the clarity of the exclusion clause and the rule that where the clause is capable of more than one interpretation it will be construed against the party who seeks to rely on it.[10] Another difficulty is in determining the nature of the liability the clause is attempting to exclude. The cases show the courts' inclination is to give the clause a narrow scope of application where possible.[11]

Where a party desires to exclude liability for negligence this may be done where the clause shows a clear intention to exclude liability for negligence and covers whose negligence is to be excluded.[12]

The final issue is whether one can have an exclusion clause which attempts to protect the proferens from any liability in the event of his not performing the contract at all, and not just an exclusion of liability for performing the contract badly. Where a party is attempting to exclude liability for a loss resulting from a fundamental breach of contract the exclusion clause must be specific and even if it is so the validity of such an exclusion clause is doubtful.[13]

4.8 Limitation period

The relevant legislation is the 1957 Act. Recent cases show a trend by defendants in certain circumstances to invoke the terms of the Constitution to attempt to avoid the statutory period of limitation in cases where it should apply.

Section 11(2)(a) of the 1957 Act provides that a party has six years to commence an action in tort from the date on which the cause of action accrued.

8 *Hill v James Crowe (Cases) Ltd* [1978] 1 All ER 812.
9 *Parker v South East Railway* [1877] 2 CPD 416.
10 *Sproule v Triumph Cycle Co* [1927] NI 83, NICA.
11 *Ronan v Midland Railway Co* (1883) 14 LR (IR) 157, QBD.
12 *Canada Steamship Lines v R* [1952] AC 192 at 208.
13 *Clayton Love v B & I Steampacket Co* (1970) 104 ILTR 157; *Photo Production Ltd v Securicor Transport* [1980] AC 827.

However, the appropriate period[14] for an action claiming damages for, inter alia, negligence on the part of the defendant where the plaintiff is claiming damages for personal injuries to any person, is three years.[15] As we shall see later, the date of accrual of a cause of action is an issue which frequently arises. It would appear that the Interpretation Act 1937, when read in conjunction with the 1957 Act, would prevent personal injury proceedings being issued on the third anniversary of the accrual of the cause of action.

When the tort alleged is actionable per se, such as in libel, the limitation period runs from the date on which the wrong was committed even though actual damage may not result for some time. Where the tort requires proof of actual damage then 'the traditional view is that time begins to run from the date on which the damage occurs'.[16]

In relation to the accrual of a cause of action a distinction was formerly drawn between injury to the person and injury to property. In relation to property, Carroll J held in *Morgan v Park Developments Ltd*[17] that the cause of action did not accrue until such damage had been discoverable by the plaintiff.

In a recent decision[18] Finlay CJ of the Supreme Court has stated that he 'must disagree with Carroll J in the conclusion reached by her in *Morgan v Park Developments*'.[19] Finlay CJ went on to hold that 'the time . . . commenced to run at the time when a provable personal injury, capable of attracting compensation, occurred to the plaintiff which was the completion of the tort alleged to be committed against her'.[20] This decision would appear to show that discoverability is no longer relevant when determining the date of accrual of a cause of action for the purposes of section 11(2)(a) or 11(2)(b) of the 1957 Act.[1]

An important decision in this area was that of *O'Domhnaill v Merrick*[2] which was summarised by Finlay CJ in *Toal v Duignan*[3] as being that:

> where there is a clear and patent unfairness in asking a defendant to defend a case after a very long lapse of time between the acts complained of and the trial, then if that defendant has not himself contributed to the delay, irrespective of whether the plaintiff has contributed to it or not, the court may as a matter of justice have to dismiss the action.

It is important to note the new discoverability rule in article 10 of the Directive. This article states that 'the limitation period shall begin to run from the day on which the plaintiff became aware, or should reasonably have become aware, of the damage, the defect and the identity of the producer'.

14 1957 Act, s 11(2)(b).
15 See p 184.
16 *Brady and Kerr* p 42.
17 [1983] ILRM 156.
18 [1990] ILRM 403.
19 [1990] ILRM 409.
20 [1990] ILRM 411.
1 Note: the Statute of Limitations (Amendment) Bill 1990, presently before the Dail, seeks to amend, inter alia, the 1957 Act by introducing discoverability before time begins to run under the 1957 Act in cases of personal injury.
2 [1984] IR 151.
3 27 November 1987, SC, at 279–286.

The Directive provides that the time of the accrual of a cause of action, and the expiry of the limitation period, depend upon the injured person having a reasonable opportunity of becoming aware of the damage which he has suffered.

4.9 Liability for third parties

4.9.1 Vicarious liability in tort

In product liability the primary question is under what circumstances a producer can be made liable for the torts of his employees? The courts have devised a number of tests to determine who are 'employees'.

The first was the 'control test'. This provided that where the employer had a degree of control over an employee in respect of the manner in which his work is to be done then the relationship of employer/employee existed and vicarious liability could be imposed upon the employer.[4] Other relevant factors are the methods of paying the employee and whether the tools used in the course of his employment are those of the employer or the employee.

Other tests favoured by the courts in deciding whether a particular person is an employee are the 'organisation' or 'integration' test, the 'mixed factor' test and the 'business on his own' test.

The 'integration' test looks to whether the work of the employee is integral or incidental to the employer's business.[5] To be deemed an employee the work done must be an integral part of the business of the employer. The 'mixed factor' test looks at all the circumstances of the employment including factors such as the keeping of accounts, the ability to delegate and the designation in the service contract.[6]

The 'business on his own' test looks at all the above factors together with the opportunities which the employee has to make profits of his own account.[7] If the person has a reasonable opportunity to control his own level of profit it is likely he will be held to be an independent contractor. Once it has been established that a particular person is an employee the liability of the employer for the torts of that person will depend upon whether the tort was committed in the course of the employment of the employee.[8] A wrongful act is done in the course of employment if:

(a) it is a wrongful act authorised by the employer; or
(b) it is a wrongful and unauthorised mode of doing some act authorised by the employer.

Clearly most liability arises under (b) above. Where the wrongful act of the employee is one which the employer has expressly warned him not to do, this factor will be taken into account.[9]

4 *Moynihan v Moynihan* [1975] IR 192, *Lynch v Palgrave Murphy* [1964] IR 150.
5 *Stevenson, Jordan and Harrison Ltd v Macdonald* [1952] TLR 101.
6 *Ready Mixed Concrete (South East) Ltd v Minister of Pensions* [1968] 2 QB 497.
7 *Market Investigations Ltd v Minister of Social Security* [1969] 2 QB 173.
8 *Poland v Parr (John) & Sons* [1927] 1 KB 236.
9 *Strong v McAuley, McIlroy & Co Ltd* 63 ILTR 39.

Whether a person is an employee is important because in tort there is a general rule that a person is not vicariously liable for the acts of his independent contractors[10] subject to cases where work involving strict liability or work of an inherently dangerous nature is involved.[11] It has been stated[12] that the reason an employer is liable in some cases for the torts of his independent contractor is not because he is liable for the contractor's breach of duty but rather the liability is imposed as the employer himself is liable for a breach of his own duty: the duty to choose a contractor who is reasonably competent to do the proposed work and to give reasonable instructions and reasonably oversee the work of the independent contractor.[13]

The employer is not liable for the collateral negligence of his independent contractor. This is illustrated in *Padbury v Holliday and Greenwood Ltd*[14] where the contractor's tool fell from a window ledge and injured a passer-by. The ultimate employers were held not liable for this collateral negligence on the part of their independent contractor.

5. LIABILITY FOR DEFECTIVE PRODUCTS BROUGHT ABOUT BY BREACH OF STATUTORY REGULATION DESIGNED TO PROTECT CONSUMERS AND/OR TO PROMOTE SAFETY

5.1 Outline of nature of protective Regulations

Certain consumer protection in Ireland is provided by Acts of the Oireachtas containing a framework under which Regulations are issued to control or regulate a range of product types. For example, production and manufacture of drugs and medicines is controlled by regulations which the Minister is enabled to implement under the provisions of the Misuse of Drugs Act 1977, as amended and the Health Acts 1947 to 1970.

The manufacture of products is controlled in Ireland by the Government standards agency, Eolas (formerly the Irish Institute for Industrial Research and Standards – IIRS) through which Regulations have been laid down under the Industrial Research and Standards Act 1961 which governs the standards to be met by such items as electrical appliances and children's night clothes.

The packaging of products is controlled by the Packaged Goods (Quantity Control) Act 1980 which enables the Minister for Industry and Commerce to make Regulations, inter alia, to apply to packages generally or to packages of a particular class or description. Where the Act is expressed to apply to certain packages, it enables inspectors appointed in accordance with the Act to carry out certain tests to ensure that the quantity of goods contained in the containers is as stated.

A final example is the Safety, Health and Welfare at Work Act 1989 which imposes a general duty upon 'any person who designs, manufactures, imports

10 *McMahon and Binchy* p 761, *Salmond and Heuston* p 544.
11 *Boylan v Northern Bank Ltd and James Corcoran Ltd* (21 July 1977, unrep), HC Costello J.
12 *Daniel v Rickett, Cockerell & Co Ltd* [1938] 2 KB 322.
13 *Sumner v William Henderson & Sons Ltd* [1964] 1 QB 450.
14 (1912) 28 TLR 494.

or supplies any article for use at work' to ensure that such is, so far as is reasonably practicable, safe and without risk to health when used by a person at a place of work and a corresponding duty upon persons who design or construct places of work. The Act also imposes upon employers and employees a duty in relation to their health and safety at work and establishes the National Authority for Occupational Safety and Health giving powers of inspection and enforcement.

5.2 Burden of proof

The burden of proof is different for civil and criminal proceedings. Where it is sought to impose criminal liability for the breach of a statutory regulation the burden of proof is the test of 'beyond reasonable doubt'. Where it is sought to impose civil liability for breach of a statutory regulation and obtain damages, the 'balance of probabilities' is the test.

5.3 Nature of liability

The liability imposed under Acts of the Oireachtas and related Regulations is, for the most part, criminal pursuant to the offences and penalties established under the relevant Acts. The question whether civil liability may flow from the breach of a statutory duty is complex and unsettled. The courts appear to ask the following two questions:

(a) Does the Act expressly allow a civil remedy? If the Act does so, the courts will respect this but if the Act does not, then the courts ask the second question which is:
(b) Is the Act for the benefit of the public as a whole or a specific class or section of the public?

Only where the courts hold that the Act was passed to benefit a specific section of the public are they likely to award damages for breach of duty imposed by the Act.[15]

Even where the court holds that damages should be available for a breach of statutory duty the plaintiff still must establish that he is one of the persons within the class of persons that the Act was designed to protect and that he has suffered loss. Further, the court then must decide whether it should award a large or a nominal amount of damages. In determining the level of damages the courts seem open to two views. Under both views the courts look to the nature of the penalty provided by the Act. One view is that if the penalty is low or if there is none at all, damages should also be low.[16] The other view is that where the penalty contained in the Act is low then damages should be high.[17]

15 *Reilly v Moore* [1935] NI 196, *O'Callaghan v Minister for Posts & Telegraphs* 81 ILTR 162.
16 *Representative Church Body v Dublin Board of Assistance* [1948] IR 287.
17 *Hughes v Dundalk Harbour Commrs* [1923] IR 38.

6. SPECIAL LIABILITIES ARISING IN RESPECT OF PARTICULAR PRODUCTS

i. Foodstuffs. The Minister for Agriculture has made a substantial number of Regulations establishing standards which certain foodstuffs must meet. Many of these Regulations are based upon EC requirements.[18] Legislation also governs the hygiene standards to be met by premises preparing certain classes of foodstuffs.[19]

ii. Radioactive products. Radioactive products are dealt with by the Nuclear Energy (An Bord Fuinnimh Nuicleigh) Act 1971 and the Nuclear Energy (General Control of Fissile Fuels, Radio-active Substances and Irradiating Apparatus) Order 1977. The 1971 Act establishes a Board whose general functions are to advise the Minister, prepare safety codes and Regulations and promote knowledge, proficiency and research. Under the 1971 Act[20] the Minister may from time to time by Order assign to the Board certain functions relating to the control, custody, use and manufacture of fissile fuel or such other radioactive substances or devices as may be specified in the Order. The Minister is also given the power under the 1971 Act[1] to regulate, restrict or prohibit the custody, use and manufacture of such radioactive fuels as may be specified in the Order.

iii. Drugs and medicines. The manufacture of and dealing in controlled drugs is regulated by Acts of the Oireachtas including the Health Acts 1947 to 1970, the Misuse of Drugs Acts 1977 and 1984, the Poisons Act 1961 and the Pharmacy Acts 1875 to 1962. The Misuse of Drugs Acts of 1977 and 1984 contain Schedules of what are described as 'controlled drugs' and give the Minister for Health the power to make Regulations prohibiting the manufacture of such drugs. The Poisons Act 1961 allows the Minister to make analogous Regulations with regard to such matters as the manufacture of poisons. Liability imposed by the legislation is primarily criminal.

7. LIABILITY FOR DEFECTIVE PRODUCTS ARISING FROM PROPOSED NATIONAL LAW IN IRELAND: IMPLEMENTATION OF THE DIRECTIVE

7.1 Introduction

As of 1 January 1991, Ireland has not yet implemented the Directive. However, the Department of Industry and Commerce issued an explanatory and

18 Examples of such Regulations are the European Communities (Fruit and Vegetable) Regulations 1973, the Food Standards (Potatoes) Regulations 1977, the Food Standards (Potatoes) (European Communities) Regulations 1978.

19 Examples of such legislation are the Dairy Produce Acts 1924 to 1941 which require the registration of certain premises to be used in the dairy industry and the Slaughter of Cattle and Sheep Act 1934 which requires the registration of premises used for the slaughtering of cattle and sheep with a view to human consumption.

20 S 5(2)(f).

1 S 6.

discussion document on the Directive outlining the possible provisions which Ireland may enact to implement the Directive. The Department has announced that a draft Bill to implement the Directive is nearing completion and is expected to be published shortly.

7.2 Outline of provisions in Ireland

As the legislation giving effect to the Directive has not yet been implemented the reader is referred to the chapter in which the Directive is discussed in this book.[2]

7.3 Descriptions of special or anomalous provisions in respect of product liability law in Ireland

7.3.1 Agricultural produce

Agricultural produce and the statutory regulation thereof has been referred to above.[3]

7.3.2 Computer software

There is no legislation specifically designed to regulate the manufacture and production of computer software. However the Department of Industry and Commerce is preparing such legislation but this has been delayed by developments at EC level proposing to extend copright to computer software.

7.3.3 Buildings and liabilities of builders

Builders' liability may arise under contract, tort or statute. Under contract law the basic principle is 'caveat emptor'. Unless the contract provides certain warranties on the part of the builder, the purchaser is assumed to have inspected the premises and purchased it 'warts and all'.[4] However, where the vendor sells a house which is not fully constructed, the courts are prepared to imply certain terms in relation to such matters as the completion of the house, materials used and the quality of workmanship.[5]

Builders are subject to the same duties as others by virtue of the 'neighbour principle' enunciated in *Donoghue v Stevenson*.[6] The one class of builder not as exposed to the rigours of the law of negligence is the person who both builds and sells the premises[7] but even his immunity for his negligent building is being eroded.[8]

The Safety, Health and Welfare at Work Act 1989 imposes a general duty on any person who designs places of work to design them so that they are, so far as

2 See Chapter 1.
3 See p 198.
4 *Otto v Bolton and Norris* [1936] 2 KB 46.
5 *Brown v Norton* [1954] IR 34.
6 *Gallagher v N McDowell Ltd* [1961] NI 26, *Colgan v Connolly Construction Co (Ireland) Ltd* [1980] ILRM 33.
7 *McMahon and Binchy* p 240.
8 *Dutton v Bognor Regis UDC* [1972] 1 QB 373, *Anns v Merton London Borough Council* [1978] AC 728, *Ward v McMaster* [1985] IR 29.

is reasonably practicable, safe and without risk to health and a corresponding duty on persons who construct places of work.

Apart from certain localised building bye-laws, there are no technical regulations governing the construction industry. The Building (Control) Act 1990 has been passed and will allow the Minister for the Environment, once he has made a commencement order, to introduce technical regulations for the construction industry.

7.3.4 Equipment lessors

The main provisions dealing with the letting of goods under hire purchase agreements are contained in Part III of the 1980 Act. Sections 26–29 imply terms dealing with such matters as title, letting by sample, implied conditions as to quality or fitness and implied conditions when there is a letting by description. As in contracts for the sale of goods, the right of the person letting the goods to restrict the hirer's right in relation to the implied conditions is either totally or partially restricted by sections 30 and 31, depending principally upon whether the hirer deals as a consumer. Part III of the 1980 Act also implies the provisions of sections 12–19 of the same Act, relating to guarantees and undertakings, into contracts for the letting of goods under hire purchase agreements in the same way as these sections apply to contracts for the sale of goods.

Section 38 of the 1980 Act[9] provides that where there is a letting of goods and the lessee deals as a consumer, as defined in section 3 of the 1980 Act, the terms implied into hire-purchase contracts under Part III of the 1980 Act, will also be implied into contracts for the letting of goods.

7.4 Optional provisions in the EC Directive

It is likely that the legislation implementing the Directive will include the 'state of the art' defence. This is apparent from the Discussion Document of the Department of Industry and Commerce.[10] The Discussion Document goes on to state that the burden of proof under the state of the art defence would fall on the producer.

From the Discussion Document it would appear that the financial limit of Ecu 70m (approximately IR£53m) will not be imposed in the implementing legislation.[11]

9 'Where goods are let, otherwise than under a hire-purchase agreement, to a person dealing as consumer the provisions of this Part, other than section 26, shall apply to the letting agreement as if it were a hire-purchase agreement and in every such agreement there is an implied warranty that the goods are free, and will remain free, from any charge or encumbrance not disclosed, before the agreement is made, to the person taking the goods and that the person will enjoy quiet possession of the goods except so far as it may be disturbed by any person entitled to the benefit of any charge or encumbrances so disclosed.'

10 'The Minister would consider that there is a case for including this defence, particularly as it is so carefully defined in the Directive.'

11 The Document states that 'the majority view (including Ireland), however, was that the financial limit, which was eventually set at a minimum of 70,000,000 Ecus (IR£53,000,000) was at such a high level that there would be no material difference from an unlimited liability system'.

The Discussion Document states that primary agricultural products and game should be excluded from the implementing legislation.[12] Agriculture is of major importance to the Irish economy and it is likely that agricultural interests would strongly oppose any attempt to include such products.

The definition in article 2 of primary agricultural products may lead to controversy as the term 'excluding products which have undergone initial processing' is undefined in the Directive.

8. PRACTICAL EFFECTS EC PRODUCT LIABILITY LAW WILL HAVE ON VARIOUS BUSINESSES IN THE CHAIN OF SUPPLY OF PRODUCTS

A discussion of the practical effects of the Directive is difficult in the absence of implementing legislation and the comments below are based on the Directive generally.

8.1 Designer

Article 3 defines producers broadly as being persons who have a manufacturing or supply role in the manufacturing process. Article 1 states that 'the producer shall be liable for damage caused by a defect in his product'. A designer may be deemed under article 3 of the Directive to be a producer of a product if he puts his 'name, trademark or other distinguishing feature' on such product.

Where a product is defective but does not cause injury then, as distinct from the position other than under the Directive, the designer would not be liable as the Directive establishes a cause of action for persons injured by a product which is unsafe and consequently defective as defined in article 6.

A designer of a defective product will still be liable in negligence to the purchaser and others injured as a result of the designer failing to fulfil his duty of care to such people. The designer may also be liable for breach of contract to the person who commissioned the design if it proves defective.

8.2 Component and accessory manufacturer

The manufacturer of a component is expressly within the definition of producer in article 3 and consequently under article 1 he will be liable for damage caused by a defect in his products. The manufacturer of an accesory might also fall within this definition.

A component manufacturer could be liable if he supplies components for a product which is held to be defective under article 6 unless he is able to avail of one of the defences under article 7. The defences most likely to be raised would be under:

12 At 21.

(a) article 7(b) which states that the defect did not exist when the product was put into circulation or that the defect came into being afterwards; or
(b) article 7(3) which is the 'state of the art' defence; or
(c) article 7(f) which is the defence that the defect is due to the design of the product in which the component was incorporated or that the defect is due to instructions given by the manufacturer.

To avoid liability under the Directive a component manufacturer should therefore ensure where his component parts are incorporated into another product that they are made strictly in accordance with the manufacturer's instructions.

8.3 Supplier of materials

Article 3 defines producers as including 'the producer of any raw material'. The recital to the Directive refers to protection of the consumer and requires liability to be extended to producers (insofar as their finished product, component part or any raw material supplied by them was defective). Although article 3 refers to a 'producer' of any raw material it might also apply to a 'supplier'. The defences open to a supplier of raw materials would be those set out in article 7.

Article 3(3) is of special relevance. This states that where the producer cannot be identified each supplier shall be treated as the producer unless he informs the injured party of the identity of the producer or party who supplied him. Thus if a supplier of raw material falls within the definition of a producer it would appear that there may be cases where the injured party will be referred to the primary supplier by the other suppliers. However, the 'state of the art' defence might more easily be invoked by the supplier of raw material than by the manufacturer.

Apart from any liability which they may have by virtue of the Directive, suppliers of materials may also have liabilities in contract and tort. The liability in contract will usually be to the manufacturer of the product, but the liability in negligence will in the usual way be potentially much wider and will include (inter alia) the manufacturers, sellers and purchasers of the product, as well as consumers.

8.4 Manufacturer or assembler

A manufacturer falls within the definition of producer in article 3 and would be liable for defective products pursuant to article 1. In certain circumstances an assembler could also fall within article 3. The liability of a manufacturer or assembler depends upon damage caused by the defective product. Whether a product is defective is determined by the 'safety which a person is entitled to expect, taking all circumstances into account'.

The use in article 6 of 'a person' rather than '*the* consumer' may indicate that the test of the safety a person can expect is to be judged by the objective standard of the reasonable man rather than by the subjective standard of the individual consumer. It will be interesting to see if the legislation makes an attempt to address this issue.

The safety which a person is entitled to expect depends on all the circumstances and the Directive states three relevant circumstances:

(a) The presentation of the product. Therefore it is possible that a person's expectation as to safety might be influenced by a form of warning on the packaging.
(b) The use to which it could reasonably be expected that the product would be put. A producer might not be liable for an unreasonable use of his product which results in injury. It may be possible to outline the products' reasonable uses on the packaging.
(c) The time when the product was put into circulation. This would suggest that the safety standards at the time of circulation may also be relevant and is supported by article 6(2) which prevents a product from being defective simply on the grounds that a better product is subsequently put into circulation.

A manufacturer or assembler may avail of the defences in article 7. In addition he may seek contribution and indemnity from another party as allowed by article 5.[13]

Article 8(2) is relevant to those involved in all stages of the manufacturing process. This article provides that the liability of the producer may be reduced or disallowed when, having regard to all the circumstances, the damage is caused both by a defect in the product and by the fault of the injured person or any person for whom the injured person is responsible.

Therefore all producers, and not just manufacturers and assemblers, would be well advised to maintain a detailed record of the dates upon which they put into circulation any products which would fall within the provisions of the Directive.[14]

As with suppliers of materials, the manufacturer and assembler may have liabilities in both contract and tort.

8.5 Importers

The effect of article 3(2)[15] is that an importer of goods into the EC is deemed to be a producer and has the same liabilities, defences and limitation periods. Importers should ensure that the goods which they import are of a reputable nature from a reputable supplier. They should also ensure that they have sufficient insurance to cover any liability under the Directive, and have provisions included in the contracts with their suppliers from outside the EC to entitle them to indemnity for any liability which they may suffer. Producers outside the EC are not covered by the Directive.

13 This leaves the provisions of the 1961 Act as amended, unchanged.

14 Art 11 provides that the liability of a producer for a product is only to survive for ten years from the date upon which the producer put the product into circulation.

15 Art 3(2) provides that 'without prejudice to the liability of the producer, any person who imports into the Community a product for sale, hire, leasing or any form of distribution in the course of his business shall be deemed to be a producer within the meaning of this Directive and shall be responsible as a producer'.

8.6 Distributors, installers, dealers and repairers

Distributors, installers, dealers and repairers are not expressly referred to in the definition of 'producer' contained in article 3 of the Directive. However, they may fall within the Directive where they put their name, trademark or other distinguishing feature on the product such as to present themselves as its producer. In addition, under article 3(3) where the producer cannot be identified these persons might be liable as the producer unless they furnish the claimant with the name of the producer or other person who supplied them.

An installer might fall within the definition of 'producer' in article 3(1) if the installation of the product amounted to an assembly. A repairer might in certain circumstances be equated with a component manufacturer and therefore fall within the definition of 'producer' in article 31(1).

Distributors', installers', dealers' and repairers' principal liability is likely to be in contract to their customers. That is not to say that they will not be liable in negligence for failing to carry out their activities in accordance with their duty. Any such liability which they may owe to their customers may extend potentially to a wide range of persons injured by their activities. Usually, however, such people will not change the product while it is in their care as much as a manufacturer may do, and so their potential to incur liability under the Directive is less.

8.7 Purchaser

Under article 4 the injured person must prove the damage, the defect and the causal relationship between defect and damage. Under article 8 the injured person may find his right to compensation reduced or disallowed if it is held that the damage is caused both by a defect in the product and the fault of the injured person himself or any person for whom the injured person is responsible. Article 9 defines damage as:

(a) damage caused by death or by personal injuries;
(b) damage to, or destruction of, any item of property other than the defective product itself, with a lower threshold of Ecu 500 (approximately IR£390) provided that the item of property:
  (i) is of a type ordinarily intended for private use or consumption; and
  (ii) was used by the injured person mainly for his own private use or consumption.

Under article 10 the plaintiff has three years to commence proceedings from the date on which he became aware or should reasonably have become aware of the damage, the defect and the identity of the producer. Under article 11 the rights of the injured party under the Directive are deemed to have been extinguished after a period of ten years from the date when the defective product was put into circulation.

Under articles 12 and 13 the producer may not exclude his liability under the Directive and the Directive purports to have no effect upon the injured party's remedies in contract or tort. Under article 3(3) the injured party, where the producer of the product cannot be identified, may treat each supplier as its producer unless such supplier informs the injured party, within a reasonable time, of the identity of the producer or the person who supplied him. A similar procedure is afforded to the injured party in the case of imported products where the product does not indicate the identity of the importer even if the name of the manufacturer is indicated.

A purchaser will, of course, have a claim in contract as against his seller for any breach of contract or any warranty if the product fails to comply with the terms, express or implied, of the contract of sale. In addition, the purchaser may have claims in negligence against other parties in the chain of supply if he can show they owed him a duty of care, that they failed in that duty and, as a result, he suffered loss or damage.

8.8 Users at work and other employees

Pursuant to article 9(b)(i) and (ii) the defective product must be of a type ordinarily intended for private use or consumption and must have been used by the injured person mainly for his own private use or consumption. Persons injured at work while using products in the course of their employment may not usually be able to claim in product liability. However, they may be able to do so if the product from which they sustained their injuries, while at work, was one which was intended for private use or consumption and was used by the injured person mainly for his own private use or consumption. Users at work and other employees' claims in addition to those brought under the Directive are likely to be based on negligence if the elements of such tort can be proved.

8.9 The general public

Members of the general public who suffer injury due to a defective product would have the same rights as are discussed above. The Directive refers to a person as opposed to the consumer.[16]

8.10 Particular problems in specific businesses or industries

The impact of the Directive and the implementing legislation will be greatest upon those industries producing goods which are capable of causing a great degree of either personal damage or damage to property. A simple example to illustrate this would be the effects of the Directive upon the manufacturer of a motor vehicle contrasted with the manufacturer of a picture frame. A defect in a motor vehicle could cause substantial damage to both persons and property and render the 'producer' liable to pay substantial sums in compensation under the terms of the Directive, whereas a defect in a picture frame may be unsightly but does not have the same potential to cause damage. The Directive is concerned with compensation for damage due to a defective product and, if there is no damage or injury caused, there is no liability. Liability may of course arise outside the Directive. The Directive will have most impact on those

16 See p 202.

producing goods containing a great potential to cause damage and those producing complex goods where in tort or contract the plaintiff might have great difficulty in establishing liability.

9. COMPARISON OF THE EFFECTS OF PRODUCT LIABILITY LAW WITH THE PREVIOUS POSITION IN CONTRACT AND TORT

As stated above, there is no implementing legislation and the following section outlines the possible differences between product liability law before the introduction of the Directive and product liability law it is likely to be thereafter.

The terms implied into contracts by the 1980 Act are concerned with the merchantability or fitness for purpose of the particular product and if the product does not live up to the standards which the 1980 Act imposes, certain remedies are available to the consumer. However, under the Directive, merchantability or fitness for purpose is not the criterion upon which liability is based. This is evident from article 1 of the Directive which states 'the producer shall be liable for *damage* caused by a defect in his product'.

Privity of contract is not relevant under the Directive. This is clear from the Directive's use of the words 'injured person'. The remedies available under the Directive are available not just to the purchaser but to any person who suffers injury as a result of a defect in the product.

The injured person no longer has to prove that the producer who caused the injury owes a duty of care to him. In tort the establishment of this duty frequently gives rise to difficulty. Article 4 provides that the injured person must prove the damage, the defect and the causal relationship between defect and damage. The injured party no longer has to prove that the producer of the defective product owed him a duty of care as article 1 states 'The producer shall be liable for damage caused by a defect in his product.'

Other areas of the Directive may compare or contrast with the existing position in tort. An example would be whether the implementing legislation or the courts will construe 'the safety which a person is entitled to expect' as involving the existence of an objective or a subjective test.[17]

Under articles 5 and 8 respectively the law in relation to joint and several liability and the right to seek contribution and indemnity is unaffected. The law on joint and several liability is contained in Part III of the 1961 Act, which defines concurrent wrongdoers as 'when both or all are wrongdoers and are responsible to a third person (in this Part called the injured person or the plaintiff) for the same damage, whether or not judgment has been recovered against some or all of them'.[18] A party may become a concurrent wrongdoer as a result of vicarious liability, breach of joint duty, conspiracy, concerted action to a common end or independent acts causing the same damage.[19] The wrong

17 See p 202.
18 S 11(1).
19 S 11(2) of the 1961 Act.

on the part of one or both may be a tort, breach of contract or breach of trust, or any combination, and it is immaterial whether the acts constituting concurrent wrongs are contemporaneous or successive.[20]

9.1 Contributory negligence

The law on contributory negligence is contained in the 1961 Act (1) Chapter III of Part III. Damages which would otherwise be awarded to a plaintiff in negligence are reduced in proportion to the amount of his contributory negligence or that of any person for whom he is responsible.

Under the Directive it would seem that an injured person would be deemed to have been contributorily negligent if he used the product in an unreasonable way and the reduction of the producer's liability would depend on the extent to which the use was unreasonable.

The defence of voluntary assumption of risk (*volenti non fit injuria*) in tort and the provisions of the 1961 Act[1] may provide a defence to the defendant where:

(a) the defendant can show that under contract he is not liable; and
(b) the plaintiff, before the act complained of, agreed to waive his legal rights in respect of it.

Article 12 of the Directive states 'that the liability of the producer arising from this Directive may not, in relation to the injured person, be limited or excluded by a provision limiting his liability or exempting him from liability'. Accordingly, it would appear that the first defence above may not be available to a producer under the forthcoming legislation.[2]

For a producer to avail himself of the defence afforded by section 34(1)(b) of the 1961 Act there would have to be some sort of communication between the parties.[3] A unilateral determination on the part of the plaintiff to give up his legal rights would not be sufficient to make the defence in section 34(1)(b) available to the defendant and might merely amount to contributory negligence under the terms of the 1961 Act.

9.2 Risk management in the new era of product liability internal risk management

9.2.1 *Quality control*

It is conceivable that the implementing legislation may have no major impact on the existing position relation to quality control if the 'state of the art' defence is based on a test of reasonableness. If a producer defends a claim in which it is alleged that his product was defective and caused injury by relying on the 'state of the art' defence, a claim may be defended by establishing that his quality control process was reasonable in all the circumstances. Where then would be

20 See *McMahon and Binchy* Ch 4.
1 1961 Act, s 34(1)(b).
2 Ibid.
3 *O'Hanlon v ESB* [1969] IR 75.

the difference between this 'new era' and the position in tort? In a recent case[4] a taxi driver who was eating in Portlaoise Prison canteen suffered injury when he ate a screw contained in his chips. He sued the manufacturer of the chips for damages for personal injury. His claim was disallowed on the basis that the manufacturer of the chips had taken all reasonable steps to ensure that the chips would be defect free. We await the legislation and subsequent judicial interpretation to determine if this case would be decided differently.

There is a form of voluntary regulation issued in the form of an international standard which has been adopted by the Irish Standards Authority, namely ISO 9000. This is a quality mark which applies to many types of manufactured goods. To obtain approval, the applicant submits a quality manual and other information. The Irish Standards Authority will amend or approve the quality manual and thereafter will inspect the production process.

9.2.2 Documentation

It will be vital that each party in the manufacturing and supply chain keeps full records of its suppliers, and the dates on which the various products were supplied, the various components were incorporated into products and various products were 'put into circulation'. In the absence of such records a defendant might lose the opportunity, inter alia, to avail of the ten-year limitation period in article 11.

9.2.3 Record-keeping

Under article 3(3), where the producer cannot be ascertained, each supplier will be deemed to have been its producer unless he informs the injured person within a reasonable time of either the name of the producer or the person who supplied him with the product. It is unclear what is a 'reasonable time'. The consequences of failing to keep records of suppliers or producers of goods supplied could be far-reaching.

Record-keeping will become increasingly important in the area of quality control where, in order to establish a defence under article 7, it will be necessary for producers to prove that the defect did not exist at the time the product was put into circulation or that the defect is due to compliance of the product with mandatory regulations issued by public authorities or that the product complied with the 'state of the art' technology.

9.2.4 Warning notices/operating instructions/service manuals

Article 6 indicates some of the circumstances to be taken into account when determining whether a product is defective.[5] The presentation of the product and the use to which it could reasonably be expected that the product would be put have direct relevance to the type of warning notices or operating instructions which should be displayed. It would seem that the notices on a product may limit the safety which a person is entitled to expect and may have a direct

4 Irish Times, 31 March 1990.

5 The presentation of the product; the use to which it could reasonably be expected that the product would be put; the time when the product was put into circulation.

relevance as to whether a product is considered defective. In the new era when a manufacturer is considering the presentation of his product he should pay particular attention to appropriate warnings the product may require, having regard to the purpose and reasonable uses of the product. The operating instructions should state as specifically as possible the uses to which the products may or may not be put.

9.3 The handling of consumer claims

9.3.1 Inspection of defective products and analysis of causes of failure

Article 1 states 'the producer shall be liable for damage caused by a defect in his product'. When a person claims under the Directive for alleged loss due to a defective product, a number of issues arise. Damage must be proved. It must be established that the defendant is a 'producer'. It may be necessary to carry out an inspection of the defective product to ascertain the reason for the defect and the party responsible. Such inspection is clearly necessary because under article 3 a party may be 'a producer' by merely putting its name on the product. If a party has had no role at all in the manufacturing process that party may endeavour to seek indemnity from another party.

9.3.2 Consequences for future, need to re-design products, cease selling products and recall of products for safety checks or replacement of defective parts

Article 6(2) states 'A product shall not be considered defective for the sole reason that a better product is subsequently put into circulation.' It would appear therefore that where a manufacturer produces an updated version of a product this will not render defective earlier versions.

Although the 'state of the art' defence under the Directive may not oblige a producer to recall a product after it had become aware of its dangerous deficiencies, a manufacturer might incur liability at common law for failure to take appropriate action.

9.3.3 Correspondence with consumers

The terms of the contract of insurance will influence the nature and content of correspondence with consumers. Certain insurers will give more autonomy than others to their insured to deal with consumer claims. In many cases it will be commercially advantageous for the producer to adopt a co-operative and sympathetic approach to consumer claims. Such producers might well be advised to have an indemnity from their suppliers. The manner in which consumer complaints are handled may assist their earlier conclusion.

9.3.4 Preservation of evidence

The preservation of evidence is important to ensure that all claims are fairly and properly dealt with, and to establish whether the consumer claim is commenced within the limitation period.

9.3.5 Problems of legal proceedings

It is likely that following the implementing legislation there will be an increase in claims. This may result in increased insurance costs, more stringent risk improvement methods and greater record-keeping requirements. Apart from the inherent risks in litigation it will take some time for the courts to consider and interpret certain phrases and words used in the Directive, for example, 'put into circulation' and the 'safety which a person is entitled to expect'. In addition there will be evidential problems associated with establishing the 'state of the art' defence. While the injured party does not have to prove negligence on the part of the producer, the producer has to produce sufficient evidence to establish one of the defences set out in article 7 of the Directive.

9.4 Exclusion of liability in claims on contracts for indemnities

By virtue of article 12[6] if you are a producer of goods effect will not be given to any provision contained in any contract which seeks to exclude or limit the terms of the Directive. However, whereas a producer may not exclude liability under the terms of the Directive it may be possible for him to offset any liability pursuant to the Directive by obtaining adequate indemnities from the manufacturer or the supplier.

A retailer, by virtue of article 3(3) may be deemed to be 'the producer' and accordingly should obtain an indemnity from the supplier against any damages resulting from a defect in the product. The retailer of a product carrying his trade mark by virtue of article 3(1) will be deemed to be 'the producer' and accordingly should obtain an indemnity from the 'actual producer' in respect of any liability arising under the Directive. A retailer who sells products manufactured by another but under the retailers' trade mark carries the risk of being deemed to be the producer.

9.5 Insurance

9.5.1 Special provisions

The Irish Insurance Federation (IIF) have issued a document entitled *Insurance Implications of the Product Liability Directive*.[7] Its major criticisms of the Directive are that, firstly, the Directive leaves the Member States with too many options, for example, to impose a financial limit for serial defects and allow or exclude the 'state of the art' defence and, secondly, that at the date of the document only three Member States had implemented the Directive and of these two were going to be proceeded against by the Commission for incorrect implementation. Since the publication of the document, most EC Member States have taken steps to implement the Directive. Of course, there is also the

6 Art 12: 'The liability of the producer arising from this Directive may not, in relation to the injured person, be limited or excluded by a provision limiting his liability or exempting him from liability.'
7 6 March 1989.

possibility that the Directive may have direct effect even before it has been legislatively implemented and insurance cover therefore may have to be maintained.

9.5.2 *Outline of the nature of cover*

The IIF[8] have stated that producers must bear three things in mind when selecting their cover. These are:

(a) that the Directive supplements but does not replace the existing liabilities in tort and contract;
(b) that no insurance policy offers unlimited indemnity against product liability;
(c) that normally the limits of the indemnity are the aggregate for the period of insurance.

9.5.3 *Limits on cover including limitation of liability paid under contractual indemnities*

Mr Michael Kemp in his address to the Irish Centre for European Law (ICEL)[9] has reminded 'producers' of the fact that 'No insurance policy offers unlimited indemnity against liability for defective products'[10] and thus it is going to be important for 'producers' to offset a portion at least of their liability under the Directive by means of effective indemnities. 'Producers' are also told that the 'new era' of product liability should not have any great effect upon the quantum of damages but will increase the number of admissible claims.

9.5.4 *Serial damages*

Although the IIF document does not specifically refer to serial damage it is worthy of note that in its submissions to the Fifth Joint Committee on the Secondary Legislation of the European Communities (Report No 1, The Implementation of the Directive on Product Liability, 18 November 1987) the IIF expressed the view that they were not 'in favour of a financial limit'.[11] Some of the reasons they gave were:

(a) fear that financial limits could become targets for claimants; and
(b) unlimited liability for defective producs will not materially affect the availability of product liability insurance at the levels currently obtained by producers under the present system of unlimited liability.

9.5.5 *Cover for recall or defective products*

The IIF document does not specifically refer to insurance cover for the recall of defective products but it does list the factors which will be of importance in deciding on insurance cover and the rate of premium.

8 Document 6.3.1989, p 2. *Insurance Implications of the Product Liability Directive*, ICEL Conference March 1989, pp 36–37.
9 At p 32.
10 At p 37.
11 At p 12.

These factors are:

(a) the nature of the product;
(b) the distribution system and shelf life of the product;
(c) the position and status of the policyholder in the supply chain;
(d) the policyholder's quality control/quality assurance procedures; and
(e) export markets.

It would seem that all these factors would also be relevant in deciding upon cover for defective products recall. A further factor which would be relevant would be the number of products in the market place at any one time and the likely user life of the product.

The IIF favour prevention to cure and see quality control as having an even more integral role under the new era. It would appear that as a condition to obtaining insurance an insured will have to allow his quality control procedure to be inspected by the insurers' loss control/risk improvement staff and operated in accordance with their recommendations.

9.6 Limitation of liability through corporate structure

9.6.1 Effect on whether a business should incorporate

The rules governing companies incorporated in Ireland are contained primarily in the Companies Acts 1963 to 1990 and the Regulations made thereunder. One of the main advantages of incorporation with limited liability is that the liability of the members is limited. As it appears that the implementing legislation will not have an upper financial limit for claims, the concept of limited liability could, in some cases, be of great importance.

9.6.2 Liabilities of companies in groups

One of the basic principles of company law is that a company is a distinct legal entity. In general a liability attaching to one company will not affect other companies within a group. However, in addition to certain statutuory inroads on this principle,[12] the courts have been prepared in certain circumstances to 'lift the veil of incorporation' in limited circumstances, including the case of fraud. The ownership and control of the structure is an important factor in determining whether the court will lift the corporate veil.

9.6.3 Splitting of high risk activities from valuable assets

i. Use of shell companies to import products from outside the EC for resale within. One reason for importing goods into the EC by a shell company is to avoid the claims for injured parties who, having claimed successfully, would

12 For example, s 140 of the Companies Act 1990 will allow the court, in certain circumstances, to order that a related company (s 140(5)) pay the whole or part of all or any of the debts provable in the winding-up of another related company. S 141 of the Companies Act 1990 will allow the court, in certain circumstances, to provide that where two or more related companies are being would up they shall be wound up as if they were one company.

find that the defendant company has no assets against which to execute. While by virtue of article 3(2) an importer of goods for sale in the course of his business is deemed to be responsible as their producer, this is expressly without prejudice to the liability of the producer. An injured party who fails to execute successfully agaisnt any importer may still be entitled to proceed against another party deemed to be a producer. An importer who chooses to import into the EC through a shell company might if he is involved in the distribution process through another entity come within the definition of 'producer' and may incur liability. Article 3(3) states that where the producer of a product cannot be identified each supplier shall be treated as its producer *unless* he informs the injured person of the identity of the producer or the person who supplied him. Accordingly, if such producer or supplier is a shell company liability may be effectively avoided.

ii. Splitting of manufacturing from the company's asset base through use of a well-endowed parent company: leasing or hiring factors of production to tightly run manufacturing company. The splitting of the manufacturing activity and assets of a group into two separate companies will not necessarily avoid liability. It would appear from recent decisions that the courts, in certain circumstances, are prepared to disregard the separate legal entity principle and hold that the businesses of two or more companies are so intertwined that in fact they are one and the same.[13]

9.7 Other practical steps to take in risk management

Obviously the best possible step in risk management is effective quality control. Perhaps what is necessary is a level of quality control sufficient to enable the 'producer' to raise the defence provided for under article 7(b):

> that, having regard to the circumstances, it is probable that the defect which caused the damage did not exist at the time when the product was put into circulation by him or that this defect came into being afterwards.

A further aid to risk management is perhaps found in article 6(a) which relates to the presentation of the product. As we have seen, the product is defective when it does not provide the degree of safety which a person is entitled to expect and one of the criteria for determining what a person is entitled to expect is the presentation of a product. Accordingly more time and attention should be spent in examining the possible uses of particular products and recording such uses in the products' presentation.

13 *Power Supermarkets Ltd v Crumlin Investments Ltd* (1981, unrep), HC, it was stated that it is 'well established . . . that a court may, if the justice of the case so requires, treat two or more related companies as a single entity so that the business notionally carried on by one will be regarded as the business of the group, or another member of the group, if this conforms to the economic and commercial realities of the situation'.

ADDENDUM

Outline of the principal features of the Liability for Defective Products Bill* 1991

On 24 April 1991 the Minister for Industry and Commerce produced a Bill which the Irish government proposes to use as the basis for the legislation which will implement the Directive. This Bill has to be considered before both houses of the Irish Parliament before it becomes law and therefore the Bill in its present form is not necessarily the Bill which will finally become domestic Irish law. The Department of Industry and Commerce are hopeful that the Bill as published will have a quick passage through both houses of the Irish Parliament and become law at the earliest possible date.

Some of the more interesting aspects of the Bill are considered below.

(1) Section 1 of the Bill defines, inter alia, 'damage'. Damage is defined as. inter alia, death or personal injury. Article 9 of the Directive defines damage as including 'damage *caused by* death or personal injuries'. It seems that to define damage as, inter alia, 'death or personal injury' is to place a more restrictive definition on the concept than appears to be envisaged under the Directive.

(2) The Bill does not include primary agricultural products within the definition of 'product' except where the primary agricultural products have undergone initial processing. As we have previously seen the concept of 'initial processing' was not defined by the Directive. The Bill, again in section 1, defines this concept in relation to primary agricultural products as 'any processing of an industrial nature of those products which could cause to show the presence of two factors before it would be held that any primary agricultural products had undergone initial processing. These factors are:
   (a) that the processing was of an industrial nature (the concept of industrial nature is not defined in the Bill); and
   (b) that the process could cause a defect in the product.

(3) Section 1 of the Bill defines 'injured person' as a person who has suffered damage caused wholly or partly by a defect in a product, or his personal representative or dependants in certain circumstances. This was another term undefined in the Directive.

(4) It would appear that primary agricultural products are defined slightly more widely in the Bill than they were in the Directive. In this regard the Bill, unlike the Directive, includes game as a primary agricultural products unless it has undergone 'initial processing'.

(5) Electricity is included in article 2 of the Directive as a 'product'. Section 1 of the Bill includes electricity as a product where damage is 'caused as a result of a failure in the process of generation of electricity'. This would appear more restrictive than the Directive.

(6) Article 3(3) of the Directive sets out the circumstances in which a supplier of goods may be deemed to be the producer thereof. As we have seen this may occur, inter alia, where the producer of a product cannot be identified, in which case each supplier of the product may be treated

as its producer unless he informs the injured person, within a reasonable time, of the identity of the producer or his supplier. Section 2(3) of the Bill is slightly more limited in its effect since it places the burden on the injured person to request the supplier to furnish him with the name of his supplier within a reasonable time after the damage occurs and at a time when it is not reasonably practical for the injured person to identify all those persons. The Directive does not require the injured person to make the request within a 'reasonable time' but perhaps such a requirement is necessary in the interests of fairness and commercial certainty.

(7) Section 3 of the Bill stipulates that, where damage to property does not exceeed IR£350, a claim in respect of such damage shall not be awarded. For damage to property greater than IR£350, only the amount in excess of IR£350 shall be awarded. As anticipated in the chapter the Bill as published does not contain an upper financial limit on liability.

(8) Article 7 of the Directive sets out certain defences which may be available to the producer under the Directive. These defences are implemented in section 6 of the Bill. According to article 7(d) there is a defence where the defect in the product is due to compliance of the product with mandatory regulations issued by public authorities which are not defined. Section 6 does not make reference to public authorities but states that it is a defence if the product is defective due to compliance of the product 'with any requirement imposed by or under any enactment or any requirement of the law of the European Communities'.

(9) The Bill includes the state of the art defence.

*As the Liability of Defective Products Act 1991 this Bill was signed by the President of the Republic of Ireland on 4 December 1991, giving it the force of law. On 9 December 1991 the Minister for Industry and Commerce made an Order under section 14(2) of the Act (Liability for Defective Products Act 1991 (Commencement) Order 1991) designating 16 December 1991 as the date upon which the Act would come into effect.

CHAPTER VIII

Italy

Gabriele Dara

Studio Consulerte Associati AD & M
Via Noto 12
90141 Palermo
Italy

Tel ++ 39 91 625 2628
Fax ++ 39 91 349600

CHAPTER VIII

Italy

1. INTRODUCTION

1.1 Introduction to the Italian legal system

Like virtually all civil law systems, the Italian legal system is chiefly based on a code which should, at least in theory, provide a comprehensive system of laws. The Civil Code ('the Code') presently in force was enacted in 1942 and was intended to regulate family, succession, property, contract, company, labour and tort law. Bankruptcy law is regulated by statutes enacted in 1942 and, for large companies, by statutes dating from the late 1970s. The structure of the Code has, however, been substantially altered by a number of statutes that have either amended it or, whilst not substituting the basic definitions contained in the Code, have introduced sweeping changes in the discipline of the area of law concerned. This is particularly true of family law,[1] of landlord and tenant law, which is now almost entirely regulated outside the Code,[2] of company law, where the code has been amended to implement some, but not all, of the EC Directives on the matter, and of labour law.

The judicial system is based on a five-tier structure of courts of which the lower three are alternatives, depending on various circumstances, of which more will be said below. The lowest court – *Conciliatore* – has jurisdiction over claims where the amount does not exceed the sum of L 750,000.[3] The *Pretura* exercises appellate review of the judgments rendered by the *Conciliatore*. It also has jurisdiction over claims where the amount involved does not exceed the sum of L 5m[4] and exclusive jurisdiction on certain other matters, amongst which the most relevant in the power to grant interlocutory injunctions, irrespective of the amount claimed or involved. The next higher ranking court – *Tribunale* – exercises appellate review on the *Pretura's* decisions and acts as court of first instance in all other cases. The *Tribunale's* judgments can be appealed to the *Corte d'Appello*. It is possible to appeal to the *Corte di Cassazione* against the decisions of the *Corte d'Appello*, the *Tribunale*, or the *Pretura* (if the last two are sitting as appellate courts) but only on questions of law.

As said before, the jurisdiction of the courts of first instance is determined by the cause of action and the amounts claimed. However, given that the judicial system is not centralised – that is to say there are a few hundred *Pretura* and

1 The 1970 Divorce Law and the 1975 Family Law Reform Law have radically altered Italian succession rules.
2 See Law 392/78 and Law 115/85.
3 Approximately £350.
4 Approximately £2,300.

Conciliatore and over 100 *Tribunale* – the venue is decided on a number of criteria which depend largely on the cause of action and take into account, eg, the place of conclusion or of performance of the contract, the domicile of the debtor or defendant etc – all of which are regulated by the Code of Civil Procedure.

The Brussels Convention of 27 September 1968 on Jurisdiction and the Enforcement of Judgments in Civil and Commercial Matters was given effect in Italy by Law 804 of 21 June 1971.

Disputes can also be solved by way of arbitration provided always that the arbitration clause is valid under Italian law (see articles 800–831 of the Code of Civil Procedure) and that the arbitrators' decision is validated on matters of form by the *Pretura* of the place where enforcement is sought.

It also has to be borne in mind that, subject to the limitations mentioned above in relation to appeals to the *Corte di Cassazione*,[5] there is an absolute right to appeal – that is, once certain formal requirements have been satisfied, there is no need to obtain leave to appeal.

The system briefly outlined above refers to the resolution of civil disputes. Criminal matters and tax matters are adjudicated under a slightly different system. The decision of any other administrative body can be challenged, although not on its merits unless the decision is patently unreasonable, before the *Tribunale Amministrativo Regionale* and, on appeal, before the *Consiglio di Stato*, the decision of which is final.

During the course of the proceedings before any of the aforementioned courts, if the constitutional validity of any provision invoked is challenged and if the judge thinks it appropriate, the matter can be brought before the *Corte Costituzionale* whose decision upon the constitutional validity of the challenged provision is final.

If the *Corte Costituzionale* finds that any provision be unconstitutional in its spirit or its effect, such provision is declared void with immediate effect. Whatever the decision of the *Corte Costituzionale*, the case is then remanded to the appropriate court.

1.2 Overview of the law relating to defective products in Italy

The liability for defective products in Italy is now regulated by Decree 224 of 24 May 1988 ('the Decree') which implemented the Directive. However, it is appropriate, before entering into a detailed examination of the Decree, to recall the general principles of Italian law on contractual and tortious liability for defective products. This is in view of the fact that the Decree does not exclude or limit any other cause of action, be it in tort or in contract, that the damaged party may have according to the law in force. Also, the Decree expressly refers to some provisions of the Code in connection with the determination of the quantum of damages. Furthermore, certain other provisions of the Decree, such as those regulating causation and remoteness of damage, should be construed in the light of the existing law.

5 Always with the possibility of appealing to the *Corte di Cassazione*.

1.3 Definition and classification of terms

The Decree uses terminology which is similar to that used in the Directive and the same as that used by Italian courts in implementing existing law. The more widely used terms are:

(a) Parties:
   (i) 'Producer'. The term is used in preference to manufacturer and includes the manufacturer of the whole product or of a part and the producer of a commodity incorporated therein;
   (ii) 'Supplier'. The term is used in the Decree and is intended to refer to wholesalers, retailers and the importer(s) of the product in the EC. The Decree further specifies that the definition includes lessors or any other person that imports the product for hire or any other form of distribution. The Decree also holds responsible for the damage caused by a defective product all those persons that put their name or trademark or other distinguishing feature on the product or on its packaging (Decree article 3(3)(4));
   (iii) 'Injured party'. The party that suffers injury or loss caused by the defective product and can claim compensation. Such party is generally referred to as 'the consumer' or 'the user'. As the Decree establishes a liability in tort, the injured party need not be the purchaser of the product but could also be a third party.

(b) 'Object'. A product is defined as any movable even if incorporated in a building. The definition expressly includes electricity. Agricultural and fish products are excluded provided always that they have not undergone any 'transformation'.
   'Transformation' is defined as 'a treatment that modifies the characteristics [of the product] or adds any substance'. Packaging and any other treatment of agricultural or fish products that make controls by the consumer difficult, or give rise to reliance as to the product's safety, are considered to be 'transformation' (Decree article 2(3)).

(c) 'Damage' means:
   (i) damages resulting from death or personal injury;
   (ii) damages to things but not to the product provided that such things were normally used by the injured party;
   (iii) consequential damages according to remedies available under general tort law.
   Compensation for pain and suffering is recoverable under strictly limited circumstances (see below).

(d) 'Defective product'. The Decree uses the term as opposed to 'defect'.

(e) 'Contributory negligence'. The negligence of the consumer or of the third party which contributes in whole or in part – eg failure to follow instructions or misuse of the product – to the damage. It may exclude liability or reduce it proportionally.

2. LIABILITY IN CONTRACT

Under the general principles of Italian contract law, a contract is legally binding if it is entered into by parties of sufficient legal capacity and has as its object the exchange of any item of economic value between the parties or otherwise the regulation of any other matter of economic value.

The Code regulates a number of contracts (eg of sale, loan, barter etc) but parties are free to enter into other kinds of contracts provided always that their structure and objectives do not conflict with the general principles of law or public policy.

2.1 Liability for pre-contractual statements

The Code does not expressly provide for liability for pre-contractual statements short of actual fraud. However, article 1337 of the Code, which imposes a general duty of good faith during the pre-contractual period, has been construed as imposing a duty on each party not to cause unreasonable or detrimental reliance by the other party on the fact of conclusion of the contract. Damages are limited to expenses suffered in reliance by one party on the other and losses consequential to foregone opportunities. There are no precedents of court decisions concerning defective products and article 1337 of the Code.

2.2 Outline of contract law relevant to defective products in Italy

The bases of the liability of the seller for defects of the product sold are set out in articles 1490–1495 of the Code. Article 1490 gives rise to a statutory warranty that the product is 'free from any defect that may make it unfit for normal use or cause a material decrease in its value' (Code article 1490). Such warranty can, however, be excluded by agreement but any such agreement would be invalid if the seller has, in bad faith, hidden the existence of defects (Code article 1490(2)). The warranty is also excluded if at the time of the contract the buyer knew of the defects or if the defects were clearly noticeable, unless in the latter case the seller had expressly stated that the product did not have any defects (Code article 1491).

2.3 Contractual warranties relating to the quality of goods and safety of goods

Apart from the statutory warranty outlined above, the seller, particularly in the case of machinery, may choose to insert a contractual warranty that the product will perform its function. The time limit of such warranty is determined by the parties (Code article 1512).

2.4 Breach of contract for supply of defective products

In the case of supply of a defective product, where the statutory warranty has not been properly excluded, the buyer has the choice between:

(a) the termination of the contract and reimbursement of the price;
(b) a reduction of the price paid proportional to the extent of the defect (Code article 1492).

The defects that give rise to such actions are those that make the product completely impossible to use for its normal purpose or otherwise unfit for use – although it could theoretically be possible to use it.

In the case of breach of a contractual warranty (of the type outlined above in section 2.2 of this chapter) the warranty usually contains an undertaking from the seller to repair or substitute the defective product in whole or in part. In the absence of such an undertaking, the buyer would be entitled to any of the other remedies described above.

2.5 Quantum of damages

In both the cases outlined above (breach of statutory or contractual warranty) the buyer can obtain redress for damages suffered. In both cases the quantum of damage is determined on the basis of the general rule concerning contract damage: the award should put the aggrieved party in the position where it would have been had the contract been properly performed.[6] Accordingly, the seller will be liable for the actual losses suffered by the buyer and any consequential loss of profit so long as they are the 'immediate and direct consequence' of the breach (Code article 1223). The concept of 'immediate and direct consequence' has been construed to include all those losses that are 'normal consequences of the breach'[7] but does not include unforeseeable damages unless the breach was a result of a wilful or grossly negligent act of the seller (Code article 1225). It is worth noting that the definition has been applied in a flexible way so as to include, eg the damage caused to the commercial reputation of a buyer who had unknowingly resold defective products.[8] Contrary to the case where a fixed sum of money is due, the sum awarded, which will refer to the value of the currency at the time of the breach, can be revalued to take into account inflation. The sum awarded can also be reduced in proportion to the contributory negligence of the buyer (Code article 1227(1)).

The redress of non-financial damages is regulated by article 2059 of the Code.[9] It is widely held that redress for non-financial damages cannot be obtained in the context of an action in contract. However, as courts have allowed the possibility of pursuing redress for damages suffered by means of concurrent actions both in tort and in contract, it is always possible to recover damages for non-financial losses. Finally, it should be noted that the buyer has

6 See *Corte di Cassazione* ('Cass') 15 April 1980, no 2458 in Massimario Giurisprudenza Italiana, 1980.
7 See Cass 19 July 1982, no 4263 in Giurisprudenza Italiana, 1983 1,1,424.
8 Cass 1512/1969.
9 Of which further in section 3.3, below.

a duty to mitigate the consequences of the breach, but such duty does not extend to include the duty to make good the loss (Code article 1227(2)).

2.6 Burden of proof

In the case of an action in contract, the purchaser of defective products must prove:

(a) the existence of a contract;
(b) the defect; and
(c) the monetary value of any damage suffered.

The seller can avoid liability if he proves that:

(a) (i) the breach depends on a fact for which he cannot be held liable. The fact must be such that the correct performance of the contract is made impossible and not merely more difficult or expensive;
(ii) the buyer knew of the defect at the time of sale; and
(iii) the damage was entirely caused by the contributory negligence of the buyer – that is, the loss would not have occurred but for the act or omission of the buyer; or
(b) there was a valid clause of exclusion or limitation of liability in the contract between the parties.

2.7 Exclusion or limitation of liability

As stated in section 2.2 of this chapter, the seller can insert in the contract a clause to the effect of excluding or limiting the liability for damages caused by a defective product. Such clause could not be invoked in an action in tort brought by the buyer or a third party. To be effective the clause has to satisfy a formal requirement which consists in its specific approval by the buyer. The requirement is, in practice, satisfied by drafting a specific clause approving limitation or exclusion of the liability which bears a separate signature of the buyer (Code article 1341(2)). The clause may completely exclude the liability of the seller or limit it to a certain amount – as in the case of liquidated damages. Despite its formal validity, however, a limitation or exclusion clause cannot be invoked when the loss arose from a wilful or grossly negligent breach of the contract (Code article 1229(1)) or where the seller has wilfully failed to disclose the existence of any defect (Code article 1490(2)).

2.8 Limitation period

An action based on the statutory warranty must be commenced within one year of delivery provided always that the seller was notified of the defect within eight days of its discovery (Code article 1495). In the case of a contractual warranty, the action must be commenced within six months of the discovery of the defect provided always that the seller was notified of the defect within 30 days of the discovery of the defect (Code article 1512).

2.9 Liability of third parties: vicarious liability

A seller is liable to third parties under the general principles of tort law. The seller is not liable when an intervening action or omission of a third party occurs, if such act or omission is by itself apt to cause the damage. The seller is liable also if the damage was caused by the act or omission of any subject which is outside his organisation and of which he has availed himself in order to perform the contract (Code article 1228).

3. LIABILITY IN TORT

3.1 Outline of relevant tort law giving rise to liability for personal and property damage in Italy

The general principle of tort law is embodied in article 2043 of the Code which states that 'any event caused by fault negligence or wilful misconduct binds its author to indemnify any damage deriving therefrom'.

Together with this article, the Code provides a number of more detailed provisions regulating the consequences of particular tortious acts, all of which have been used by the courts to impose liability on producers or suppliers of defective products. In this respect, the most relevant provisions are:

(a) article 2050 which holds that whoever carries out an activity that, because of its nature or the means used is potentially 'dangerous', is liable for any damage caused by a defective product unless he proves that 'all the appropriate measures to avoid the loss had been taken' (Code article 2050);

(b) article 2051 which holds liable a bailee for damage caused by things in his possession. This article has been used to establish the liability of suppliers in cases where it was not possible to sue the producer.[10]

3.2 Causation: remoteness of loss and damage

The Code article 1223, which regulates the principle of causation for actions in contract, can also be applied to actions in tort. All that is required therefore is that the damage caused be the 'immediate and direct consequence' of the tortious act. In addition, the Code does not limit the recoverable damages to those that were foreseeable at the time of the event but includes any unforeseeable damages. Liability is, however, excluded or reduced in the case of contributory negligence (Code article 1227). Courts have applied this provision in cases where the consumer had not followed the instructions or the

10 *Corte d'Appello* of Rome, 8 October 1986 in Foro Italiano, 1987 1, 1590.

warnings for the use of the product.[11] Finally, the courts have held jointly and severally liable in tort both the producer of a single part of a product and the assembler. The rationale given by the courts is that the producer is at fault for having manufactured a defective product whilst the assembler is negligent for not having properly inspected the part and therefore having failed to detect the defect.[12]

3.3 Quantum of damages

Damages in tort should restore the aggrieved party to the position where it was before the tortious act. Damages should cover not only the expenses incurred and the losses suffered, but also loss of earnings and other consequential losses suffered as a result of the tortious act.

As for moral damages – that is, all those losses that do not have a prima facie economic value – article 2059 states that they can only be recovered if the tortious act is criminal.

The article, however, has been construed by the courts as having a rather narrow scope. It has in fact been held that its provisions intend to cover only the so-called 'subjective moral damages' – that is, only those damages to which no economic value can be attributed, such as pain and suffering. On the other hand, the redress of other kinds of damages which do not have an immediate economic value, such as damages to health or reputation, have been recognised as being outside the scope of article 2059[13] and can therefore be compensated even if the tortious act is not relevant with respect to criminal law.

3.4 Burden of proof

In an action in tort, the plaintiff has to prove:

(a) an act or omission on the part of the defendant;
(b) its unlawfulness;
(c) negligence (the degree of which may vary);
(d) damage; and
(e) a causal link between the act or omission and the damage.

In practice, however, particularly in the case of actions in tort for damage caused by defective products, the courts have practically reversed the burden of proof in relation to the proof of negligence. In a leading case decided in 1964, the *Corte di Cassazione* held that the proof of the negligence of the producer was in the fact that the product was defective.[14] In other cases, the courts have applied article 2050 of the Code which places on the producer engaged in

11 Cass 6 February 1978 no 595 in Foro Italiano, 1979, 1, 422.
12 Cass 13 March 1980 no 1696 in Giustizia Civile, 1980, 1, 1914.
13 A leading case on the matter is the judgment of the *Corte Costituzionale* of 14 July 1986 no 184 in Foro Italiano, 1986, 1, 2053 which clearly stated the principle that damage to health is regulated by article 2043 of the Code and not by article 2059.
14 See Cass 25 May 1964 no 1270 in Foro Italiano, 1965, 1, 2098. In that case, the plaintiff had eaten some biscuits which were unfit for human consumption. The court held that the mere fact that the biscuits had deteriorated was sufficient proof of the negligence of the producer. See also Cass 28 October 1980 no 5795 in Repertorio Foro Italiano 1981.

activities defined as dangerous the burden of proving that he had adopted all the appropriate measures to avoid the damage – a burden of proof which in most cases has been impossible to discharge. The courts have, for example, qualified as dangerous the sale of children's balloons filled with helium,[15] the sale of bottled gas[16] and the manufacture of pharmaceutical products which were based on or contained human blood.[17]

3.5 Exclusion or limitation of liability

Article 1229 of the Code has been applied to causes of action in tort. Therefore clauses that exclude or limit liability of the producer have been held to be invalid in the case of gross negligence or wilful misconduct. In general, however, as most actions in tort are brought by and against parties amongst which there is no contractual relationship (eg the producer of soft drinks and the ultimate consumer) it is unlikely that such problems may arise.

3.6 Limitation period

The limitation period for an action in tort is five years (Code article 2947) from the day of the tortious action, or the day when the damage occurred if later. If the tortious act qualifies as a crime, then the limitation period is the same as the one for the commencement of the criminal proceedings (Code article 2947(3)). If the crime is pardoned or a final judgment given on the matter, the limitation period runs from the date of the pardon or of the final judgment.

3.7 Liability for third parties

Vicarious liability is established by article 2049 of the Code which holds employers liable for damage caused by their servants and employees if the tort was committed in the course of their employment. The rule has been held to encompass the liability of the state for acts of civil servants. As in the case of contractual liability, liability is excluded if an intervening act or omission of a third party occurs, provided always that such act or omission by itself is apt to cause the damage.

4. LIABILITY FOR DEFECTIVE PRODUCTS BROUGHT ABOUT BY BREACH OF STATUTORY REGULATION DESIGNED TO PROTECT CONSUMERS AND/OR TO PROMOTE SAFETY

The Italian legal system provides a number of statutory regulations that are designed to promote safety and/or protect consumers.

15 *Pretura* of Genoa 15 February 1974 in Repertorio Foro Italiano, 1974.
16 Cass 13 January 1981 no 294 in Foro Italiano, 1981, 1, 1326.
17 Cass 15 July 1987 no 6241 in Foro Italiano, 1988, 1, 144.

Examples are Law 547 of 1955, which lays out the necessary precautions to ensure safety at work, or Decree 927 of 1981, which imposes a duty of placing a health warning on the packaging of dangerous substances. Another interesting example is provided by Law 592 of 1967 and the Decree of 15 September 1972 which discipline the manufacturing and importing of medicines based on or containing human blood. Specifically, Law 592 prescribes that any medicine should, before being distributed, be approved by the Ministry of Health. Such approval, however, was held not to exclude the liability of the manufacturer for damage suffered by consumers.[18]

The Decree of 15 September 1972 states that in the case of imported medicines the importer can also be held liable for damages. A general duty of information on medicines is imposed upon the National Health Service (*Servizio Sanitario Nazionale*) by Law 833 of 1978 but any failure to do so does not seem to result in liability on the part of the Health Service.

Finally, it is worth noting that the manufacture, distribution or importation of defective medicines gives rise, in certain cases, to criminal liability pursuant to articles 443 and 452 of the Italian Penal Code.

In general, however, all the above-mentioned regulations, whilst envisaging different forms of criminal liability for the case of non-compliance, do not provide any specific provision for the redress of damage caused to third parties. This is consistent with the widely held opinion that the principles of tort law contained in the Code are applicable to any case of tortious liability.

5. SPECIAL LIABILITIES ARISING IN RESPECT OF PARTICULAR PRODUCTS

Italian law does not generally make particular provision for special liability in respect of any particular product. In a related field, however, it is appropriate to mention Law 1860 of 1962 which regulates liability for the case of accidents in nuclear power stations.

6. LIABILITY FOR DEFECTIVE PRODUCTS ARISING FROM NATIONAL LAW IN ITALY: IMPLEMENTATION OF EC DIRECTIVE 85/324 ON PRODUCT LIABILITY

6.1 Introduction

The implementation of the Directive by means of the Decree has introduced some relevant modifications to the pre-Directive position with regard to liability for defective products.

Whilst the Directive and the Decree are consistent with the general principles of Italian tort law, the new legislation has introduced material changes in a number of areas, such as the identity of the defendants, the burden of proof, the quantum of damages, the limitation period and the defences that the producer can raise.

18 Cass 15 July 1987 no 6241 in Foro Italiano, 1988, 1, 144.

6.2 Outline of the provisions in Italy

The basic principle introduced by the Decree is that the producer is liable for the damages caused by the defects of his product as a consequence of the mere fact of having put it into circulation.

We shall now examine in more detail the most relevant provisions of the Decree:

6.2.1 Defendants

The provisions of the Decree differ from those of the Directive with respect to the release from liability of the supplier upon disclosure of the identity of the producer or of the importer. According to the Decree, the consumer must ask the seller in writing to disclose the name of the producer or importer. The supplier has a term of three months from the date of the request to disclose the identity of the producer or of the importer. The request must contain information on the product and the date and the place of purchase and can be made before commencing the proceedings. If the injured party fails to ask the seller to disclose the name of the producer or importer, the supplier can disclose it within three months of commencement of the proceedings. The supplier may also at the first hearing ask the court to grant a further three-month term within which the seller may disclose the name of the producer. The disclosure of the name of the producer or the importer will mean that the producer or importer will be joined in the case as defendant pursuant to article 106 of the Italian Code of Civil Procedure.

The effect of the application of article 106, however, is not immediately to release the supplier. The scope of article 106 is to prevent related causes of action from being decided in different proceedings, but it does not go so far as to release any of the parties involved.

The Decree does not provide for cases in which the producer does not appear in court or is outside the reach of the jurisdiction.

In the light of the general scope of the Decree – that is, to ensure the protection of the consumer – it could be argued that, if the producer cannot be brought before the court, the liability should be borne entirely by the supplier.

6.2.2 Defective product

The Decree, unlike the Directive, specifies that a product is to be considered defective when it does not provide the same degree of safety as that 'normally offered by any other product of the same series' (Decree article 5(3)). On the other hand, whilst article 6(2) of the Directive does not allow a product to be considered defective 'for the sole reason that a better product is subsequently put into circulation', the Decree seems to expand such exception. In fact, the corresponding provision refers to a 'better product that has, at any time, been put into circulation' (Decree article 5(2)). The wording of the Decree seems, however, to be consistent with the principle, stated in article 6 of the Directive and article 5 of the Decree, that a product is defective when it does not provide the level of safety which a person is entitled to expect – this is different from the level of safety which it is technically possible to obtain.

6.2.3 Damages

The Decree does not put a ceiling on the amount of damages that can be awarded thus exercising the option granted by article 17(1) of the Directive. The Decree also states that the recovery of damages to property is limited by a lower threshold of L 750,000.

6.2.4 Defences

Article 6 of the Decree contains a list of exclusions of producers' liability which mainly reflect the provisions of the Directive. There are, however, some differences.

(1) Whilst article 7(b) of the Directive excludes the liability of the producer if the latter proves that '*it is probable* that the defect *did not exist* at the time when the product was put into circulation by him or that the defect came into being afterwards', article 6(b) of the Decree requires that 'the defect did not exist at the time when the product was put into circulation by [the producer]'. The difference would appear to be substantial. However, in article 8(2) the Decree seems to reintroduce the wording of the Directive when it states that, in order to exclude the liability pursuant to article 6, 'it is sufficient to prove that, in the circumstances, it is probable that the defect did not yet exist at the time when the product was put into circulation'. It would therefore appear that, albeit in a rather contorted way, the Decree substantially adheres to the wording of the Directive in connection with the exclusion of liability as stated by the latter in article 7(b).

The second part of the provision of article 6(b) of the Directive is excluded from the Decree which would bring into play any defect that came into being after the product was put into circulation.

(2) Article 6(d) of the Decree (which reproduces the corresponding provision of the Directive) is consistent with a general principle of Italian law according to which no one can be held liable for the detrimental consequences of his act or omission if such act or omission were due to compliance with an existing law or regulation.

It is, however, worth noting that such provision could contradict article 6(e) which excludes the liability of the producer if it is proved that the defect could not have been discovered taking into consideration the existing 'state of the art'.

In fact, it is not uncommon that laws and regulations are not regularly updated to take into account any change in scientific and technological knowledge and therefore it could well happen that a product, though it would formally satisfy the conditions laid down by para (d), would be considered defective and give rise to liability under para (e). Although courts have not yet been called to decide on the issue, it is possible that they will allow a defence under para (d) to stand only if the producer can prove that existing laws or regulations compelled him to manufacture the product in only one possible way.

(3) Article 6(e) of the Decree adopts a wording which is not altogether the same as that of article 7(e) of the Directive. In fact, whilst the latter excludes liability when 'the state of scientific and technical knowledge at the time when

he [the producer] put the product into circulation was not such as to enable the existence of the defect to be discovered', the former refers to the fact that scientific and technical knowledge did 'not yet allow the product to be considered as defective'. The different wording seems to introduce a 'subjective' element in the appraisal of the state of scientific and technical knowledge and such an approach would appear to be in contrast with the more objective one that is suggested by the wording of the Directive.

Finally, it should be noted that the Decree has accepted the broad principle contained in article 7(e) of the Directive – even if in a slightly different wording, and possibly in an even softer form – rejecting the stricter option provided by article 15(1)(b) of the same.

6.3 Description of special or anomalous provisions in respect of product liability law in Italy

6.3.1 Notion of 'product put into circulation'

The Decree, unlike the Directive, specifies when a product is considered as 'put into circulation'. Article 7 of the Decree states that a product is to be considered as put into circulation when:

(a) it is delivered to the purchaser or the user, or an employee or agent of the former, even if such delivery is made for the sole purpose of testing or otherwise inspecting the product (Decree article 7(1));
(b) the product is not delivered directly to the purchaser or user but is delivered to a carrier or forwarding agent for delivery (Decree article 8(2));
(c) in the case of forced sale, the debtor has not specifically indicated the defect to the bailiff at the time of the attachment or within 15 days of the attachment by lodging in court appropriate notice or by notifying the creditor (Decree article 7(3)).

6.3.2 Third party liability

The Decree does not reproduce article 8(1) of the Directive which states that the liability of the producer is not excluded by the contributory act or omission of a third party. The absence of such provision reinforces the liability of the producer, but it would not seem to prejudice its right of contribution against a third party.

6.3.3 Contributory negligence

Article 8(2) of the Directive provides for reduction or exclusion of the liability of the producer in the case of contributory negligence on the part of the consumer. In the corresponding provision of the Decree (article 10) it is stated that contributory negligence should be evaluated in the light of article 1227 of the Code. Also, the said article 10 provides for exclusion of the liability of the producer in the case of there being a willing assumption of the risk – as in the case of a consumer who, although not acting negligently in using the product, had knowledge of the defect and had nevertheless willingly exposed himself to the risk of damage (Decree article 10(2)). Finally, article 10(3) of the Decree states that, to the limited extent of the compensation for damage to property, the contributory negligence of whoever is in possession of the defective product is to be construed as contributory negligence of the injured party.

6.4 Optional provisions in the EC Directive

The Directive allowed for a number of optional provisions to be inserted in the national implementing laws.

6.4.1 Agricultural produce

With respect to agricultural produce, the Decree has implemented the Directive in its main formulation, rejecting the option provided in article 15(1) of the Directive – that is, choosing not to include 'primary agricultural products and game' in the definition of a product. In this respect, it is appropriate to recall that the Decree also contains an elaborate description of what is a 'primary agricultural product which has undergone initial processing' (see above in section 1.3(b) of this chapter).

6.4.2 'State of the art' defence

The Decree includes 'the state of the art' defence – albeit in a slightly different wording (see section 6.2.3(d) of this chapter).

6.4.3 Limitation of the total liability for damage

The Directive gave the option of limiting the total liability for damages caused by identical products and resulting in death or personal injuries. The Decree does not contain any such limitation.

6.4.4 Extinction of the right to compensation

The Directive provides that the right to obtain compensation should be extinguished within ten years of the date when the defective product was put into circulation. Such extinction would be avoided only if the injured party commenced proceedings against the producer. In the Decree, the extinction of the right is avoided not only by the commencing of proceedings – if the case is not then abandoned – but also by the admission of the party which is liable or the presentation of a statement of claim in the liquidation of the producer or any other liable party (Decree article 14(1)(2)). Article 14(3) of the Decree also states that any such act mentioned before, which would avoid the extinction of the right, would have effect only with regard to the liability of the party (defendant) concerned.

7. PRACTICAL EFFECTS EC PRODUCT LIABILITY LAW WILL HAVE ON VARIOUS BUSINESSES IN THE CHAIN OF SUPPLY OF PRODUCTS

The main practical effect of the implementation of the Directive in Italy is that the injured party will stand a better chance of obtaining compensation for damage. This is due to the fact that it seems likely that the supplier would be held liable in all those cases where the producer is out of the jurisdiction or cannot otherwise be brought to court.

On the other hand, the liability of the assembler or the supplier of a single part or the supplier of raw material does not seem to be different now from what it was under the previous law. The only difference is that the producer of a single part can now use the defence set out in article 7(f) of the Directive and article 6(f) of the Decree that allows him to escape liability if he shows that the defect is attributable to the design of the product. Although Italian courts had not been called to decide such a case in the pre-Decree period, a degree of clarity on the matter is certainly beneficial.

In the case of damage caused by a product which has been manufactured by more than one party, the Decree clearly states that all the parties concerned are to be held jointly and severally liable for the damage caused. As for the relationship between the various parties who can be held responsible for the damage, the Decree states that any party that pays in full has the right to be indemnified by the others. The amount of such indemnity is determined having regard to 'the risk that can be traced to each party, the degree of culpability and the consequences' (Decree article 9(2)).

This principle may be difficult to apply when the liability arises from a case in which there was no negligent act or omission. In that case it could be argued that the apportionment of liability should be made with reference to the part played by each party in the manufacture of the product. From the comments of the Parliamentary Commission which drafted the Decree, it would appear that the foreseeability of the damage could also be a relevant criterion for the determination of the indemnity. If the liability of each single party cannot be clearly ascertained, the total amounts of damage shall be shared equally.

8. COMPARISON OF THE EFFECTS OF PRODUCT LIABILITY LAW WITH THE PREVIOUS POSITION IN CONTRACT AND TORT

Although the Decree expressly states that its introduction does not affect the pre-Directive position with regard to causes of action in tort and in contract which would derive from damages caused by a defective product, the Decree has brought a number of material changes to the position of the parties in a product liability case. In fact, it would seem that the concept of defect contained in the Decree is not comparable to the concept of defect which would give rise to an action in contract. Whilst the former is focused on the concept of safety, the latter would seem to be centred on the idea of aptness to perform a particular function and hence on its limited use or decreased economic value.

Of great importance also is the introduction of a form of strict liability where the consumer has been relieved from the burden of proving the negligence of the producer, although the same result had in practice been reached by case law. On the other hand, the consumer is now left with a shorter limitation period, at least if compared with the five-year limitation period which is in force for normal tort actions. In this last respect, however, the discipline is also different with regard to the start of the limitation period. In the case of an action in tort it runs from the date of the tortious action or of the damage, if different; in an action under the Decree, the limitation period starts to run from the day when the consumer knew or should have known of the damage, the defect and the identity of the producer. In the case of damage which will worsen during the course of time, it is not unreasonable to argue that the limitation period would start from the day when the injured party has or should have knowledge of a sufficiently serious damage (Decree article 13(2)) that would 'justify the commencing of proceedings'.

Another main difference from the previous legislation is the absolute invalidity provided by the Decree of any clause which tends to exclude or otherwise limit the liability of the producer.

On the other hand, as the Decree restricts the action for damages only to things and personal injuries or death, it is not clear whether a clause of exclusion or limitation of liability for consequential financial losses would be caught by the prohibition of the Decree.

Finally, it is worth noting how the Decree introduces, in the Italian system, the concept of willing assumption of the risk which is different from the traditional contributory negligence hitherto known in Italy.

9. RISK MANAGEMENT IN THE NEW ERA OF PRODUCT LIABILITY

9.1 Limitation of liability through corporate structure

The implementation of the Directive in Italy could facilitate the beginning of actions which could lead to potentially large awards against manufacturers or suppliers of consumer products. In the circumstances, therefore, it would be appropriate to try and limit as much as possible the exposure to such liability.

The first, and most obvious, step is incorporation in the form of a limited liability company (*Società per Azioni or Società a responsabilità limitata*). In addition, it could be advisable to try and protect valuable assets by splitting the manufacture of high risk products or their import into the EC from the parent company in which most of the group's assets would be vested.

These solutions, however, would not necessarily lead to a complete insulation of the parent company from the liabilities incurred by the manufacturing or importing subsidiary. Indeed, article 2362 of the Code states that in the case of insolvency of a company, when the corresponding liabilities arose during a period when there was only one shareholder or stakeholder, such shareholder or stakeholder bears unlimited liability for the obligations of the company.

Although it is not clear whether such unlimited liability arises in the case where the only shareholder is another company,[19] still there is a sizeable risk that

19 In favour Cass no 1088 of 1986 and no 6594 of 1981. In the sense that there would not be any liability see Cass no 73 of 1987.

courts will be inclined to 'pierce the corporate veil'. The relevant criterion seems to be whether or not the intention of the parties concerned was or was not fraudulent – that is, if their only or main scope was to avoid liability.[20] In this context it was held that liability was not excluded by the fact that the only shareholder was a foreign company[1] and/or the purchase of the shares of the subsidiary was made abroad.[2] The courts have not been consistent in applying article 2362 to cases where the shares of the subsidiary were held by more than one subject although one clearly exercised actual control.[3] In those cases it would be advisable to proceed on a case-by-case basis.

9.2 Translation of the articles of the Italian Civil Code frequently referred to in the chapter

9.2.1 Article 1223: Quantum of damages

The quantum of damages for breach or delayed performance must include both the loss suffered by the creditor and the lost earnings so long as they are the immediate and direct consequence of the breach.

9.2.2 Article 1225: Foreseeability of the loss

If the breach or the delay in performing is not the result of a wilful action of the debtor, damages are limited to the loss that was foreseeable at the time of the conclusion of the contract.

9.2.3 Article 1227: Contributory negligence

If the loss is caused by the concurrent negligent behaviour of the creditor, damages are reduced proportionally to the degree of negligence and the consequences thereof.

Damages are not due for losses that the creditor could have avoided by using reasonable diligence.

9.2.4 Article 1229: Limitation or exclusion of liability

Any clause which limits or excludes the liability of the debtor for losses deriving from his gross negligence or wilful act or omission is null and void.

Any clause which limits or excludes the liability of the debtor in cases where his act or omission or those of his agents or employees constitute a violation of existing laws, is also null and void.

20 Applying this criterion it was held that the fact that a certain stake was settled in trust did not exclude the liability of the beneficial owner (Cass 29 November 1983 no 7152 in Giurisprudenza Commerciale, 1964, II, 694).

1 See Cass no 6594 of 1981.

2 See Cass no 1088 of 1986.

3 It was held that when the shares in a company were held by two subjects and the minority holding was in turn wholly owned by the majority shareholder, there was unlimited liability on the part of the majority shareholder (see Cass no 5143 of 1982). A similar case, however, was resolved in the opposite way applying the fraudulent scope test (see Cass 9 May 1985 no 2879 in Le Società 1985, 717).

9.2.5 *Article 1337: Negotiations and pre-contractual liability*

The parties, during negotiations and the formation of the contract, must behave in good faith.

9.2.6 *Article 1341: Standard contract terms*

Standard contract terms prepared by one party bind the other party if the latter knew of them or should have known of them at the time when the contract was entered into.

In any case, all those clauses that stipulate, in favour of the party that inserted them, limitation of liability, the facility to suspend the execution of the contract, or impose on the other party limitation periods, limitation of the possibility to raise exceptions, restriction of the facility to contract with third parties, automatic renewal of the contract, arbitration clauses or clauses that otherwise derogate from the jurisdiction of Italian courts, are not valid unless specifically approved in writing.

9.2.7 *Article 1490: Warranties for defects of the goods sold*

The seller is obliged to warrant that the goods sold are free from defects that may make them unfit for normal use or cause a material decrease of their value.

A clause that excludes or limits such warranty is null and void if the seller has in bad faith hidden the existence of defects.

9.2.8 *Article 1491: Exclusion of the warranty*

A warranty is excluded if at the time of the contract the buyer knew of the defects or if the defect was clearly noticeable unless, in the latter case, the seller had expressly stated that the goods did not have any defect.

9.2.9 *Article 1492: Effects of the warranty*

In the cases indicated in article 1490, the buyer can choose between termination of the contract or reduction of the price unless, for certain defects, commercial custom excludes termination.

The choice becomes irrevocable when inserted in the statement of claims.

If the goods were delivered and perished as a result of the defects, the buyer has the right to terminate the contract; if instead they perished because of natural causes or fault of the buyer, or if the buyer has resold or transformed them, he can only claim a reduction of the price.

9.2.10 *Article 1495: Terms and conditions for the action in damages*

The buyer is estopped from acting on the warranty if he does not notify the seller of the defect within eight days from discovery, unless otherwise provided by the law or the parties. Such notification is not necessary if the seller has acknowledged the existence of the defect or has hidden it.

In any case the action is precluded within one year of delivery; however, if the seller commences an action on the contract, the buyer can always oppose the warranty provided that the seller has been notified of the defect within eight days of discovery and one year of delivery.

9.2.11 *Article 1512: Warranty of merchantability*

If the seller has warranted that the goods will perform their function for a certain period of time, the buyer, unless otherwise provided, must notify the seller of the defect within 30 days of discovery. The action must be commenced within six months of discovery.

The court can allow the seller a fixed term within which to substitute or repair the goods but remains liable for any damage.

The warranty need not be expressed but can also consist of an implied condition according to commercial custom.

9.2.12 *Article 2043: Damage in tort*

Any event caused by fault or negligence or wilful misconduct binds its author to indemnify any damage deriving therefrom.

9.2.13 *Article 2049: Vicarious liability*

Employers are liable for damage caused by their servants or employees if the tortious act was committed in the course of their employment.

9.2.14 *Article 2050: Liability for dangerous activities*

Whoever whilst exercising an activity which, because of its nature or the means used is dangerous, causes damage to third parties, is bound to redress such damage unless he proves that all appropriate measures to avoid the loss have been taken.

9.2.15 *Article 2051: Liability of the bailor*

A person is liable for damage caused by things in his custody unless he proves that the damage was caused by an Act of God.

9.2.16 *Article 2059: Moral damages*

Any damage which is not economically valuable must be redressed only in the cases determined by the law.

9.2.17 *Article 2362: Sole shareholder*

In case of insolvency of the company, a single shareholder has unlimited liability for all the obligations which were entered into during the time when all the shares belonged to a single shareholder.

9.2.18 Article 2947: Limitation for actions in tort

The right to obtain damages for tortious actions cannot be enforced after five years from the day of the tortious act.

Damages deriving from tortious actions involving vehicles cannot be claimed after two years from the day of the tortious act.

In any case, if the tortious act is also a crime, and the commencement of the criminal action has a longer limitation period, then such longer period will apply to the civil action. However, if the crime is pardoned or a final judgment given on the matter, the limitation period applicable is the one indicated in paragraphs 1 and 2 of this article and shall run from the date of the pardon or of the final judgment.

CHAPTER IX

Luxembourg

René Diederich Esq

Loesch & Wolter
Avocats – Avoués
8 Rue Zithe
Boîte postale 1107
L-1011 Luxembourg

Tel ++ 352 494 015
Fax ++ 352 494 944

CHAPTER IX

Luxembourg

1. INTRODUCTION

(1) Prior to the implementation of the Directive, Luxembourg did not have any comprehensive product liability legislation.

As in France and Belgium, the product liability rules in Luxembourg were based mainly on the provisions contained in articles 1641–1649 of the Luxembourg Civil Code dealing with liability for latent defects in products under sales contracts.

The Luxembourg courts have traditionally and repeatedly expressed the view that the provisions of articles 1641–1649 of the Luxembourg Civil Code can be applied to sales contracts as general principles of law. Similar rules have also been applied by the Luxembourg courts to other kinds of contracts as, for instance, building contracts, lease contracts, etc.

The courts developed the seller's and the manufacturer's obligations under these kinds of contracts to supply a product which had to conform with the provisions of the contract. A number of ancillary obligations were also developed by the courts which were imposed on the seller and the manufacturer, in particular the obligation to inform, advise and warn the purchaser of the conditions of use of the product and its potential dangers.

Apart from the liability deriving from the contract in the case of a defective product, the seller or the manufacturer of a product may also be held liable in tort in the event that the defects of a product have caused injury or loss to an unrelated third person.

(2) The Directive was implemented in Luxembourg by a law of 21 April 1989, regarding the liability deriving from defective products (the 'Law on Defective Products').

In accordance with article 8 of the Law on Defective Products, the legal provisions implementing the Directive do not prejudice the rights of the plaintiff to claim compensation for the damage suffered on the basis of the 'common' law of contractual or extra-contractual liability or on the basis of any other specific laws on liability.

This means that the Law on Defective Products supplements, rather than amends, the provisions of Luxembourg law governing the liability in contract or the liability in tort of the seller or the manufacturer of the defective product or of any other professional contractor.

It goes without saying, however, that this choice of the Luxembourg legislator presents a number of difficulties and it is foreseeable that the co-existence of the general rules of liability in contract and liability in tort with respect to defective products and the specific rules contained in the Law on Defective Products will give rise to conflict.

2. LIABILITY IN CONTRACT

2.1 Introduction

As indicated above, the legal provisions relating to the seller's liability under a sales contract are mainly, but not exclusively, set out in articles 1641–1649 of the Luxembourg Civil Code. These articles of the Civil Code deal with the seller's warranty for latent defects in the products sold and the provisions relating to this warranty will be examined in detail below. As it is, however, of some importance to understand these provisions relating to the warranty for hidden defects in the more general context of the seller's liability towards the purchaser or the potential purchaser under a sales contract, it is useful to summarise briefly the provisions of Luxembourg law governing this liability.

2.2 Liability for pre-contractual statements or representations

(1) According to article 1602 of the Luxembourg Civil Code, the seller is bound to explain to the purchaser clearly what his obligations will be under the sales contract. An obscure or ambiguous agreement will be construed against the seller.

The liability of the seller under this provision of the Civil Code is a contractual one.

(2) Although the Luxembourg Civil Code does not contain any specific provisions with respect to a duty of information which could be binding upon the parties prior to the conclusion of a contract, Luxembourg case law provides that professional sellers are bound to inform their potential customers of the advantages and dangers of a contemplated measure or action and of any circumstances which might influence the other party to enter into an agreement.

The professional seller has to give full information to his potential customers so they may decide whether or not to buy the product with full knowledge of the facts. The professional seller does not, however, have to act as adviser to his potential customer.

It remains that the liability in respect to this duty of information is considered to be a liability in tort and not a liability in contract.

2.3 The vendor's liability in a sales contract

(1) According to article 1603 of the Civil Code, the seller has two main obligations under a sales contract: the first is to deliver the product, meaning that the seller has to place within the actual control of the purchaser a product which conforms to the object sold, and the second is to warrant the object sold.

(2) The warranty to be given by a seller under a sales contract is twofold: first, the seller has to ensure that the purchaser has 'peaceful and untroubled possession' of the object sold and, secondly, the seller must give a warranty to the purchaser against hidden defects in the object sold or redhibitory defects. The breach of the obligation to deliver the product may lead to the rescission of

the sales contract and may entitle the purchaser to claim further damages, unless the purchaser accepted the object acquired.

2.4 Contractual warranties relating to the quality of products and the safety of products

(1) As indicated above, the seller has to ensure that the purchaser has peaceful or untroubled possession of the product which has been sold. This warranty is mandatory and perpetual. The seller is bound to this warranty unless he can give evidence that the non-performance of his obligation under the sales contract is due to an external cause.

A breach of this warranty may lead to the reimbursement of the price paid by the purchaser and the payment of further damages, as the case may be.

(2) Although the Civil Code does not contain any specific provision imposing a warranty on the seller for the safety of the products sold by him, Belgian jurisprudence has developed in many types of contracts an ancillary safety obligation which is binding upon professional sellers.

Numerous court decisions have admitted that the seller is liable under the sales contract for accidents caused to the purchaser by a product which has been sold.

To a certain extent, this warranty of the seller relating to the safety of the products sold and the warranty of the seller for hidden defects may merge into one another.

However, this may not be completely the situation and the warranty deriving from the safety obligation may complete the effects of the warranty for hidden defects. A seller may, indeed, be held liable to the purchaser on the basis of this safety obligation without the necessity for the purchaser to give evidence that the hidden defect has caused the damage.

2.5 The warranty for hidden defects

2.5.1 Definition

(1) Article 1641 of the Civil Code provides that the seller is bound to give a warranty for hidden defects in the product sold which render the product unsuitable for its intended use or which restricts that use to such a degree that the purchaser would not have bought it or would have paid a lesser price had he known of the defects.

According to article 1642 of the Civil Code, the seller is not bound to give a warranty for visible defects which could have been detected by the purchaser himself.

The purchaser discovering a latent defect may sue the seller if:

(a) the product under consideration cannot be used for the purpose for which it has normally been designed; and
(b) the defect is latent or hidden, which means that the purchaser was not able to notice it at the moment of the purchase; and
(c) the defect existed prior to the purchase; and
(d) the defect is within the product itself.

(2) It is generally admitted that a defect is deemed to be latent if it was not reasonably possible to discover it at the very moment when the purchaser took possession of the product and the existence of the defect could not be revealed by any circumstance. For a purchaser having no technical knowledge, the defect is deemed to be hidden if only a qualified technician could have detected it. The defect is, however, deemed to have been visible if a normally skilled person could have discovered it by an elementary but not superficial examination.

(3) Subject to the above-mentioned conditions, the seller will be liable for any hidden defect which has been discovered.

(4) However, the Civil Code makes a distinction with respect to the extent of liability incurred between a seller who was unaware of the defect in the product and who, as a consequence, acted in good faith, and a seller who knew of the defect in the product at the very moment of the sale and who therefore acted in bad faith.

Whereas the seller who has acted in good faith may, on the one hand, have to repay the price of the defective product and reimburse the purchaser for the costs of the sale and may also be entitled to take advantage of a provision of the contract limiting his liability, the seller who has or is deemed to have acted in bad faith will have to repay the price and will also be bound to compensate the purchaser against any and all damages suffered by the purchaser.

(5) The seller having, or deemed to have, acted in bad faith may not avail himself of any provision of the contract limiting his liability.

(6) Pursuant to well-established law, professional sellers are presumed to have knowledge of all hidden defects and the professional seller therefore has the same liability as a seller having acted in bad faith. This rule applies equally to manufacturers, suppliers and retailers.

Luxembourg jurisprudence considers that this presumption is irrebutable and the professional seller (or the manufacturer) may not escape his liability by pleading that it was technically impossible to discover the defect or to avoid the appearance of the defect.

Indeed, the Luxembourg courts have decided that, as a professional, the seller is liable for the quality of the product used, even though he did not know of the defect or the characteristics of the product. The 'development risks' defence is not therefore available under Luxembourg contract law.

2.5.2 Sanctions

(1) Where the requirements of article 1641 of the Civil Code are fulfilled, the purchaser may either sue the seller in order to have the contract rescinded ('redhibitory action'), or he may sue the seller in order to obtain a reduction of the sale price ('estimatory action').

The Luxembourg courts have also admitted that apart from these two actions the purchaser can also claim from the seller other types of performance, such as the replacement of the product or the repair of the defect. The court will not order a seller to repair a product where the repair is impossible, or if the repair will run up costs which are out of all proportion to the value of the object which has been sold.

The purchaser may only sue the seller on the basis of the redhibitory action if the object sold is absolutely unusable for the purpose for which it is intended. If, however, the defects may easily be repaired and the repairing of the object does not deprive the purchaser of the use of the object for a long period, the purchaser may only make a claim for the repair of the product.

(2) It should be noted that the warranty for hidden defects is transferred together with the product if it is sold several times. The ultimate purchaser may bring a direct action based on this warranty for latent defects against a remote seller or even against the manufacturer.

The manufacturer and the successive sellers will be held jointly and severally liable towards the ultimate purchaser, save that in this chain only the persons who sold the product after the hidden defects came into existence will be liable.

(3) Besides rescission of the contract or reduction of the price, further compensation as indicated above can be sought by the purchaser if the seller acted in bad faith.

2.6 Damages

(1) According to article 1150 of the Civil Code, contractual compensation is only available for foreseeable damage, that is to say, for damage which was or could be foreseen when the contract was concluded. This principle does not apply however if the non-performance of the contractual obligation is a consequence of fraud or wilful misrepresentation.

Even in the latter case, the amount of damages which will have to be paid to the plaintiff may only be in compensation for the damage suffered (*damnum emergens*) by the person entitled to performance of the contractual obligation and of the profit of which such person has been deprived (*lucrum cessans*), that is to say, for all those damages which can be seen as an immediate and direct consequence of the non-performance of the contractual obligation.

It is indeed a general rule under Luxembourg law that a plaintiff has to be compensated for the entire damage he has suffered, no more and no less.

As far as the principle of foreseeability is concerned, it has been ruled that the damage must be foreseeable only as to its possibility not as to its amount.

On the other hand, immediate and direct damage means that the plaintiff will have to give evidence of a direct relationship between the breach of contract and the damage.

(2) The plaintiff may recover either for material or immaterial losses. These damages include all losses suffered by the purchaser of a defective product either to his property or to his person, such as physical harm, loss of income and of ability or earning capacity.

Immaterial losses which may be claimed include moral and aesthetic sufferings, including pain and suffering.

The damage suffered by the plaintiff must be actual. The plaintiff may not be compensated for a potential damage.

(3) As far as parties who may claim compensation are concerned, besides the plaintiff himself and his relatives (if they can give evidence of their indirect material or immaterial loss and if they can demonstrate that their claim is based on negligence), legal insurers for injuries to workers, property insurers and

employers may, to a certain extent, recover sums paid to the plaintiff whether under an employment agreement or under an insurance contract.

(4) Pursuant to article 1152 of the Civil Code, if the agreement stipulates that the party failing to perform its obligation under the contract has to pay a specific sum of money to the other party in order to compensate for the damage suffered by the party, it will not be possible to allocate to the recipient of the contractual obligation either a greater or a lesser sum of money.

The recent Law of 15 May 1987 has introduced a second paragraph to article 1152 of the Civil Code. This paragraph provides that the court may reduce or increase the agreed penalty if this penalty obviously appears to be excessive or ridiculous. This legal provision contained in paragraph 2 of article 1152 is a mandatory provision of Luxembourg law.

2.7 Causation

As indicated above, contractual compensation is only due for foreseeable damage. In this respect, it is important to make a distinction between the nature and the extent of the damage on the one hand, and the monetary equivalent which has to be paid in order to compensate for this damage on the other hand.

The seller will, of course, only be held liable for foreseeable damage which is a consequence of the non-performance by the seller of a contractual obligation.

Compensation for all other kinds of damage may only be sought against the seller on the basis of a liability in tort, even though the defendant and the plaintiff are contractually bound.

As a consequence, the seller will have to compensate the purchaser for any foreseeable damage resulting from the non-performance by the seller of any of his contractual obligations and it will be for the seller to prove that certain damage claimed by the purchaser was not foreseeable at the moment of the conclusion of the contract.

It follows that, in this context of liability in contract, the main question to be solved will not be that of causation but foreseeability of a certain damage.

2.8 Exclusion or limitation of liability

(1) Generally speaking, provisions contained in a contract limiting or excluding the liability of one of the contracting parties are deemed to be valid unless they are expressly excluded by mandatory legal provisions or they cover fraud or wilful misconduct.

(2) It should also be noted, in this context, that according to article 1135–1 of the Luxembourg Civil Code, a clause in a contract which includes a limitation of the liability of the person who has prepared standard pre-established terms and conditions (ie normally the seller) has to be accepted by a special signature of the other contracting party.

(3) Provisions limiting the seller's liability in respect of either his delivery obligations or his obligations with respect to the conformity of the product sold, have traditionally been deemed valid.

(4) However, as the professional seller is presumed to know the defect latent in his product, where such clauses limit the duration of the liability, the types of defect or the kinds of damage for which the seller will be responsible, they are considered to be invalid.

In the case of contracts entered into between professionals, the seller may produce evidence to show that the purchaser had the same kind of professional skill and expertise as himself and therefore had the technical knowledge and capability to discover the defect at the time of the sale. In this event, a contractual provision excluding or limiting the liability of the seller would be effective.

(5) According to article 1645 of the Civil Code, if the purchaser is a non-professional end-consumer a contractual provision limiting or excluding the liability of the seller is considered to be null and void.

2.9 Limitation period

(1) Pursuant to article 1648 of the Civil Code, in respect of the appearance of latent defects, the purchaser must declare the latent defect to the seller within a short period from the time when the purchaser discovered or should have discovered the hidden defect.

Article 1648 gives no clear-cut definition of this short period. The acceptable length of such period will therefore be left to the discretionary powers of the courts, which will come to a decision taking into consideration the circumstances of a given case and the kind of defect.

(2) The purchaser loses his right to sue the seller after the expiry of a period of one year starting on the date the purchaser disclosed the latent defect to the seller, in the event the purchaser was not in a position to start the proceedings due to a fraud committed by the seller.

This limitation period may be suspended by negotiations with a view to an amicable settlement between the seller and the purchaser, and may also be interrupted by summary proceedings or by any other judicial means with respect to the latent defect.

A new limitation period of one year will then start at the moment when the seller notifies the purchaser by registered mail that he has decided to break off negotiations or at the moment when the purchaser has been informed at the end of the judicial proceedings initiated in order to establish the alleged latent defect.

After the expiry of this further period of one year, the purchaser will no longer have the right to protection in respect of the latent defect, even by way of defence or counterclaim to an action by the seller. However, according to article 1648(5) of the Civil Code, the purchaser, who has not yet paid the price of the product and who has complained of the latent defect within the short period mentioned above, has the right to put it to the seller, as a defence to a claim for the payment of the price, and a counterclaim in order to obtain a reduction of the price or compensation for further damages.

(3) An action for lack of conformity of the product sold to specification or to the provisions of the sale contract is not subject to the limitation period provided under article 1648 of the Civil Code.

In accordance with the general rules of liability in contract, the limitation period is either:

(a) ten years for actions taken against a manufacturer or professional seller; or
(b) thirty years for actions taken against a private seller.

However, clauses contained in a contract providing for a shorter limitation period are valid:

(a) if they are agreed between professionals having the same kind of expertise; and
(b) to the extent that the shorter limitation period provided for leaves a sufficient and reasonable period of time for the plaintiff to initiate proceedings in order to enforce his rights.

2.10 Burden of proof

Under Luxembourg law, the onus is normally on the plaintiff to establish the merits of his claim.

The burden of proof, however, is reversed to a certain extent insofar as product liability is concerned, since the law almost presumes the manufacturer's liability unless the seller proves an 'act of God' (*cas de force majeure*).

2.11 The liability of a building contractor

(1) Pursuant to article 1792 of the Civil Code 'if the building is destroyed totally or partially by reason of the defect [whether apparent or latent] affecting the construction, or even by reason of a defect affecting the ground, the architect and the building contractors and other persons bound by a building contract will be responsible for ten years in respect thereof'.

The defect referred to by article 1792 is a defect which (a) affects a major part of the building, and (b) endangers the strength of the building in whole or in part.

The warranty of ten years will only apply if both these conditions are fulfilled.

Sometimes court decisions have adopted a very restrictive view and have retained the liability of the building contractors only on the basis of this warranty for ten years if and to the extent that the defect under consideration endangered the strength of the building. Some other court decisions have adopted a more liberal position and admitted liability of the building contractors on the basis of article 1792 if it appeared that the defects were sufficiently major to render the building unfit for its normal purpose.

Other more recent decisions have applied new criteria for assessing the seriousness of the defect, namely the extent of the damage and the cost of the repairs.

It appears from the foregoing that the courts have adopted a case-by-case approach.

(2) Article 2270 of the Civil Code repeats that architects, building contractors and other persons bound to the principal by a building contract are liable for the main parts of the building during a warranty period of ten years and for the smaller parts of the building during a warranty period of two years.

In this context, the question has been raised whether court proceedings have to be initiated within a short period from the date of the discovery of the latent defect.

This question has been thoroughly discussed. Many court decisions have admitted that in the realm of the defects covered by the ten-year warranty, it is sufficient to initiate proceedings within this period of ten years.

Other court decisions have maintained that court proceedings have to be initiated within a shorter period, both if the latent defect qualified as a defect affecting a major part of the building and if the defect qualified as a defect affecting a minor part of the building.

It seems for the moment that there is no clear-cut solution. It would appear, however, that the courts are tending to relax the requirement that an action should be brought within a short period from the discovery of the latent defect.

(3) Difficulties have also appeared with respect to those latent defects which affect main parts of the building but do not appear to endanger the strength of the building. In this respect also the law has not up to now taken a clear-cut position.

There are, however, a certain number of arguments that the limitation period during which court proceedings could be initiated in connection with this kind of defect is thirty years, with the additional requirement that the court action has to be brought within a short period from the date of discovery of the defect.

(4) As far as the ten-year and two-year warranty periods are concerned, it is generally admitted that the limitation period may only be interrupted by starting court proceedings or by an acknowledgment of liability on behalf of the architect or the building contractor.

(5) Similar solutions exist with respect to the liability of a seller in the case of the sale of a building that is due to be constructed (*vente d'immeubles à construire*).

Article 1646–1 of the Civil Code provides that the seller of a building which is due to be constructed is liable for latent defects covered by the liability of the architects, building contractors and other persons bound by a building contract during a period of ten years from the date of the taking over of the work by the purchaser and that he is liable for latent defects relating to the minor parts of the building for a period of two years from the date of the taking over of the work by the purchaser.

According to the same article of the Civil Code, these warranties will accrue to successive owners of the building.

If the seller undertakes to repair the defect, the purchaser (or the successive owners) will not be entitled to sue the seller in order to have the contract rescinded or in order to obtain a reduction of the price.

The action deriving from article 1646–1 of the Civil Code may be exercised by successive purchasers only against the original seller.

2.12 Guarantee concerning services

Since services are excluded from the Directive, contracts for services will continue to be governed by the normal rules relating to contracts for services.

The rules of liability which govern this matter are similar to those examined in relation to sales contracts.

Professional contractors are therefore under an obligation to comply with the technical standards applicable in the field of their activity, to inform and advise their customers and to anticipate and, where necessary, to warn against, any possible damage.

As explained above, the Luxembourg courts have expressed the opinion that the warranty for latent defects provided for under article 1641 of the Civil Code is the specific application to sales contracts of more general principles of law. The rules governing the warranty for latent defects will therefore also apply to contracts concluded for the supply of services.

3. LIABILITY IN TORT

(1) Provisions relating to extra-contractual liability are contained in articles 1382–1386 of the Civil Code.

(2) As a rule, the victim of damage is not free to choose between liability in contract and liability in tort in order to recover in respect of the damage suffered. Under Luxembourg law, the liability in contract and the liability in tort are both mutually exclusive.

Where there has been a contractual relationship between the person who is held liable and the plaintiff, the plaintiff should start proceedings against the responsible person on the basis of the contract, even though this rule is not a mandatory one.

This means that normally only third persons may sue the manufacturer of a defective product on the basis of liability in tort. Third persons are defined as being all those who are not parties to or beneficiaries of a contract.

(3) The manufacturer of a defective product may be held liable in tort either on the grounds of articles 1382 and 1383 of the Civil Code, which provide for the liability of those who cause injury to others as a result of a tortious breach or negligence, or on the grounds of article 1384(1) of the Civil Code, which provides that a person may be held liable for an injury caused by a product or an object which he has in his custody (*garde*).

3.1 Liability in tort based on articles 1382 and 1383 of the Civil Code

The plaintiff harmed by a defective product must establish fault or negligence on the manufacturer's part. This fault or negligence may relate to design or manufacturing defects and also includes the failure of the manufacturer to inform or warn consumers of the possible dangers of the product.

The French courts have been very liberal and have considered that a manufacturer has, in fact, an obligation to deliver products free of defects and to know all the possible defects of his products. This means that the mere fact that the manufacturer has carried out quality control procedures and the necessary checks to ensure the maximum safety of his products will not necessarily exclude him from liability.

This also means that the plaintiff will only have to give evidence that the product under consideration was defective. To date, the Luxembourg courts have not reached similar judgments. However, as the Luxembourg courts tend to follow the jurisprudence of the French courts in such matters, it can be expected that in a similar situation the Luxembourg courts will adopt the same kind of solution.

3.2 Liability in tort based on the Civil Code article 1384(1)

(1) The Luxembourg courts have developed from article 1384(1) a principle of strict liability in respect of injury caused by products which a person has in his custody (*garde*). In most cases, this person is the legal owner of the product.

Article 1384(1) of the Civil Code applies generally to all kinds of products, whether dangerous or not, whether defective or not. For instance, electricity is considered in this respect as being a 'product'.

Article 1384(1) of the Civil Code relates to the rules of evidence which have been developed: a person is not only held liable for products in his custody, but also for damage caused by the products.

(2) The following distinctions have been made:

(a) If there has been no physical contact between the inanimate product and the injured party, the injured party has to give evidence:
   (i) of the intervention of the product in causing the damage; and
   (ii) the abnormal character of the inanimate product.

   Possible defences are: evidence either of the interference of the injured party or of a third party, or of the occurrence of an extraneous cause (as, for example, 'force majeure').

   However, the defence of interference of a third party is only possible provided that such interference has the characteristics of a 'cas de force majeure'. In order for an event to be considered as being a 'cas de force majeure', it has to be unforseeable, irrefutable (incontrovertible) and extraneous to the injured party.

(b) If there has been contact between an inanimate product and the injured party, the injured party has to give evidence of the abnormal character of the product, ie of the abnormal position, installation or behaviour of the said product.

   Possible defences are: evidence of the passive role of the product, or of an extraneous cause.

(c) If the product was in movement and there has been no contact between the product and the injured party, the injured party will have to give evidence:
   (i) of the intervention of the product in the occurrence of the damage; and
   (ii) that the movement of the product is the cause of the damage.

   Possible defences are: evidence either of the interference of the injured party or of a third party, or of an extraneous cause.

(d) If the product was moving and came into contact with the injured party, it is presumed that the injured party has given evidence of the existence of the causal link between the damage and the accident.

Possible defences are: evidence of the passive role of the product, or the intervention of a third person or the injured party.

(3) In order to indemnify a plaintiff who has no direct contractual link with the seller or the manufacturer, the courts have developed the concept of custody of the structure of the product (*garde de la structure*) by which the manufacturer's or the manufacturer's liability continues after delivery of the product.

The manufacturer is deemed to be able to control the internal structure of the product and check whether the product could be used without danger, even though he no longer owns or possesses the product. This concept of custody has been applied only to products with inherent internal dynamic forces capable of becoming dangerous by exploding or imploding, such as bottled gas, television sets, soft drink bottles, etc.

The plaintiff will only have to show a causal relationship between the damage suffered and the product.

The 'custodian' of the product may exonerate himself in proving that the damage was due to an external cause, such as a mistake committed by the plaintiff. His liability will be reduced if he shows that the plaintiff has contributed to the damage.

3.3 Exclusion or limitation of liability

Clauses excluding or limiting the liability of the manufacturer have no effect on an action based on tort liability.

3.4 Limitation period

The limitation period for tort action is the general limitation period of 30 years from the date the damage occurred.

4. VICARIOUS LIABILITY

In accordance with article 1384(3) of the Civil Code, employers who may be manufacturers are liable for the damage caused by their employees in the course of the employees' duties.

They may disclaim this liability by proving that they were vigilant in exercising their authority or in choosing their employees.

They are also discharged if the fault or negligence occurred outside the course of the employees' functions.

In any case, employers have recourse against such employees and may recover all the damages they have had to pay on behalf of the employees provided the employees can be found guilty of wilful misconduct or of gross negligence (article 47 of the Law of 24 May 1989 on Work Contracts).

5. CRIMINAL LIABILITY

In the case of an accident resulting in death or personal injury caused by a defective product, the manufacturer may be subject to criminal liability, for instance, if he is found guilty of gross negligence or non-compliance with regulations.

The manufacturer of a dangerous product (and consequently also the seller who is aware of the danger) who does not warn the purchaser of the product's dangers or who does not withdraw the product from the market when it has caused personal injury, may be subject to criminal sanction.

In this respect it should, however, be stressed that only individuals are liable to criminal sanction.

The managers of a firm may be held liable either for their personal acts and decisions or for their failure to organise manufacture in such a way as to avoid a breach by an employee.

6. SPECIAL REGULATIONS

The Luxembourg legislature has adopted a series of specific regulations in the field of, amongst others, foodstuffs, cosmetics, drugs and medicines, environment, consumer protection etc.

We do not purport to be exhaustive in describing these various specific regulations, we will only briefly summarise some of these provisions and highlight their main features.

6.1 Law of 25 August 1983 on Consumer Protection

(1) Pursuant to article 1 of the Law of 25 August 1983, a clause or clauses contained in a contract entered into between a professional supplier of consumer goods, whether durable or not, or a professional supplier of services and a private end-consumer, which will unevenly balance the contract to the prejudice of the consumer, is considered to be excessive and as such is presumed to be null and void.

(2) The Law of 1983 lists clauses which in particular are to be considered as being excessive. These include clauses:

- (a) excluding or limiting the legal warranty for hidden defects;
- (b) increasing the amount of the claim of the professional supplier in the event of possible court proceedings;
- (c) prohibiting the consumer from suspending the whole or part of the payment of amounts due to the professional supplier if the latter does not fulfil his obligations under the contract; in particular, and according to article 2 of the Law of 25 August 1983, clauses excluding or limiting the legal warranty for hidden defects;

(d) authorising the professional supplier of products or services to amend or to terminate unilaterally the contract without any specific and valid reason stipulated in the contract;
(e) authorising the professional supplier of products or services to determine unilaterally whether or not the products or the services are to be considered as conforming to the contract;
(f) excluding the right of the consumer to terminate the contract if the product has not been delivered or the service has not been rendered within the time promised or within a reasonable or a customary time if no period has been specified;
(g) authorising the professional supplier to determine unilaterally and without any valid and specified (in the contract) reason the date of performance of his obligation;
(h) providing that the products may not correspond to specifications for the consumer or to the sample or to the use which has been specified by the consumer and accepted by the supplier or to their normal use, if no specification has been given;
(i) extending the duration of the contract for more than one year if the consumer does not terminate the contract at a given date;
(j) providing that the price will be determined at the moment of delivery or at the moment of successive deliveries or authorising the professional supplier to increase the price, even with regard to objective criteria, if the consumer does not at the same time have the right to terminate the agreement if it appears that the final price will be excessive for the consumer compared to the price which could be expected by the consumer at the conclusion of the contract;
(k) forcing the consumer to submit his complaints to the supplier within a period which appears to be unreasonably short;
(l) excluding the right of the consumer to terminate the agreement if the supplier is under the obligation to repair the product and he does not comply with this obligation within a reasonable time;
(m) excluding the right of the consumer to sue the supplier in the normal jurisdiction;
(n) authorising the supplier to substitute for the product or the service promised in the contract a different product or service, save if this has been specified in the contract and been formally and explicitly accepted by the consumer;
(o) placing on the consumer the burden of proof which normally has to be borne by the supplier;
(p) forbidding the consumer to set off his obligation to pay against the obligations of the supplier;
(q) imposing on the consumer a minimum consumption obligation in a contract providing for the delivery of gas, electricity or fuel;
(r) which, in relation to the liability of the professional supplier, who commits himself to accomplish a specified work on a product sent to him for that purpose, exclude or limit his obligation to take care of the product which has been remitted to him and to return this product to the consumer after the completion of the work;
(s) pursuant to which the consumer waives his rights to file a claim against the repairer of the product or against the person having done work on

this product, on the basis of the legal warranty of the professional seller with respect to the work which has been accomplished by him and the new spare parts supplied by him;

(t) pursuant to which a private end-consumer consents to a transfer of the supplier's claim to a third person and gives a waiver with respect to the rights and defences which he could assert against the third party.

(3) Notwithstanding any clause providing to the contrary, the provisions of the Luxembourg Law of 25 August 1983 apply to sales contracts and to contracts for the supply of services entered into between professionals, whether established in Luxembourg or not, and private end-consumers having their normal residence in Luxembourg:

(a) if the conclusion of the contract has been preceded in Luxembourg by a specific proposal or by advertisement, and if the consumer has accomplished in Luxembourg all the requisite acts for the conclusion of the contract; or

(b) if the contracting party, being a consumer or his representative, has received the order in Luxembourg; or

(c) if the contract qualifies as a sale of products and if the consumer, being resident in Luxembourg, has travelled to a foreign country and has placed the order in this foreign country, subject to the condition that the journey has been organised by the seller with the purpose of inciting the consumer to enter into a sales agreement.

(4) If the parties to the contract did not specifically designate the applicable law, the agreement will be governed by Luxembourg law if the consumer has his normal residence in Luxembourg and if the contract has been concluded in the circumstances described above under 3(a) to (c), above.

However, these provisions do not apply:

(a) to transportation contracts; and

(b) to contracts for the supply of services if the services to the consumer are to be rendered exclusively in a country other than the country of the consumer's normal residence.

The provisions do, however, apply to those contracts offering a global price for combined services of transport and accommodation, ie package tour holidays.

(5) The professional supplier who has been successfully sued in proceedings initiated by a private end-consumer, where the application of a clause or of a combination of clauses has been declared excessive and null and void by a final judgment, may be sentenced to a fine between LUF 3,000 and 100,000.

(6) According to article 11 of the Law of 25 August 1983, descriptions of the main features and characteristics of a product or of a service provided in written form and in advertisements, as well as any kind of warranty offered, are deemed to be part of the contract relating to the product or to the service, even though the information or publicity originates from the manufacturer, the holder or the operator of the trademark, or any other professional person at a prior stage in the supply chain to the seller or the supplier of the product or services concerned.

If the product or the service does not conform to the description provided, the consumer is entitled to ask for the rescission of the agreement or a reduction of the price.

6.2 Law of 25 September 1953 relating to the Reorganisation of the Control of Foodstuffs, Drinks and Common Products

By virtue of this law, the manufacturing, preparation, transformation, trade and distribution of all kinds of foodstuffs, drinks or drugs used by men and animals, all kinds of consumer products and clothes, cosmetic products etc are submitted to control by the Luxembourg authorities in the interests of public health.

In pursuance of the provisions contained in the Law of 25 September 1953, a certain number of decrees have been adopted.

6.3 Specific regulations relating to pharmaceutical products and drugs

(1) The manufacture, preparation, import and sale of pharmaceutical products are subject in Luxembourg to authorisation obtained in advance from the Ministry of Health.

On the one hand, the manufacturer or the importing body needs to obtain a licence and on the other hand, each product needs to be approved separately by the Ministry of Health.

(2) The manufacture of medicines has to be done under the effective control of a responsible pharmacist, who has been approved by the Ministry of Health. The entity having obtained an authorisation to import medicines into Luxembourg has to entrust either a pharmacist or an approved laboratory with the control of the conformity to specifications of each and every portion of medicine imported. This condition is, however, not applicable if medicines are imported from another Member State of the EC.

The manufacturing or the importing entity must also comply with a series of conditions in order to ensure that the authorised operations are made under irreproachable conditions regarding employees, premises and equipment.

(3) An information sheet has to be enclosed with every medicine which is distributed in Luxembourg which has to state the counter-indications, the side effects and the kind of precautions the recipients of the medicines need to take.

However, there is no formal requirement to appoint a specific person in Luxembourg or elsewhere to report to the Ministry of Health on the recipients' medical reactions.

(4) Although the development risk defence is not permissible under Luxembourg law, the possibility cannot be excluded that the Luxembourg courts might follow French jurisprudence with respect to damage caused by pharmaceutical products and might consequently admit that a manufacturer may not be held liable for damage caused by a pharmaceutical product if it was the only one to enable a certain kind of medical treatment.

6.4 Liability in the nuclear field

The Paris Convention of 29 July 1960, as well as all subsequent international treaties and conventions regarding liability in the nuclear field, have not yet been ratified by the Grand Duchy of Luxembourg.

6.5 Liability arising from certain industrial activities

(1) A Grand-ducal Decree of 10 April 1987 has implemented EC Directive 82/501/EEC of 24 June 1982, as amended by Directive 87/216/EEC of 19 March 1987 relating to the risks of major accidents deriving from certain industrial activities.

The Grand-ducal Decree gives a list of activities which make use of one or several dangerous substances and which present a risk of major accident.

(2) According to article 3 of the Grand-ducal Decree of 10 April 1987, a manufacturer is under an obligation to take all the requisite actions in order to avoid major accidents and in order to limit the possible consequences of such accidents for persons and the environment. The manufacturer must at any time be in a position to show that he has determined the existing risks of major accidents, that he has taken all the appropriate safety measures and informed, trained and equipped all persons working on the site to ensure their safety.

(3) The manufacturer is also under an obligation to inform the authorities immediately of any major accident and he must communicate to the authorities all the circumstances of the accident and the dangerous substances which have been used. He must also give the authorities any information which might be of help in evaluating the significance of the accident and its effect on people and the environment.

7. LAW ON DEFECTIVE PRODUCTS OF 21 APRIL 1989

(1) The basic principle of the Law on Defective Products is contained in article 1, which is worded as follows: 'The manufacturer is liable for the damage which has been caused by a defect of his product.'

(a) Article 2.2. gives a more explicit definition of 'the producer' as being the producer of a final product, the producer of a raw material or the producer of a component, as well as any person presenting himself as the producer in affixing to the product his name and trademark, or another distinguishing sign. For all products which have been manufactured in a non-EC country, the importing person or entity is considered, for the purpose of this law, as 'the producer'.

If, however, it is not possible to identify the producer of the product, each and every supplier is deemed to be the producer save if he can indicate the identity of the producer or of his own supplier to the plaintiff within a reasonable time. The same applies with respect to a product which has been imported from a non-EC country, if this product does not indicate the identity of the importer, even though the name of the producer is indicated on the product.

(b) Article 2.1 of the Law on Defective Products defines the product as any movable product even if it is incorporated in another item of movable or immovable property. The same article specifies that the term 'product' also includes electricity.

As a consequence of this definition of the product, it is important to stress that the Law on Defective Products does not apply to immovable or to intangible products.

(c) A product is defective if it does not offer the safety which could reasonably be expected with regard to all the circumstances and in particular with regard to:

(i) the presentation of the product;
(ii) the use of the product which one could reasonably expect;
(iii) the time of putting the product into circulation.

The law specifies that a product may not be regarded as being a defective product by the mere fact that later on a more sophisticated product has been put into circulation.

(d) The damage which will be taken into consideration is defined as each and every type of damage save:

(i) damage deriving from nuclear accidents;
(ii) damage caused to the defective product itself;
(iii) damage caused to a product or the destruction of a product where this product:
- is of a kind which is not normally aimed at private use or consumption; and
- has not been used by the plaintiff mainly for private use or consumption.

(2) As a consequence, it appears from the foregoing that the main purpose of the Law on Defective Products is to grant protection to private end-consumers.

(3) On the basis of the Law on Defective Products, the plaintiff may seek compensation of the entire corporal damage he has suffered without any restriction and of damage to his property with a deduction of an amount of approximately LUF 22,500.

(4) Pursuant to article 3 of the Law on Defective Products, the plaintiff will have to prove the damage, the defect of the product and the causal link between this defect and the damage.

(5) The producer will not be held liable in accordance with the Law on Defective Products if he succeeds in establishing:

(a) that he did not put the product under consideration into circulation;
(b) that, with regard to the circumstances of the matter, it would be admitted that:
(i) the defect that caused the damage did not exist at the very moment when the product was put into circulation by him; or
(ii) that the defect appeared at a later stage;
(c) that the product has neither been manufactured for sale or for any other means of distribution with an aim to profit on the part of the producer nor has it been manufactured or distributed within the parameters of the producer's professional activity;

(d) that the defect is due to the conformity of the product to mandatory rules established by the authorities; and
(e) where the person qualifying as the producer is the producer of a component, that the defect is attributable to the conception of the final product of which the product under consideration is only a component, or is attributable to the instructions which have been provided by the producer of the final product.

(6) If the damage has been caused jointly by a defect of the product and by the mistake of the plaintiff or of a person under his responsibility, the producer will only be held liable to the extent the defect of the product has contributed to the damage.

The producer may not, however, be relieved totally from his liability if he establishes that the damage has been caused jointly by a defect of the product and by the intervention of a third party.

(7) According to article 5(3) of the Law on Defective Products, the liability of the producer in accordance with the provisions of this law may not be restricted or excluded by a contractual clause.

The Law on Defective Products does not require the existence of a contractual relationship between the plaintiff and the producer.

The liability of the producer will only pass through the existence of a contractual relationship between the producer and some other person. Putting a product into circulation can therefore be seen as putting it on the market through a contract transferring its ownership.

(8) Finally, if, on the basis of the provisions of the Law on Defective Products, several persons are liable for the same damage, they will be held liable jointly and severally according to article 6 of the Law on Defective Products.

(9) Article 7 of the Law on Defective Products provides for the following *limitation periods*:

(a) an action for compensation on the basis of the Law on Defective Products has to be started within three years from the date when the plaintiff has or should have discovered the damage, the defect and the identity of the producer (this limitation period may be suspended or interrupted in accordance with the general rules contained in the Civil Code);
(b) the right of the plaintiff to obtain compensation under the Law on Defective Products will expire at the end of a period of ten years from the date on which the producer put into circulation the defective product which caused the damage, except if during this period the plaintiff has started court proceedings against the producer.

(10) Since, in accordance with article 8 of the Law on Defective Products, the provisions of this law do not prejudice the rights of the plaintiff to claim compensation for the damages suffered on the basis of the common law of contractual or extra-contractual liability or on the basis of any other specific laws on liability, it seems obvious that the provisions of the Law on Defective Products will give rise to a certain number of difficulties. At the time of writing, the Luxembourg courts have not yet had the opportunity to examine and address the questions raised by these new legal provisions.

(a) On the one hand, it is clear that all matters other than those related to the safety of a product will only be subject to the rules governing liability in contract or liability in tort. As has been explained above, certain products do not qualify as products as defined by the Law on Defective Products and the rules laid down by the Law on Defective Products do not apply to damage caused by a product which has not been put into circulation. The main purpose of the Law on Defective Products appears to be the protection of the private end-consumer against the defects of a product which is intended for private use or private consumption.

(b) On the other hand, it appears also that the provisions of the Law on Defective Products will only constitute a part of the more general rules governing liability for defective products.

However, there may be situations where compensation for damage caused by a defective product may not be possible pursuant to the general or the specific provisions contained in the Civil Code and a plaintiff might, therefore, sue the producer on the basis of the Law on Defective Products.

(c) Finally, it is not yet clear whether and to what extent it will be possible to take advantage of both the provisions contained in the Civil Code relating to liability in contract and liability in tort for latent defects and the provisions contained in the Law on Defective Products.

(d) As the rules and principles governing liability in contract and liability in tort are highly developed in Luxembourg, it is possible that the provisions contained in the Law on Defective Products will be of only limited practical interest and impact. In any case, it seems for the time being premature to make final statements in this respect.

CHAPTER X

Netherlands

S S H Wibbens Esq

A M G M Mallant Esq
R Stoeckart Esq
Van der Kroft cs
Keizersgracht 561–563
1017 DR Amsterdam
Netherlands

Tel ++ 31 20 626 48 47
Fax ++ 31 20 620 36 58

CHAPTER X

Netherlands

1. INTRODUCTION

The introduction of new legislation on product liability in the Kingdom of the Netherlands is taking place at the same time as a comprehensive renewal and restructuring of the Civil Code, which is transforming it into an up-to-date system relevant to the modern world.

The Dutch Civil Code was based directly on the French Civil Code, which was introduced into this country by Napoleon Bonaparte's brother Louis Napoleon. It is a long way, however, from there to the introduction of the new legal rules which will henceforth govern the general area of the law of property and of obligations, which will enter into effect in the Netherlands by 1 January 1992. These new rules will contain a separate section dealing with product liability based on the provisions of the Directive.

The section which follows will deal exclusively with the present rules.

1.1 Overview of legal provisions relating to defective products in the Netherlands

As in most other European States, the law and practice relating to defective products is dealt with through the law of contract, tort and product safety, together with industrial self-regulation schemes and the criminal law.

In contract law, the rules governing damage caused by a defective product are found, in so far as they relate to inadequate performance, in articles 1279 ff of the Civil Code and, in respect of hidden defects, in articles 1540 ff of the Civil Code. Where compensation is payable for defects arising from a third party's demands or any legal restriction on the product in question, articles 1528 ff of the Civil Code apply. All these rules come into effect, of course, where the purchaser, hire-purchaser or exchanger of the product has a direct contractual relationship with the manufacturer or the supplier of that product.

In principle, it is also possible for the contracting party, if he succeeds in proving negligence or fault resulting in damage on the part of the seller, to invoke the rules relating to tort liability, which are currently contained in article 1401 of the Civil Code. In this case, an obligation also comes into being, but instead of arising from a contract, it arises from the Civil Code. It was as a direct result of a long-running series of decisions by the Supreme Court (*Hoge Raad*), that the aforementioned system of tort liability was also made available to those persons who have not had a direct contractual relationship with the manufacturer or seller. The various implications of this system are dealt with later in this chapter in section 3.

Since 1935, the Dutch Government has caused a number of laws to be adopted for the purpose of protecting the consumer, the most relevant of which is the Goods Act 1935. This provides a mechanism enabling the Government on a legal basis to adopt general executive measures in order to ensure that all products meet certain standards of health and safety and, under the provisions of the 1935 law, regulations governing cosmetics, toys and many other specific products have been brought into effect.

The Goods Act places obligations on both manufacturers and suppliers to take the necessary preventative measures and imposes criminal sanctions for breach of obligations through the law relating to economic offences (*Wet Economische Delicten*). As this law now stands, traders in dangerous products can be required to issue appropriate warnings to the public and, where the authorities issue the warnings, in the event of their failing to comply with this obligation traders can be required to bear the cost. The legal system of the Netherlands also includes specific laws concerning the safety of persons in many other situations.

A system of self-regulation applies to quite a large degree in the business world of the Netherlands, the establishment of the Travel Industry Guarantee Fund by those involved in that particular line of business being a case in point. Many other sectoral arrangements have come into being as a result of pressure exercised with varying degrees of flexibility by the authorities, such as the system of self-regulation which applies in the advertising of cigarettes and of alcoholic beverages, and arrangements which constitute a natural corollary to certain rules contained in the Goods Act, such as the product-recall system.

Provisions can be found in the Penal Code concerning:

(a) the distribution of products which are harmful as a result of their defects; and
(b) the knowledge of such defects by those involved.

Article 174 lays down penalties ranging from a maximum of 15 years imprisonment to relatively high fines in respect of the person who sells, offers for sale, supplies or distributes goods in the knowledge that these are harmful to human life or health, and who fails to draw attention to their harmful nature. The criminal intent and guilt on the part of the person concerned must be proved by the public prosecutor.

Article 175 of the Penal Code lays down penalties for the person who is to blame for selling or supplying or distributing faulty products which are harmful to human life or health without the buyer and/or the recipient being aware of these harmful effects. Since this offence is related mainly to criminal negligence, the penalties reflect this, ie imprisonment or custody of a maximum of six months or moderate fines. In the case of both types of offence, the penalty is increased where the person affected dies as a result. This criminal negligence is expressed in more general terms in articles 307 and 308 of the Penal Code. Article 307 provides that the person through whose fault the death of another person has occurred shall be punishable by imprisonment for a maximum period of nine months. Serious injury sustained through the fault of another person is punishable by imprisonment of that person for a maximum of six months.

2. LIABILITY IN CONTRACT

2.1 Liability for statements made at the offer stage prior to the conclusion of the contract

The conclusion of a contract is normally preceded by a certain period in which negotiations take place. For the vast majority of purchases made by consumers, negotiations are confined to the unilateral announcement of an offer, whereupon the other party makes his acceptance coincide with the conclusion of the contract. Dutch case law accepts that the statements and the conduct of the parties during this pre-contract stage can be relevant to the relationship between the parties, regardless of whether the contract is eventually concluded or not. Thus it is possible to establish, in the light of these (mutual) statements, whether or not there actually exists a particular obligation between the parties. It is also possible for the terms of a contract between the parties to be analysed by a judge in the light of the statements which were made and the events which occurred during the pre-contract stage.

More generally still, the Civil Code provides that relations between the negotiating parties are governed by the principle of good faith and by the rule that the negotiating parties must conduct themselves in a manner which is compatible with their mutual legitimate interests.

Given the history of the importance attached in the Netherlands to the pre-contract stage, it is appropriate that the question of liability for certain statements made or information given at the time of offering goods for sale should be governed by the law of obligations. The reason for this is that even though the basis for liability laid down by the Directive remains articles 1407a ff of the current Civil Code, an action for damages arising from certain statements can also be based on the pre-contractual relations between the parties.

2.2 Outline of contract law, relevant to defective products in the Netherlands

Book Four of the current Civil Code regulates a wide variety of day-to-day transactions which involve products such as the sale of goods, hire-purchase agreements and rental agreements. The transactions in question are each based on agreements made between two or more parties.

The two main obligations that rest on the seller are (a) to supply the product sold, and (b) to provide the necessary guarantees relating to the burdens or defects to which the product in question might be subject. Article 1527 of the current Civil Code further defines this guarantee. It has two aspects: the purchaser is entitled (a) to quiet and undisturbed possession of the article sold, and (b) for the product to be free from hidden defects or, where such hidden defects exist, to claim that the sale is void.

Whenever defects with varying degrees of seriousness occur in the goods which are sold, exchanged or rented, the possibility arises of unsatisfactory performance on the part of the party who supplied, exchanged or rented out the product in question. This concept of unsatisfactory performance, by virtue of article 1302 of the Civil Code, is a nullifying condition of the contract which is always deemed to arise in the case of contracts if one of the parties fails to perform his obligations. This does not lead to the automatic rescission of the contract, although this is a remedy that the dissatisfied party may ask for on the hearing of his case. This nullifying condition may arise as a result of a failure to supply the goods within the agreed time limit or, in the case of a combination of products, as a result of supplying part of the goods only. The supplying of a defective product is therefore to be regarded in Dutch contract law as a failure on the part of the supplier to fulfil his contractual obligations. Where the defects are noticeable immediately, the nullifying condition contained in article 1302 of the current Civil Code may be directly relied upon as a result of which the contract in question can be rescinded by the courts or by agreement between the parties. Other options available for the purchaser are to request repair of the defective product, delivery of replacement goods or the payment of compensation for the defect.

The distinction that is made in the Netherlands between goods that are defined by their type ('unascertained' goods) and goods that have been clearly selected by the contracting parties is relevant to a purchaser in deciding which compensation option to select. Such individually defined goods are mostly secondhand goods, unique products, such as antique vases, paintings and the like, and mass-produced goods which have been singled out by the contracting parties.

Where an individually selected product is defective so as to make it unsuitable for the purpose for which it is intended, the purchaser has the option either to return the product and reclaim the sale price, or to retain the product and reclaim part of the sale price. Only in the event that the purchaser can prove that the seller was aware of the defects in the product can the seller be required to indemnify the purchaser for all expenses, damages and interest which arise from these defects. This is the so-called 'hidden defect' rule. Dutch case law has established that complaints concerning hidden defects must be lodged within a very short period after the discovery of the defect.

It is a further requirement that the defect must exist, at least embryonically, at the moment of sale. Essentially this rule protects the selling party, since the compensation payable is restricted to specific circumstances and such losses as can be proved by the purchaser, and also the purchaser may only lodge his complaint within a short period. Accordingly, case law only allows the 'hidden defects' exception to be raised by the seller where the sale concerns an individual item. Only when the product bought is identifiable as such – and therefore not interchangeable – does the case law allow such defence to be raised.[1]

2.3 Contractual warranties relating to quality of goods and safety of goods

The extent to which the seller incurs certain obligations relating to the quality of the product sold by him is subject to whether the transaction in question

1 Supreme Court (*Hoge Raad*), 16/5/1952, Nederlandse Jurisprudentie ('NJ') 1953, 459.

concerns the sale of 'unascertained' goods – such as mass-produced goods – or the sale of individually selected goods.

In relation to unascertained goods, the rule is that such goods must satisfy such standards as are normally required for the purpose of normal use.[2] In a well-known Dutch case involving the defective performance of a washing machine, the court sought to reflect the type of terms found in the Vienna Convention concerning International Sales of Goods and stated that:

> 'there can only be held to be unsatisfactory performance where the goods supplied, even though they do not differ from other goods of this type, do not correspond to the substance of the agreement because they do not possess the properties which the purchaser was entitled to expect on the basis of the agreement.'

The wide scope for invoking the doctrine of unsatisfactory performance is not open to the purchaser in the case of individually selected products, where the product has hidden defects making it impossible for it to be used for the purpose for which it was intended, or where it has defects which reduce the possibility of using it to such an extent that the purchaser would never have purchased the article had he been aware of them. Unless it is expressly excluded by the selling party in the sales contract, the purchaser may rely upon the hidden defects provisions in article 1540 of the current Civil Code mentioned above, in which case the purchaser may choose between giving back the product (and getting his money back) or keeping the product and making the seller repay part of the price. The rule stated in article 1540 is not mandatory, and accordingly the seller may exclude his liability by means of an appropriate exclusion clause.

On the other hand, the seller may also increase his liability by means of a warranty or guarantee, sometimes referred to as a 'positive warranty'. In this way the 'hidden defects' rule can be circumvented in respect of individually selected goods, and the purchaser may invoke the doctrine of 'unsatisfactory performance' where the relevant guarantee obligation is not fulfilled. Exercising the latter option will give him more opportunities to act against the seller from the point of view of both the time limits and the possible remedies involved,[3] as in the case of mass-produced 'unascertained' goods.

Another situation where case law has developed eminently practical remedies is that of the duty of the seller to provide information. Depending on the professional involvement of the seller and the expertise of the purchaser, the courts decide on the extent to which the seller is under an obligation to draw the purchaser's attention to certain potential defects and aspects which denote inferior quality. It will come as no surprise to learn that this case law has resulted mainly from the sale of secondhand cars.

2.4 Breach of contract for supply of defective products

The seller's duty to provide the relevant guarantees extends to both legal and actual defects in the product sold. Thus, the seller must indemnify the

2 Supreme Court, 29/1/1971, NJ 1971, 221.
3 Supreme Court, 10/5/1963, NJ 1963, 288: folding machines.

purchaser of the product in relation to third parties who claim to have certain rights or claims on the product or on part of it. It is possible as a matter of contract for the seller to exclude this guarantee of good title. However, the seller remains liable for any claims by third parties which result directly from his own previous acts or omissions.

The supply of a defective product is generally treated in Dutch law as constituting a form of unsatisfactory performance, since a seller who fails to fulfil his obligations (within any agreed time limit) infringes the buyer's rights and has consequently unsatisfactorily performed the contract. In principle, the seller of a defective product is automatically held to be in default. An order requiring the proper performance of the agreement is unnecessary in such cases. The fact that the seller is in default opens the way for payment of compensation.

Each shortfall in the performance of an obligation compels the seller to compensate the purchaser for the damage incurred as a result – unless the shortfall cannot be ascribed to the seller, as is the case with an event of *force majeure*.

The seller may invoke the doctrine of *force majeure* if a shortfall in the performance of the contract arose which was not his fault and for which he is not liable. However, it has already been noted that, in the case of the supply of 'unascertained' goods which contain hidden defects, there can be no question of shortfalls within the meaning attributed to it here, ie that of an absolute impossibility to perform the obligation. It is perfectly possible for the manufacturer or seller of industrially mass-produced goods (ie 'unascertained' goods) to replace the product which has not been properly supplied and therefore fulfil his obligations.

It is clear that, as one writer puts it:

> 'a defendant cannot rely upon *force majeure* in cases where, as a result of the agreement concluded between parties, he is held liable for the occurrence of the event which prevents performance. This is the case, for example, where the seller of a product warrants the absence of a certain harmful property and it appears, subsequent to delivery, that the product supplied actually does possess that harmful property.'[4]

Where a purchaser incurs costs in preventing damage arising from a defective product, he can claim this in addition to claiming a replacement product. Also, where it is impossible for the supplier to replace the product, the purchaser will have a claim in damages. If replacing the article is completely impossible, any damage suffered can be compensated or, if no damage has been incurred, the agreement can be rescinded. If the latter occurs, the sale price must be reimbursed to the consumer.

In summary, depending on the circumstances of the case, the purchaser of a defective product has a choice between various possibilities:

(a) he may apply to the courts for

4 Hartkamp, Asser-Rutten I, p 264.

(i) the performance of the obligation by repair;
(ii) compensation by way of replacement for unsatisfactory performance; or
(iii) both performance and payment of additional compensation;

(b) he may apply to the court for the rescission of the sale on grounds of unsatisfactory performance plus compensation.

The rules in the Civil Code on the subject of compensation in cases of unsatisfactory performance are in part the same as those which apply in the case of tort liability.

2.5 Damages for breach of contract

The term 'damage' is understood as meaning the disadvantage which the purchaser suffers from the unsatisfactory performance of a defective product. The principle adopted in assessing damage is that the purchaser should be put back as closely as possible into the state he would have been in if the damage-causing event had not occurred. The damage for which the seller has to indemnify the purchaser will include material damage and any other disadvantage to the extent that the law makes provision for such compensation. As well as in destruction, damage and business loss (ie reduced competitiveness), unsatisfactory performance may also result in immaterial damage. The person affected must, in the present state of the law, be compensated for such damage within certain limits. These limits are not closely defined and are open to judicial interpretation.

Material damage includes both losses which the disadvantaged person has actually suffered and loss of earnings. In addition, compensation may also be obtained in respect of any reasonable expenses incurred in attempting to prevent or restrict the damage which has occurred precisely as a result of the event on which liability is based. Reasonable expenses incurred in establishing damage and liability or in obtaining a settlement out of court, as well as costs lost by the product being defective, must also be compensated.

The extent of the loss to be compensated is established by a valuation carried out by the court. The court will compare the situation resulting from the defect with that which would have prevailed if the product had not been defective.

The Dutch system of compensation is very precise and it has been said that literally every penny and/or item of damage suffered must be stated and proved. Such items of compensation are calculated on the basis of invoices, declared expenses and costs of repair, as well as generally accepted flat rates in relation to current market value, as is the case with cars.

In view of the difficulties inherent in calculating earnings or expected earnings, the lawyers and the injured plaintiff will be at the mercy of the damage assessment by the court, which will determine the amounts *ex aequo et bono*. This compensation can be spread over many years by means of payment by instalments on the part of the defendant or his insurer.

2.6 Burden of proof

When it comes to allocating the burden of proof, the general principle is applied that the person who alleges damage must prove it in its entirety. As a result, the plaintiff must, in the case of unsatisfactory performance, make sure that all the elements of the damage are attributable to the defect, and at the same time he must, if he brings an action for compensation, state and prove the damage in question. These elements include the extent of the damage and the defective nature of the product, in addition to which the so-called 'causal link' between the damage and the defect will need to be proved by the plaintiff. In most cases, unsatisfactory performance consisting of a failure to supply within the agreed time limit, or of partial supply, will be relatively easy to prove, whereas damage resulting from unsatisfactory performance will be more difficult to prove. Further, the purchaser, whether he is a consumer or not, may experience considerable difficulties in proving the causal link between the defect and the damage. As will be discussed later, the draftsmen of the Directive have made an individual consumer's task easier on this point. Moreover, this process of easing the burden of proof on the part of the consumer had already started in the shape of a series of judgments in the Dutch courts which had, incidentally, been developed in the context of statutory liability under article 1401 of the current Civil Code.

2.7 Exclusion or limitation of liability

In the context of the attribution of the damage to the person who supplied the defective product or who performed the contract in an unsatisfactory manner, a doctrine based on the degree to which the consequences were reasonably foreseeable was invariably applied by the Supreme Court in cases of unsatisfactory performance from 1927–1970. Gradually, this theory was replaced by a more modern doctrine under which the person who unsatisfactorily performs the contract is liable for the damage caused if this damage, taking into account the circumstances of each particular case, could be reasonably attributed to him. This theory of attribution sought to give the courts the necessary degree of freedom to judge each case on its merits when determining liability and the extent of the damage to be compensated.

Having discussed above the general trends as they appear in cases where the parties made no agreement amongst themselves concerning unsatisfactory performance and the resultant damage, it is necessary to take a closer look at the world of business, where the parties involved frequently agree not to invoke unsatisfactory performance or to claim the resulting compensation.

The principle of freedom of contract leaves all traders free to exclude their own liability. Such an exclusion or limitation of liability requires the consent of both parties and, in the absence of such consent being given, the non-mandatory provisions of the Civil Code will apply.

The businessman obviously tries to limit or completely exclude the implications of any damage caused by his products whether they arise in contract or tort. Nevertheless, such exclusion or limitation of liability requires the consent of the other party, and it is precisely on this point that the present-day manufacturer can be faced with problems. Such exclusions must be clearly worded, and in practice usually arise by means of a written notice, either on the packaging itself or on an insert. If the exclusion clause is to be enforced, this clause must be addressed in a very precise manner to the purchaser, as a result of which the latter may be deemed to have given his consent. It is precisely in this area of so-called standard terms and conditions that there exists a conflict between the interests of the producer and those of the consumer. It has been remarked that:

> 'it hardly appears to be an exaggeration to state that it is precisely the clauses limiting liability, as they regularly appear in standard terms and conditions, which have resulted in the standard terms and conditions being regarded as a problem area. Moreover, the proposed new Civil Code contains provisions in relation to consumer purchases which represent a real danger for such unilateral exclusions or limitations.'[5]

In the meantime the Supreme Court has ruled that the exclusion of the guarantee against any hidden defects is not valid in respect of defects which were known to the seller.[6] More recently, the court gave a ruling which went even further[7] which concerned a defect not known to the seller, but one of which he should have been aware in view of his expert knowledge. In that case, in spite of the existence of an exclusion clause, the seller was held to be liable by the Supreme Court.

2.8 Limitation period

Under the principle of freedom of contract, it is possible to exclude or limit liability for claims brought within a shorter period of time than that prescribed as the limitation period in the Civil Code.

The judicial concept of legal prescription of an obligation arising from a contract or from the law is specifically regulated in articles 2004 ff of the current Civil Code. The general period of negative prescription after which proceedings cannot be brought used to be 30 years. In the new version of the Civil Code, this period is reduced to 20 years. The prescription period begins at the time when the claim becomes defined or with effect from the day following that on which the event triggering the start of the prescription period took place.

More especially with regard to product liability, article 1407g of the new law states that a legal claim in respect of product liability may not be brought after the expiry of three years. This expiry date does not depend on the attitude of the parties, but is a statutory limit which is mandatory in law. In view of the short period of product liability, it appears reasonable that this period only begins as of the moment when the victim gains or is able to gain a clear understanding of the damage and the identity of the producer responsible. The term 'producer' should be understood to have the widest possible meaning. After the passing of this three-year limit, an injured party can still invoke the tort liability for several more years.

5 Van Empel, *Produktaansprakelijkheid*, p 40.
6 Supreme Court, 26/5/1950, NJ 1951, 18.
7 Supreme Court, 7/5/1982, NJ 1983, 509.

Especially in the new Civil Code, a large number of specific rules exist relating to limitation of actions, particularly under consumer legislation. Furthermore, claimants have a number of means at their disposal of interrupting a period of limitation once it has started, such as writing a warning, serving a writ or taking legal proceedings. Acknowledgment of fault by the defendant also interrupts the period of limitation. Where the exercise of a certain right is not subject to a compulsory legal expiry date as is the case in articles 1407a ff of the Civil Code, the producer can contractually specify in his standard conditions or elsewhere that this right must be exercised within a certain period, or else it will expire.

Lastly, it is important to mention here that under article 1407g the right of an injured party to lodge a complaint lapses after ten years from the day following the day that the defective product was brought into circulation.

2.9 Liabilities for third parties and vicarious liability

2.9.1 Vicarious liability

In principle a defendant is liable for any breach of contract or for any tort caused by sub-contractors, employees and agents that he has used to perform his contract. If the defendant has excluded his liability in contract, he cannot be held liable for the breach of contract of one of his helpers, collaborators and/or employees.

In the case of a breach of contract, the party not in breach can claim the loss and damage he has suffered from the party in breach and can also require him to perform the contract in accordance with its terms. The circumstances in which the party that has committed the breach can hold a third party liable will depend on the type of contract between these two parties. Exclusions of liability between the first two parties in the form of a 'force majeure' clause are very common but do not always take into account the non-performance of a third party. Trading companies may often use conditions of purchase in which they preserve the right to attribute responsibility and liability for defects to their suppliers, in case they themselves are summoned to perform and find themselves in a position that they cannot do so as a result of a breach of contract by their suppliers.

The liability of a third party may be important where non-performance of an obligation goes together with an obligation arising from the law, eg in the case of a reckless fault by a subordinate or a third party engaged to execute a contract. Where an employee or a contract carrier recklessly damages products in transit to a retailer, the supplier can be held liable for deficient supply (non-performance) and the executing employee or carrier can be personally liable for negligence (tort). If the supplier has excluded his liability for non-performance in the contract, the employee or carrier can be held liable. To avoid such an unsatisfactory outcome for the consumer, the new Civil Code contains rules which prevent such exclusion of liability.

Where liability is based principally on non-performance, a defence that the third party has caused the non-performance seems reasonable. In section 3.8, below, we shall see that in other circumstances the relevant employee or third party contractor can be held liable.

3. LIABILITY IN TORT

3.1 Introduction

The new product liability legislation has been implemented in the sections following article 1407 of the Civil Code, therefore close to the other articles which provide for compensation to be paid in specific situations: under article 1406, where death by fault or intent occurs, the surviving spouse, children or parents are entitled to compensation. Article 1407 entitles the injured persons to compensation for serious injuries. In both situations the obligations of the party causing the death or injury arise directly from statute law, of which the principal source is article 1401.

The specific compensation rules set out in articles 1401 ff of the current Civil Code complement the more general compensation rules and provisions which are given in the Civil Code regarding breach of contract. These last provisions also apply in tort.

The new Civil Code of 1992 will contain only one general section, concerning indemnification and compensation, for liability in both contract and tort.

3.2 Outline of relevant tort law giving rise to liability for personal and property damage

Article 1401 of the current Civil Code states:

> 'Each unfair deed, by which another has been damaged, brings the person by whose fault the damage has been caused in the obligatory position to indemnify the damage.'

Article 1402 of the current Civil Code adds:

> 'Any person is responsible not only for the damage that he has caused by his deed but also for the damage which has been caused by his neglect or carelessness.'

The meaning of the term 'unfair deed' has been greatly expanded through jurisprudential developments in the twentieth century. The well-known *Lindenbaum v Cohen* judgment of the Supreme Court in 1919 defined an 'unfair deed' as:

> 'Any act or negligence, that either infringes another's right, or is in contravention of the perpetrator's legal duty or goes against good custom or against the carefulness that should be observed in society with regard to other persons or goods.'

As demonstrated above, the growth of product liability is part of this broad trend, and concepts such as 'conflict with normal legal duty' and 'misuse of rights' also form part of the trend.

Article 1403 of the Civil Code mentions several situations in which liability in tort is imposed on a person who is held responsible in a particular situation: for example, parents or guardians for their minor children who live with them; employers for their servants and employees; teachers for their pupils.

Article 1405 of the Civil Code states that the owner of a building is liable for the damage that may be caused by its partial or total collapse, if this arises as a result of his lack of maintenance or due to a fault in construction or internal decoration. Article 1407 of the current Civil Code contains a provision that gives a person with physical injuries a right to claim material and immaterial damage that has been caused by the injury. Such damage is assessed by the court in the light of the circumstances and the wealth of the persons concerned.

3.3 Causation and remoteness of loss and damage

The principles applying to causation in contract cases apply equally in tort cases. Therefore, the defendant has to compensate the damage resulting from his breach of contract or tort, which means that between the tort and the damage the causal connection has to be proved by the plaintiff. The theory of 'adequate causation' is also important here (see section 2.7, above).

During the 1970s this theory of adequate causation in tort liability was removed from its dominant position and replaced by the ruling that the person who commits a tortious act is liable for the damage caused by that act, so long as the damage can be logically attributed to the tortfeasor. As can be expected, there is a multitude of case law on this topic.

Historically the Dutch courts have held that even where the damage has been caused by an extremely dangerous product, all the elements of the tort, including fault, have to be established in full by the injured party and proved. In modern product liability cases though, the judges have decided that the producer's liability is almost strict.

In the famous *Ford* case, a production fault in the steering mechanism of a car was established and Ford was held liable for all the consequences arising from such defect. The production error by Ford was such as to be contrary to the degree of 'carefulness, that should be observed in society'. Also instruction faults or errors, non-deliberate as they may be, are by now regarded as elements that make a producer and/or the vendor strictly liable.

3.4 Quantum of damage

The basic principles for the assessment of damages in tort cases are the same as apply in contract cases and have been described in sections 2.5 and 2.6, above. When injuries or death occur, the statutory tort rules of articles 1401 ff of the Civil Code automatically apply and bring about an obligation for the party causing the damage to pay compensation.

Torts resulting in personal injury give rise to an obligation to pay compensation for the transport of the injured person, medical and surgical assistance, medicines, hospital expenses, damage to clothing, loss of future income, physiotherapy treatment etc. Immaterial damages can be claimed by an injured person to compensate pain, mental suffering, fear and loss of enjoyment of life.

Torts resulting in death give rise to an entitlement to the direct relatives, such as parents, spouse and children, insofar as they depend on the deceased for income. In the Netherlands, such relatives are not entitled to compensation for immaterial damages, which remain attributable only to the injured person himself.

In the case of damage to property belonging to a person who was not contracting with the party causing the damage, the tort rules of articles 1404 ff of the Civil Code also apply. This damage, including loss of income, is compensated through the rules of contract law on the non-performance of an obligation (see section 2.5, above).

The leading principle in Dutch tort law is that the court should award damages of a sufficient measure to put the injured party back in the position that he would have been in, so far as possible, had the injury or loss not occurred. Again, the assessment of the extent of the damage is to be estimated by the court. The damage not only includes the actual damage, but also future loss and damage.

3.5 Burden of proof

As we have seen above, the general principle remains that the injured party has to provide the proof of all the elements of tort as set out in article 1401 of the current Civil Code. During recent years a gradual shift of the burden of proof in product liability cases has come about in case law, notably concerning the element of fault. Further, in the Netherlands it remains accepted that consumers of industrial products have to prove that the cause of damage was in the product itself.

3.6 Exclusion of limitation of liability

As in many other countries, it is possible in the Netherlands to contract so as to exclude liability in tort. There are certain non-excludable elements such as gross neglect or malicious intention and criminal intention. Considering that much liability in tort arises between parties who have not entered into contracts, this point remains rather academic.

For the manufacturer, however, it is of the greatest importance to protect his interest by introducing as many exclusions as possible into his contract and/or conditions of sale. Many manufacturers try to exclude carelessness and neglect of employees and other collaborators through the use of guarantee documents, although these are frequently ineffective if the provisions of the guarantee contradict a supplier's statutory obligations to a consumer.

A widely known technique for the exclusion of liability is for a manufacturer to point out in writing on the product or its packaging that a particular use of the product concerned may be dangerous and that the user must take precautionary measures. The validity of such warnings will depend on the nature, skill and experience of the user and the means of giving the warning.

In one case a manufacturer of roof insulation material was held liable for damage resulting from his incomplete instructions. Further, it was held that the manufacturer has a duty to inform his distributors of revisions of the instructions for use, where they are up-dated as a result of new information.[8]

8 The Hague Court, 7/12/1979, NJ 1981, 670.

3.7 Limitation period

Currently, the limitation period for tort claims expires 30 years from the moment that the damage occurs. The new Civil Code provides that from 1 January 1992 this period will be reduced to 20 years.

Pursuant to paragraph 2004 of the Civil Code the provisions regarding the limitation period, its suspension and interruption apply in the same way for tort as for breaches of contract. Paragraphs 1407 ff of the Civil Code provide that in product liability cases a limitation period for making claims of three years will apply and such limitation period will run from the moment when the injured person knew or ought reasonably to have known of the damage, the defect and the person(s) liable in this respect.

3.8 Liabilities for third parties

A principal is liable for the fault of any person he uses to perform any of his obligations if such person is unfit or the principal knows that the person might be reckless in certain conditions.

Further, legal theory and practice generally impose a liability on the owners of dangerous installations, products or heavy equipment for the gross neglect or carelessness of their personnel.

4. LIABILITY FOR DEFECTIVE PRODUCTS BROUGHT ABOUT BY BREACH OF STATUTORY REGULATION DESIGNED TO PROTECT CONSUMERS AND/OR TO PROMOTE SAFETY

4.1 Outline of protective regulations

The Netherlands have for a long time adopted administrative regulations to control the socio-economic activities of producers and specify requirements that must be adhered to by different industrial groups such as meat producers, farmers, toy producers and electricity suppliers. The most important Act amongst this legislation is the Goods Act 1935. An important paragraph of this Act is paragraph 14 which gives a clear-cut authorisation to the Dutch Cabinet to designate 'General Decrees' in which very specific requirements for the quality, design and safety of certain products may be laid down. These Decrees also contain rules on the marking and description of food and drinks as well as non-food products, in the interest of the public health or for reasons of fair trading. Nowadays, many of these decrees are greatly influenced by EC regulations.

Together with this very general Goods Act there exists a variety of protective regulations, including the Act on Butchers Inspection, the Act on Agricultural Quality, the Electricity Act and environmental laws such as the Act on Chemical Disposals, the Act on Insecticides and Pesticides, the Act on Dangerous Materials and the Act on Air Pollution. In view of the multitude of these laws it is important to take into account that the Netherlands, after Hong Kong and Monaco, is one of the most densely populated countries in the world.

The enforcement of this socio-economic legislation is mainly in the hands of diverse administrative bodies, such as the Inspectorate for Public Health. These inspectorates work in regional areas with inspectors in order to avoid the sale, consumption and use of goods which are dangerous for public health or are of poor quality and/or composition. The import and transit of dangerous products can be officially forbidden on the same grounds.

The system of public health inspectors and diverse local inspection laboratories is designed to control and detect breaches of statutory regulations. The Goods Act sets out very specific regulations concerning the taking of samples, including a rule that at the request of the producer or supplier a duplicate sample must be taken by the inspector and given to the producer or supplier. Also on the basis of the quality of such a specimen, the head of the local laboratory can take the decision to request the local public prosecutor to commence criminal proceedings.

The public prosecutor will base his prosecution on the Economic Offences Act (*Wet Economische Delicten – WED*). All breaches of the Decrees concerning the denomination, quality and requirements of products, or their import and transit are deemed offences. This means that they are not considered criminal misdemeanours. This important penal distinction means that the defendants, whether they are persons or legal entities, cannot be punished with imprisonment (in the latter case, of their directors) for more than six months or a fine higher than that of the so-called third category – a sum of Hfl 10,000 – or these two punishments combined. Only on rare occasions is the judge entitled to award a higher fine.

In addition to these punishments other socio-economic forms of redress for the situation may be ordered by the judge, such as the payment of the amount of money that the offender has gained as a result of his breach of the Decree. Another measure is to place the enterprise of the defendant under administration. A much more apt measure is that the defendant can be sentenced to perform that which he has unlawfully neglected, nullifying that which has been unlawfully performed, and such action as will remedy the situation, all at the expense of the defendant, unless the judge rules otherwise.

Gradually, some ministerial or cabinet Decrees are being replaced by self-regulatory measures introduced by trade and industry bodies. This gives manufacturers and retailers the benefit of the possibility of a maximum say in the establishment of the Decrees and measures. As a result of European unification, some important Decrees made under the Goods Act are products of Community harmonisation, such as the General Indication Decree and the Quantity Indication Decree.

Exceptionally precise regulations operate in relation to the production and sale of medicines in the Law on Medical Supplies where, logically, the consumer is more protected than under other law. Other laws in this field are the Law on Serums and Vaccines, the Opium Law and also the Law on Human Blood.

4.2 Burden of proof

Since breaches of these statutory regulations on consumer safety generally fall under the scope of the Economic Offences Act, the basic rules and stipulations of the penal law system apply. Therefore the public prosecutor's office will have to construct the case and provide proof of all the elements of the offence on which it bases its claims against the defendant producer or trader.

In the Dutch penal system it is possible for victims or injured persons to join in the procedure by putting themselves forward as the aggrieved person. The penal judge can award the victim an amount of money, which has to be paid by the defendant where he is found guilty and sentenced. The maximum sum that can be awarded to the injured person is nevertheless rather low: Hfl 1,500. This, however, is expected to change in the coming years.

The possibility of joining in criminal proceedings is therefore mostly used by the injured party's lawyers, who automatically receive all the documents concerning the criminal case and with the help thereof can construct their own civil case before the civil court against the same defendants. It is important to keep in mind that in the latter case, the injured's lawyer will have officially to withdraw his claim in the penal case; for once a defendant has been sentenced to pay the maximum penal sum of Hfl 1,500, it is no longer possible to file a civil suit against him.

4.3 Nature of liability, damages or criminal sanctions

The liability of a manufacturer who fails to comply with the regulations or requirements imposed under the various administrative measures on the basis of the Goods Act or other socio-economic laws is in essence no different from liability for tort. Certainly a civil judge having to deal with a civil claim is more likely to assume that accountability and blame lie with the defaulting manufacturer. In addition to the above, the manufacturer can be criminally charged with this offence and suffer penalties, including the withdrawal of a licence. With the introduction of articles 1407a ff of the Civil Code and the reversal of the burden of proof, an injured party in future is likely to refrain from a civil suit in a penal case as described above, whereas earlier he would have tended to make his own civil claim with reference to the possible penal judgment on the basis of the Economic Offences Act.

5. SPECIAL LIABILITIES ARISING IN RESPECT OF PARTICULAR PRODUCTS

Most of the above-mentioned Acts take the safety of the human being and, in a broader sense, the environment into consideration. In order to protect the consumer, laws such as the Goods Act force producers to fulfil many requirements as to the quantity and quality of products as well as diverse labelling requirements in respect of the composition and quality of products. In case such requirements are not met, the import, trade and transport of such products can be forbidden, while in the case of gross neglect the public prosecutor's office can take the producer to court to have the producer sentenced to pay a fine, have his licence withdrawn and/or the condemnatory judgment publicised. When the non-fulfilment of vital requirements causes injury, the public prosecutor can institute proceedings under the general Penal Code, which provides for more severe punishments and higher fines (see section 1.1, above).

It is important to mention here the Act on Nuclear Energy and the Act on Waste Disposal, which emphasise the safety of human beings, flora and fauna and the environment, much more than the consumer as such. It is beyond the scope of this book to describe these and the many other environmental laws in detail.

6. LIABILITY FOR DEFECTIVE PRODUCTS ARISING FROM NATIONAL LAW IN THE NETHERLANDS

6.1 Outline of provisions in the Netherlands

The adaptation of Dutch legislation to the requirements of the Directive was formulated in a Bill that was submitted to Parliament on 11 September 1986 (no 19636). This Bill was accepted in amended form after lengthy discussions on 20 March 1990. It passed into law with effect from 1 November 1990. Bill 19636 has thus taken its place in amending article 1407 of the Civil Code which will be renumbered 1407a–1407j of the Civil Code.

In view of the current changes to the Civil Code and the uncertainty at that time as to the implementation of the new articles, in 1995 an evaluation of the law will be made to see whether it accords with the terms of the Directive.

The law does not contain any interpretation of concepts in cases where the Directive does not itself give an explanation or does not expressly leave the interpretation to Dutch legislation. According to the legislators, interpretation is reserved for the European Court of Justice.

The amendments to article 1407 of the Civil Code are summarised below.

6.1.1 Article 1407a

The producer is liable for the damages caused by a defect in his product, unless:

(a) he did not bring the product into circulation;
(b) he can show that the defect that caused the damage did not exist at the time he brought the product into circulation or the defect arose later;
(c) the product was not manufactured for sale or for any other form of distribution having a commercial objective, nor was it manufactured or distributed in the normal course of trade;
(d) the defect arose as a consequence of the producer making the product conform with compulsory government regulations;
(e) given the state of scientific and technical knowledge at the time of bringing the product into circulation, it was impossible to discover the existence of the defect; and
(f) in the case of a manufacturer of a component, the defect is attributable to the design of the product of which the component forms a part.

The producer's liability may be reduced or eliminated if the damage is caused both by a defect in the product and by the fault of the aggrieved party or a person for whom the latter is responsible.

The liability of the producer is not reduced where the damage is caused both by a defect in the product and by the action of a third party.

6.1.2 Article 1407b

A product is defective where it does not offer the safety that one might expect, taking into consideration:

(a) the presentation of the product;
(b) a reasonable expectation of its use; and
(c) the time at which the product was brought into circulation.

A product is not to be regarded as defective simply because a better product is subsequently brought into circulation.

6.1.3 Article 1407c

The term:

(a) 'Product' means any movable property including electricity, with the exception of agricultural products and game;
(b) 'Agricultural products' means products of the soil, of stock-breeding and of fisheries, with the exception of products which have undergone initial preparation or processing;
(c) 'Producer' means the manufacturer of the finished product, as shall be the producer of a raw material or the manufacturer of a component, or anyone presenting himself as the producer by affixing his name, his trademark or some other distinguishing sign on the product.

Without prejudice to the liability of the producer, anyone importing a product into the EC in order to sell it or lease it out or to supply it in some other way, is regarded as the producer; his liability is the same as that of a producer.

Where it is not possible to determine the identity of the producer, any supplier of the product shall be regarded as the producer, unless he is able within a reasonable time to inform the aggrieved party of the identity of the producer or of the party who has supplied him with the product. In the case of a product imported into the EC, if it is not possible to ascertain the identity of the importer into the EC of that product, any supplier shall likewise be regarded as the producer, unless he is able within a reasonble time to inform the aggrieved party of the identity of the importer into the EC or of a supplier who has supplied him with the product.

6.1.4 Article 1407d

The aggrieved party must prove the damage, the defect and the causal connection between the defect and the damage.

6.1.5 Article 1407e

In the event that by virtue of article 1407a(1), different persons are responsible for the same damage, each of them is responsible for the whole.

6.1.6 Article 1407f

The liability referred to in article 1407a(1) exists for damage due to death or physical injury and damage caused by the product to another object which is normally intended for use or consumption in the private sphere and is chiefly used as such, with the proviso that the damages must amount to at least Hfl 1,236.85.

6.1.7 Article 1407g

The limitation period for making claims is three years; this period starts to run on the day when the aggrieved party becomes aware of the damage, the defect and the identity of the producer. The right to damage compensation lapses ten years after the start of the day following the day on which the producer brought the object which caused the damage into circulation. The same applies to the right of a third party jointly responsible for the damage to seek redress against the producer.

6.1.8 Article 1407h

The liability of a producer towards an aggrieved party cannot be excluded or limited. If a third party who does not use the product in the exercise of a profession or business is also liable to the aggrieved party, the duty of redress of the producer against the third party cannot be limited or excluded.

6.1.9 Article 1407i

The aggrieved party is entitled to damage compensation from the producer without prejudice to any other rights or claims.

6.1.10 Article 1407j

Article 1407a, first section, is not applicable inter alia in case of determination of the amount which may be derived from provisions of any disability insurance policy, the Health Law, the National Health Service Act and the law on disability provision for servicemen.

The right to damage compensation from the producer cannot be subrogated pursuant to article 284 of the Commercial Code, except where the benefit paid by the insurer relates to the liability of the insured party, and another party is jointly liable by virtue of this article. Nor can a party for whom redress or subrogation is ruled out by the first and second paragraphs obtain the rights referred to in the second paragraph according to an agreement or have these rights exercised on his behalf by the entitled party in his name.

Finally, the implementing law of articles 1407a–i contains a second article which states, in so many words, that the liability of producers in respect of products brought into circulation before such law came into effect is regulated by the law that was in effect at that time.

6.2 Description of special or anomalous provisions in respect of product liability law in the Netherlands

6.2.1 Agricultural products

Agricultural products as defined in article 1407c and which have not undergone an initial preparation or processing, fall outside the product liability regulations, such as glasshouse products, vegetables and typical Dutch products such as herrings – not kippers!

6.2.2 Computer software

It remains unclear whether software is to be seen as a product and as such falling within the scope of the new regulations. The view is widespread that software should be seen as information as such, and therefore as a service and consequently cannot fall within the scope of the new regulations. On the other hand, software is easily brought within the scope of the new regulations if it is closely connected with the PC-Board or any kind of component that carries software in it. It seems that in the making of the new product liability regulations, the complexity of software was not clearly considered.

The European Commission recently answered a question put in the European Parliament expressing its view that software is to be considered a product in the sense of the Directive.[9]

6.2.3 Buildings and the liabilities of the constructors thereof

In the Netherlands a specific provision was enacted in the tort section of the Civil Code.[10] It reads:

> 'The owner of a building is liable for the damages caused by the whole or partial collapse thereof, in case this has been caused by a lack of maintenance, or by a defect in the construction or internal decoration.'

As can be seen, the legislators chose to make the owner of the building directly liable; this of course does not prevent the owner starting an action against the builder or decorator of the building for defects brought about by their activities. Such a guarantee procedure may be based on product liability in the future, namely in claims against the manufacturer of a defective component that has become part of an immovable property, eg sash windows, spiral staircases and revolving doors as well as joists and rafters.

So far as buildings and engineering works constructed prior to the adoption of the amendments to article 1407 are concerned the old tort rules will continue to apply in the situation, where no specific cause of the defect in the construction can be found.

6.2.4 Equipment

Defects of a product liability nature could fall within the scope of the Act on Dangerous Equipment of 1952. This Act prohibits the possession, delivery and exhibition of dangerous equipment and the like, which has not been approved and marked with a sign of approval by the appropriate authorities. This Act further provides a basis for regulations concerning the production, import and use of dangerous equipment. For instance, the import has to be notified to the proper authorities. In respect of equipment such as lifts, baling machines and grinding machines, specific control methods and safety requirements are required by this Act.

9 Pub EC 8/5/1990, no C 114, 142.
10 Article 1405 Civil Code.

6.3 Optional provisions in the Directive

The Directive enables divergent national rulings on certain optional points. We set out below the options chosen by the Netherlands listed by articles of the Directive.

6.3.1 Article 2

In the Netherlands, the option to include agricultural produce and game was not taken up, so agricultural produce and game were excluded from the definition of a product in Dutch law. This was contrary to a considerable volume of advice given to the Government.

6.3.2 Article 5

Where, as a result of this part of the Directive, different persons are liable for the same damage, each of them is severally liable, without prejudice to the terms of the national law regarding redress. The redress rules are contained in article 1407j of the Civil Code.

6.3.3 Article 7(e)

The option not to adopt the 'state of the art' defence has not been taken up by the Dutch. This defence has been incorporated by the Dutch Government into the proposed article 1407a(1)(e) of the Civil Code. Therefore where the producer can prove that on the basis of scientific and technical knowledge at the time when the product was brought into circulation it was impossible to discover the existence of the defect, he cannot be held liable. Moreover, the word 'impossible' indicates that heavy demands are made in terms of the furnishing of proof.

6.3.4 Article 8

Without prejudice to Dutch legal provisions regarding the right of redress, the liability of the producer is not reduced where the damage was caused both by the defect in the product and by the action of a third party, where this party uses the product as a private person. But this does not apply to traders and professional persons.

Where national law concedes the validity and scope of an agreement sharing liability between the various producers or links in the chain of production and distribution, they are free to proceed with such an agreement. Liability exclusions are valid, as these may be used by suppliers of components.

6.3.5 Article 9

Compensation arrangements are left to the national legislators. The amount of financial compensation for pain, suffering and reduced enjoyment of life is very difficult to determine under Dutch law. The normal practice here is to fall back on precedents. Every three years, a fairly complete review is given in the monthly journal *Verkeersrecht* (Traffic Law) published by the General Dutch Motorists' Association.

6.3.6 Article 10

The first paragraph of this article states that a claim for damage compensation is excluded after three years. It will be necessary on the basis of applicable national legislation to see whether there can be any question of suspending or interrupting the limitation period, as detailed in article 1407g of the Civil Code.

6.3.7 Article 13

The rights which the aggrieved party can derive from national legal rules are left unimpaired insofar as these go beyond the Directive in terms of the protection afforded. The producer must therefore continue to take account of the rules which apply in the Netherlands.

This is specified in article 1407i, which states that without prejudice to articles 1407a–1407j, all the other national rights and claims to damages remain available to the injured party. According to circumstances, claims may be made for: damage to the defective product itself; damage to other products in a public environment such as offices, factories, etc and damage of a value lower than Ecu 500. Therefore the new legislation does not affect the existing possibility of claiming damages based on contract liability or tort liability, both with limitation periods of 30 years.

It is possible for business parties to contract to share the relation to the burden of product liability. It is also possible to insert a clause providing for liquidated damages for product liability.

6.3.8 Article 16

This article leaves it for each Member State to determine the maximum amount to which the liability of the producer for damages resulting from death or physical injury caused by identical articles exhibiting the defect should be limited. In the Netherlands there is no upper limit.

The Parliament was of the opinion that a reasonable elaboration of article 16(1) will lead to a system of apportionment. This will result in all timely claims being divided proportionally.

7. PRACTICAL EFFECTS EC PRODUCT LIABILITY LAW WILL HAVE ON VARIOUS BUSINESSES IN THE CHAIN OF SUPPLY OF PRODUCTS

7.1 Liability of the various producers

The definition of 'producer' in article 1407c increases the number of persons and businesses which may be held liable for defective products and their resulting damage.

In the process between development of the product and its final distribution, the following persons or institutions are involved:

(a) The designer is not mentioned amongst the persons or institutions that might be held responsible as producer in paragraph 2 of article 1407c.

As design defects are probably more difficult to establish than production defects, the exclusion of the designer seems to be a just choice, also taking into account the Dutch legal system in which an employer is responsible for his employees and/or collaborators.

The possibility of holding a designer or architect liable for tort in case of damage resulting from professional faults remains.

(b) The supplier of component parts or any other sub-contractor is considered a producer in the sense of article 1407c(1). It is likely that between these and the producer of the final product some contractual arrangements on the apportionment of product liability will be made.

(c) Anyone who presents himself as the producer, by attaching his name, his trademark or any other distinctive sign to the defective product is also listed as a producer in the sense of article 1407c. It has been made clear that trademark licensors or franchisors are not considered producers on the ground that they themselves do not bring the disputed product into circulation, nor do they attach their names to the products. This is undertaken by other persons and they receive royalties or other means of income from this arrangement.

In order to prevent claims and liability, it is advisable that the product itself is labelled with the names of the licensor and the licensee, and the actual producer.

(d) The producer of the finished product is always liable. It is completely immaterial whether he makes the component parts himself or buys them from others. Therefore, the assembler is also considered a producer of the finished product.

Nevertheless, an assembler of imported pieces, working under close instruction and supervision of a foreign producer, whose trademark is attached to the product, is likely to have contracted with the foreign producer concerning product liability issues. However, such a contract does not prevent the assembler from being held liable if a defective product is produced.

(e) The above-mentioned producer is often a person or institution that presents itself as the producer by fixing its trademark or name to the product. Where the product, often bought from contractors in developing countries, is brought into circulation by himself, then there is no legal problem. Such a problem might arise, however, in a case where the producer is granted a licence by a third party. It will not always be easy to detect who the liable producer is. In such cases, however, the local distributors, wholesalers or retailers can be held liable.

(f) In the new legislation, the importer of products into the Community is to be held liable in the same way as the producer. This is despite the fact that an importer is purely a trader and may have nothing to do with the actual manufacturing of the product. As a result of this new legislation the importer needs to spend a considerable amount of his time record-keeping. Further, he must pay great attention to the quality, safety, storage and transportation of the products imported by him. Also, he will have particular responsibilities concerning instructions and labels and the languages in which they appear.

(g) The new legislation also indicates that anyone who distributes a defective product can be held liable in a case where it is difficult or impossible to establish the real producer. Such distributors are entitled to communicate the identity of the producer or their supplier within a reasonable period.

The same rule applies in the case of a product that has been imported into the Community, but where the importer's identity is impossible to establish. Any supplier of such product may be held liable and it will be for him to provide the identity of his preceding supplier.

Again, in the above-mentioned cases, the importance of record-keeping must be emphasised.

It has also been said that, in connection with the limitation period of ten years, an accurate check will have to be kept as to which products have been brought into circulation and when. It would be advisable to keep such records for an even longer period to provide a basis for contesting claims based on the strict liability of the producer lodged after the expiry date. Further, importers and distributors should keep records for at least ten years of the identity of those preceding or following them in the chain of supply. This information can be used if necessary to pass liability along the chain or to contest any claimed liability.

Whether a producer can recover damage compensation from whoever precedes him in the chain of supply or from some other party might have to be decided under the rules of international contract law. The distribution of the burden of proof among the parties concerned will therefore often be a deciding factor. To avoid problems regarding the question of how and to what extent possible damage shall be borne, contracts usually contain limitation clauses. Business enterprises, in contrast to consumers, are considered to be adequately capable of fending for themselves and contract law offers the scope to agree on limitations by taking them up in general conditions of purchase or of delivery.

It is possible under the new legislation, albeit to a limited extent, to exclude liability for certain damages, eg by means of a perpetual exemption clause, even in the relationship with the consumer. In particular, this can be in relation to damage to real estate, damage to the product itself and damage below the amount of the damage threshold, as well as damage claimed after the three or ten-year limitation period.

When the new Civil Code comes into effect on 1 January 1992, a set of rules on general conditions will be introduced. This forthcoming legislation will be clearer on the question of which clauses will or will not be acceptable in the general conditions of supply. In essence, the law states that oppressive clauses in general conditions which are unreasonable can be nullified. This flexible concept of oppressive clauses is elaborated into a black list of unreasonably oppressive clauses and a grey list of clauses which are suspected of being unreasonably oppressive. A consequence of the introduction of these new rules is that businesses will have to reconsider their general conditions.

8. COMPARISON OF THE EFFECTS OF PRODUCT LIABILITY LAW WITH THE PREVIOUS POSITION IN CONTRACT AND TORT

Under legislation prior to articles 1407a ff, liability for defective products was derived from the contract between the parties or from tort law. In the absence of fault or neglect by the producer, an aggrieved party could bring a claim where the selling party had made exaggerated statements about the characteristics or qualities of the product.

A typical feature in tort is gross neglect or an element of fault. The aggrieved party must prove this. With the introduction of the Directive into Dutch law, three important changes will occur, namely:

(a) The required gross negligence on the part of the producer is replaced by risk liability. Therefore, in proceedings against a producer the aggrieved party merely has to show the defect, the damage and the causal link between them. No longer is blame or negligence on the part of the producer a precondition for establishing the latter's liability.
(b) The aggrieved party has a wider choice of legal and natural persons whom he can approach for financial compensation, since the term 'Producer' is considerably widened under the Directive.
(c) The defectiveness of a product is more widely interpreted. A product is already defective where it does not offer the degree of safety expected of it, and this depends on the presentation of the product, on the use that may reasonably be expected to be made of it and on the time at which it was brought into circulation.

Where the new legislation is not applicable, liability for defective products in contract and tort still undoubtedly has a role to play. In the first place, this will apply to damage caused by products used outside the consumer sphere. The product liability rules do not apply, for example, to damage inflicted on machines in commercial use and to damage to the defective product itself. Further, the tort rules can be invoked in the case of damage suffered by defective agricultural products which has not yet undergone initial processing. The same applies to damage caused by defects which were not foreseeable when the product was brought into circulation given the state of technical and scientific knowledge at the time. Finally, the damage claim cannot be based on the new product liability rules where the limitation period under the Directive is exceeded or where the damage is below the threshold level or the damage is damage to real estate and damage to the defective product itself.

The aim of the Directive is to improve the position of the consumer and not that of the insurance company. The insurer compensating the damage caused by the defective product to the victim cannot therefore derive any rights from the product liability law (article 1407j of the Civil Code) or take the place of the policyholder (subrogation). After paying out compensation to the injured party, the insurer will have to claim this amount from the producer on the basis of the general law of contract or tort, with a proportionately heavier burden of proof. In practice it is possible that the judge may tend to apply a more flexible distribution of the burden of proof where an insurance company participates in such a damage compensation process. For the time being, however, no certainty can be given in this respect.

With regard to aspects of the damage that are not compensatable or not covered by the insurer, the producer may have to take into account the possibility of claims being brought against him directly by the injured person, rather than by the insurer.

As a rule, the producer will be held liable by means of receipt of a registered letter in which the aggrieved party states his damage and the claimed amount of compensation and in which the producer is requested – and insofar as necessary summoned – to pay this amount before a certain date, failing which he will also be held liable for further costs and interest. Where the producer fails to comply, the aggrieved party can serve a writ of summons.

At this point, one may conclude that the forthcoming introduction of the new liability regime is not expected to lead to dramatic changes. Rather, there is the prospect of a shift of emphasis, as a result of which producers will be more conscious than hitherto of the possible risks of bringing products onto the market. One can also make the observation that consumer lawyers specialising in product liability will generally be more prepared to take harsher procedural measures, such as levying attachments, than the insurance companies are at present.

9. RISK MANAGEMENT IN THE NEW ERA OF PRODUCT LIABILITY

9.1 Internal risk management

In an industrialised world, the seriousness of the possible consequences of a defective product and the responsibility of the producer are such that producers must continuously and systematically examine, monitor and remedy the possible causes of defects in their products. They should realise that time and again human factors and changes to the daily routine appear to be the major internal causes of product defects within the production process.

Furthermore, recent events, accidents and occurrences with defective products have shown that besides the damage to the directly injured parties there is also a danger of damage rebounding on the producer in the form of a severely impaired reputation, sometimes drastic negative publicity and loss of business, which may result in a loss of market share and a heavy drop in share value.

The following contains a number of general indications as to how a producer can take internal measures to reduce the risks of defective products.

9.1.1 Quality control

Obviously, dealing with manufacturing and quality defects in products is a first priority. Good quality control, whether or not involving sampling, either during or at the end of the production process, is clearly very important. It is also advisable to check the quality of incoming raw materials, additives, semi-finished products and the like immediately upon arrival. Recently there has been a tendency in the foodstuffs industry to provide product components with a 'history' description, similar to that found in the aviation industry, for example.

As a rule, the last check before the product is finally dispatched and brought into circulation is a thorough outgoing inspection, which means not only a check to see whether its quality has been affected by storage but also verification that products have the correct labelling for the intended customer.

Strict internal quality control of this kind will undoubtedly place the producer in a stronger position in the arduous process of furnishing evidence that must be expected in legal proceedings relating to product liability.

9.1.2 Documentation

A possible defence of the producer against liability for damage caused by a fault in its product may be that, given the state of scientific and technical knowledge at the time when the product was brought into circulation, it was impossible to foresee or discover the existence of the fault. Therefore it is essential that the producer should itself keep pace with and store documentation on the state of scientific and technical knowledge at the time of manufacture and supply of the product.

Taking external advice on the matter will undoubtedly strengthen the producer's position when employing this defence based on state of the art.

Documentation on inspections carried out during the production process and on outgoing inspections for, for example, the keeping of sample analyses or texts of product specifications, may also serve as proof to support the argument that the product was not defective at the time it was brought into circulation.

9.1.3 Record-keeping

In connection with the various limitation period expiry dates, the producer is advised to keep an accurate check of when it brought the product into circulation. In view of the period of limitation specified in the Directive, such records should be kept for a minimum of ten years. Indeed it is advisable to keep records for a longer period, so that claims made after the expiry of ten years based on the risk liability of the producer can be contested on a sound basis.

In order to pass liability along the chain or to contest it, the supplier and producer should keep records for at least ten years of the names of those that precede or follow them in the chain of supply. It may also be possible to indicate the name of the producer or importer on the product, so that it is possible to name a prior link in the distribution chain to third parties without difficulty.

9.1.4 Warning notices, operating instructions and service manuals

The presentation of the product and the use to which it may reasonably be expected to be put are two factors in particular which may be of importance in answering the question of whether the product offers the level of safety which one is entitled to expect. Information relating to a product must therefore correspond as far as possible to reality.

Operating instructions may play an important role in causing accidents due to incorrect or deviant use or use not intended by the producer. Therefore these must be written in the appropriate national language, in unambiguous terms, and at the same time must closely correspond with the producer's aims and the consumer's expectations.

9.2 The handling of consumer claims

In the event that, despite good quality control and clear information, a defective product is brought into circulation and causes damage to the consumer, the producer should ask itself what the best means of remedying the situation might be.

Generally speaking, when an incident occurs, it should be possible to settle the matter of the damage by amicable means. The producer should certainly ask itself whether the method of production is capable of being improved. In this sense, a good complaints procedure is very important to the development and improvement of products.

Where, however, the damage and the number of interested parties appear to be significantly more extensive, then other measures will be unavoidable. One must look into the question of whether there is a serial defect. If this may be the case, irrespective of official requirements, it will be necessary to consider whether the products in question will have to be recalled. It goes without saying that it is highly important to keep a strategy to hand to cope with such situations, and to keep good records in order that distributors and customers can be traced. The codes or serial numbers which are now customary can be used to trace customers, so as to be able to recall a series of products reasonably easily.

9.3 Exclusion of liability and claims under indemnity contracts

As we have seen, it is possible for producers and dealers to agree on mutual exclusion clauses relating to product liability. This will determine in advance who is liable for damage, regardless of who is sued. Where such a distribution of damage is made, the insurance cover and the premiums of the various producers should be in line with the risk to be borne.

The new product liability rules also provide the possibility, albeit to a limited extent, of excluding liability towards consumers. In particular, this might concern transactions relating to real estate, economic damage outside the private sphere, damage to the product itself and damage below the damage threshold, as well as damage claimed for after the three or ten-year limitation periods. It is necessary to bear in mind in the case of exclusion clauses in the relationship with the consumer that the extent to which these are admissible depends, amongst other things, on the mutual commercial positions and relationships between the parties and the consumer's and consumer organisations' degree of awareness of the scope of the clause.

Otherwise, trading partners are free to pass liability on to one another; it may even be agreed that a low level of blame on the part of one of the parties has no effect on the exclusion. Generally speaking, the limit of exclusion of liability lies at the level of gross negligence bordering on deliberate intent.

A new section in the Civil Code concerning general conditions is expected to be introduced on 1 January 1992. This law will deal with the question of which clauses will or will not be acceptable in general conditions in relation to consumers. In brief, oppressive clauses which are unreasonable can in principle be nullified at the request of interested consumer organisations.

As regards the question of which national law is applicable to the content of international agreements, the conflict rules in force in the Netherlands leave it up to the parties to determine, within certain and not unreasonable limits, the law that is applicable to their agreement. Where no choice of law is made, the applicable law shall be the law of the country where the party executing the principle feature of the contract has its residence or its place of establishment. Where no principal feature of the contract can be discerned, or where it appears from the circumstances of the case that the agreement is more closely connected with a third country, the applicable law shall be the law of the country with which the agreement is more closely connected, taking all the circumstances into account.

9.4 Insurance

9.4.1 Special provisions

A separate insurance policy covering product liability risks is not customary in the Netherlands. In return for payment of an additional premium, cover for the risk of damage caused by a defective product may in most cases be incorporated into the usual business liability policy.

Following the introduction of the new product liability regime, as regards the product liability risk, three risk groups will be defined, based on factors such as the nature of the product, the production process, the current extent of the product liability risk and the nature of the business. The amount of the premium will depend on the group to which the producer belongs. It is expected that the premium for the group with the highest risk factor will increase by 15%.

9.4.2 Outline of the nature of cover

In general, the insurance will cover the consequences of both contractual liability and tort liability. However, damage limited to the product itself is not covered, nor is economic loss resulting from that damage. The latter damage category includes damage resulting from the recalling, replacement, improvement and repair of the product. These damages come under normal business risk.

As regards the territory covered by the insurance, one may choose, for example, the Netherlands, Europe or worldwide. In the case of worldwide cover, the US and Canada will almost always be excluded, because of the high risk of costly damage awards which are common there. For exports to these countries, special arrangements have to be agreed which are usually on the basis that cover of this specific export risk is provided on condition that premiums are payable at the same level as those demanded by local insurers for cover of the same risk.

Between the moment of the occurrence of damage and the time of claiming under the product liability insurance, a considerable time-lag is not unusual. The most common form of policy for overcoming problems relating to this time-lag is the 'claims-made' policy. This covers the damages occurring during the period of the insurance and within a specified earlier period where such claims are reported during the period. Variations are possible, such as extra cover for damage occurring before the starting date of the insurance or for damage not occurring until after the end date.

9.4.3 Limits on cover excluding limitation of liability paid under contractual indemnities

The sum assured is the maximum amount that can be paid out per damage-causing event. Generally speaking, an insurance policy should contain limitations as to the maximum number of claims, and the total amount resulting therefrom, that are covered in a certain period. In principle, the limitation of cover is based on three issues:

(a) a limit per event;
(b) a limit on the cover of a complex event in the form of a serial damage clause;
(c) a limit per insurance period.

9.4.4 Serial damages

Where a number of damage claims have the same cause, the insurance company will in principle cover the overall damage as if it were the result of a single damage-causing event. The insurance policy will usually contain a maximum limit for damages resulting from a complex event of this sort.

9.4.5 Cover for recall of defective products

The costs of measures for recalling products because of identified faults or as a precaution are generally regarded as normal business risks and are not covered by the insurance. However, taking such steps can be regarded as damage-limiting action, so that these costs could indeed be compensated by the insurer under the normal business liability insurance. The extent to which the recall of defective products is a damage-limiting action, and therefore covered by the insurance, should be considered according to circumstances.

9.5 Limitation of liability through corporate structure

A common legal form of company in the Netherlands is the so-called *besloten vennootschap met beperkte aansprakelijkheid* (BV) – private company with limited liability. The most important characteristics of this form of company are that the shares are registered shares and not freely transferrable, that paid-up capital of at least Hfl 40,000 is required and that the liability of shareholders is limited. The last of these characteristics is of particular importance in this context. The shareholders can be called upon to pay up their shares in full, but in principle are not liable for the debts of the company. Even those acting on behalf of the company, such as directors and others, are in principle not personally liable for claims against the company. Only the company itself is fully liable for its debts.

Such limited liability, especially of shareholders, makes the legal form of the BV highly suitable for conducting business to which risk is attached. Since there is nearly always some risk involved in bringing products onto the market, certainly in the case of imports from outside the EC, it is advisable to make use of this legal form. In the case of claims against a subsidiary BV, the parent company is in principle not involved, even if the subsidiary BV goes bankrupt. Valuable goods which are used by the subsidiary BV can in principle be safeguarded by leaving ownership of such goods with the parent company.

In connection with the foregoing it should be pointed out that the legislation on abuse of these rules in the Commercial Code has been considerably extended since 1987. Since then an administrator can be held severally liable for the company's debts where the administration or the administrator has performed its, his or her task in an improper manner and it may rightfully be assumed that this was a significant cause of the bankruptcy.

Shareholders, members of the supervisory board or other persons who are closely involved in company policy and who thus act as if they were directors likewise run the risk of being claimed against in the event of improper administration. In certain circumstances the parent company may be regarded as the policymaker of a bankrupt subsidiary and can be claimed against on this basis.

In general it can be said that where the parent company is closely involved in the policy of the subsidiary or where the possibilities of redress against the subsidiary are reduced because of its actions, such as withdrawing goods from the subsidiary, the parent company can be held liable for the debts or shortcomings of the subsidiary. A connection is then established between the extent of its influence on policy and liability for damage.

CHAPTER XI

Norway

Wilhelm Matheson Esq

Wiersholm, Mellbye & Bech
PO Box 400 Sentrum
0103 Oslo 1
Norway

Tel ++ 47 2 410 600
Fax ++ 47 2 400 600

CHAPTER XI

Norway

1. INTRODUCTION

1.1 Overview of the law relating to defective products in Norway

In Norway, liability for defective products is governed by three areas of law: the Product Liability Act, the Purchases Act and the common law. These three areas of law are not mutually exclusive and overlap in some instances of their application.

The Norwegian Product Liability Act (*Produktansvarsloven*) was passed in 1988 (Act 104 of 23 December 1988, governing product liability) ('PLA') and came into force in 1989. The PLA regulates questions of liability for damage caused by defects in general products and medicines sold or made available for distribution after its coming into force.

The Purchases Act (*Kjopsloven*) (Act 27 of 13 May 1988, governing the sale of goods) ('PA') also regulates a vendor's liability for any items he may sell. The provisions of the PA governing liability for damage caused by defective products can be applied to only a limited extent in cases where the product damages the environment.

Product liability is not a new concept in Norwegian Law. Liability for damage caused by defective products derived from the early so-called common law relating to damages. Producers, wholesalers and retailers of products can be made liable for any injurious characteristics the product may have which result from negligence or a breach of duty imposed on manufacturers to check the product is free from defects prior to distribution. The common law is still of importance in fields which are not regulated by the PLA.

1.2 Definition and classification of terms

In general usage, the term 'product liability' is defined as the rules regulating a producer's, retailer's or other party's (eg importer's) liability for damage resulting from a defective product he has put into circulation. This liability is, however, regarded as different from the liability for defects regulated by legislation governing purchases. The latter liability exists, for example, if a new washing machine fails to start when turned on, having been satisfactorily delivered and installed. If, however, the clothes in a washing machine are torn to shreds by a defect in the machine, a claim for damage to the clothes will be covered by the product liability law. The boundary between the two types of liability can sometimes be difficult to define. In Norwegian law, product liability is generally understood to apply to movable property and not to real estate. It does, however, apply to building and construction materials incorporated into land and buildings.

2. LIABILITY IN CONTRACT

2.1 Introduction

As already mentioned, the PLA is the key Act governing liability for compensation as a result of damage caused by products. This applies regardless of whether a contract exists between the parties or not. Where a contractual relationship exists, however, limited product liability can be claimed against the vendor pursuant to the PA. Contractual liability deriving from the PA is supplemental to and, in some cases an alternative to, a liability deriving from the PLA.

2.2 Outline of contract law relevant to defective products in Norway

Apart from the PLA, generally only the PA is relevant in relation to contractual claims for product liability. Provisions of the PLA will be dealt with in greater detail under section 6 below. The following paragraphs will therefore concentrate on the provisions of the PA.

The PA primarily deals with claims for damage to and defects in the product itself.

The PA has limited scope for application where damage is caused to items other than the product itself. For example, the PA cannot be applied where a defective product has caused personal injury. Further, damage to property which affects the item's environment generally lies outside the scope of the PA.

There will, however, be a small area which is covered by both the PLA and the PA. Provisions of the PA governing liability can be applied if damage is caused to items which have a close physical or functional relationship with the product. For example, if clothes are damaged by a defective washing machine, a claim can be made against the vendor to replace these. Furthermore, the damage must be of an extent which could be reasonably predicted at the time of the sales agreement. Where a sale of a defective product is made to a consumer, the consumer can also claim under section 84 of the PA against the producer, the wholesaler, the distributor and other parties providing a link in the sales chain. Such a claim is made upon the basis of a right to take over the seller's recourse/claim for reimbursement against any person or business who was at a prior stage in the distribution chain. The injured person is entitled to make his claim directly to the party at the prior stage in the distribution chain provided the seller could have made a claim for reimbursement from the party at the prior stage in the distribution chain. None of the businesses in the distribution chain can exclude their liability to the consumer for any claims made against it in contract law. In practice, the only way a producer can reduce his liability for such claims is for him to claim an indemnity from someone higher up the distribution chain. In this instance the two sets of regulations supplement each other – but the injured party will only be entitled to receive compensation once.

This being the case, the possibilities for applying the PA to matters of product liability are very limited in practice. This limitation must be borne in mind quite clearly when reading the following explanations of the provisions of the PA governing damages.

2.3 Liability for pre-contractual statements or representations

According to the PA, the vendor can be held liable for damages vis-à-vis the purchaser if the sales item does not correspond to the conditions of delivery, correspondence, contract negotiations and other preconditions upon which the agreement is based (cf PA section 17).

The vendor can also be liable if the goods, their characteristics or their use do not correspond to the statements which the vendor made in his publicity materials or elsewhere which can be assumed to have exerted an influence on the purchaser (cf PA section 18). Such statements do not have to be in writing. However, in order for the statements to provide a basis for liability, they must take a concrete form and be proved adequately. Many of the statements given in conjunction with the marketing of a product will be so general and vague that it will be difficult to use them as a basis for claiming liability for damages.

2.4 Breach of contract for supply of defective products

The purchaser's right to claim damages in the event of defects is regulated by section 40 of the PA. This provision imposes a strict liability for defects. However, the strict liability does not apply if the purchaser proves that the failure was due to an impediment beyond his control. This liability relates solely to direct losses. Damages for indirect losses can only be claimed according to the general liability (cf PA section 67(2); see below). Alternatively, it is possible to claim that the damage has resulted from the fact that the goods did not possess the claimed characteristics (cf PA section 40(3); see section 5, below).

2.5 Contractual warranties relating to the quality of goods and safety of goods

Section 40(3)(b) of the PA regulates instances in which the vendor has guaranteed the product's quality or safety characteristics for a warranty period. The Act stipulates in this respect that the purchaser can claim damages in all instances if, at the time of the agreement, the products differed from the description of them given by the vendor.

The question of whether such warranty exists on the part of the vendor must be determined through an interpretation of the sales agreement. If an expression such as 'guarantee' or 'assurance' is used, this would tend to indicate that a warranty exists as defined by the Act. The vendor's warranty or guarantee must normally refer to specific concrete characteristics of the product if the warranty or guarantee is to be enforced as a contractual liability.

2.6 Quantum of damage

Section 67 of the PA lays down the main provisions for the scope of the damages. The provisions are constructed on the principle that the injured party is to be compensated fully for losses and expenses attributable to the breach of contract. Only those actual losses which could reasonably have been foreseen as the possible consequence of the breach of contract can be claimed.

2.7 Burden of proof

In a claim for damages, the general provisions governing the burden of proof are applied (cf section 3.6, below).

2.8 Exclusion on limitation of liability

The application of the PA is obligatory where consumers are involved (section 4). Where a businessman is supplying goods to a consumer he cannot supply them on terms and conditions which exclude the supplier's liability under the Act. Businesses when dealing together, however, can freely conclude agreements deviating from the provisions of the Act and excluding the seller's liability under the Act.

2.9 Limitation period

According to section 32 of the PA, the purchaser looses his right to put forward a contractual claim relating to a defect if he does not submit a complaint to the vendor within a reasonable time after he has discovered, or ought to have discovered, it. The question of what is understood by 'reasonable time' depends, among other things, on who the purchaser is. A quicker reaction is required from businesses than from private consumers.

The Act also lays down an absolute deadline for complaints of two years from the date on which the goods were actually handed to the purchaser (cf section 32–2(1)). The vendor incurs no liability if defects are not revealed or complaints not made until after this period has expired. The vendor may extend the limitation period through his guarantee.

3. LIABILITY IN TORT

3.1 Outline of relevant tort law giving rise to liability for personal injury and property damage in Norway

3.1.1 Product Liability Act

As mentioned above in sections 1 and 2 and also in section 6 below, the PLA applies both within and outside contractual relationships. Provided the relationship is between businesses the Act does not cover damage to goods belonging to the business undertakings, which are covered by the common law of damages (see below) or contractual liability. The PLA always applies in respect of personal injuries, however.

3.1.2 Jurisprudence relating to damages

The jurisprudence relating to damages has developed over a long period of time. This law provides that a vendor, producer etc is liable for damage caused by a product he has put into the distribution chain. The liability can derive from negligence.

Negligence can relate to either the manufacture or distribution of the product, whether in the form of the choice of raw materials, the design, the production or inadequate information given to the user regarding dangerous aspects of the product. The key question is whether the producer, vendor, etc is at fault for the damage which has occurred and whether this could have been prevented by alternative action.

In certain instances, the producer can also be liable for the products' injurious characteristics on the basis of strict liability, ie liability regardless of fault. Liability of this kind may be applicable if the product involves an extraordinary or continuous risk that it will cause damage and, from an evaluation of the risk, it is natural to place liability with the producer who produced a product involving an extraordinary or continuous risk or the part thereof which caused such an extraordinary or continuous risk to arise.

In principle, there are no limits to which a party can be held liable regardless of fault. However, in practice the injured person will claim against the principal producer who actually put the product into circulation (or the vendor if he acted negligently when selling the product and this negligence has a causal link to the damage). The parties referred to above will claim reimbursement on an indemnity basis from the relevant party in the chain who is actually liable. In cases of the producers'/vendors' insolvency etc the claimant may have a relevant interest in bringing the claim against, eg the manufacturer of the defective component.

The PLA in many ways incorporates an unwritten basis for claiming damages. The injured party does not have the right to raise a claim for damages in addition to, or as an alternative to, the liability deriving from the provisions of the PLA. As already stated, the PLA cannot be applied to commercial damage which does not involve personal injury. Such instances are fully covered by the existing jurisprudence.

3.2 Causation

Norwegian law governing damages is built on what is known as the causation principle. The need to establish a causal relationship between the action leading to the damage and the damage itself is structured on common law and a long period of legal practice. Furthermore, a logical causal relationship will be sufficiently substantiated if it can be shown to exist in the balance of probabilities.

The question as to what can be legally regarded as the cause of damage can be problematic where there are several proven causal relationships. If the damage is the result of several causes, each one will normally be regarded as the cause of the damage. In some instances, however, it may be natural to differentiate between significant and completely insignificant aspects of the causal picture and to make the main cause of the damage the reason for the liability.

3.3 Remoteness of loss and damage

The loss must be reasonable for it to justify a claim for damages. In other words, a producer is not liable for the consequences of a defect in a product if these could not be envisaged. This applies irrespective of whether the liability derives from the PLA or from jurisprudence. Norwegian law has no written provisions regarding reasonableness. The provisions derive from general principles of law (judicial rulings) governing damages.

If the relationship between the product defect and the concrete damage/loss which has arisen is too remote, the result can be either reduced liability or no liability for the producer, vendor etc.

3.4 Quantum of damages

The rules for calculating the quantum of damages in claims under the PLA are the same as generally apply in Norwegian law regarding damages: the injured party is entitled to claim compensation for the entire financial loss he has suffered under the Norwegian Compensation for Damages Act (cf Act 26 of 13 June 1969 sections 3–1 and 4–2 governing compensation for damages). In addition, certain non-financial damage can be recovered, including damages for personal injury. These assessment principles apply regardless of the basis for damages; see, amongst others, PLA section 2–5.

If the claimant as a consequence of the damage, in addition to all financial losses, suffers permanent disablement, pain and suffering, he may receive compensation for his suffering, eg inability to sleep well or to enjoy his usual hobbies.

In the event of personal injury, the occupational damage/disability is of decisive importance for determining the magnitude of the damages.

The consequential losses resulting from product damage (eg loss of income in the event of suspension of production) is covered only to the extent that the consequential loss is reasonable and can be compensated in accordance with the general rules of the law governing damages.

With regard to section 5–2 of the Compensation for Damages Act, liability for damages can be alleviated if the court, taking account of the extent of the damage, the financial capacity of the party responsible, insurance policies and the opportunities to take out insurance, the apportionment of blame and other relevant matters, finds the burden of liability weighs unreasonably heavily on the party responsible. The same applies when, in special cases, it is reasonable for the injured party to bear the damage either wholly or in part.

3.5 Burden of proof

The Compensation for Damages Act does not include any provisions relating to the burden of proof. In principle, the injured party must prove fault and the causal relationship between the product's damaging characteristics and the damage itself. The injured party must also prove the losses to be compensated. The proof required may depend to some extent on the position of the parties. Stricter requirements regarding the provision of evidence or counter-evidence can be made on a producer than on a general consumer as regards a product's characteristics etc.

As regards who must prove that the loss is not too remote, it is incorrect to talk about a 'burden of proof'. The Norwegian system is that the defendant alleges the claim is too remote and the defendant opposes such an application. The court at its discretion decides whether, according to the relevant situation, it will rule on the question of remoteness or not.

3.6 Exclusion on limitation of liability

Agreements which restrict or limit liability of any person who may be held liable for a claim relating to a defective product under the provisions of the PLA are invalid (cf section 2–6). In practice it is difficult for a manufacturer to limit his liability to an end-user in respect of a product liability claim as he mainly sells direct to the end-user and cannot get the consumer to agree to limit his liability. Beyond the scope of the Act, agreements which waive liabilities can (in theory) be set aside in accordance with section 36 of the Contract Act (Act 14 of 31 May 1918 on Contracts) relating to the prohibition of unreasonable business terms and conditions.

3.7 Limitation period

The provisions of the Act of Limitation of 18 May 1979, no 18, also apply to questions of product liability, irrespective of whether liability ensues from the PLA or from jurisprudence or common law. This is stated expressly in section 2–7 of the PLA, though with the further stipulation that the limitation period is calculated from the day the product leaves the producer's supervision.

The limitation period for claims under the common law and the PLA is normally three years from the time the injured party learned of the damage and the party responsible (cf Act of Limitation section 9(1)). This first rule is subject to an overriding rule that liability is statute-barred ten years from the day the damage occurred, ie from the time the damage manifests itself, even if the injured party is not aware of this (Act of Limitation section 9(2)).

The limitation period for claims under the common law and the PLA is subject to a further rule that in no circumstances can a claim be brought more than 20 years after the date the product left the producer's supervision. If the damage has not occurred within this period, the right to claim damages is lost even if the damage manifests itself at a later date.

As a result of the Directive, a maximum limitation period of ten years from the product leaving the producer's supervision applies for so-called 'development faults'. The prerequisite, however, is that on the basis of the technical and scientific knowledge which existed prior to the expiry of this period, the producer was unable to know about the risk which resulted in the damage.

However, no limitation period applies if the damage results from a commercial activity and if, before the product left his supervision, the producer knew or ought to have known that it could endanger life or represent a serious danger to health.

3.8 Liability for third parties

In certain circumstances, intervention from a third party may result in the producer being relieved of liability. For example, this may occur where damage is attributable to a third party being negligent in performing modifications to a product.

The producer can also be held jointly liable with a third party, depending upon the other party's 'contribution' to the damage. The issue here is one of joint causation of damage. The principal rule in such cases is that the producer and the third party are held jointly and severally liable for the damage (Compensation for Damages Act section 5–3).

It is important to appreciate that 'third party' here refers to persons who are not defined as 'sub-producers' within the terms of the PLA. A sub-producer and a principal producer are treated as jointly and severally liable vis-à-vis the injured party. This does not apply if the sub-producer can prove that the safety defect of the sub-product is attributable to a planning design or specification by the principal producer and that the sub-producer cannot be blamed for having followed instructions.

4. LIABILITY FOR DEFECTIVE PRODUCTS BROUGHT ABOUT BY BREACH OF STATUTORY REGULATION DESIGNED TO PROTECT CONSUMERS AND/OR TO PROMOTE SAFETY

4.1 Outline of nature of protective regulations

Act 79 of 11 June 1976, governing product supervision (*Lov om produktkontroll*) has the object of preventing the manufacture of products causing damage to health or environmental pollution. According to section 3 of the Act, a producer, importer, vendor, etc of a product which can damage health, etc is obliged to exercise caution and pursue measures directed at preventing and restricting such damage. These parties undertake to obtain the knowledge necessary to assess whether the product can have effects which are damaging to health.

According to section 4 of the Act, the Government is empowered to adopt measures relating to how a product is to be manufactured, marketed, distributed, identified, used or handled, etc. It is also empowered to adopt measures covering the composition of a product or prohibiting a product from being manufactured, marketed, distributed or used.

Official identification standards have been laid down for, eg, power saws, motor mowers, detergents and certain chemicals. Certain standards also apply for child-proof packaging.

In addition to the above, Norway has adopted a number of international product standards (eg SENELEC). The regulations for approved electrical products are particularly prominent in this respect.

4.2 Burden of proof

The Product Supervision Act does not include any provision for any claims for damages to be made by anyone who suffers loss as a result of any producer, importer etc being in breach of its provisions. As discussed below, the failure of a manufacturer or importer etc to produce or sell products that conform to the requirements of the Product Supervision Act may result in claims under contract product liability law or under common law being more likely to succeed, as well as criminal sanctions. Nor does the Act contain any provisions relating to the burden of proof of liability which can be attributed in the event of a breach of the Act. The burden of proof relating to actions for damages is subject to the same regulations as other claims for damages (cf section 3.6 above).

4.3 Nature of liability, damages or criminal sanctions

Official approval or compliance with product standards in accordance with the Product Supervision Act or international standards can be a key issue for determining liability in claims based in contract law under the PLA or pursuant to the terms of the common law on damages. The general principle adopted is that official approval does not free the producer from liability. The producer is subject to independent liability for defective products which is separate from any such approval. Where production is performed in compliance with officially defined production standards, the producer is relieved of liability only if the standard is mandatory and provides the producer with no possibility of deviating from the principal standard. Insofar as deviation is permissible, the producer bears independent liability for deviations he undertakes.

Violation of the Product Supervision Act is punishable by fines or imprisonment of up to three months.

If the distribution of a dangerous product results in personal injury, this is (in theory) punishable as a violation of the provisions of the General Civil Penal Code relating to bodily harm caused through negligence. This can be punished by fines or imprisonment of up to three years.

5. SPECIAL LIABILITIES ARISING IN RESPECT OF PARTICULAR PRODUCTS

5.1 Radioactive products

Damage and injury caused by radioactivity (radioactive substances) are covered by special legal provisions providing for strict liability, obligatory insurance for product liability involving very high coverage and channelling of liability towards the operator of the nuclear plant, cf Act 28 of 12 May 1972. The Act implements the Paris Convention on Third Party Liability in the Field of Nuclear Energy of 29 July 1960 with subsequent amendments.

5.2 Drugs and medicines

As stated in the introduction, the PLA contains special provisions governing liability for drugs and medicines. This liability also extends to substances which are tested in medical experiments on humans as part of the process of developing drugs.

The party which is liable according to these special provisions is not the producer of the drugs or medicines, but the underwriters of insurance policies. As laid down by the Act, it is compulsory for manufacturers of the drugs in question to take out insurance policies. Liability for damage to health caused by drugs and medicines is thus channelled to a special insurance arrangement which is directly liable to the injured parties.

This arrangement is based on an obligatory insurance which must be taken out for all medicines sold in Norway. A special association for liability in the field of drugs and medicines known as the Association of Liable Medicine Producers (*Legemiddelansvarsforeningen*) is responsible for ensuring that the obligatory insurance is taken out.

The PLA imposes strict liability for damage to health caused by drugs and medicines (cf section 3–3(1)). It is sufficient to demonstrate that damage to health has occurred and that a causal relationship exists between the consumption of the product and the damage to health.

The section on drugs and medicines includes various exceptions from liability. These include instances where the course of the illness can be attributed to the person's own state of health. Limitations are also laid down as to the maximum indemnities which can be paid out under the insurance per year/per illness. According to section 3–6 of the Act, the total volume of damages relating to this section must not exceed NOK 80m for illnesses ascertained in the same calendar year. The total compensation for serial damage to health resulting from the same substance in one or more drugs or medicines is further limited to NOK 100m. If the indemnity sums laid down in the Act are insufficient to cover the losses of everyone entitled to damages, the level of these damages is reduced in accordance with section 3–7 of the Act.

6. LIABILITY FOR DEFECTIVE PRODUCTS ARISING FROM NATIONAL LAW IN NORWAY: HARMONISATION OF THE DIRECTIVE WITH NORWEGIAN LAW

6.1 Introduction

Endeavours have been made to harmonise the Norwegian PLA with the Directive. Even though Norway is not a member of the EC, harmonisation has been essential due to the needs of international trade.

The PLA lays down rules aimed primarily at protecting the consumer. Damage to property resulting from business enterprises falls outside the scope of the Act. Commercial damage which does not involve personal injury continues to be covered by jurisprudence relating to damages and by contractual agreements between the parties involved.

6.2 Outline of provisions in Norway

6.2.1 The products covered by the Act

The PLA covers all types of goods and movables, whether they are raw materials or finished goods, sub-products or main products (cf PLA section 1–2(1)). Indeed, the Act can only be applied where products which fall within the scope of the Act are manufactured or distributed as a link in the commercial chain, starting with the initial manufacturers and ending with the consumer (PLA section 1–1).

The term 'products' also includes those items incorporated into other movables or into real estate (eg machine parts, electrical components, concrete, supporting structures). Waste from the production process is also covered if it is distributed as a link in the commercial chain where, for instance, the waste from one manufacturing process may be used as a raw material in another production process. Water, gas, oil etc are also included in the term 'product' – not only where these are supplied in packaged quantities, but also when supplied via pipeline.

However, the term 'product' excludes real estate from the scope of the Act. This means that, among other things, building and construction contracts are not automatically included in the provisions of the Act. It must be noted, however, that the Act applies to building and construction materials which are incorporated into real estate. It is therefore necessary to resort to jurisprudence/contractual provisions to determine liability for building and construction work.

Electricity is not encompassed by the provisions of the Act. The PLA could not be applied if, for example, property was damaged as a result of a technical fault in which a low-voltage system was supplied with high-voltage current.

6.2.2 Which producers are liable?

The Act does not restrict liability to producers as such, but extends to importers and, to a certain degree, vendors.

As regards goods produced in Norway, the principal liability for defective products is borne by the manufacturer (cf PLA section 1–3(1, a)). Parties other than the manufacturer can be held liable if the party concerned presents the product as his own by attaching his name or trademark etc to it (PLA section 1–3(1, b)). Agents bear a secondary product liability if the producer is unknown (PLA section 1–3(1, c)).

In the case of goods produced abroad, product liability will always be borne by the importer (PLA section 1–3(1, e)). Secondary product liability also applies to agents of importers of products if the actual importer is unknown (PLA section 1–3(1, f)).

6.2.3 Basis for liability

Section 2–1 of the PLA sets out a special basis for liability. According to this provision, the party responsible for the product is liable to pay damages if the product does not provide the safety which a user or the general public could reasonably expect. In assessing the safety which can be expected, consideration must be taken of all aspects related to the product, such as its presentation, marketing and envisaged use. The Act defines the absence of the safety which a user could reasonably expect as a safety defect.

The basis for liability introduced by the PLA is new in Norwegian law. The point of focus is no longer the circumstances relating to the producer but rather the product itself. The question of what the producer could have done differently to prevent the injurious characteristic is no longer posed. Instead, the Act concentrates solely on whether the product provided the safety the user could have reasonably expected of it for the envisaged area of application. It is important here to understand that it is not the user's concrete safety expectations which are decisive. In other words, if the subjective safety expectations exceed what are otherwise generally expected, the producer cannot be held liable, ie an objective safety standard applies. The safety standard implies, for example, that one can expect a child's toy not to react explosively when brought into contact with a naked flame. On the other hand, however, one cannot expect vehicles, for example, to be completely safe from accident.

A special problem arises in conjunction with the safety standard in cases where safety equipment (eg smoke detectors, emergency radio beacons, inflatable life rafts, etc) fails to work. Such failure would represent a safety defect of crucial importance. There is nevertheless a problem in recovering damages since there must always be a causal relationship between the failure and the damage which occurs. It is, for example, not certain that a drowning accident could have been prevented in the event of a shipwreck if the emergency radio beacon had worked and a rescue operation could therefore have been mounted. However, the causal relationship is much more apparent where, for example, a life raft fails to inflate as expected or a fire extinguishing system fails.

The safety standard means that development faults fall within the scope of product liability. Norwegian law makes no exceptions in this regard. A development fault is present if, on the basis of known and optimal technological know-how and scientific knowledge, there was, at the time of production, no way of foreseeing the defective characteristic resulting in the damage. The producer is not freed of liability even if, on the basis of known technology, he has done all he can to optimise the product.

6.2.4 The circumstance triggering liability

According to section 2–2(1) of the PLA the circumstance triggering liability is the actual act of distributing the product. Distribution here is also taken to include providing samples of goods and transferring the product to shipping agents.

6.2.5 The damages covered

The Act encompasses personal injury and damage to property (cf PLA section 2–3(1)). As mentioned earlier, however, damage to property occurring between business enterprises does not fall within the scope of the Act.

6.2.6 Exemption from liability due to the kind of damage

Damage caused to the product itself is exempted from product liability (cf PLA section 2–3(1, a)). Compensation for damage of this type must be claimed under the PA or contractual agreements.

Furthermore, all damage which a sub-product causes to a main product before the latter is distributed to a user will be exempted from liability (cf PLA section 2–3(2, b)). On the other hand, all damage to the main product occurring after the user himself (possibly with specialist assistance) has incorporated the sub-product causing the damage will be covered.

As already outlined above, liability for damage to property occurring between business enterprises is exempted from the Act's provisions (cf PLA section 2–3(2, c)). Liability in such circumstances must be resolved through the provisions of the common law on damages and contractual agreements. The decisive issue here is the kind of enterprise the damaged object was used in.

6.2.7 Exemptions from liability due to delineations to other regulations governing damages

Section 1–5 of the PLA exempts damage covered by the following Acts or resulting in the following situations:

(a) Act Governing Third Party Liability for Motor Vehicles;
(b) Act Governing Road-Freight Agreements;
(c) damage to property caused by railways;
(d) damage to property caused by a boat, ship, hovercraft or aircraft, or by permanent or mobile equipment on the Norwegian continental shelf;
(e) third party liability in the field of nuclear energy;
(f) Petroleum Act.

If, for example, a motor vehicle causes damage due to a safety defect, the injured party must claim damages through the Act Governing Third Party Liability for Motor Vehicles and not through the PLA. If circumstances exist for claiming damages, the insurance company covering this liability can, however, make an indemnity claim from the motor vehicle manufacturer at common law.

6.2.8 Exemption from liability

According to section 2–6 of the PLA, agreements which restrict or limit liability under the PLA are void.

6.3 Description of special or anomalous provisions in respect of product liability law in Norway

6.3.1 Agricultural produce

Agricultural produce constitutes a 'product' within the terms of the PLA and is subject to the same liability regulations as every other product.

6.3.2 Computer software

Product liability within the terms of the Act is limited to material products only. The Act does not encompass computer software.

6.4 Optional provisions in the EC Directive

The Norwegian PLA encompasses both agricultural produce and development faults. There are no de minimis levels for damage claims by an injured party. Furthermore, with the exception of the limitations which apply for liability relating to drugs and medicines, no other restrictions have been laid down as regards the maximum damages recoverable. The Norwegian Act has therefore chosen the most severe options laid down by the Directive.

7. PRACTICAL EFFECTS EC PRODUCT LIABILITY LAW WILL HAVE ON VARIOUS BUSINESSES IN THE CHAIN OF SUPPLY OF PRODUCTS

As compared to the former legal situation, the PLA is of only minor significance as regards liability in the distribution sector. It must be presumed that the Act has had a particularly beneficial effect on clarifying the product liability which can be attached to the various links in a chain of agents in which no manufacturer is known.

8. COMPARISON OF THE EFFECTS OF PRODUCT LIABILITY LAW WITH THE PREVIOUS POSITION IN CONTRACT AND TORT

The PLA has had the effect of somewhat extending the product liability derived earlier from the common law, except where the liability related to an area involving so-called objective liability. This is due to the fact that the question of possible negligence on the part of the producer is no longer an issue, the point in question being solely whether the product satisfied the user's safety expectations.

There is also a certain practical consequence that clauses limiting or renouncing the mandatory liability instituted by the PLA will not apply in cases where damage is regulated by the Act. In view of the fact that damage to property used essentially for business activities does not fall within the scope of the Act, exemption from liability between business enterprises will continue to apply. The Act is therefore of reduced effect where relationships between business enterprises are concerned.

9. RISK MANAGEMENT IN THE NEW ERA OF PRODUCT LIABILITY

9.1 Introduction

It is important to understand that the elimination or reduction of risk is not always a question of insurance.

Risk can be minimised through *quality monitoring* as early as the design stage by employing reasonable safety margins and by complying with national and international standards. Quality monitoring of this type must also be practised at the production site and through the supervision of sub-contractors and purchased components.

It is equally important to ensure that quality monitoring involves the monitoring of finished goods and packaging.

Risk management can also be performed at the *contract draft* stage. By using standard or individual contracts for relationships between business enterprises, one can attempt to limit one's exposure to risk to the extent that the law allows exemptions and limitations of liability. This will always apply in a chain of business links, but not vis-à-vis consumers who have suffered damage or vis-à-vis injured persons. As already mentioned, the PLA does not recognise any exemptions from liability.

In order to be best prepared to deal with a claim for damages, the business concerned must employ good *documentation routines* for the product. Where industrial supplies are concerned, subsequent modifications might be encountered, for example, which have been performed by parties other than the producer. It is important in such instances to establish fully comprehensive documentation routines so as to be able to prove the technical standard of the supplied product. It may also be important to be able to verify which user information has accompanied the product.

It can also be important for risk management purposes to have an overview of the product's distribution channels so that where goods need to be recalled, this can be done as practically and inexpensively as possible.

9.2 Insurance

Each producer requires product liability insurance to cover liability deriving from both the PLA and common law. In the case of damage caused by consumer products, these will often be found to be covered initially by combined household contents insurances taken out by the injured party. It is nevertheless evident that insurance companies can and will make a claim of recourse against the producer liable for the product in accordance with the provisions of the PLA. The extent of insurance cover taken out by the injured party therefore should not be taken into account by producers in assessing their insurance requirements.

Three different principles are applied in Norwegian liability insurance, namely, the occurrence principle, the damage-assessment principle and the claims-made principle. Two principles are employed in international liability insurance, namely the occurrence principle and the claims-made principle.

Where the same insurance company has been used for several years and the insurance amount and other terms and conditions have remained unchanged and have been adequate, the question of which principle is employed is of only minor importance. The principle becomes important in particular when a change is made to another insurance company or business operations have ceased.

If the producer changes his insurance company, it should be remembered there is a risk that products distributed a long time ago may not be covered if damage occurs at some point in the future.

It should also be remembered with regard to product liability insurance that, in the event of liability being established, there are many different costs which need to be compensated which are not covered by any general product liability insurance.

These costs are, firstly, the cost of repairing, re-delivering, removing, discarding and scrapping the product – the so-called 'product guarantee' or 'liability for complaints'.

Secondly, costs or damages necessarily involved in supplementary work required for repairing or exchanging the supplied product.

Thirdly, costs of withdrawing the product from the market, such as expenses sustained in tracing the product or informing customers or the general public – the so-called 'recall liability'.

All this can be insured on the Norwegian and, to some extent, foreign markets. Coverage is characterised by high own risk levels and high premiums.

As regards future developments, it seems quite evident that the situation surrounding claims and damages will change substantially within a number of years. This applies particularly to exported products.

A number of general recommendations can be made to Norwegian producers on the aspect of insurance. These include routine reviews of policies and in particular ensuring that the indemnity sum is adequate and that all types of liability/loss items are covered/insured separately.

A routine check also ought to be performed to assess the need for recall coverage.

9.3 Limitation of liability through corporate structure

The question may arise of who is to bear product liability when the product is manufactured by a company or another legal entity which forms part of a corporate group or other group of enterprises which has a more complex ownership structure. The question is whether liability of this type can be directed solely against the company which is directly responsible for causing the damage or whether the parent company also bears responsibility. Such questions of liability can also arise where a physical person holds all or most of the shares in the company.

This problem is particularly relevant for joint-stock and other companies having limited liability. In the case of general partnerships, it will follow from the form of liability that the participants bear direct responsibility for product liability (cf section 2–4 of the Act relating to general partnerships).

According to section 15–1(2)(cf (1)) of the Companies Act, the shareholders can be made liable if they contribute either wilfully or negligently to a company causing damage. This provision is particularly important for groups of companies and means that the injured party can advance a claim for damages against the parent company. The prerequisite for this is that the parent company has acted wilfully or negligently.

The provision applies to liability vis-à-vis both the company itself and third parties. On the basis of this provision, a parent company – in instances when the necessary blame has been demonstrated on the part of the owners – can thus be held liable for the product damage caused by a subsidiary. The same applies for a physical person who, through his shareholding, has a decisive influence over a joint-stock company.

An example of a situation in which it may be possible to advance a claim for liability in accordance with section 15–1(2) (cf (1)) is where a parent company exerts real control over a subsidiary and instructs the latter to start production of damaging/dangerous products without taking account of official production standards or any form of quality monitoring. Another example could be a subsidiary which is under-financed to the extent that it has insufficient funds to implement the product supervision measures which such operations demand.

Apart from the Companies Act there are no other regulations governing the transfer of liability between companies. In other words, such transfer is excluded if the company causing the damage does not itself have funds to cover the claim for compensation and the parent company/shareholders cannot be blamed.

CHAPTER XII

Portugal

Jorge Santiago Neves Esq

Menezes Falcao e Associados
Assessores em Direito
Av Da Republica 48–B, 5–D
1000 Lisbon
Portugal

Tel ++ 351 1 793 8524
Fax ++ 351 1 793 8541

CHAPTER XII

Portugal

1. INTRODUCTION

1.1 Overview of the law relating to defective products in Portugal

Until the enactment of Decree Law 383/89 (henceforth referred to as 'DL 383/89') implementing the Directive, there was no product liability law as such in Portugal. It is, however, possible to find various pieces of legislation dealing with matters related to liability resulting from defective products, the most important being the Portuguese Constitution, the Consumer Protection Law and the Civil Code (governing liability in contract and tort). It is noteworthy that these are mainly concerned with a person's right to purchase products which are not defective or unsuitable for their stated purpose, and his right to redress if they are. The introduction of legislation which creates a general no-fault liability for damage caused by a defect in a product is a substantial innovation in Portuguese law, and one which was, no doubt, overdue.

1.2 Consumer protection in the Portuguese Constitution

In article 60(1) the Portuguese Constitution establishes the general principle that 'All consumers are entitled to [a reasonable degree of] quality of goods and services consumed, to training and information, to the protection of their health, safety and economic interests and to the recovery of damages.'

This rather vague statement gives no indication of what can be expected in terms of 'quality' of goods and services, and is of no use in determining whether the consumer is entitled to the recovery of damages according to the usual rules of contract or tort, or whether, failing these, he can rely on no-fault liability. There is also no indication from whom the consumer can expect to recover his damages – the manufacturer, the distributor or the State as guarantor of the consumer's constitutional rights?

In short, this express constitutional principle appears to be of little practical use. In a more positive vein it may be said that this constitutional reference to consumer rights inspired the Consumer Protection Law of 1981 but, as we shall see further on, this Law produced no substantial change to the rules consumers could already rely on, namely those included in the Civil Code.

1.3 Definition and classification of terms

Civil (as opposed to *criminal*) liability is usually classified as contractual or non-contractual. In Portuguese law contractual liability is something of a misnomer since it is not limited to contractual performance, but covers the breach of any obligation to perform. Non-contractual liability or, more precisely, liability for illicit acts (which for the purposes of this study, we shall later refer to as liability in tort) refers to the breach of a duty of care (ie through negligence) or abstention (ie causing damage by violating the rights of another person or breaching a rule of law designed to protect the interests of other persons). The Portuguese Civil Code divides civil liability into three areas: non-contractual liability at articles 483ff; contractual liability at articles 798ff and the obligation to repair damages irrespective of their nature, at articles 562ff. A particular category of non-contractual liability, and one which is of special interest to product liability, is no-fault liability, which the Portuguese Civil Code deals with at articles 499ff. Articles referred to in this chapter, where not otherwise identified, are those of the Portuguese Civil Code. All translations of the provisions of Portuguese law used in this chapter are the author's own.

In section 2 below we shall cover contractual liability, and in section 3 we shall look at liability in tort. The rules on the obligation to repair damages irrespective of their nature (articles 562ff) govern both forms of liability, in particular as to the quantum and payment of damages, and regarding the fault of the injured party, and shall be analysed concurrently with contractual and tortious liability. No-fault liability, to which many of the rules for tortious liability apply, will also be dealt with in section 3.

In the analysis which follows our references will be largely statutory rather than judicial, as can be expected when analysing the law of a civil law system such as that which exists in Portugal. Some references will, however, be made to the rulings of the higher courts (ie appeals courts and Supreme Court) where these help to clarify a point of law or give useful indications as to its practical application. These rulings are identified by their date and the law report in which they appear – *Boletim do Ministério da Justiça* ('BMJ') or *Colectânea de Jurisprudência* ('CJ'), followed by the identification of the volume number in the case of the BMJ, year and number of volume in the case of the CJ, and the page number.

2. LIABILITY IN CONTRACT

2.1 Introduction and outline of contract law relevant to defective products in Portugal

As in most other Western European legal systems the principle of privity of contract (identified in Portuguese law as the 'principle of relativity') limits the effects of a contract to its respective parties. The only recognised exceptions to this principle are those contracts concluded expressly for the benefit of a third party, or contracts where one of the parties is later to be substituted by a third party (and it is arguable whether the latter is truly an exception). Various attempts have been made over the years to import foreign doctrines, such as the French 'action directe', or the American 'implied warranties', to establish a contractual relationship between the producer and the consumer, but these have been rejected. Liability in contract is therefore only possible as between the parties to the contract, eg in the distributive chain, between a manufacturer and his distributor, or between a dealer and a purchaser.

2.2 Liability for pre-contractual statements or representations

In what is basically an adaptation of the Italian Civil Code's article 1337, the Portuguese Civil Code at article 227(1) states that 'Whosoever negotiates with another person with a view to concluding a contract shall, both in its preliminaries and in its formation, proceed in accordance with the rules of good faith, failing which he shall be liable for any damages he causes to the other party'.

The general rule, therefore, is one of bargaining in good faith, so that a liability is created for the party who through deeds, acts or artifices, or through ignoring a duty to inform, leads another party into believing that a contract will be concluded when that is not, in fact, the intention, or leads the other party into concluding an invalid contract.

This is the extent of pre-contractual liability in Portuguese law, which means that only so-called 'negative damages' may be claimed, ie damages which would not have arisen if negotiations had not taken place, or if an invalid contract had not been concluded. So-called 'positive damages', ie for breach of contractual obligations, may only be claimed on the basis of the contract which is eventually concluded.

Portuguese law does therefore recognise the possibility of liability for damages arising from misrepresentations which are prior to a contract. These may occur as the result of non-serious statements and those which are intentionally misleading.

At article 245 it is stated that:

> '(1) A non-serious statement made in the belief that the lack of seriousness is known, does not produce any effects;
> (2) If, however, the statement is made in circumstances which lead the party receiving the statement into justifiably accepting the seriousness of the statement he will have a right to compensation for damage incurred.'

The non-serious statement referred to in both paragraphs of the article is made in the belief that the other party is aware of the unserious nature of the statement, and in both cases the party making the statement has no intention to mislead. This is an essential distinction between this form of misrepresentation and the other form mentioned, ie that which is intentionally misleading. Only when the unserious statement is made in circumstances which justify the other party's belief that it is serious, will liability for damages arise.

When, on the other hand, the statement is intentionally misleading, and influences the acts of the party receiving the statement, these acts may be annulled (article 254(1)) and give rise to tortious liability. It is, however, difficult to draw the line between deliberately misleading statements which produce such effects, the so-called *dolus malus*, and the legally tolerated *dolus bonus* to which the Civil Code expressly consents. Article 253(2) states that 'suggestions or usual artifices considered legitimate according to [society's] dominant concepts, [or] the dissimulation of error, when no duty to elucidate the other party arises from the law, contractual agreement or [society's] dominant concept' will not produce the effects attributed to *dolus malus*, ie will neither be voidable nor give rise to liability for damages.

Judicial rulings on this topic of any authority are rather scant. It is clear that a dishwasher advertised as 'the best on the market', when the manufacturer is aware it occupies a more modest position in the dishwasher league, will be a case of *dolus bonus*, whereas if a retailer sells a used dishwasher claiming that it is brand new, this will be a case of *dolus malus*, but a lot may lie in between, and may not be so easily classified.

Another situation is that of mental reservation, described in article 244(1) as 'a statement contrary to the party's real intention with a view to misleading the other party'. Such statements do not affect the validity of a contract except where the other party is aware of the mental reservation, in which case the law treats them in the same way as simulation between parties, with the consequence that the agreement concluded is null and void (articles 244(2) and 240).

2.3 Contractual warranties relating to the 'proper functioning' of goods

The law implies a general warranty for the vendor as regards the 'proper functioning' of goods sold, so long as a warranty has been agreed to by the parties or is usual in the circumstances of the sale (ie this will always be the case if the sale occurs through the usual retail channels, but it may not be the case if one neighbour sells his used television set to another). Such a warranty creates an obligation for the vendor, irrespective of any fault on his part, to repair the goods sold or to substitute them when such substitution is necessary, and the goods are of such a nature as to make the substitution possible (article 921 of the Portuguese Civil Code, in turn based on article 1512 of the Italian Civil Code).

When the warranty period has not been established contractually, or cannot be determined in accordance with custom, it is legally fixed as six months after the delivery of the product, although within this period, the failure of the product to 'function properly' must be communicated to the vendor within 30 days of the purchaser's knowledge of the defect arising. An action at law for satisfaction of the warranty must be brought within the six months following delivery, or within six months of the date on which the communication of the failure of the product to function properly was made to the vendor.

The warranty covers only the 'proper functioning' of the goods sold, so that the warranty will not apply if the goods are used improperly. A further limitation to the warranty results from a 1984 ruling by the Portuguese Supreme Court when, in interpreting article 921, it stated that it resulted from the clauses of the contract in question that only manufacturing defects are covered by the warranty, and not defects which may result from imperfect conception of the goods' design (4.10.1984, BMJ, 340–364).

The limitation of warranties of proper functioning are, however, mitigated by the general understanding that they do not exclude the purchaser's rights based on breach of contract, which is described in section 2.4, below.

2.4 Breach of contract for supply of defective products

The law recognises a limited number of defects in products which give rise to breach of contract (article 913):

(a) a defect which devalues the product;
(b) a defect which prevents the product from fulfilling the purpose for which it is sold;
(c) the non-existence of characteristics specified by the vendor; and
(d) the non-existence of characteristics necessary for the fulfilment of the purpose for which the product is sold.

Where such defects arise, certain rules must be satisfied before it can be concluded that a breach of contract has occurred. Namely, it will be necessary that the purchaser has acquired the defective product mistakenly believing it not to be defective, or has been misled by the vendor into believing that the product is not defective. For the purchaser's error regarding the defect of the product to be relevant, it must be one which the vendor should or could have recognised as essential to the purchaser's decision to buy.

Once the defect has been detected, various outcomes are possible:

(a) the purchaser may opt for the rescission of the contract;
(b) the vendor may, of his own initiative, repair the defect, so that it is no longer possible for the purchaser to rescind the contract, unless he has already suffered damages as a result of the defect, or has already brought an action at law to rescind the contract;
(c) the purchaser may demand that the vendor repair damages, although the extent of such a right will depend on:
    (i) whether the purchase was made because the vendor deliberately misled the purchaser as to the characteristics of the product, in which case the purchaser is entitled to damages; or
    (ii) if the purchase was made because the purchaser was mistaken in assessing the characteristics of the product, in which case, the purchaser will not be entitled to damages if the vendor through no fault of his own was unaware of the product's defect;
(d) the purchaser may demand that the defect be repaired, or that, where this is not possible, the product be substituted, if it is of such a nature as to make substitution possible, but this will no longer be the case if the vendor, through no fault of his own, was unaware of the product's defect (in which case the purchaser may only exercise his right to rescind the contract, and liability for damages will not occur, (c)(ii), above);
(e) given the circumstances, the vendor may prove that, if the purchaser had not been mistaken or misled, he would still have acquired the product, but at a lower price, in which case the purchaser will only be entitled to a reduction of the purchase price, although this will not affect his right to recover damages (cf (c), above).

2.5 Quantum, causation and reparation of damage

As was mentioned in the introduction to this chapter, the Portuguese Civil Code deals with the obligation to repair damages irrespective of their nature, consequently such rules apply to both contractual and tortious liability. We shall therefore analyse in this section the various aspects of damage, namely quantum, causation and reparation, bearing in mind that the same rules apply to tortious liability which will be dealt with in the following section.

Article 562 establishes the general rule that the obligation to pay damages implies the reconstitution of the situation which would have existed if the event which created the liability for damages had not occurred. This covers not only the damage actually caused, but also the benefits lost as a result of such damage, and where these are foreseeable it is also possible to recover losses which will be incurred in the future as a result of the breach of contract (article 564).

However, the obligation to pay damages does not cover all and any form of damage directly or indirectly resulting from the event giving rise to the liability. Of the various doctrines which have attempted to establish the limit of damages to those actually caused by an event, the Portuguese Civil Code opted for the doctrine of 'adequate causation' according to which the obligation to repair damages will only exist in relation to the damages that the injured party would probably not have suffered if such an event had not occurred (article 563). The Civil Code thus bases causation on the idea of the probability of the damage. Given that the Civil Code expresses the matter in terms of 'probabilities' it has become the topic for much academic musing, and since this gives rise essentially to questions of fact, the matter has been largely left to the first instance courts to decide, with often conflicting results. It is, nevertheless, possible to state that the doctrine adopted, when applied in practice, means that the cause of damage is an act which in abstract terms is enough to have produced the damage. If an act actually caused the damage, but would not in the usual course of events in everyday life have been expected to have caused such damage, then no causal link is established, eg if a person is highly susceptible to shock and dies of a heart attack on seeing his television set explode, the explosion of the television set cannot be considered as adequate cause of his death. On the other hand, it is important to take into account the knowledge of the agent of the action, eg if, in the above example, the explosion of the television set was provoked by the victim's wife, who was fully aware of his susceptibility, then the explosion would be adequate cause of death.

As to reparation of damage, the law establishes that reparation should bring about the 'natural restoration' of the situation which existed before the damage occurred, and only when this is not possible or insufficient to redress fully the damage, or proves itself excessively burdensome for the liable party, should the damage be redressed in money (article 566(1)). In accordance with the general principles of contractual freedom, however, the parties may agree differently, eg to redress the damage in money even when 'natural restoration' would have been possible.

The quantum of damages to be paid by the person causing the damage may, however, be reduced or disallowed entirely, if the damage has also been caused or aggravated by the fault of the injured person (article 570(1)). In such cases, if the liability is based on a presumption of fault (ie in certain cases of tortious liability (qv section 3.3, below) then, notwithstanding any rule to the contrary, it shall be disallowed entirely (article 570(2)).

2.6 Exclusion or limitation of liability

By article 809, any exclusion clause relating to contractual liability is null and void. This does not exclude the possibility of waiving a right to damages once this right has come about as a result of breach of contract, but it does categorically preclude the possibility of waiving such a right before the breach has occurred. The only exception to this rule is in the case of vicarious liability (section 2.9, below).

Limitation of liability is not clearly forbidden in the law, nor is it clearly permitted. The Portuguese Supreme Court (ruling of 2 July 1981, BMJ, 309–319) and leading academics generally believe that limitation clauses in contracts are valid so long as they do not:

(a) conflict with public welfare;
(b) limit liability to a negligible or insufficient sum, so as to amount, in fact, to an exclusion of liability;
(c) cover cases of serious fault or intentional breach by the liable party.

This view is based on general rules of law, in particular that of contractual freedom, and on the fact that article 602 allows a debtor to agree with his creditor that only a certain part of his property may guarantee a debt, which is in effect a limitation of liability.

2.7 Limitation period

Liability in contract is subject to the usual limitation period of Portuguese Civil Law, which is 20 years from when the damage occurred (article 309). One point of controversy is the situation which may arise when liability results from both contract and tort (eg damage arising from the supply of a defective gas canister which subsequently explodes). Tortious liability is subject to a much shorter limitation period of three years from the injured party becoming aware of his right to compensation, which gives rise to the question of which limitation period prevails. Different rulings of the Portuguese Supreme Court have gone in opposite directions, but the appeal courts have consistently viewed such situations as essentially cases of contractual liability and subject to the longer limitation period of 20 years (eg Lisbon Court of Appeals, ruling of 25 June 1985, CJ, 1985, 3–173).

2.8 Burden of proof

The general rule regarding the burden of proof is that whoever claims a right must prove the facts giving rise to such a right (article 342(1)). However, in the case of breach of contract it is for the party whose obligation it is to perform to prove that the breach or defective performance is not that party's fault (article 799(1)), although the burden of proof regarding the existence of breach or defective performance shall, in accordance with the general rules above, rest on the party claiming breach or defective performance.

2.9 Vicarious liability

A party to a contract shall be liable for the acts of his legal representatives or of the persons he engages in performing his contractual obligations, in the same way as if such acts were carried out by that party (article 800(1)).

The only concession made by the law to limit such liability is the possibility of its being limited or excluded by prior agreement of the parties to the contract, so long as this is not contrary to mandatory rules (article 800(2)). It is, however, the view of the courts that this exclusion of liability is limited to cases where contracts are actually negotiated by the parties, and does not extend to standard agreements where one party is limited to accepting the clauses drafted by the other (ruling of 11 May 1981 of the Appeals Court of Coimbra, CJ 1982, 3–90).

3. LIABILITY IN TORT

Tortious liability arises when the law creates an obligation for one person to redress the damage suffered by another resulting from an illicit act for which the first person is responsible. The illicit acts giving rise to such an obligation are classified as intentional or arising from mere fault. Intentional acts are those carried out in the knowledge that they will produce a damaging result, whereas those in the second category are the result of negligence or lack of care on the part of the person responsible. The Portuguese Civil Code establishes some practical consequences based on this distinction, which are considered later (section 3.3).

The general principle governing tortious liability is to be found in article 483(1) which states that 'whoever, intentionally, or through mere fault, illicitly violates the rights of another person or breaches any rule of law designed to protect the interests of other persons shall be under an obligation to compensate the injured person for the damage arising from such violation or breach'. In article 483(2) it is added that no-fault liability for damages will only arise in those cases expressly foreseen in the law.

The rule of 483(1) presupposes tortious liability will only arise where there is a voluntary act on the part of the agent and there is a link of causation between the act and the resulting damage. The fact that the injured party may only claim damages if the act was intentional or arose through 'mere fault', ie negligence, distinguishes this form of liability from that introduced by DL 383/89 in implementation of the Directive.

3.1 Voluntary acts

Only acts which represent voluntary human conduct may give rise to tortious liability. This excludes cases of *force majeure* and of fortuitous circumstances (lightning, floods, etc).

The conduct in question may consist either in committing an act which violates a duty not to interfere with another person's rights or an omission which causes damage. Omissions are dealt with by article 486 which states that 'omissions give rise to liability for damage when, without prejudice to other requirements of the law, an obligation to carry out the omitted act existed in law or covenant'. Taking into account the general requirement of causation, this means that omissions will only be relevant where there was a legally binding obligation to commit the omitted act and, if it had been carried out, it would, at least probably, have avoided the damage.

One particular form of omission relevant to product liability is that foreseen in article 485(2), where a liability is established for those cases where there is a legal obligation to 'counsel, make recommendations or inform and the agent has proceeded with negligence or the intention to cause harm, or when the agent's action is punishable by [criminal] law'. In certain cases the law does establish an obligation to inform, eg instructions which must accompany pharmaceutical products, labelling of food products, etc. Unfortunately, no judicial precedent has been developed around this rule and given the practical difficulties of proving intent or negligence, it can be expected that persons suffering injury as a result of such an omission will prefer to base their claim on the no-fault liability created by DL 383/89.

3.2 Illicit acts

As stated above, an act is illicit when it involves the violation of rights of another person or the breach of a rule of law designed to protect the interests of other persons (article 483(1)). The rights in question are considered by Portuguese legal doctrine to include, generally, all personal rights (the rights to physical and moral integrity, ie right to life, to physical well-being and health, to freedom, honour, good name and reputation) and property rights. As to rules of law designed to protect the interests of other persons, these are to be found in laws relating to specific matters, such as laws regulating the production and sale of toys, foodstuffs and pharmaceutical products.

Liability for certain acts may be precluded. Generally speaking, such liability will be precluded when a right is exercised in a regular and acceptable manner or in fulfilling a duty. Apart from these two situations, the law deals with special cases of justification for acts which might otherwise give rise to a liability:

(a) *direct action* (article 336): the use of force to protect certain rights;
(b) *legitimate defence* (article 337): acts designed to fend off aggression;
(c) *necessity* (article 339): destruction or damage to a third party's property in order to remove the danger of a more serious form of damage or injury;
(d) *consent of the injured party* (article 340): generally, an act which violates the rights of another party is licit if that other party consents, unless such consent is contrary to a prohibition of law or custom.

3.3 Intent and mere fault

Tortious liability, as a rule, presupposes some sort of intent or psychological connection between the act giving rise to the damage and the agent, and it is only in the limited cases of no-fault liability that a simple material connection will suffice. The psychological connection may be established as *intent* or *mere fault* in producing the damaging act.

In Portuguese legal doctrine intent is classified as:

(a) direct;
(b) indirect or necessary; and
(c) eventual.

In the case of *direct intent* the agent acts with the intention of producing the illicit result, eg he deliberately sets fire to another person's car. When the intent is *indirect* or *necessary* the agent's objective is not to cause the illicit act, but he is aware that it is likely to result as a consequence of the course of action he has chosen, eg a manufacturer of fire-resistant suits uses inferior materials to reduce production costs after tests have proved that such materials will not tolerate temperatures over X degrees which are likely to occur in the case of chemically fuelled fires. Eventual intent occurs when the agent foresees the possibility of an illicit result but acts in the hope that it will not occur, eg a boiler is manufactured to withstand X pressure, it being possible, but technically unlikely, that it may, for its intended purposes, have to withstand greater pressure.

In practice it may be difficult to draw a line between these different forms of intent, but the object of legal doctrine in creating such forms is not to extract different legal consequences from them, but rather to extend the concept of intent to cover all situations other than mere fault or negligence, which may produce different consequences for the liable party.

Mere fault or negligence will arise through a lack of diligence which can be expected of the agent, and as a result of which he does not foresee the occurrence of an illicit act, eg a manufacturer of foodstuffs, through lack of verification, uses ingredients which are past their prime and, on being consumed, these foodstuffs produce effects of ill health for consumers.

In the case of both intent and mere fault the obligation will arise for the agent to redress the damage caused (article 483(1)). However, in the case of mere fault it is possible that the agent may only have to partially redress the damage caused, and this will depend on the degree of fault of the party responsible, the economic situation of both the agent and the injured party, and other circumstances pertinent to the matter (article 494). Further, in certain very particular cases (which fall outside the object of our analysis), the obligation to repair damages will only arise when the agent has acted with intent (articles 814(1), 815(1) and 1681(1)).

3.4 Burden of proof

The burden of proof of the fault of the agent (be it through intent or mere fault, as discussed above), lies with the injured party, except where the law establishes a presumption to the contrary (Article 587(1)) (as explained in the next paragraph). The fault itself is to be assessed in the light of the diligence of a good 'paterfamilias', taking into account the circumstances of the case (article 487(2)). In other words, it is usually for the injured party to prove that the agent was at fault in causing the damage, in the sense that he did not act diligently and reasonably in the circumstances of the case.

The law does, however, establish a number of situations where the agent is presumed to be at fault, unless he is able to prove otherwise. For example, if damage is caused by incapacitated persons, those responsible for their care shall be liable, unless they prove that they satisfied their duty of vigilance, or that the damage would have occurred even if they had fulfilled such a duty (article 491). The same rule is established in article 492 for those who own or possess buildings or other forms of construction, which cause damage as a result of collapse arising from a defect in construction or conservation. One further instance of legal presumption of fault of the agent occurs where damage is caused by a movable or fixed object, or animal, which is in a person's possession and which he has a duty to invigilate, in which case that person must prove that there was no fault on his part, or that the damage would have occurred even if he was exempt from fault (article 493(1)). An extension of this situation, and one of great practical significance, is the presumption of fault for those who cause damage when carrying out an activity which is considered dangerous by its very nature or as a result of the means used in such activity. In this instance the agent is under an obligation to pay damages for harm caused except where he can prove that he undertook every precaution that could be expected in the circumstances with the object of avoiding the damage (article 493(2)). This rule has led to a large number of decisions by the Appeal and Supreme Courts, particularly with regard to the definition of 'dangerous activities', which have been held to include such situations as the storage of inflammable materials, the use of explosives in quarrying and even the transport of cotton (given the possibility of spontaneous combustion).

3.5 Damage

Damage covers damage to both property and persons. Damage to property occurs when property is destroyed or when its possessor is deprived of its use. Personal damage is a more abstract notion which refers to a negative effect on a person's moral or spiritual values, eg the physical pain suffered as a result of an injury or the suffering caused by the death of a relative. As regards personal damage, the Civil Code states that in establishing compensation the courts must take into account personal damage which, because of its gravity, deserves the protection of the law. This allows the courts a certain degree of discretion so that they will not be obliged to consider all claims, although they will always consider claims for physical injury and serious offences to a person's honour.

In calculating the quantum of damages the same rules apply as those discussed above in connection with contractual liability (section 2.5, above), although special rules apply in the case of personal damage. For personal damage the sum of compensation shall be established on an equitable basis and taking into account the degree of fault of the agent, his economic situation and that of the injured party, as well as the circumstances of the case (article 496(3)). In the case of death, not only the suffering of the victim, but also the suffering of his close relatives (wife and descendants, or in cases where these do not exist, parents and other ascendants, or, failing these, siblings or nephews) shall be taken into account (article 496(3)). Apart from redress for the suffering inflicted in the case of death or personal injury, both the injured party and his dependants shall have a right to compensation for loss of earnings resulting from the death or injury. It should be stated, however, that Portuguese courts are notorious for awarding extremely low sums of compensation for death and personal injury, except in cases where it can be shown that the injured party was prevented from earning substantial sums through death or injury. It is possible that the courts are influenced by the very low legal limits applicable to the special case of no-fault liability for accidents caused by vehicles (qv section 3.9, below), so it is hoped that the much higher limits introduced by the Product Liability Directive will change this attitude. Whatever the reason, and even taking into account Portugal's relatively low standard of living, there can be no doubt that awards of 500,000 Escudos for loss of life, which are not uncommon, are far from granting suitable compensation.

3.6 Causation

As stated previously, article 483(1) obliges the agent of the illicit act to repair 'the damage arising from' violation of the rights of a third party or breach of any rule of law designed to protect a third party's interests. This clearly means that the agent is only liable for the damage caused by the illicit act and only to the extent that it has been produced by the illicit act. To establish causation the Civil Code then relies on the general rules foreseen at article 563, and which have already been discussed under contractual liability (qv section 2.5, above).

3.7 Limitation period

Article 498(1) establishes a limitation period of three years counting from the date on which the injured party became aware of his right to compensation (if the three years are to be counted from a date after the act, however, it is for the injured party to prove that he was not aware of his right to compensation until that date), as well as a maximum limitation period of 20 years from the time when the damage occurred, irrespective of the injured party's knowledge of his right to compensation. If, however, a longer limitation period is established in criminal law, that will be the period applicable (eg five years in the case of homicide through negligence: Portuguese Criminal Code article 117).

3.8 Joint and several liability

When several people are liable for damage, they are jointly and severally liable (article 497(1)), and a right of recourse is available to the person who redresses the damage against the parties at fault (article 497(2)). The proportion of liability depends on the degree of fault of the parties concerned, although the law presumes, unless proven otherwise, that all the parties liable are equally at fault.

3.9 No-fault liability

In Portuguese law liability is contractual or tortious, and in the latter case it always presupposes the existence of intent or mere fault. The only exceptions to this rule are clearly laid down in law, and the implementation of the Directive adds one more such exception to the list. Of those in existence before the Directive, because of the light they may shed on product liability, it is worth considering the following cases of no-fault liability: vicarious liability, accidents caused by road vehicles and damage caused by electrical or gas installations. Except where otherwise foreseen, the rules of tortious liability analysed above apply to cases of no-fault liability (article 499).

3.9.1 Vicarious liability

This is dealt with in the Civil Code as a specific case of no-fault liability whereby 'whoever charges another person with the commission of an act shall be liable, irrespective of any fault, for damages caused by that person, so long as that person is also liable' (article 500(1)). Such liability shall, however, only occur in cases where the person carrying out the act, the agent, is in some way subordinated to, or dependent on, the person commissioning the act, the commissioner, and the act giving rise to the liability was carried out in the course of the functions assigned to that agent.

Once the commissioner has redressed the damage he shall have a right of recourse against the agent, except to the extent that the commissioner is also at fault, either through the choice of agent, through the instructions given or through defective control of the agent's activity. In such cases, depending on the degree of fault of the two parties, the commissioner may have no right of recourse, or may have a right of recourse to only a part of the compensation he has satisfied.

3.9.2 Accidents caused by road vehicles

The cases most frequently decided in Portuguese courts are those connected with motor vehicle accidents, and it is useful that where intent or mere fault cannot be proven it is possible to fall back on the no-fault liability foreseen in article 503 for those who, in their own interest, have effective control over, or use of, a road vehicle of any sort. Such liability may only be excluded when the accident has been caused by the injured party, by a third party, or is the result of *force majeure* unrelated to the functioning of the vehicle (article 505).

The maximum limits for such liability are established in article 508 as:

(a) 4 million Escudos in the case of death or injury of one person;
(b) 4 million Escudos per person, in the case of death or injury of more than one person, up to a maximum of 12 million Escudos;
(c) three times the amounts stated in (a) and (b), ie 12 million Escudos or 36 million Escudos in the case of accidents caused by vehicles used in public transport (ie to passengers);

(d) ten times the amounts stated in (a) and (b), ie 40 million Escudos or 120 million Escudos in the case of accidents caused by trains;

(e) 2, 6 or 20 million Escudos for damage to property, depending respectively on whether the accident is caused by a road vehicle generally, or by a vehicle used in public transport or a train.

3.9.3 Damage caused by electrical or gas installations

In this particular case of no-fault liability, those responsible for the production, storage, transport and distribution of gas or electricity are liable for damage caused by these forms of energy, unless the installations used are in accordance with the technical rules applicable and in a perfect state of conservation (article 509(1)). (Before DL 383/89 was implemented liability was excluded in the case of *force majeure* which covered all exterior causes unrelated to the functioning or use of the installations: Article 509(2), and damage caused by utensils which use gas or electrical energy: Article 509(3).)

4. THE CONSUMER PROTECTION LAW

Law 29/81 of 22 August ('the Law') was published with the intention of satisfying the constitutional requirements of consumer protection (Portuguese Constitution article 60(1)). It has proved to be an abject failure.

The Law establishes a number of principles, including the right of consumers to protection against risks of damage to their interests, the effective prevention and reparation of individual or collective damage and active participation in the legal and administrative definition of consumer rights and interests (article 3).

As far as protection against risks of damage is concerned, the Law foresees, amongst other actions, the need to regulate the sale of an extensive list of products of particular importance to the protection of the health and safety of users, such as pre-packaged foodstuffs, cosmetics and detergents, toys, textiles and pharmaceutical products. In fact little or nothing was done in this context following the adoption of the Law in 1981 until Portugal's accession to the European Community in 1986, following which various laws have been adopted in implementation of EC Directives on consumer protection, such as Directive 79/112 on the labelling, presentation and advertising of food products and Directive 88/379 on the classification, packaging and labelling of dangerous substances.

As to the prevention and reparation of individual or collective damage, the Law did not develop any particular form of producer liability, and limited itself to stating that the consumer has a right to 'the reparation of damage [to his interests] which has been caused by defective goods or services, or defective post-sales service, or, in general, breach of the contract of supply' (article 7(e)). The Law is silent as to the manner in which such reparation is to be obtained, which means that it leaves the consumer in exactly the same position he was in before the adoption of the Law, ie the need to base his claim on contractual or tortious liability, as described above.

5. LIABILITY FOR DEFECTIVE PRODUCTS ARISING FROM DECREE LAW 383/89 OF 6 NOVEMBER: IMPLEMENTATION OF THE DIRECTIVE

5.1 Introduction

The Directive was published in the Official Journal of 25 July 1985, which was some months before Portugal's accession to the European Community on 1 January 1986. Article 19 of the Directive stipulates that Member States would bring into force national measures for the implementation of the Directive not later than three years from the date of notification. Given the principle of *aquis communautaire*, embodied in article 2 of the Treaty of Accession of Portugal and Spain, and according to which new Member States are bound by Community law in the same way as existing Member States, it was expected that Portugal would implement the Directive by 25 July 1988. In fact, following successive delays, the Directive was finally implemented on 6 November 1989. The insurance lobby in Portugal was, in part, responsible for these delays, having strongly resisted the implementation of the Directive which it considered was not adaptable to local circumstances, in particular, in relation to the maximum limit provided for in article 16(1).

Despite these objections, the Decree Law which finally implemented the Directive is an almost faithful reproduction of its provisions, with one important exception in relation to the maximum limit mentioned above, and which we shall deal with in section 5.2, below, outlining DL 383/89.

5.2 Outline of Decree Law 383/89

Article 1 of the Decree Law establishes that the producer is liable, irrespective of intent or mere fault, for damage caused by defects in his products. The producer is defined in article 2 in a manner which includes both the definition of 'producer' foreseen in article 3(1) of the Directive (the manufacturer of a finished product, of a component part or of any raw material, and any person who represents himself as a producer by placing his name, trademark or other distinguishing feature on the product) and the importer and supplier of the product as provided for in article 3(1) and 3(2) of the Directive.

The 'product' is defined in article 3 in the exact terms used in article 2 of the Directive, and excludes primary agricultural products, ie no use is made of the possibility of derogation provided for in article 15(1)(a) of the Directive allowing Member States to include 'agricultural products and game'. However, in a departure from article 2 of the Directive, no mention is made of electricity, but the accepted view in Portuguese law, taking into account the definition of movables and immovables given in articles 204 and 205 of the Portuguese Civil Code, is that electricity is classified as a movable object, so such a specific inclusion in DL 383/89 would have been superfluous.

The definition of defect is provided for in article 4 and reproduces the definition in article 7 of the Directive. The same is true of article 5 which reproduces verbatim the list of cases of exclusion of liability foreseen in article 7 of the Directive and includes the 'state of the art' defence of article 7(e) of the

Directive. Therefore, no use has been made of the possibility of derogation provided for in article 15(1)(e) of the Directive.

The rule of joint and several liability is established in article 6(1). In articles 6(2) and 6(3) it is stated that in apportioning liability between the jointly and severally liable parties, it shall be necessary to take into account the circumstances of the case, in particular, the risk created by each liable party, the gravity of fault with which the party may have acted and the party's contribution to the damage. In cases of doubt, the liability shall be apportioned equally between the parties.

Article 7(1) provides that the liability of the producer may be reduced or disallowed when, taking into account all the circumstances, the damage has also been caused by the fault of the injured person, but this has not been drafted also to include 'any person for whom the injured person is responsible'. The reason for this omission on the part of the Portuguese legislator probably lies in the fact that he deemed the inclusion of persons for whom the injured person is responsible as superfluous in the light of the rule of article 491 of the Portuguese Civil Code. This article states that those responsible for invigilating others are responsible for the damage they cause to third parties, so that the damage caused by a person the injured person is responsible for would be the same as damage caused by the injured person himself and consequently any reference in DL 383/89 to persons for whom the injured person is responsible would be unnecessary. The flaw in this logic, however, is the caveat provided for in article 491, which excludes the liability of the invigilator if he can prove that he fulfilled his duty to invigilate, or that the damage would have occurred even if such a duty had been fulfilled. Such a caveat definitely falls outside the scope of the Directive and, in keeping with the *Von Colson* principle must be considered inapplicable (Case 14/83 *Von Colson and Kamman v Land Nordrhein-Wesfalen* [1984] ECR 1981, ECJ, according to which courts of a Member State are obliged to interpret national legislation passed to implement an EC Directive so as to give effect to it).

Article 7(2) lays down the rule that the liability of the producer shall not be reduced when the damage is also caused by the intervention in any way of a third party (this must be presumed to include omissions, if article 8(1) of the Directive is taken into account), without prejudice to the rules of article 6(2) and 6(3), described above, on the apportioning of liability.

The definition of damage in article 8 is the same as that contained in article 9 of the Directive, namely damage resulting from death or personal injury, and property damage, other than to the defective product itself. The lower threshold of Ecu 500 provided for in article 9 of the Directive appears as 70,000 Escudos in article 8(2), and a maximum limit for damage is established in article 9(1) at 10,000 million Escudos. It appears from the amounts of the lower threshold and maximum limit that the Portuguese legislator had some difficulty in informing himself of the exchange rate for the Ecu. Article 18(1) of the Directive provides that the equivalent in national currency of the amounts stated in the Directive in Ecu 'shall initially be calculated at the rate obtaining on the date of adoption of this Directive'. On 11 November 1989, the day on which DL 383/89 came into force, the Ecu was quoted, in round figures, at 175 Escudos. At this rate the lower threshold of Ecu 500 would have been 87,500 Escudos and the maximum limit of Ecu 70 million foreseen in article 16(1) of the Directive would have been 12,250 million Escudos, ie more than 20 per cent higher than the limit established in DL 383/89. A party seeking damages under DL 383/89 which exceeded the 10,000 million Escudos limit might attempt to overcome such a limitation by involving the *Von Colson* principle, but it is possible that the courts would consider such an attempt as more than simply a matter of construction of the law, and rather as an effort to establish (horizontal) direct effect for a Directive, ie invoking the rules of a Directive to create rights and obligations between private parties, something which the European Court of Justice has never accepted (eg Case 152/84 *Marshall v Southampton & West Hampshire Area Health Authority (Teaching)* [1986] 1 CMLR 688).

The remaining articles of DL 383/89 (articles 10–15) transcribe almost literally the Directive's provisions on the prohibition of the producer's exemption or limitation of liability (Directive article 12); limitation period (Directive article 10(1)); extinction of the rights conferred on the injured person (Directive article 11); the safeguarding of rights of the injured person conferred by national rules on contractual and non-contractual liability (Directive article 13); the exclusion of nuclear accidents covered by international conventions (Directive article 14) and the non-application of the Directive to products put into circulation before the entry into force of DL 383/89 (Directive article 17).

5.3 Comparison of the effects of Decree Law 383/89 with the previous position in contract and tort

As can be concluded from the preceding analysis, DL 383/89 represents a major improvement for the consumer who has suffered damage resulting from a defective product, as compared with his situation before the adoption of the law. On the one hand, he can overcome the limitations of contract law which restrict the effect of contracts to the parties who conclude them, on the other hand, he no longer has to face the sometimes formidable hurdle of proving the intent or mere fault of the agent who caused the damage.

The need for such protection of the consumer has been recognised in a number of western countries, indeed the topic had been the subject of debate in Portugal for some time, and it was disappointing that the legislator did not choose to introduce no-fault product liability when Law 29/81 on consumer protection (section 4, above) was adopted.

The reverse of the situation is that Portuguese manufacturers and insurers have suddenly been faced with potential liabilities which are beyond the means of many of them to satisfy. If Law 29/81 had included no-fault product liability with lower maximum limits, more suitable to Portuguese economic conditions, then manufacturers and insurers may have had some time to adapt and develop experience in risk management. As it is, most companies in Portugal are woefully unprepared for the levels of liability foreseen in DL 383/89. However, it must be said that even if the Directive had not been implemented in Portugal, Portuguese economic agents would still be subject to the product liability it establishes whenever they exported their products to another Member State which had implemented the Directive, and with Portugal's eventual ratification of the Brussels Convention on Jurisdiction and the Enforcement of Judgments in Civil and Commercial Matters, it would always be a relatively simple matter to enforce, in Portuguese courts, the judgments on claims brought before the courts of other Member States.

6. RISK MANAGEMENT IN THE NEW ERA OF PRODUCT LIABILITY

6.1 Insurance

Having fiercely opposed the implementation of the Directive in Portugal, a year later the insurance companies appear to be continuing to adopt their 'ostrich' approach. At the time of writing the Association of Portuguese Insurers (*Associação Portuguesa de Seguradores*) refused to disclose the standard insurance policy it has been drafting for its members to cover no-fault product liability. It can only be hoped that this situation will change soon.

6.2 Limitation on liability through corporate structure

The principle of companies as distinct legal entities in their own right is one which is enshrined in Portuguese law, and recognises very few exceptions outside the realms of tax law and rules of accounting. The liability of the shareholder, whether physical person or body corporate, of a limited company (in Portuguese company law these are *sociedade por quotas, sociedade anonima* and, far less common, the *sociedade em comandita por accoes*) is limited to the value of his shares, or in the peculiar case of the *sociedade por quotas*, the value of his shares plus, jointly and severally with other shareholders, the value of other shares not fully paid up. There is no tradition on the part of Portuguese courts of 'lifting the veil' of incorporation or disqualifying shell companies. The only situations where this is possible are clearly laid down in the law.

In connection with this matter, the Portuguese Companies Code of 1986 introduced various innovative provisions on relationships between companies. Of the various ways in which such relationships may occur, two are of particular interest to our subject, and these are the cases of 'total domination' and 'contracts of subordination'.

(a) Total domination (Companies Code articles 489 and 490) can occur either if a company is set up by another company which is its only shareholder (Companies Code article 488), or if more than 90% of a company's shares are acquired directly or indirectly by another company.

(b) Contracts of subordination (Companies Code articles 493ff) are contracts concluded between companies under the terms of which one company (the subordinated company) subordinates its management to that of another (the directing company). This may occur irrespective of whether one company already has control over the other (through a majority shareholding or direct or indirect control of its management).

Following the conclusion of such a contract the independent shareholders are permitted to choose between the sale of their shares or a guarantee of profits provided by the directing company.

In both of these situations the Companies Code provides that the dominant, or directing, company shall be liable for the obligations of the dominated, or subordinated, company for as long as the domination or subordination exists (article 501). An added liability is established at article 502, which states that the subordinated, or dominated, company may require its master company to compensate annual losses which cannot be covered by the former's reserves. Put very simply, a company may be held liable both by the creditors of its wholly-owned subsidiary and the company whose management it controls contractually, or it may be held liable by that company itself for its losses.

Apart from these situations, which are easily avoidable, a company, or person, with a controlling interest in another company cannot be held liable for the debts of the latter. Therefore, for businesses in high risk activities of any kind, incorporation and the use of shell companies is always an advantage under Portuguese law, as long as total domination and contracts of subordination are avoided.

7. FURTHER READING

Almeida, C *Mario Julio Obrigações* (Coimbra Editora, 4th edn 1984).
Lima, P & Varela, A *Código Civil Anotado* (Coimbra Editora), vol I (4th edn, 1984) and vol II (3rd edn, 1986).
Neto, A and Martins, H *Código Civil Anotado* (Livraria Petrony, 7th edn, 1990).
Neto, A *Notas Práticas ao Código das Sociedades Comerciais* (Livraria Petrony, 1989).
Rodrigues, J V C *A Responsabilidade Civil do Produtor Face a Terceiros* (Associação Académic da Faculdade de Direito de Lisboa, 1990).
Galvao Telles, I *Direito das Obrigações* (Coimbra Editora, 6th edn, 1989).
Varela, A *Das Obrigações em Geral* (Almedina) vol I (6th edn, 1989) and vol II (4th edn, 1990).

following the conclusion of such a contract the [illegible] [illegible] the [illegible] to choose between the [illegible] and [illegible] provided by the [illegible]

[illegible]

FURTHER READING

[illegible]

CHAPTER XIII

Spain

Mr Ramon Mullerat
Ms Sonia Cortes

Bufete Mullerat & Rosell
Paseo de Gracia 81
08008 Barcelona
Spain

Tel ++ 34 3 215 0233
Fax ++ 34 3 215 8602

CHAPTER XIII

Spain

1. INTRODUCTION

1.1 Overview of the law relating to defective products in Spain

As with most civil law systems, Spanish legislation contains provisions expressly dealing with liability for defective products. For a long time, the legal basis for product liability was found in several provisions enacted in the nineteenth century: the Commercial Code (1885) ('Cco') and the Civil Code (1889) ('Cc'). These provisions contained two main hurdles as regards bringing a claim for product liability, namely (a) the principle of privity of contract, which prevented a victim who was not a party to a contract (eg a bystander) from obtaining a contractual remedy, and (b) the need for the plaintiff to prove that there was fault or negligence by the seller.

Product liability law was thus not properly developed and the courts failed to provide case law that could create a modern system in this field. One of the reasons for this lack of evolution in civil liability must be found in the fact that in most cases where a defective product has caused injuries, the plaintiff generally institutes criminal proceedings which may be more efficient since the judge has a more active part ('ex officio') and his judgment also covers civil damages.

More recently, the General Act on Defence of Consumers and Users 26/84 approved on 19 July 1984 ('GAC') introduced the principles of the producer's liability for damage caused by his product to consumers and users as a consequence of his negligent behaviour, and strict liability (regardless of the existence of negligence) for certain categories of products. Even if described as incomplete and technically deficient, the GAC has provided the basis for future legislation on the matter and thus represents an undeniable development in this field, with the resulting increased risk of exposure to product liability claims for producers, suppliers and others.

It should be borne in mind that the Spanish Central Parliament has basic jurisdiction on consumer protection policy, but most Spanish Regional Parliaments have jurisdiction to develop any legislation enacted on such a basis (eg Catalan Act 1/1990 of 8 January).

As provided in article 149.1.13 of the Spanish Constitution, the Spanish Central Legislature has exclusive jurisdiction to set forth the basis and co-ordination of the economy's general planning, which includes consumer protection policy. However, most Regional Parliaments have exclusive jurisdiction to develop the legislation enacted by the Central Parliament, by approving Regional Acts and Regulations within the scope of such national basic legislation, since most Autonomous Regions have included such a jurisdiction in their Statutes of Autonomy. The Constitutional Court shall decide whenever there is a conflict of jurisdiction between Central and Regional legislative bodies.

The Directive has not yet been implemented in Spanish law despite the three-year term for implementation having long since expired. The Department of Commercial Law of the General Commission of Codification in the Ministry of Justice prepared a draft which was presented on 26 January 1988. Unfortunately, the approval of this draft has been delayed and it is thus uncertain when the Directive is to be implemented. At the time of writing the Government recently declared its intention to implement most of the outstanding EC Directives shortly, and a new draft prepared earlier in 1991 is being studied by the Central Government before taking it to Parliament.

1.2 Definition and classification of terms

This area has traditionally been referred to in Spain as the 'Manufacturer's Liability' (*responsabilidad del fabricante*), stressing the subjective aspect as in other countries with a civil law system instead of 'Product Liability' (*responsabilidad de los productos*), although the latter is used increasingly. Spanish legal authors normally use terms relating to product liability with the same meaning and scope as employed in the Directive. The GAC uses a terminology of its own that does not always coincide with the one employed in the Directive.

The main terms used in this area of the law in Spain are:

i. Subjects.

(a) *Producer*: Strictly speaking, the party manufacturing the product and in a broad sense, any party participating in the chain of supply (supplier, importer, assembler, etc). The term 'manufacturer' (*fabricante*) is more widely used than that of 'producer' (*productor*) which in Spanish law used to have a social connotation.
(b) *Injured person*: The party who suffers injury caused by the defective product. Spanish law does not generally refer to this term but rather to a 'consumer' or 'user', thus a person who acquires, uses or enjoys a product other than for a business purpose (GAC articles 1.2 and 3).
(c) *Other subjects*: The GAC, which at present is the main legislation regulating this matter, refers to a number of other parties, who are not considered in the Directive, such as the 'holder' (*tenedor*) who is the party in the chain of supply holding the product.

ii. Product. Any kind of product that may cause damage to any consumer or user. Certain products that entail a higher risk are subject to a more strict product liability system as described in section 5 of this chapter.

iii. Damage. Death, personal injury or moral damage caused by the use or consumption of the defective product, as well as other damages that may also be covered by the compensation such as non-physical damage (physical effects such as phobias, death of a child, etc) and financial loss. Since the GAC makes no restrictions or delimitation, it seems that any kind of damage is susceptible of being grounds for a claim.

Spanish law does not provide a definition of non-physical damage ('moral damage'); this concept includes any damage related to personal rights (health, freedom, reputation, etc) that does not cause an immediate economic loss, eg discrediting of a businessman, pain, damage to a woman's reputation, suffering on the death of a close relative, damage caused when infringing morals or damage to a person's physical appearance, thus hindering social life, etc. Loss thus covers not only pure economic damage but also subjective and moral consequences that compensation should help to overcome.[1]

iv. *Defect.* Any irregularity in the product that causes the damage. This element is not specifically contemplated in the GAC but it may be an implicit element.

v. *Compensation.* An amount awarded to the victim for the damage caused by the defective product, which consists of an amount of money which is meant to place the victim, to the extent possible, in the situation he was in before the damage occurred.

vi. *Contributory negligence.* The negligence of the injured or third person besides the defective product which has also contributed to the damage, eg misuse of the product or failure to follow the warning on the label. Exclusion of liability only arises when the damage is exclusively attributable to the negligence of the injured or third party.

2. LIABILITY IN CONTRACT

Spanish law has traditionally been based on privity of contract (*relatividad de los contratos*), in the sense that only the parties to a contract may reciprocally claim enforcement of its clauses, since as provided by Cc article 1257, 'contracts only entail effects for the parties who execute them'.

To be legally valid, contracts require the consent of the parties (who must have sufficient legal capacity), an object and a consideration.[2]

2.1 Liability for pre-contractual statements or representations

Any statements made before the contract is agreed to that may be the basis on which a party enters into the agreement is deemed representation. Spanish contract law makes no particular reference to pre-contractual misrepresentations and the case law is somewhat contradictory.[3]

1 Judgment of the Supreme Court of 7 February 1962.
2 Cc 1261.
3 Supreme Court judgment of 12 December 1976, 30 October 1984, 13 December 1984, 16 May 1988, 30 October 1988.

However, GAC article 10 provides that all clauses, conditions or stipulations which in a general manner are applied to the offer, promotion or sale of products or services to consumers, shall fulfil the following requirements:

(a) Concrete, clear and simple wording should be used which is easily understood and references to other texts or documents that are not provided should be avoided. The contract shall make express reference to such documents.
(b) A receipt, voucher, copy of the transaction or budget must be delivered to the consumer unless expressly waived.
(c) Good faith and fair balance of the consideration including the avoidance of a number of unfair trade practices listed in the GAC, eg omitting the rate of interest applied when payment is deferred, including abusive clauses that place the consumer in a blatantly disadvantageous situation or abusive credit conditions, unfairly limiting liability, etc.

2.2 Outline of contract law relevant to defective products in Spain

The vendor is liable to the purchaser for the product's latent defects (*saneamiento por vicios ocultos*),[4] if the product is not fit for its purpose (to the extent such purpose was obvious or clearly stated by the purchaser) or when its usefulness is reduced to such an extent that if the purchaser would have known, he would not have acquired the product or would have paid less for it.

Conversely, the vendor is not liable for any disclosed defects, nor for those which the purchaser could have ascertained upon inspection. If the purchaser is an expert in the field a higher degree of knowledge is expected, since the vendor will not be liable for undisclosed defects that the purchaser could have easily spotted due to his profession or job.

On that basis, the vendor may be found liable for any defects in the product he did not disclose to the purchaser. It is no defence for the supplier to state that the defect was due to the manufacturer's fault if the vendor could have noticed the defect if he had acted with sufficient diligence.

A specific liability is provided for building constructors and architects in case of collapse (*ruina*) of a building due to construction or engineering defects.[5] This liability may never be contractually excluded by the parties (*jus cogens*). The action to claim damages expires after a term of ten years or fifteen years if the damage is due to the constructors' breach of the contract. There is an overwhelming amount of case law on this matter as a result of the construction boom which has occurred in Spain in the last thirty years. The courts have set up a complete system of construction liability based on this provision of the Cc. There is also at the time of writing a draft Bill on construction contemplating liability without fault of the building agents (promoter, constructor, architect, sub-contractor, supplier, manufacturer of materials, etc).

4 Cc 1484 and Cco arts 336.2 and342.
5 Cc 1591.

2.3 Contractual warranties relating to quality and safety of goods

Under Spanish law the general principle of freedom of the parties to agree is only subject to compliance with the law, morality and public order (Cc article 1255). The vendor's liability for the latent defects can be the object of different agreements by the parties as long as the vendor is not aware of the existence of such defects at the moment the agreements are made (Cc article 1485). However, the parties to a contract frequently agree on certain warranties provided by the vendor to the purchaser.

The parties to a consumer contract may, in principle, agree on the covenants they deem appropriate. However, there are certain rules with which they should comply and may not be excluded. According to GAC article 3.1, no products launched on the market may entail risks for the consumer's health or safety, except for those usually or statutorily accepted in normal and foreseeable conditions of use.

2.4 Breach of contract for supply of defective products

When the vendor supplies a defective product, the purchaser has the right to choose between either (a) terminating the contract (returning the product and collecting the purchase price), with reimbursement of the expenses incurred as part of the remedy of termination, or (b) having the purchase price promotionally reduced according to expert judgment.[6]

If the vendor knew of the hidden defects, the purchaser will have not only the rights described above, but also the right to claim damages if he chooses to rescind the contract. If the transaction is deemed to be commercial (ie when the parties are acting within the sphere of their respective businesses), the purchaser shall have the right to receive damages in any case, even when the vendor was not aware of the defect.

2.5 Quantum of damage

The behaviour of the vendor must be taken into account:

(a) If he acted in good faith (ie was not aware of the defect and acted diligently), the purchaser may either terminate the contract and claim the expenses incurred or reduce the purchase price in proportion to the gravity of the defect.[7] Compensation shall cover loss of the purchased object and expenses incurred, but not damages suffered.

(b) If he acted in bad faith (ie if he was aware of the defects and did not reveal them to the purchaser) the latter shall have the same choice as in

6 Cc art 1486.
7 Cc art 1488.

the above paragraph, but he shall be entitled to damages if he chooses termination of the contract.[8]

Compensation shall cover loss of the purchased object and any expenses and damages incurred. If loss of the product is due to *force majeure* (unforeseeable cause), the vendor will also be liable for damages and interest.

Compensation for damages includes the value of the actual damage and any loss of profits, even if they were not foreseeable at the time of the agreement. As stated above, evidence should be provided of the defect of the product and the causal relationship, ie the link between the defect and the resulting damage. Further, a claim to obtain compensation should contain sufficient elements in order to quantify damages and loss profits.

Damages for personal injury are generally calculated on the basis of a particular amount per day the victim has not been able to work, in addition to any moral and physical damage or costs incurred (eg medical expenses) etc.

2.6 Burden of proof

The burden of proof is on the purchaser, who as plaintiff has to prove the existence of the contract between the parties, the defect of the purchased product, the fact that it makes the product useless for its purpose, the damage caused and the causal relationship, according to the rule that the burden of proof of the contractual obligations rests with the party claiming their fulfilment.[9] However, in civil cases the courts have frequently accepted the shifting of the burden of proof from the plaintiff to the defendant.

2.7 Exclusion or limitation of liability

The level of diligence for the obligations arising out of a contract can be agreed by the parties.[10]

In a standard contract the parties may exclude the liability of the supplier as long as this agreement is not contrary to law, morality or public order.[11] This agreed exclusion of liability shall be effective as long as the vendor was not aware of the defects in the products.[12] However, if the agreement is considered to be a consumer contract, it falls within the GAC and thus no absolute exclusion of liability may be agreed to.[13]

8 Cc art 1486.
9 Cc art 1214.
10 Cc art 1104.
11 Cc art 1255.
12 Cc art 1485.
13 Art 10.c.6.

2.8 Limitation period

Under Spanish contract law personal actions in general must be commenced within 15 years of the date when the harm occurred or the date when the plaintiff discovered the harm.[14] Actions for claims relating to defective products have a time limit of six months, starting from the date of delivery of the product.[15] If the transaction is subject to commercial law (the parties are traders acting in the scope of their business), actions for defective products have a time limit of 30 days[16] or 4 days when furnished in packages.[17]

2.9 Liability for third parties

The intervention of a third party may avoid liability of the vendor whenever the intervention can be considered to have been of such a degree that the link between the defect of the product and the damage caused is broken.

2.10 Conclusion

The provisions described above regarding contractual liability under traditional Spanish law entail major disadvantages for the consumer injured by a defective product, ie:

(a) If a person suffers injury caused by a defective product, he can only claim against the vendor (generally the retailer) who sold him the product and not against the wholesaler, the distributor or the producer, since he holds no contractual relationship with them.

(b) If the transaction is not a commercial one, the purchaser will only have the right to receive damages if he can prove that the vendor was aware of the defects and he did not reveal them to the purchaser. This rule is based on the principle of subjective or fault liability, which in terms of contractual obligations is established in Cc article 1101 in the sense that a party shall be deemed liable for damages whenever he has acted negligently (*negligencia* or *culpa*). On this basis, proper redress of the damage can only be obtained by the person injured by a defective product if he can furnish proof that the producer acted negligently in the manufacture of the defective product.

(c) The burden of proof is on the plaintiff (purchaser) and not on the defendant (vendor), so the purchaser must provide any required evidence.

(d) The purchaser fails to obtain damages if the vendor becomes insolvent. Indeed, in the case of insolvency the creditor holds the same right which is not extinguished by this reason and is thus added to the claims of

14 Cc arts 1964 and 1969.
15 Cc art 1490.
16 Cco art 342.
17 Cco art 336.

creditors in the liquidation of the vendor. However, in practical terms he shall seldom receive any compensation.

(e) The above-mentioned rights only protect the purchaser but not his relatives, friends or any bystanders who (unless they are heirs of a deceased purchaser) have no action against the vendor for liability in contract.

(f) The action of the purchaser to claim his rights usually expires six months after delivery of the object of the agreement for the sale and purchase. Furthermore, whenever the contract is deemed to be commercial, the Cco reduces this term to 30 or even 4 days.

3. LIABILITY IN TORT

3.1 Introduction

Extra-contractual liability (liability in tort) is mainly based on the Civil Code pursuant to which 'whomsoever causes damage to another person by an act or omission and with negligence or fault is liable for the damage caused'.[18] This provision is broad enough to grant protection to any injured person who suffers damage by any kind of tort. The courts have constantly repeated that the following requirements are necessary for the existence of extra-contractual liability:

(a) action or omission;
(b) unlawfulness;
(c) negligence;
(d) damage; and
(e) causal link between the act or omission and the damage.

It should be borne in mind that Spanish law does not provide different 'torts' as is the case in the common law countries (negligence, nuisance, etc). The above broadly worded provision, however, may include any such situation.

3.2 Outline of the law of tort giving rise to liability for personal and property damage

Spanish law is traditionally founded on subjective or fault-based liability in the sense that such liability only arises when the tortfeasor has acted negligently or with *dolus* (malicious intent). According to the traditional system if a manufacturer is not aware of the defect in a product and acted diligently enough to avoid any such defect, he shall not be liable in tort for damage caused by the product.

This principle, summarised in the expression 'no liability without fault', has been confirmed by a large number of court judgments. Besides proving the existence of an unlawful act or omission, the damage caused and the causal relationship between the act or omission and the damage, the consumer must

18 Cc art 1902.

give sufficient evidence that the manufacturer acted negligently when manufacturing the product, which is a very heavy burden of proof.

Prior to the GAC, the Spanish courts developed the relevant case law so as to mitigate this harsh situation for the consumer by introducing certain elements of a strict liability system (not essentially depending on the behaviour of the defendant), although the principle of subjective liability was never completely set aside.

3.3 Causation

For there to be liability in tort, the damage caused must be a direct result of the negligent action of the producer (supplier, importer, etc). Such causal relationship (*nexo causal*) is examined on a case-by-case basis using certain criteria such as reasonable consequence, sufficiency of cause to give rise to the damage etc. For instance, a judgment of the Supreme Court of 30 December 1981 found a company supplying electric power liable for the death of a person due to electrocution as a result of the lowering of certain overhead electricity cables.

3.4 Remoteness of loss and damage

No liability shall be found whenever the relationship between loss and damage on the one hand and the negligent act or omission on the other is too remote. In this sense, any element that is considered to break the causal relationship exempts the defendant from liability, whenever it is unforeseeable or inevitable. The case law has not defined unforeseeability, and thus has found liability in cases where a child threw a firecracker at a girl causing her to become blind,[19] and also where a company left chemical material near a river bank polluting nearby cultivated land when the river rose.

The following may be causes allowing exclusion of liability: *force majeure* (eg earthquake),[20] intervention of a third party (eg the supplier introduces essential amendments to the design of a product which entail a substantial degree of risk, thus excluding the liability of the manufacturer if he was not to blame as well) or negligence of the victim (eg a pedestrian suddenly walks onto the road without checking whether any cars are coming and in a way that the driver could never have foreseen, or avoided, even having acted diligently).

3.5 Quantum of damage

Damages in tort cover all damages directly caused by the negligent act and those that may be deemed to have been caused by the act, but not those that are too remote. In particular, they include the replacement of the product, damage effectively caused and an amount for compensation for damage to property and other prejudices and non-physical damage (*pretium doloris*) including pain and

19 A judgment of the Supreme Court of 4 May 1984.

20 Which is contemplated by Cc art 1105: 'nobody is liable for such events which cannot be foreseen or which, if foreseen, were unavoidable'.

suffering, reputation, etc. They cover not only the damage (*damnum emergens*) but also lost profits (*lucrum cessans*) if there is sufficient evidence of the loss. In general, Spanish case law provides for a lump sum to be paid for all the heads of damage. On some occasions these sums are not as high as those awarded by courts in other countries, although the Spanish courts are gradually taking a more realistic attitude. The Court of Appeal of Girona recently awarded compensation of 40m pesetas to an unfortunate child who lost both legs in an incident involving a cultivator.

3.6 Burden of proof

According to the strict letter of the law, the victim must establish the main elements of the action (unlawful act or omission, damage, link between act or omission and damage and negligence of the defendant). However, Spanish case law has in practice altered this situation by introducing a presumption of negligence by the defendant, thus inverting the burden of proof. Important case law concerning extra-contractual liability has been based upon a presumption of negligence of the person causing the damage, such presumption being susceptible to being overturned by means of conclusive evidence (*juris tantum* presumption).[1]

3.7 Exclusion of limitation of liability

Liability arising in tort may not be restricted.[2]

3.8 Limitation period

A claim for damages in tort must be brought within one year from the moment the plaintiff was aware of the damage.[3]

However, whenever the plaintiff's fault qualifies as a crime, the victim's claim in civil liability may be brought within 15 years of the time when the plaintiff was aware of the damage.[4]

3.9 Liability for third parties

Spanish law provides reference to certain particular cases of liability involving third parties in tort. The employer or manager is liable for damage caused by his employees within the scope of their jobs; parents, teachers and tutors are liable for damage caused by children under their responsibility and the State is liable in some cases for the acts or omissions of civil servants, except when they

1 Judgments of the Supreme Court of 22 June 1931, 10 July 1943, 23 December 1952, 24 March 1953, 14 May 1963, 20 October 1963, 11 March 1971, 9 March 1974, 20 December 1982 etc.
2 Cc art 1255.
3 Cc art 1968.2
4 117 Criminal Code and Cc art 1964, a judgment of the Supreme Court of 1 April 1990.

can prove that they acted with the required diligence to avoid the damage (Cc article 1903). The recent Act of 7 January 1991 has amended Cmc article 22 and Cc articles 1903 and 1904 which declared the liability of teachers with respect to their pupils, and declares instead the liability of owners of schools for the damage caused by the pupils as minors under the control of the teachers.

The law provides for liability of owners of machines that expel polluting fumes, owners of land whose trees fall and cause damage, owners of buildings which fall etc. In the case of buildings, the architect or the builder shall be liable if damage is caused due to a construction defect.[5]

3.10 Implications for producers and defendants

Although the requirements to be fulfilled by a consumer in order to sue a producer or a supplier for liability in tort are difficult to comply with, Spanish case law has mitigated the situation in the following way:

(a) reversal of burden of proof, as described in section 3.6, above;

(b) relaxation of the requirement of proving the facts ('principle of expansion'), whereby the courts have sometimes accepted weak evidence in order to protect the weaker party;[6]

(c) requirement of a higher degree of diligence, in the sense that some judgments have been based on the fact that the defendant should have acted with a higher level of diligence according to the nature of the obligations and the circumstances of persons, time and place as provided in Cc article 1104 for contractual liability;[7]

(d) relaxation of the requirement of unlawful behaviour (*antijuridicidad*), since it has been found in certain cases that even lawful behaviour causing damage may give rise to compensation whenever the defendant has not acted with sufficient diligence;[8]

(e) non-acceptance of the justification that regulatory provisions have been complied with, since it has been found that such a defence is not enough to relieve a person from liability.[9] A judgment of the Supreme Court of 20 December 1982 held in a case concerning a manufacturing business whose easily flammable products were set on fire, that mere compliance with regulations was not sufficient to relieve from liability when the duty to foresee and thus avoid the foreseeable and avoidable damages had failed, thus showing insufficient care;

(f) acceptance of liability for the creation of risks, close to strict liability, in the sense that whoever develops a business activity that involves risks for others is liable for any damages arising therefrom.[10]

5 Cc arts 1908 and 1909.

6 Judgment of the Supreme Court of 5 April 1963.

7 Judgments of the Supreme Court of 14 February 1974, 14 April 1962, 9 April 1963, 28 June 1974, 10 October 1975, 22 October 1977.

8 Judgments of the Supreme Court of 14 February 1944, 23 February 1950, 23 December 1952, 24 March 1953, 30 June 1959, 14 March 1963, 28 June 1974.

9 Judgments of the Supreme Court of 14 May 1963, 30 October 1963.

10 Judgments of the Supreme Court of 30 October 1963, 15 June 1967, 25 October 1973.

A judgment of the Supreme Court of 20 December 1982 declared that 'even if originally based on fault-based *liability*, the case law has developed extra-contractual liability towards strict liability, although the moral or psychological factor and the evaluation of the subject's behaviour have not been completely disregarded'. This new approach has been due to the increase in dangerous activities and is based on the principle that those who obtain the profit from a dangerous activity are liable for the compensation for damages resulting therefrom. This trend is based on the general principle[11] that the provisions are to be interpreted within the scope of the social sphere in which they operate.

The evolution referred to relates to liability in tort in general and not only to product liability. Decisions on product liability have been very scarce. A judgment of the Supreme Court 14 November 1984 declared that liability of the producer for damages caused to consumers and users by the product he manufactured should either be based on a negligent manufacturing of a defective product launched on the market[12] or on the failure to provide the required specific information and instructions for the use of the product and warning on the dangers involved therefrom.[13] In spite of the efforts of the courts, there has been no decisive case law for product liability in Spain as in some other countries like the USA or the German Federal Republic.

As indicated earlier, plaintiffs prefer on many occasions to bring actions in the criminal courts instead of the civil courts. The reason is that the criminal jurisdiction is often more effective and cheaper. Furthermore, the criminal courts have a more important role in the proceedings since they act *ex officio*, enabling them to consider any necessary evidence (in civil procedures they can only consider evidence put forward by the parties). The criminal judgments also cover any civil damages. This was the situation in a case for compensation of the effects of a toxic oil, which caused more than one hundred deaths and hundreds of serious injuries. This is the reason why case law in civil product liability has not expanded sufficiently.

4. LIABILITY FOR DEFECTIVE PRODUCTS BROUGHT ABOUT BY BREACH OF STATUTORY REGULATION DESIGNED TO PROTECT CONSUMERS AND/OR TO PROMOTE SAFETY

4.1 Outline of nature of protective regulations

4.1.1 Evolution towards the GAC

Spanish law has slowly begun to evolve towards a concept of liability based on the risk rather than the fault of the producer, thus gradually introducing into Spanish law the principle of strict liability.

11 Cc art 3.1.
12 Judgment of the Supreme Court of 26 March 1982 and 29 March 1983.
13 Judgment of the Supreme Court of 20 October 1983.

There have been several legislative developments in the field of strict liability, such as:

i. Motor vehicles. The Act of 21 December 1962 laid down that:

> 'The motor vehicle driver who, as a consequence of traffic, causes damage to persons or property, shall be obliged to compensate the damage caused, unless it is evidenced that the event was due solely to fault or negligence on the part of the injured person or to *force majeure* . . .' (article 1).

ii. Air navigation. The Act of 21 July 1960 introduced strict liability for a carrier for damage involving death or injuries suffered by the passengers and involving the destruction of merchandise and luggage (article 116), as well as for damage to persons or property on the land surface caused by airplanes (article 119).

iii. Nuclear energy. Under the Paris Convention of 1960 and the Spanish Act of 29 June 1964 and its Regulations of 22 July 1967, a company running a plant which produces or deals with radioactive materials is strictly liable for the damage it may cause.

iv. Hunting. Under the Hunting Act of 4 April 1979 and its Regulations of 25 March 1971, the hunter shall compensate for the damage caused by the hunting activity, except for that due to *force majeure* or to the negligence of the injured person.

4.1.2 Spanish Constitution of 1978

The legal basis for the protection of consumers is set forth in the Spanish Constitution ('SC') approved on 27 December 1978, which provides that 'the public bodies shall guarantee the defence of consumers and users by protecting their safety, health and lawful economic interests through efficient procedures' (SC article 51.1).

4.1.3 Precedents of the General Act for Consumers

Subsequently there were two main legislative precedents leading to the approval of the General Act in the Defence of Consumers and Users, namely the Basque Consumers Statute and the ratification of The Hague Convention on Product Liability.

(a) the Basque Consumer Statute (Basque Act of 18 November 1981) represented an important advance in the field of product liability, though the Constitutional Court declared that the legal provisions regarding product liability were unconstitutional on the grounds of the lack of determination of some essential elements (Judgment of 30 November 1982);
(b) on 7 November 1988 Spain ratified The Hague Convention on the Law Applicable to Product Liability dated 2 October 1973.

4.1.4 General Act for the Defence of Consumers and Users

The General Act for the Defence of Consumers and Users of 19 July 1984 was approved in order to enforce the constitutional principle set forth in SC article 51.1. Although it was intended to give protection to all consumers, as far as product liability is concerned it broadly surpassed the position taken by the Spanish codes, which up until then had still been anchored in the subjective liability system, and tried to approach modern concepts of product liability. Nevertheless, this approach was hesitant and confused and the GAC is far from having brought a clear and coherent system of liability without fault (strict liability) and from offering technical solutions close to those provided for by the Council of Europe Convention of 27 January 1977 and by the Directive. In many aspects the GAC goes beyond simple protection in the field of product liability but in others it reveals important shortcomings.

It is unfortunate that although the GAC was approved on 19 July 1984 when the proposal for the Directive was very advanced, the GAC did not follow the proposed general principles. It is also unfortunate that the Directive, which was approved on 25 June 1985, did not refer to the product liability of a Member State that would join the EEC the following 1 January 1986 after the signature of the Adhesion Treaty on 12 June 1985.

The GAC is an incoherent and technically defective system of product liability. However, it has represented a step forward as regards the protection of consumers since it has overcome the difficulties stemming from:

(a) subjective liability, by introducing specific cases where liability is found even when no negligence has been involved and disregarding the fact that the producer acted diligently; and
(b) privity of contracts, by granting consumers direct action against the manufacturer, importer, supplier, etc.

The GAC starts its Chapter VIII ('Guarantees and liabilities') with a general principle of consumer law: 'the consumer and user have the right to be compensated for the proven damage caused by the consumption of goods or the use of products or services . . .' (article 25). Indeed, the GAC takes the principle of fault as the basis for liability of the producer. The negligence is presumed but this presumption may be overturned if it is shown that the relevant regulations were complied with and that the producer acted diligently (article 26). This principle is subject to an important exception: liability without fault is established for a long list of 'vital' products or, in the terms of the GAC, those including a warranty of pureness, efficacy or safety and involving quality controls (article 28.1).

The system of exceptions – subject to strict liability – is so broad that it almost does not leave room for the application of the general system – subject to liability with fault. The main articles of the GAC in which product liability is regulated are the following:

'*Article 25*
Consumers and users have a right to be compensated for proven damage resulting from the consumption of goods or the use of products or services unless the damage is caused by their exclusive fault or that of any person for whom the consumer is responsible under civil law.

Article 26
Acts or omissions for those who manufacture, import, supply or provide products or services to consumers or users, which cause damage to them shall give rise to liability unless it appears or is evidenced that all statutory demands and requirements, as well as other care and diligence required by the nature of the product, service or activity, have been set.

Article 27
1. The following criteria in the field of liability shall apply as a general rule and without prejudice to other legal provisions or conventions more favourable to consumers or users:
   (a) The producer, importer, seller or supplier of products or services to consumers or users are responsible as to the origin, identity or suitability of these products or services, in accordance with their nature and purpose as well as with the regulations governing the same;
   (b) In the case of products in bulk the person holding them is liable, without prejudice to the possibility of identifying and proving the liability of the former holder or supplier;
   (c) In the case of packaged, labelled and fully enclosed products, the firm or company appearing on the label, display or advertising is liable. The firm or company may be exempted from liability by proving that the product has been opened or unduly handled by third parties who will then be liable.
2. If several persons were involved in causing the damage, they shall be jointly and severally liable vis-à-vis the injured persons. The person who compensates the injured person shall be entitled to claim payment from the other liable persons according to their participation in the causation of the damage.

Article 28
1. Notwithstanding the provisions of the previous articles, damage caused in the correct use and consumption of goods and services, shall give rise to liability whenever, whether because of their nature or on the ground of this being expressly provided for by administrative regulations, they necessarily contain a warranty of specific standards of purity, efficacy or safety, under objective conditions of determination, and involve technical, professional or systematical quality controls, until they reach the consumers or users in the proper conditions.
2. In any case, the following products shall be considered to be subject to this type of liability: food products, hygienic and cleaning products, cosmetic, pharmaceutical specialities and products, sanitary services, gas and electricity services, domestic appliances, lifts, transport means, motor vehicles, toys and products aimed at children.
3. Without prejudice to the provisions contained in other legal provisions, the liabilities stemming from this article shall have a limit of 500 million pesetas. This amount shall be revised and adjusted from time to time by the Government in accordance with the index of consumption prices.

Article 29
1. The consumer or user has a right to compensation, calculated on the basis of the indemnities for contractual and non-contractual damage during the time which elapses from the moment of the court judgment deciding on the existence of liability to the moment of final payment.
2. Said compensation shall be determined in accordance with the provisions of the Civil Procedure Act.'

4.2 Burden of proof

The GAC takes the principle of fault as the basis for liability of the producer. Negligence is, however, presumed, resulting from a reversal of the burden of proof. Consequently, it is the producer's task to overturn such presumption by proving that he complied with all legal requirements provided for in all applicable regulations and that he acted diligently according to the nature of the product, service or activity (article 27), in order to avoid being found liable.

Conversely, as described in section 5, below, this defence is not available whenever the products involved require 'a warranty of a certain level of purity, efficiency and safety' (strict or absolute liability: article 28).

4.3 Nature of liability, damages or criminal sanctions

The GAC clearly establishes the right of consumers and users to be indemnified for the duly evidenced damage that the consumption of goods or the use of products or services may have entailed, only excluding the damage for which they exclusively are to be blamed or which was caused by the negligence of persons for whom they are responsible.[14]

As regards compliance with legal requirements, the points to be covered by provisions regulating products, services and activities are clearly listed, including conditions of installation and qualified personnel, qualities of authorised production processes, lists of authorised additives, methods for quality control and analysis, registration etc.[15]

As for the diligence demanded according to the nature of the product, service or activity, GAC article 5 provides specific rules in certain cases, eg obligation to comply with the list of additives for manufacturing and treatment of foodstuffs; prohibition to store certain products where foodstuffs or beverages are manufactured, processed, stored or transported; prohibition to supply or sell packaged foodstuffs where the Health Registration Number is not shown; obligation to withdraw from the market by way of efficient procedures any product not complying with legal requirements or that entail a foreseeable risk to human health and safety; the obligation to market pharmaceutical products in closed packages containing a fully informative brochure etc.

Although the GAC does not clearly state it, the application of the general principle provided in Cc article 1105 results in no liability arising for the producer when the damage has been caused due to *force majeure* or when circumstances breaking the chain of liability have intervened. Besides, the doctrine deems that *force majeure* may not be raised as a defence by the manufacturer when products included in the strict liability system of GAC article 28 (see section 5 of this chapter) are involved.

The GAC makes no particular reference to the items the compensation is to cover. Personal injury, death and food poisoning would seem likely. Further examples will depend on the judge's criteria in each particular case.

14 GAC art 25.
15 GAC art 4.

Sanctions provided for violation of regulations on protection of consumers are mainly administrative, ranging from 500,000 pesetas (maximum for less serious violations) to 100m pesetas (maximum for very serious violations) or up to five times the value of the products or services which are the object of the violation, including the eventual closing down of the establishment, installation or service during a maximum term of five years.

However, this does not prejudice the possibility of civil, criminal or other liabilities arising,[16] as long as there is no double sanction covering the same facts and protecting the same public interests.[17] The Criminal Code ('Cmc') describes as criminal offences, eg, the sale of spoiled or damaged pharmaceutical products;[18] the sale of basic products where their substance, quality or quantity have been altered;[19] the sale of foodstuffs without complying with legal regulations regarding expiry and composition and entailing a risk to public health.[20]

In practice many cases of product liability are submitted by the injured party to the criminal courts since, in addition to the criminal penalties (fines, imprisonment etc), such courts may grant damages derived from criminal offences. One of the most outstanding cases of product liability is the toxic oil (*aceite de colza* case see section 9.4.2) which was resolved by the criminal courts.

5. SPECIAL LIABILITIES ARISING IN RESPECT OF PARTICULAR PRODUCTS

As stated above, the GAC is based on the principle of fault (article 26). However, an important exception is provided for what could be described as vital products, where liability arises even without fault by the producer, supplier etc. Indeed, the GAC provides a strict liability for producers of particular defective products, not granting any legal defence thereto (unlike the Directive), even if such producers acted with the required diligence and following all legal requirements. It could thus be qualified as strict liability, ie a 'legal and direct obligation of liability' rather than a *juris tantum* presumption of fault.[1]

A manufacturer of these products may only base his defence on the grounds that damage was caused due to the exclusive negligence of the injured person, ie an incorrect and unforeseeable use of the product.

Pursuant to article 28 (see section 4.1.4) the products in question are those that due to their nature or to specific regulations 'require a warranty of certain standards of pureness, efficacy or safety and involve quality controls'. Article 28.2 includes in this group foodstuffs, sanitary and cleaning products, pharmaceutical products, health services, gas and electricity services, cosmetics, lifts, electrical appliances, means of transport, motor vehicles, toys and products designed for children. The wide scope of this article means that what was intended to be a rule applicable only in exceptional cases, turns out to be the

16 Art 32.
17 Art 33.
18 Cmc art 343.
19 Cmc art 529.
20 Cmc art 346.
1 Judgment of the Provincial Court of Valencia, Section 7, of 23 January 1990.

general rule and unlike other national legislations or the Directive, Spanish law grants no legal defence at all to the producer in this wide sphere. The GAC, however, provides a maximum liability arising out of this article of 500m pesetas to be annually revised by the Government.

The general reference to these products, which are not defined as such, may lead to difficulty in ascertaining into which category certain items fall, particularly bearing in mind that the application of the different liability systems depends on such classification. In this sense, the judge will have to decide on the basis of several undefined criteria whether certain products are to be deemed included in article 28 (in which case strict liability applies if they are defective) as shall be requested by the plaintiff, or otherwise, as requested by the manufacturer (in which case subjective liability will apply).

The above-mentioned legal structure – general systems of fault liability with the exception of strict liability in certain cases – although imperfect and giving rise to conflicting interpretations, represents a considerable improvement on the previous legal codes but has resulted in legislation with little protection for producers, particularly those who manufacture the 'vital' products listed in article 28.2. The Directive's regime is, however, still a long way off.

By basing the system of product liability on liability for negligence, the GAC differs from the strict liability concept of modern legislation and more particularly the concept of the Directive. However, by submitting a substantial number of products to a liability system (article 28.2) where no defences in favour of the producer are provided, the GAC goes too far.

6. LIABILITY FOR DEFECTIVE PRODUCTS ARISING FROM NATIONAL LAW IN SPAIN: IMPLEMENTATION OF THE DIRECTIVE

6.1 Introduction

At the time of writing, the Directive has not yet been adopted by Spanish law, although the implementation period expired on 30 July 1988. The Government recently declared its intention to implement most of the EC Directive pending implementation by the end of 1990, by approving the relevant provisions. It is therefore expected that the Directive will be approved shortly.

There are several methods by which the Directive may be implemented in Spanish legislation:

(a) modification of the liability system of the civil and commercial codes; or
(b) modification of the GAC (directly or through regulations); or
(c) enactment of a specific Act for product liability, which is the method preferred by the legal experts.

Spain has not yet selected which option is to be followed, although there has been some preliminary work for a new Act to introduce the Directive into Spanish law. One of them is a draft Bill (*propuesta de anteproyecto de ley*) that the Ministry of Justice prepared in 1987, which was approved by the Commercial Law Section of the General Commission for Codification in 1988. This draft never obtained the approval of the Council of Ministers. The

Government is now studying a new draft Bill that was prepared in early 1991. Approval of this new Bill requires prior approval of the Council of Ministers and formal approval by the Central Parliament. Therefore the GAC, approved only one year before the Directive, is the legislation in force until such implementation takes place.

6.2 GAC: outline of provisions in Spain

Although the preamble of the GAC states that it follows the principles of the European Community in this field (the proposal for the Directive under discussion at that time) the GAC differs from the Directive, since the essence of the latter is liability without fault on the part of the producer whereas the Spanish Act, although containing a wide number of exceptions for which strict liability is imposed, is based on subjective liability.

6.2.1 Subject

i. Producer. GAC article 27.1(a) clearly makes manufacturers, importers, vendors and suppliers of products or services liable for the origin, identity and adequacy of such products or services pursuant to their nature and purpose and the rules which regulate them. If several persons (individuals or companies) are involved in the damage, they shall jointly be liable for it.[2]

The supplier is treated at the same level as the manufacturer or importer, independently of the manufacturer having been identified or the identity of the importer having been indicated on the product.[3]

In the case of bulk products (*productos a granel*), the holder of them shall be deemed liable for their defects, without prejudice that the previous holder or supplier has been identified.[4] This can be criticised since:

(a) these products cover a more reduced sphere than that covered by products not showing the identity of manufacturers or importers and it is difficult to understand why the holder in this case is not jointly liable with the previous holder or supplier as in the other cases;

(b) the term 'holder' (*tenedor*) is confusing and should have been replaced by 'supplier'; and

(c) it disregards the event in which the manufacturer (who may in fact be the person responsible for the defect) is identified.

In the case of packaged, bottled, labelled and sealed products, the individual or company identified on the label, display or advertising shall be deemed liable unless evidence is given that the products have been forged or unduly manipulated by third parties, who shall then eventually be held liable therefor.[5] The reference to products which at the same time are packaged, labelled and sealed is extremely restrictive and may lead to the belief that the person

2 GAC art 27.2.
3 See Directive art 3(3).
4 Art 27.1(b).
5 Art 27.1(c).

who presents itself as the producer may not be held liable for products which are not packaged, labelled and sealed. Besides, the exemption of liability for such persons in cases of forgery or manipulation could have been worded in a more efficient way by referring to defects not existing at the time the product was put into circulation.[6]

ii. Injured person. The GAC only protects the consumer (article 1.2) and thus contains a narrower concept of the range of protected persons than that provided in the Directive (which gives rights to an injured person, whether defined as a consumer or not). In addition, as the consumer is defined as the end-user of the product, the GAC does not protect the manufacturer's employees, the bystander or third parties.

6.2.2 Product

The GAC is very broad as regards the objects it covers, since it includes all kinds of products and *services*, by referring to movable goods or *immovables*, products, services, activities or functions, either of a public or private nature and independently of their being manufactured, provided or supplied by individuals or legal entities.[7] Articles 26 and 28 of the GAC provide a distinction between two groups of products, but this is not to exclude liability for certain products, but rather to delimit subjective or strict liability.

This broad definition of product in the GAC differs from the restrictive approach adopted by the Directive, which includes only movables which have been industrially produced and excludes agricultural products and game except where they have undergone industrial processing (Directive article 2). In fact, the GAC does not include any exception at all as to the products which product liability protection is to cover.

6.2.3 Defect

Unlike the Directive, where defect is an essential element of product liability ('liability for *defective* products' as the very title of the Directive reads), the GAC does not, surprisingly, refer to defects as a requirement of liability and it provides no definition thereof. The GAC provides that the consumer has the right to claim compensation for the damage caused by the consumption of goods or the use of products and services (article 25) and that the liability of those producing, importing or supplying specific products shall arise as a result of damage caused in the proper use and consumption of such products (article 28). But there is, however, no reference to the defect in the injuring product.

The GAC declares that any damage caused in the correct use or consumption of goods and services will give rise to liability whenever the goods contain a warranty of specific standards of purity, efficacy or safety and imply technical quality controls[8] (section 5 of this chapter), which appears to imply that products not including such warranty nor involving such controls need to be defective in order to give rise to liability. This is, of course, absurd.

6 See Directive art 7(b).
7 Art 1.2.
8 Art 28.1.

The only reasonable explanation is that the GAC assumes that only products containing defects can cause damage and that it is thus not necessary to mention the defect as a requirement of product liability. The defect would consequently be deemed an implicit characteristic of any harmful product, which implies that the injured person should only be required to prove the damage and the causal relationship between the product and the damage in order to claim for compensation, without having to prove the existence of a defect.

6.2.4 Damages

The GAC grants the consumer the right to obtain compensation for the damages (*daños y perjuicios*) incurred[9] but, unlike the Directive, no definition is provided. Death and personal injuries certainly give rise to damages, according to the GAC.[10] However, since no exclusion or delimitation of damage is provided, it seems that any kind of damage can be covered (personal injury, physical damage, non-physical damage – *pretium doloris* etc) as long as it is duly evidenced and quantified. In this sense, the GAC has a wider scope than the Directive, which only considers death, personal injury and damage or destruction of property (subject to certain conditions in the last case), without prejudice to national provisions relating to non-material damage. Nevertheless, since there is practically no case law, the extent to which damages can be recovered under the GAC will eventually depend upon its interpretation by the courts.

6.2.5 Causes of exclusion of liability

There is one defence the producer can raise in order to avoid being found liable for damages caused by defects in his product. This defence has two cumulative requirements, namely (GAC article 26):

(a) that all the relevant legal requirements were complied with; and
(b) that the diligence required by the nature of the product, service or activity were observed.

Conversely, no defence is provided when particular products requiring warranties for certain standards of pureness, efficacy and safety are involved (strict liability: see section 5), except for the case where damage may be attributed to the exclusive negligence of the consumer.

In spite of the GAC's silence in this matter, it is obvious that in the event of *force majeure* or in the event no causal relationship between the product and the damage exists, there is no product liability.

6.2.6 Contributory negligence

According to the GAC, the consumer shall not have the right to claim for compensation when the damage is caused exclusively by his own negligence or that of a person for whom he is responsible (article 25), ie parents and

9 Art 2.1(c).
10 Arts 7, 30 and 31.

guardians of children under their custody; owners or managers of a business and their employees; school-owners and their pupils; the Government and civil servants acting as special agents, etc.[11] This provision is in line with the Directive.

No specific rule is provided in the GAC for a situation where the damage is caused as a consequence of the negligence of both the producer and the consumer. The solution to this case should thus be looked for in case law, which supports a similar solution to that provided for in the Directive,[12] ie the producer's liability may be reduced or even disallowed having regard to all the circumstances.

A judgment rendered by the Supreme Court on 23 January 1970 distinguishes three different situations: in the first place, absolution of the fault of the injured person by that of the agent on the grounds of the seriousness of the fault; in the second place, absolution of the agent's fault by that of the injured person, on the grounds of the importance of the latter's fault; and, finally, a reduction of the claim when both faults are similar or equivalent.

Where damage is caused both by a defect in the product and by the act or omission of a third party, no specific rule is provided by the GAC either. Spanish case law on criminal liability deems that whenever the intervention of a third party is such that it breaks the chain of liability, the cause of the damage is to be seen as beyond the control of the producer and he shall thus not be found liable. Since civil and criminal matters are, generally, dealt with by the same judge, it is possible to make analogies between civil case law and criminal case law in Spain.

6.2.7 *Period of limitation*

The Directive provides a limitation period of three years for proceedings for the recovery of damages and a period of ten years from the date on which the product was put into circulation for the extinction of all rights pursuant to the Directive[13].

The GAC does not provide any specific period of limitation and the general ones already mentioned for the sale of goods (six months, 30 days and four days), contractual liability (15 years) and extra-contractual liability (one year)[14] should be applicable.

6.2.8 *Financial ceiling*

The Directive provides that the total liability for damage resulting from death or personal injury and caused by identical items with the same defects shall be limited to an amount which may not be less than Ecu 70m.[15]

Article 28.3 provides a financial ceiling of 500m pesetas (less than Ecus 4m) as the maximum liability that may be imposed on manufacturers of products subject to GAC article 28 (strict liability). The GAC does not specify whether this maximum liability is to be applied for all claims arising in respect of the

11 Cc art 1903, Cmc arts 20 and 22.
12 Art 8.2.
13 Directive arts 10.1 and 11.
14 Cc Arts 1964 and 1968.
15 Art 16.1.

same defect or to each claim; however, bearing in mind that the wording of this article refers to 'the liabilities [plural] stemming from this article', it is the writer's view that it provides the maximum liability to be applied for all the claims arising from the same defect.

6.3 Draft to implement the Directive

From 1988 to 1990, two drafts were prepared, one by the Commercial Law Section of the General Commission on Codification of 26 January 1988 and another one by the National Institute for Consumption (*Instituto Nacional de Consumo*). However, the procedures to adopt the Directive in Spanish law were suspended for some time.

Apparently, the reasons for these preparatory works not being developed and for Spain not fulfilling its obligation to adapt its legislation to the Directive lie in the difference of opinion between the Ministry of Justice and the Ministry of Health and Consumption with regard to some major aspects of the legislation.

One of the main discrepancies stems from article 13 of the Directive which provides that the Directive shall not affect any rights which an injured person may have according to the rules of the law of contractual or non-contractual liability or any special liability system existing at the time of notification of the Directive; there is discord on whether Spain may keep a product liability system (ie the one contained in the GAC) which conflicts with that of the Directive.

Another important discrepancy appears to arise in connection with the minimum amount of the producer's total liability for damage which the Directive sets at Ecus 70m for damage caused by identical items with the same defect involving death or corporal injury, while the GAC provides a total amount of 500m pesetas (less than Ecus 4m) for damage caused by products described in GAC article 28.2 as subject to strict liability. The EC Commission has taken a rather tolerant attitude, probably because Spain was one of the last members to join the EC.

The Spanish Government undertook to fulfil the obligations to adopt the legislative by the end of 1991. The draft Bill (*propuesta de anteproyecto de ley*) prepared in early 1991 has the following main features:

(a) As in the Directive, 'product' is defined as all movables, either in their natural condition or incorporated into another movable (not immovable as the Directive) including gas and electricity. Products from the soil, of stock-farming, hunting and fisheries that have not undergone any processing are excluded (arts 1 and 2 draft).
(b) The supplier of the product shall be liable unless he informs the injured person of the identity of the producer or person who supplied him with the product within one month from the date it is requested.
(c) The defect and causal relationship shall be deemed proved when it has been duly established that their existence is more likely than not.

(d) The draft follows the lines of the Directive in relation to the defences available to producers, including the defence of the state of scientific and technical knowledge.
(e) The producer's total liability for damage resulting from a death or personal injury and caused by identical items with the same defect shall be limited to an amount of 10,500m pesetas.
(f) The scope of the coverage is enlarged in that not only consumers and users are protected, as provided for by the GAC, but any person who has suffered damage as a consequence of a defective product (as in the Directive).
(g) Damages include compensation for personal injury (physical and psychological) and death, as well as damage to property or destruction of goods directed to private use or consumption if these goods were mainly used in this sense by the injured person.
(h) Contributory negligence of the injured person may reduce the liability of the producer unless the injured person is incapable of ascertaining the risk of his own behaviour due to his age or his mental capacity.

6.4 Description of special provisions

A Royal Decree 1945/83 of 22 June 1983 regulates infringements and sanctions in relation to consumer protection and the production of primary agricultural products (including products of stock-farming) for human consumption and use (foodstuff, drugs, beverages, woollen clothes, etc). This regulation, which was not superseded by the GAC, was meant to merge with and update the piecemeal provisions in this area.

Infringements related to these issues are classified as follows:

(a) *Health infringements*: Non-compliance with regulations regarding the manufacturing and quality of particular products; acts or omissions creating risk or damage to consumers' health; non-compliance with regulations regarding pollution; the promotion or sale of foodstuffs containing non-authorised additives; the manufacturing, supply or sale of foodstuffs with misleading presentation regarding its health or nutritional characteristics; the distribution, supply or sale of foodstuffs containing toxic substances etc.
(b) *Consumer protection infringements*: Selling, supplying or manufacturing products fraudulent as to quality, weight etc, or with misleading labels; selling at higher prices than those legally authorised and other acts of unfair competition etc.
(c) *Infringements to regulations regarding the protection of the quality of agricultural and farming foodstuffs*: The sale of products without the required authorisation; the ownership of machines not having the required authorisation; fraud in quality, weight etc of such products; sale of counterfeited products etc.

Serious sanctions are imposed on any participants for infringements of the above-mentioned provisions and wide powers are granted to the authorities in order to carry out inquiries. An action to sanction such behaviour is subject to a time limit of five years from the date of infringement.

7. PRACTICAL EFFECTS EC PRODUCT LIABILITY LAW WILL HAVE ON VARIOUS BUSINESSES IN THE CHAIN OF SUPPLY OF PRODUCTS

7.1 General practical effects

The enforcement of the Directive in Spain will mean that producers and other parties in the chain of supply will be subject to strict liability and no longer to the fault-based liability of the general system of liability. However, producers and other parties in relation to certain products (those described in section 5 of this chapter), which the GAC subjected to a liability that was close to an absolute one, will have available certain defences that they were not able to use under the GAC.

Spanish importers and suppliers of products subject to the general system will feel the effects of the stricter liability imposed by the Directive. Businesses such as supermarket chains and department stores will face strict liability claims for defective products that they have not manufactured, since they will no longer have as a defence the fact that they acted diligently, unless they can identify who supplied the product to them,[16] as article 12 of the Directive expressly declares contractual limitations of liability as null and void.

In other cases, the Directive will represent a more favourable situation for certain manufacturers and other traders than that provided in the GAC since, as stated above, additional defences will be available. The following should be highlighted:

(a) manufacturers of particular products, such as foodstuffs, cosmetics, drugs etc (article 28(e)) will no longer be subject to an almost absolute liability as in the GAC (hardly any defences are available) but to a strict liability subject to certain defences;

(b) while, according to the GAC, suppliers may be found liable for damage caused by a product if they did not act with sufficient diligence, the Directive will enable them to avoid liability by identifying the producer who in fact created the risk by manufacturing a defective product.

Implementation of the Directive will also place importers in Spain in a better position than under the GAC whenever they are importing from an EC country, since they will be able to base their defence on the grounds that the defective product was supplied to them by another supplier in the EC, whereas they are currently liable themselves.

7.2 Particular problems in specific businesses or industries

As stated above, the Spanish GAC stipulates a strict liability for manufacturers of certain products which, due to their nature, or on the basis of regulations,

16 EC Directive art 3(2).

require a certain standard warranty of pureness, efficacy and safety and require technical, professional and systematic quality controls. Producers of such products have currently no defence to a claim by a consumer except for substantial contributory negligence by the consumer. The implementation of the Directive will mean that these businesses will be included in the general system of product liability and thus the relevant defences provided by the Directive will also be available to these producers.

8. COMPARISON OF THE EFFECTS OF PRODUCT LIABILITY LAW WITH THE PREVIOUS POSITION IN CONTRACT AND TORT

As described above, the main feature of product liability law in Spain will be, when the Directive is implemented, the overcoming of two main legal obstacles faced in contract and tort under the Cc and the Cco, namely:

(a) privity of contract which prevented the injured person from suing others except the party which whom he had contracted; and
(b) the difficulty faced by the plaintiff in proving that the defendant has acted negligently.

These hurdles have been partially overcome by the GAC. Indeed, this Act provides for the liability of the producer and the importer (besides that of the supplier) for damage caused by the product and it is their task to prove that they acted without negligence by proving that they complied with all the legal requirements and acted with the required diligence.[17]

The main innovations that implementation of the Directive will entail in relation to the current system provided in the GAC are as follows:

(a) The Directive will impose strict liability (instead of the GAC system which is based upon liability with fault with some exceptions);
(b) The definition of products that may entail liability according to the Directive is narrower than that provided by the GAC which covers immovables and agricultural products.
(c) The Directive provides a subsidiary system to identify the liable party in the chain of supply (article 3.3) by enabling the supplier to avoid liability if he informs the consumer of the identity of his own supplier, whereas the GAC, which gives no definition of producer, provides for the joint liability of all persons in the chain of supply (producer, importer and supplier).
(d) The Directive defines the concept of defect and provides grounds of defence related to it (article 7) which are not currently contemplated in the legislation in force.
(e) The Directive is also precise as regards damage. Spanish law, which currently makes no precise reference to damage, will have to include a similar definition to that of the Directive, thus limiting damage to

17 Art 26.

death, personal injury, property and possibly non-material damage shall depend upon the national criteria.

(f) As regards grounds for defence, the Directive provides a list of defences available to the producer. Spanish law will have to introduce these defences. These defences will enable manufacturers of products requiring a warranty of safety, currently listed in GAC article 28, to avoid liability in certain cases, which were not available under the GAC.

(g) The implementation of the Directive will cause a reduction or exclusion of the producer's liability to occur not only when damage is due to the exclusive fault of the consumer or of the persons he is responsible for, as is the case now in the GAC, but also when damage is caused by both the consumer's fault and a defect in the product.

(h) The introduction into Spanish law of the time limitations laid down in the Directive (three years to institute proceedings and ten years for rights conferred upon the injured person) will represent a considerable change to the provisions in existing legislation that currently enable Spanish consumers to bring an action against a producer.

9. RISK MANAGEMENT IN THE NEW ERA OF PRODUCT LIABILITY

9.1 Internal risk management

Enforcement of product liability provisions entails a global exposure to risk for manufacturing corporations and other enterprises taking part in a chain of supply. There are many regulations on specific products which provide certain minimum conditions of safety, strict compliance with which must be closely ensured by management, who normally establish internal policies to reduce the risk of product liability. Such policies cover product design and specification, packaging, instructions for use and quality control.

Dealing with product liability risks implies:

(a) reducing the risk by complying with all safety requirements related to design, manufacture and marketing of the product; complying with safety regulations and international standards, and ensuring the quality standards of suppliers;

(b) transferring the risks where possible by entering into adequate insurance arrangements and ensuring that suppliers may be easily identified.

Managements of businesses should stress their commitment to procuring safe products so that their employees become involved and familiar with their importance, since the action or omission of a single employee may involve the company and make it face serious claims for liability. To this extent, it is advisable to draw up a product safety policy statement which should be made available to all employees, suppliers and customers.

The appointment of an effective risk manager may be a worthwhile aspect of effecting a management risk policy. It might also be helpful to create a committee for product safety. Such a committee, to whom the risk manager would report, could periodically discuss cases of defects found in products, deal with customer complaints, etc. Ongoing training for staff which provides information on legislative developments, case law and potential claims is also a constructive system to be considered.

With a view to reducing any potential risks related to product liability to a minimum, company policy should encompass the following aspects.

9.1.1 *Quality control*

Quality should be linked to safety; any potential hazard created by the product should be eliminated to avoid eventual liabilities.

9.1.2 *Documentation*

Documentation and record-keeping on previous claims may be very helpful to provide a valuable background of the effects of the product. Documentary evidence is the main form of evidence in Spanish judicial practice. Thus documentation can be of vital importance for the producer in defending a case, particularly due to the fact that he may be discharged from liability under the GAC (prior to implementation of the Directive) if he can prove that he acted with the required diligence (subjective liability), eg tests of the product were carried out, potential safety improvement was assessed etc.

9.1.3 *Record-keeping*

Article 30 of the Cco obliges corporations and other undertakings to keep records of their business for a period of six years. However, it is advisable that, once the Directive is implemented, record-keeping should cover the period of limitation of liability, ie ten years. It is important to keep records of any relevant matters relating to the product: identification of suppliers, tests carried out to check safety, designs etc.

9.1.4 *Warning notices, operating instructions, service manuals*

The GAC provides that any risks stemming from a foreseeable use of the product, taking into account its nature and the persons it is addressed to, should be duly notified to consumers through warning labels, operating instructions and service manuals (GAC articles 3.2 and 13 ff).

A safe product in inexperienced hands may be harmful if not properly used. Therefore, warning notices, operating instructions and service manuals are essential to reduce potential risks and to help to defend a claim that the corporation has been negligent. Revealing certain risks may slightly reduce the volume of sales of a product, but a claim in respect of a defective product may damage the commercial situation to a greater extent. Warnings should cover instructions for the correct use of the product, any dangers of the product and risks arising from an incorrect or unsafe use of it.

In a judgment of the Supreme Court of 14 November 1984, a producer was discharged from any liability for damage caused by a dangerous pesticide for having included a warning in the labelling and packaging of the product. The exclusive distributor was, however, found liable for failure to ensure compliance with safety warning requirements.

9.2 The handling of consumer claims

9.2.1 Inspection of defective products and analysis of causes of failure

It is advisable to create a department responsible for consumer claims. An active role played by this department may be very useful to avoid potential claims before the court since it may obtain information of great value regarding the safety of the product that tests carried out by the company have not disclosed. This may enable the company to avoid potential hazards in future models of the product.

9.2.2 Consequences of the future and the need to re-design products, cease selling products and recall products for safety checks or replacement of defective parts

When facing a defect in a product that entails a risk, management should take the decision as to what measure should be followed: enforcing a measure when not really required implies high commercial costs, but failure to take such a decision while being aware of the defect may result in the court finding the company liable for any resulting damage.

If the defect implies no danger whatsoever, re-designing future products may be enough. However, if there is in fact a significant risk of personal injury, recall systems should be enforced. Recall systems consist in the recovery of all the products from the market in order to avoid any potential risks stemming from a defective product. However, this measure implies high costs for the personnel and strategems required to recover the products in the shortest possible period of time.

Recall may more easily be enforced when the purchasers of a product can be identified, eg cars, where personalised recall through phone calls or letters with acknowledged receipts may be carried out. Records of ownership of a product are essential in order to be able to trace it. Otherwise a media compaign may be a reasonable solution, if advisable once the advantages and disadvantages have been carefully balanced. Consumer organisations, trade associations, treasury authorities and safety authorities could be of constructive help.

9.2.3 Requirements of insurers

With regard to risk exposure, the corporation must determine the levels at which it is prepared to be exposed. When choosing what kind of insurance, to take out, several issues should be borne in mind. These are, chiefly, the kind of product and the risks involved, the volume of sales, the number of users involved, the importing or exporting countries etc. Product liability insurance is a rather new kind of insurance in Spain, though it is quickly developing. Not all insurers are sufficiently experienced in these kinds of policies, thus a specialist should be appointed in order to obtain sufficient cover at a reasonable premium.

9.2.4 *Correspondence with consumers*

Maintaining correspondence with consumers may be very useful in certain cases to preclude the possibility of claims. Valuable information is provided through such correspondence that makes it possible to forecast potential risks. It is a matter of collaborating with users to improve safety policy.

9.2.5 *Preservation of evidence*

As stated above, preserving evidence and record-keeping is of utmost importance to be able to prepare a defence when required. This implies not only keeping existing documents, but also trying to put into writing all facts that could support the company's defence.

9.2.6 *Problems of legal proceedings*

Spanish proceedings are usually slow and very formal. This sometimes deters consumers from attempting to claim damages in court proceedings. Indeed, proceedings of this kind may take from one to seven years. In addition, the lack of sufficient case law makes it difficult to predict the result of a claim. Moreover, the Spanish procedural system does not, in contrast to the common law system and in particular the American procedural pre-trial discovery rules, allow for a thorough and extensive preparation of the trial, making the gathering of evidence against the guilty party more burdensome.

However, it should be borne in mind that courts tend to protect consumers, over powerful companies, since they sometimes deem them to be in an inferior situation. Therefore, such companies would be wise to prevent such claims and to be aware that a risk safety policy is advisable in order to be able to prepare a good defence before the court and to try and cover eventual liabilities.

9.3 Exclusion of liability and claims on contract for indemnities

The GAC is very strict as regards the exclusion of liability (as is the Directive), since the right to obtain remedies for damage caused by a defective product is a basic right of consumers. The GAC recognises the priority of the consumers' rights related to products of common, ordinary and generalised use[18] and declares that all waivers of consumers' rights are null and void.[19]

18 Art 2.2.
19 Art 2.3

9.4 Insurance

9.4.1 Special provisions

The Spanish Constitution of 1978 established the grounds for the approval of the General Insurance Act 50/1980 of 8 October ('GIA'). This legislation, also influenced by the enactment of compulsory insurance for vehicles (1980), introduces an essential innovation as regards the regulation of insurance contract. The previous system, whose main characteristic was the wide scope it granted to the parties to agree on the covenants of the contract, was substituted by a detailed regulation that leaves little freedom to the parties on the basis that it mainly aims at ensuring an effective protection for the insured party.

9.4.2 Outline of nature of cover

One of the main innovations of the GIA is the fact that it grants the injured person a direct action against the defendant's insurer and it restricts the possibilities of defences raised by the latter. Besides, it provides that the responsible party is bound to inform the injured person of the existence of the insurance policy. Furthermore, the insurer is bound to pay compensation for damages intentionally (*dolus*) caused by the insured party, even if such risk is excluded from the cover. Finally, this Act enables the Government to require by Decree compulsory insurance cover to be taken out by those carrying on certain manufacturing processes, etc, although the Spanish Government has not agreed any compulsory subscription of insurance policies for manufacturers.

The enforcement of the GIA coincided with two major judgments that set out a general concern regarding product liability:

(a) *Accident in Los Alfaques* case (*Sinisestro de Los Alfaques*) 1978: The explosion of a truck carrying an excessive amount of a dangerous sustance (*propileno*) caused 215 deaths and a high number of injured persons at a camping site close to the site of the explosion.

(b) *Toxic oil* case (*Sindrome Toxico*) 1981, judgment on 20 May 1989, still pending appeal: The marketing for human consumption of oil manufactured for industrial purposes caused a great number of deaths and affected hundreds of people.

Such judgments, although dealing with criminal rather than civil matters, entailed high compensation on the whole and greatly influenced public opinion, and represented an important step towards product liability.

As regards the GAC, it provides that the Government shall adopt the required measures to enforce a compulsory insurance system covering certain risks which shall be taken out by all producers of certain products. This has not been adopted at the time of writing. The GAC also provides for the creation of a guarantee fund.[20] Such products are those referred to in

20 Art 30.

article 28, ie those where an absolute liability is provided (foodstuffs, pharmaceutical products etc). No such compulsory insurance has been provided yet the draft for the implementation of the Directive does not supersede GAC article 30. Furthermore, it removes the limitation that this kind of insurance shall only be applied to certain sectors, thus enforcement of such a provision would be certain to entail an increase in the insurance sector.

The enforcement of product liability by the GAC has increased the volume of turnover in the insurance sector, though not to the expected extent. Enforcement of the Directive will entail an increase in the risk to be covered by insurance policies that will probably give rise to a substantial increase in premiums. It can be expected that multiple risks insurance (*multiriesgo*) will become a more common suitable solution. This sector may experience a considerable increase if compulsory insurance is enforced.

9.4.3 Limits of coverage

In delimiting coverage in time, Spanish insurance policies are usually based upon the principle of loss occurrence, ie according to the moment when damage is caused, and not upon that of claims made. It is also usually required that the defective products were delivered within the period of cover of the insurance contract and that the damage and the claim take place in the said period. However, coverage is extended to a period of two years where claims for undisclosed damages may be filed.

In general terms, insurance policies in Spain usually cover material and immaterial damage. As regards damage caused abroad, insurance contracts usually provide that the insurer shall pay the insured party the amount in pesetas awarded by the foreign court.

The system of quantitative limit of coverage is generally in line with those systems implemented in other countries, ie limit per accident and limit of aggregate amount per year. There is a trend to restrict serial damages by considering the various types of damage resulting from one accident as stemming from the same cause.

The most frequent clauses giving rise to exclusion of liability under the insurance policy are: expenses for repair, replacement and compensation of defective products; nuclear risks; damage caused by products when the insured company was aware of the defects before taking out the insurance policy; unsuitability of the product for its purpose or damage derived from a lack of suitable operating instructions.

9.4.4 Serial damages

Damage which is not linked to the producer's negligent act or omission will probably be found not to fall within his product liability, and thus not to be covered by the insurance company.

9.4.5 Cover for recall of defective products

Recently, the practice of insuring losses for recall of products has become more frequent, but it is generally subject to taking out insurance for general product liability and for liabilities stemming from the operation of the business.

CHAPTER XIV

Sweden

Christer Wagenius Esq

Brenner & Wagenius HB
Kullagatan 8–10
252 20 Helsingborg
Sweden

Tel ++ 46 42 18 01 30
Fax ++ 46 42 12 21 54

CHAPTER XIV

Sweden

1. INTRODUCTION

The law in Sweden relating to liability for defective products is currently undergoing substantial change. Accordingly this chapter will outline the new situation (in January 1991) as well as describe the further changes that are likely to be brought about.

Owing to the range of this subject, only a brief summary of Swedish legislation can be provided in this chapter. Therefore, the survey must not be regarded as a full and comprehensive statement of Swedish law regarding defective products.

1.1 Definitions

Product liability under Swedish law usually means liability – irrespective of negligence – arising from:

(a) either personal damage caused by a product; or
(b) property damage caused by a product to other items.

In this chapter the term 'product liability' is used in this sense.

This means that the normal contractual liability of the seller towards the buyer regarding defects in goods sold is not regarded as *product liability* unless it involves consequential damage to persons or to property other than the product itself. The contractual liability under the Swedish Sale of Goods Acts as described below is largely restricted to matters arising between the seller and the buyer regarding *the goods as such*. In this chapter the term 'goods' will be used when referring to contractual liability.

1.2 Overview of laws relating to defective products in Sweden

1.2.1 Current situation (January 1991)

i. Product liability. There is no specific product liability law in force in Sweden. Product liability is based on the Tort Liability Act (*Skadeståndslagen*), on certain provisions in the Consumer Sale of Goods Act (*Konsumentköplagen*) and in the Consumer Service Act (*Konsumenttjänstlagen*) as well as on specific laws, mainly regarding various dangerous activities. The said Consumer Acts are applicable when professionals as part of their business activity sell goods or services to consumers; that is to say, goods mainly intended for consumers' private use.

There is also a Product Safety Law (*Produktsäkerhetslag*), which has been in force since mid-1989, aimed at preventing personal and property damage being caused by unsafe products and services. This law enables the authorities to act against the suppliers of products and services which are deemed unsafe. It is not a law establishing product liability for the suppliers of the said products and services.

ii. Contractual liability for goods. There is a new Sale of Goods Act and a new Consumer Sale of Goods Act, both of which came into force on 1 January 1991. Furthermore, a Consumer Service Act has been in force since mid-1986.

1.2.2 Laws in the making

i. Product liability. A Memorandum on Product Liability Law (*Produktskadelag*) has been prepared by the Swedish Ministry of Justice and recently submitted to various bodies for consideration. It is anticipated that a law in this respect will be proposed during 1991 (which may possibly come into force on 1 July 1992) unless delayed. As reactions to the Memorandum have not yet been published it is difficult to judge whether the law will be adopted in due course without major changes or if substantial amendments will prove necessary. However, during the course of its work, the Ministry of Justice held a 'hearing' with about 70 representatives of various bodies concerned, at which it presented a basic draft, and it also met with representatives from the corresponding ministries of the other Nordic countries.

In fact, the discussions in Sweden regarding a Product Liability Law have been going on for many years. In 1972 a committee was formed and in 1979 it presented its suggestions regarding a Product Liability Law. There was, however, no legislative result in accordance with these suggestions, mainly due to a desire to wait for the outcome of EC initiatives regarding product liability legislation. Now, when the EC Directive of 1985 is showing results in national laws among the Member States of the EC, the issue has been brought up again in Sweden and has resulted in the Memorandum mentioned above. According to the Ministry, the Memorandum has been prepared against the background of what is known about the legislative situation worldwide, but especially in Western Europe, and of what has come out of discussions with the corresponding ministries in the other Nordic countries.

Since this chapter was written, a bill relating to product liability (referred to in this chapter as 'the Bill') has been proposed by the Swedish Government to the Swedish Parliament for its consideration during autumn 1991. The major changes made to the Memorandum by the Bill are referred to in the footnotes to this chapter.

2. LIABILITY IN CONTRACT

2.1 Introduction

As mentioned earlier, the Swedish Sale of Goods Acts are largely restricted to matters arising between buyers and sellers concerning the goods as such. Liability of sellers/manufacturers in a more general sense, as in product liability, is left for other legislation, mainly for the planned Product Liability Law. However, the Acts specially relating to consumers contain provisions extending liability beyond the goods sold or serviced (see section 2.2.1, below).

Regarding the international sale of goods it should be observed that Sweden has adopted articles 1–13 and 25–88 of the UN Convention of 11 April 1980 on Contract for the International Sale of Goods, with the exception of sales where both seller and buyer have their place of business in Sweden, Denmark, Norway, Finland or Iceland. The question of applicable law regarding the international sale of goods is dealt with in a Swedish law of 1964. If the parties have not agreed upon a governing law, the law of the country where the seller receives the order from the buyer will normally apply.

2.2 Outline of contract law relevant to defective products in Sweden

2.2.1 Product liability under contract law

The Sale of Goods Act does not contain any provisions regarding product liability as defined above, ie liability for personal damage or damage to property other than the goods. On the contrary, in section 67 it is expressly stated that *damages under the Act do not comprise compensation for loss due to damage to anything other than the goods sold*. See the Appendix to this chapter for a translation of the Sale of Goods Act.

The Consumer Sale of Goods Act contains, however, a provision similar to that of the Consumer Service Act (see the next paragraph) namely that *the liability of the seller also extends to damage caused by the product to other property, provided that the property damaged is intended for personal use and belongs to the purchaser or a member of his household*. The reasons for extending the seller's liability when the buyer is a consumer are mainly the following: it is natural for the consumer to claim compensation for all the damage (eg not only for the malfunctioning deep-freeze as such but also for any stored products damaged therein), the damage is usually compensated by a small sum (the damage is restricted to items for personal use by household members), and the liability of the seller is also limited to what falls under his power of control (see section 2.6.2 below).

Under the Consumer Service Act anyone who is commercially rendering services to consumers will be liable for damage caused by faults therein not only to the object of the service but also to *any other goods owned by the consumer or by a member of his household*.

2.2.2 *Liability for the goods as such under contract law*

Under Swedish contract law goods sold (as well as services provided) are required to be defect free and the liability of the seller (or the provider of the service) is closely related to the type of defect.

In order not to be defective the goods/services should – as further specified in section 2.4, below – primarily be in conformity with what is expressly stated or implied in the contract. But they can also be regarded as defective under a broader interpretation, eg if they vary from what could reasonably be expected by the buyer, such a defect still being regarded as a defect under the contract.

As further specified in sections 2.5 and 2.6, below, the consequences of liability involve the right for the buyer to have the goods/services remedied, to get a reduction in price or to cancel the contract and claim damages. He may also withhold his payment for the goods or services (to a certain extent).

2.3 Pre-contractual liability

Concerning a seller's/provider's pre-contractual liability for statements and representations made, it can generally be said that such statements and representations still apply under the contract if they can be deemed to have had an influence on the buyer's/consumer's decision. Misrepresentations in this respect are regarded as defects in the goods sold or the services rendered. The consequences of such defects are the same as of other defects in the goods (see sections 2.5 and 2.6, below).

In the Sale of Goods Act these principles are laid down in sections 18 and 19 and similar provisions are found in section 16 of the Consumer Sale of Goods Act as well as in section 10 of the Consumer Service Act.

2.4 Contractual requirements relating to quality of goods and safety of goods

2.4.1 *Sale of Goods Act*

In order not to be defective, the goods must conform to the contract between the seller and the buyer in respect to:

(a) character;
(b) quantity;
(c) quality;
(d) other properties; and
(e) packaging.

Unless otherwise provided for in the contract, the goods should also be suitable for their normal or intended use. Furthermore, the goods should have those properties which the seller may have referred to by showing a sample or model, and they should also be properly packaged, if packaging is needed to keep or protect them. Finally, if the goods vary from what could reasonably be expected by the buyer, they may also be regarded as defective.

2.4.2 *Consumer Sale of Goods Act*

In order not to be defective under the terms of the Act, the goods must first comply with the corresponding requirements under the Sale of Goods Act.

Furthermore, necessary instructions regarding:

(a) assembly;
(b) use;
(c) storage; and
(d) handling

must be delivered with the goods.

If the seller has omitted to inform the buyer of circumstances regarding the goods which the buyer could reasonably have expected to be informed of, and if this omission can be assumed to have had an influence on the purchase, the goods may also be regarded as defective.

Under this Act the goods are expressly regarded as defective due to *safety* reasons:

(a) if they are sold despite a prohibition due to safety reasons (eg a prohibition declared by the authorities under the Product Safety Law, see section 3.2, below); or
(b) if their use clearly endangers life or health.

2.4.3 *Consumer Service Act*

Under the Consumer Service Act a service is defective if:

(a) the result is not in conformity with what the consumer had reason to expect regarding professional skill and due respect for the consumer's interests;
(b) the result is not in conformity with regulations mainly aiming at the service being safe; or
(c) if the service has been performed despite prohibitions due to safety reasons.

2.5 Breach of contract for supply of defective goods

By defective goods or services are meant those which are defective according to Swedish contract law (see sections 2.2–2.4, above).

Regarding damages, see section 2.6, below.

2.5.1 *Sale of Goods Act*

In case of a defect in the delivered goods the buyer is entitled to:

(a) remedy of the defect; or
(b) delivery of a replacement without defects; or
(c) reduction of the price; or
(d) cancellation of the delivery;
(e) and damages.

The buyer may also withhold payment by way of set off (in order to bring some pressure on the seller to remedy etc).

The buyer has the right to demand that the seller shall remedy the defect without any cost to the buyer, if this can be made without unreasonable cost or inconvenience for the seller. The seller is free to replace the goods instead, if he so prefers.

The buyer has the right to demand a replacement delivery of the goods if the breach of contract is of substantial importance to him and the seller was or should have been aware of this. (This is not applicable if a new delivery would mean an unreasonable burden on the seller.)

The buyer may demand a price reduction if remedy of the defect or replacement delivery is not of issue or not fulfilled within a reasonable time.

The buyer may cancel the delivery if the breach of contract is of great enough importance to him and the seller was aware or should have been aware of this.

2.5.2 Consumer Sale of Goods Act

In case of defect in the delivered product, the consumer is – in a similar way to buyers under the Sale of Goods Act – entitled to:

(a) remedy of the defect; or
(b) delivery of a replacement without defects; or
(c) reduction of the price; or
(d) cancellation of the delivery;
(e) and damages.

The consumer may also withhold payment by way of set off.

In detail the provisions regarding these alternatives for consumers are somewhat different from those referred to regarding the Sale of Goods Act, mainly because they put the consumer in a better position than other buyers. For example, the consumer may cancel the contract if the defect is of great enough importance to him; there is no requirement of the seller's awareness of this importance.

2.5.3 Consumer Service Act

If the service is defective, and such defect is not due to acts or omissions by the consumer, the consumer is entitled to:

(a) have the defect remedied; or
(b) have a reduction in price; or
(c) cancel the contract;
(d) and claim damages.

The consumer may also withhold payment corresponding to what is needed to safeguard his claim.

2.6 Damages

2.6.1 Sale of Goods Act

The buyer is entitled to damages due to any defect in the goods unless the seller proves that the defect is caused by a circumstance outside his control and which he could not reasonably have expected, avoided or overcome. Thus, the scope of 'seller's control' plays an important role in this new legislation, forming a basic principle for liability.

Damages for breach of contract comprise compensation for expenses, difference in price and loss of profits as well as other direct or indirect losses due to the breach of contract. Certain indirect losses, eg loss of production, loss of contract, are however not compensated in the circumstances described in the paragraph above.

The buyer is, however, always entitled to compensation if the defect or loss is due to the seller's *negligence* or if the product differs from what the seller expressly promised.

Damages according to this Act do not include compensation for loss or damage caused to goods other than the goods sold.

The buyer is obliged to minimise his losses.

Furthermore, if the damages in the circumstances are deemed by the court to be unreasonably high, they can be lowered.

2.6.2 Consumer Sale of Goods Act

The consumer is entitled to damages in respect of any defect in the goods except where the seller is able to prove that the defect is caused by circumstances outside his control which he could not reasonably have expected, avoided or overcome. Thus, the same principle about 'seller's control' as under the Sale of Goods Act is found in this Act.

The consumer is always entitled to compensation if the goods differ from that which the seller expressly promised. Damages comprise compensation for expenses, loss of income and difference in price as well as other losses due to the delay or the defect.

Damages according to this Act do not comprise compensation for damage caused to other goods, with the exception of damage to such other goods that belong to the buyer or a member of his household and are intended mainly for private use.

2.6.3 Consumer Service Act

The consumer is entitled to compensation for loss caused to the consumer due to defect in services rendered unless the provider of the service proves that the loss is not caused by his or his representatives' negligence.

2.7 Burden of proof

Following general principles of law, the burden of proof rests with the plaintiff.

Accordingly, the burden of proof regarding

(a) the existence of a defect rests with the buyer/consumer;
(b) the excuse for a defect rests with the seller/provider;
(c) the extent of loss due to a defect rests with the buyer/consumer.

If a price has not been agreed, the burden of proof whether a price is reasonable or not rests with the seller/provider (at least towards a consumer).

2.8 Limitation period

The buyer/consumer must complain within a reasonable time after discovering the defect. If he fails to complain within two years from receiving the goods or services he loses his right to complain unless otherwise stipulated in the contract. Under certain circumstances (eg gross negligence) the limitation period will be extended.

2.9 Liability for third parties

Regarding damages due to defective goods/services, the seller/provider is in principle liable for his representatives/sub-suppliers/sub-contractors as for himself (Sale of Goods Act sections 40 and 27; Consumer Sale of Goods Act section 30; Consumer Service Act section 31).

3. LIABILITY IN TORT

3.1 Outline of relevant tort law giving rise to liability for personal and property damage in Sweden

3.1.1 Introduction

As pointed out earlier in this chapter, there is no specific product liability law in force in Sweden. Product Liability – as liability in tort – is based on the Tort Liability Act (*Skadeståndslagen*), and on special laws, mainly regarding various dangerous activities.

3.1.2 Tort Liability Act (Skadeståndslagen)

Liability under the Tort Liability Act is based on *negligence* (*culpa*). However, under court practice, the degree of fault required for the establishment of 'negligence' has been diminished increasingly over the years.

In a decision by the Supreme Court (NJA 1986 s 712) the manufacturer of a safety device for a crane was held responsible for a defect in the safety device (part of which was provided by a sub-contractor) causing damage to property (the crane turned over due to overload). The Supreme Court argued that the safety *device* was an important item and that insufficient *control* must have been exercised either by the manufacturer or by his sub-contractor.

In another case (NJA 1989 s 389) the Supreme Court clearly acknowledged strict liability. A schoolteacher was granted compensation for personal damage caused by food served to her at school, although the court expressly recognised that no negligence could be shown. Thus, at least regarding food causing personal damage strict product liability already exists in Sweden today.

3.1.3 Special laws

Strict liability for damage caused can be found in laws regarding certain dangerous activities, namely:

(a) Nuclear Liability Law (*Atomansvarighetslagen*);
(b) Environmental Liability Law (*Miljöskadelagen*);
(c) Railroad Traffic Law (*Järnvägstrafiklagen*);
(d) Air Traffic Law (*Luftfartslagen*);
(e) Electrical Power Plant Law (*Elanläggningslagen*).

Provisions of strict liability can also be found in the

(a) Maritime Act (*Sjölagen*);
(b) Law regarding Oil Damage at Sea (*Lag om oljeskada till sjöss*).

3.1.4 Insurance coverage

The provisions regarding product liability which can be found in the special laws referred to above do not give the full picture of how product liability issues are in reality currently dealt with in Sweden. Various insurance arrangements play a far more important role regarding compensation for personal damage and damage to property.

Liability under the Motor Traffic Damage Law (*Trafikskadelagen*) is connected to a mandatory insurance coverage. For personal injury or damage to property occurring due to motor vehicle in Sweden, compensation shall be paid out under the mandatory traffic insurance for the vehicle concerned. (If no traffic insurance has been taken out for the vehicle in question, compensation will nevertheless be paid out – based on joint responsibility amongst all the insurance companies.) The insurance company paying may claim compensation from the person actually causing the accident only if it was caused wilfully or by gross negligence.

For personal injury there is basic coverage under social security provisions, namely under the Law of General Insurance (*Lagen om allmän försäkring*). This insurance is mandatory and automatic, covering in principle everybody domiciled in Sweden. Regardless of the cause of personal injury, compensation will be paid out under the insurance (mainly for medical care and for loss of income).

It is very common for insurance coverage offered by the general insurance to be increased by various group insurance schemes offered to employees etc.

Furthermore, there is Occupational Injury Insurance (*Arbetsskadeförsäkring*) financed by social security contributions and covering all those gainfully employed. Compensation is paid out for occupational injury and disease (mainly for medical care and loss of income). The coverage is increased by the Security Insurance for Work Connected Injuries (*Trygghetsförsäkringen vid arbetsskada*) which is based on an agreed strict liability for the employer in respect of the employees' occupational injuries and is an arrangement agreed between trade unions and employers' associations in collective agreements. This insurance is underwritten by a consortium of Swedish insurance companies. As mentioned, the insurance covers strict liability: the employee is compensated even if no negligence of the employer can be shown.

Another insurance offered by a consortium of Swedish insurance companies is the Maltreatment Insurance (*Patientförsäkringen*) covering liability of governmental, county and municipal bodies for maltreatment in hospitals or by other medical staff employed by them. The liability covered by the insurance lies very close to strict liability, an exemption being the unavoidable consequence of a necessary treatment. On a voluntary basis many other doctors, dentists etc have taken out the same insurance cover. There is a maximum of MSEK 20 for each occurrence of injury, of MSEK 3 per person injured, and of MSEK 125 in total compensation under the insurance per calendar year.

Finally there is the Pharmaceutical Injuries Insurance (*Läkemedelsförsäkringen*) also offered by a consortium of Swedish insurance companies, covering the liability of producers or importers of pharmaceutical products for injuries caused by their products. Nearly all such producers and importers in Sweden have taken out this insurance. There is a maximum of MSEK 3 per person injured, of MSEK 100 for each series of injuries due to the same cause and of MSEK 150 in total per calendar year.

3.2 Laws to prevent personal injury and property damage

3.2.1 Product Safety Law (Produktsäkerhetslagen)

In July 1989 the Swedish Product Safety Law entered into force. The purpose of the law is to prevent products and services from causing personal injury or property damage. Under the law anyone conducting a business can:

- (a) be ordered to give safety information regarding his products and services;
- (b) be prohibited from selling products and providing services;
- (c) be ordered to provide warnings regarding his products and services; or
- (d) be ordered to withdraw his products and services.

Products and services provided as a business activity fall under the Product Safety Law if the products and services are or can be expected to be used by consumers to a substantial extent (private use only).

The National Board for Consumer Policies (*Konsumentverket*) is the main supervising authority in respect of matters falling under the Product Safety Law.

The Supervising Authority is supposed to take action *ex officio* under this Act. Nevertheless, anybody may initiate such actions by raising the issue in a complaint to the National Board for Consumer Policies.

The Supervising Authority shall primarily negotiate with the supplier of the product or service in order to obtain a voluntary remedy. Failing this, the Supervising Authority may turn to the Consumer Ombudsman (*Konsumentombudsman*) who may ask the Market Court (*Marknadsdomstolen*) for a mandatory decision. In minor cases the Consumer Ombudsman may present his own decision to the supplier of the product or service but such a decision is only valid if it is accepted by the supplier within a certain period of time.

The decision of the Market Court shall normally be combined with a directive on penalty of fine, falling due if the decision by the court is not duly observed. The fine is normally set at SEK 100,000, but it can be varied.

3.2.2 Special laws

The Pharmaceutical Act (*Läkemedelsförordningen*) contains provisions regarding the production, import and distribution of pharmaceutical products. The National Board of Health and Welfare (*Socialstyrelsen*) has the supervising responsibility regarding observance of the act.

The Law regarding Foods (*Livsmedelslagen*) contains stipulations regarding the handling and care of food. Various governmental bodies have supervising responsibilities regarding the law. There is also a Law regarding Animal Feed (*Lagen om foder*).

The Act regarding Chemical Products (*Lagen om kemiska produkter*) concerns producers importers and other providers of chemical products. The supervising responsibilities rest mainly with the National Inspection Board for Chemical Products (*Kemikalieinspektionen*) and with the National Board of Health and Welfare.

Other laws and regulations containing provisions to promote safety are the Working Environment Act (*Arbetsmiljölagen*), the Act regarding Transportation of Hazardous Goods (*Lagen om transport av farligt gods*), the Act regarding Explosives and Inflammable Goods (*Lagen om explosiva och brandfarliga varor*) and the Radiation Safety Act (*Strålskyddslagen*).

3.3 Laws in the making: Product Liability Law (*Produktskadelag*)

3.3.1 Introduction

As mentioned above, a Memorandum regarding a Product Liability Law has been prepared by the Swedish Ministry of Justice and submitted to various bodies for consideration.

3.3.2 Causation

Liability under the Product Liability Law suggested in the Memorandum arises:

(a) for personal injury caused by a product; and
(b) for property damage caused by a product for private use; damage to the product itself is, however, excluded;

always provided that the product, when it was put into circulation, was not as safe as could be reasonably expected at that time.

3.3.3 *Exceptions*

The following are excluded from the ambit of the Product Liability Law:

(a) any damage falling under the
  (i) Nuclear Liability Law (*Atomansvarighetslagen*);
  (ii) Traffic Liability Law (*Trafikskadelagen*);
  (iii) Insurance (Motoring Competition) Act (*Lagen om motortävlingsförsäkring*); or

(b) any occupational injury covered by Collective Agreement Insurance (*kollektivavtalsgrundad försäkring*).

3.3.4 *Definitions*

Product means all movables, even though incorporated into another movable or into an immovable.

The safety of the product shall be judged based on the foreseeable use of the product, the marketing of the product, directions for use and other circumstances.

3.3.5 *Liability*

The following may be liable:

(a) the person who has manufactured, produced or collected the defective product;

(b) the person who has imported the product in order to put it into circulation in Sweden; and

(c) the person who has marketed the product as his product and has furnished the product with his name or brand or any other distinctive mark.

Furthermore, liability will extend to *anyone* who has made the defective product available *if*:

(a) the product fails to show who is/are liable according to (a), (b) or (c), above; or

(b) whoever is liable under (a), (b) or (c), above has/have no domicile in Sweden;

always provided that the person who is held liable does not, within one month after receiving the claim, identify somebody domiciled in Sweden who has manufactured, developed or collected the product or supplied him with the product.

However, liability is avoided if a person:

(a) *proves* that he has not put the product into circulation in the course of a business activity; or

(b) can *plausibly* claim that the safety defect did not exist when he put the product into circulation.

3.3.6 *Mandatory provisions*

The provisions of the Product Liability Law are *mandatory*. Any contractual stipulations restricting this liability are invalid.

3.3.7 *Damages*

Damages under the Product Liability Law shall include compensation for *personal injury*.

Furthermore, damages under the Product Liability Law shall include compensation for *damage to property for personal use but not for damage to the product itself*.

There is *no limitation* to the amount of compensation for damages under the Product Liability Law. (Nevertheless, under the general provisions of the Tort Liability Act damages can be modified if the liability to pay full damages is regarded as an unreasonable burden, taking into account the economic situation of the respective parties and other circumstances involved.)

3.3.8 *Burden of proof*

The general principle is that the burden of proof rests with the plaintiff. This means that the plaintiff must prove not only the existence of the defect but also that the damage was caused by the defect.

Nevertheless, the Memorandum on the Product Liability Law emphasises that it is often very difficult to prove these circumstances, especially product liability cases, and that court practice has recognised and somewhat lessened the standard of proof needed. On the other hand, as pointed out above, the defendant can avoid liability if he proves that he did not put the product into circulation pursuant to business activity or if he proves that the safety defect did not exist when he put the product into circulation.

Regarding the amount of damages to be considered as full compensation, the burden of proof also rests with the claimant. However, under the Swedish Code of Judicial Procedure (*Rättegångsbalken*) the court may estimate the reasonable amount of compensation if it is impossible, difficult or unreasonably expensive to establish beyond reasonable doubt the full extent of damage caused.

3.3.9 *Limitation period*

Anybody claiming damages under the Product Liability Law must file his claim in court within three years of learning of the right to claim.

Furthermore, claims regarding compensation must be filed:

(a) for personal injury within 25 years[1] of the day when the defective product ceased to be in the possession of the liable party;
(b) for damage to property within 10 years of the day when the defective product ceased to be in the possession of the liable party.

1 The Bill proposes a time limit of ten years.

3.3.10 *Major differences in comparison with EC Directive*

Liability under the Product Liability Law of the Memorandum differs from that under the Directive in the following main aspects:

(a) the Swedish law makes no exception for primary agricultural products and game;
(b) the Swedish law makes no exception in liability due to the state of scientific and technical knowledge at the time when the product was put into circulation;
(c) the Swedish law has no lower threshold of Ecu 500,[2] nor any limit for total liability;
(d) the Swedish law only permits a reduction of liability owing to the fault of the injured person if the fault was wilful or due to gross negligence;
(e) the Swedish law contains no limitation of liability due to defects occurring under mandatory regulations made by public authorities;
(f) the Swedish law has a maximum limitation period of 25 years[3] in case of personal injury (the Directive maximum is 10 years).

3.3.11 *Entering into force*

It must be emphasised that the Product Liability Law has not yet been passed by the Swedish *Riksdag*. Therefore, it is still uncertain when and in what final form the law will be accepted. In no event can such a law be expected to enter into force earlier than 1 July 1992.[4]

4. RISK MANAGEMENT IN THE NEW ERA OF PRODUCT LIABILITY

4.1 General principles

4.1.1 *Product liability*

Due to the fact that product liability in Sweden still is based on the principle of *negligence*, the main objective of any risk management must be to ensure that the seller/manufacturer of the product is acting with due diligence.

As already pointed out earlier in this chapter, the degree of fault needed for 'negligence' may in many cases be very low, closing the gap to 'strict liability'. In general it can be said that the more dangerous an activity is, the closer to strict liability will the responsibility of the seller/manufacturer be.

Especially in cases where the seller/manufacturer has received some indication that his product can cause damage, it is essential that he immediately makes all reasonable efforts to avoid further damage and risk of damage. Otherwise he will most certainly be found negligent and liable.

Recently, the Swedish car manufacturer Volvo, having discovered that four

2 A threshold of SEK 3,000 has been proposed in the Bill.
3 The Bill proposes a maximum of ten years.
4 This date has been proposed in the Bill.

of its cars in Japan had leakage at the petrol intake, recalled all cars of the same model throughout the world for checking.

Records and documentation regarding the products as well as regarding decisions and actions by the seller/manufacturer are of course of great value whenever a product liability claim must be met.

4.1.2 Contractual liability

In order to avoid goods being regarded as defective, the seller must ensure that – in so far as the contract does not clearly state otherwise – they meet all the requirements under the Sale of Goods Act or the Consumer Sale of Goods Act respectively (see section 2.4, above). This includes what the buyer/consumer had 'reason to expect' regarding the goods and – in respect of consumers – also information from the seller about the goods.

Therefore, effective risk management must involve

(a) the forming of sales contracts reflecting the true characteristics of the goods and any reservations made by the seller;
(b) an analysis of what a buyer has 'reason to believe' in the respective case; and
(c) necessary documentation to confirm the compliance of the goods with these requirements.

Furthermore, regarding the liability to pay damages for defects in the goods, under the Sale of Goods Acts it is a question of (see sections 2.4 and 2.6, above):

(a) what the seller specifically promised;
(b) whether the seller can be regarded as negligent or not; and
(c) what the seller can prove lay 'outside of his control' and could not be foreseen, avoided or overcome.

Therefore, clarifying sales contracts as well as records and documentation regarding any promises made or any problems arising in respect of defects, will be of value when handling demands for damages due to defects in the goods.

4.2 Insurance

Swedish insurance companies offer product liability insurances at premiums which compare favourably with European levels.

The normally applied principle for insurance coverage is the *occurrence principle*, ie the insurance covers damage occurring during the insurance period. However, in international matters concerning substantial insurance amounts, and especially if the US market is involved, the *'claims made' principle* prevails.

According to the normal basic terms the liability insurance does *not* cover:

(a) damage to the product delivered, if the damage is caused by a defect in the product;
(b) the costs of taking back a defective product;

(c) damage which can be remedied by the delivery of a non-defective replacement;
(d) damage due to the inadequacy of a product under expressed or implied warranties;
(e) liability accepted by the insured in excess of normal liability in tort and normal (standard) contract terms.

Thus, the liability covered by the insurance under its normal basic terms is the liability to pay damages due to damage to persons or to property other than the product itself.

The product liability insurance offered by Swedish insurance companies normally consists of basic general terms amended by additional general terms applicable for the field of business concerned and, finally, if needed or of interest, amended by special terms individually negotiated and agreed.

4.3 Limitation of liability through corporate structure

4.3.1 Introduction

A highly recommended method of limiting liability is to establish an appropriate corporate structure, but it must be noted that business activities under the chosen structure should still be handled with due diligence and not contrary to equitable business principles.

4.3.2 Company forms

Two forms of company offering a limited liability are the joint stock company (*Aktiebolag*) and the limited partnership company (*Kommanditbolag*).

In an *Aktiebolag*, which is the most common form, the shareholders' liability is limited to the amount paid into the company as share capital.

In a *Kommanditbolag* one partner, the general partner (*komplementären*), has unrestricted liability but the liability of the other partners, the silent partners (*kommanditdelägarna*), is restricted to the amount they have agreed to put up as capital for the company. Normally an *Aktiebolag* (offering in itself limited responsibility for the shareholders as stated above) is the general partner of a *Kommanditbolag*.

4.3.3 Corporate veil: liability for shareholders

The fundamental principle of the *Aktiebolag*, laid down in the first article of the Companies Act (*Aktiebolagslagen*) is that the shareholders are not personally liable for the company's obligations. This principle also applies for the respective *Aktiebolag* in a group of companies, thus limiting the responsibility of a parent company or of another company holding shares.

It can, therefore, in general be said that the corporate veil is not easily lifted in Sweden.

Still, there has been much discussion as to whether, and under what circumstances, the corporate veil could and should be lifted. A special committee was formed in 1984 to study this issue and it reported in 1987. The committee recommended that the 'corporate veil should be lifted if a shareholder had used his influence on the company in a manner which was unfair to the creditors'. In the committee's opinion there were powerful reasons for making an action for lifting the corporate veil conditional on the company having been declared bankrupt.

The legislative recommendations of the committee have, however, so far not resulted in modification of the Companies Act.

There are some cases regarding the corporate veil that have been tried in the Supreme Court. In those decisions where the court found the shareholder(s) liable, the reason, generally speaking, was that the true business activities and interests lay with the shareholder(s) and that the company up front was not a normally active company managing on its own behalf with its own financial resources.

The minimum requisites for lifting the corporate veil have, in the legal literature, been said to be:

(a) that the company's activities have been carried out in the interests of the parent company (or in the interests of other shareholders); and
(b) that the assets of the company have been clearly insufficient for the foreseeable risks and obligations.

4.3.4 Liability towards shareholders

The founder, the managing director and the board member of the *Aktiebolag* can always be held liable by the shareholders for damage caused to the company by their 'negligence or intent' in fulfilling their duties. Damage caused to the shareholders or others shall be compensated if the Companies Act or the Articles of Association have not been observed.

A shareholder who is involved in the non-observance of the Companies Act or the Articles of Association can also be held liable by other shareholders for damage to the company, to the shareholders or to others caused by his 'gross negligence or intent' in this respect.

4.3.5 Splitting of high risk activities from valuable assets

Taking into account:

(a) the principle of each *Aktiebolag* being its own legal entity with limited responsibility for the shareholders; as well as
(b) the difficulties in lifting the corporate veil regarding companies that are carrying out normal business activities with due diligence,

the possibility of dividing operations between two or more *Aktiebolag* should be noted and considered.

This could, for example, lead to the establishment of various companies locally and abroad, eg one company owning patents, trademarks and other immaterial rights and issuing licences, a second company handling the manufacturing, a third company being the main marketing company, a fourth company being the local distributor etc, always provided that the division is made in a reasonable way, enabling each company to carry out normal business activities within its specific field of business.

APPENDIX

SALE OF GOODS ACT

(Issued on 6 September 1990; Swedish Code of Statutes 1990:931)

In accordance with a decision of the *Riksdag* (Parliament), the following is hereby ordained.

Introductory provisions

Sphere of application

1. This Act applies to the sale of all types of property other than real property.

Where applicable this Act also applies to exchanges of all types of property other than real property.

This Act does not apply to transfer of site leaseholds.

In the case of the sale of a building constructed for permanent use, the provisions contained in Chapter 4, sections 11, 12 and 18–19d of the Real Property Code apply instead of the provisions in sections 3, 13, 17–21 and also 30–40 of this Act. If a transfer of a site leasehold in accordance with Chapter 13, section 5 of the Real Property Code has included transfer of a building, the said provisions in the Real Property Code do not apply if other provisions apply under Chapter 13, section 8 of the Real Property Code.

2. This Act applies to orders for goods which are to be manufactured, except where the party ordering the goods undertakes to supply a substantial proportion of the materials. This Act does not apply to contracts for construction of buildings or other permanent construction on land or over water or under water.

This Act does not apply to contracts in which the party furnishing the goods shall also supply labour or other services, if the services comprise the predominant part of the obligations of this party.

Contractual freedom

3. The provisions of this Act do not apply where other provisions result from the contract, by practices which the parties have established between themselves or by commercial usages or other customs which must be considered binding on the parties.

Consumer sales

4. This Act does not apply in cases where the Consumer Sales Act (1990:932) is applicable.

International sales

5. This Act does not apply in cases where the International Sale of Goods Act (1987:822) is applicable.

Delivery of goods

Collected goods

6. The goods shall be kept at the buyer's disposal at the place where the seller had his place of business at the time of concluding the contract or, if he did not have a place of business which was connected with the sale, at his place of residence. If the parties knew, when the contract was concluded, that the goods or the consignment from which the goods were to be drawn were located elsewhere, the goods shall be kept at the buyer's disposal for collection at this location.

Goods have been delivered when they have been taken over by the buyer.

Carriage of goods sold

7. If the goods are to be transported to the buyer within one and the same locality or within an area in which the seller usually arranges the carriage of similar goods, delivery takes place when the goods are handed over to the buyer.

If the goods are to be transported to the buyer in other cases and where there are no obligations under the terms of delivery or otherwise under the contract, delivery takes place when the goods are handed over to the carrier who has undertaken to transport the goods from the place of dispatch. If the seller transports the goods himself, delivery does not take place until the goods are handed over to the buyer.

If the goods have been sold 'free', 'delivered' or 'free delivered' and a specific locality is specified, they are not considered to be delivered until they have arrived at this locality.

8. If the seller is to arrange for carriage of the goods, he shall enter into such contracts as are necessary for carriage to the place of destination by means of appropriate transportation and in accordance with the customary conditions for such transportation.

Time of delivery

9. If the goods are not to be delivered on demand or without delay, and if the time of delivery is not otherwise determined by the contract, the goods shall be delivered within a reasonable time after the conclusion of the contract.

If the goods are to be delivered within a specific period of time and it is not clear in the circumstances that the buyer is to determine the time for the delivery, the time for the delivery shall be determined by the seller.

If the goods are to be collected by the buyer and the seller is to decide the date of delivery, the seller shall inform the buyer in good time concerning when the goods will be at the buyer's disposal for collection.

The right to retain the goods

10. If the seller has not allowed credit or an extension of time for payment, he is not obliged to hand over the goods or, by transfer of documents or in any other way, to relinquish the right of disposition of the goods until payment has been made.

If the seller is to send the goods from the place where they are to be delivered, he is not entitled by virtue of the preceding paragraph to fail to dispatch the goods. However, the seller may prevent the handing over of the goods or documents concerning the goods to the buyer before payment has been made.

Costs arising from the goods

11. The seller is responsible for costs for the goods which arise prior to their delivery and which are not incurred by delay in the delivery of the goods as a result of circumstances attributable to the buyer.

Risk

What risk means

12. If the buyer bears the risk for the goods, he is liable to pay for the goods even if they have been spoiled, lost, have deteriorated or are diminished through events which are not attributable to the seller.

Transfer of risk

13. The risk passes to the buyer when the goods are delivered in accordance with the contract or in accordance with sections 6 or 7 of this Act.

If the goods are not delivered at the right time and this is attributable to the buyer or some circumstance attributable to the buyer, the risk passes to the buyer when the seller has fulfilled his obligations to enable delivery to take place.

If the buyer is to collect the goods from a place other than at the seller's place of business or residence, the risk passes to the buyer at the time delivery is due and when the buyer has been informed that the goods are at his disposal for collection.

14. The risk never passes to the buyer until it has been made clear, whether by markings on the goods, by notation in the transportation documents or in some other way, that the goods are clearly intended for the buyer.

Goods in transit

15. The risk in respect of goods sold in transit passes to the buyer at the time of sale, unless it is clear from the circumstances that the buyer has undertaken to bear the risk from the time the goods were handed over to the carrier who issued the transport documents. However, the seller always bears the risk for goods if, at the time of the sale, the seller knew or should have known that the goods had been spoiled, lost, had deteriorated or were diminished and did not inform the buyer of this.

Sale with option to return

16. If sale with option to return has been agreed and the goods have been handed over, the buyer bears the risk until the goods have been returned.

Status of the goods

Conformity with the contract etc

17. The goods must conform with what is implied by the contract as regards type, quantity, quality, other characteristics and also the packing or packaging.

Unless otherwise implied by the contract, the goods

(1) shall be fit for the purposes for which goods of the same description would ordinarily be used;
(2) shall be fit for the specific purposes for which the goods were intended to be used, if the seller at the time of the sale must have understood such specific purposes and the buyer had reasonable cause to rely on the seller's skill and judgment;
(3) shall possess the qualities of goods which the seller has referred to in providing samples or models; and
(4) shall be contained or packaged in a customary or otherwise adequate manner, if packaging is required to preserve or protect the goods.

If the goods do not comply with the provisions set out in the preceding paragraphs or do not conform in any other way with what the buyer can justifiably assume, it is to be considered that the goods do not conform with the contract.

18. It shall also be considered that the goods do not conform with the contract if they do not comply with descriptions of the qualities (characteristics) or use of the goods provided by the seller in marketing the goods or in other contexts prior to the sale and which may be assumed to have influenced the sale.

It shall also be considered that the goods do not conform with the contract if they do not comply with descriptions of the qualities or use of the goods which a party other than the seller has given, at an earlier stage in the sales transaction or on behalf of the seller, in marketing the goods, and which can be assumed to have affected the sale. However, non-conformity does not apply if the seller neither was aware nor should have been aware of these descriptions.

The first and second paragraphs do not apply if the descriptions have been corrected in time and in a clear manner.

Goods sold in existing condition

19. Notwithstanding the fact that the goods have been sold 'in their existing condition' or with any other similar general reservations, it shall be considered that they do not conform with the contract:

(1) if the goods do not conform with descriptions of their qualities or use which the seller has provided prior to the sale and which can be assumed to have influenced the contract;
(2) if, prior to the sale, the seller has failed to inform the buyer of a significant circumstance concerning the qualities or use of the goods which it must be assumed he was aware of and which the buyer could with good reason expect to be informed of, on condition that the omission can be assumed to have affected the sale; or
(3) the goods are in a condition which is considerably inferior to that which the buyer had good reason to expect with regard to the price of the goods and other circumstances.

When second-hand goods have been sold by auction, they are considered to be sold 'in their existing condition'. Where sub-section 3 of the preceding paragraph applies, regard shall be paid to the price estimated or indicated by the auctioneer.

Examination of the goods prior to sale

20. The buyer may not claim lack of conformity if it may be assumed he must have been aware of the lack of conformity at the time of the sale.

If the buyer has examined the goods before the sale or without giving acceptable reason has failed to follow the seller's exhortation to examine the goods, he may not claim what he should have noticed upon examination as a lack of conformity, unless the seller has acted in breach of faith and honour.

The preceding paragraph also applies when the buyer has had an opportunity to examine a sample of the goods before the sale and the lack of conformity relates to qualities which would have been revealed in the sample.

Relevant time factors in judging whether there is a lack of conformity

21. When judging the question of whether there is lack of conformity, heed shall be paid to the condition of the goods at the time when the risk for the goods passes to the buyer. The seller is responsible for any failure to conform with the contract which existed at this time, even though such non-conformity does not appear until later.

If deterioration of the goods occurs after the risk has passed to the buyer, it shall be considered that the goods do not conform with the contract if the deterioration is a consequence of a breach of contract on the part of the seller. This also applies if the seller has undertaken by guarantee or a similar pledge to be responsible for the usefulness or other qualities of the goods during a certain period and the deterioration relates to a quality covered by such a pledge.

Remedies in the case of delay in delivering the goods

Remedies

22. If the goods are not delivered or if they are delivered too late and this is not attributable to the buyer or to circumstances which are attributable to the buyer, under sections 23–29, the buyer may claim performance by the seller or may declare the contract avoided (cancel the contract) and in addition claim damages. He may also withhold payment by virtue of section 42.

Performance

23. The buyer may adhere to the contract and demand performance by the seller. However, the seller is not liable to fulfil the contract if there is an impediment to his performance which he cannot overcome or if performance would require sacrifices which are unreasonable in view of the buyer's interest in fulfilment of the contract by the seller.

However, if the above-mentioned circumstances cease within reasonable time, the buyer may require that the seller fulfil the contract.

The buyer loses the right to require that the seller fulfil the contract, if he waits for an unreasonably long time before presenting his claim.

24. If the seller asks the buyer whether, despite the delay, he will accept delivery within a specified period of time or if the seller notifies the buyer that he will fulfil the contract within a specified period of time, and if the buyer does not reply in reasonable time after receiving the inquiry or notification, the buyer may not declare the contract avoided if the seller fulfils his obligations within the time he has specified.

Declaring the contract avoided

25. The buyer may declare the contract avoided on grounds of the seller's delay, if the breach of contract is of substantial importance to the buyer and the seller was aware of this or should have been aware of this.

If the buyer has prescribed a specified additional period of time for delivery of the goods for the seller and if this period of time is not unreasonably short, the buyer may also declare the contract avoided if the goods are not handed over within the additional period of time.

During the additional period for delivery, the buyer may only declare the contract avoided if the seller declares that he will not fulfil the contract within the additional period.

26. If the sale refers to goods which are to be manufacturered or acquired especially for the buyer in accordance with the buyer's instructions or wishes, and if the seller cannot make use of the goods in any other way without substantial losses, the buyer may only declare the contract avoided on grounds of delay if his purpose in signing the contract is essentially frustrated by the delay.

Damages

27. The buyer has the right to compensation for the damage he suffers as a result of the seller's delay, unless the seller proves that the delay is due to an impediment beyond his control and that he could not reasonably be expected to have taken the impediment into account at the time of the conclusion of the contract or to have avoided it or overcome it or its consequences.

If the delay is caused by a party the seller has engaged to wholly or partly fulfil the contract, the seller is only exempt from liability for damages if the party he has engaged is also exempt from liability for damages under the preceding paragraph. This also applies if the delay is caused by a supplier who has been engaged by the seller or by any other party at an earlier stage in the sales transaction.

In accordance with the preceding paragraphs, the indirect loss referred to in section 67, paragraph (2), is not compensated.

The buyer always has a right to compensation if delay or loss is due to negligence on the part of the seller.

28. If the seller is prevented from fulfilling the contract on time, he shall notify the buyer of the impediment and its effect on his performance. If the buyer does not receive such notification within reasonable time after the seller was aware of or should have been aware of the impediment, the buyer has a right to compensation for the loss which could have been avoided if he had been notified in time.

Notice of avoidance and damages

29. If the goods have been delivered too late, the buyer may not declare the contract avoided or make a claim for damages on grounds of the delay, unless he notifies the seller, within reasonable time after he has learnt that the delivery has taken place, that he is declaring the contract avoided or wishes to claim damages. However, if the buyer declares the contract avoided, he does not need to specially notify the seller that he wishes to claim damages.

Remedies in the case of goods which do not conform with the contract

Remedies

30. If the goods do not conform with the contract and this is not attributable to the buyer or to circumstances which are attributable to the buyer, under sections 31–40 the buyer may require the seller to remedy the lack of conformity by rectification, delivery of substitute goods, or price reduction, or to declare the contract avoided and in addition he may claim damages. The buyer may also withhold payment in accordance with section 42.

Examination of the goods after delivery

31. When the goods have been delivered, as soon as circumstances so permit, the buyer shall examine the goods in accordance with generally accepted business practices.

If it is apparent that the goods are to be transported from the place of delivery, the buyer may postpone the examination until the goods have arrived at their destination.

If the buyer changes the destination of the goods while they are in transit or sends on the goods without having had a reasonable opportunity to examine them and the seller was aware of or should have been aware of such redirection or forwarding when the contract was concluded, the examination may be postponed until the goods have arrived at their new destination.

Complaint

32. The buyer may not claim that the goods do not conform with the contract unless he has notified the seller of the lack of conformity within a reasonable time after he noticed or should have noticed the lack of conformity (complaint).

If the buyer does not complain about lack of conformity in the goods within two years of having received them, he forfeits the right to do so unless other provisions are contained in a guarantee or similar pledge.

33. Notwithstanding sections 31 and 32, the buyer may claim that the goods do not conform with the contract, if the seller has acted with gross negligence or in breach of faith and honour.

Rectification and delivery of substitute goods

34. The buyer has the right to demand that the seller rectify lack of conformity free of charge if rectification can be carried out without unreasonable cost or inconvenience to the seller. Instead of rectifying the lack of conformity, the seller may deliver substitute goods in accordance with section 36.

The buyer has the right to demand delivery of substitute goods, if the breach of contract is of substantial importance to him and the seller was aware of this or should have been aware of this. However, the buyer does not have the right to demand delivery of substitute goods if the circumstances referred to in section 23 apply. Nor does the buyer have the right to demand delivery of substitute goods if it is a question of goods which were available at the time of the sale and which, in view of their qualities and what the parties must be presumed to have assumed, cannot be substituted by any other goods.

If the seller does not fulfil his obligations to rectify the lack of conformity, the buyer has the right to compensation for legitimate costs for rectification.

35. The buyer may not demand rectification of non-conformity or delivery of substitute goods if he does not notify the seller of his demand when he makes his complaint or within reasonable time thereafter. This does not apply, however, if the seller has acted with gross negligence or in breach of faith and honour.

36. Even though the buyer does not so demand, the seller has the right to rectify non-conformity at his own expense or deliver substitute goods if he can do so without substantial inconvenience to the buyer or without the risk that the buyer will not receive compensation for his own costs from the seller.

The seller may not claim that he was not given an opportunity to rectify non-conformity or deliver substitute goods if the buyer has rectified the non-conformity and, in view of the circumstances, the buyer could not reasonably be required to wait for rectification or delivery of substitute goods by the seller.

Price reduction and contractual avoidance

37. If the question of rectification of lack of conformity or delivery of substitute goods has not been raised or if rectification of lack of conformity or delivery of substitute goods does not take place within reasonable time after complaint, the buyer may demand a price reduction calculated in accordance with section 38 or may declare the contract avoided under section 39. However, the buyer is not entitled to a price reduction in the case of second-hand goods sold by auction.

38. If the buyer demands a price reduction, the price reduction shall be calculated in such a way that the relationship between the reduced price and the contractual price corresponds to the relationship at the time of delivery between the value of the goods in non-conforming and in contractual condition.

39. The buyer may declare the contract avoided on grounds of a lack of conformity if the breach of contract is of substantial importance to him and the seller was aware of this or should have been aware of this.

The buyer may not declare the contract avoided on grounds of lack of conformity, unless he notifies the seller within reasonable time after he noticed or should have noticed the lack of conformity, or after the time required to rectify the lack of conformity or deliver substitute goods under section 37, that he is declaring the contract avoided. However, this does not apply if the seller has acted with gross negligence or in breach of faith and honour.

Damages

40. The buyer is entitled to compensation for the damage he suffers because the goods lack conformity unless the seller proves that the lack of conformity is due to an impediment as described in paragraphs one and two of section 27. The provisions in section 28 regarding the seller's obligation to notify the buyer of impediments to fulfilling the contract on time apply correspondingly to impediments to delivering goods which conform with the contract.

In accordance with the preceding paragraph, no compensation may be claimed for the indirect losses referred to in paragraph two of section 67.

The buyer is always entitled to compensation if the lack of conformity or loss is the result of negligence on the part of the seller or if the goods did not conform with what the seller had especially pledged when the contract was concluded.

Remedies in the case of defective title to goods

41. If a third party has title to the goods or lien or any other similar right to them (defective title to goods) and the contract does not provide that the buyer shall take over the goods with the limitations due to the rights of third parties, the provisions on complaint in the first paragraph of section 32 and section 33, on rectification and delivery of substitute goods in sections 34–36, on price reduction and contractual avoidance in section 37–39, on damages in section 40 and on the buyer's right to withhold payment in section 42 shall apply.

The buyer is always entitled to compensation for the damage he suffers as a consequence of defective title to the goods which existed at the time of the conclusion of the contract, if he was neither aware of such defective title to the goods nor should have been aware of it.

Remedies for defective title to goods may also apply if a third party claims that he has the right described in the first paragraph above and there are probable grounds for the claim.

Common provisions concerning remedies for breach of contract by the seller

The right to withhold payment

42. If the buyer has the right to claim compensation on grounds of the seller's delay or of non-conforming goods, the buyer may withhold as much of the payment as corresponds to his claims.

Partial breach of contract

43. If only part of the delivery is delayed or lacks conformity, the provisions concerning the breach of contract in question shall be applied in respect of this part. The buyer may declare the contract avoided in its entirety if the breach of contract is of substantial importance to him with regard to the total contract and the seller was aware of this or should have been aware of this.

If it can be assumed that the seller considers he has fulfilled the contract in its entirety despite the fact that not all the goods have been delivered, the provisions regarding lack of conformity apply.

Contractual avoidance in the case of successive delivery

44. If delivery is to take place successively and if a part delivery is delayed or lacks conformity, the buyer may declare the contract avoided in respect of the part delivery in accordance with the provisions which otherwise apply for avoidance.

If the delay or lack of conformity gives reasons to assume that a breach of contract giving the right to avoidance will take place regarding any later part delivery, the buyer may on these grounds declare the contract avoided in respect of such later part deliveries, if he does so within reasonable time.

If the buyer declares the contract avoided regarding a part delivery, he may at the same time declare the contract avoided regarding earlier or later deliveries if, due to the interdependence of these deliveries, he would be caused considerable inconvenience by adhering to the contract regarding these deliveries.

The buyer's obligations

Determination of the price

45. If the price is not implied or stated in the contract, the buyer shall pay what is reasonable with regard to the nature and condition of the goods, the current price at the time of the conclusion of the contract and other circumstances.

46. If the price is to be calculated according to the number, dimensions or weight of the goods, the calculation shall be based on the quantity of the goods at the time when the risk for the goods passes to the buyer.

If the price is to be calculated according to the weight of the goods, the weight of packaging/packing shall be deducted first.

47. If the buyer has received an invoice, he is bound by the price stated in the invoice. However, this does not apply if he notifies the seller within a reasonable time that he does not accept the price, if the contract implies a lower price or if the sum required is unreasonable.

Payment

48. Payment shall be made at the seller's place of business or residence. However, if payment is to be made against the transfer of the goods or documents, payment shall be made at the place where such transfer occurs.

The obligation to pay also includes the obligation under the contract to accept bills of exchange and issue letters of credit, bank guarantees or other securities and to take other measures necessary to make payment possible.

49. If the time for payment is not implied or stated in the contract, the buyer shall pay when the seller requests payment. However, the buyer is not obliged to pay before the goods are made available or they have been placed at his disposal in accordance with the contract.

Before the buyer makes payment, he has the right to examine the goods in the manner which is customary, or which should be allowed in view of the circumstances, unless the form of delivery and payment which has been agreed is not compatible with such examination.

Notwithstanding the preceding paragraphs, if a bill of lading has been issued for transportation of the goods to their place of destination or if the goods are otherwise transported under conditions which prevent the seller from having disposal of the goods before payment has been made, payment may be required against the bill of lading or when the buyer has received the consignment note or other proof that the goods have been transported under such conditions.

Co-operation on the part of the buyer etc

50. The buyer shall

(1) co-operate in the sale in such a manner as may be reasonably expected of him if the seller is to fulfil the contract; and
(2) collect or receive the goods.

Remedies for breach of contract by the buyer

Remedies

51. If the buyer does not pay in time or does not co-operate in the sale in accordance with section 50, sub-section 1, and where this is not due to the seller or any circumstance attributable to the seller, in accordance with sections 52–59 the seller may require payment or other performance or may declare the contract avoided and may, in addition, claim damages. The seller may also withhold the goods in accordance with section 10 and demand interest in accordance with section 71.

If the buyer does not fulfil his obligation to collect or receive the goods and where this is not due to the seller or any circumstance attributable to the seller, section 55, section 57, paragraphs 2–4, and section 58 apply.

Demand for payment and other fulfilment of the contract

52. The seller may adhere to the contract and demand payment.

However, if the buyer cancels an order for goods which are to be manufactured or supplied especially for him, the seller may not adhere to the sale by completing the manufacture, making preparations for delivery and demanding payment. However, this does not apply if a cancellation would result in substantial difficulty for the seller or risk that the seller's loss as a result of cancellation would not be reimbursed. Damages on the grounds of cancellation are estimated in accordance with sections 67–70.

If the goods have not yet been delivered, the seller forfeits the right to demand payment if he waits an unreasonably long time before demanding payment.

53. The seller may adhere to the contract and require the buyer's co-operation in accordance with section 50, sub-section 1. However, the buyer is not obliged to co-operate in the sale if there is an impediment which he cannot overcome or if his co-operation would require unreasonable sacrifices with regard to the seller's interest in the buyer's co-operation.

However, if the circumstances mentioned above cease to apply within a reasonable time, the seller may require the buyer's co-operation.

The seller forfeits the right to require the buyer's co-operation if the seller waits an unreasonably long time before presenting such a requirement.

Contractual avoidance due to delay in payment

54. The seller may declare the contract avoided on the grounds of delay in payment on the part of the buyer, if such delay constitutes a substantial breach of contract.

If the seller has specified a fixed additional period of time for payment and this period is not unreasonably brief, the contract may also be declared avoided if the buyer fails to make payment within the additional time allowed.

While the additional period applies, the seller may only declare the contract avoided if the buyer states that the payment will not be made within this period.

If the goods have come into the buyer's possession, the seller may only declare the contract avoided if he has reserved the right to avoidance or if the buyer has rejected the goods.

Contractual avoidance on the grounds of lack of co-operation

55. The seller may declare the contract avoided if the buyer does not co-operate in the sale in accordance with section 50, sub-section 1, and if the breach of contract is not of substantial importance for the seller and the buyer had been aware of this or should have been aware of it. Similarly, the seller may declare the contract avoided if the buyer did not collect or receive the goods in time where it is stated or implied by the contract or the circumstances that the seller has a special interest in disposing of what he has sold.

Moreover, the seller may declare the contract avoided if, within a fixed additional time period which the seller specifies for the buyer and which is not unreasonably brief, the buyer fails to

(1) co-operate in the sale in accordance with section 50, sub-section 1; or
(2) collect or receive the goods in cases where it is stated or implied by the contract or the circumstances that the seller has a special interest in disposing of what he has sold.

While the additional period applies, the seller may only declare the contract avoided if the buyer states that he will not fulfil his obligations within this additional period.

Contractual avoidance in the case of successive deliveries

56. If payment is to be made in stages, in special part payments, as deliveries take place, and if there is delay in payment for any delivery, the seller may declare the contract avoided as regards such a delivery in accordance with the provisions which otherwise apply for avoidance.

The seller may also declare the contract avoided as regards a subsequent delivery if there is reason to suppose that delay in making payment which would justify avoidance will be repeated.

Damages

57. The seller has the right to compensation for the damage he suffers as a result of the buyer's delay in making payment, unless the buyer proves that the delay is due to the law, to a failure or breakdown in transport or communications facilities or means of effecting payment or other similar hindrance which the buyer could not reasonably have been expected to take into account at the time of the conclusion of the contract and the results of which he could not have reasonably avoided or overcome.

The seller is also entitled to compensation for the damage he suffers if the buyer does not co-operate in accordance with section 50, sub-section 1, or if the buyer fails to collect the goods in time or receive the goods in cases where it is stated or implied by the contract or the circumstances that the seller has a particular interest in disposing of what he has sold. However, there is no right to compensation in such cases if the buyer proves that there has been an impediment of the type specified in section 27, paragraph 1 or 2, preventing him from co-operating or from collecting or receiving the goods.

In accordance with the second paragraph, indirect loss as covered by section 67, paragraph 2, is not compensated.

The seller always has a right to compensation if the breach of contract or the loss is due to negligence on the part of the buyer.

58. If the buyer is prevented from fulfilling the contract in time, he shall notify the seller of the impediment and its effect on the possibilities of fulfilling the contract. If the seller does not receive such notification within a reasonable time after the buyer was aware of or should have been aware of the impediment, the seller has a right to compensation for the loss which could have been avoided if he had been notified in time.

Notice of avoidance and damages

59. The seller may not declare the contract avoided on the grounds of the buyer's delay in paying, collecting or taking over the goods if he does not notify the buyer of his avoidance before fulfilment of the contract has taken place.

If the buyer has co-operated in accordance with section 50, sub-section 1, but such co-operation has occurred too late, the seller may not declare the contract avoided or claim damages on the grounds of delay if he fails to notify the buyer of his avoidance or that he wishes to claim damages within a reasonable time after he was aware that the buyer has co-operated. However, if the seller declares the contract avoided, he does not need to especially notify the buyer that he intends to claim damages.

Specifications

60. If the buyer is to specify the form, dimensions or other qualities of the goods and if he fails to do so at the time agreed or within a reasonable period after the seller has requested such specification, the seller may draw up the specifications in accordance with what may be assumed to be the buyer's interest. However, this does not prevent the seller from applying other remedies.

The seller shall notify the buyer of the specifications he draws up and prescribe for the buyer a reasonable time within which the buyer may change the specifications. If the buyer does not change the specifications within the prescribed period, the seller's specifications become binding.

Anticipated breach of contract

Right to stop performance under the contract

61. If it appears after the conclusion of the contract that the actions or financial situation of one of the parties give every reason to anticipate that he will not fulfil a substantial proportion of his obligations, the other party may for his part suspend fulfilment of the contract and withhold his performance.

If the seller has already dispatched the goods and if it appears that circumstances such as those covered by the first paragraph exist in respect of the buyer, the seller may prevent the handing over of the goods to the buyer. This also applies where the buyer has received transport documents in respect of the goods.

The party suspending fulfilment of the contract or preventing the handing over of the goods shall immediately notify the other party to this effect. If he does not do so, the other party has the right to compensation for the damage he suffers because such notification has not been given in time.

The party who has suspended his fulfilment of the contract or prevented the handing over of the goods shall continue to implement the contract if the other party provides acceptable security for his fulfilment of the contract.

Contractual avoidance

62. If it is clear that a breach of contract will occur which gives one party the right to declare the contract avoided, this party may declare the contract avoided prior to the time for performance. However, such avoidance is without effect if the other party immediately provides acceptable security for his fulfilment of the contract.

Bankruptcy etc

63. If one party has been declared bankrupt, the estate of the bankrupt party may enter into the contract. The other party may require that, within a reasonable period, the estate notifies its entry into the contract.

If the estate of the bankrupt party enters into the contract and if the time for fulfilment of the contract by the other party is due, the other party may require that the estate complete its performance or, if an extension of time has been granted, that the estate provide acceptable security without unreasonable delay for the fulfilment of the contract. If the time for the fulfilment of the contract by the other party is not yet due, the other party may require security if such security is necessary to protect this party against loss.

If the estate does not enter into the contract within a reasonable period of time after the other party has required entry into the contract in accordance with the first paragraph, or if the estate does not comply with the other party's requirement in accordance with the second paragraph, the other party may declare the contract avoided.

If the goods are handed over to the buyer or to his estate after the buyer has applied for the appointment of a trustee in accordance with the Composition with Creditors Act (1970:847) or has been declared bankrupt and payment has not been made, the seller may require that the goods are returned. However, it is not necessary for the goods to be returned if payment is made immediately or, where payment for the sale is not yet due, the buyer or the estate provides acceptable security for payment within a reasonable time after being required to return the goods.

If the estate has sold the goods or otherwise has utilised or disposed of them so that they cannot be returned in a substantially unchanged and undiminished state, the estate shall be considered to have entered into the contract.

Joint provisions regarding avoidance and delivery of substitute goods

The effects of avoidance and delivery of substitute goods

64. If the contract is declared void, the seller's obligation to hand over the goods and the buyer's obligation to pay and to co-operate no longer apply.

To the extent that the contract has been fulfilled, either party may require the other party to return what he has received. In this connection, each party may retain what he has received until the other party supplies what he is to return and also makes payment or provides acceptable security for damages and interest for which he may be liable.

If the seller is to undertake delivery of substitute goods, the buyer may retain what he has received until delivery of substitute goods takes place.

65. If the contract is declared void, the buyer shall pay for any gain from the goods and also pay reasonable compensation if he has had any other benefit from the goods.

If the seller is to return payment made, he shall pay interest from the day on which he received payment.

Lapse of the right to compensation and delivery of substitute goods

66. The buyer may only declare the contract avoided or require delivery of substitute goods if he can return the goods substantially unchanged or undiminished.

However, the right to declare the contract avoided or require delivery of substitute goods is not forfeited if

(1) the goods have been spoiled, lost, impaired or diminished as a result of their nature or of any other circumstance which is not attributable to the buyer;
(2) the goods have been spoiled, impaired or diminished as a result of a measure which was required to investigate whether the goods were without fault; or
(3) the goods have been sold in part or in their entirety to a third party in a normal manner or have been used by the buyer for anticipated usage before he noticed or should have noticed the lack of conformity which gives him cause to declare the contract avoided or to require delivery of substitute goods.

Furthermore, the right to declare the contract avoided or to require delivery of substitute goods is not forfeited if the buyer compensates the seller for the loss in the value of the goods which is the result of the impairment or the diminution of the goods.

The extent of damages

General

67. Damages on the grounds of breach of contract cover compensation for expenditure, price difference, loss of profits and other direct or indirect loss due to the breach of the contract. However, damages under this Act do not cover compensation for loss suffered by the buyer as a result of damage to anything other than the goods which have been sold.

Indirect loss is considered to comprise

(1) loss as a result of reduction or loss of production or turnover;
(2) other loss because the goods cannot be used in the manner intended;
(3) loss of profits as the result of the lapse of a contract with a third party or because such a contract has not been properly fulfilled; and
(4) other similar loss, if such loss was difficult to foresee.

However, a loss which the injured party has suffered in order to limit a loss of a kind which is not covered by the second paragraph is not to be considered an indirect loss in accordance with the second paragraph.

Difference in price

68. If the contract has been declared avoided and the buyer has made a replacement purchase or the seller has again sold the goods (resale) and if such a measure has been taken with due consideration and within a reasonable time after the avoidance of the contract, the basis for calculating the price difference is the price under the terms of sale and the price for the replacement purchase or the resale of the goods.

69. If the contract has been declared avoided and if there has been no replacement purchase or resale in accordance with section 68 and if there is an accepted and current price for such goods as are covered by the contract, the basis for calculation of the price difference is the price under the terms of contract and the accepted and current price at the time of avoidance.

Limitation of damage and reduction of damages

70. The injured party shall take reasonable measures to limit his damage. If he fails to take such measures, he must himself bear a corresponding proportion of the loss.

If the damages are unreasonable with regard to the opportunities of the person liable for damages to foresee and prevent the occurrence of damage, and with regard to other circumstances, the damages may be adjusted.

Interest

71. The Interest Act (1975:635) applies as regards the interest on the price and other claims which are not paid in time.

However, where the seller may require payment in exchange for supplying the goods, interest is payable in accordance with section 6 of the Act (1975:635) from the day when the seller makes such a demand, even if the due date of payment has not been determined in advance. This also applies where the seller may require payment against documents or verification which means that the seller may not have disposal of the goods when such documents or verifications have been handed over to the buyer.

However, the second paragraph does not apply if the seller supplies the goods, documents or verification despite failure to make payment.

Preservation of the goods

The seller's obligations

72. If the goods are not collected or received in time or if they are not handed over to the buyer as a result of some other circumstance attributable to the buyer, the seller shall, on behalf of the buyer, take reasonable measures as regards preservation of the goods if he has them in his possession or can otherwise take charge of them.

The buyer's obligations

73. If the buyer wishes to reject goods which he has received, he shall take reasonable measures on behalf of the seller as regards preservation of the goods.

If the buyer wishes to reject goods which have been dispatched to him and kept available for him at the place of destination, he shall take charge of them on behalf of the seller if this can be achieved without payment taking place and without unreasonable cost or inconvenience. However, there is no such obligation if the seller or some other person who is acting on his behalf and who can take charge of the goods is at the place of destination.

Storage with a third party

74. If the party who is to preserve the goods has transferred the goods to a third party for storage on behalf of the other party and if the storer has been chosen with due care, the party responsible for preservation of the goods is not held responsible for the goods after the storer has received them.

Compensation for preservation

75. The party who is to preserve the goods on behalf of the other party is entitled to compensation for reasonable expenses and costs due to such preservation. He may retain the goods until compensation has been paid or acceptable security has been given for such compensation.

Resale of the goods

76. The party who is to preserve the goods may sell them if he cannot continue to preserve the goods without substantial costs of inconvenience or if the other party makes unreasonable delay in taking charge of the goods or in paying for the goods or in compensating the cost of preservation.

If the goods are subjected to rapid spoiling or deterioration or if preservation of the goods is unduly costly, they shall be sold if this is possible.

The goods shall be sold with due care. If possible, the other party shall be notified prior to such sale.

77. If a party has the right to sell the goods in accordance with section 76, but they cannot be sold or it is obvious that the price would not cover the costs of such a sale, this party may have disposal of the goods in some other reasonable manner. Before this occurs, the other party shall be notified, if this is possible.

78. The proceeds of such a sale and other benefit that a party has received from the goods, together with the costs incurred, shall be accounted for to the other party. Any surplus shall accrue to the other party.

Gain

79. Any gain yielded by the goods before the time agreed for delivery accrues to the seller unless there was good reason to consider that such gain would occur later. The gain which the goods yield after they are to be delivered accrues to the buyer unless there was good reason to consider that such gain would occur later.

80. The sale of shares includes dividends which are not yet due for payment prior to the conclusion of the contract and any such preferential rights for shareholders to participate in a share issue which it has been impossible to exercise prior to the conclusion of the contract.

81. The sale of an interest-bearing claim includes interest which has accrued but which is not yet due for payment at the agreed time for delivery of such a claim. In addition to the price to be paid for such a claim, the buyer shall pay the seller a sum corresponding to such interest unless the claim was sold as a doubtful claim.

Notifications

82. If a notification which the buyer shall make to the seller in accordance with sections 23, 24, 29, 32, 35, 39, 47 or 61 has been dispatched in an appropriate manner, the notification may be cited, even if it has been delayed, distorted or has not arrived.

This also applies to notification which the seller shall make to the buyer in accordance with sections 52, 53, 59 or 61.

* * *

This Act comes into force on 1 January 1991.

This Act revokes the Act relating to the Purchase and Exchange of Goods (1905:38 s 1) with the limitation that the references in the Act found in the Act on Commission, Commercial Agencies and Commercial Travellers continue to apply.

However, previous provisions apply as regards contracts entered into before this Act came into force.

On behalf of the Government
ODD ENGSTRÖM

LAILA FREIVALDS
(Ministry of Justice)

CHAPTER XV

Switzerland

Dr Peter Honegger

Niederer Kraft & Frey
Bahnhofstrasse 13
8001 Zürich
Switzerland

Tel ++ 41 1 217 1000
Fax ++ 41 1 217 1400

CHAPTER XV

Switzerland[1]

1. INTRODUCTION

1.1 Definition and classification of terms

i. Product liability. The term product liability encompasses the liability for damage caused by products which are defective, dangerous, unhealthy or otherwise unsafe.

Product liability is intended to cover loss arising from physical injury, damage to property, economic loss (eg medical expenses or lost earnings) and mental distress, but not damage to the product itself.

ii. Producer. The producer is an individual/entity who manufactures and/or assembles a product or any part thereof.

iii. Distributor. The distributor is an individual/entity who distributes a product to the user either directly (eg as a retailer) or indirectly (eg as a wholesaler).

iv. Consumer. The consumer is an individual/entity who uses a product. He may or may not have a contractual relationship with a distributor or a producer.

1.2 Abbreviations

CO	Swiss Code of Obligations
The Convention	Convention on Jurisdiction and Enforcement of Judgments in Civil and Commercial Matters made in Lugano on 16 September 1989
The Directive	EC Directive 85/324 on Product Liability
EC	European Community
EFTA	European Free Trade Association
FCR	Swiss Federal Court Reporter
PILA	Swiss Private International Law Act
SFr	Swiss Francs
USA	United States of America

1 The author wishes to thank Dr Adolf E Kammerer and Dr Alexander von Ziegler for their valuable advice and assistance in the preparation of this article.

2. OVERVIEW

2.1 Overview of the law relating to defective products

Under Swiss law there is no specific law on product liability. In particular, Switzerland – which is not an EC country – has not implemented EC Directive 85/324 on Product Liability (the Directive).

Producers and distributors can be sued in Switzerland under traditional rules of contract and tort only (see sections 2.2 and 2.3, below). Under both contract and tort law the consumer will have to establish that the damage was caused by the use of the product (see section 2.4, below). In addition, he will have to substantiate in detail the quantum of the damage (see section 2.5, below). These rules are laid down in the Swiss Code of Obligations (CO).

2.2 Liability in contract

The delivery chain (eg producer–wholesaler–retailer–consumer) consists of a series of contracts, most of which are contracts of sale (CO articles 184 ff). Typically, there is no direct contractual link between the producer and the consumer. However, there is usually a contract of sale between the consumer and the retailer. Accordingly, a consumer can only sue the retailer in contract, and not the producer, with whom he has no direct contractual relationship.

This at least is the current view of the Swiss Federal Court (the highest Swiss court). The German concept of construing privity of contract between a producer and a consumer (on the basis that the contract between the producer and its immediate contractual partner, eg a wholesaler, contains an implied warranty in favour of the consumer and the consumer can sue the producer on such warranty in contract) is not followed by the Swiss courts. Further, there is no indication that this argument will be accepted by Swiss courts in the near future.

Contractual liability based on a contract of sale can be twofold: it may be for a breach of a warranty or a breach of contract. The seller can exclude any warranty and disclaim its contractual liabilities. Claims against the seller are barred one year after delivery of the product (see section 4, below).

2.3 Liability in tort

Since there is usually no contractual relationship between the consumer and the producer, claims against the producer can generally only be made in tort (CO articles 41 ff).

An action in tort can be based on the so-called danger rule (*Gefahrensatz/principe du risque*) or on liability of the principal (*Geschäftsherrenhaftung/responsabilité de l'employeur*). Disclaimers are not possible under tort law. Claims in tort are barred one year after the consumer has been injured or suffered damage (see section 3, below).

2.4 Causation

Under both contract and tort law, the consumer has to prove that the damage was, in the specific instance, caused by the product and that, according to general experience of life, the use of the product can reasonably be expected to cause the damage in question.

However, a producer or distributor will not be liable for damage caused by an event which was highly unlikely to occur. That is, the producer is not responsible for unforeseeable events and the concept of remoteness of damage applies.

Further, under special circumstances, a court can reduce or even refuse compensation, if the consumer is contributorily negligent.

If the damage was caused by different producers and/or distributors, eg by a component manufacturer and by the assembler, the consumer may recover full compensation from either party, ie either from the component manufacturer or from the assembler (joint and several liability). However, the consumer may only receive full compensation once. Further, the producer or distributor paying full compensation may have the right to recover in part or in full from other producers/distributors.

2.5 Quantum of damage

Under both contract and tort law, the consumer may recover damage arising from physical harm, property damage, economic loss (eg medical expenses or lost earnings) and mental distress.

In the case of contributory negligence of the consumer, the court may reduce the damages recovered or deny them altogether (CO article 44(1)). Other reasons for reductions are the fact that the producer or distributor was negligent to a minor extent only, or that the injured consumer was particularly disposed to be struck by the injury or disease in question (eg weak heart in case of heart attack). This differs from the 'egg shell skull' rule in English common law, which provides that a defendant 'takes a plaintiff as he finds him'; that is, that a plaintiff is entitled in principle to recover damages in full for a physical injury, even if he was already particularly disposed of that injury.

If the product causes the death of a consumer, the costs in connection with death, including the costs caused prior to death, eg hospitalisation costs, lost earnings etc have to be compensated (CO article 45(2)). The claimants in this case are the descendants of the deceased.

If the deceased consumer was responsible for supporting other persons (for example, his spouse or children), these persons have a claim against the producer or distributor for survivors' benefits, ie compensation for the support they could have expected to get from the deceased person, taking into account his and their life expectancy, their chance to find an alternative supporter (eg to remarry), and the economic potential of the deceased person.

Although the amount of damages is neither limited by the Swiss Code of Obligations nor by reasons of foreseeability, the Swiss courts adopt a conservative approach. They require the consumer to substantiate in great detail all recoverable damage arising from physical harm and economic loss. Punitive damages do not exist at all under Swiss law.

Pursuant to CO article 47 the injured consumer or, if he dies, his close relations can, at the Swiss court's discretion, be awarded additional compensation for mental distress. Unlike in the USA, such damages are likely to be small.

Some examples may illustrate the reluctance of the Swiss courts in awarding compensation for mental distress.

(a) Airplane crash: two children dying in front of their parents; SFr 40,000 each for the mother and for the father (FCR 112 II pp 118 ff [1986]).
(b) Car accident: death of husband; SFr 13,000 for the wife and SFr 5,000 for each of the two children (FCR 90 II pp 184 ff [1964]).
(c) Explosion: total blindness of 43-year-old man: SFr 25,000, reduced to SFr 20,000 due to contributory negligence (FCR 89 II pp 24 ff [1963]).
(d) Burn of 50% of the skin, loss of all fingers, hair of the head and one ear, distorted face, painful suffering; SFr 40,000 (62 Schweizerische Juristen–Zeitung p 384 [1966]).
(e) X-ray burn: distorted face of 54-year-old man, long-lasting, painful suffering; SFr 15,000 (FCR 53 II pp 419 ff [1927]).

3. CLAIMS AGAINST PRODUCERS

As stated above, the consumer's claim against the producer is usually based in tort, either on the so-called danger rule (see section 3.1, below) or on liability of the principal (see section 3.2, below).

If the consumer bought the product directly from the producer, the consumer would also have a contractual claim, as against the retailer (see section 4, below).

3.1 Danger rule (*Gefahrensatz/principe du risque*)

About 50 years ago, the Swiss Federal Court established – under the principles of negligence (CO article 41) – the so-called 'danger rule' according to which whoever creates a dangerous condition will be deemed to have been negligent unless he proves that he took the necessary safety measures to prevent injury or loss (FCR 66 II pp 114 ff [1940], FCR 79 II pp 66 ff [1953]). Only after considerable time was the rule applied to product liability claims. In this context the danger rule says that the producer is liable in negligence if it fails to take reasonable steps to avoid damage to the consumer of its products.

The first time the danger rule was explicitly mentioned in a product liability case was in 1961 (Basler Juristische Mitteilungen pp 180 ff [1961]). In this case a wine-grower had applied a plant-growth agent to his grapevines. About 70,000 grapevines were damaged by a frost as the agent caused a hyper-susceptibility to frost. When the wine-grower sued the seller and the producer of the plant-growth agent, the Basle Court of Appeal ruled that the producer had created a dangerous condition and failed to take the necessary safety measures to avoid damage to the consumer. The court held that, despite the fact that the *Agricultural Yearbook* had mentioned such danger, the producer in particular failed to give warnings that the plant-growth agent should not be used for grapevines. Therefore, the producer was held negligent and liable to the wine-grower. The parties settled out of court when the case went to the Swiss Federal Court, so the point was never decided by the highest Swiss Court.

Under the danger rule, the producer must therefore either make its products safe or, if this is not possible, give sufficient warnings to the consumer.

3.2 Liability of the principal (*Geschäftsherrenhaftung/responsabilité de l'employeur*)

A producer may also be sued in his capacity as principal (CO article 55). As such he is liable for the damage caused by his employees or other support staff in the course of their employment, whether they acted negligently or not. If the consumer shows that he was injured or suffered loss when using a dangerous product, the producer will be held liable unless he shows that he carefully selected, instructed and supervised the employees who manufactured the product.

In 1984, the Swiss Frederal Court restricted the producer's ability to furnish such exonerating proof (FCR 110 II pp 456 ff [1984]). In the given case, a construction worker was heavily injured when a 700 kg reinforced concrete frame, lifted by a building dredger, was dropped on his right foot due to a faulty fixing set in the concrete. The Swiss Federal Court ruled that the producer was liable as principal – regardless of whether his employees were carefully selected, instructed and supervised – as the producer could not show that he had made a final quality control inspection of the fixings set in the concrete frame. The court held that a producer of dangerous products must be able to show that he made a final quality control inspection or that the producer designed a product that, in all probability and almost certainly, excludes damage to the consumer. The court did not rule on the question whether the producer was also liable under the danger rule. The effect of the case is that since by definition it is impossible to design an inherently dangerous product so that it will definitely not cause damage to consumers, quality control inspections of dangerous products made available in Switzerland are of tremendous importance to any producer wishing to limit or exclude its liability.

Following this decision, the burden of proof on the producer is very difficult to discharge and the liability of the principal is all but strict. It follows that consumers tend to base their claims against producers primarily on liability of the principal.

3.3 Disclaimer

Disclaimers are only possible in Swiss contract law, not under Swiss tort law. As there is usually no contract between the consumer and the producer, the producer's disclaimer, whether in general business conditions, in instruction manuals, or in warranty forms, is not generally effective as against the consumer.

3.4 Limitation period

All claims in tort, including claims under the danger rule and claims against a principal, are subject in Switzerland to a relatively short limitation period of one year commencing on the date on which the essential elements of damage as well as the identity of the producer liable for the damage are known to the injured consumer. In any event, the limitation period expires ten years after the date of the unlawful act, ie in the case of product liability, after the dangerous product has been manufactured (CO article 60).

3.5 Consumer's burden of proof and producer's defences

Under the danger rule, the consumer seeking recovery from the producer must prove:

(a) the damage; and
(b) that the product was dangerous; and
(c) that his damage was caused by the product.

Under the rule of liability of the principal, the consumer must prove:

(a) the damage; and
(b) that the product was dangerous due to an act or omission of the producer's employees; and
(c) that his damage was caused by the product (more precisely, by the employees' act or omission).

The producer has, inter alia, the following defences:

(a) the consumer did not sufficiently substantiate his damage – in practice a very important defence; or
(b) the producer took the necessary safety measures to prevent damage to the consumer; or
(c) the producer carefully selected, instructed and supervised the employees who manufactured the product; or
(d) the scientific and technical knowledge at the time did not permit the product to be seen as dangerous ('state of the art'); or
(e) the consumer was contributorily negligent; or
(f) the consumer was inclined to the injury or disease in question; or
(g) the limitation period expired.

4. CLAIMS AGAINST RETAILERS/DISTRIBUTORS

Typically, the consumer enters into a sales contract with the retailer, but not with the wholesaler.

Against the *wholesaler*, the consumer can claim in tort only and such claims are extremely rare in Switzerland. If the wholesaler is sued at all, he would usually be sued together with the producer, in tort (see section 3, above), based on the concept of joint and several liability.

Against the *retailer*, the consumer can claim for breach of warranty (see section 4.1, below), breach of contract (see section 4.2, below), or in tort (see section 4.3, below).

4.1 Warranty claim

Under Swiss sales law, the retailer must supply the consumer with a product that not only accords with any express representations, but also shows the physical and legal qualities that are necessary for its intended use (CO article 197).

However, the retailer will not be liable if the consumer was aware, or should have been aware, of the deficiency of the product (CO article 200).

The consumer must notify the retailer as soon as he discovers the product's deficiency. Ordinarily, this means within a couple of days. Otherwise, the deficiency is presumed to be accepted, save the case in which its existence was intentionally concealed or its disclosure withheld by the retailer (CO article 201).

The retailer selling the defective product is strictly liable for the damage directly arising from the breach of warranty, such as medical and litigation expenses and lost earnings (CO article 208(2). As for further damages, the retailer is put under an obligation to show that he was not blameworthy (CO article 208(3)). There is an ongoing controversy as to where the borderline between direct damage and further damage has to be set.

4.2 Breach of contract claim

Alternatively, a consumer has the possibility of suing the retailer for breach of contract (CO articles 97 ff)).

The Swiss Federal Court has held that the consumer must not only prove the breach of contract by the retailer, causation and the quantum of damage, but also that he immediately complained to the retailer once he discovered the defect. The retailer is not strictly liable and may prove that he was not blameworthy.

Thus, if the consumer is not successful in a warranty claim against the retailer, it is unlikely that he will succeed in a breach of contract claim, the latter not holding the retailer strictly liable, but allowing him the opportunity to prove that he was not blameworthy.

4.3 Tort claim

In theory a claim in tort, comparable to the one against the producer, can also be brought against the retailer.

The retailer might be negligent in selling a dangerous product, thereby creating a dangerous situation. But a retailer is usually under a lesser obligation to take safety measures than a producer, since typically he has no influence on the technical safety measures and warnings of the product.

4.4 Disclaimer

A retailer who sells a product to a consumer can exclude any and all warranties (CO article 199). In addition, the retailer may, in the absence of wilful misconduct or gross negligence, on the part of himself or his employees, disclaim its contractual liabilities (CO articles 100/101).

Such disclaimer under a contract of sale is also effective against tort claims made in the context of contractual liability.

4.5 Limitation period

The period of limitation for contractual warranty claims against a retailer is one year after delivery of the product. If the retailer intentionally deceives the consumer, the limitation period is ten years (CO article 210).

The period of limitation for breach of contract claims is ten years (CO article 127). However, if a breach of contract claim is made in the context of a product purchased from a retailer, the one-year limitation period for a warranty claim applies (FCR 77 II p 249 [1951], FCR 63 II p 407 [1937]).

At the time of writing, the Swiss Federal Court has not decided whether the one-year limitation period for warranty claims (starting with delivery of the product to the consumer) applies equally to tort claims against the retailer.

4.6 Consumer's burden of proof and retailer's defences

The consumer seeking recovery from the retailer under sales law must prove:

(a) his damage; and
(b) a breach of warranty or of a contractual obligation; and
(c) that his damage was caused by the product (more precisely; by the breach of warranty or of the contractual obligation).

The retailer has, inter alia, the following defences:

(a) the consumer did not sufficiently substantiate his damage – in practice a very important defence; or
(b) the consumer did not promptly notify the retailer of the product's deficiency – also a very important defence; or
(c) the consumer was aware, or should have been aware, of the deficiency; or
(d) the retailer has disclaimed warranties and contractual liabilities; or
(e) the retailer is not blameworthy for the breach of the contractual obligation; or
(f) the consumer was contributorily negligent; or
(g) the consumer was inclined to the injury or disease in question; or
(h) the limitation period has expired.

5. INTERNATIONAL CONSIDERATIONS

5.1 Attempt to introduce the Directive

The current Swiss law governing product liability is in many ways outdated. Landmark decisions by EC courts might be taken note of as a matter of comparison, but they would under no circumstances have a guaranteed impact on the Swiss courts' decisions.

Attempts to introduce special product liability legislation were made in 1979, but were soon abandoned. There is nevertheless a call for a complete revision of the law of tort, including product liability, and a Special Commission has been dealing with this since the autumn of 1988. In March 1991, a new attempt to introduce specific product liability legislation – de facto implementing the Directive – has been made in the Swiss Parliament. It is too early to predict what form the future Swiss tort law, and especially product liability law, will take. The report of the Special Commission was completed in July 1991 and the revised product liability law might be enacted in 1994 or 1995. The legislative process would be accelerated if the EC and the EFTA – including Switzerland – could come to an agreement on the 'European Economic Space' (EES) in the near future.

5.2 EC producers subject to the Directive in Switzerland

The Swiss Private International Law Act (PILA) expressly deals with product liability, providing for a choice by the consumer between the law of the producer's domicile and the law of the place where the product was purchased (PILA article 135(1)). A consumer seeking recovery from an EC (or US) producer or distributor before a Swiss court may therefore choose, instead of Swiss law, the law of the EC country (or the US state law) where the product has been manufactured or where he has purchased the product. This will most likely put him in a more favourable position.

However, the Act also explicitly states that the awards rendered by a Swiss court based on foreign product liability law may not exceed the amount that could be awarded under Swiss law (PILA article 135(2)). Thus, if US law is applied by a Swiss court, Swiss public policy would probably prevent the court from awarding punitive damages.

5.3 Swiss producers subject to the Directive in EC countries

On the other hand, products manufactured in Switzerland will be subject to stringent product liability rules whenever imported into and sold in the EC (Directive article 3(2)).

Given this internationalisation of product liability laws, the producer-friendly Swiss law will only apply throughout where products have been both manufactured and sold to the consumer in Switzerland.

5.4 Impact of the Lugano Convention

Under present Swiss law, Swiss producers and distributors can be sued at their Swiss domicile only (article 59 of the Swiss Constitution). However, Switzerland has recently signed the Lugano Convention and it seems likely that Switzerland will implement the Convention on 1 January 1992. Under the Lugano Convention, producers and distributors can be sued both in their place of domicile and at the place where the product causes harm (articles 2(1) and 5(3)). Accordingly, Swiss producers and distributors may be sued in any EC or EFTA country where their products cause harm. In addition, Swiss courts will recognise and enforce foreign judgments rendered against Swiss producers and distributors under the Lugano Convention (articles 26(1) and 34(2) of the Convention).

On the other hand, under the Swiss Private International Law Act, foreign producers and distributors can be sued at their foreign domicile or, if the product causes damage in Switzerland, at the place where the product causes harm (PILA article 129). The jurisdiction to deal with product liability claims lies with the ordinary cantonal courts. Their judgment can generally be appealed to the Swiss Federal Court, ie the highest Swiss court.

5.5 Other Conventions: judicial assistance

A Swiss court may call a witness from abroad, however he may not have to travel to Switzerland. He can request to be questioned by a court at his domicile. The Swiss court will, in this case, apply for judicial assistance to the respective country, based on applicable treaties or established practices between the two countries. Switzerland is a member of the 1954 Hague Convention on Civil Procedure but has not yet ratified the succeeding 1965 Hague Convention on the Service Abroad of Judicial and Extrajudicial Documents or the 1970 Hague Convention on the Taking of Evidence in Civil and Commercial Matters, respectively.

6. RISK MANAGEMENT IN THE NEW ERA OF PRODUCT LIABILITY

6.1 Quality control

Under the danger rule, the producer of a dangerous product has to take the necessary safety measures to prevent injury and loss. One of the safety measures is quality control. In addition, the Swiss Federal Court has ruled that a producer of dangerous products will be held liable as principal, if he has not made a final quality control inspection.

Where possible, the producer must examine the component parts of the product, especially if they are manufactured by a third party. If the producer wants to have recourse to a component manufacturer, he must be able to prove that the necessary quality checks were made before the components were installed. The producer should also keep appropriate documentation evidencing control of the components.

It is clear that the main way to avoid delivery of defective products is final quality control. It is the last opportunity to check a product before it leaves the plant and is put into the streams of commerce and finally sold to the consumer. The best control is to check each and every product, eg checking every bottle of mineral water by refraction of light. If the product is likely to cause serious damage more rigorous checks may be necessary, eg safety controls in the car industry. Further, it might be advisable to test the product under extreme conditions or by durability and solidity control. If it is not possible to check each product, final quality control should be effected by spot-checks.

Final quality control must guarantee that all safety standards are met, that warnings are on the product itself or attached thereto and that the instruction manuals are delivered with the product. If the number of products is small, the product should be photographed with safety measures, warnings and manuals before packaging.

Final quality control is primarily the producer's task and the producer cannot disclaim liability by claiming that the distributor should have made its own checks.

6.2 Documentation

Under the danger rule, the producer will be requested to furnish evidence as to his having taken the necessary safety measures to prevent injury and loss. Further, the producer in its capacity as a principal has to show that it has carefully selected, instructed and supervised the employee who manufactured the defective product.

Therefore the producer should keep all documents in connection with the development and the manufacturing of a product. It seems somewhat paradoxical to give such advice at a time when most companies are trying to rationalise production by limiting the paperwork. At least, microfilm and other storing possibilities facilitate record-keeping by the producer.

Firstly, complete documentation is essential to mount an effective defence in a product liability case. Secondly, documentation can prove valuable in efforts to improve a product that has caused damage, irrespective of whether or not a product liability claim has been filed. Thirdly, it is important that the documents are systematically recorded and that they never have to be laboriously pieced together at short notice.

Record-keeping must have already begun before the development of the product. During this time, the producer may inquire to various component manufacturers and they may give answers as to the feasibility and risks of such component parts. Such correspondence, particularly any kind of assurances by component manufacturers, must be recorded. Consumers of pharmaceutical products especially may make claims after many years that the producer commenced production trading in a field which was not sufficiently researched at that time. The documentation might then reveal how the producer coped with the particular problem and whether he received assurances from component manufacturers, scientists or other third parties. During the time before the development of the product, it can also be necessary to keep records of the statutory provisions countrywide or worldwide.

During the development of the product, the following documents should be kept and recorded: internal regulations with duties of various employees, protocols of accident possibilities, test results including tests of alternative components or products, and all documents evidencing which changes of the product have been considered and why they have or have not been realised. During the time of the development it may be necessary to appoint a risk manager. It is obvious that the work of such a person has to be carefully documented and recorded.

During manufacturing of the product it is necessary to keep the following documents: market tests, evaluation of consumer complaints and internal reports of defects of the product, results of quality control, including control of the products of component manufacturers and final quality control of the product. If possible, final quality control may be recorded by photo or by video evidencing, eg, that warnings and instruction manuals have been attached to the product. During the time of manufacturing it may also be necessary to record which employee worked at what place/machine at which time, especially if a safety measure of a product is installed or controlled. Further, it will be helpful to record how employees have been instructed and continuously educated. Such documents can be used by the producer as exonerating proof if he is sued in his capacity as a principal.

If potentially highly dangerous products, eg cars or pharmaceutical products, are manufactured, the producer must develop a concept that gives clear instructions as to which documents have to be made and collected and how, how long and where they have to be recorded and how, by whom and when they may be destroyed.

6.3 Warnings

Wherever possible, the producer should install technical safety measures on its products and thus avoid liability under the danger rule in the first place.

Childsafe/foolproof construction, safety boxes that prevent direct contact of a consumer with dangerous parts of the product, or automatic security systems, eg circuit breakers which interrupt power supply when the casing is opened, are always preferable to mere warnings.

Where technical safety measures are not possible, the danger rule requires that warnings be placed on the product itself, on the packing material or in the instruction manual.

Warnings must be:

(a) complete (the consequences of wrongful use must be explained); and
(b) comprehensible (symbols are better than text; written warnings should be made at least in all the national languages of Swiss consumers, ie in German, French and Italian); and
(c) perceptible (warnings on the product itself are always preferable to warnings on the packing materials or in the instruction manual); and
(d) proportional (danger to life and limb must be pointed out by colour or bold type).

6.4 Disclaimers

Under Swiss law, disclaimers are only possible under contract law, but not under tort law.

Disclaimers of the producer are generally null and void, as there is no contractual relationship between producer and consumer. Nevertheless, a disclaimer may be of some value as it may take the function of a warning.

Only the retailer selling the product to the consumer may disclaim its liability. However, such a disclaimer is not comprehensive. Liability for wilful misconduct and gross negligence cannot validly be disclaimed. The retailer may only disclaim liability for its 'slight negligence'.

Disclaimers are thus not a safeguard against product liability claims.

6.5 Recall of products

Another safety measure that may have to be taken under the danger rule is the recall of products.

To date, the Swiss authorities have not asked producers in spectacular ways to recall their products as, eg, in the USA. A recall may nevertheless be necessary in Switzerland based on management decisions, especially if a product is recalled worldwide.

The recall of products which are prone to create risks, eg cars, tyres, pharmaceutical products, children's toys etc, should be planned in advance. The planning must deal with the various possible scenarios of a recall and should especially address the problem of how to inform customers, either directly or through the mass media.

Most recalls require that a crisis manager be appointed who has to select a planned recall scenario and organise the recall step by step. The producer will have to inquire on the defect of the product and improve the product, eg its safety measures, at this point.

6.6 Corporate structure

Most individuals limit their liability by trading through a company. Further limitation of liability through the use of corporate structure has not been seen to be necessary in Switzerland for various reasons.

Generally speaking, limitation of liability seems of lesser importance in Switzerland than in the EC or USA, as the Swiss courts take a conservative attitude and do not award excessive damages in product liability claims. In particular, punitive damages do not exist in Switzerland. Second, product liability claims can be insured in Switzerland without major problems and there is no reluctance of insurance companies in this field as, for example, in the USA. Third, Swiss courts may impose liability on affiliated companies by piercing the corporate veil (or by considering one company to be the other's principal under CO article 55). However, at the time of writing there is no precedent in which liability has been imposed on an affiliated company in the field of product liability. Finally, limitation of liability by corporate structure might be criticised by the media and lead to poor public relations.

Accordingly, the concept of limitation of liability by corporate structure is generally not recommended in Switzerland. Nevertheless, it is no secret that several Swiss producers have established subsidiaries for performing especially risky business which is separate from the main objects of the company.

6.7 Insurance

A producer who has taken all possible safety measures (technical safety measures, warnings, quality control etc), as required by the danger rule, and which, in his capacity as a principal, has carefully selected, instructed and supervised his employees, is likely to avoid liability.

However, there remains a certain risk which calls for insurance. In Switzerland, the appropriate insurance coverage is known as enterprise liability insurance (*Betriebshaftpflichtversicherung/assurance responsabilité civile d'entreprise*).

Enterprise liability insurance may cover damage arising from personal injury, property damage, economic loss and mental distress. However, economic loss and mental distress are usually only covered if they are a result of personal injury or property damage.

EC and USA importers usually ask the Swiss producer for their vendor's liability to be included by vendor's endorsement in the producer's enterprise liability insurance. Such insurance cover is possible in Switzerland, so long as the EC or USA importer is not negligent himself (eg by delivering the incorrect product or by imprudently labelling the product). The following points should be borne in mind when an enterprise liability insurance policy is taken out in Switzerland:

(a) Switzerland is a very small market. The possibility that a product manufactured in Switzerland will be used in one of the surrounding EC countries or, for example, in the USA is obvious. Worldwide insurance coverage is, therefore, recommended for most products.

(b) For the same reason, insurance companies with branches worldwide are to be preferred.

(c) Worldwide insurance should be made on one and the same insurance principle (eg insurance cover based on causation, based on damage, or based on consumer claims). Missing insurance and double insurance must be avoided.

(d) It should be borne in mind that worldwide insurance may be very expensive as certain countries much more readily award high damages for personal injury and mental distress. In this context it is important to reiterate that the producer may be sued by the consumer for the entire damage, even if component manufacturers or other third parties are equally liable (joint and several liability).

(e) It is not possible to insure criminal liability in the Swiss insurance market.

(f) It is, as a rule, not possible to insure against punitive damages in the Swiss insurance market.

(g) However, the costs of a recall of products can be insured to a certain extent.

7. SUMMARY

Switzerland is not an EC member and therefore is not required to implement the Directive.

Product liability claims can be based on traditional rules of contract and tort only. Claims against the producer can be made only in tort (unless the product is directly sold to the consumer). The unique Swiss legal construction making producers liable under the danger rule (for dangerous products) together with their liability as principals (for damage caused by their employees) are quite effective tools for consumers.

Nevertheless, product liability has not been given much public attention in Switzerland, as the Swiss courts are very reluctant to award large damages to consumers. The low awards may be explained by the following facts: Swiss consumers are generally very well insured against personal injury and property damage, compensation is granted by professional judges rather than by lay juries, and lawyers may not be paid contingent fees.

On an international level, foreign producers importing their products into Switzerland may be sued in Switzerland either under Swiss law or under the law where the product has been manufactured. On the other hand, Swiss producers exporting their products into the EC or USA may be sued in the country where the product is finally sold to the consumer either under Swiss law or under the foreign law. As a consequence, although Switzerland may, at first sight, appear to be a 'producers' heaven', producers should comply with the more stringent product liability laws of the EC countries and of the USA.

8. BIBLIOGRAPHY

Borer P 'Haftpflichtrecht, insbesondere Produktehaftpflichtrecht' in *Die Europaverträglichkeit des schweizerischen Rechts* Schriften zum Europarecht vol 1 pp 495 ff (Zürich 1990).

Borer, Kramer, Posch, Schwander and Widmer *Produktehaftung, Schweiz-Europa-USA* Schweizerische Beiträge zum Europarecht vol 29 (Berne 1986).

Bühler R 'Die EG-Produktehaftung: Eine Einführung aus schweizerischer Sicht' Der Schweizer Treuhänder 1–2/90 pp 29 ff, 3/90 pp 130 ff (Zürich 1990).

Culemann H J 'Produktehaftpflicht für schweizerische Lieferungen in die EG' in *Beziehungen Schweiz-EG* (1. Lieferung) s 10.7 (Zürich 1989).

Egli and Hartmann 'EG-Produktehaftpflichtrecht: Folgen des Lugano-Uebereinkommens, Abbau eines prozessualen Damms für die Schweiz' Neue Zürcher Zeitung no 147, 28 June 1989, p 69.

Fellmann W 'Produzentenhaftung in der Schweiz' 107 Zeitschrift für Schweizerisches Recht pp 275 ff (Basle 1988).

Fischer, Girsberger and Stark 'Wer haftet für Produkteschäden?' NZZ-Schriften zur Zeit vol 40 (Zürich 1978).

Heini A 'Direkte Gewährleistungshaftung gegenüber dem Endabnehmer' in *Festschrift für Max Keller zum 65 Geburtstag* pp 175 ff (Zürich 1989).

Hohloch G 'Harmonisierung der Produkthaftung in der EG und Kollisionsrecht' in *Festschrift für Max Keller zum 65 Geburtstag* pp 433 ff (Zürich 1989).

Holliger-Hagmann E *Produktehaftung* (Diessenhofen 1989).

Kummer M 'Produktehaftung – Modewort, sozialpolitischer Druck, Notwendigkeit?' 35 Wirtschaft und Recht pp 29 ff (Zürich 1983).

Lörtscher T 'Internationales Produkthaftungsrecht der Schweiz, Sonderstatut im Regulativ des ordre public' 88 Zeitschrift für vergleichende Rechtswissenschaft pp 76 ff (1989).

Nater H 'Zur Entwicklung der Produktehaftpflicht in der Schweiz' 85 Schweizerische Juristen-Zeitung pp 389 ff (Zürich 1989).

Prager M 'Zur Produktehaftpflicht im internationalen Privatrecht' Schweizer Schriften zum Handels- und Wirtschaftsrecht vol 10 (Zürich 1975).

Rust P *Produktehaftpflicht und Defensivstrategien* (Zürich 1983).

Schmid N 'Von der zivilrechtlichen zur strafrechtlichen Produktehaftung' in *Festschrift für Max Keller zum 65 Geburtstag* pp 647 ff (Zürich 1989).

Spiro K 'Zur Haftung für gesundheitsschädigende Produkte' in *Revolution der Technik, Evolution des Rechts, Festgabe für Karl Oftinger* pp 255 ff (Zürich 1969).

Stauder B 'Schweizerische Produktehaftung im europäischen Umfeld' 109 Zeitschrift für Schweizerisches Recht p 363 (Basle 1990).

Stucki and Altenburger 'Product Liability in Switzerland' in *Product Liability: A Manual of Practice in Selected Nations* (Oceana Publications Inc, London/Rome/New York 1981).

Vischer F 'Das Deliktsrecht des IPR-Gesetzes unter besonderer Berücksichtigung der Regelung der Produktehaftung' in *Beiträge zum neuen IPR des Sachen-, Schuld- und Gesellschaftsrechts, Festschrift für Prof Rudolf Moser,* Schweizer Studien zum Internationalen Recht vol 51, pp 119 ff (Zürich 1987).

Widmer P 'Produktehaftungrecht' pp 50 ff (Zürich 1986).

Widmer and Jäggi 'Erwachtes Interesse an vernachlässigtem Thema: Anstehende Revision des Haftpflichtrechts, Gesetzgebung und Rechtsprechung in der Schweiz' Neue Zürcher Zeitung no 147, 28 June 1989, p 67.

CHAPTER XVI

United Kingdom

Michael Thornton
Tom Ellis

Laytons
Sunlight House
Quay Street
Manchester M3 3LD
England

Tel ++ 44 61 834 2100
Fax ++ 44 61 834 6862

CHAPTER XVI

United Kingdom

1. INTRODUCTION

1.1 Introduction to the law of the United Kingdom

Our present legal system has steadily developed from the reforms of Henry II in the twelfth century. This has led to a system of law based upon two concepts which have come to be interlinked, common law and statute law.

By the fourteenth century judges were despatched from the King's Court to sit in local courts. These judges became known as circuit judges and began the process of adopting the local laws and decisions and out of them creating the certainty of laws which were 'common' to the whole kingdom.

Alongside this common law has developed the legislation passed by monarchs, and later, governments. Today the English courts consider both common and statute law as well as the relatively new element of the law of the European Communities.

Judges must now decide cases giving precedence to European law, then statute law and finally decided cases or common law.

1.2 Overview of the law relating to defective products in the United Kingdom

At present in the UK there are four areas of law under which manufacturers of goods may have liability imposed on them in respect of producing defective goods. Liability may be imposed by virtue of:

(a) the law of contract,
(b) the law of tort,
(c) the law of product safety, and/or
(d) product liability law,

each of which will be considered in greater detail during the course of this chapter. However, the following is a brief summary of the main principles involved.

1.2.1 Contract

In addition to the terms on which a manufacturer or retailer of goods and the purchaser of such goods agree their contract, legislation also imposes certain conditions (for example, as to merchantability and fitness for purpose in consumer contracts) and restricts the manufacturer or retailer's ability to exclude many such terms. However, the establishment of liability under contract may be difficult because of the doctrine of privity of contract which means that for a party to have either obligations or rights under a contract it is necessary for him to be a party to the contract. So, if a person is injured by defective goods, but does not have a contractual relationship with the manufacturer or retailer, he may find that he does not have a claim under contract law.

1.2.2 Tort

To establish a claim for liability in tort for negligence in the manufacture of goods the three following factors must be established:

(a) that the manufacturer owed the injured person a duty of care when producing his goods (this is sometimes called in the UK the 'neighbour' principle);
(b) that the manufacturer failed in this duty of care; and
(c) that as a result of this failure the injured person suffered the injury of which he complains.

These three factors can cause an injured party considerable difficulties when seeking to establish a claim that a manufacturer was negligent. Can the injured party show that the manufacturer owed him a duty of care in the circumstances in which the injury occurred? If he can, can the manufacturer then exclude his liability? A further limitation upon the injured party's ability to claim is that damages for purely economic loss may not be recoverable at all. These topics are dealt with in greater detail later in this chapter.

1.2.3 Statute

Manufacturers and suppliers may also have liabilities in respect of defective products because of statute law and regulations made by government departments. Prior to CPA 1987 which implements the Directive, a large body of safety law had been passed. This body of law makes the statutory protections for defective products some of the most complex in Europe.

Breaches of this body of statute law can lead to claims for damages or criminal penalties. These will be dealt with in detail later in this chapter.

1.3 Definition and classification of terms

In this chapter the following definitions and abbreviations have been used:

CPA 1987	Consumer Protection Act 1967
SGA 1893	Sale of Goods Act 1893
SGA 1979	Sale of Goods Act 1979
UCTA 1977	Unfair Contracts Terms Act 1977
SGSA 1982	Supply of Goods and Services Act 1982
SG(IT)A 1973	Supply of Goods (Implied Terms) Act 1973
CCA 1974	Consumer Credit Act 1974
MR 1967	Misrepresentation Act 1967

the 1987 Act	Consumer Protection Act 1987
QB	Queen's Bench Division
KB	King's Bench Division
CH	Chancery Division
TLR	Times Law Reports
AC	Appeal Cases
All ER	All England Law Reports
New LJ	New Law Journal
Lloyds Rep	Lloyds Reports
Build LR	Building Law Reports
ST	Scottish Times

2. LIABILITY IN CONTRACT

2.1 Introduction

The law relating to defective products has undergone a radical change in recent years with the passing of CPA 1987 which has provided a code for liability for defective products which cause damage or personal injury, though it is still necessary to consider the existing position in contract as CPA 1987 does not take away any of the consumer's rights under the contract. As will be seen later, in some cases it will be better for a consumer to bring his claim in contract rather than under the CPA. In others, a consumer will only obtain damages if he brings his claim in contract.

The basic principle is freedom of contract. That is, that the parties are free to enter into an agreement upon the best possible terms they can negotiate and the courts may not interfere to repair a bad bargain. In a contract for the sale or supply of goods the rule is 'caveat emptor', ie let the buyer beware.

This principle of freedom of contract has slowly been eroded by a series of decisions by judges and consumer protection statutes so far as it relates to contracts for sale or supply of goods.

The first major piece of legislation affecting the principle was SGA 1893 which codified the existing common law relating to contracts for the sale of goods. This statute implied into such contracts certain terms relating to the quality and fitness of goods. Subsequent statutes made further in-roads into this principle and the whole statutory law was consolidated in SGA 1979 (as amended by UCTA 1977). In the case of contracts of supply, hire and exchange similar provisions relating to implied terms are found in SGSA 1982. Hire purchase contracts are dealt with by SG(IT)A 1973 (as amended by CCA 1974). SGA 1979 did give the parties the right to exclude the implied terms by express agreement but this right has been restricted by UCTA 1977. The provisions of UCTA 1977 are considered later.

The purpose of the next two sections in this chapter is to consider liability for defective products in contract and tort and later on to compare this liability under CPA 1987 generally. Although not strictly contractual in nature it is convenient to deal with liability for pre-contractual representations at this point.

2.2 Liability for pre-contractual statements

An agreement will usually only be reached after negotiations during which various statements of intention or requirement will be made. Some of these statements become express terms in the contract, others may not become a part of the contract but may nevertheless have contractual effect as a warranty collateral to the contract if the maker of the statement guarantees or promises that it is true; others still may not have any contractual effect at all but will be a statement which induces a party to enter into an agreement.

This latter category of statement is covered by MR 1967. For a statement to be a misrepresentation, and therefore give rise to liability, it must be a false statement which induces a party to enter into a contract. It must be a statement of fact and not an expression of opinion or an advertising slogan which, generally, will not give rise to any liability. So advertisements such as 'probably the best beer in the world' are considered to be nothing more than 'mere puffs', as the courts call them, and will not be actionable although the expression of an opinion could be if there were no reasonable grounds to believe it, for example, where the vendor of a property described a tenant as 'a most desirable tenant', when his rent was continually in arrears.

If a misrepresentation is contrary to MR 1967 then the contract is voidable at the option of the party misled, ie the misled party has the right to be restored to the pre-contractual position. This remedy, called rescission, is an equitable remedy which means that it is granted at the court's discretion and will not be granted if the parties cannot be restored to their original position. In addition, CPA 1987 confers upon the injured party the right to damages as well as rescission for fraudulent and negligent misrepresentations. Except in cases of fraud, the court has a discretion to award damages in lieu of rescission.

2.3 Outline of contract law

A contract for the sale of goods will contain various terms relating to the supply and delivery of the goods. Some will be essential to the contract, others less important. A term may be either expressed by the parties, or implied by statute or custom. In simple sales of consumer articles such as a television set, the expressed terms will usually relate to the physical characteristics of the goods, such as the type, its price, model, colour etc, while the implied terms will relate to the quality and fitness of the goods.

The legal consequences of breach of contractual terms in contracts for the sale of goods are discussed in greater detail below.

A condition is the most important type of term and relates to the main purpose of the contract. A breach of a condition gives rise to the right to treat the contract as at an end and to reject the goods.

A warranty is a less important term than a condition. If a new motor car had a defective cigarette lighter this would be a breach of a warranty and would only give the buyer the right to claim damages (the cost of repair) and not the right to reject the motor car. However, if a new motor car was supplied without any wheels or an engine that would constitute a breach of condition.

Two interesting cases provide a good illustration as to how the courts categorise a term. In one[1] an actress was to play the leading role in an operetta. She was unable to take up her role until one week after its opening. It was held that her promise to perform was a condition. By contrast, in another case[2] a singer arrived three days late for rehearsals. The theatre company sought to terminate the contract. The court held that the rehearsal clause was subsidiary to the main purpose of the contract and, therefore, a warranty.

In recent years, a third classification, known as an intermediate or innominate term, has appeared. The legal remedies following a breach of an intermediate term will depend upon the consequences of the breach. If the damage suffered is relatively minor and capable of remedy the injured party's claim will be in damages alone. If, however, the damage is more serious the effect will be to treat the breach as a right for the innocent party to terminate the contract.

The disadvantage in English contract law that the ultimate consumer may not be the buyer may be overcome in some circumstances by the device known as 'the collateral contract'. This is what was decided in the case of *Shanklin Pier Ltd v Detel Products Ltd*,[3] the plaintiffs being the owners of an amusement pier at a place called Shanklin in Southern England. The defendants, who were paint manufacturers, assured the plaintiffs, who owned the pier, that their paint was suitable for the pier, so a clause was inserted in the contract for the repair of the pier that the defendant's paint had to be used. The paint proved unsuitable and the plaintiffs successfully sued the defendants for a breach of warranty in the collateral contract which the court decided existed between the pier company and the paint manufacturers.

2.4 Implied terms

As already mentioned, English law, through various consumer protection statutes, implies into contracts for the sale and supply of goods (including contracts for hire, exchange, and hire purchase) terms relating to title, description, quality, fitness and sale by sample. So far as defective goods are concerned the most important of these will be the implied term of quality and fitness.

2.4.1 Implied condition as to description

Section 13 of SGA 1979 states:

> Where this is a contract for the sale of goods by description there is an implied condition that the goods will correspond with the description.

A sale by description takes place where the buyer identifies the goods by reference to their description. A buyer may identify a particular type of refrigerator he wishes to buy, perhaps, by reference to a particular model on

1 *Poussard v Spiers and Pond* [1876] 1 QBD 410.
2 *Bettini v Gye* [1876] 1 QBD 183.
3 *Shanklin Pier Ltd v Detel Productions Ltd* [1951] 2 KB 854.

display in the shop, or in a catalogue. It might be thought that a contract for specific goods can never be a sale by description as the buyer is purchasing a specific item and not relying upon its description. However, this is not always the case, as is illustrated by the following case.[4]

A buyer, after having inspected it, purchased a car described as a 'Herald convertible white 1961'. Unfortunately, only the back half of the car corresponded with the description as the front was a totally different car which had been welded on to it.

The main difficulty is to know which of the particular statements used to identify and describe the goods form part of the description. It is essentially a question of construction in each case although the courts have construed 'description' widely and, therefore, it may include not only the particular type of goods involved, but also the purpose and use to which the goods might be put as, for example, hair shampoo or baby food.

Once it has been established that there has been a sale by description and what the description attached to the goods is, it is necessary to consider whether the goods correspond with the description or not. As the courts have held:[5]

> if the written contract specifies conditions of weight measurement and the like, those conditions must be complied with. A tonne does not mean about a tonne or a yard about a yard.

2.4.2 *Implied condition as to merchantable quality*

The condition of merchantable quality is set out in SGA 1979 s 14. Section 14(1) provides:

> except as provided by this section and section 15 below and subject to any other enactment, there is no implied condition or warranty about the quality or fitness for any particular purpose of goods supplied under a contract for sale.

Section 14(2) goes on to provide:

> Where the seller sells goods in the course of a business there is an implied condition that the goods supplied under the contract are of merchantable quality.

This section only applies to goods which are supplied 'in the course of a business'. A business is defined so as to include a profession and also the activities of any government department or local or public authority although the goods sold need not be of the type normally sold in that business. So, for instance, if a firm of architects sold some of its office equipment this would be a sale in the course of a business and the condition of merchantable quality would be implied.

SGA 1979 also extends to goods 'supplied under the contract' and therefore includes not only the goods themselves but their packaging, containers and instructions. So even if the goods are not defective the seller may still be in breach of the implied condition of merchantable quality if the packaging is faulty.

4 *Beale v Taylor* [1967] 1 WLR 1193.
5 *Acrow Ltd v E A Ronaasen & Son* [1933] AC 470.

Illustrations of the principle are shown in a case[6] where inadequate packaging allowed corn solvent to escape and cause injury, and in another[7] where a farmer bought a herbicide to kill wild oats. The instructions for use were misleading. Although on the particular facts of the case there was no breach of the implied condition, the court held that the instructions supplied with goods are one of the factors to be taken into account to determine whether or not there has been a breach of the implied term of merchantable quality.

Merchantable quality is defined in SGA 1979 s 14(6) as:

> Goods of any kind are of merchantable quality if they are as fit for the purpose or purposes for which goods of that kind are commonly bought as it is reasonable to expect having regard to the description applied to them, the price (if relevant) and all other relevant circumstances.

No single judicial definition of merchantable quality has emerged from the cases though this is, perhaps, to be expected when one considers the vast range of transactions that come under the umbrella of contracts for sale of goods. The courts have expressed doubt whether an 'all-embracing definition of merchantable quality could ever be made' and it has been decided that the statutory definition was left in the widest possible terms 'in order to cater for the great variety of situations which may occur'.[8]

Some cases will not cause any legal difficulty: If an engine of a motor vehicle blows up after only a few miles the vehicle is clearly not of merchantable quality but what if the bodywork of the vehicle has a slight dent? Does this render the vehicle unmerchantable? The use of the vehicle has not been affected but is the buyer entitled to a vehicle in perfect condition? In a vast number of cases it may be very difficult to know where to draw the line between merchantability and non-merchantability. The starting-point is the wording of the statutory definition itself.

2.4.3 'Fit for the purpose or purposes'

Where goods have only one function and they do not perform that function they are without question, unmerchantable. But many goods have defects which do not affect the function or general fitness of the goods but nevertheless affect the general quality or expectation of the goods, such as dents and scratches. Upon a strict interpretation of the statutory definition these cosmetic defect would not render goods unmerchantable as the goods would still be fit for the purpose for which they were bought. Consider the purchase of a new motor vehicle: it has generally come to be expected that there may be a few minor teething problems but that such problems will be put right by the car dealer. To what extent should the buyer put up with such defects? Further, where is the line drawn between teething problems and defects which render a vehicle unmerchantable?

6 *Devilez v Boots Pure Drug Company Ltd* [1962] 106 SJ 552.
7 *Wormell v RHM Agriculture (East) Ltd* [1987] 1 WLR 1091.
8 *Bernstein v Pamsons Motors (Golders Green) Ltd* [1987] 2 All ER 220.

In one case[9] a buyer had bought a new Range Rover generally considered to be a quality motor vehicle. The vehicle had many minor mechanical and bodywork defects which remained despite attempts by the dealer to remedy them. The court found that the vehicle was not of merchantable quality and considered the definition included, in respect of motor vehicles, 'comfort, ease of handling and reliability, and pride in the vehicle's outward and interior appearance'.

If the goods are multi-purpose do they have to be fit for all their purposes? The courts have considered the meaning of the phrase 'purpose or purposes' in a case involving quantities of a roofing compound packed in plastic pails which collapsed when stored at very high temperatures in Kuwait.[10] The buyers argued that the goods had to be fit for all common purposes for which such goods could be used and, therefore, would be unmerchantable if they were only fit for some of its uses. This would mean, in this case, that the plastic pails would have to be fit for use in hot countries, such as Kuwait, as well as for use in colder climates. The court decided, after reviewing the existing case law, that provided the goods were fit for one purpose for which they were commonly bought they were merchantable even if they were not fit for all of its common purposes.

2.4.4 'Description and price'

According to the statutory definition, factors to be taken into account when determining merchantability are their description and price which, when applied to goods, will have a significant effect on the standard of quality required. These factors take on particular significance when dealing with secondhand goods. Although the same principles will apply to secondhand goods as to new ones, a buyer can hardly expect secondhand goods to be in perfect condition but equally the buyer does not expect them to be useless.

A recent case illustrates this point.[11] It concerned the sale of a secondhand Mercedes motor car for the price of £14,850. After a few months defects appeared which required repairs at a cost of £635.00. The court accepted evidence that such faults were rare in a Mercedes car of that age and mileage but, nevertheless, came to the conclusion that the vehicle was merchantable.

Quite often price can be an indication of the quality of goods expected. A consumer wishing to purchase, say, a television set will have a whole range to choose from – different types, sizes, functions, and so on – but, perhaps, the most important factor will be the price. The buyer expects better quality from the more expensive models and would, quite rightly, have more reason to complain if the picture was not in sharp focus or the sound distorted. Of course, one has to remember that we are all subject to the advertisers' skill to make us believe that because a product is more expensive than its rival it has to be better. This is reinforced by the consumer's own belief that 'you pay for what you get'.

9 *Rogers v Parish (Scarborough) Ltd* [1987] QB 933.
10 *M/S Aswan Engineering Establishment Co v Lupdine Ltd* [1987] 1 WLR 1.
11 *Business Application Specialists Ltd v Nationwide Credit Corporation Ltd* (1988) Times, 27 April.

Price may also be relevant to the question, for how long must goods remain merchantable? Clearly, goods must be merchantable at the time of delivery, but what about products, particularly electrical or household appliances, which initially work satisfactorily then, after a short time, break down? It was said by the House of Lords[12] that goods must remain fit for 'a reasonable time'. How long is 'reasonable' is a question of fact based on the circumstances of each case. Perhaps, as a rule of thumb, more expensive goods will have a greater life expectancy than the cheaper equivalent.

2.4.5 *Exceptions to the implied term of merchantable quality*

There are, however, two exceptions to the implied terms of merchantable quality, namely:

(a) as regards defects specifically drawn to the buyer's attention before the contract is made; or

(b) if the buyer examines the goods before the contract is made, as regards defects which that examination ought to reveal'.

The first exception is a matter of common sense and one would not expect a buyer to be able to sue for defects brought to his attention. The use of the word 'specifically' would prevent a seller being able to escape the condition of merchantable quality by using such phrases as 'bought as seen'.

The second exception is not so straightforward. The test would appear to be subjective and relates to defects which that particular buyer with his knowledge and ability ought to have discovered, and not, in the case of a motor vehicle, a reasonable mechanic. It can be seen that the provision only relates to examinations carried out, and therefore, if the buyer does not carry out an examination at all the exception cannot apply.

2.4.6 *Implied condition as to fitness for specified purpose*

Section 14(3) of SGA 1979 provides:

> 'Where the seller sells goods in the course of a business and the buyer expressly or by implication, makes known
> (a) to the seller, or
> (b) where the purchase price or part of it is payable by instalments and the goods were previously sold by a credit-broker to the seller, to that credit broker
> any particular purpose for which the goods are being bought, there is an implied condition that the goods supplied under the contract are reasonably fit for that purpose, whether or not that is a purpose for which such goods are commonly supplied, except where the circumstances show that the buyer does not rely, or that it is unreasonable for him to rely, on the skill or judgment of the seller or credit-broker.'

In cases where the goods have only one purpose then the buyer will normally, by implication, make known the particular purpose to the seller. This is particularly true of consumer transactions where, for instance, a buyer wishing to buy a cooker hardly has to specify to the seller the particular purpose for which the cooker is being bought. Any breach by the seller in this type of case would give rise to a claim both under both s 14(2) and s14(3) of SGA 1979.

12 *Lambert v Lewis* [1982] AC 225.

Where, however, s 14(3) of SGA 1979 does come into its own is where goods have more than one purpose and the buyer requires goods for a particular purpose which is different than, perhaps, the common purpose. An example of this is provided by the case of the lady who bought a tweed coat.[13] She had very sensitive skin and contracted dermatitis after wearing the coat. Unfortunately for the buyer, she did not tell the seller of her condition, and as the coat was fit to be worn by a person with normal skin, her claim failed. Of course, had she made known her condition and then been told it was fit to wear she would have succeeded in her claim.

Once the buyer has made known his particular purpose whether by implication or expressly then the goods must be reasonably fit for that purpose. Although there is no statutory definition of 'reasonably fit' as there is for 'merchantable quality', the courts have treated it in the same way, and therefore, for instance in cases concerning secondhand motor cars, the same factors, such as description, price and age would be considered.

As in s 14(2) of SGA 1979 there is an exception to the implied condition and that is where the buyer does not rely, or it is unreasonable for him to rely, upon the seller's judgment.

So if the goods are made to a specification provided by the buyer he can hardly complain if the goods are not fit for their purpose if the fault lies in the specification, but if the fault is due to some part of the specification left to the seller's skill and judgment, such as a manufacturing process, the buyer can complain about the goods' lack of fitness for purpose. In a case which involved two propellers to be made according to the specification of the buyer, certain matters, such as the thickness of the blades, were left to the seller's skill and judgment, which proved to be inadequate. The court found that the seller was in breach of the implied condition as to fitness.[14]

2.4.7 *Implied condition as to sale by sample*

SGA 1979 s 15 provides:

(1) A contract of sale is a contract for sale by sample where there is an express or implied term to that effect in the contract.
(2) In the case of a contract for sale by sample there is an implied condition—
  (a) that the bulk will correspond with the sample in quality;
  (b) that the buyer will have a reasonable opportunity of comparing the bulk with the sample;
  (c) that the goods will be free from any defect, rendering them unmerchantable which would not be apparent on reasonable examination of the sample.
(3) In subsection (2)(c) above 'unmerchantable' is to be construed in accordance with section 14(6) above.

Sale by sample is relatively rare in consumer transactions, an example would be where one chooses a suit of clothing from a book of sample cloths or wallpaper from a book of sample wallpapers.

13 *Griffiths v Peter Conway Ltd* [1939] 1 All ER 685.
14 *Cammell Laird Co Ltd v Maganese Bronze & Glass Co Ltd* [1934] AC 402.

2.4.8 Conditions implied by custom of trade

Terms may be implied by a local custom or usage of a particular trade. Although this is a general principle which affects all contracts SGA 1979 s 14(4) gives it statutory recognition for contracts for sale by providing that: 'an implied condition or warranty about quality or fitness for a particular purpose may be annexed to a contract of sale by usage'.

2.5 Breach of contract for supply of defective products

As we have already seen, a term may be classified as either a condition, a warranty or an intermediate term. A buyer's rights following a breach of contract depends upon which type of term has been breached.

Under the SGA 1979 the implied terms as to quality and fitness are classified as conditions and any breach enables the buyer to treat the breach as a repudiation which allows him to reject the goods; or, alternatively, he can affirm the contract, keep the goods and claim damages.

The right to reject the goods in the event of a breach of a condition is limited by s 11(4) of the SGA 1979 which provides:

> Where a contract of sale is not severable, and the buyer has accepted the goods or part of them, the breach of any condition to be fulfilled by the seller can only be treated as a breach of warranty, and not as a ground for rejecting the goods and treating the contract as repudiated, unless there is an express or implied term of the contract to that effect.

It can be seen from this subsection that a buyer loses his right of rejection if he has accepted the goods.

If the contract is able to be split into smaller contracts, such as the delivery and payment of goods by instalments, then acceptance of one or more of the instalments will not stop a buyer from rejecting future instalments but if the contract cannot be severed in this way then acceptance of any part of the goods will. So, for example, if a buyer agrees to purchase a vehicle to be delivered in parts for assembly by the buyer acceptance of some of the parts will prevent the buyer from rejecting the vehicle if some of the parts subsequently delivered are defective.

Acceptance is dealt with by s 35(1) of SGA 1979:

> The buyer is deemed to have accepted the goods when he intimates to the seller that he has accepted them, or (except where section 34 otherwise provides) when the goods have been delivered to him, and he does any act in relation to them which is inconsistent with the ownership of the seller, or when after the lapse of a reasonable time he retains the goods without intimating to the seller that he has rejected them.

Acceptance can be in one of three ways:

(a) by intimating to the seller that he has accepted them;
(b) by doing any act in relation to the goods which is inconsistent with the seller's title to them (eg, a sub-sale); or
(c) by retaining the goods for longer than a reasonable time without telling the seller that he has rejected them.

Dealing with each of these three methods of acceptance in turn:

i. Intimation of acceptance. It is uncertain exactly how a buyer can accept goods in this way. It may be that a buyer who signs a note on delivery which acknowledges that the goods conform with the contract intimates acceptance, although this is probably doubtful; or where a buyer returns faulty goods to the seller for repair. The UK law review body, the Law Commission, has suggested that the law be changed by allowing a buyer an opportunity to examine the goods before he can accept in this way. This would mean that the signing of an 'acceptance note' could be no more than confirmation that the goods were delivered.

ii. An act inconsistent with the seller's ownership. This method of acceptance is subject to s 34 of SGA 1979:

> (1) Where goods are delivered to the buyer, and he has not previously examined them, he is not deemed to have accepted them until he has had a reasonable opportunity of examining them for the purpose of ascertaining whether they are in conformity with the contract.
> (2) Unless otherwise agreed, when the seller tenders delivery of the goods to the buyer, he is bound, on request, to afford the buyer a reasonable opportunity of examining the goods for the purpose of ascertaining whether they are in conformity with the contract.

A difficulty with SGA 1979 s 35 is that in the majority of cases ownership of the goods passes at the time the contract is made and, therefore, at the time of delivery the goods belong to the buyer and it is difficult to see how any act by the buyer can affect the seller's ownership. The only apparent explanation, and one which has some judicial support, is that the buyer loses his right to reject if he does any act which would affect the seller's ownership if those goods were revested in the seller.

iii. Lapse of a reasonable time. This method of acceptance has caused more disputes than any other method. Obviously, the difficulty is what is meant by a 'a reasonable time'. Clearly, the longer the buyer keeps the goods the less likely he will be able to reject them. Goods such as fruit and vegetables will have a relatively short life span, and for a buyer to reject such goods he will have to act very quickly. Others, such as motor vehicles or electrical goods, have a much greater life expectancy and it is this type of case which has caused the most difficulty.

Does the word 'reasonable' in s 35 relate to the time to inspect the goods or to a time to discover the defect? The answer was provided in a case involving a motor car.[15] The court held that the buyer had lost his right to reject having driven it for 140 miles since a 'reasonable time' meant sufficient time to give the vehicle a general try out. The court made the point that what is reasonable will depend upon the nature and function of the goods. The more complex the intended function of the goods is the longer the buyer will have to reject the

15 *Bernstein v Pamsons Motors (Golders Green) Ltd* [1987] 2 All ER 220.

goods. What does seem clear is that in the majority of consumer transactions the buyer does not have a great deal of time in which to try out the goods and, if faulty, reject them.

2.6 Causation and damages

Before a buyer can succeed in a claim for damages arising out of a breach of contract he must show that the product was defective and that the defect was the cause of damage suffered. There must be a direct link between the defect and the damage. This is known as the chain of causation and any break in the chain by, for example, an intervening event, will prevent a buyer from succeeding.

In the case of *Grant v Australian Knitting Mills Limited*[16] a buyer purchased a pair of underpants and later contracted dermatitis after wearing them. It was discovered that an excess of a particular chemical had been allowed to remain in the garment. The seller argued that the attack of dermatitis was not caused by the wearing of the garment but was a pre-existing condition. The court found that the wearing of the garment was the cause of the dermatitis.

The longer the period between the sale of the goods and the damage occurring the harder it will be for the buyer to prove the damage was caused by a defect in the goods present at the time of delivery.

2.6.1 Remoteness of damage

Even if the buyer can prove a causal link between the damage caused and the defect in the goods the seller will not be liable for all the loss which the buyer may suffer. A simple breach of contract may trigger off a series of events each linked with each other causing immense damage.

The general principle was laid down in the case of *Hadley v Baxendale*:[17]

> Where two parties have made a contract which one of them has broken, the damages which the other party ought to receive in respect of such breach of contract should be such as may fairly and reasonably be considered either arising naturally, ie according to the usual course of things from such breach of contract itself, or such as may reasonably be supposed to have been in the contemplation of both parties, at the time they made the contract, as the probable result of the breach of it.

This has become known as the rule in *Hadley v Baxendale*. The rule has two parts to it:

(a) loss which flows naturally as a result of the breach; and
(b) loss which although it might not be a natural consequence of the breach was contemplated by the parties as likely in the event of a breach.

A look at some of the cases will illustrate the two parts of the rule.

In the *Hadley v Baxendale* case the plaintiff claimed loss of profits following the late delivery of a crankshaft which meant the plaintiff's mill could not

16 *Grant v Australian Knitting Mills Ltd* [1936] AC 85.
17 *Hadley v Baxendale* [1854] 9 Exch 341.

operate. The court had to decide whether to include loss of profits in awarding damages for breach of contract.

The court held that the loss of profit was not a consequence which was foreseeable at the time of the contract. The court found that the plaintiff could not rely upon the second limb of the rule as the special circumstance was not communicated to the defendant, so the loss was not in the contemplation of the parties at the time the contract was made.

2.6.2 Damage recoverable

The types of damage recoverable in practice are:

(a) Damage to property: this will include not only the cost of repair or replacement of the product itself but also damage caused to any other property.
(b) Personal injury to the buyer: If the goods cause personal injury to the buyer then he will be able to recover damages for the injuries caused by the goods.
(c) Economic loss not related to any physical damage to property or person, eg loss of profits.

2.6.3 Measure of damages

A buyer may have an action against a seller for damages for non-delivery of the goods. With respect to delivered goods, which are defective, a buyer can either reject the goods, if that option is still open to him, or keep the goods and sue the seller for damages. On the other hand, a seller may have a claim against the buyer for non-acceptance.

The measure of damages in respect of non-delivery and non-acceptance of goods is laid down in ss 50 and 51 of SGA 1979 and is framed in similar terms. It is:

> the estimated loss directly and naturally resulting in the ordinary course of events . . . from the breach of contract.

Take, for example, the case where a seller has agreed to sell and deliver to a buyer a box of soap at a contract price of £12 a box but fails to deliver the soap on the agreed date by which time the market price has risen to £15. The buyer can recover as damages for non-delivery the difference between the contract price and the market price, in this example £3 a box. If the market price falls below the contract price the buyer will still have a claim for damages for non-delivery but it will only be for nominal damages.

Where the seller is late in delivering goods bought for the buyer's own use, damages will be the additional costs incurred by the buyer as a result of the delay. Where the goods are bought to be resold the damage will be the difference between the market price when the goods ought to have been delivered and the market price when the goods were, in fact, delivered.

The seller's measure of damages for non-acceptance, although framed in the same terms as non-delivery, is given a different interpretation by the courts. In a case where[18] the buyers wrongfully refused to accept a motor vehicle from the sellers who were car dealers, the sellers were able to return the vehicle to the manufacturer but sued the buyer for their loss of profit on the sale. The buyer contended that as the market price, set by the manufacturer, was the same as the contract price, the seller was only entitled to nominal damages. The court held that the seller was entitled to his loss of profit on the transaction. This case can be contrasted with another[19] where the court came to the opposite view and only awarded the seller nominal damages. The rationale between the two decisions appears to be that in the first case supply of the particular vehicle exceeded demand whilst in the latter case there was an adequate supply of vehicles and no shortage of buyers.

The buyer's remedy for breach of warranty is set out in s 53 of SGA 1979.

(1) Where there is a breach of warranty by the seller, or where the buyer elects (or is compelled) to treat any breach of a condition on the part of the seller as a breach of warranty, the buyer is not by reason only of such breach of warranty entitled to reject the goods; but he may:
  (a) set up against the seller the breach of warranty in diminution or extinction of the price; or
  (b) maintain an action against the seller for damages for the breach of warranty.

(2) The measure of damages for breach of warranty is the estimated loss directly and naturally resulting, in the ordinary course of events, from the breach of warranty.

(3) In the case of breach of warranty of quality such loss is prima facie the difference between the value of the goods at the time of delivery to the buyer and the value they would have had if they had fulfilled the warranty.

With respect to breaches of warranty of quality (which, confusingly, means breaches of condition of quality but where the buyer elects or is compelled to carry on with the contract) the measure of damages under SGA 1979 s 53 is the difference between the value of goods actually delivered and the value of the goods without the faults. In simple consumer sales the difference between the value of the goods delivered and the actual value of the goods will be an amount equal to the cost of putting the defect right.

In addition, the buyer is entitled to recover consequential loss, subject, as we have already seen, to the principle of remoteness. So, for instance, in the case of *Grant v Australian Knitting Mills* discussed above the buyer was able to recover damages for personal injury as a consequence of the underwear being unmerchantable. The English courts are becoming more willing to award damages for inconvenience and disappointment although, in general, this will only be in consumer cases. In a recent example a buyer recovered damages for disappointment and general inconvenience for a ruined holiday caused by the continual breakdown of the buyer's new motor vehicle.[20]

In a commercial contract where the goods are brought for the purposes of making a profit and the goods fall below the warranted performance, the buyer must choose whether to claim damages for the difference in value between the goods supplied and goods conforming to the contract or loss of profit.

18 *W L Thompson Ltd v Robinson (Gunmakers) Ltd* [1955] Ch 177.
19 *Charter v Sullivan* [1957] 2 QB 117.
20 *Jackson v Chrysler Acceptances Ltd, Minories Garages Ltd (Third Party)* [1978] RTR 474.

2.6.4 Mitigation

As a general rule the injured party must take reasonable steps to mitigate or lessen his loss. If he fails to do so then the defendant will only be liable for the loss the plaintiff would have suffered had he mitigated his loss. This was illustrated in a case[1] where an employee's contract of employment was terminated following a reorganisation. The employers offered him new employment on the same terms but the employee rejected their offer. The court held that he failed to mitigate his loss by unreasonably refusing to accept their offer of employment.

2.6.5 Burden of proof

As will be seen later, one of the principle advantages of bringing a claim for defective products in contract rather than tort, is that once it has been shown that the goods are not of the right quality or fitness he need not go on and show fault on the part of the seller. The seller's liability is strict: that the seller has no defence to argue that it was not his fault.

2.7 Exclusion of liability

A seller may attempt to escape or limit liability by the insertion of an exclusion clause into the contract. Such a clause seeks to limit, exclude or modify a liability arising out of a breach of a contractual obligation.

To be valid an exclusion clause must be incorporated into the contract. Although this might seem an obvious point not all terms of a contract are contained in a single written document, and many of the cases involving exclusion clauses focus on whether the exclusion clause is incorporated into the contract. In one case[2] where the plaintiff stayed at the defendant's hotel, on the back of the door in his room was a notice which read:

> 'The proprietors will not hold themselves responsible for articles lost or stolen unless handed in to the manageress for safe custody.'

Owing to the negligence of the hotel staff the plaintiff's furs were stolen. The defendant sought to rely upon the exclusion clause to avoid liability contending that the clause was incorporated into the contract by notice. The court held that the contract was made at the reception desk, and as the clause had not been brought to the plaintiff's notice before or at the time that the contract was made, they could not rely upon it.

As notice may be given either before or at the time the contract was made, it is particularly important to know exactly when the contract is made. In *Thornton v Shoe Lane Parking Ltd*[3] the plaintiff drove his motor vehicle up to an automatic barrier at the entrance to a car park. The machine produced a

1 *Brace v Calder* [1895] 2 QB 253.
2 *Olley v Marlborough Court Ltd* [1949] 1 KB 532.
3 *Thornton v Shoe Lane Parking Ltd* [1971] 2 QB 163.

ticket and the plaintiff drove in and parked his vehicle. Upon his return he was injured through the negligence of the owners of the car park. The defendants sought to rely upon a notice on the ticket which read: 'issued subject to conditions displayed on the premises'. Just inside the car park was a notice displaying lengthy conditions, one of which said the owners would not be responsible for injury to customers. The court concluded that notice of the conditions came after the contract was made.

One of the relevant factors in determining whether sufficient notice has been given is the type of document in which the exclusion clause appears.

For example, a cloakroom ticket would not normally have conditions printed on it and therefore any conditions printed on the reverse might not be sufficient.

This is illustrated by a case[4] where the plaintiff hired a deck chair and received a ticket in return. The ticket contained an exclusion clause which the defendant sought to rely upon to escape liability to the plaintiff for injury caused by the defendant's negligence. The court was of the view that the ticket was simply a receipt and not a contractual document where one would expect to find printed conditions.

Once the seller had overcome the hurdle of incorporation he still had to face the court's strict interpretation as to whether the clause covered the type of breach which the seller had committed and was seeking to avoid liability from. A clause excluding liability for implied terms will not cover express terms; a clause excluding liability for breach of warranty will not cover a breach of conditions. The courts generally strain to construe exclusion clauses so as to prevent a seller from escaping liability.

The need for the court to safeguard the consumer from oppressive exclusion clauses has, to a large extent, been taken over by statute through the enactment of UCTA 1977, but it will still be necessary to have regard to the existing case law as a party seeking to rely upon an exclusion clause will first have to show the clause has been incorporated into the contract and, on a true construction, covers the breach which has occurred. Perhaps the only difference is that the court no longer needs to rely upon strained constructions to defeat an unreasonable exclusion clause because, once the clause has survived both common law tests, it then has to meet the requirements of UCTA 1977.

2.7.1 Statutory controls

UCTA 1977 was passed to control the effectiveness of exclusion clauses. In some cases liability cannot be excluded or restricted by reference to a term in the contract and in others it can only be excluded or restricted if it is 'reasonable' as defined in the Act. Certain contracts are specially excluded, such as international supply contracts, contracts of insurance and contracts of employment.

2.7.2 Sale and hire purchase

So far as contracts for the sale of goods and hire purchase are concerned, s 6 of UCTA 1977 is the most important section. As against a 'Consumer', a seller

4 *Chapelbon v Barry Urban District Council* [1940] 1 KB 532.

cannot exclude or restrict liability for breach of the obligations arising from ss 12–15 of SGA 1979 dealing with implied conditions as to the vendor's right to sell, that the goods correspond with their description, are of 'merchantable quality' and fit for their intended purpose, and correspondence with any samples. As against a 'non-consumer' a seller cannot exclude or restrict his obligation under s 12 for having to have the right to sell and can only exclude or restrict his obligations under ss 13–15 dealing with the aforementioned if the clause is reasonable according to the standard laid down in UCTA 1977.

A 'consumer' in UCTA 1977 is given an extended meaning by s 12(1):

> A party to a contract 'deals as consumer' in relation to another party if:
> (a) he neither makes the contract in the course of a business nor holds himself out as doing so; and
> (b) the other party does make the contract in the course of a business; and
> (c) in the case of a contract governed by the law of sale of goods . . . the goods passing under or in pursuance of the contract are of a type ordinarily supplied for private use or consumption.

Consider the following three examples:

(a) a firm of solicitors buys an ordinary domestic electric kettle for use in their staff kitchen;
(b) a car enthusiast buys a secondhand classic sports car from his neighbour;
(c) a private individual (keen on home improvements) buys a large quantity of materials from a builder's merchant to build an extension to his house.

Which of the above examples is a 'consumer' deal?

Certainly the first is a 'consumer' deal. Although it is a purchase by a business it is not in the course of business and the goods in question are of a type ordinarily supplied for private use. The courts have defined a purchase to be 'in the course of a business' if it was an 'integral part of the business'.

The second example above is not a consumer deal as neither party makes the contract in the course of business.

The third example is the most difficult to categorise. Clearly, the materials are sold 'in the course of business' but s 12(1)(c) of SGA 1979 would probably prevent it from being a 'consumer' deal as the goods are not of a type normally sold for private use. It is a question of degree; no doubt, the purchase of a handful of small nails from the same builder's merchant would be a 'consumer' deal.

2.7.3 *Liability arising in contract*

Section 3 of UCTA 1977 provides a general control over liability in contract. It provides:

> (1) . . . as between contracting parties where one of them deals as consumer or on the other's written standard terms of business.

(2) As against that party, the other cannot by reference to any contract term
 (a) when himself in breach of contract, exclude or restrict any liability of his in respect of the breach; or
 (b) claim to be entitled—
  (i) to render a contractual performance substantially different from that which was reasonably expected of him, or
  (ii) in respect of the whole or any part of his contractual obligation, to render no performance at all except in so far as . . . the contract term satisfies the requirement of reasonableness.

This section applies, not only to contracts of sale and hire purchase, as does s 6 of UCTA 1977, but to all types of contracts (except those specifically excluded from the Act). Furthermore, it applies where one person deals as 'consumer' or on the other's written standard terms of business. It is, therefore, wide enough to include, not only a 'consumer' sale, but also a commercial transaction where the contract is based on one of the party's written standard terms.

The control imposed by s 3 of UCTA 1977 is twofold:

(a) a party cannot, by reference to a contract term, unless such term is reasonable, when in breach, exclude or restrict his liability; and
(b) claim to be entitled to render a performance substantially different from that which was expected, or, render no performance at all in respect of any part of his obligation.

It will be seen that the second part of sub-s 3(2)(b)(ii) of UCTA 1977 does not require a party to be in breach of contract, but that a party claims to be able to perform the contract in a manner different than was agreed.

2.7.4 The reasonableness test

Where a contract term is required to satisfy the requirements of reasonableness, the test is laid down in s 11 of UCTA 1977.

In relation to a contract term generally s 11(1) of UCTA 1977 provides:

> . . . the term shall have been a fair and reasonable one to be included having regard to the circumstances which were, or ought reasonably to have been, known to or in the contemplation of the parties when the contract was made.

In addition to the general test of s 11(1) of UCTA 1977, particular attention is to be paid to the matters referred to in Sch 2 of UCTA 1977 when considering an exclusion clause in a contract for sale or supply; they are:

(a) the strength of the bargaining position of the parties relative to each other, taking into account (amongst other things) alternative means by which the customer's requirements could have been met;
(b) whether the customer received an inducement to agree to the term, or in accepting it had an opportunity of entering into a similar contract with other persons, but without having to accept a similar term;
(c) whether the customer knew or ought reasonably to have known of the existence and extent of the term (having regard, amongst other things, to any custom of the trade and any previous course of dealing between the parties);
(d) where the term excludes or restricts any relevant liability if some condition is not complied with, whether it was reasonable at the time of the contract to expect that compliance with that condition would be practicable:

(e) whether the goods were manufactured, processed or adapted to the special order of the customer.

The highest English Court of Appeal, the House of Lords, had the opportunity of considering the criteria in the case of *George Mitchell (Chesterhall) Ltd v Finney Lock Seeds Ltd*.[5] The facts were: a seed merchant agreed to sell to a farmer 30lbs of 'Finney Late Dutch special cabbage seed'. The seed supplied was, in fact, a variety of cabbage seeds and of poor quality. The farmer sued for damages and the sellers relied upon a clause of the contract restricting their liability to the price of the seed itself and contended that the clause was fair and reasonable. The court decided that the clause was unreasonable, making it quite clear that the relative strength of each party's bargaining position had played an important part in their decision.

If the court considers the clause to be unreasonable they will not substitute a reasonable clause in its place but will strike out the offending clause.

2.7.5 Limitation period

The right to bring an action for breach of contract does not last indefinitely. Statute imposes limitations: the principle statutes are the Limitation Act 1980 and the Latent Damage Act 1986.

For a contract not under seal or expressed to be by way of deed, an action must be brought within six years from the date the cause of action arose. On a contract under seal, or expressed to be by way of deed, this time is extended to 12 years from when the cause of action arose.

In an action based on contract the cause of action accrues when the breach occurs and not when the plaintiff suffers damage.

The courts have decided that where there is a continuing breach the latest date can be taken. Thus, in a case concerning a building contract,[6] engineers were engaged to design and supervise the construction of a building. The work was completed in 1978 and in 1982 the plaintiffs brought an action for faulty design. The engineers claimed that the action was statute-barred as the breach relating to the design occurred more than six years before the action was begun. The court held that the engineers' duties in respect of the design and supervision were a continuing contractual obligation and, therefore, the six years would not have started to run until 1978.

3. LIABILITY IN TORT

3.1 Introduction

From the section above dealing with English contract law it can be readily seen that only a party to a contract can sue upon that contract. Consequently, many people who suffer harm caused by a defective product do not have a remedy in contract. Take the following examples:

5 *George Mitchell (Chesterhall) Ltd v Finney Lock Seeds Ltd* [1983] 2 All ER 337.
6 *Chelmsford District Council v T J Evers* [1984] 25 Build LR 99.

(a) A buys an electric toaster and gives it to B as a gift. The toaster blows up causing damage to B's property.
(b) A buys a bottle of lemonade and gives the bottle to B to drink it. Unknown to both, a decomposed snail had found its way into the bottle during the manufacturing process. B becomes violently ill.

In both examples B would not have a remedy in contract and unless he were able to sue under a manufacturer's guarantee, his only remedies will lie in tort and product liability.

3.2 Negligence

To meet the rising need for better consumer protection from defective and unsafe products in an age of increasing mechanisation and industrialisation there developed an area of law known as the tort of negligence. Surprisingly, it was not until 1932 that the English courts came to a landmark decision. In the case of *Donoghue v Stevenson*,[7] the tort of negligence was recognised in its own right as a separate tort. The importance of this decision lay in the fact that it was the first time that the courts had attempted to formulate a principle for universal application for liability in negligence which could be used in all situations and, at the same time, remain flexible to suit the changing needs of society. This principle became known as the 'neighbour principle'.

Mrs Donoghue was bought a bottle of ginger beer by a friend. She drank some of the contents and allegedly found the remains of a decomposed snail. It was held that:

> A manufacturer of products which he sells in such a form has to show that he intends them to reach the ultimate consumer in the form in which they left him with no reasonable possibility of intermediate examination, and with the knowledge that the absence of reasonable care in the preparation or putting up of the products will result in an injury to the consumer's life or property, owes a duty to the consumer to take reasonable care.

The breakthrough in the case was that the decision did not simply add manufacturer and consumer to the list of relationships which involved a duty to take care, but that it laid down a principle much wider than the facts of the case which could be used as a test in all cases to determine whether a duty of care exists or not:

> You must take reasonable care to avoid acts or omissions which you can reasonably foresee would be likely to injure your neighbour. Who, then, in law, is my neighbour? The answer seems to be – persons who are so closely and directly affected by my act that I ought reasonably to have them in contemplation as being so affected when I am directing my mind to the acts or omissions which are called in question.

In order to succeed in establishing liability in negligence, the plaintiff must show:

(a) the existence of a duty of care;
(b) breach of that duty; and
(c) consequential damage which is not too remote.

7 *Donoghue v Stephenson* [1932] AC 562.

Once a duty of care has been established it is a question of fact whether the defendant has breached that duty by falling below the standard of care required. The legal standard is not that of the defendant himself but of a reasonable man using ordinary care and skill.

In relation to the supply of goods, a manufacturer owes a duty to take reasonable care in their design and manufacture, and in providing adequate warnings so as not to cause injury to the buyer or his property provided the manufacturer has sold the goods in such a manner as to show that he intended them to reach the user in the form in which it left him without any reasonable prospect of an intermediate examination which would reveal any defects. A manufacturer may be in breach of his duty if a warning on the goods on how to use the product is misleading or, simply, inadequate. A good example of this is provided by the case[8] where the defendant sold ampoules of a chemical which were marked 'harmful vapour'. The chemical came into contact with water and an explosion occurred. The manufacturer was found to be in breach of his duty to take reasonable care as the ampoules should have been marked with a specific warning of the dangers of an explosion occurring. The warning given was clearly inadequate.

A design defect may become apparent after the manufacturer has sold his product and, in some cases, it may affect hundreds of buyers as, for instance, where a new model of motor vehicle is recalled due to a design fault being discovered. Provided the design fault itself was not as a result of the manufacturer's failure to take reasonable care, whether he is in breach of duty or not will depend upon what steps he takes after becoming aware of the fault.

3.3 Causation

It has to be shown that the product was defective when it was put into circulation, and the manufacturer's breach caused the damage suffered. In a large number of cases this is by far the most difficult problem faced by the buyer. It was said by the court in *Donoghue v Stevenson* that the manufacturer's responsibility ceases once he no longer has control over the product. The burden of proof, as will be seen later, is on the buyers to prove the manufacturer's action or omission caused, or contributed to, the damage. The legal test adopted by the courts is the 'but for' test; in other words: the damage would not have occurred 'but for' the manufacturer's breach of duty to take care.

In one case[9] an employee had been injured in an accident at work. His employers had been in breach of their duty in not providing a safety belt which could have prevented the accident. However, the action failed because he could not prove, on a balance of probabilities, that he would have worn the belt if it had been supplied.

The principle decided by the court is that the burden is on the plaintiff to prove that the defendant's actions or omissions caused the harm suffered, which means that causation will be the major stumbling block for a plaintiff trying to pursue a claim in negligence.

8 *Vacwell Engineering Co Ltd v BDH Chemicals* [1969] 3 All ER 1681.
9 *McWilliams v Arrol Ltd* [1962] 1 WLR 295.

3.4 Nova causa interveniens

The chain of causation between breach of duty of care and damage caused may be broken by the wrongful act of another person.

An example of an act which breaks the chain of causation is found in a case[10] where the plaintiff sustained a leg injury due to the defendant's negligence. The plaintiff attempted to climb down stairs without assistance which was nearby. The court refused to hold the defendant liable for the plaintiff's further injury because his act intervened.

3.5 Contributory negligence

If the plaintiff has contributed in some way to the damage suffered his claim will not be defeated but any damages recoverable will be reduced according to his share of the blame.

If the plaintiff's negligence is so great it may be a nova causa interveniens.

3.6 Remoteness of loss and damage

The basic principle on remoteness is to be found in the decision of the court in *The Wagon Mound*.[11] A defendant who is in breach of his duty to take care will be liable for the damage that was reasonably foreseeable as likely to happen at the time the breach occurred. It is not the exact damage which has to be foreseen, but the type of harm generally. The court in another case[12] put it this way: 'It is not necessary that the precise concatenation of circumstances should be envisaged. If the consequence was one within the general range which any reasonable person might foresee then it is within the rule that a person . . . is liable for the consequences'.

In other words, what is needed then is to foresee the general type of harm as a result of a breach of duty to take care, but not, necessarily, the exact harm.

Whilst the principle, itself, may be clear, a look at the cases reveals a difficulty in applying the principle. In one case[13] a boy aged eight tripped over a paraffin lamp and fell into a hole left unattended by the defendant, and the boy suffered severe burns as a result of an explosion. Although it could not be foreseen that the lamp would explode, nevertheless the House of Lords held the defendant liable for the boy's injuries as they had created a foreseeable risk of injury by burning which was sufficiently similar in nature to the harm suffered.

10 *McKew v Holland & Hannen & Cubitts (Scotland) Ltd* [1969] 3 All ER 1621.
11 *The Wagon Mound* [1961] AC 388.
12 *Stewart v West African Terminals Ltd* [1964] 2 Lloyd's Rep 371, CA.
13 *Hughes v Lord Advocate* [1963] 2 WLR 779.

3.7 Measure of damage

Since the *Donoghue v Stevenson* decision it has been established that a manufacturer who puts into circulation a defective product will be liable in negligence for personal injury or damage to property which the product causes, but will not be liable in tort for any defect in the product itself.

The product is either capable of repair or it is worthless. In either case the loss is purely economic and is normally only recoverable in contract. 'Pure economic loss' is a term used to describe loss which occurs independently of any other physical damage either to the plaintiff or his property and is only recoverable in tort for negligent misstatement under the principles set out in the case of *Hedley Byrne v Heller*[14] or where there is a special relationship or proximity between the plaintiff and defendant.[15]

This principle that economic loss cannot be claimed in tort has been firmly established in a variety of recent cases.[16]

3.8 Burden of proof

The burden of proof in an action for negligence rests primarily on the plaintiff which, in a claim for defective products, means that the plaintiff must show that a product was defective at the time it left the control of the manufacturer and that the defect in the product was the cause of the plaintiff's loss or damage. In *Donoghue v Stevenson* the manufacturer was treated as being in control of the ginger beer bottle until such time as it was opened by the customer. This difficulty increases for the plaintiff the longer the time between when the manufacturer puts the goods into circulation and the time the damage occurs, particularly in cases where there is an opportunity for interference with the goods.

There is, however, one very important exception to this basic rule: where the plaintiff proves damage in circumstances which can only be attributable to a breach of duty to take care on the part of the manufacturer. In this case the burden shifts to the manufacturer to prove that he has taken reasonable care.

This is known as the doctrine of 'res ipsa loquitor' which literally means 'the thing speaks for itself'. Under this maxim the plaintiff establishes a prima facie case of negligence where it is not possible for him to know what caused the loss but it would not have happened had it not been for the negligence of the manufacturer. In other words, the plaintiff is able to treat the actual facts of the case as evidence of the negligence.

The rule has been used to establish a prima facie case of negligence in cases, for example, where objects have fallen from buildings and where motor vehicles have gone out of control and a stone was found in a cake.

If, of course, the manufacturer is able to offer an explanation which is consistent with having taken reasonable care, the manufacturer will not be liable.

14 *Hedley Byrne v Heller* [1964] AC 465.

15 *Junior Books Ltd v Veitchi Co Ltd* [1983] AC 520.

16 *Muirhead v Industrial Tank Specialities Ltd* [1986] QB 507; *Murphy v Brentwood District Council* [1990] 3 WLR 414; *Department of the Environment v Thomas Bates & Son Ltd* [1990] 3 WLR 457.

3.9 Exclusion or limitation of liability

Before the passing of UCTA 1977 a manufacturer of a defective product could exclude or restrict liability for any damage caused by his product to the ultimate consumer provided he could show that the plaintiff was aware of the risk and had consented to an expressed exclusion of the manufacturer's duty. Normally such expressed exclusion would be by way of a notice or warning, and the manufacturer could rely upon this to set up the defence of 'volenti non fit injuria', ie the plaintiff had consented to the risk of injury. However, in cases involving defective goods the fact that a warning or notice is given is more likely to be relevant to the manufacturer's duty to give adequate warnings to render the product safe than purporting to exclude liability.

Since UCTA 1977 any notice purporting to exclude liability for negligence is subject to the provisions of the Act. As in contract the Act only relates to business liability.

Section 2 of UCTA 1977 provides:

(1) A person cannot by reference to any other contract term or to a notice given to persons generally or to particular persons exclude or restrict his liability for death or injury resulting from negligence.
(2) In the case of other loss or damage a person cannot exclude or restrict his liability for negligence except in so far as the term or notice satisfies the requirement of reasonableness.
(3) Where a contract term or notice purports to exclude or restrict liability for negligence a person's agreement to or awareness of it is not of itself to be taken as indicating his voluntary acceptance of any risk.

The test to determine reasonableness in relation to a notice is that it should be fair and reasonable to allow reliance upon it, having regard to all the circumstances when the liability arose.

3.10 Limitation period

A claim will be statute barred unless it is brought within the statutory time limits. A plaintiff has six years from the date the case of action accrued in which to bring a claim in negligence, although claims involving personal injury must be brought within three years. The time limits mean that a manufacturer is exposed to liability for a considerable time after the product was manufactured. In one case[17] a defective chisel splintered and caused injury to a mechanic seven years after the chisel was manufactured. The mechanic had three years after this to bring a claim which meant that in this particular case the manufacturer had an exposure to liability for ten years.

17 *Davie v New Merton Board Mills Ltd* [1959] AC 604.

For actions involving latent defects the limitation period is either six years from the date when the cause of action arose or, if later, three years from the date when the plaintiff (or any person in whom the cause of action was vested before the plaintiff) had both knowledge of the damage and a right to bring the action. There is, however, an overriding time limit of 15 years from the date of the alleged negligent act or omission.

3.11 Liability for third parties

A manufacturer will be vicariously liable for the negligent acts or omissions of his employees during the course of their employment. Even if the manufacturer has taken all reasonable precautions and installed a safe system of work he will still be liable for the acts or omissions of his employees. In *Grant v Australian Knitting Mills* the court accepted that the manufacturer had a very good safety record with an allegedly foolproof system of production; nevertheless, he was still held liable as a result of the negligence of one of his operatives on the production line.

3.12 Breach of statutory duty

An injured party may be able to bring a claim for breach of a statutory duty. For example, s 41(1) of CPA 1987 provides:

> An obligation owed by safety regulations shall be a duty owed to any person who may be affected by a contravention of the obligation, and . . . a contravention of any such enactment shall be actionable accordingly.

4. LIABILITY FOR DEFECTIVE PRODUCTS BROUGHT ABOUT BY BREACH OF STATUTORY REGULATION DESIGNED TO PROTECT CONSUMERS AND/OR TO PROMOTE SAFETY

4.1 Outline of nature of protective regulations

Apart from CPA 1987, which will be examined later, UK law has many Acts and regulations directed at the subject of product and consumer safety.

CPA 1987 consolidated much previous legislation, as well as implementing the Directive. More importantly, in the area of product safety CPA 1987 specifically adopted existing safety regulations. These regulations are made on the authority of the UK Government to impose safety requirements where it is considered necessary to reduce the risk of death and personal injury from products.

Apart from CPA 1987 there are powers under the Health and Safety at Work Act 1974, the Food Safety Act 1990 and the Medicines Act 1968 which enable enforcing authorities to take action in relation to unsafe products.

In particular, under CPA 1987 the Secretary of State can issue Prohibition Notices to prohibit a particular person or group of persons from supplying a particular product (s 13) or issue a Limited Duration Safety Regulation to prohibit the supply of a product or class of products which are considered unsafe (s 11).

The Limited Duration Safety Regulation replaces an existing power (the prohibition order) which was used with great effect to ban the supply of dangerous products such as children's pyjamas and nightdresses which had been treated with a carcinogenic flame-proofing material.

Apart from the Acts mentioned above there are statutory provisions to deal with a wide range of potentially dangerous products such as aircraft and radioactive material.

The Secretary of State is able to create regulations to cover dangerous, or potentially dangerous products. The present list of safety regulations covers a variety of products from asbestos, bicycles, bunk beds and cosmetic products to snuff, toys, fireworks and many others.

4.2 Burden of proof

Because of the criminal nature of the enforcement of these provisions it is necessary for the government department or local authority bringing the prosecution to prove its case to the standard required in all criminal matters, namely, beyond reasonable doubt.

4.3 Nature of liability, damages or criminal sanctions

A person who contravenes a prohibition notice, a notice to warn, or a Limited Duration Safety Regulation, may be liable to criminal penalties. If the case is proved 'beyond reasonable doubt' then upon conviction that person would be liable to a fine and/or imprisonment.

Similarly, where safety regulations prohibit a person from supplying or offering or agreeing to supply any product, any failure to comply with the prohibition may also result in a criminal penalty. The criminal penalty can range from a fine to a term of imprisonment.

Non-compliance with safety regulations may also give rise to a civil action for breach of statutory duty.

Such claims are not easy to bring unless the Act in question specifically allows a civil remedy.

5. SPECIAL LIABILITIES ARISING IN RESPECT OF PARTICULAR PRODUCTS

Under UK law a series of protective measures has been implemented from time to time in relation to specific products, including foodstuffs, drugs and chemicals, furniture and motor vehicles, to ensure that such products are safe. These regulations are now subsumed in CPA 1987 and are therefore subject to the legal principles which will be discussed later in this chapter. However, there are certain categories of product for which it has been considered necessary to introduce special rules.

5.1 Nuclear power

Items relating to nuclear power installations are, as a matter of public policy, dealt with under a separate scheme. The Nuclear Installations Act 1965 is designed to deal with injury or damage which results from nuclear accidents. Under the scheme of the Nuclear Installations Act only a licence holder is permitted to operate a nuclear plant. The victims of emitted radiation have a claim against the licensee. The UK Atomic Energy Commission and government departments are also liable for omissions from sites operated by them.

If a duty imposed by the Act is breached the licence holder, UK Atomic Energy Commission, or government department incurs the liability in respect of that injury or disaster. This means that if a manufacturer supplies a faulty component to a nuclear installation, which is then shown to have caused the disaster, the licensee or operator of the installation is liable and is unable to claim an indemnity from the negligent manufacturer.

The sale of substances containing a radioactive chemical element are also controlled. The Ionising Radiation Regulations 1985 impose a duty to protect employees and other persons against ionising radiation arising from working with radioactive substances.

5.2 Foodstuffs

The UK has had food safety law since the thirteenth century when legislation was passed in relation to bread and ale.

Apart from liabilities in contract or tort foodstuffs are governed by the Food Safety Act 1990 and regulations made under it. These regulations control quality, composition, packaging and labelling of food. Such regulations are policed by local authorities through their environmental health and trading standards departments. Breach of such regulations can result in fines or prison sentences.

The Food Safety Act 1990 makes it an offence to treat or process food so as to render it injurious to health, or to sell food which is not of the nature or of the substance or of the quality demanded by the purchaser, or which is unfit for human consumption.

5.3 Chemicals

There are also regulations to control the transport of dangerous chemicals, to impose a duty to report new dangerous chemicals to the Health and Safety Executive (an officially appointed body), to control the labelling and packaging of dangerous chemicals and to control any substance considered hazardous to health.

Similarly, there is a specific Act governing medicines, the Medicines Act 1968. Under the Medicines Act 1968 all dealings with medicinal products are controlled and the contravention of the major provisions of the Act is a criminal offence.

The Medicines Act imposes the duty that no person may, to the prejudice of the purchaser, sell any medicinal product which is not of the nature or quality demanded by the purchaser.

A system of licensing is in force for medicinal products and in general no such product may be manufactured or assembled without a licence. In addition, particular medicines may be prohibited from sale, supply or importation in the interests of public safety.

Reference to Her Majesty's Inspectorate of Pollution or the relevant local authority regarding 'relevant proscribed substances or processes' will need to be considered when the relevant regulations under the Environmental Protection Act 1990 are brought into force.

6. LIABILITY FOR DEFECTIVE PRODUCTS ARISING FROM NATIONAL LAW IN THE UK: IMPLEMENTATION OF EC DIRECTIVE 85/324 ON PRODUCT LIABILITY

6.1 Introduction

When CPA 1987 was brought into full effect in March 1988 it brought about an extension of the liability of manufacturers and suppliers to members of the public who are injured or suffer loss as a consequence of coming into contact with harmful or defective goods.

The liability upon manufacturers and suppliers under CPA 1987 is in addition to their responsibilities under the law of contract and tort and other existing statutory obligations such as the Health and Safety at Work Act 1974 and SGA 1979 described above.

A new liability arises under CPA 1987 from the fact of the supply of defective goods, whether or not the manufacturer/supplier can be said to be 'at fault' and whether or not there was a contractual relationship with the person using the goods.

CPA 1987 was introduced as a result of the Directive which requires all EC countries to bring into effect product liability law based upon the detailed terms of that directive. The Act also reflects the position which has existed in US law for the last decade.

As a result of CPA 1987, a person who is injured or whose personal property is damaged by a product ('the claimant') will be able to claim against the manufacturer/supplier of that product ('the producer') if it can be shown that the product was defective.

'Producer' is a very wide term. It includes the producer of the finished product as well as of any material or component contained in it, and also any person who, by putting their name, trade mark, or other distinguishing feature on the product, represents himself as being the producer of the product. This latter class of producer is often known by the collective term 'own branders'.

If a producer of a product cannot be identified, each supplier will be treated as its producer. This is to protect the claimant from producers hiding behind chains of suppliers. However, provided a supplier informs the claimant within a reasonable time of the identity of the real producer of the product or of the person from whom the product was obtained, the liability is passed along the chain. Clearly complaints and claims must be handled by potential defendants speedily and accurately to avoid being treated as a producer by the courts when they have only acted as a supplier.

The European dimension is also very important when considering the liability of the producer. Anyone who imports a product into the EC for re-sale, hire, leasing or any other form of distribution, is to be treated as its producer.

Consider Tom, Dick and Harry, that well-known trio of television set manufacturers, wholesalers and retailers. Tom manufactures the television set and Dick wholesales it to Harry who retails it to the claimant, who is injured when the set explodes. The claimant can claim against Harry unless he tells him that Dick supplied it, and can claim against Dick unless Dick tells him Tom manufactured it. Additionally, as we have seen, the claimant may have causes of action under common law in contract or tort against Harry as the supplier. However, if two or more persons are liable for the same damage then they are jointly and severally liable. This joint liability would occur where a defective component was also defectively installed in a product. Once liability has been established both the component producer and the installer would be equally liable but if one was unable to pay, the other could be made to pay all compensation under s 2(5) of CPA 1987.

6.1.1 Defences to a claim for product liability

A producer has six defences upon which to rely, namely:

(a) if he proves that he did not put the product into circulation; or
(b) having regard to all the circumstances, the product was not defective when he put it into circulation; or
(c) that the product was not produced for sale, hire, or any other distribution for commercial purposes, or that the producer has not produced and distributed the product within the course of his business activities; or
(d) the defect in the product is due to compliance of the product with mandatory public authority regulations; or
(e) if the product is a component, that the defect is attributable to the design of the product in which the component has been fitted and not to the component; or
(f) that the state of scientific and technical knowledge at the time when the product was put into circulation was not such as to enable the producer to know the existence of the defect or discover it ('the state of the art defence').

The state of the art defence, for which we can largely thank the pharmaceutical industry's lobbying, will only be available to producers who can satisfy a court that the state of scientific and technical knowledge available in the world at the time the product was put on the market was insufficient to reveal the existence of the defect at that time.

No proceedings may be commenced after ten years from the date that the producer brought into circulation the actual product which caused the damage.

Although the Directive permits each EC country to impose a ceiling for liability for multiple design defects, no such ceiling has been provided under CPA 1987.

Liability under CPA 1987 is not retrospective and does not extend to products in circulation before the date upon which it came into force.

6.2 Description of special or anomalous provisions in respect of product liability law in the UK

Because of the existing framework of statute law certain products remain a risk business for the producer even if not specifically covered by CPA 1987. However, as has been demonstrated most products, unless specifically excluded, are potentially caught by the Act.

CPA 1987 defines 'product' as any 'goods or electricity' and also includes the term 'substances'. This raises the possibility that computer software will be caught by CPA 1987. Opinion is divided as to whether such claims will be successful but it is arguable that defective software provided on a tangible medium such as a computer disk can be treated as a product. If that defective software then causes injury or damage to property CPA 1987 would appear to apply. However, it is only likely that such software will be caught where it amounts to a defective component in a product. With the increasing control of high voltage/high risk technology by software care must be taken to ensure that adequate safety checks and de-bugging have been carried out on the software being incorporated.

It is quite likely that the 'state of the art' defence would be of help to producers of software provided they can demonstrate through documentation that full de-bugging and testing has been carried out.

Natural agricultural produce will not be caught by the Act, although beware the Food Safety Act 1990. This is because natural agricultural produce will not have been subject to a process. However, food processing will bring such produce back within CPA 1987.

The building industry provides another example of how the Act produces surprising results. CPA 1987 has been drafted in such a way as to create a liability for defects in buildings which the Directive did not necessarily intend. Obviously components in buildings such as windows and doors are caught by CPA 1987.

It would appear that the liability of a contract builder who builds for someone else on land that he does not own is different to the liability of a speculative builder who builds houses on land that he does own and subsequently sells or leases. It would appear that the contract builder may only be liable as a supplier or producer in respect of defective products supplied or produced by him and incorporated into the building, whereas the speculative builder may be liable as a producer of the defective building as a whole, although exempted from liability as a supplier of any defective product comprised in the building.

6.3 Optional provisions in the EEC Directive

There are three optional provisions in the Directive and they are concerned with agricultural products (art 15(a)), the so-called 'state of the art' defence (art 15(b)) and the question of whether a ceiling should be put on a producer's liability (art 16).

The UK has adopted the 'state of the art' defence but has not chosen to place a ceiling upon liability. With regard to agricultural products untreated produce is not caught by the Act, but processed food would be.

7. PRACTICAL EFFECTS EC PRODUCT LIABILITY LAW WILL HAVE ON VARIOUS BUSINESSES IN THE CHAIN OF SUPPLY OF PRODUCTS

As we have seen above, the term 'producer' embraces many different people. In our exploding television set example the manufacturer, Tom, wholesaler Dick, and retailer Harry, are all potentially liable to the claimant. However, ascertaining who is the manufacturer of a product is seldom that simple. It is usual to involve designers, component manufacturers, assemblers, importers, distributors and others before a retailer supplies the product to the potential claimant.

We must also consider those who work on the factory lines, employees of the firms who handled the product during its passage along the chain of supply, together with the installers of products and repairers. A product may be safe when designed but become defective due to faulty assembly or manufacture.

CPA 1987 is all about ensuring that someone is accountable for injury or damage arising from a defective product, and to this end the previous common law principles of privity of contract, duty of care and remoteness of damage have been amended to increase accountability.

The effects of this accountability by way of strict liability must be carefully considered by each person in the chain of supply.

If a product is defective because of a design defect then it will be a liability upon the designer. However, the defect may have been caused by a component in the design. Was the component defective, or was it rendered defective by its design application? If the former then the designer is liable, if the latter it is the component manufacturer who is liable. However, under CPA 1987 the liability will fall upon the first importer of the product into an EC country. Such importer must ensure that he has appropriate contract terms with his suppliers and has confidence in the safety of the products being handled.

A designer must take great care to ensure that the product is safe. The component supplier needs to know, not only that the product he supplies is safe, but also that its application is safe. The prudent component supplier will want to know exactly how his product is going to be used, and what it is to be used in conjunction with, and should ensure that it is suitable for that purpose.

The manufacturer will want to ensure that the design and manufacture of the component supplied is safe and that the process of manufacture does not render either the design or the component defective. He would also need to know that other materials used in manufacture are free from defects.

8. COMPARISON OF THE EFFECTS OF PRODUCT LIABILITY LAW WITH THE PREVIOUS POSITION IN CONTRACT AND TORT

CPA 1987 clearly imposes a much stricter control upon the producer of a defective product. Once the claimant has shown that a product is defective and has caused damage then (subject to the defences above) he will obtain damages. The common law principles of privity of contract and foreseeability of damage and remoteness have been swept away.

With the implementation of CPA 1987 significant extensions have been introduced to the law relating to defective products. These extensions produce some fundamental differences in the way a claim relating to a product can be dealt with and the legal result of that claim.

CPA 1987 creates numerous different results to that which would be achieved under the existing law of contract and tort.

8.1 Contract

In contract law SGA 1979 implies the term that goods will be of merchantable quality and fit for their purpose, if they are not, the consumer will have remedies. However, under CPA 1987 merchantability and fitness of purpose are not the criteria upon which liability is based. The liability is much broader and more straightforward because it is based on the concept of 'defect'.

As has been seen earlier in this chapter, for a claim to succeed in contract law there must be privity of contract. However, under CPA 1987 privity of contract plays no part. This means that the remedies under CPA 1987 are available to an injured person whether or not that person has a contract with manufacturer or supplier.

8.2 Tort

The main difference between the law of tort and CPA 1987 is that the injured person no longer has to prove that the producer of the article owed a duty of care to the injured party. However, the injured person does still have to prove that damage has occurred (in excess of £275), that there is a defect, and that there is a causal relationship between the defect and the damage. Nevertheless, it is proving a duty of care which has been argued to be the most difficult element of such a claim in tort. In this respect CPA 1987 provides a much more user friendly framework for the claimant.

One area of comparison which will not become clear until cases under CPA 1987 have been determined by the courts in the UK is the concept of the 'safety which a person is entitled to expect' (CPA 1987 s 3(1)). If the courts adopt an objective test, that of the reasonable person in the circumstances, then the position will be analogous to that which already existed in tort, but if the test is adopted subjectively the law will have changed.

CPA 1987 preserves the concept of contributory negligence dealt with earlier in this chapter. Under CPA 1987 an injured person would be liable to have his claim reduced if he had contributed to his own injury by his misuse of the defective product.

8.3 Risk management in the new era of product liability

8.3.1 Internal risk management

i. Quality control. Quality control is of vital importance for the manufacturer or producer, who must take the necessary safety measures to prevent injury and loss. It is advisable for checks to be made upon all component parts of a product, especially where components have been manufactured by a third party. If the necessary quality controls have not been made before a third party's components are installed the manufacturer may not have recourse against that third party in the event of a defect causing injury or damage. It is not enough for the checks to be done, they must also be adequately documented.

It is advisable that big risk products be double checked, and/or tested under extreme conditions. Some products may be subject to final spot checks, others may need a check to be made on every item to be despatched, such as the refraction of light test on bottles of drink.

ii. Documentation. Full documentation of all control inspections, as well as of all developmental and pre-production testing, is vital if a liability claim is to be successfully defended. Further, the documentation should be readily retrievable. Obviously with the advent of computerisation in the manufacturing industry documentation will be easier to retrieve. Remember such documentation will need to be kept for a minimum of ten years.

iii. Record-keeping. The type of records that need to be kept will vary from product to product. However, as the importance of record-keeping cannot be stressed too highly producers should try to ensure that records reflect the entire process of manufacture from design through to the finished product and it is as well to put these record-keeping practices in place at the earliest possible stage.

Additionally, those who sell products but do not manufacture them will need to be able to identify the manufacturer in the event of a claim being made. Remember, no records, no defence!

iv. Warning notices/operating instructions/service manuals: 'Loose lips sink ships'. An otherwise safe product may be rendered unsafe by the producer providing insufficient information about its operation, or through failure to display adequate warning notices.

Such notices and information should be prominently displayed and, in particular, care should be taken that warning notices cannot be easily removed.

Importers of goods to the EC, in particular, should ensure that the translations of instructions and notices are accurate. Everyone has a favourite nonsense translation of foreign instruction – today such a mistake could give rise to a liability that might not otherwise exist.

As the existence of a warning which is ignored may give rise to a defence of contributory negligence (that, is, that the user was partly or completely to blame), every effort must be made to ensure that the user of the product reads the instruction manual and is aware of any potential dangers in operating the product.

As many users will not have access to, or will not read, the user's manual, it is necessary to have the main warning on the product itself where possible. This may not always be appropriate so warning notices, lights and control devices should be placed in a position where they are most likely to come to the attention of users or products or persons who come into contact with the product.

Clearly, rotor blades in a lawn mower or a helicopter are inherently dangerous. However, it is necessary for a producer to ensure that all reasonable practical steps have been taken to highlight the danger.

Particular points to be borne in mind with regard to warning notices are that they should be proportional to the size of the product and the degree of risk and that they should be clearly visible. They should also be in a form that cannot be easily removed, tampered with or obscured and their message should be in clear and unambiguous language. Appropriate lettering and colouring should also be adopted so that the notice captures the attention of the user, such as red for danger. If possible international symbols should be used, for example, on a label for a dangerous substance the symbol of a skull and cross bones should be used to warn of a potential fatality if the product is consumed.

However, it is not enough simply to include a warning notice, the wording used is also important. The word 'Warning' may be considered stronger than the word 'Caution' and both would probably be considered less effective than the word 'Danger'.

The producer would also be well advised to give consideration to the persons who are most likely to come into contact with or use the products supplied, and also the circumstances in which the products are most likely to be used. All foreseeable danger should be assessed and the warnings directed accordingly.

Wherever appropriate, safety devices should be incorporated. An example might be that in high voltage electrical goods a circuit breaker should be built in. Warning lights and alarms may also be considered as necessary safety devices upon certain products. The new law under CPA 1987 gives rise to an argument that where a safety device could have prevented an injury and was not fitted, the lack of it could be considered a design defect.

Where safety standards are in force all labels, warnings and safety devices should be prepared in accordance with government regulations, industry standards and custom and practice. As we have seen, the goverment is able to create regulations under CPA 1987 and breach of these regulations can amount to a criminal offence.

It is important to review advertising and promotional material to consider whether warnings should be used in them and whether any claims about the product, or examples of its use, have inherent dangers for the user.

8.4 The handling of consumer claims

8.4.1 Inspection of defective products and analysis of causes of failure

When a claim has been made it is necessary to inspect thoroughly the class of products involved and analyse the cause of failure. This is particularly important if the product is made up of components and/or raw materials supplied to the producer.

As a result of the inspection, careful consideration must be given to the consequences of the failure of the product on the future of that product. Will it be necessary to redesign, should the product be withdrawn from the market, or should the products that have already been sold be recalled for safety checks or replacement of defective parts? Motorists, in particular, are familiar with the letter inviting them to return their car to their dealer for a safety check.

Later in the chapter we will consider the question of insurance for product liability claims. However, when handling a claim it is important to bear in mind the requirements that an insurer may have of the insured. There may be particular requirements with regard to documentation of the claim, notification of the claim, as well as the requirements in relation to the future of the product.

Because of the possibility that liability for the damage or injury may be passed on down the line of supply, it is very important that when a claimant requests information about the product and its producer that that information is supplied accurately and speedily.

It is vital to preserve evidence in relation to a claim. It is no good having thoroughly tested a product to establish that it would be safe in any foreseeable operating environment if that evidence is then lost. Similarly, if recalled parts have been tested and found to be safe they should be stored somewhere other than the scrap heap.

In a subsequent chapter (Chapter 17) some of the problems of legal proceedings will be considered in greater detail. In particular, the producer must be aware of the variety of different jurisdictions in which he may find himself being sued. An individual claimant will, in many instances, be able to bring his claim in courts outside the country in which the producer is domiciled.

As we have seen, there are limitation periods within which proceedings can be brought, but the effect of these is that a claimant may legitimately be able to bring a claim some years after the manufacture of the product in question. Again, this raises the question of how long records and products should be kept available. As mentioned earlier, ten years should be the minimum length of retention.

8.4.2 Consequences of failure and need to re-design products for safety checks or replacement of defective parts

A potential area of claim for a defective product may arise where a product has been recalled or is subsequently re-issued on the market having been re-designed or having had a component replaced with a safer one. Clearly if this has been done as a result of a product failure which has given rise to a claim the re-design and redevelopment may support the argument that the original product was defective. However, by virtue of s 3(2) of CPA 1987 which implements art 6.2 of the Directive, a product will not be considered defective simply because a better product is subsequently put into circulation. Therefore, if a producer finds a competitor is able to market a product incorporating new safety features, that will not of itself render the original product defective.

The 'state of the art' defence will also be relevant in this area, it may be possible for a producer to argue that at the time the first product was put into circulation the new safety feature incorporated by a competitor went beyond the scientific or practical knowledge available at the time of the original launch.

8.4.3 Requirements of evidence

In English law all relevant evidence must be disclosed to the other side in legal proceedings unless it can be classed as privileged. Privileged documents generally comprise communications with lawyers and experts about a particular case for the purposes of that case. However, a report obtained before a claim has been made might not be privileged.

This means that documentation that is relevant to a claim *must* be disclosed in an action, whether it helps or damages your case, unless it can be argued that the documents are privileged.

8.4.4 Correspondence with consumers

Corresponding with consumers must, of course, be handled carefully. In particular, due regard must be given to the requirement of a producer's insurers with regard to dealing with potential claims. Different controls are operated by different insurance companies. Some insurers may, for instance, allow a great deal of autonomy to those dealing with potential claims, particularly if those claims are below certain monetary limits. Other insurers may take the attitude that no correspondence should be entered into with potential claimants except where it has been previously cleared by that insurer.

It will also be relevant when considering correspondence to look at where the writer is in the chain of supply. A retailer may be more predisposed towards settling a claim with regard to a particular product than the producer. The retailer may have only dealt in a small number of the products and might consider a particular claim to be of a minor nature. However, documentary evidence obtained from the retailer may become relevant and be used in subsequent actions brought against the producer of the product. Careful examination should be given of any indemnities existing between producers and retailers in such circumstances.

8.4.5 Preservation of evidence

In English law, as has been stated above, it is necessary in court actions to produce all relevant documentary evidence whether it helps or damages the case of the person holding that evidence. It is also a rule of law in England that documentary evidence which was once in the possession of a party to an action, but is no longer in that party's possession, must also be included in any relevant list of documents. Clearly it is necessary to ensure that proper records are maintained until at least the expiry of the relevant limitation period. This is three years from the date the claimant became aware or should reasonably have become aware of the damage, the defect *and* the identity of the producer. Further, there is a secondary bar to a claim, namely that an injured person's rights are extinguished once a period of ten years has elapsed from the date on which the producer put into circulation the actual product which caused the damage.

8.4.6 Problems of legal proceedings

There have not at the time of writing been a great number of product liability cases brought to court under CPA 1987. Therefore, it is difficult to assess any particular problems which will be posed when proceeding under that Act. Clearly claimants will experience considerable difficulties in proving their cases where the 'state of the art' defence is raised by a producer and it is likely that the court will have a fruitful time dealing with the concept of phrases such as when a product is 'put into circulation'. With the ten-year limitation period upon claims from the date upon which a product was put into circulation, considerable argument is likely to arise. It is likely that a producer would want to show the earliest possible date for a product having been put into circulation, relying perhaps on the earliest documentary evidence of the product being available. A claimant, on the other hand, may because of the limitation period need to satisfy the court that a product only physically appeared on the market or become available to be purchased, at a considerably later date.

A problem for the producer of a defective product, although of benefit for the claimant, is that whilst the claimant must prove the damage, the defect and the causal relationship between defect and damage, that claimant no longer has to prove that the producer owes a duty of care or has, indeed, been negligent.

8.5 Exclusion of liability and claims on contracts for indemnities

It is important to review all contractual relationships in the light of CPA 1987. Where manufacturers are not in direct contact with the ultimate users of their product then they are not likely to be in a position to control the display of warnings and accordingly may need to require contractually that the appropriate persons maintain and display the necessary warnings and indemnify them against any loss which arises from a failure to display those warnings. Further, it may be useful for them to impose upon people below them in the chain of supply, an obligation to observe their own safety policy. As a consequence, conditions of business for both the inward purchase and the outward sale of products would have to be reviewed to ensure that the careful steps that have been taken to protect, for example, a manufacturer, are being observed by those around them in the chain of supply.

Whilst it is possible to seek indemnities from the people with whom a party contracts, and warranties as to the fitness and safety of their products, it is expressly forbidden by CPA 1987 to exclude or seek to exclude liability for a claim in relation to a product defect.

8.6 Insurance

Product liability insurance may be provided as part of a general public liability policy or as a separate policy. Product liability insurance covers the insured against the legal liability to pay to third parties compensation for bodily injury and loss or damage to personal property arising out of defect in any product sold, supplied, serviced, repaired or tested by that insured.

Public liability insurance does not, however, provide the insured with a 'carte blanche' to act and manufacture as he pleases. The insurer will require certain standards to be adopted in the design, manufacture and supply of products and if these standards are materially breached the policy of insurance may be negated.

When a product causes injury or damage there is no limit in law on the level of damages that may be claimed in the UK, although in certain other European countries, as we shall see later in this book, financial limits have been imposed. One product may cause injury or damage to more than one person. The obvious example of a multiple or 'serial' claim will be a defective drug manufactured by a pharmaceutical company. If claims exceed the amount insured then the insured will have to bear the excess loss.

The insurer will usually pay the cost of investigating and defending a claim, but if those costs are included in the indemnity provided the actual cover will have been significantly reduced.

The costs of recalling defective products will not be covered by a public liability policy. Indeed, such cover goes beyond the typical 'products guarantee policies' available. Product guarantee policies protect the insured when his product fails to do what it is intended to do. It covers the cost of repair or replacement and consequential loss that results from a defective product even where no injury occurs. By an extension of such a policy it is possible to provide cover for the costs of recall of defective products. However, insurers are not keen to provide such cover, premiums are high and very considerable investigations will be undertaken by the underwriters before such cover will be provided. No insurer will be prepared to risk providing cover for an unlimited amount and so liability will probably be limited to a set figure. That figure will be negotiable, but if large sums of cover are required the insurer will want to spread the risk either by co-insurance with other insurers or by accepting the first portion of risk and passing the balance of the risk to a consortium by way of excess of loss cover.

If the risk is considered hazardous the insurer will not provide cover without undertaking rigorous underwriting enquiries which may take some time. Such delays must be planned for.

British courts tend to construe exclusion clauses against the insurer where doubts about the meaning of a clause arise. However, careful examination of the cover being offered should be carried out in any event to avoid protracted litigation.

8.7 Limitation of liability through corporate structure

8.7.1 Effect on whether a business should incorporate

Trading through a limited liability company has always been regarded as advantageous. Limited liability means exactly that. The shareholders of a company will have limited their indebtedness to those who deal with the company to the value of their share capital contribution. Of course, in practice, if a company has little share capital the directors or shareholders of a company will be asked to enter into separate agreements with those with whom a company trades to indemnify or guarantee the company's position. Such limited liability will be very important in relation to product liability cases, particularly as under CPA 1987 there is no upper limit upon the damages which can be awarded. This would be particularly so in relation to producers whose products are inherently dangerous and could cause great damage.

Naturally there are other advantages to incorporation such as tax benefits, but it should not be forgotten that there are also disadvantages, not the least of which are the rules requiring the disclosure of accounts and other relevant information with regard to shareholders and changes in the company's memorandum and articles of association.

8.7.2 Liabilities of companies in groups

A company is a legal person, and a group of companies is the result of grouping together a number of legal persons. If there are very close links between companies within a group and one of those companies becomes liable to a claimant for a large sum of damages which it cannot meet then it may be possible for the claimant to persuade a court that another company within the group, or indeed the group as a whole, should be responsible for those damages.

8.7.3 Splitting of high risk activities and valuable assets

i. Use of shell companies to import products from EC for resale within the UK. It may be prudent for those involved in the chain of supply to set up distinct companies in different jurisdictions to deal with various aspects of their business. For instance, the intellectual property rights in a product having a value might be owned by Company A, whilst the manufacture of that product was dealt with by Company B and the importation of that product dealt with by Company C. If Company C has no assets, other than the goods which pass through it, a claimant would be in some difficulties in recovering damages if the claim were brought against the shell Company C as the importer. This does not necessarily stop the claimant from chasing his claim back further to the actual producer.

Whilst there are obviously advantages in seeking to protect the position of producers and importers it must not be forgotten that there are also disadvantages in operating through shell companies. A company without assets, unless part of a more substantial group of companies, may have great difficulties in dealing with others in the marketplace because of its apparent lack of substance.

ii. Splitting off manufacturing from the companies asset base through use of a well-endowed parent company: leasing or hiring factors of production to tightly run manufacturing company. It may be prudent to seek to reduce the assets available to a prospective claimant by means of having a parent company manufacture the product and a shell company import the product. However, as has been suggested earlier in the chapter, companies which are in groups may not succeed in defeating a claim in this way and, indeed, if the shell company were treated as being the subsidiary of the parent company this might result in the failure of the attempt to keep the parent company's assets away from the claimant.

One prudent method of proceeding might be to keep the intellectual property rights in a product in one's own company and then lease or hire out the rights to produce that product to independent companies. If the design of the product does not have inherent defects and the product itself is not naturally hazardous, then much of the production risk will have been passed on. The disadvantage of this may be that the profit made on the leasing or hiring of the design is less than the profit upon the manufactured article. However, the risk can usually be measured against the potential level of profit.

8.3 Other practical steps to take in risk management

Clearly, a prudent producer or supplier will want to ensure that his business is as fully protected as possible. Now more than ever producers and suppliers should consider the benefits of trading through a corporate structure such as the UK Limited Company ('ltd') or Public Limited Company ('plc') with their in-built protections for the shareholders.

However, it is increasingly likely that if you have a group of companies which are ultimately under the same control that a judgment against one member of the group will have a knock-on effect upon the rest of that group.

For example, does a particular product or company have a good or bad record on product safety? Are appropriate insurance policies in place? Do you have an insurable interest which could be noted on such a policy?

If you are importing goods to the EC have you obtained an appropriate warranty and/or indemnity from the manufacturer? Have you had the product independently checked for safety? Will you be able to monitor manufacture?

If a large quantity of goods is to be imported, how many will you physically check on arrival?

It is extremely important to know the product you are dealing with. Where has it been? Where is it going? What will it be used for, and is that use both appropriate and safe?

Most people concerned with the manufacturing industry want to be associated with good quality products. Now more than ever there is a positive need to ensure that you are associated with safe products. The days of the mad scientist creating wonderful labour-saving inventions in his garden shed from a design on the back of an envelope are gone. Whether we like it or not consumer safety is king and manufacturers must spend the time and money to audit their systems and review their products. If they do not they may spend even more time and money on their lawyers.

CHAPTER XVII

Jurisdiction, enforcement of judgments and conflicts of laws

Miss Rebecca Attree

Laytons
16 Lincoln's Inn Fields
London WC2A 3ED
England

Tel ++ 44 71 404 5177
Fax ++ 44 71 405 1883

CHAPTER XVII

Jurisdiction, enforcement of judgments and conflicts of laws

INTRODUCTION

Many claims of product liability will be between victims and defendants from more than one country. The defective product itself may comprise components from different countries. It may, for example, have been made or assembled in Germany, exported to France, and then transported to Italy, where it may cause harm. These situations raise questions of where and against whom a plaintiff may bring his claim and which law will govern the determination of such claim.

This chapter is divided into three sections. Section 1 will deal with the principal international conventions which may govern a product liability claim in Europe. Section 2 will deal largely with issues of when a court will have jurisdiction to hear a claim, and section 3 with which national law will be applied in determining the claim.

1. THE INTERNATIONAL CONVENTIONS

The law relating to jurisdiction and choice of law as between European Member States is largely set out in a series of international Conventions. The adoption of the text of a treaty does not, by itself, create any obligations. A treaty does not come into being until two or more States consent to be bound by it, and the expression of such consent is usually by signature, exchange of instruments constituting a treaty, ratification, acceptance, approval or accession.

A treaty normally enters into force as soon as all the negotiating States have expressed their consent to be bound by it, but the negotiating States are always free to depart from this general rule by inserting an appropriate provision in the treaty itself. For example, a treaty may provide that it shall enter into force only when it has been ratified by a specified number of States.

Further, in some countries there is a very clear difference between the effects of a treaty in international law and the effects of a treaty in domestic law. In the Netherlands, Portugal and France, a treaty becomes effective in domestic law following its publication. In the UK, Sweden and Denmark, a treaty becomes effective in international law when it is ratified, but it usually has no effect in national law until appropriate national legislation is passed. Indeed, the English House of Lords recently held that UK ministers are not obliged to take the European Convention on Human Rights into consideration before issuing Directives, since to impose such an obligation 'would be to incorporate the Convention into domestic law by the back door'.[1] In Austria, the effect of a treaty

1 *R v Secretary of State for the Home Department, ex p Brind* (1991) Times, 8 February.

depends on its terms. If it contains no provisions to the contrary, it will be effective in national law upon signature or ratification. Otherwise, an Act of Parliament is required to give it effect.

International treaties require prior authorisation of the Spanish Parliament whenever they refer to political, military, financial or fundamental rights or territorial issues, or whenever they entail the amendment or superseding of an act or regulation or require the approval of legislation for its implementation. In any other case, a treaty may become effective in Spain by the signature of the representative, promulgation by the King and publication in the Official Gazette; no passing of national legislation is required. In these latter cases, Parliament should be immediately informed of the signature of the treaty.

1.1 Convention on Jurisdiction and the Enforcement of Judgments in Civil and Commercial Matters 1968 ('the Brussels Convention')

This Convention contains detailed rules on jurisdiction and defines which country will have jurisdiction over a particular action. Its aim is to reduce the possibility of 'forum shopping', that is, the multiplicity of jurisdictions in which a plaintiff may choose to commence proceedings. It also introduces an expeditious procedure for the recognition and enforcement of judgments of certain courts of Member States throughout the EC.

The Convention was adopted by the six original members of the EC, namely Belgium, France, West Germany, Italy, Luxembourg and the Netherlands and was acceded to by Denmark, the Irish Republic, the UK and Northern Ireland in 1978. In recent years, the pace of developments has quickened, with Greece, Spain and Portugal having acceded to the Convention.

In countries where the Brussels Convention is not in force, for example, Austria, existing national law and any relevant Conventions and bilateral agreements will continue to apply.

In the UK, the Brussels Convention was implemented in 1987 by way of the Civil Jurisdiction and Judgments Act 1982. Indeed, the Convention is annexed as a Schedule to the Act and accordingly has the force of law in the United Kingdom. The Convention has also become law in Belgium, Denmark, France, Italy, Luxembourg, the Netherlands, the Republic of Ireland and West Germany. Spain ratified the Brussels Convention on 1 February 1991. Although at the time of writing no national law has been implemented in Spain in relation to the Brussels Convention, its terms are in force.

The 1991 Protocol relating to the Brussels Convention on Jurisdiction and Enforcement of Judgments in Civil and Commercial Matters 1968 (Luxembourg) gives the EC Court of Justice jurisdiction to interpret the Brussels Convention. Each of the countries who signed or acceded to the Brussels Convention have signed and ratified this Protocol.

1.2 Parallel Convention

On 16 September 1988 in Lugano the EFTA countries (Austria, Finland, Iceland, Norway, Sweden and Switzerland) entered into a Convention on

Jurisdiction and the Enforcement of Judgments in Civil and Commercial matters with the Member States of the EC ('the Lugano Convention'). The Lugano Convention contains materially the same provisions as those of the Brussels Convention. The Convention will not come into force until it has been ratified by one EC country and one EFTA country. At the time of writing France has ratified it and it seems likely that the Netherlands and Switzerland will implement it on 1 January 1992.

1.3 Hague Convention on the Law applicable to Product Liability 1973 ('the Product Liability Convention')

This Convention applies to international cases of product liability and designates the applicable law whether or not this is the law of the State party to the Convention. At the time of writing, the Convention is in force in France, Luxembourg, the Netherlands, Norway, Spain and Yugoslavia.

The Product Liability Convention sets out choice of law rules which constitute a rather complex system consisting of traditional conflict rules with certain refinements aiming to balance the interests of each party to a product liability case. It applies to claims brought by any legal person irrespective of whether or not they are a consumer. The provisions of the Product Liability Convention stand side by side with those of the Brussels Convention, the former dealing with choice of law and the latter dealing with jurisdiction and enforcement of judgments.

1.4 Unification of International Sales Law (the Hague Conventions and the Vienna Convention)

The Uniform Law on the International Sale of Goods (ULIS) and the Uniform Law on the Formation of Contracts (ULFC) for the International Sale of Goods were adopted at the Hague in 1964 (together referred to as 'the Hague Conventions'). The former seeks to unify the substantive law of international sales, in particular the obligations of the buyer and seller, and the passing of risk. The latter attempts to reconcile the differences of the common and civil law on offer and acceptance leading to the conclusion of an international contract.

One of the defects of the ULIS from an international conflicts of law standpoint is that article 17 provides that where the Convention does not expressly settle questions concerning matters it is intended to govern, the courts must decide them 'in conformity with the general principles on which the Convention is based'. With respect to private international law, article 2 prohibits the courts from applying this except under special circumstances. Since this Convention is not as comprehensive as other civil codes, and fails to lay down an explicit statement of the general principles upon which it is supposedly based, the courts have been unable to promulgate general principles which are essential for analogy to their particular systems of law.

The Hague Conventions are given effect in the UK by the Uniform Laws on International Sales Act 1967. Since the Vienna Convention does not apply in the UK, this Act will apply to cases of international sales of goods brought before the UK courts.

The number of countries which have ratified the Hague Conventions is disappointingly small.[2] As a result a further Convention, namely the Convention for the International Sale of Goods, was approved in Vienna in 1980 ('the Vienna Convention'). The Vienna Convention came into effect on 1 January 1988 between (inter alia) the USA, France and Italy, but, at the time of writing, has not been signed by the UK nor introduced into English law by way of an Act of Parliament. It has been acceded to or ratified by Austria, Denmark,[3] West Germany, Norway and Sweden (in part).[4] The Vienna Convention shall enter into force in Spain on 1 August 1991. It is intended to be the centrepiece of international harmonisation of trade laws, setting out to provide a unified system of law which attempts to meet the many demands of international commerce. In particular, it governs the formation of contracts for international sales, controls the transfer of goods, lays down the obligations of seller and buyer and addresses the issue of allocation of risk. Unlike the Hague Conventions, the Vienna Convention provides that national law is to be referred to wherever possible, but that it is to be supplemented, where necessary, by the rules of private international law.

1.5 UN Convention on the Limitation Period on the International Sale of Goods ('the Limitation Convention')

This Convention was signed on 14 June 1974 in New York. It was amended by a Protocol on 11 April 1980, the same day that the Vienna Convention was approved. The Protocol aligns the provisions of the Limitation Convention with those of the Vienna Convention. Of the European countries, only West Germany and Norway have ratified or acceded to the Limitation Convention at the time of writing.

The Limitation Convention will replace in the countries which sign and enforce it a variety of conflicting national laws which provide limitation periods ranging from six months to 30 years. The basic aim of the Convention is to establish a uniform time limit that prevents the pressing of claims at such a late date that evidence has become unreliable.

The Convention limits to four years the period in which a buyer or seller may bring an action based on a contract for the International Sale of Goods. However, the Convention, as amended by the 1980 Protocol, does not apply to sales to which the Vienna Convention does not apply, which will continue to be governed by relevant national periods of limitation.

The Convention sets out when the limitation period begins and ceases, when it can be extended, how it can be modified by the parties, and how it is

2 Notably Belgium, West Germany, Italy, Luxembourg, the Netherlands and the UK.

3 The Vienna Convention was brought into force in Denmark on 1 March 1990, except for Part II which concerns formation of the contract. The Convention shall not, however, apply where both contracting parties have their places of business in Denmark, Finland, Iceland, Norway or Sweden.

4 Arts 1–13 and 25–88 apply as Swedish law from 1 January 1989, except in cases where both parties have their place of business within the Nordic countries.

calculated. In the case of a breach of contract of sale, the limitation period begins on the date of the breach. When the buyer finds a defect in the goods supplied or discovers that they do not otherwise conform to the terms of the contract, the limitation period starts from the date of delivery or when he refused to accept delivery.

The Convention provides that the limitation period ceases to run when one party brings judicial proceedings against the other. When a party making a claim is prevented by circumstances beyond his control from starting legal proceedings, he may have a one-year extension from the time when those circumstances cease to exist. The overall limit for extensions of the limitation period is ten years from the date when the period began to run.

1.6 EC Convention on the Law applicable to Contractual Obligations ('the Rome Convention')

This was adopted by the Council of the EC on 19 June 1980 in Rome. Its object is to provide in all Member States of the EC uniform rules for the ascertainment of the law governing an international contract. The Rome Convention will apply from April 1991 to France, Italy, Luxembourg and West Germany. It is already in force in Belgium and Denmark. The provisions of the Rome Convention were introduced into UK law in April 1991 by the Contracts (Applicable Law) Act 1990.

The Convention regulates not only conflict situations between the laws of the Member States but also cases in which the law of a Member State conflicts with that of a non-Member State. It establishes two principles:

(a) if the parties agree at the outset which country's law should apply, then that choice will be upheld;

(b) if no such choice has been made, the law of the country which is the most closely connected with the contract will apply. A set of principles has been established to make this work in practice.

1.7 Summary of international Conventions

The practical result of the current state of play of enforcement of the abovementioned Conventions is that most questions of jurisdiction, recognition and enforcement will be governed as between Member States of the EC by the Brussels Convention and as between EFTA countries by the Parallel Convention. The choice of law in tort will be governed by the private international law of the relevant country which may be a party to the Product Liability Convention. The 'proper law' of a contract will increasingly be ascertained pursuant to the Rome Convention, as more states implement its provisions in their national law. Until a state does so implement, the 'proper law' of a contract will be determined in accordance with the private international rules of the country in question.

Many international sales contracts will be governed by the Vienna Convention and national laws relating to periods of limitation. Certain such contracts will be governed by the Hague Conventions and the Limitation Convention.

2. THE CONSIDERATIONS WHEN BRINGING AN INTERNATIONAL CLAIM

If a plaintiff is injured by a defective product which has been, for example, manufactured in France, he may be faced with a choice of countries in which to bring his claim.

The four principal considerations which a plaintiff should bear in mind when deciding in which court to bring his action are:

(a) Does the court in question have jurisdiction to hear his claim?
(b) Will that court accept jurisdiction (or will it grant a stay of those proceedings)?
(c) Will a judgment obtained from that court be enforceable elsewhere? and
(d) Which law will the court apply in deciding the claim?

A consideration of these questions will dictate the most appropriate forum in which the plaintiff should bring his claim.

The first consideration is dealt with in section 2.2, below; the second is dealt with in section 2.7, below. The third question is dealt with in section 2.8, below and the fourth question is dealt with in section 3 of this chapter.

2.1 Choosing the forum in which to bring the claim

The plaintiff's choice of forum may be affected by various procedural and substantive factors such as:

(a) How much will it cost and might I have to pay the cost of the defendant's lawyers if I lose?
In Belgium, the legal costs are never recoverable from the unsuccessful party, whereas in England a proportion of them may well be. In France, the awards for legal costs are minimal and bear no real relationship to the actual fees paid to lawyers. Further, before French appellate courts, the parties must retain an 'avoué' in addition to an 'avocat'. Avoués are intermediaries having a monopoly as regards procedural aspects of the appellate proceedings. Avoués are by statute paid a percentage of the amount involved in the litigation and their costs are always borne by the losing party.
In Switzerland, the practice of solicitors charging their clients is regulated by Cantonal law preventing lawyers from charging excessively. As a general principle, the losing party before a Swiss court will have to pay court costs and the winner's lawyer's fees.
(b) Am I eligible for legal aid or is there any other means available of financing my claim? *In Switzerland, persons in financial difficulties may be relieved from paying court costs.*

(c) What type of damages are recoverable and are awards for those heads of damages usually substantial in the court in question?
For example, damages granted by Belgian and Swedish courts are relatively low.
The Swiss Private International Law Act expressly provides that an award rendered by a Swiss court based on foreign product liability may not exceed the amount that could be awarded under Swiss law.

(d) Is my case likely to be heard before a jury or a judge?
Many believe that a claim brought by an individual against a corporate defendant is more likely to be treated sympathetically by a jury.

(e) How long will it take for my case to be heard?
In Belgium and Italy, the 'judicial overdue' has become critical.

(f) To what extent will I be able to appeal against any decision made?

(g) How good are the lawyers and the judges considered to be in the country in question?

(h) How much tactical advantage can I gain by causing inconvenience to the defendant?

(i) What are the private international laws of the country in question and, perhaps more importantly, is the court likely to consider at length whether it is the appropriate place to conduct the litigation?

(j) Which, if any, of the international Conventions described earlier are in force in the country in question?
For example, the Product Liability Convention may enable a claimant in the Netherlands to recover interim damages within approximately one month of initiating the claim.

(k) What are the rules relating to obtaining information before the trial?
In England, there are usually no opportunities to ask a court to order disclosure of information to see whether legal action may be worthwhile. However, in a product liability case brought before the English courts, an application can be made to the court for an order for inspection of property, which may become the subject of legal action. A potential plaintiff may also apply to the court for disclosure of documents, such as medical and hospital records, before the action starts.[5]
In Switzerland, the earliest moment a party can generally be forced to produce documents or disclose information is during evidence procedures, taking place after both parties have completely filed their written statements. Exceptions to this rule are where a contract relied on the disclosure of certain specific information, or if certain evidence is in danger of being lost.
In France, it is quite common for an expert to be appointed prior to the action on the merits, who will carry out an adversary investigation often involving all parties to the litigation and their legal advisers. The expert usually submits a written report to the court which, although not binding, normally carries considerable weight.

(l) What are the rules relating to discovery of documents?
In product liability actions, discovery is a burden mainly on defendants. While it is useful to have details of a plaintiff's financial claims and his

5 Supreme Court Act 1981 s 33, RSC Ord 24, r 7A and Ord 29, r 7A.

medical record, this task is small compared to the duty of, for example, the manufacturer, who must disclose all documents relating to the development of a product over many years. The court will only order further discovery where it is necessary in the interests of justice or to save costs but a manufacturer's data will almost always be seen to be centrally relevant.

The common law jurisdictions in Europe in general allow for greater discovery than civil law jurisdictions. For example, a party to litigation in France must 'spontaneously' submit to the other parties all documents which he intends to use at a trial. Although there are rules whereby a judge may subpoena a party to produce a specific document and impose fines upon him if he fails to comply, in practice this procedure is rarely used. In Switzerland, subpoena orders are available against both the other party to the action and third parties, although they must be very specific. A party's refusal to comply with such an order may be taken into account by the court when making judgment.

In an English product liability claim, the court may order third parties who are not defendants to give discovery.[6] *This contrasts with other English litigation where third parties can only be required by a subpoena to produce material to bring to the trial.*

In the German civil procedure law, no party has an affirmative duty to help inform the court or the other party of the objective facts of the case. There are a few statutory provisions which grant a right to obtain information explicitly, but none of these provisions is of importance with respect to product liability cases.

(m) To what extent will my claim be reported in the press or other media?

(n) If there are other individuals with similar claims, can I bring a 'class action' in one jurisdiction?
For example, in England and Switzerland, class actions cannot be brought to claim damages. In England, a 'representative' plaintiff can act where numerous people 'have the same interest' but not where the claim is by plaintiffs to recover damages for themselves individually, rather than for the group as a whole.

(o) Will any experts and any other persons I wish to call as witnesses be available in the country in question?

(p) Are the courts in the country in question generally sympathetic towards the kind of claim I am going to bring? How predictable is the result of my claim?
In Germany, it is generally considered that the success or failure of a claim is fairly predictable.

(q) Has the country in question implemented the Directive by way of national law? If so:
   (i) When was the defective product put into circulation?
   The Directive does not apply to products put into circulation before the date on which the national implementing law came into force. Until that date, existing national law will apply. As can be seen from the foregoing chapters, there are many differences between these

6 Supreme Court Act 1981 s 34.

laws. For example, in France, Luxembourg and Belgium, the producer is strictly liable for any defects in his product. In Ireland and the United Kingdom, the consumer must prove negligence. In Austria, Belgium, Denmark and West Germany, the burden of proof is reversed in the consumer's favour. In Danish law, the distributor of a product has a right of indemnity against its manufacturer, which cannot be excluded for product liability falling under the national legislation implementing the Directive. A distributor may therefore seek to insist on Danish law applying to his contract with the manufacturer, and the manufacturer on the other hand may wish to resist this.

(ii) Has the national implementing law derogated in one of the three ways permitted by the Directive? (See the 'compare and contrast' Schedule on p 523 for details of derogation, if any, by the countries dealt with in this book.)
Namely, does the national law permit liability for primary agricultural produce and game, has the 'development risks' defence been provided for and has a financial ceiling on damages payable for death or injury caused by the same defect been adopted? The effect of implementing legislation in relation to this last derogation will be reviewed in 1995 and there is a possibility that Member States will be required to change their substantive laws at that time.

(r) If the country in question has not implemented the Directive by way of national law, what are the national laws relating to contract, tort and product liability?
For example, the Spanish General Act for Consumers (GAC), unlike the Directive, does not expressly provide that the retailer may avoid liability by informing the consumer of the identity of the producer or the person who supplied him with the product. Furthermore, GAC article 28 provides a very strict liability system for certain products which leaves the producer with few, if any, grounds for defence. Also, the GAC does not expressly provide the defences set out in article 7 of the Directive; moreover, the producer must prove he acted with sufficient diligence and that he complied with all the relevant regulations.

(s) Has the limitation period for bringing my claim expired in the country in question?
In Norway, the limitation period can be up to 20 years from the date when the product left the producer's control. In France, the designation of a court-appointed expert will often interrupt the limitation period.

2.2 Jurisdiction

Since most of the countries dealt with in this book have adopted or acceded to the Brussels Convention, its provisions will be considered in some detail. The jurisdiction of the courts of those countries which have not implemented the Brussels Convention or the Lugano Convention will be determined by the private international laws of the country in question. For example, under the Swiss Private International Law Act, foreign producers and distributors can be sued at their foreign domicile or, if the product causes damage in Switzerland, at the place where the product causes harm. However, there is no specific Swiss jurisdiction for contract claims against foreign sellers and therefore no such claim can be brought in the Swiss courts in the absence of an applicable treaty or the foreign defendant having a domicile or branch in Switzerland.

In the new system for establishing jurisdiction provided by the Brussels Convention, there is very little scope for judicial discretion, which previously played a significant role in common law jurisdictions. Thus, for example, if a plaintiff brings proceedings before an English court of competent jurisdiction, that court is not permitted to decline to hear the case on the grounds of *forum non conveniens* – ie that some other forum is more 'appropriate', in the sense of more suitable for the ends of justice. Incidentally, most continental European jurisdictions never accepted this doctrine, although Dutch appellate courts are obliged to apply it.

2.2.1. Domicile

The cornerstone rule on jurisdiction contained in the Brussels Convention is that a defendant may be sued in the State where he is domiciled. The Convention does not provide any definition of domicle. The domicile of an individual and a company is broadly ascertained as follows.

i. Individual. The question of whether an individual is domiciled in a particular country is determined by the national laws of that country. Since the laws relating to domicile have not been harmonised throughout Europe, a person could be held to be domiciled in two countries simultaneously according to each of the relevant laws.

In the UK, a person will be domiciled there if he has been resident for a period of three months or more prior to the commencement of proceedings.

In France, the domicile of a citizen is the place where he has his 'main establishment'.

In Belgium, the domicile of a citizen is separately defined for judicial purposes as the place where he is principally registered as resident in the local population register. Belgian law requires all persons resident in Belgium to be so registered, although the place where they are registered may not necessarily be the place where they are actually resident.

In Germany a person is domiciled in the city where he lives for most of the time. In practice, this is usually the city where the person is registered with the police, as required by law.

In Denmark, Norway and Sweden, a person is domiciled where his permanent home is situated (ie the place where his belongings are normally situated and where he usually lives).

In Austria, a person's domicile is the place where he has settled down with the proven intention, or the intention which results from his circumstances, of permanently residing.

ii. Company. Article 53 of the Brussels Convention provides that the seat of a company shall be treated as its domicile. However, in order to determine that seat, the court shall apply rules of private international law. The seat of a company in English law is defined in broad terms as being where it has its registered office, or where its central management and control are exercised. However, a corporation is not to be regarded as having its seat in a contracting State other than the UK if it is shown that the courts of that State would not regard it as having its seat there.[7]

In Denmark, the domicile of a company is where its main office is situated. If the domicile of a company has to be determined pursuant to the Brussels Convention, the Danish court will refer to the judicial system according to which the company was founded for the answer.

In Italy, France, Norway and Portugal, the mere fact of a company having its registered office (and conducting business) in the relevant country will mean it is considered domiciled there.

In Austria, a company is domiciled where it has its seat, which will normally be entered on the commercial register. If it is not so registered, the seat of a company is where its administration is located.

In Spain, a company is domiciled in the place stated in its byelaws. In the absence of such statement, it is domiciled in the place of its headquarters.

In Germany, a company is domiciled where it has its seat. If the company has a branch, then there is a choice between the place of the branch and the place of the seat, if the branch was involved in the claim.

In Norway, in addition to bringing claims based on domicile, it is possible to bring a claim against a person or company that owns any property in the country.

The imposition of the 'domicile' of the defendant principle can, in certain cases, actually lead to a restriction in the plaintiff's choice of forum. For example, French courts could, in the past, take jurisdiction over a non-resident manufacturer on the grounds of the French nationality of the plaintiff under article 14 of the French Civil Code unless precluded under a binding international Convention. Article 3 of the Brussels Convention specifically excludes this rule in cases involving parties domiciled in a contracting State, and therefore this exorbitant jurisdiction can only be taken in relation to manufacturers not domiciled in a contracting State (as construed by the French courts). Further, a French plaintiff may be considered as having expressly waived the benefit of article 14 through the effect of a valid jurisdiction or arbitration clause. An implied waiver could be established, for instance, on the ground that the plaintiff had instituted action or voluntarily entered a counterclaim before a foreign court on the same cause of action as the one before the French court.

2.2.2 Jurisdiction clauses

Article 17 of the Brussels Convention permits the use of choice of jurisdiction clauses and sets out the formal requirements for their validity. The agreement of a specific jurisdiction must be in writing, or evidenced in writing, or agreed by way of commercial practice of which the parties are or ought to have been aware. The effect of this article is that a valid jurisdiction clause confers exclusive jurisdiction on the chosen court or courts, provided at least one of

7 Civil Jurisdiction and Judgments Act 1982 s 42.

the parties is domiciled within the EC. However, if the jurisdiction clause was for the benefit of only one of the parties then that party will have the right to bring proceedings in another Member State's courts if it has jurisdiction by virtue of the Brussels Convention. Certain national laws preclude the exclusion of their own jurisdiction. For example, article 2 of the Italian *Codice di Procedura Civile* provides that jurisdiction can only be excluded for disputes between a non-national and a national non-resident.

In Portuguese law, the choice of jurisdiction must be expressed in writing, in the same form as is required of the contract it relates to (for example, since a contractual loan must be notarised, the choice of forum clause must also be notarised).

2.2.3 *Jurisdiction if no jurisdiction clause*

The Brussels Convention provides that, if there is no agreement as to jurisdiction, the courts may exercise:

(a) general direct jurisdiction;
(b) special jurisdiction;
(c) additional jurisdiction; or
(d) exclusive jurisdiction.

i. General jurisdiction. As stated above, the fundamental principle set out in the Brussels Convention is that, if a defendant is domiciled in the EC, the court of the country of his domicile will be the only one competent to entertain claims in civil and commercial matters. The rule of only one court being competent to entertain a claim is extended so that if proceedings involving the same cause of action between the same parties are pending in the courts of one contracting State, any court in another contracting State shall decline jurisdiction over that case on its own motion. If 'related actions' are brought in the courts of different Member States, the second court has a discretion to order a stay (see section 2.7, below). Actions are 'related' if there is a risk of irreconcilable judgments of the two courts concerned with the same matter.

A victim within the EC of a defective product manufactured outside the EC will always be able to bring an action in the EC provided the relevant country has implemented the Directive and is a party to the Brussels Convention, as there will be an importer treated as a producer for the purpose of the Directive. If the plaintiff cannot identify the importer, then the supplier becomes liable unless he in turn can identify the importer.

Plaintiffs outside the EC seeking to sue EC producers will have to look at their national rules and Conventions to establish whether they can bring those producers into their own jurisdiction. In the case of EFTA countries, the Parallel Convention may be applicable. In Austria, the Act on Consumer Protection provides that the parties to a contract can only agree upon the jurisdiction of a court where the consumer either lives or works.[8] However, the consumer is free to choose any other forum which is provided for by private international law if he wishes to institute proceedings against a producer.

8 Konsumentenschutzgesetz-KSchG s 14.

ii. Special jurisdiction. Under article 5 of the Brussels Convention, in certain circumstances the plaintiff will have alternative fora available in which to bring his claim.

(a) *In contract*, the courts for the place of performance of the obligation in question will also have jurisdiction. The national court, using its own rules of private international law, must decide upon the place of the performance. It would appear that the word 'obligation' is given a wide meaning with the result that a company entering into a contract to be performed in a Member State accepts the jurisdiction of that Member State's courts over any dispute arising out of the contract, whether it be for a primary or secondary obligation. In a product liability claim, this probably means the place of sale or, if different, the place of delivery.

(b) *In tort*, the courts for the place where the harmful event occurred will also have jurisdiction. The European court has interpreted 'harmful event' in the widest possible way[9] to refer both to the place where the damage occurred and the place of the event giving rise to it. Accordingly, it seems that where the act occurs in one Member State and the damage occurs in another Member State, the plaintiff has the option of suing the defendant in the courts of either State, as well as the State where the defendant was domiciled, if this happened to be different. For example, a Dutch court assumed jurisdiction on the basis of article 5(3) of the Brussels Convention in a product liability case over a German manufacturer who had shipped rolls of underfelt to a wholesaler in the Netherlands, where the goods caused damage to a Dutch business purchaser.[10]

iii. Additional jurisdiction. Additional fora are available in matters relating to insurance and to consumer transactions involving the grant of credit to the consumer.

iv. Exclusive jurisdiction. Certain cases in which the national courts of the contracting states to the Brussels Convention have exclusive jurisdiction, regardless of domicile, are listed in article 16 of the Convention. They include, among others, any proceedings concerning the enforcement of foreign judgments.

2.2.4 Consumer claims

Article 14 of the Brussels Convention makes a special provision for jurisdiction when a consumer brings proceedings. This provides that a consumer may bring proceedings against the other party to a contract either in the courts of the contracting State in which the latter is domiciled or in the courts of the contracting State in which he is himself domiciled. So, for example, a Dutchman who buys an English manufactured toaster which causes a fire in his home could bring proceedings in either the Netherlands or England against the manufacturer.

9 Case 21/76 *Bier v Mines Des Potasse European Court* [1976] ECR 1735 (30 November 1976).
10 Zwolle 18 February 1976, (1976) 23 NILR 364.

It follows that a component supplier may not even be aware of the destination of the final product, yet faces possible liability under less favourable laws than either in his own domicile or in that of the manufacturer of the finished product. For example, the 'development risk' defence may be ineffective when a victim uses the Convention rules to bring his case in a country such as Luxembourg, which has not adopted that defence.

2.2.5 *Civil jurisdiction when criminal proceedings are brought against a defendant*

A 'civil action' procedure exists in many European countries (most notably France, but also Austria, West Germany, England and the Netherlands, where it seems to be of far less practical significance) whereby an aggrieved party may intervene in the course of a criminal trial in order to claim damages or other civil law remedy from the accused, in respect of the latter's alleged civil wrong. This civil wrong, which may be negligence, must have arisen from the same facts as those on which the criminal charge is based. The courts seem to have favoured a negligence per se approach in this type of action, namely that the victim need only establish the causal relationship between non-compliance with the statute and the damage. This civil procedure allows the plaintiff to avoid undergoing the procedural burdens of mounting separate civil proceedings in that country's courts, and to enjoy certain evidential benefits through the criminal and inquisitorial nature of the main action (the court eventually delivering judgment in the civil action at the same time as deciding on the criminal cause). It follows that, for example, English defendants prosecuted elsewhere within the EC, may find themselves doubly in jeopardy through civil proceedings being mounted on the back of criminal prosecutions brought by the State.

In the UK, victims of a crime who have sustained personal injury as a result of the crime may in certain circumstances be able to recover relatively small amounts of compensation.[11]

2.2.6 *Interim jurisdiction*

Article 24 of the Brussels Convention provides that a plaintiff may apply to the courts of the contracting State for provisional, including protective, measures even if, under the Convention, the courts of another contracting State have jurisdiction as to the substance of the matter. This means that courts of all contracting States possess jurisdiction to exercise their national law powers to grant the protective measures – for example, Mareva injunctions – notwithstanding that jurisdiction to do so would otherwise be lacking on other Convention grounds. For example, if a Belgian takes certain medicines when on holiday in Portugal which have been manufactured in Spain by a Spanish company, he may choose to bring his main claim against the manufacturer in

11 Such a claim is formally made to the Criminal Injury Compensation Board. If a victim has sustained other types of damage as a result of a crime, the prosecutor may ask the judge to make an award for damages against the defendant to compensate the victim. However, it would appear rare for the manufacture or supply of a defective product which causes injury to constitute a crime, and therefore the occasions upon which a plaintiff might recover on this basis in the UK are limited.

Spain. However, he may, pending the determination of the main action, seek an injunction in Portugal to prevent the distribution of the dangerous drug.

2.3 Branch/agency considerations

Article 5(5) of the Brussels Convention provides that a person domiciled in a contracting State may, in another contracting State, be sued as regards a dispute arising out of the operations of a branch, agency or other establishment, in the courts of the place in which the branch, agency or other establishment is situated. It is the location (and appearance of permanence) of the branch, agency or other establishment, and the fact that its operations gave rise to the claim, which form the connecting factors justifying the jurisdiction of the court for that place. It is irrelevant whether or not the subject matter of the dispute has any direct connection with the courts.

The words 'branch, agency or other establishment' have been held to imply an undertaking which must have the appearance of permanency, management and be 'materially equipped' to negotiate business with third parties so that they would not have to deal direct with head office.[12] An independent distributor or sales representative would not come within this rule.

2.4 Co-defendants

Article 6 of the Brussels Convention provides that if there are ongoing proceedings in a State, a party domiciled in another contracting State can be made a joint defendant or third party to those proceedings. However, the proceedings cannot be used solely with the object of obtaining jurisdiction over a target defendant.

In a product liability claim, the manufacturer and original supplier of the product or its components might be joined as a defendant or third party in the same proceedings. Jurisdiction over the manufacturer or original supplier of products will be established by article 6 irrespective of whether the person or company in question is domiciled in that jurisdiction in accordance with the domestic law of that jurisdiction. For example, if an Italian buys a French car in Italy which is defective, he may choose to sue the Italian car dealer in Italy. It may not be clear before initiating proceedings whether the car was defective as a result of the Italian car dealer improperly servicing it before sale, or whether the fault lay with its original French manufacturer. The Italian plaintiff may in these circumstances consider suing both the Italian car dealer and the French manufacturer as potentially liable suppliers of the defective car. For such a combined action to lie, it is not necessary that each defendant be charged with a tort: the Italian could sue the car dealer on the contract in Italy and obtain jurisdiction in Italy in tort over the foreign manufacturer.

The effects of articles 5 and 6 of the Brussels Convention may be substantial, not only on jurisdiction but also through the private international laws of the forum, on choice of law. Further, these articles may have a significant effect

12 *Somafer SA v Ferngas* [1978] ECR 2183.

under the Convention's enforcement rules (see later), on enforcement of a judgment given, for example, in Belgium against an Irish manufacturer, in Ireland or, indeed, any other EC country.

It may often be the case that since in many product liability cases at least one prospective defendant is established within the EC country in which the plaintiff is domiciled, the Convention will often permit litigation of the whole case in that country.

2.5 Insurance

Articles 7–12 of the Brussels Convention make specific provisions in relation to the insurance industry. Insurers domiciled in a contracting State may be sued in that State, or the courts of the contracting State where the policyholder is domiciled, or if he is a co-insurer, the courts of the contracting Start in which proceedings are being brought against the leading insurer. When the insurer is the plaintiff, he may only bring proceedings in the courts of the contracting State where the insured is domiciled. However, in the UK, Schedule 4 to the Civil Jurisdiction and Judgments Act 1982 contains no equivalent to these specific provisions. It follows that internal UK jurisdiction in direct insurance actions is governed by the same rules of Schedule 4 as apply to non-insurance proceedings brought under the Civil Jurisdiction and Judgments Act 1982.

2.6 Summary

The practical effect of the Directive and the Brussels Convention is that when there are alternative jurisdictions available, a plaintiff will have a choice as to the court in which he brings his claim for product liability. Once judgment is obtained, it can be enforced in any other Member State, even though no judgment could have been realistically anticipated against that defendant had the proceedings originally been brought in the country where the enforcement is to be undertaken. So, for example, a French plaintiff injured in Luxembourg by an exploding television manufactured in Germany, might choose to sue the German manufacturer in Luxembourg (as being the place where the harmful event occurred), since the 'developments risk' defence is not available there. If he were to obtain judgment, it could be enforced against the defendant in Germany, irrespective of whether the defendant could have avoided the claim by successfully pleading the 'developments risk' defence, had the claim originally been brought there.

2.7 Restraint of proceedings

In certain circumstances, a Member State court may stay an action brought in that court or may restrain the prosecution of foreign proceedings. The principles upon which the English court will either grant a stay of English proceedings or an injunction to restrain a party from prosecuting outside England are now quite distinct.

The English court will only grant a stay of proceedings where it is satisfied that there is some other available forum in which justice can be done between the parties at substantially less expense or inconvenience. The stay must not deprive the plaintiff of a legitimate personal or juridical advantage which would be available to him if he involved the jurisdiction of an English court.

The Brussels Convention provides that once a court of an EC Member State is seized with a dispute, no other court of an EC Member State shall accept or issue proceedings related to the same dispute.

In most cases, even where the Convention applies, the courts of more than one state will have jurisdiction. However, the Convention was designed to avoid such duplicity of proceedings. Article 21 provides that, in such circumstances, the court 'first seized' with the action shall have jurisdiction. The question when a court was 'first seized' will depend upon the law of the State in which the court is situated and different rules can apply. Thus, for example, an English court is seized of an action when the writ is issued in the court offices, whereas the French court is not seized of the action until proceedings are served on the defendant. The matter is further complicated by the rule that a party domiciled in a contracting EC State may also be sued in the courts of another contracting State which would not have jurisdiction save that the party concerned is one of a number of defendants, one of which is domiciled in that state. The outcome is that an inventive plaintiff can obtain a tactical advantage by foisting proceedings on an opponent in an unexpected European court.

Where the case falls within the Brussels Convention, the English court *must* decline jurisdiction if the proceedings involve the same cause of action and are between the same parties and the courts of another contracting State have been first seized of the action. The English courts *may* stay its proceedings where the courts of another contracting State have been first seized of a related action which has not been the subject of a judgment.

It is unclear whether an English court which has jurisdiction under the Brussels Convention and in which proceedings have commenced may stay those proceedings on the ground that a court in another contracting State is more appropriate. It is generally thought that where the Convention confers jurisdiction on the English courts, there is no question of a discretion to stay the proceedings in favour of the courts of another contracting State except pursuant to the specific rules relating to pending actions in the Convention. However, in a recent Court of Appeal case[13] where the defendant to proceedings initiated in England whose subject matter came within the Brussels Convention was domiciled in England, but there was a conflict of jurisdiction between the English court and a State which was not party to the Convention, the English court retained its discretion to stay or strike out the proceedings before it on the basis of the doctrine '*forum non conveniens*'. This doctrine is not generally accepted in civil law jurisdictions, although certain Dutch cases have applied it and, indeed, Dutch legislation specifically applies it in appeal cases.

In general the burden of proof of a more appropriate forum rests on the defendant who is seeking the stay of proceedings but the evidentual burden rests on the party who asserts the matter; if the plaintiff asserts a legitimate, personal or juridical advantage, the burden to prove this falls on him. If the

13 *Harrods (Buenos Aires) Ltd* (1991) Times, 11 January.

court decides that no other available forum is clearly more appropriate, then it will usually refuse to grant a stay. Where the English court has jurisdiction it is usually reluctant to disturb it without good reason. If the court concludes that there is some other available forum that is clearly more appropriate, a stay will be granted unless justice requires otherwise, in which case it must be established that the plaintiff would not obtain justice in a foreign jurisdiction.

To satisfy the English courts that there is a more appropriate forum it is not enough merely to show that England is neither the natural nor appropriate forum but another forum must be clearly and distinctly established as more appropriate. The factors which point to another forum being more convenient and less expensive may be the availability of witnesses, the location of parties and their business, and the law governing the transaction. This list is not exhaustive; the fundamental test is with which forum 'did the action have the most real and substantial connection?'

Once the defendant has proved that a more appropriate forum exists, the plaintiff may oppose the stay on the grounds that he will not obtain justice in the foreign jurisdiction. The plaintiff must overcome the burden of proof and show that he has 'a legitimate personal or juridical advantage'. This in itself is not decisive as the case must be tried in the light of the interests of all the parties and for the ends of justice. Typical of the advantages that plaintiffs have pleaded under this heading include damages being awarded on a higher scale, more complete procedural discovery, and a more generous time limitation period, but the mere fact that the plaintiff has a procedural advantage in England is not always sufficient in the light of the interests of all the parties.

In Portugal, the courts will not give up jurisdiction in matters regarding real property rights in connection with property situated in Portugal, actions for insolvency and bankruptcy, actions concerning industrial relations and actions regarding rights of which the parties may not freely dispose (eg political rights).

The basic principle which determines whether an injunction may be granted by an English court to restrain a party from pursuing foreign proceedings is that if the interests of justice so require, an injunction will be granted. The court does not consider the appropriateness of either forum but for a substantial degree of hardship contrary to the interests of justice. The parameters of the 'interests of justice' are not fixed; however it has been stated that the English court will 'restrain the plaintiff from pursuing proceedings in the foreign court if such pursuit will be vexatious or oppressive'. Mere unreasonableness will not do.

2.8 Recognition and enforcement of judgments

Under the Brussels Convention, a judgment given in a contracting State shall in general be recognised in the other contracting States without any special procedure being required. However, a judgment shall not be recognised if such recognition is contrary to public policy in the State in which recognition is sought. The cases when a decision is considered to be contrary to public policy are rare. Under no circumstances may the foreign judgment enforced pursuant to the Brussels Convention be reviewed as to its substance.

The Brussels Convention provides for a standard procedure by which a judgment given in one contracting State may be automatically enforced in another contracting State. This additional element of Convention regulation is as vital as that concerning jurisdiction discussed earlier, since ability to proceed against foreign producers and importers under the Brussels Convention would be significantly reduced in impact, if it were not also possible to have a judgment obtained against them in the national courts enforced against their assets situated in other contracting States.

The Brussels Convention is very wide in its scope and is not limited to judgments of superior courts or to money judgments. It also appears that the Convention covers any judgment of a contracting State whether the defendant is domiciled inside or outside the contracting State. So, a judgment rendered by a French court against a German defendant could, if appropriate, be enforced against its assets in Spain.

In order to enforce a judgment, the plaintiff must apply to the court of competent jurisdiction. The procedure for obtaining enforcement in a particular country usually depends upon whether the Brussels Convention applies, whether some reciprocal enforcement Convention applies or whether no Convention applies. For example, Norway has entered into bilateral agreements relating to enforcement of judgments with Great Britain, Germany and Austria.

In England, an application for the enforcement of a judgment to which the Brussels Convention applies is made first to a procedural judge known as a Master on an *ex parte* basis. The application must be accompanied by an affidavit supporting the registration of the judgment, together with a copy of the judgment and proof that it can be enforced in the country in which it was made. Execution on a foreign judgment registered in the High Court in England may issue in the same way as on an English judgment. Where the foreign judgment is not enforceable under an international Convention or bilateral agreement, a fresh cause of action will be the foreign judgment itself.

In Spain, whenever there is no particular applicable Convention and no reciprocity with the country whose courts have issued the relevant judgment, an application for enforcement of a foreign judgment should be filed before the Supreme Court. This court reviews whether the relevant requirements are fulfilled and decides upon whether the judgment should be enforced. An application may take up to one year to be determined.

In Belgium, foreign judgments are enforceable once their execution has been authorised by the endorsement of a *formule exécutoire*. An application to enforce a judgment to which the Brussels Convention applies must be made to the *Tribunal de Première Instance*. A copy of the foreign judgment must be produced, together with the translation into the language of the court. Once the judge has satisfied himself that the requirements of the Brussels Convention have been fulfilled, he will grant an order for enforcement in the form of a judgment of the Belgian court. If the Brussels Convention does not apply, the precise procedure to be followed will depend upon whether or not another convention applies and, if so, its terms. If there is no applicable enforcement convention, the Belgian court will re-examine the merits of the case and refuse to allow enforcement if the trial judge appears to have erred in fact or law.

In Denmark, foreign judgments are enforceable once their execution has been authorised. If a foreign judgment falls within the Brussels Convention, the judgment creditor applies in the first instance to the *Fogedret*. The documentation lodged with the application will often be accepted in English. Before the Brussels Convention came into force in Denmark, the only foreign judgments that were directly enforceable were those of other Nordic countries. Judgments of the courts of other countries were enforceable only by bringing a fresh action in the Danish courts. This is still the case for judgments not falling within the Brussels Convention. In such an action, the foreign judgment has only an evidential effect.

In France, foreign judgments are enforceable once their execution has been authorised by the endorsement of a *formule exécutoire*. If the Brussels Convention applies, the judgment creditor makes an application for an order that the judgment be endorsed. The application is made to the President of the *Tribunal de Grand Instance* for the district in which the defendant is domiciled or, if he is not domiciled in France, the district in which the assets to be seized are located. The original judgment or an authenticated copy of it must be produced together with proof that the judgment is enforceable in the country in which it was pronounced and that it has been served on the judgment debtor. The judgment and other documents need to be translated only if the judge so requires. If the Brussels Convention does not apply, nor any other bilateral or multilateral convention, a foreign judgment can only be enforced if an order for its enforcement is obtained from the *Tribunal de Grand Instance*. The other documents required are the original judgment, or an authenticated copy, evidence of service, and evidence that the judgment is enforceable in the country of origin. Certain conditions must be shown, including that the foreign court had jurisdiction in respect of the subject matter. Provided that these conditions are satisfied, there is no examination of the factual or legal merits of the foreign judgment.

In Germany, foreign judgments are enforceable by the same means as are available in respect of German judgments once their execution has been authorised by the endorsement of a *Vollstreckungsklausel*. If the Brussels Convention applies, the judgment creditor applies in writing for the judgment to be enforced. The application will usually be decided without an oral hearing by the presiding judge of the relevant Chamber of the *Landgericht*. The foreign judgment and supporting documentation must be accompanied by a German translation. If the Brussels Convention does not apply, the foreign judgment may be enforced after proceedings for an order for its enforcement have been brought in the *Amstgericht* or the *Landgericht* for the area of the defendant's domicile or where the assets are located. If there is no enforcement Convention with the country in which the judgment was given, the foreign court has jurisdiction according to German rules of private international law and if the judgment was final. The German court will authorise the judgment's enforcement if a German judgment would be enforced in that country. The court will also examine the judgment process both as to its form and its content, but will not reconsider the merits of the case.

In Ireland, a foreign judgment to which the Brussels Convention applies is enforced by obtaining an order for its enforcement on an *ex parte* application to a procedural judge known as a Master of the High Court. The person against whom the judgment is given is then served with notice of enforcement together with a copy of the order. If the Brussels Convention does not apply, Irish law does not provide any special procedure for the enforcement of foreign judgments, and Ireland is not a party to any other Convention providing for the recognition or enforcement of foreign judgments in civil and commercial matters. The defences to an action for enforcement are limited, the most important of which is that the foreign court does not have jurisdiction.

Foreign judgments are enforceable in Italy by all means available in respect of Italian judgments once their execution has been authorised by the endorsement of a *formula esecutiva*. If the Brussels Convention applies, a certified copy of the foreign judgment is filed with the *corte d'appello* for the district of the defendant's domicile or, if he is not domiciled in Italy, the *corte d'appello* for the district where execution is to take place, together with certified copies of the other documents required by the Convention. A sworn translation of the judgment and other documents must be attached. In the absence of multilateral or bilateral Conventions, the recognition and enforcement of foreign judgments is governed by the provisions of the *Codice di Procedura Civile*, which lays down certain requirements, the most important of which is that the foreign judgment has been given by a court which had jurisdiction over the case according to the principles of Italian law and jurisdiction.

In Luxembourg, foreign judgments are enforceable by the same methods as are available in respect of Luxembourg judgments, once their execution has been authorised by the endorsement of a *formule exécutoire*. If the Brussels Convention applies, this can be obtained by means of a request to the President of the *Tribunal d'Arrondissement* of the area in which the debtor is domiciled. The judgment which is to be enforced and its accompanying documentation must be in French or German, or be accompanied by a translation into one of those languages. This procedure has been extended to the enforcement of judgments from any country with which Luxembourg has a bilateral Convention. If a judgment is not covered by the Convention, nor any other bilateral or multilateral Convention, proceedings for enforcement of a foreign judgment are brought in the *Tribunal d'Arrondissement* for the area in which the defendant is domiciled, by serving an assignation on the defendant, as in an ordinary action. Certain conditions apply for recognition. If these are satisfied, the court is precluded from considering the merits of the foreign judgment and will authorise its enforcement.

Foreign judgments are enforceable in the Netherlands by all the means available in respect of Dutch judgments, once their execution has been authorised by an order of the court (an *exequatur*). When the foreign judgment is covered by the Brussels Convention, the judgment creditor must apply for permission to enforce the judgment to the President of the *Arrondissementsrechtbank* for the place either of the debtor's domicile or, if the debtor has no domicile in the Netherlands, where the judgment is to be enforced. Once the judge has authorised enforcement, the creditor is given notice of the *exequatur* by means of a letter. The foreign judgment with the *exequatur* is then served on the judgment debtor. A foreign judgment cannot be enforced in the Netherlands unless it is covered by the terms of an appropriate enforcement Convention. If no such Convention applies, a fresh action must be brought in respect of an original claim, but the foreign judgment may have evidential effect in that action.

The system of recognition and enforcement of judgments provided by the Brussels Convention has many advantages over national enforcement rules and those contained in bilateral enforcement Conventions. These can be summarised as follows:

(a) An application for enforcement is *ex parte*, which means that the other party is not summoned to appear. This preserves the element of surprise in favour of the applicant (article 34(1)).
(b) Courts of contracting States requested to recognise and enforce a judgment are not generally required, nor even entitled, to examine whether the judgment court properly exercised jurisdiction, nor to question the substantive correctness of the judgment requested to be enforced (articles 28(3), 29 and 34).
(c) The grounds upon which a court may refuse to recognise or enforce a judgment are limited. The list of grounds includes recognition being contrary to public policy, lack of proper service of process on the defendant and irreconcilability of judgments sought to be recognised (articles 27 and 28). The courts of most European countries, and in particular West Germany, France and Norway, are reluctant to refuse to enforce a judgment on the grounds of public policy. Indeed, in France the courts will generally refuse to recognise a judgment only where the result of the application of the foreign law would be particularly unjust. The courts in Italy, by contrast, frequently invoke the doctrine of public policy, which is embodied in article 31 *Preleggi* to the Civil Code.
(d) The documents in support of an application for recognition and enforcement are specified, and where possible, reduced in number and simplified (articles 46 and 47).
(e) Possibilities of appeal against a decision in relation to enforcement are limited (articles 37, 40 and 41).

3. CONFLICT OF LAWS

Once a plaintiff has settled on a jurisdiction in which to bring a claim, the court seized with the action must then determine which law it will apply in determining the claim. The rules relating to choice of law will depend upon whether the claim is brought in contract, tort or product liability.

As a result of the implementation of the Directive in Europe, with its near strict liability, it is likely that most claims brought by individuals for personal injury resulting from defective products will in the future be brought in product liability or tort, rather than in contract. However, in certain jurisdictions, the availability of an action in contract may preclude one in tort or product liability. In English law, a claim under Part 1 of the Consumer Protection Act 1987 is in tort (section 6(7)).

In English, Danish, Spanish and Swedish law, even if it is clear that a claim is governed by a foreign system of law, the judge or arbitrator has no obligation to ascertain the rules of that legal system. They regard foreign law as a question of fact which has to be proved to their satisfaction by expert witnesses or other admissible evidence. If a party fails to produce such evidence, national law will be applied. Consequently, a party to proceedings brought in any of these countries will plead foreign law only if this is to his advantage; otherwise it is cheaper for him to have the issue decided in accordance with domestic law. This is unlike the position in many continental European countries, such as, for example, Austria, the Netherlands and Portugal, where judges and arbitrators have to ascertain the foreign law, which in their view applies, *ex officio*.

3.1 The law governing product liability

The law applicable to a claim brought in respect of a defective product will be determined either by the rules set out in the Product Liability Convention (if the country in question has signed, acceded to or ratified the Convention) or by the rules of private international law in respect of tort of the relevant country.

3.1.1 The Product Liability Convention

As stated earlier, the Product Liability Convention sets out choice of law rules. The system of choice contained in the Product Liability Convention provides that a supplier's product liability is determined by the law of the country where certain pairs of connecting factors are located. These pairs are selected from among four connections, viz the place of injury, the victim's habitual residence, the place of business of the supplier and the place of acquisition of the product. If no relevant coincidence of factors is found, the law of the defendant's place of business applies, unless the claimant prefers the place where the harmful event occurred. The Convention provides that the place where the harmful event occurred shall be the place of injury, thereby excluding the possibility of interpreting this to mean the place where the defendant's action occurred which caused the harm. Unfortunately the meaning of the term 'place of injury' is left open. It may be that the place of the first impact of the act on the victim is regarded as material if subsequent elements of the tortious occurrence as a whole are located in different countries, although this is not conclusive.

A supplier may, however, challenge the applicability of either a place of injury combination or a habitual residence combination if he establishes that he could not reasonably have foreseen that the product would be marketed in the relevant state. The interpretation of this rather novel notion is entrusted by the Product Liability Convention to national courts. Furthermore, safety standards of the country of marketing may be taken into account.

The Convention applies whether the proceedings are brought in contract or in tort. However, the Product Liability Convention does not overcome the traditional tort/contract dichotomy whereby claims in tort and contract are treated differently. As a result, concurrent claims in contract and tort are regulated by different conflict rules even if both claims were to result from the same product damage and were to involve the same parties in the same proceedings. The other major defect of the Convention is it makes no provision for plurality of litigants. The procedural complications of the application of different laws in regard to different defendants in the same proceedings are obvious.

3.1.2 Specific product liability rules

The Swiss Private International Law Act expressly deals with the law governing a product liability claim, allowing the consumer the choice between the law of the producer's domicile and the law of the place where the product was purchased.

3.1.3 Product safety standards

Another question which may be raised in an international product liability context is 'which country's product safety standard should apply?' For example, the State in which production takes place may completely prohibit the use of a certain chemical substance in a food product, whereas the State to which such food is exported may only require that a maximum content be observed. To the extent that there is a conflict of applicable standards, it may be resolved by considering the class of persons whom the statutory rule on its construction intends to protect, and giving only those persons the benefit of its safety standards. So, for example, the UK Health and Safety at Work etc Act 1974 is intended to protect those persons who use articles 'at work'; it seems that a reasonable construction would be to give effect to the statute wherever the incriminated article was so used or destined for such use, ie England.

3.2 Choice of law in tort

A wrongful act abroad can be actionable in England if it is both a tort in the law of the country where the act was done and in English law. This private international law differs from that of many other countries, including France and Germany, where the act need only be a tort in the place in which the wrongful act was committed.

However, a particular issue between the parties may be governed by the law of the country which, in respect of that issue, has the most significant relationship with the occurrence and the parties. For example, in *Boys v Chaplin*,[14] the plaintiff and defendant were both normally resident in England but were involved in a motor accident while temporarily stationed in Malta in the British Armed Forces. Under Maltese law, the plaintiff could only recover special damages for his expenses and proved loss of earnings, which in the circumstances were minimal. By English law, he could also recover general damages for pain and suffering, which were quite significant. The House of Lords granted damages for pain and suffering, albeit their reasons for doing so were conflicting. Lord Wilberforce stressed the need to segregate the relevant issue of heads of damage and consider whether, in relation to that issue, the general rule stated above should be departed from. In this case, it was held such grounds existed as both parties were normally resident in England and only temporarily present in Malta. If both parties, or only the defendant, had been Maltese residents, the decision would probably have been different.

14 [1971] AC 365.

4.2.1 The place of wrong

It may not always be easy to ascertain in which country the act is done. For example, if a company negligently manufactures dangerous pharmaceutical products in Spain which are used with harmful results in Portugal, where has the tortious act occurred? At one time, the tort was held to have been located at the place where the defendant acted[15] (ie in this example, Spain). It was later held to be located at the place where the harm ensued (ie in this example, Portugal). The modern English approach appears to be to look at the sequence of events constituting the tort and to ask: 'Where in substance did the cause of action arise'?

For example, in *Distillers Co (Biochemicals) Ltd v Thompson*,[16] the Privy Council in England, sitting as an appeal court from New South Wales, was faced with the question of jurisdiction of the Supreme Court of New South Wales, over the English manufacturers of a sedative containing Thalidomide. The facts assumed for the purposes of the appeal were broadly that Distillers Co (Biochemicals) Ltd was an English company carrying on business in Great Britain, one of whose products was a sedative and sleep-inducing tablet, the principal ingredient of which was thalidomide. The thalidomide had been obtained in bulk by Distillers from German manufacturers. The tablets were sold to an Australian distributor which marketed and sold them in Australia with the advertising matter and in the form supplied by Distillers. The accompanying printed matter described the drug as a sedative with no side effects.

The plaintiff was the infant daughter of a woman who had taken the drug; the child had been born with certain physical defects. The plaintiff claimed damages against Distillers and the Australian distributor.

The characterisation by the court of the alleged tort in this case is rather hard to support logically. The tablets, printed matter and the package were supplied as a unit by Distillers to the distributor in a form in which they were to reach the ultimate consumer. Yet the Privy Council was forced by its formulation of the jurisdictional rule to characterise the act of negligence as the failure to give a warning that the tablets could be dangerous if taken by an expectant mother in the first three months of pregnancy. The failure, the court said, had taken place in both England and in New South Wales and therefore the plaintiff's cause of action arose within the jurisdiction of New South Wales. Thus, the tort was characterised as negligent failure to warn, rather than negligent manufacture. This case has since been applied by the Court of Appeal in England.[17]

Although it is not clearly established, the English courts tend to apply the 'substance' test to determine the place of the tort. Adoption of such a test avoids the mechanical solution inherent in an outright choice between the place of acting and the place of harm. It is also sufficiently flexible to take account of factors such as the nature of the tort alleged to have been committed and the material elements of the relevant tort, and will, without undue rigidity, enable the court to locate the tort in one place with a choice of law.

European case law reflecting trends in general tort choice of law is somewhat sparse. The lack of international cases reported in highly industrialised

15 *Abbot-Smith v University of Toronto* (1964) 45 DLR (2d) 672.
16 [1971] AC 458.
17 *Castree v E R Squibb & Sons Ltd* [1980] 2 All ER 589, [1980] 1 WLR 1248.

Western Europe suggests that the great part of such product liability claims are settled out of court. The Norwegian Supreme Court decided a case involving a Norwegian woman who allegedly died through using a contraceptive pill made by a German pharmaceutical drugs manufacturer.[18] Lengthy discussions were devoted to the medical evidence and the claim ultimately failed for lack of a reasonable likelihood that the injury and death were caused by the use of the drug. Since no consideration appears to have been given to the choice of law issue, it must be assumed that Norwegian law was tacitly deemed applicable.

In Germany, a statutory rule applies if the plaintiff is a German national, namely that torts committed abroad between Germans are subject to German law.[19] The highest German court has upheld this rule in postwar cases involving collisions between German ships outside German territorial waters.[20] It is disputed whether the rule is generally still valid, notably if the German parties involved do not, or one of them does not, habitually reside in Germany. If both do, then German law is deemed to apply. This rule is analogous to the one in English private international law established by *Boys v Chaplin* discussed earlier.

In Portugal, Italy, and usually in the Netherlands, an action brought in tort will be determined in accordance with the law of the place where the principal act which caused the damage occurred.[1]

In Belgium, the applicable law for a claim in tort is the law of the place where the defendant acted.

3.3 The law governing the contract

3.3.1 Introduction

According to English law, a contract is governed by the law which the parties intend to apply to their agreement or, if they have not formed such an intention, the law with which the contract is most closely connected. The international Conventions mentioned earlier do not exclude the possibility of a conflict of national laws in the field of international commercial transactions. To solve such conflicts, the courts must turn to private international law. Private international law differs from one country to another (for example, in Portugal, in the absence of any express intention, the law of the common habitual residence of the parties or, failing that, the law of the place where the contract is concluded, shall apply) and it is not within the scope of this chapter to deal in detail with those laws of each of the countries discussed in the earlier chapters of this book. Expert legal advice should be sought in the relevant jurisdiction.

Incidentally, submission to the law of a particular legal system does not necessarily mean that there is a submission to the jurisdiction of the courts of that country.

18 Hoyesterettsdom, 14 November 1974, (1974) NRr 1160.
19 *Verordnung* of 7 December 1942, RGB1 1, 706.
20 BGH, 2 February 1961, 34 BGH 7 222.
1 Portuguese Code of Civil Procedure art 45(1).

Although it is usual to talk of the proper law of the contract, it may be that one particular aspect of the contract is governed by one legal system and another aspect governed by another law. The proper law of the contract may thus be split by applying the laws of different countries to various aspects of the same contract.

3.3.2 Express choice of law

It is advisable for parties to a contract to provide expressly which legal system they desire to be applied to their contract to avoid ambiguity. The parties may submit their contract to any legal system which they choose and, in particular, they are not limited to a legal system with which the circumstances surrounding their contract have an actual connnection. In certain civil law jurisdictions, such as Italy, any clause which purports to exclude Italian law or the jurisdiction of the Italian courts must be specifically agreed to in writing by the parties. In practice, words acknowledging specific agreement to the relevant clause are added at the end of the contract and the parties sign after these words of acknowledgment, in addition to signing the main contract.

However, the discretion of the parties to elect the law applicable to the contract is not usually entirely unlimited. The parties must exercise this discretion bona fide and for a legal purpose. Although in theory parties to a contract in Italy may agree to any applicable law, in practice, particularly in the case of a contract between Italian nationals, the *Cassazione* has declared a foreign choice of law clause invalid for reasons of public policy. French law allows its nationals to contract out of applying domestic law, provided that the reason for their so doing is not to avoid the application of certain mandatory rules.

In the UK, the mandatory provisions of the Unfair Contract Terms Act 1977 cannot be contracted out by a choice of law clause adopting foreign law in certain circumstances. Also, in Denmark certain acts, for example, in relation to maritime and transport law, cannot be contracted out of by the parties. In Austria, a choice of foreign law shall not apply if it is incompatible with the basic principles of Austrian law, which in practice is considered by the Austrian courts to occur very rarely. The mere fact of a foreign law deviating from certain mandatory Austrian regulations will not render the foreign law inapplicable. Certain regulations cannot be contracted out of in Austria, such as restrictions on the transfer of money, import-export restrictions, and the requirement that the sale of land to a foreigner has to be approved by the Austrian authority.

In Germany, there are no restrictions with regard to choice of law clauses in contract except where they are used in consumer agreements. In Belgium, the 'Belgian international public policy' sets out rules which are defined as essential for moral, political and economic security and which necessarily exclude the application of a different or contrary provision. However, there have, in practice, been few cases where public policy has been applied. In Switzerland, Swiss law will apply if the seller is domiciled in Switzerland or if the parties have chosen Swiss law.

Incidentally, a recent UK Court of Appeal case held that a provision that disputes arising under a contract should be referred to 'British' courts was an unequivocal reference to English courts, and inferred that the parties intended that the proper law of the contract should be English law.[2]

3.3.3 *Inferred choice of law*

Where the parties do not expressly state which law shall govern their contract, it may be possible to gather their intention from other contract clauses. For example, in a contract for insurance of ships where the insurance is effected in the USA, and the policies contained a 'follow London' clause which began 'assurers herein shall follow Lloyd's Underwriters and/or British insurance companies in regard to amounts, terms, conditions, alterations, additions, extensions, endorsements, cancellations, surveys and settlements of claims hereunder', the English Court of Appeal held that this clause revealed the intention that English law should apply.

3.3.4 *The most close connection*

If the parties have not stated the law which is to govern their contract and if their intention cannot be gathered from the terms of the contract itself, the courts will ascertain the legal system with which the contract is most closely connected. All the circumstances surrounding the contract have to be examined to ascertain that law, including the form of the contract, the place where the contract was concluded, the place where the contract is to be performed, a submission to arbitration, the situation of the funds which are liable for the discharge, a connection with a preceding transaction and the effect attributed to the transaction by a particular legal system.

3.3.5 *The Rome Convention*

This Convention will replace the national rules of the signatory States on what is the 'proper law of the contract'. It will effect both domestic contracts and international contracts worldwide. It regulates not only conflicting situations between the laws of the Member States (including, for example, conflicts between the laws of England and Scotland), but also cases in which the law of a Member State conflicts with that of a non-Member State. The Rome Convention does not apply to certain commercial transactions such as questions relating to bills of exchange, cheques and promissory notes, to agreements for arbitration or the choice of a court, to insurance contracts covering risks situated in an EC country, to the internal law of companies or to trusts. It also does not apply to the determination of certain legal questions, the most important of which for the purposes of this chapter is whether an agent is liable to bind a principal to a third party.

2 Komninos FT Law Reports, 16 January 1991.

As stated earlier, two basic principles are adopted by the Rome Convention. The first is that the proper law of the contract shall be the law intended by the parties. The second is that, if the parties have failed to choose the proper law, it shall be the law with which the contract is most closely connected. These two principles are the same as those outlined earlier as developed by the English courts. However, since the rules provided by the Rome Convention for the application of these principles may sometimes lead to results different from those at which current English law would arrive, its forthcoming enforcement in the UK will result in certain changes in the law taking place.

With regard to the first basic principle, the Rome Convention imposes similar restraints on the freedom of choice as exist in English law, for example, the parties cannot contract out of the mandatory provisions of the law of a particular country if all the other elements at the time of the choice are connected with that country only.

With regard to the ascertainment of the law of the closest connection, the Rome Convention establishes a rebuttable presumption that the law shall be the law of the 'characteristic performance'. This is a concept so far unknown in most common and civil law jurisdictions although it has been impliedly accepted in the Netherlands by certain decisions of the *Hoge Raad*. The law of characteristic performance is not the law where performance has to be carried out but is the law of the place where the party who has to effect the characteristic performance has his seat of business. For example, in a contract of sale, the characteristic performance is effected by the seller who has to deliver the goods, and not by the buyer who has to pay the price, and therefore the law of the seller's country will apply.

It appears that the Rome Convention will not enhance legal certainty, as was no doubt intended. For example, article 4(2) provides that if a contract, in which no choice of law is made by the parties, is to be performed by a branch office, the applicable law will be that of the country where the branch office is situated. This can lead to considerable uncertainty, particularly when dealing with multi-national companies who use contracts which leave it open to the multi-national to use any of its branch offices or subsidiaries for the performance of the contract.

Articles 5 and 6 of the Rome Convention provide special rules relating to certain consumer contracts and individual employment contracts. A consumer or an employee shall not be deprived by a choice of law of the parties of the protection afforded by the mandatory rules of the country in which he has his habitual residence. The Convention also provides that the application of a rule of foreign law, which by virtue of the Convention would generally apply, may be refused if such application is 'manifestly incompatible' with the public policy of the forum.

A controversial provision of the Rome Convention is article 7(1) which states that, when applying the law of the country, the judge may give effect to the mandatory rules of another country with which the situation has a close connection 'if and so far as, under the law of the latter country, those rules must be applied whatever the law applicable to the contract'. The extension of the effect of mandatory rules goes beyond the effect of those rules in the law of the country with the closest connection and might even admit the extra-territorial effect of mandatory rules of the third country. The justification for this is the 'public interest' of the domestic law. The far-reaching provisions of the US with regard to anti-trust embargoes, the freezing of assets and restrictions of resale to foreign countries may be given further effect.

The Convention allows contracting States to reserve the right not to apply this controversial article and the UK exercised the right of reservation when signing the Convention. The UK Contracts (Applicable Law) Act 1990 and the Luxembourg Law of 27 March 1986, which implement the Rome Convention in the respective national laws, exclude article 7(1). However, neither Denmark or France exclude article 7(1).

Whatever law is applicable by choice of the parties or otherwise, consumers will remain protected by the mandatory rules of their country of residence in respect of purchases which were made at home from a foreign supplier's agent or on the strength of his local advertisement or direct offer, and even in respect of purchases made abroad if their shopping visit to another country was arranged by the seller.

3.4 Tort and contract

In some cases, the defendant may be liable for breach of contract as well as in tort, and then it may be possible for the plaintiff to bypass the question of where the tort was committed by framing his claim in contract. For example, in England, a railway passenger who has paid for his ticket and is injured in a railway accident can sue the British Railways Board either in contract or in tort. The plaintiff cannot, of course, rely on a contract, for example, if at the time of a motor accident he was the driver's guest. However, in certain jurisdictions, such as France, a plaintiff cannot sue both in tort and in contract. If the plaintiff has a contractual link with the defendant his action must be founded solely in contract. In fact, even where the plaintiff is an end-user with no direct contractual link with the defendant producer, it is now settled case law that his claim will also lie in contract if brought in France.

3.5 Renvoi

When any of the above private international rules, applied to the circumstances of a given case, direct that the case be determined in accordance with the law, for example, of Germany, then the term 'law of Germany' usually means the domestic law of Germany. However, it may sometimes mean any system of law which the German courts would hold applicable to the particular case. This ambiguity in the expression 'law of Germany' gives rise to the difficult problem of renvoi. There are in practice very few cases on the point and it is rarely specifically pleaded in international cases. Indeed, renvoi is expressly excluded by the Vienna Convention. However, Austrian courts are obliged by section 5 of the Austrian Law on International Private Law (IPRG) to apply the doctrine of double renvoi (that is, they will look to the private international law of the country to whose law they refer).

4. SHOULD FORUM SHOPPING BE ALLOWED?

Disquiet has been expressed by English judges[3] as to the amount of litigation which the subject of forum shopping has created. It has been pointed out that parties to a dispute may choose to litigate in order to determine where they shall litigate.

Forum shopping has been defined as 'a plaintiff bypassing his natural forum and bringing his action in some alien forum which would give him relief or benefits which would not be available to him in his natural forum'. Unfortunately this definition raises as many questions as it answers. What is the natural forum? Is it the forum with which the dispute is most closely connected or the forum in which it can be resolved most conveniently? Is it necessarily objectionable to bring proceedings in an alien forum if that forum is one of the established centres for the resolution of disputes and offers specialised services or facilities not available in the natural forum? Is there any need to control forum shopping unless the plaintiff's principal object is to harrass the defendant or the alien forum is, in normal circumstances, highly inappropriate?

Outside the courts, two main arguments have been advanced for controlling forum shopping.

The first is that it may result in unfairness to the defendant. This implies that it is always the defendant who must be protected from abuse of the system by the plaintiff. This is not always the case. Defendants who try to put off the day of judgment, or drive the proceedings to a forum where they will have an advantage, are not unknown.

The second argument against forum shopping is based on public interest. It is said to be wasteful of the time of witnesses and others. It is also said to be unfair to the interests of local inhabitants whose actions may be delayed as a result of the courts being clogged with foreign actions.

The advantage of forum shopping in the area of product liability is that it increases the protection of consumers and other plaintiffs by giving them a greater scope of recourse against defendants.

5. CONCLUSION

It has been seen that the Directive imposes liability upon a number of parties, namely producers, own branders, importers from outside the EC and, in certain cases, suppliers. The national laws of most EC states implementing the Directive provide that where two or more persons are liable for the same damage, their liability is joint and several. The availability of jurisdiction in respect of joint defendants, who may not otherwise be capable of being proceeded against, may therefore be of special importance in bringing claims for defective goods.

The relatively recent regulation of both product liability on the one hand and jurisdiction and recognition and enforcement of judgments in Europe on the other, form part of a broader process of improving and harmonising legal protection and recourse to remedies for consumers within the EC. This is of

3 For example, Lord Templeman in *The Spiliada* [1985] 2 Lloyds Rep 116.

increasing importance as national barriers to trade and commerce are being removed as part of the process of creating the 'four freedoms' in the European Community, namely free movement of goods, capital, services and workers, which is often referred to as '1992'.[4]

4 I would like to thank each of the contributors to this book for their assistance in preparing this chapter by advising me in relation to the laws and legal systems of their countries.

CHAPTER XVIII

Product liability insurance

D A Thomas Esq

Willis Corroon Limited
Willis Wrightson House
Wood Street
Kingston-upon-Thames
Surrey KT1 1UG
England

Tel ++ 44 81 787 6290
Fax ++ 44 81 943 4297

CHAPTER XVIII

Product liability insurance

1. INTRODUCTION

Product liability law is complex and the responsibilities faced by those who introduce products to the marketplace are great.

Product liability insurance has a key role in risk management strategy in relation to the product liability exposure.

A clear understanding of the scope and limitations of product liability insurance is necessary if risk management planning is to achieve its objectives.

This chapter will outline the cover available from the insurance market and will explore some practical aspects of placing, underwriting and structuring a product liability insurance programme.

The viewpoint from which this is written is that of the London insurance market, which is still the most influential in Europe. There are differences in insurance practice within different countries in Europe. These are highlighted in the relevant country chapters. There are, however, many factors which are working to reduce or eliminate these differences. Product liability law is converging within the European Community. Many businesses operate across borders and wish to purchase insurance on the same basis in all territories. Many insurers do business in more than one country.

A product liability policy is a contractual promise made by an insurer in return for a premium payment to make good certain defined losses suffered by the insured.

In addition to the normal legal rules governing the making of contracts, there are some important principles which apply to insurance contracts including product liability insurance.

First, there must be an insurable interest, that is, the insured must be at risk of some financial loss in the event of the circumstances insured by the policy arising.

This does not usually cause problems in the case of liability policies as the establishment of a legal liability in respect of any event gives the insured an insurable interest in that event.

A liability insurance policy is a contract of indemnity. The insured may not recover more than his actual loss. This again does not cause difficulties as the measure of loss is an award or agreed settlement with a third party.

There is in connection with all insurance contracts a duty of disclosure. When asking an insurer to provide a quotation for product liability insurance all facts which are material to the risk must be disclosed. Information will be considered material if it can be demonstrated that it would have affected an insurer's acceptance of the risk or the terms and conditions of the quotation. Failure to disclose material information could allow the insurer to avoid the policy.

The duty of disclosure revives at each renewal of the policy. In addition there may be specific conditions within the policy requiring notification of certain changes of risk during the policy period.

The principle of subrogation applies and may often be significant in product liability insurance. Where an insured receives an indemnity from an insurer the insurer may then take over the insured's rights against any other parties that may be responsible for the loss. For example, the manufacturer or supplier of a defective product may be liable for an injury under the Consumer Protection Act and have to pay compensation. However, the defect in the product may have been the result of a defective component supplied by a sub-contractor. The insurer would then be subrogated to the insurer's rights and could endeavour to recover his outlay from the supplier.

2. THE PRODUCT LIABILITY POLICY

Product liability insurance normally forms part of a general liability policy covering public, product, and sometimes in the UK, employers' liability claims. The product liability insurance may be a separate section within the policy or the public and product liability insurance may be integrated.

For the purpose of examining the cover it will be more straightforward to treat the product liability insurance as if a separate policy had been issued. There is not, however, a standard product liability policy used by all insurers. Each insurer will have their own form and indeed many individual insured may have specially negotiated wordings. There are therefore many variations of cover to be found. Current practice also varies considerably in different European countries.

Whatever the detailed variations a product liability policy will tend to follow the same basic construction. A typical policy will have:

(a) a schedule;
(b) a recital clause;
(c) an operative clause;
(d) policy definitions;
(e) policy exceptions;
(f) policy conditions.

Each of these will be examined in turn in relation to the specimen policy.

The recital clause in one form or another appears in all policies and usually makes reference to a proposal form. The wording of this clause makes the proposal the basis of the contract. In practice, particularly with large and complex risks, a proposal form may not be completed and the insurer will rely on detailed information supplied by the proposer or his broker. This is examined in more detail under the section dealing with practical aspects of placing and underwriting. The recital clause will also make reference to the payment of premium by the insured.

The operative clause defines the scope of the policy indemnity. There are two alternative forms of operative clause which affect the way in which the product liability cover operates. These are usually referred to as the occurrence form and the claims made form. The occurrence form of cover, which is the most common, will be examined first. The way in which the claims made form of cover operates and its impact will be examined in a later section.

The product liability policy is concerned with the insured's legal liability for injuries and property damage.

Financial losses suffered by a claimant which flow directly from such injury or damage will also be covered. For example, if a piece of equipment is supplied to a factory and because of a defect causes a fire, the product liability policy would provide an indemnity both for the direct property damage to the factory and the consequential losses suffered by the owner of the factory because production is brought to a halt. The policy would not cover a situation where the equipment caused no damage but due to a defect did not function resulting in consequential losses.

A product liability policy is applicable to insureds who may be involved at any point in the chain of supply and who may incur a liability.

The injury or damage for which indemnity is provided by the policy must happen during the period of insurance. The time when an injured third party brings a claim is not relevant, what matters is when the injury or damage complained of took place. Some types of injury and damage may take many years to become apparent and for third parties to realise that they have a cause of action. An example in the area of production liability would be asbestos-related diseases. Exposure to the substance may cause injury which remains latent for 20 or 30 years. Insurers may find themselves paying claims on policies which are many years old in relation to such exposures. The insured on the other hand knows that once he has affected a product liability policy on this 'occurrence' basis he has protection against injury or damage that may be caused during that policy period even if cover is subsequently cancelled or not renewed.

2.1 Legal costs

The policy also provides cover for legal and other costs incurred in defending any claim and the costs of a successful claimant. This is not the least important part of the cover as costs may be very substantial. Even where a claim is successfully defended it may not be possible to recover all costs from the plaintiff.

3. DEFINITIONS

A product liability policy will contain definitions of certain words and phrases. The significant definitions that may be found in a product liability policy and their effect are described below.

3.1 The product

The definition of product will usually include containers' instructions and advice given in connection with the supply. This is important as a product may be correctly designed and manufactured and not in itself defective but may be rendered defective by inadequate or inaccurate instructions or advice.

3.2 The insured

The Schedule of the policy will include the name of the insured. This definition may be extended to bring others under the protection of the policy. For example, directors and employees of the insured. In some cases it may be necessary further to extend the definition by endorsement to include other categories of additional insured. For example, distributors of products may ask to be included as an insured.

3.3 Territorial limit

The territorial limit of the policy defines the geographical area within which injury or damage insured by the policy must occur. It is usual in the case of product liability for the territorial limit to be worldwide in respect of products manufactured or supplied by the insured businesses.

Occasionally insurers may seek to impose restrictions on the territorial limit. If this is the case the insured would have to consider carefully whether this is acceptable.

The geographical area most likely to be excluded is the USA. This is because of the particular problems associated with product liability in that jurisdiction. When assessing the impact of such an exclusion it is necessary to consider not only whether products are exported directly to any excluded territory by the insured but whether the insured's products could find their way to that area by some other route. The product may have been supplied to another manufacturer for incorporation into, for example, a motor vehicle. It may then be exported without the insured's knowledge. It is not unknown for companies to be involved in a product's liability action in the USA having never knowingly exported there.

3.4 Jurisdiction

The policy jurisdiction defines the geographical area within which the insurers will respond to legal actions. In most cases this will be the same as the territorial limits on the policy. It is possible, however, for the jurisdictional limit to be narrower.

It may be that injury or damage occurring anywhere in the world is covered but only if the legal action is commenced within the insured's domicile. This restriction would in some cases not provide adequate protection as a claimant may be able to bring a claim in particular circumstances in another jurisdiction (see Chapter 17).

It is more common for insurers to include a clause limiting the jurisdiction within which actions between the insured and the insurers may be heard in relation to disputes on policy cover.

3.5 The business

The business description is usually contained in the policy Schedule. The cover is limited to the described business and it is therefore vital that it is accurate and complete. The nature of the business undertaken is a major consideration in underwriting product liability insurance and any inaccuracy could result in insurers denying coverage. In many cases it is desirable to agree as general a business description as possible. For example, 'any activity undertaken by the insured'.

This does not, however, negate the duty of material disclosure. It is necessary to give insurers full information as to the business undertaken when cover is placed.

4. INDEMNITY LIMITS

There is usually in law no limit to the monetary amount of a claim that may be brought. A court award would reflect the legally recoverable losses of the claimant. A product liability policy, however, does have an indemnity limit which is the maximum sum the insurer will pay.

The product liability limit is usually expressed as being 'any one claim and in the aggregate during the period of insurance'. The indemnity limit is thus the maximum amount the insurer will pay during the policy period without regard to the number of claims. This is in contrast to public liability cover where the limit is usually expressed as 'each and every claim' with no limit on the number of claims. Insurers limit their exposure on product liability insurance because there could be many different claims arising from one defect which is reproduced in a product which is widely distributed. In the absence of an aggregate limit insurers are concerned that in these circumstances they could be liable for a multiple of the basic indemnity limit.

Legal costs incurred in defending claims are usually paid in addition to the limit of indemnity. On occasion, however, insurers may make the limit inclusive of costs, particularly where there is a North American exposure. This reflects the very high cost of litigation in that territory. In some circumstances the legal costs could equal or exceed the limit of indemnity being given under the policy.

The range of indemnities offered by one insurer may vary between £1m and £5m.

For many risks the indemnity limit offered by any one insurer may be insufficient.

Larger indemnities may be achieved by arranging for a number of insurers to accept part of the risk. This may be by co-insurance where each insurer writes a percentage of the whole limit or more usually by arranging excess layer policies.

Excess layer policies are separate insurance contracts that provide cover for claims which exceed the indemnity limit on the primary policy or on the total of the layers below. The excess layer policies should normally be arranged to follow the same terms and conditions as the underlying policies. Substantial limits may be built up with a series of excess layer policies; some insureds may buy limits exceeding £100m.

5. EXCLUSIONS

The limitations of cover or exclusions that appear in a product liability policy are of considerable importance in defining the cover provided by the underwriter. The insured has to demonstrate that a particular claim falls within the scope of the operative clause of the policy and it is for the insurer to prove the application of the exclusions.

Exclusions fall into three broad categories:

(a) those risks which underwriters consider are uninsurable or for which governments accept responsibility;
(b) those risks which are normally insured under separate policies by different segments of the insurance market;
(c) those risks which underwriters view as particularly hazardous. These exclusions may be negotiable on provision of additional information and possibly the payment of an additional premium.

The exclusions likely to be met in a product liability policy are described below. They are given in full in the specimen wording in the Appendix. The wordings can vary considerably from insurer to insurer with important differences in the effect of the exclusions.

5.1 War

This is the only exclusion which falls under the first category mentioned above. Its relevance to the product liability cover is limited.

5.2 Radio-active contamination

If products are supplied to nuclear installations a liability could arise to the operators of the site. In most countries the site operator would be responsible for any injury or damage occurring off site. Product liability cover is available from nuclear pool arrangements in most European countries. In the UK the British Insurers Atomic Energy Committee issues such policies.

5.3 Contractual liability

The product liability policy is a legal liability policy. The phrase legal liability encompasses all forms of liability at law including tort, statute and liability accepted in contract. It is usual for insurers' standard policies to contain a contractual liability exclusion. This is because the range and scope of agreements entered into by the insured could be very wide, exposing the insurer to extensive additional liabilities. It is usually possible to negotiate the elimination of this exclusion if information is provided as to the type of contracts normally entered into. There may be an additional premium charged and in some cases insurers might wish to see each contract before providing cover.

5.4 Repair, replacement and recall

Insurers will not pay for the repair, replacement or recall of the product which gives rise to injury and damage. This exclusion can give rise to difficulties, particularly where complex products which may consist of separate units are concerned. For example, a complete production line system may be supplied for a factory. An electrical failure in one small component could cause damage to the rest of the product supplied as well as the third party's building. A dispute may arise with insurers as to whether it is only the defective component which is excluded or the complete product supplied which is excluded. When placing cover it is important that the situation is addressed and agreement reached with insurers as to how such claims will be dealt with. It is sometimes possible to amend the exclusion so that only 'that part of the product' which gives rise to the claim is excluded.

5.5 Aviation products

Most product liability policies will have an exclusion of injury and damage caused by aviation products. This may be qualified by restricting its application to those products supplied knowingly by the insured for such purpose. Separate aviation product liability cover is needed where such products are involved.

The aviation insurance market has developed the special forms of cover and the capacity needed to deal with the extensive exposures presented by aviation products.

5.6 Advice, design and specification

Many policies will have an exclusion of legal liability arising out of the giving of advice, design work or specification for a fee where no product is supplied. This cover is normally available in a professional indemnity policy. The exclusion does not, however, apply where a product is actually supplied.

Even a manufacturer would need to scrutinise carefully his range of activities to ensure that this exclusion would not have an impact. It is increasingly the case that many contracts, particularly with Government organisations, fall into a number of stages. The potential manufacturer may at stage one have to submit design work for a new product and then at the second stage tender for the manufacture. It might be that the design is accepted but that the tender for manufacture goes elsewhere. If such an exposure does exist then a professional liability policy can be effected. It is however possible in some cases to negotiate with the product liability insurer to remove the exclusion and therefore provide the injury and damage element of the cover. There would still, of course, be no cover for pure financial losses which would still need to be insured in the professional indemnity market.

5.7 Other exclusions

There are a number of exclusions which appear in specific circumstances. For example, where there is an exposure in the USA or Canada punitive and exemplary damages may be excluded.

It would be usual where these territories are concerned to exclude all claims arising out of pollution. Where products are concerned it is sometimes possible to negotiate the retention of this cover.

Even where there is not a North American exposure insurers are becoming increasingly concerned about pollution exposures. Primarily this is in relation to public liability cover but certain products do represent a particular exposure. These may be potentially polluting chemicals or there may be equipment such as valves and tanks where failure could result in pollution damage. It is becoming increasingly common for coverage to be restricted to injury and damage caused by sudden and unintended pollution. This removes cover where there is a gradually operating cause.

There are circumstances in which insurers would apply exclusions of specific products. This arises where there is a known and substantial problem associated with that product and in effect insurers feel the exposure is uninsurable or is one that they in particular do not wish to underwrite. Many insurers would not be prepared to provide cover for claims arising from asbestos-related diseases. Certain pharmaceutical products with known problems are usually excluded.

Some types of product can cause injury and damage by remaining passive. A pharmaceutical product may fail to provide a cure. Equipment that is designed to provide a response in certain circumstances may not. Examples might be fire and burglar alarms and other warning equipment. In the case of pharmaceutical products it is extremely difficult, if not impossible, to obtain what is termed 'efficacy cover'. With other types of products there are insurers who are prepared to provide cover without an efficacy exclusion at additional premium.

6. POLICY CONDITIONS

Most, if not all, liability policies contain further clauses under the general heading of Conditions. Most conditions contained in the policy relate to particular circumstances in connection with claims and are therefore conditions precedent to liability and breach of the condition would not void the policy but enable insurers to avoid the particular claim. The most important conditions are as follows:

i. Reasonable precautions. This condition appears in most liability policies. Whilst it may appear out of place in a liability policy, which is designed to cover the insured's negligence, it could only be relied on by insurers in the case of reckless behaviour by the insured.

ii. Notice of claims. This condition is important since it requires that details of claims of circumstances which might result in a claim are reported quickly to insurers. It also stipulates that the insured should not admit liability or enter into negotiations in relation to the claim independently.

It makes it clear that the insurers are entitled to negotiate a settlement on behalf of the insured. A breach of this condition which would prejudice the insurer's position would be treated seriously. Late reporting of a claim could mean that important information becomes unavailable or witnesses are not traced and interviewed at an early stage.

The admission of liability and the negotiation of claims by the insured can result in settlements having to be made in circumstances where there might have been a defence if the claim had been handled properly from the beginning.

iii. *Cancellation*. This condition is rarely invoked. It would only be used in circumstances where perhaps insurers become aware of behaviour by the insured which may amount to a breach of one of the other conditions or a material non-disclosure and where they do not want to wait for a claim to arise before taking the point. It could, however, be invoked where the claims record deteriorates rapidly and unexpectedly and insurers simply want to avoid further involvement without waiting until expiry of the policy period. When negotiating policy cover it is a good idea if possible to extend the normal 30 days notice to perhaps 60 or 90 days. This would give adequate time to try and secure a replacement cover in the event of notice of cancellation being given.

7. THE 'CLAIMS MADE' PRODUCT LIABILITY POLICY

The operative clause described above is the occurrence form. The alternative basis is referred to as 'claims made'. Insurers have become concerned with the exposure represented by some types of product particularly, but not exclusively, where there is exposure in the US. Some products may cause undetected or latent damage over a long period of time. This has led to claims being made under occurrence product liability policies many years after the policy was written.

The claims made form of policy is designed to enable insurers to control their exposure to latent claim more effectively. On this basis the policy provides an indemnity in respect of injury and damage for claims which are made by third parties during the currency of the policy.

The injury or damage does not have to have occurred during the policy period. The policy may be subject to a retroactive date. There would then be no cover for claims made in respect of an injury and damage occurring prior to the retroactive date. The major disadvantage of this form of cover is that in the event of insurers not renewing cover there would be no insurance for events which may have already occurred but have not yet come to light.

From the insured's point of view a claims made policy does mean that the current limit of indemnity applies to claims even when the damage which resulted in a claim occurred many years ago. With an occurrence form the limit of indemnity in force at that time may have been totally inadequate.

The use of the claims made form for products liability in the UK is still relatively rare except in the case of pharmaceutical products, chemical products and certain heavy exposures in North America. It is more common in some European countries.

It is likely that in the long term insurers will endeavour to make more use of the claims made form of cover and limit their exposure to the open-ended occurrence form.

With a claims made form the claims reporting additions are particularly critical. If the insured is aware of a claim and does not report it within the policy period cover could be lost.

8. PLACING AND UNDERWRITING THE PRODUCT LIABILITY RISK

It has already been said that product liability insurance normally forms part of a policy including the public liability risk.

It is true to say, however, that in many cases it is the product liability aspect of the risk which will be the focus of the insurer's attention when underwriting. It is still common with smaller risks for a proposal form to be completed by the insured giving the information required by the underwriter. With larger and more complex risks it is often the case that an underwriting submission is prepared by the insured's broker who will have carried out a thorough investigation of the insured's business and identified those areas which are of most interest to the underwriter.

The underwriter will be seeking to understand the nature of the business and to assess the premium he requires for future risks based on past experience of the proposed risk and his product liability account as a whole. Within Europe there is no marketwide statistical base which can assist the underwriter. Each insurer has to rely on the information he holds himself.

In forming a view of any particular risk there are a number of key areas of information which the underwriter needs. This information will form the basis of the contract and as has already been seen it must be accurate and complete.

The business description and details of the products manufactured or supplied is perhaps the most important information. The insurer will want to see product brochures and, in some cases, technical descriptions. The range of hazards that need to be assessed are considerable.

One proposer may be merely distributing a relatively low hazard product such as office furniture. He may have a liability for the products as he is in the chain of distribution but the main liability may well rest either with the manufacturer or the final seller. On the other hand, the proposer may be the manufacturer of hazardous chemicals which represents a quite different risk exposure.

The turnover of the proposer is important and should be supplied broken down between products. In some cases large companies may have subsidiaries manufacturing products ranging through the whole spectrum of potential hazards. It is also necessary to identify export turnover, in particular to North America, because of the high incidence of product liability claims and the higher awards in that territory.

The previous claims experience of the proposer is of obvious importance. Normally insurers would seek information for at least three previous years and in some cases five. They would want full details of any large claims. The claims experience gives a view of past costs which may be a guide to the future and in addition it can be helpful in identifying particular problems. It may show that there have been a large number of small claims involving a particular product. If these claims are continuing to happen insurers may form a view that sooner or later the particular product will be the cause of a much more substantial loss.

The contractual arrangements entered into by the proposer are important, particularly where it is desired to delete or modify the contractual liability exclusion which has been discussed earlier.

Insurers will wish to know the size of the indemnity limit required and what, if any, deductables or self insurance the proposer is prepared to carry.

On the basis of this information the insurer will form a view as to whether the risk is acceptable. If the risk is acceptable a premium will be quoted together with any modification to the standard wording. When the insurer has arrived at a premium it would be normal to express this as a percentage rate of the turnover of the company. As indicated above, there may be differential rates for particular products and for exports to North America. Indeed, in some cases the rate for North America exports may be ten times that for identical products sold in other territories.

8.1 Risk control

It is by and large true to say that product liability underwriting has in the past been a desk exercise and very few insurers in the UK and Europe had become involved with physical risk assessment and control. This contrasts markedly with experience in the US where product liability insurance in many cases requires risk assessment surveys, both when risks are proposed and at continuing intervals. Insurers in the US have taken this path because of the particular circumstances there. Strict liability for injury and damage caused by products has a longer history. Americans are on the whole more willing to commence proceedings and juries inject a certain element of uncertainty into the outcome.

It is possible to see the beginnings of a more active approach to risk control by insurers in Europe. It is becoming rather more common for insurers to seek specialists' reports on particular high hazard product risks or risks where there have been past problems.

A number of large European insurers do employ specialist engineers and a number of specialist product liability risk assessment organisations do exist. In the future there will perhaps be more involvement by insurers in this respect. This would bring benefits both to the insurer who would have a much better view of the particular risk and to the insured, who would have the benefit of risk control advice in relation to his product exposure.

9. MULTI-NATIONAL POLICIES

Many companies who require product liability insurance have operations located in more than one country.

Such multi-national companies often wish to take a global view of the various insurable risks faced by the company and of the insurance protection required to meet those exposures.

The traditional approach of each subsidiary buying a product liability policy in its own territory on the basis of decisions made by local management may not meet group objectives.

The parent company may have a number of aims when considering the way in which product liability and indeed other types of insurance are arranged, such as:

(a) The protection of the group to a common standard. There may be a concern that individual arrangements made by subsidiary companies are inadequate, exposing them to potential insolvency in the event of uninsured claims. This impacts on the value of the group as a whole.
(b) Cost effectiveness. Focusing premium expenditure with one insurer may result in worthwhile discounts as against expenditure with large numbers of different insurers on an unco-ordinated basis.
(c) Large corporations operating in many territories with different subsidiaries may actually have a large degree of interdependence. Components may be supplied from one subsidiary to another for final manufacture.

    Sales and marketing functions may be centralised or carried out in different parts of the group. In the event of product liability claims arising it may be difficult to identify which subsidiary is responsible. On a non-global basis it might be that the insurers of each subsidiary could be involved in legal action against each other establishing where the responsibility lies.

These objectives can be met by the issue of a global liability policy for all territories in which the insured operate. In theory this could be a single policy document for all territories. However, there are practical and legal difficulties with this approach. In many countries it is a requirement that insurance policies for local subsidiaries must be placed with locally regulated insurers.

Local subsidiaries may want a policy document in the local language and their customers may wish to see proof of insurance locally. It may be necessary to identify premia paid locally so that appropriate premium taxes are accounted for.

In practice there are number of insurers who themselves operate on a worldwide basis and have offices in many countries. These insurers issue multi-national policies with locally admitted documentation.

The approach is to issue a 'Master' policy to the parent company containing all the terms and conditions negotiated centrally. The insurers would then issue local policies, sometimes on a more restrictive basis, following local practice in each territory. The premium again will be agreed centrally but the insurer would collect a proportion of that figure for each of the insured subsidiaries.

There are a number of large insurance brokers who operate on a worldwide basis and would provide local broking services in parallel with the insurance protection provided by the insurer. They are also able to provide services in relation to the control of the programme and the flow of information to ensure that such arrangements operate smoothly across national boundaries.

Within the European Community regulatory barriers to purchasing insurance across borders are being removed in two stages. The first stage, which took place in July 1990, involves large companies. This means that at least within the European Community it is possible for an insurer to issue a single policy covering all the subsidiaries of a multi-national company. The second stage of implementation will extend this freedom to smaller companies.

It is likely that practical considerations will mean that local policy documentation in local language will still be required in some cases. This means that in the future a combination of approaches will be seen. At the very least the choice is available to the insured. Even where local policies are issued it would no longer be necessary for the insurer issuing the policy to be based in the territory concerned, although if local service, including claims handling, is required some local presence would be necessary.

10. THE EC PRODUCT LIABILITY DIRECTIVE AND PRODUCT LIABILITY INSURANCE

The legal effect of the implementation of the Product Liability Directive in each European Community country is discussed elsewhere.

The insurance industry has been concerned with assessing the likely impact of the Directive on the number and level of product liability claims in the future and the effect this will have on their underwriting.

It should perhaps be reiterated at this point that the product liability policy in common with other liability policies does not need to be endorsed or reworded to provide cover for claims brought under the new legislation. It responds to the insured's legal liability which includes liabilities introduced by statute. There has been no move at the time of writing by any product liability insurer to try and restrict cover because of the implementation of the Directive.

The intuitive view of the insurance industry is that the legislation will increase the number of smaller claims. The assessment is that where serious personal injuries have been suffered in the past claims have been brought notwithstanding the difficulties of proving negligence. People may have been more reluctant to try to pursue smaller claims. However, the effect of the legislation in terms of claims frequency and cost is going to be difficult to disentangle from other factors.

Potential claimants are becoming more aware of the rights and are more willing to bring claims.

There are still uncertainties within the legislation itself. The way in which the Consumer Protection Act 1987 in the UK has implemented the 'state of the art' defence arguably does not comply with the Directive. There are at the time of writing no authoritative court decisions in the United Kingdom dealing with any important aspect of the Act.

The liability insurance industry does not keep centralised statistics and each insurer has to rely on his own statistical base as a guide to development. Emerging trends will thus be more difficult to identify.

Some liability insurers believe that premium increases should be implemented now in anticipation of rising claims costs in the future. Various percentages have been ascribed to the necessary increases but it is difficult to see from what base these have been calculated. In practice the insurance market throughout Europe is at the time of writing in a very competitive state and insurers find it difficult, if not impossible, to achieve premium increases.

The reality is likely to be that insurance costs will be affected if and when increased claims costs make their presence felt. This process will almost certainly take a number of years.

Schedule comparing and contrasting the law on product liability in Europe

(As at 21 July 1991)

SCHEDULE COMPARING AND CONTRASTING THE LAW ON PRODUCT LIABILITY IN EUROPE

(As at 21 July 1991)

UNITED KINGDOM	REPUBLIC OF IRELAND
EXISTING PRODUCT LIABILITY LEGISLATION:	
New law in force.	No specific product liability law.
Supplements existing contract and tort law.	
DATE NEW LEGISLATION FOLLOWING EC DIRECTIVE COMES INTO FORCE:	
The Consumer Protection Act 1987 ('CPA') came into effect on 1 March 1988.	Directive not yet implemented at time of writing. A Bill to implement the directive has been published.
NATURE OF LIABILITY – CONTRACT:	
The new CPA does not affect the existing position in contract as between the actual parties to the contract, eg seller and buyer.	The 1980 Sale of Goods Act ('1980 Act') does not affect the basic contractual relationship. It does, however, imply terms and conditions into contracts.
Absolute liability under Sale of Goods Act 1979 for failure to provide goods of merchantable quality and fit for the purpose for which they were bought.	*Absolute* liability under the 1980 Act for goods not of merchantable quality and fit for the purpose for which they were bought.
Quantum of damage in contract All loss which is a likely consequence of the breach – would include loss on the purchase of the product itself, compensation for any illness, medical expenses, damage to property and pure economic loss.	*Quantum of damage in contract* The loss which may be recovered is the loss which was at the time of the contract a reasonably foreseeable consequence of the breach.
Injured party is under a duty to mitigate his loss.	The injured party is under a duty to mitigate his loss.

Exclusion clauses
Exclusion clauses in consumer contracts and otherwise in respect of death and personal injury are not enforceable but exclusion clauses in respect of commercial contracts involving persons other than consumers are enforceable insofar as they are reasonable.

Limitation periods in contract claims
Six-year time limit from the date on which the cause of action occurred.

NATURE OF LIABILITY – TORT: NEGLIGENCE

Negligence claims
A claim may lie in negligence against a manufacturer or supplier if fault can be proved.

Plaintiff must prove:
(1) That the defendant owed him a duty to take reasonable care.
(2) A breach of that duty.
(3) That he suffered loss.
(4) A causal connection between that breach and the loss.

Quantum of damage in negligence
The general principle is that the plaintiff should be placed in the same position as if the tort had not occurred. Damages may be special or general. Nominal, contemptuous or exemplary damages may be awarded.

Limitation period in negligence
Generally six years from the date of action accruing but three years from date of action accruing for personal injury.

Exclusion clauses
Where a purchaser of goods does not deal as a consumer and where the exclusion is fair and reasonable certain implied warranties relating to the sale of goods may be excluded.

Limitation periods in contract claims
Six-year time limit from the date on which the cause of action occurred.

Negligence claims
A claim may lie in negligence against a manufacturer or supplier if fault can be proved.

Plaintiff must prove:
(1) That the defendant owed him a duty to take reasonable care.
(2) A breach of that duty.
(3) That he suffered loss.
(4) A causal connection between that breach and the loss.

Quantum of damage in negligence
The general principle is that the plaintiff should be placed in the same position as if the tort had not occurred. Damages may be special or general. Nominal, contemptuous or exemplary damages may be awarded.

Limitation period in negligence
Generally six years from the date of action accruing but three years from date of action accruing for personal injury.

UNITED KINGDOM	REPUBLIC OF IRELAND
NATURE OF LIABILITY – TORT: PRODUCT LIABILITY	
Strict liability under the Consumer Protection Act 1987.	*Strict liability* under the Directive Products Bill 1991.
	Includes many of EEC Directive's recommendations.
The producer of a product is liable to the claimant in respect of damage caused by a defect in his product.	The producer of a product is liable to the claimant in respect of damage caused by a defect in his product.
Plaintiff must prove: (1) Defect. (2) Damage. (3) Causation.	*Plaintiff must prove*: (1) Defect. (2) Damage. (3) Causation.
'*Producer*' includes: (1) the manufacturer; (2) a person who puts his trade mark on a product; (3) importer into the EC; (4) supplier where the manufacturer cannot be traced.	'*Producer*' will include: (1) the manufacturer; (2) a person who puts his trade mark on a product; (3) importer into the EC; (4) supplier where the manufacturer cannot be traced.
'*Product*' excludes primary agricultural products unless they have undergone initial processing.	'*Product*' excludes primary agricultural products unless they have undergone initial processing.
'*Defect*' exists if the safety of the product is not such as persons generally are entitled to expect. In considering this, regard is had to marketing of the product, presentation and packaging, use of marks, instructions for use and warnings, and what might reasonably be expected to be done with and in relation to the product at the time the product was supplied by the producer. The fact that a later product may have higher safety standards is irrelevant (provided the producer took all due care to use the latest technology).	'*Defect*' similar to UK position.
'*Damage*' means death or personal injury or loss of or damage to any property including land *not* damage to the product itself, and not purely financial loss.	'*Damage*' means damage caused by death or personal injury.
'*Causation*' Plaintiff must show the defect caused the damage	'*Causation*' Plaintiff must show the defect caused the damage

Defences (inter alia): (1) Defect attributable to compliance with statute or EC obligation. (2) Supply of product was other than in the course of business. (3) Defect did not exist at the relevant time. (4) The defect is in the final product of which the product is a component part. (5) *Development risks defence ('state of the art')* That the state of scientific and technical knowledge at the relevant time was not such that a producer of products of the same description might be expected to have discovered the defect if it had existed in his products while they were under his control (note: arguably wider than under the Directive).	*Defences* Proposed defences which may be available include: (1) Defect attributable to compliance with statute or EC obligation. (2) Supply of product was other than in the course of business. (3) Defect did not exist at the relevant time. (4) The defect is in the final product of which the product is a component part. (5) *Development risks defence ('state of the art')* That the state of scientific and technical knowledge at the relevant time was not such that a producer of products of the same description might be expected to have discovered the defect if it had existed in his products while they were under his control (note: arguably wider than under the Directive).
Quantum of damages Minimum of £275. No maximum. All loss reasonably foreseeable. May be reduced by contributory negligence of the claimant.	*Quantum of damages* Minimum claim for damage to property is IR £350.
Limitation period Three years from the date of knowledge of relevant facts, eg damage, causation and identity of defendant, with a 'cut off' point of ten years from the date the product was brought into circulation.	*Limitation period* Three years.
WARNINGS:	
Essential to consider: (1) Warning notices on product. (2) Warning lights and/or alarm. (3) Product safety information in the User Manual. (4) Fail-safe devices on the equipment, eg circuit breaker and guard around dangerous parts.	Essential to consider: (1) Warning notices on product. (2) Warning lights and/or alarm. (3) Product safety information in the User Manual. (4) Fail-safe devices on the equipment, eg circuit breaker and guard around dangerous parts.

UNITED KINGDOM	REPUBLIC OF IRELAND
SPECIFIC SAFETY LEGISLATION:	
CPA Part II Ths part of the Act which deals with consumer safety makes it a criminal offence to supply consumer goods which fail to comply with 'the general safety requirement' defined by reference to reasonable safety in all the circumstances including the manner of marketing, packaging, instructions and warnings. The Government may publish standards which must be complied with.	*Safety Health and Welfare Act 1989* This creates a general duty upon 'Any person who designs, manufactures, imports or supplies any articles for use at work' to ensure so far as is reasonably practical that it is safe without risk to health when used by a person at a place of work.
Health and Safety at Work Act 1974 Duty on manufacturer who supplies an article for use at work to (inter alia) ensure the article is designed to be safe and provide adequate information on safety.	This can give rise to an action in either criminal or civil proceedings. Mainly this Act gives rise only to criminal liability. Civil actions can be grounded in this Act but the requirements are complex.
Special regulations for specific products Certain safety regulations are in force for particular products, eg domestic electrical equipment, products containing asbestos, packaging and labelling of dangerous substances, childrens' toys, foodstuffs, radioactive products, drugs and medicines.	*Special regulations for specific products* In particular for: (1) Foodstuffs. (2) Radioactive products. (3) Drugs and medicines.

LUXEMBOURG	FRANCE	BELGIUM
EXISTING PRODUCT LIABILITY LEGISLATION:		
New Product liability law in force. Co-exists with the general provisions of Luxembourg law governing the liability in contract and the liability in tort.	Existing contract and tort law remains effective. It is based mostly on jurisprudence which interprets extensively the provisions of the Civil Code.	Existing contract and tort law still applies for foreseeable future. Much based on jurisprudence. No comprehensive legislation on product liability.
DATE NEW LEGISLATION FOLLOWING EC DIRECTIVE COMES INTO FORCE:		
Directive implemented by law of 21 April 1989. Took effect on 2 May 1989.	Proposal on 23 May 1990 of the French government to incorporate EC Directive into French law ('The Proposal') should be discussed and adopted by the Parliament in 1991.	Directive was implemented by law of 25 February 1991, published in the Belgian Official Gazette of 22 March 1991 and came into force on 1 April 1991.
NATURE OF LIABILITY – CONTRACT:		
1 Hidden defects	**1 Hidden defects**	**1 Hidden defects**
A vendor warrants against *hidden defects*. Buyer may return the goods or claim a reduction in price, and if the vendor has acted in 'bad faith' he must compensate the buyer for all losses. *Retailers* practically as liable as manufacturers if they are specialists. *Professional vendors* are presumed to know the defects affecting the products they sell and are thus compelled to compensate all harm suffered by the buyer. *Purchaser needs not to prove fault of vendor*. Needs only to prove that at the time of the sale there was a hidden defect, unknown to purchaser, which caused harm. The defect, however, will be considered to be apparent if it should have been discovered by a summary inspection.	Action against the seller and any prior seller in the distribution chain (including the manufacturer) may be brought for hidden defects according to Civil Code art 1641. The purchaser will have to prove that the defects were *hidden* and existed prior to or, at the latest, at the time of the purchase. The Proposal provides that any defect occurring within the period of a contractual warranty (or within a year from delivery when there is no warranty) is presumed to have existed at the time of the sale. Such a presumption will not be effective in a contract between professionals. For a non-professional purchaser, case law provides that the defect is hidden if it could not have been discovered through preliminary inspection. Professional purchasers are required to undertake a more thorough check of the product. The seller is not liable for the defect when the purchaser shares the same area of expertise.	A seller warrants against *hidden defects*. Buyer may return the goods or claim a reduction in price, and if the seller has acted in 'bad faith' he must compensate the buyer for all losses. RETAILERS Under present law a retailer is practically as liable as a manufacturer if he is a specialist. *Professional sellers* are presumed to know the defects affecting the products they sell and are thus compelled to compensate all harm suffered by the buyer. PURCHASER *Need not prove fault of seller*, if at the time of sale there was a hidden defect, unknown to purchaser, which caused harm. The defect, however will be considered to be apparent if it should have been discovered by a summary inspection.

LUXEMBOURG	FRANCE	BELGIUM
Quantum of damages Compensation includes all foreseeable losses.	*Quantum of damages* Purchase price may be reduced or reimbursed. The Proposal provides for repair or replacement of the product. A professional seller is presumed to know about the defect and is liable to pay damages which include all loss suffered as a direct consequence of the defect.	*Quantum of damages* Compensation includes all direct and indirect losses.
Limitation period Purchaser has to declare the hidden defect within a 'short period' from the discovery of the defect. The purchaser loses his right to sue the vendor after expiry of a period of one year from the date of the declaration. The limitation period may be interrupted by negotiations, summary proceedings or by any other judicial means.	*Limitation period* The plaintiff must start proceedings within a short period of time from discovery of the defect. The Proposal provides that purchaser must inform the seller within one year from the date the defect is (or should have been) discovered.	*Limitation period* Proceedings must be brought within 'a brief period'. No specific limitation period.
Exclusion clauses *Disclaimers of liability* are usually upheld if reasonable except for a 'professional vendor'. Disclosure of the defect may have a wider application than simply based on safety.	*Exclusion clauses* *Exclusion or limitation* clauses are valid between professionals only.	*Exclusion clauses* *Disclaimers of liability* are usually upheld if reasonable except for a 'Professional seller'.
	2 Lack of conformity An action against the seller and the producer can also be brought under the provisions of art 1184 of the Civil Code for the non-performance by the seller of his	

obligation to deliver a product conforming to the purchaser's order. The *product is defective when it does not conform to normal use*. The defect may be an apparent defect and may constitute an unauthorised change to the quality of the product.

Quantum of damage
The purchase price may be reduced or reimbursed.

Limitation period
Ten years starting from the day when the damage occurred when the seller is a professional; 30 years for a private seller.

Exclusion or limitation clauses in respect of claims for lack of conformity are valid between professionals only.

3 Mistake on the substantive qualities of the product

The buyer may also bring an action to have the contract declared void for lack of consent, on the ground of a mistake as to the substantive qualities of the product (Civil Code art 1110).

Quantum of damages
Damages can only be claimed if the seller has wilfully misled the purchaser. Only available remedy is repayment of the price.

NATURE OF LIABILITY – TORT:

LUXEMBOURG	FRANCE	BELGIUM
1 Civil Code art 1382	**1 Civil Code art 1382**	**1 Civil Code art 1382**
A producer may be held liable for damages caused by a defective product where the defect was caused by the producer's fault or negligence. Breach includes situations where the manufacturer has failed to inform or warn the purchaser of the possible dangers of the product. Fault or negligence may be interpreted widely so that a producer may be held liable if it can be evidenced that his product was defective.	A manufacturer is liable for personal and property damage caused by a design or manufacturing defect in its product under art 1382 of the Civil Code. Breach also includes situations where the manufacturer has failed to inform or warn the purchaser of the possible dangers of the product.	A manufacturer is liable in negligence if through 'fault' he makes or designs a defective product although 'fault' may be interpreted widely so that a manufacturer is at fault if he puts into circulation a product which becomes dangerous because of a defect or because of lack of information, ie close to strict liability. *Manufacturers must*: (1) Take care and diligence. (2) Avoid producing products threatening to life, health or property. (3) Be aware of technical and scientific progress. (4) Comply with public safety regulations. (5) Display appropriate warnings. There is a duty to inform of danger and advise on safety. (6) Do everything to reduce risk of accident, eg recall defective goods. Failure to do any of these is negligence. Defect and damage alone is not enough.
Limitation period Thirty years.		*Limitation period* Thirty years maximum.

2 Article 1384 para 1	**2 Article 1384 para 1**	**2 Art 1384 para 1**
Liability under art 1384 para 1 of the Civil Code in respect of injury caused by products which a person has in their custody ('garde'). The liability in this case is a strict liability with a certain number of distinctions developed by the jurisprudence. An action based on tort will often be dismissed if the plaintiff and the defendant were contracting parties. Clauses limiting or excluding the liability of the producer are invalid.	Liability under art 1384 para 1 of the Civil Code in respect of injury caused by products which a person has in their custody ('garde'). Case law concept of 'custody of the structure' by which the manufacturer's liability continues after delivery since he is deemed to be able to control the internal structure of the product and check whether the product could be used without danger. The victim will only have to show a causal relationship between the damage suffered and the product. Exoneration of the manufacturer if he proves that the damage was due to an external cause. His liability will be reduced if he shows that the victim has contributed to the damage. Clauses limiting or excluding the liability of the producer are invalid. **3 Civil Code art 1384 para 5** Pursuant to art 1384 para 5 of the Civil Code, the manufacturer will also be liable for damages caused by his employees in the course of employment. Clauses limiting or excluding the liability of the producer will be invalid in the case of an action based on tort. Exoneration of the manufacturer if he proves that the injury is due to an external cause.	Liability under art 1384 para 1 of the Civil Code in respect of injury caused by products which a person has in their custody ('garde'). An action based on tort will often be dismissed if the plaintiff and the defendant were contracting parties.

LUXEMBOURG	FRANCE	BELGIUM
Limitation period Thirty years from the date the damage occurred.	*Limitation period* Ten years from when the damage occurred or the loss was further aggravated.	*Limitation period* Thirty years maximum.
	Plaintiff must prove: Plaintiff must prove that the product was defective.	*Plaintiff must prove*: (1) failure to meet general duty of care; or (2) breach of a legal obligation; and (3) a casual link.

NATURE OF LIABILITY – TORT – PRODUCT LIABILITY

LUXEMBOURG	FRANCE	BELGIUM
New Product liability law.	No product liability law is yet in force under the Directive.	New Product liability law.
Directive has imposed strict liability on the 'producer' for damage caused by defect in the product.		Directive has imposed strict liability on the 'producer' for damage caused by defect in the product.
Plaintiff must prove: (1) Defect. (2) Damage. (3) Causation. (4) Size of loss.		*Plaintiff must prove*: (1) Defect. (2) Damage. (3) Causation. (4) Size of loss.
'*Producer*' includes: (1) The manufacturer of the final product. (2) Producer of raw material or component. (3) A person affixing his name or trade mark to the product.		'*Producer*' includes: (1) The manufacturer of the final product. (2) Producer of raw material or component. (3) A person affixing his name or trade mark to the product.

'*Product*' Widely defined as any movable product even if incorporated in any other immovable or movable product.		'*Product*' Widely defined as any movable product even if incorporated in any other immovable or movable product.
'*Defect*' A product is defective if it does not provide the safety that could legitimately be expected with regard to all the circumstances.		'*Defect*' A product is defective if it does not provide the safety that could legitimately be expected with regard to all the circumstances.
'*Damage*' The damage is each and every type of damage except damage: (1) from nuclear accidents; (2) to the defective product; (3) to property not used for private purposes on consumption.		'*Damage*' The damage resulting from nuclear accidents is not covered.
'*Causation*' Causation must be proved.		'*Causation*' Causation must be proved.
Defences (1) Producer did not put the product into circulation. (2) Defect did not exist when the producer put the product into circulation. (3) Product not been manufactured for sale or for means of distribution within an economic scope nor has it been manufactured or distributed within the frame of producer's professional activity. (4) Defect due to the conformity of product to mandatory rules established by authorities. (5) If the producer is the manufacturer of a component, a defect attributable to the concept of the final product or to the instructions given by manufacturer of the final product.		*Defences* (1) Producer did not put the product into circulation. (2) Defect did not exist when the producer put the product into circulation. (3) Product not been manufactured for sale or for means of distribution within an economic scope nor has it been manufactured or distributed within the frame of producer's professional activity.

LUXEMBOURG	FRANCE	BELGIUM
The development risks defence does not apply.		The development risks defence does apply.
Quantum of damages Compensation without any restriction and compensation of the damage to property with deduction of an amount of approximately LUF 22,500.		
Where two or more parties responsible for defect, joint and several liability.		Where two or more parties responsible for defect, joint and several liability.
Liability period Three years from the date of discovery of the damage which must in any case be no later than ten years from the date when the product was put into circulation.		*Liability period* Three years from the date of discovery of the damage which must in any case be no later than ten years from the date when the product was put into circulation.
WARNINGS:		**WARNINGS:**
As the producer is due to inform the consumers of possible dangers of the product, a clear notice in the national language (French or German) should be affixed to the equipment. Full instructions and advice on safety should be included in the user instructions materials.		Because of the duty on the manufacturer to inform of danger, a clear notice in the national language and English should be affixed to the dangerous part of the equipment. Full instructions and advice on safety should be included in the user instructions materials.
SPECIFIC SAFETY LEGISLATION:		
No specific legislation.		

SPAIN	PORTUGAL	ITALY
EXISTING PRODUCT LIABILITY LEGISLATION:		
1984 General Act for the Defence of Consumers and Users (GAC) applies for the foreseeable future.	New law in force. Decree Law 383/89 supplements existing contract and tort law.	New law in force. Supplements existing contract and tort law.
DATE NEW LEGISLATION FOLLOWING EC DIRECTIVE COMES INTO FORCE:		
No date fixed at the time of writing for the Directive to be implemented.	Decree Law 383/89 implemented on 6 November 1989.	The Directive has been implemented through a presidential decree of 24 May 1988.
NATURE OF LIABILITY – CONTRACT:		
Vendor is liable to the purchaser for hidden defects or if the product is not fit for its purpose.	Vendor liable to the purchaser if the product does not function properly or is defective.	Vendor is liable to the purchaser if defects make the product unfit for the intended use.
Usually there is no contractual relationship between the purchaser and the manufacturer.	Usually there is no contractual relationship between the purchaser and the manufacturer.	Usually there is no contractual relationship between the purchaser and the manufacturer.
Only parties to the contract can claim. Plaintiff must prove defect, damage and causation.	Generally only the parties to the contract can claim. Plaintiffs must prove defect, damage and causation.	Only parties to the contract can claim. Plaintiff must prove contractual obligation, defect and damage.
Quantum of damage in contract If vendor acted in good faith, buyer can claim for termination of contract, and reimbursement for losses or price reduction.	*Quantum of damage in contract* Vendor must repair damage that the purchaser probably would not have suffered if the product had not been defective.	*Quantum of damage in contract* Quantum of damage in contract is all loss suffered as a direct consequence of the breach, therefore including purely financial loss.

SPAIN	PORTUGAL	ITALY
Not liable for disclosed defects or those discoverable on summary inspection. If the vendor acted in 'bad faith' (ie the vendor knew of hidden defects) plaintiff can claim damages including loss of income, medical costs etc. All commercial contracts are liable for damages.	Vendor not liable if purchaser mistaken in assessing the characteristics of the product and the Vendor, through no fault of his own was unaware of the defect. Damages may be reduced or disallowed entirely if the damage has been caused or aggravated by the purchaser.	
Limitation period in contractual claims Six months after delivery of product; except if contract is deemed commercial when the limitation period is four days.	*Limitation period in contractual claims* Twenty years after the damage occurred.	*Limitation period in contractual claims* One year after delivery provided that the seller is notified of the defect within eight days of discovery.
Exclusion clauses Exclusion clauses permitted.	*Exclusion clauses* Exclusion clauses void. Certain limitation clauses permissible.	*Exclusion clauses* Reasonable exclusion clauses may be upheld in certain cases.
NATURE OF LIABILITY – TORT:		
Whoever causes damage to another person by an act or omission and with negligence or fault is liable for the damage caused.	Whoever, intentionally or through mere fault, illicitly violates the rights of another person or breaches any rule of law designed to protect the interests of other persons shall be under an obligation to compensate the injured person for the damage arising from such violation or breach.	Any event caused by fault, negligence or wilful misconduct binds its author to indemnify any damage deriving therefrom.

Plaintiff must prove: (1) Action or omission. (2) Unlawfulness. (3) Negligence. (4) Damage not too remote. (5) Causal link between the act or omission and the damage.	*Plaintiff must prove*: (1) (a) Fault (unless it is presumed by law); or (b) Illicit violation of rights. (2) Damage not too remote. (3) Causation.	*Plaintiff must prove*: (1) An act or omission on behalf of the defendant. (2) Its unlawfulness. (3) Negligence. (4) Damage. (5) A causal link between the act or omission and the damage.
Quantum of damages in tort Damages in tort to cover all damages directly caused, or deemed to have been caused by that act. They include replacing defective products, damage caused damage to property and non-material or moral damage.	*Quantum of damages in tort* Defendant must pay damages to reconstitute the situation if the event which caused the damage had not occurred. Actual and potential damage is taken into account. Portuguese courts are very conservative in their awards.	*Quantum of damages in tort* Damages should restore the aggrieved party to the position it was in before the tortious act occurred. Damages cover expenses losses and consequential losses. Moral loss cannot usually be claimed.
Limitation period One year from when aware of damage. Fifteen years when criminal offences are involved.	*Limitation period* Three years from when aware of right to compensation. Twenty years maximum limitation from when damage occurred.	*Limitation period* Five years from the day of the tortious action or the day the damage was done if earlier. If the tortious act is a crime the limitation period is the same as for the crime.

NATURE OF LIABILITY – PRODUCT LIABILITY:

Subjective liability under the General Act for the Defence of Consumers and Users of 19 July 1984 contains a wide number of exceptions for which *strict liability* is imposed.	*Strict liability* under the decree of 383/89 of 6 November. The producer is liable irrespective of intent or mere fault for damage caused by defects in his product.	*Strict liability* under the decree of 24 May 1988. The producer of a product is liable for the damages caused by the defects of his product as a consequence of having put it into circulation.

SPAIN	PORTUGAL	ITALY
Plaintiff must prove: (1) Unlawful act or omission. (2) Damage. (3) Causation. (4) Negligence except for products subject to strict liability.	*Plaintiff must prove*: (1) Defect. (2) Damage. (3) Causation.	*Plaintiff must prove*: (1) Defect. (2) Damage. (3) Causation.
'*Producer*' Manufacturers, importers, vendors and suppliers of products are liable for the origin, identity and adequacy pursuant to their nature and purpose. In the case of packaged, bottled, labelled or enclosed products the individual or company on the label is usually liable. '*Injured person*' Consumers only.	'*Producer*' Includes: (1) The manufacturer of a finished product on a component part of any new material; and (2) any person who represents himself as a producer by placing his name, trademark or other distinguishing feature on the product; and (3) the importer and supplier of the Product.	'*Producer*' Is quite widely defined but may include a seller when the identity of the producer is unknown or is outside the jurisdiction.
'*Product*' Wide definition but *strict liability* for foodstuffs, sanitary and cleaning products, cosmetics, drugs, health services, gas and electricity services, lifts, electrical appliances, transport, sport, toys and products designed for children.	'*Product*' Excludes primary agricultural products. No mention is made expressly to electricity but it is considered to be implied in the definition.	'*Product*' Excludes primary agricultural products. A detailed definition of 'primary agricultural products that have undergone initial processing' is included.
'*Defect*' There is no definition of 'defect'.	'*Defect*' The definition follows the directive in that a product is defective when it does not provide the safey which a person is entitled to expect taking all the circumstances into account.	'*Defect*' This differs from Directive. A product is to be considered defective when it does not provide the same degree of safety as that 'normally offered by any other product of the same series'.

'*Damages*' There is no definition of 'damages' although a consumer has a right to compensation for damages and therefore damages will include personal injury, physical damage, non-physical damage duly evidenced and quantified.	'*Damage*' Damage is damage resulting from death or personal injury and property damage other than to the defective product itself. Damage may be reduced by the extent to which it was caused by the injured person but not 'any person for whom the injured person is responsible'.	'*Damage*' See *Quantum of damage* below.
Causation The plaintiff must show causation.	*Causation* The plaintiff must show the defect caused the damage.	*Causation* The plaintiff must show the defect caused the damage.
Defences There is only one defence for a producer, namely: (1) that all the relevant legal requirements had been complied with; and (2) That the diligence required by the nature of the product, service or activity had been complied with.	*Defences* (1) The producer did not put the product into circulation. (2) The defect did not exist at the time the product was put into circulation. (3) Defect attributable to compliance with statute and mandatory regulations. (4) The product was not manufactured for sale or for any form of distribution. (5) *Development risk defence*, ie scientific and technical knowledge at the time did not permit the product to be seen as defective.	*Defences* (1) Defective product was not put into circulation, ie on the market. (2) The defect did not exist at the time the product was put into circulation. (Manufacturer has the burden of proof.) (3) Defect attributable to compliance with statute and mandatory regulations. (4) The defect is in the final product of which the product is only a minor component. (5) *Development risk defence*, ie scientific and technical knowledge at the time did not permit the product to be seen as defective.

SPAIN	PORTUGAL	ITALY
	Quantum of damages Minimum of PTE $70,000.	*Quantum of damages* Minimum of L 750,000.
	Maximum of PTE $10,000,000,000.	No maximum.
		Decree says producer must pay damages due to death, damage to health and personal injury. Damages to goods must be paid if they are normally intended for private use or consumption and were used in this manner. Claims can also be made for non-material damages, eg shock, mental distress, pain and suffering.
		Other claims, including the value of the defective goods themselves, must be made using the general Italian law of tort based on negligence.
		Damages are reduced if the injured person significantly participated in damages or denied if he did not try to avoid the damage occurring.
Limitation period One year from when aware of damage.	*Limitation period* Three years.	*Limitation period* Three years from date of knowledge of relevant facts.
WARNINGS:		
Failure to provide warnings and instructions on use is classed as 'negligence'.	Warning notices and instructions on safety advisable to comply with the Directive.	Warning notices and instructions on safety advisable to comply with the Directive.

SWEDEN	DENMARK	NORWAY
EXISTING PRODUCT LIABILITY LEGISLATION:		
No specific product liability law in force in Sweden. Existing contract and tort laws will remain in effect. New law, which includes many of the provisions to be found in the Directive, to be proposed in 1991 for entry into force on 1 July 1992.	New law incorporating the Directive in force. Few changes from the existing practices in contract and tort law.	New product liability law in force. Few changes from the existing law.
DATE NEW LEGISLATION FOLLOWING EC DIRECTIVE COMES INTO FORCE:		
No date fixed at the time of writing. **From 1 January 1991** *Sale of Goods Act* For defects, buyer is entitled to repair, replacement, price reduction or cancellation with compensation. A defect exists if product lacks quality, quantity, character etc agreed *or* if unsuitable for normal or intended use. *Consumer Sale of Goods Act* For defects, consumer is entitled to repair, replacement, price reduction or cancellation with compensation. A defect exists if product lacks quality, quantity, character etc agreed *or* if unsuitable for normal or intended use. Also if necessary instructions are missing or if use clearly endangers life or health.	Directive implemented with Act No 371 of 7 June 1989. Took effect on 10 June 1989. Product liability very rarely based on contract law. Sales of Goods Act 1906 does not govern the right to compensation for damage caused by the product or to the product.	EC Directive has been the 'Godfather' to Act No 104 of 23 December 1988. The Product Liability Law came into effect on 1 January 1989 (chapter 1 and 2) and on 1 July 1989 (chapter 3). Product liability very rarely based on contract law. Purchasers Act 1988 does not govern the right to compensation for personal injury caused by the product. *The Purchasers Act of 13 May 1988* This Act deals with claims for damage to and defects in the product itself. The vendor of products and manufacturers and those in the distribution chain have *strict liability* as against consumers for defects extending to direct losses only. Damage for indirect losses can be claimed in certain circumstances. Contractual claims can be made if the goods do not possess expressly warranted characteristics.

SWEDEN	DENMARK	NORWAY
Quantum of Damage *Under the Sale of Goods Act* Compensation for direct and indirect loss, however not for loss to other property than the product. *Under the Consumer Sale of Goods Act* Compensation for expenses, loss of income, difference in price etc. Compensation also for damage caused by the product to other property provided the property damaged is intended for private use and belongs to the consumer or member of his household.	*Quantum of damage* Assessed according to general principals of law.	*Quantum of damage in contract* The injured party should be fully compensated for losses and expenses attributable to breach of contract which could have been reasonably foreseen.
Exclusion clauses Exclusion clauses possible in non-consumer sales.	*Exclusion clauses* Certain exclusion clauses are valid so far as they are reasonable but no exclusion possible in product liability cases.	*Exclusion clauses* Businessmen supplying goods to consumers cannot exclude liability.
Limitation period in contract claims Within 'reasonable time' from discovering defect; or within two years from receiving product unless longer guarantee period or gross negligence. NB *International Sale of Goods* Sweden has adopted art 1–13 and 25–88 of the UN Convention of 11 April 1980 on Contracts for the International Sale of Goods; except in cases where both seller and buyer have their place of business in Sweden, Denmark, Norway, Finland or Iceland.	*Limitation period in contract claims* One year.	*Limitation period in contract claims* A claim must be brought within a reasonable period of time of it being discovered and, in any event, within two years of the goods being delivered.

NATURE OF LIABILITY – TORT: NEGLIGENCE

Negligence claims Claims founded in negligence under the Tort Liability Act. However, court practice requires little or even no negligence to have occurred. Strict liability is provided in laws regarding certain dangerous activities, eg Nuclear Liability Law, Air Traffic Law and Electrical Power Plant Law.	*Negligence claims* Liability for damage requires negligence of the tortfeasor. The low degree of fault approaches strict liability.	*Negligence claims* Liability will arise where the manufacturer/vendor etc are at fault for the damage that has occurred or which could have been prevented by alternative action. Strict liability exists for producers of products involving continuous risk that they will cause damage.
Plaintiff must prove: (1) Negligence (slight). (2) Causation.	*Plaintiff must prove*: (1) Negligence (slight). (2) Causation. (3) Damage that is not too remote.	*Plaintiff must prove*: (1) Negligence or product involves continuous risk. (2) Damage (must be foreseeable). (3) Causation.
Quantum of damage in negligence Compensation for all losses of an economic nature and to some extent for pain and suffering.	*Quantum of damage in negligence* Compensation awarded under basic tort law principles and excludes personal injury and property damage and consequential damage.	*Quantum of damage in negligence* Compensation for entire financial loss and damages for personal injury, pain and suffering together with consequential loss.
Limitation period in Negligence Normally ten years.	*Limitation period in negligence* Three years.	*Limitation period in negligence* Claims must be brought within three years from date of knowledge of possible claim but in any event within 20 years of circulation of the product.

SWEDEN	DENMARK	NORWAY
NATURE OF LIABILITY – TORT: PRODUCT LIABILITY		
Product Liability Law proposed in 1991 Suggested liability for personal damage caused by product and for property damage caused by a product on goods for private use. Damage to the product itself is excluded. Liability will include manufacturer, importer, retailer or those who marketed product with own trademark.	The Directive has imposed strict liability on the 'producer' for damage caused by a defective product.	The Product Liability Act has imposed strict liability on the 'producer' for damage caused by a defective product.
Plaintiff must prove: (1) Defect. (2) Damage. (3) Causation.	*Plaintiff must prove*: (1) Defect. (2) Damage. (3) Causation. (4) Size of loss.	*Plaintiff must prove*: (1) Defect. (2) Damage. (3) Causation. (4) Size of loss.
Under the proposed Product Liability Law '*Producer*' includes: (1) Manufacturer. (2) Importer. (3) A person who has sold the product as his own and sold it under his trademark. (4) Any supplier if nobody under (1)–(3) can be held responsible.	'*Producer*' includes: (1) Manufacturer. (2) A person who puts his trademark on the product. (3) Importers to the EC. (4) Supplier when the manufacturer cannot be traced.	'*Producer*' includes: (1) Manufacturer. (2) Importers. (3) Vendors.
'*Product*' All movables (including primary agricultural products and game) even though incorporated into another product or movable.	'*Product*' Excludes primary agricultural products unless they have undergone initial processing.	'*Product*' Includes all items incorporated into other products or real estate and waste products. Electricity is excluded. Agricultural products are included.

'Defect' Exists if the product when put into circulation was not as safe as could reasonably be expected at that time. *'Damage'* Damage means compensation for damage to property for personal use but not damage to the product and damage for personal injury.	*'Defect'* Exists if the safety of the product is not such as persons generally are entitled to expect. *'Damage'* Damage means death or personal injury or loss or damage to personal property and not damage to the product.	*'Defect'* Exists if the product does not have the degree of safety which a user or the general public would expect. *'Damage'* Damage means personal injury and damage to personal property. Damages to business property is excluded.
Causation The plaintiff must prove causation.	*Causation* The plaintiff must prove causation.	*Causation* The plaintiff must prove causation.
Proposed defences (1) Product was as safe as could be reasonably expected at the time. (2) Manufacturer did not put product into circulation under a business activity. (3) Defect did not exist when put into market. The development risks defence does *not apply*.	*Defences* (1) Defect attributable to compliance with statute or EC obligation. (2) Supply of product otherwise than in the course of business. (3) Defect did not exist at the relevant time. (4) The producer did not put the product into circulation. (5) *Development risks defence*.	*Defences* (1) Defect attributable to compliance with statute. (2) Supply of product otherwise in the course of business. (3) Defect did not exist at the relevant time. (4) The producer did not put the product into circulation. The *Development risk defence* does *not apply*.
Quantum of damages No limit BUT burden of proof in relation to damages with claimant.	*Quantum of damages* Minimum claim of DK 4,000. No maximum. If the loss is less than the minimum the plaintiff must use existing jurisprudence based on negligence. The defendant is liable for damages due to death, injury, harm to health and property (other than product itself), eg loss of income, loss of possibility to earn, medical expenses, compensation for invalidation, compensation for loss of breadwinner etc.	*Quantum of damages* No minimum claim. No maximum. Liability for damages due to death, injury, harm to health and property (other than product itself), eg loss of income, loss of possibility to earn, medical expenses, compensation for invalidation, compensation for loss of breadwinner. Where two or more parties responsible for defect, shared liability.

SWEDEN	DENMARK	NORWAY
	Existing jurisprudence provides for reclaiming value of product itself. Where two or more parties responsible for defect, shared liability.	
Limitation period Proposed to be three years from learning of the possibility of a claim; or maximum 10 years from the day when product ceased to be in the possession of the liable party.	*Limitation period* Three years from date of knowledge of a possible claim. Ten-year cut off period has practically no effect.	*Limitation period* Claims must be brought within three years from the date of knowledge of the possible claim but in any event within 20 years of circulation of the product. In cases of development faults a maximum limitation period of ten years from the product leaving the producer's supervision.
WARNINGS:		
Warning notices advisable.	Warning notices and instructions on safety similar to UK to comply with Directive. Failure to do so will make producer liable.	Warning notices and safety instructions similar to UK to comply with Directive. Failure to do so will make producer liable.
SPECIFIC SAFETY REGULATIONS:		
Under the 1989 Product Safety Law any business can be ordered to give safety information regarding its products and services, be prohibited from trading, be ordered to provide warnings or be ordered to withdraw products from the marketplace. Also fine of SEK 100,000. Certain legislation for specific products and services, eg Nuclear Liability Law etc.	Certain legislation for specific products, eg Act on Drugs, Act on Chemicals, Act on Foodstuffs etc.	Certain legislation for specific products, eg Act on Drugs, Act on Nuclear Energy, Act on Petroleum, Act on Product Supervision.

NETHERLANDS	GERMANY	SWITZERLAND	AUSTRIA
EXISTING PRODUCT LIABILITY LEGISLATION:			
New Product Liability Law in force.	New Product Liability Law in force. No fundamental changes to the existing position under contract and tort law.	Existing contract and tort law remains effective. No specific law on product liability. The Swiss Private International Law Act enables a claimant to choose between the law of the producer's residence (which could be, for example, US or EC) and Swiss law. Therefore, although Swiss law is more lax, producers should comply with EC law. In the near future Switzerland is expected to implement the Lugano Convention which will mean that Swiss producers can be sued more effectively abroad in EC courts.	New Product Liability Law in force to supplement contract and tort law under the civil code.
DATE NEW LEGISLATION FOLLOWING EC DIRECTIVE COMES INTO FORCE:			
Directive came into effect on 1 November 1990, implemented by art 1407a–1407j of current Civil Code.	New Product Liability Act came into force on 1 January 1990.	Switzerland did not incorporate the Directive on Product Liability into Swiss law.	The Federal Act of 21 January 1988 is based on the Directive which took effect on 1 July 1988.

NATURE OF LIABILITY – CONTRACT:

NETHERLANDS	GERMANY	SWITZERLAND	AUSTRIA
Existing contract law remains unaffected. Applicable where there is a direct contract between the manufacturer/seller and the buyer. Any product must be fit for the purpose of the contract, and shall be free from any hidden defects, if not, then a claim for unsatisfactory performance arises.	Warranties relating to the product being free from defects may exist, remedies for breach are normally limited to repair or replacement. Damages can only be claimed where buyer wilfully deceived or if qualities are guaranteed. Where there is a positive violation of contractual duty there is a requirement to prove negligence.	An action against the producer is rare since the consumer typically has no direct contractual relation. Usually a consumer can only invoke liability in contract against the retailer. The claims under contract law may be a warranty claim and/or a breach of contract claim. In a warranty claim the retailer has strict liability for the damage directly caused by the deficiency, eg lost earnings, medical costs. For further damages and in breach of contract claims the retailer is allowed an exculpatory proof. Warranty claims will fail if the consumer was or should have been aware of the deficiency at time of sale.	The seller warrants that the product has the stipulated or customary character, quality and safety. Depending on the defect the buyer has the right for the defect to be converted or to claim a price reduction or cancellation of contract. Cannot claim for damages based only on the provisions of warranty. Chain of contract goes back to *producer*. It is a breach of contract to supply defective goods whether due to design, insufficient instructions and warning or manufacturing errors.
Quantum of damage in contract Quantum of damage in contract is all loss suffered as a direct and/or foreseeable consequence of the breach. Losses include loss of the possibility to purchase the product itself, compensation for any illness, medical expenses, damage to property and purely economic loss. The injured party is under a	*Quantum of damage in contract claims* Quantum of damage in contract is all loss suffered as a direct consequence of the breach. Unlike tort, this includes pure financial loss.	*Quantum of damage in contract* Includes damage from physical harm, property damage, economic loss and mental distress.	*Quantum of damage in contract* Claims are limited to damage caused by the unlawful Act that were not too remote. Damages may include claims for loss of earnings and pain and suffering.

Limitation period In case of 'hidden defects' the buyer must notify the seller within two days after discovery.	*Limitation period* Where: (1) wilfully deceived; 30 years; (2) guarantee qualities do not exist or a positive violation of contractual duties; 6 months.	*Limitation period* Deficiency or violation of contractual duty claims had to have been notified to retailer within a couple of days. One year after delivery of product.	*Limitation period* Three years from the time plaintiff knew or ought to have known of liability. Thirty years shut-off period.
Exclusion clauses Between professional traders, exclusion clauses are possible.	*Exclusion clauses* In cases where the contract is *not* entered into or the vendor's standard terms exclusion clauses are permissible to some extent, however, in cases involving standard terms exclusion is limited.	*Exclusion clauses* Warranty exclusion clauses are possible.	*Exclusion clauses* Exclusion clauses are possible to a limited extent.
NATURE OF LIABILITY – TORT: NEGLIGENCE			
Liability in negligence Each unfair deed by which another has been damaged, by a person through whose fault the damage has been caused has an obligation to indemnify for the damage so caused.	*Liability in negligence* Anyone who wilfully or negligently and without justification infringes upon the life, body, health, liberty, property or other right of another person is obliged to compensate the other person for the damage resulting from such infringement.	*Liability in negligence* A 'producer' is liable in *negligence* if his product is dangerous and if he fails to take reasonable steps to avoid foreseeable damage to the user of the product. If the product is dangerous, negligence is proved unless the producer shows he took necessary safety measures to prevent any injury or loss. (Warnings are important.) Also kind of *strict liability* for damage caused by employees of the producer. BUT: The producer is not liable if he carefully selected instructed and supervised the employee who caused the damage.	*Liability in negligence* If a party has breached an absolute right enforceable against everyone or a protective law a claim in tort will arise if fault can be proved.

NETHERLANDS	GERMANY	SWITZERLAND	AUSTRIA
Plaintiff must prove: (1) Unfair deed or negligence. (2) Causation. (3) Damage not too remote.	*Plaintiff must prove*: (1) Infringement of a right. (2) Unlawful conduct. (3) Causation. (4) Damage.	*Plaintiff must prove*: (1) Product was dangerous. (2) Damage. (3) Causation. OR: (1) Employee of producer. (2) Damage. (3) Causation.	*Plaintiff must prove*: (1) Breach of absolute right. (2) Fault. (3) Causation. (4) Damage not too remote.
Quantum of damage The injured party should be put back into the position he would have been in had the damage not occurred.	*Quantum of damage* Claimant must be put in the financial position that would have existed if the damaging event had not occurred.	*Quantum of damage* The consumer may recover damages arising from physical harm, death, property damage, economic loss (eg lost earnings, medical expenses and litigation costs) and mental distress. Although the quantum is unlimited, the Swiss courts tend to be conservative in their awards.	*Quantum of damage* Includes damage from physical harm, property damage and mental distress but pure financial loss can only be recovered if a protective law seeks to prevent such damage.
Limitation period Thirty years from the moment the damage occurs. From 1 January 1991 this will become 20 years.	*Limitation period* Three years from when claimant became aware of the damage.	*Limitation period* Claims in tort subject to a limitation period of one year after claimant has knowledge of relevant facts with 'cut off' of ten years after production.	*Limitation period* Three years from time

NATURE OF LIABILITY – TORT: PRODUCT LIABILITY

Strict liability A producer is liable for the damage caused by a defect in the product.	*Strict liability* A producer is liable for the damage caused by a defect in the product.	There is no specific product liability law currently in force in Switzerland.	*Strict liability* A producer is liable for the damage caused by a defect in the product.
Plaintiff must prove: (1) Defect. (2) Damage. (3) Causation.	*Plaintiff must prove*: (1) Defect. (2) Damage. (3) Causation.		*Plaintiff must prove*: (1) Defect. (2) Damage. (3) Causation.
'*Producer*' Includes: (1) Manufacturer. (2) Importer to the EC. (3) Person who applies his own trademark to the product.	'*Producer*' Includes: (1) Manufacturer. (2) Importer to the EC. (3) Person who applies his own trademark to the product.		'*Producer*' Includes: (1) Manufacturer. (2) Importer to the EC. (3) Person who applies his own trade mark to the Product.
'*Damage*' Means personal injury and personal private property damage.	'*Damage*' Means personal injury and personal property.		'*Damage*' Means personal injury and personal property damage.
'*Defect*' A product is defective if it does not offer the safety that one might reasonably expect.	'*Defect*' A product is defective if it does not offer the safety that one might reasonably expect.		'*Defect*' A product is defective if it does not offer the safety that one might reasonably expect.
'*Product*' Means any movable property with the exception of agricultural products and game that have not undergone initial processing.	'*Product*' Any movable thing, including part of any movable or immovable thing, including electricity. Excluding primary agricultural products that have not undergone initial processing.		'*Product*' Any movable property, including energy but excluding agricultural products and game that have not been initially processed.
'*Causation*' The plaintiff must prove causation.	'*Causation*' The plaintiff must prove causation.		'*Causation*' The plaintiff must prove causation.

NETHERLANDS	GERMANY	SWITZERLAND	AUSTRIA
Quantum of damage Minimum Dfl 1,263.85. No maximum. Dutch courts tend to be conservative in their awards.	*Quantum of damage* Damages can be claimed for death, physical damage etc but not for damage to the product itself or for pure financial loss. Minimum liability: DM 1,125. Maximum liability: DM 160,000,000.		*Quantum of damage* Minimum AS 5,000 claim. If less must use old rules based on 'negligence'. No maximum. Must repay damages due to death, injury, harm to health and property (other than product itself). Includes medical costs, loss of earnings and pain and suffering. Where two or more parties involved they share liability.
Defences (1) Defective product was not put into circulation by producer. (2) The defect did not exist at the time the product was put into circulation. (3) The product was not for sale nor had any commercial objective. (4) Defect attributable to compliance with statute and mandatory regulations. (5) Scientific and technical knowledge at the time did not permit the product to be seen as defective. (6) The defect is in the final product of which the product in question is only a competent part.	*Manufacturer's defences* (1) Not responsible for introducing the product onto the market. (2) The defect did not exist when the product was brought onto the market. (3) The defect results from complying with legal requirements. (4) The defect is in the final product of which its product is a component part. (5) *Development risk defence* ('*state of the art*') The defect could not be ascertained according to scientific and technical knowledge available at the time of marketing the product.	*Defences* (inter alia) (1) Producer took necessary safety measures to prevent damage to the consumer. (2) Producer carefully selected, instructed and supervised employee who caused the damage. (3) Consumer is 'contributorily negligent'. (4) Injured consumer was inclined to the injury or disease in question. (5) *Development risk defence* ('*state of the art*') Scientific and technical knowledge at the time did not permit the product to be seen as dangerous. However, the producer of a component is liable to compensate in full, ie there is joint and several liability	*Defences* (1) The defect did not exist at the time the product was put into circulation by the defendant. (2) Defect attributable to compliance with statute. (3) *Development risk defence*. (4) Defendant did not distribute the product as a business person.

Limitation period Three years or later of knowledge of relevant facts and within ten years of the product being distributed.	*Limitation period* The years from the date of relevant knowledge. Ten years from the date of distribution (30 years under existing laws).		*Limitation period* Three years from date of knowledge of relevant facts.
WARNINGS:			
(1) Warning notices on product. (2) Product safety information, eg in the User Manual. (3) Fail-safe devices on the equipment, eg circuit breaker and guard around dangerous parts.	Same considerations apply as for UK, ie it is essential to provide warnings on the product, warnings on the marketing material, warnings in the packaging, warnings in the instruction manual, fail-safe devices where possible. Must also include warnings of dangers that arise from the combination of products with those of other manufacturers.	A producer of dangerous products will be held negligent unless he proves he took the necessary safety measures to prevent injury or loss. A producer should therefore take safety measures, eg warnings on the packaging and on the product and in the instructions for use, safety devices, quality control and the recall of goods if needed.	Warning notices and instructions on safety similar to UK to comply with EC directive. Any error in this is classed as a 'defect'.
SAFETY LEGISLATION:			
The Goods Act attaches duties to manufacturers, eg to include warnings, perform safety measures, give instructions etc literature/use instructions. Decrees, based on the Goods Act, provide various safety measures for toys, motorcycle helmets, cosmetics etc. Law on Medical Supplies, Law on Serums and Vaccines, the Opium Law and the Law on Human Blood.	Specific safety regulations attach duties to manufacturers, eg to perform safety tests, to include warnings in sales Officially approved standards and/or protective regulations exist for certain products. Under the Equipment Safety Act 1968 all machines, work equipment, toys etc imported into Germany must safeguard against risks to life and health.		1983 Product Safety Act allows public intervention if a product threatens life and health. Apart from the resulting liability in tort, producer is subject to a fine of up to AS 100,000. Certain legislation for specific products, eg nuclear energy.

APPENDIX

EC Product Liability Directive

EC Product Liability Directive

COUNCIL DIRECTIVE OF 25 JULY 1985

On the approximation of the laws, regulations and administrative provisions of the Member States concerning liability for defective products.

(No 85/374/EEC)

THE COUNCIL OF THE EUROPEAN COMMUNITIES

Having regard to the Treaty establishing the European Economic Community, and in particular Article 100 thereof,
Having regard to the proposal from the Commission,
Having regard to the opinion of the European Parliament,
Having regard to the opinion of the Economic and Social Committee,

Whereas approximation of the laws of the Member States concerning the liability of the producer for damage caused by the defectiveness of his products is necessary because the existing divergencies may distort competition and affect the movement of goods within the common market and entail a differing degree of protection of the consumer against damage caused by a defective product to his health or property;

Whereas liability without fault on the part of the producer is the sole means of adequately solving the problem, peculiar to our age of increasing technicality, of a fair apportionment of the risks inherent in modern technological production;

Whereas liability without fault should apply only to movables which have been industrially produced; whereas, as a result, it is appropriate to exclude liability for agricultural products and game, except where they have undergone a processing of an industrial nature which could cause a defect in these products; whereas the liability provided for in this Directive should also apply to movables which are used in the construction of immovables or are installed in immovables;

Whereas protection of the consumer requires that all producers involved in the production process should be made liable, in so far as their finished product, component part or any raw material supplied by them was defective; whereas, for the same reason, liability should extend to importers of products into the Community and to persons who present themselves as producers by affixing their name, trade mark or other distinguishing feature or who supply a product the producer of which cannot be identified;

Whereas, in situations where several persons are liable for the same damage, the protection of the consumer requires that the injured person should be able to claim full compensation for the damage from any one of them;

Whereas, to protect the physical well-being and property of the consumer, the defectiveness of the product should be determined by reference not to its fitness for use but to the lack of the safety which the public at large is entitled to expect; whereas the safety is assessed by excluding any misuse of the product not reasonable under the circumstances;

Whereas a fair apportionment of risk between the injured person and the producer implies that the producer should be able to free himself from liability if he furnishes proof as to the existence of certain exonerating circumstances;

Whereas the protection of the consumer requires that the liability of the producer remains unaffected by acts or omissions of other persons having contributed to cause the damage; whereas, however, the contributory negligence of the injured person may be taken into account to reduce or disallow such liability;

Whereas the protection of the consumer requires compensation for death and personal injury as well as compensation for damage to property; whereas the latter should nevertheless be limited to goods for private use or consumption and be subject to a deduction of a lower threshold of a fixed amount in order to avoid litigation in an excessive number of cases; whereas this Directive should not prejudice compensation for pain and suffering and other non-material damages payable, where appropriate, under the law applicable to the case;

Whereas a uniform period of limitation for the bringing of action for compensation is in the interests both of the injured person and of the producer;

Whereas products age in the course of time, higher safety standards are developed and the state of science and technology progresses; whereas, therefore, it would not be reasonable to make the producer liable for an unlimited period for the defectiveness of his product; whereas, therefore, liability should expire after a reasonable length of time, without prejudice to claims pending at law;

Whereas, to achieve effective protection of consumers, no contractual derogation should be permitted as regards the liability of the producer in relation to the injured person;

Whereas under the legal systems of the Member States an injured party may have a claim for damages based on grounds of contractual liability or on grounds of non-contractual liability other than that provided for in this Directive; in so far as these provisions also serve to attain the objective of effective protection of consumers, they should remain unaffected by this Directive; whereas, in so far as effective protection of consumers in the sector of pharmaceutical products is already also attained in a Member State under a special liability system, claims based on this system should similarly remain possible;

Whereas, to the extent that liability for nuclear injury or damage is already covered in all Member States by adequate special rules, it has been possible to exclude damage of this type from the scope of this Directive;

Whereas, since the exclusion of primary agricultural products and game from the scope of this Directive may be felt, in certain Member States, in view of what is expected for the protection of consumers, to restrict unduly such protection, it should be possible for a Member State to extend liability to such products;

Whereas, for similar reasons, the possibility offered to a producer to free himself from liability if he proves that the state of scientific and technical knowledge at the time when he put the product into circulation was not such as to enable the existence of a defect to be discovered may be felt in certain Member States to restrict unduly the protection of the consumer; whereas it should therefore be possible for a Member State to maintain in its legislation or to provide by new legislation that this exonerating circumstance is not admitted; whereas, in the case of new legislation, making use of this derogation should, however, be subject to a Community stand-still procedure, in order to raise, if possible, the level of protection in a uniform manner throughout the Community;

Whereas, taking into account the legal traditions in most of the Member States, it is inappropriate to set any financial ceiling on the producer's liability without fault; whereas, in so far as there are, however, differing traditions, it seems possible to admit that a Member State may derogate from the principle of unlimited liability by providing a limit for the total liability of the product for damage resulting from a death or personal injury and caused by identical items with the same defect, provided that this limit is established at a level sufficiently high to guarantee adequate protection of the consumer and the correct functioning of the common market;

Whereas the harmonisation resulting from this cannot be total at the present stage, but opens the way towards greater harmonisation; whereas it is therefore necessary that the Council receive at regular intervals, reports from the Commission on the application of this Directive, accompanied, as the case may be, by appropriate proposals.

Whereas it is particularly important in this respect that a re-examination be carried out of those parts of the Directive relating to the derogations open to the Member States, at the expiry of a period of sufficient length to gather practical experience on the effects of these derogations on the protection of consumers and on the functioning of the common market.

Article 1
The producer shall be liable for damage caused by a defect in his product.

Article 2
For the purpose of this Directive 'product' means all movables, with the exception of primary agricultural products and game, even though incorporated into another movable or into an immovable. 'Primary agricultural products' means the products of the soil, of stock-farming and of fisheries, excluding products which have undergone initial processing. 'Product' includes electricity.

Article 3
(1) 'Producer' means the manufacturer of a finished product, the producer of any raw material or the manufacturer of a component part and any person who, by putting his name, trade mark or other distinguishing feature on the product presents himself as its producer.
(2) Without prejudice to the liability of the producer, any person who imports into the Community a product for sale, hire, leasing or any form of distribution in the course of his business shall be deemed to be a producer within the meaning of this Directive and shall be responsible as a producer.
(3) Where the producer of the product cannot be identified, each supplier of the product shall be treated as its producer unless he informs the injured person, within a reasonable time, of the identity of the producer or of the person who supplied him with the product. The same shall apply, in the case of

an imported product, if this product does not indicate the identity of the importer referred to in paragraph 2, even if the name of the producer is indicated.

Article 4
The injured person shall be required to prove the damage, the defect and the causal relationship between defect and damage.

Article 5
Where, as a result of the provision of this Directive, two or more persons are liable for the same damage, they shall be liable jointly and severally, without prejudice to the provisions of national law concerning the rights of contribution or recourse.

Article 6
(1) A product is defective when it does not provide the safety which a person is entitled to expect, taking all circumstances into account, including:
 (a) the presentation of the product;
 (b) the use to which it could reasonably be expected that the product would be put;
 (c) the time when the product was put into circulation.
(2) A product shall not be considered defective for the sole reason that a better product is subsequently put into circulation.

Article 7
The producer shall not be liable as a result of this Directive if he proves:
 (a) that he did not put the product into circulation; or
 (b) that, having regard to the circumstances, it is probable that the defect which caused the damage did not exist at the time when the product was put into circulation by him or that this defect came into being afterwards; or
 (c) that the product was neither manufactured by him for sale or any form of distribution for economic purpose nor manufactured or distributed by him in the course of his business; or
 (d) that the defect is due to compliance of the product with mandatory regulations issued by the public authorities; or
 (e) that the state of scientific and technical knowledge at the time when he put the product into circulation was not such as to enable the existence of the defect to be discovered; or
 (f) in the case of a manufacturer of a component, that the defect is attributable to the design of the product in which the component has been fitted or to the instructions given by the manufacturer of the product.

Article 8
(1) Without prejudice to the provisions of national law concerning the right of contribution or recourse, the liability of the producer shall not be reduced when the damage is caused both by a defect in product and by the act or omission of a third party.

(2) The liability of the producer may be reduced or disallowed when, having regard to all the circumstances, the damage is caused both by a defect in the product and by the fault of the injured person or any person for whom the injured person is responsible.

Article 9

For the purpose of Article 1, 'damage' means:

(a) damage caused by death or by personal injuries;

(b) damage to, or destruction of, any item of property other than the defective product itself, with a lower threshold of 500 ECU, provided that the item of property:

  (i) is of a type ordinarily intended for private use or consumption, and

  (ii) was used by the injured person mainly for his own private use or consumption.

This Article shall be without prejudice to national provisions relating to non-material damage.

Article 10

(1) Member States shall provide in their legislation that a limitation period of three years shall apply to proceedings for the recovery of damages as provided for in this Directive. The limitation period shall begin to run from the day on which the plaintiff became aware, or should reasonably have become aware, of the damage, the defect and the identity of the producer.

(2) The laws of Member States regulating suspension or interruption of the limitation period shall not be affected by this Directive.

Article 11

Member States shall provide in their legislation that the rights conferred upon the injured person pursuant to this Directive shall be extinguished upon the expiry of a period of 10 years from the date on which the producer put into circulation the actual product which caused the damage, unless the injured person has in the meantime instituted proceedings against the producer.

Article 12

The liability of the producer arising from this Directive may not, in relation to the injured person, be limited or excluded by a provision limiting his liability or exempting him from liability.

Article 13

This Directive shall not affect any rights which an injured person may have according to the rules of the law of contractual or non-contractual liability or a special liability system existing at the moment when this Directive is notified.

Article 14

This Directive shall not apply to injury or damage arising from nuclear accidents and covered by international conventions ratified by the Member States.

Article 15

(1) Each Member State may:

(a) by way of derogation from Article 2, provide in its legislation that within the meaning of Article 1 of this Directive 'product' also means primary agricultural products and game;

(b) by way of derogation from Article 7(e), maintain or, subject to the procedure set out in paragraph 2 of this Article, provide in this legislation that the producer shall be liable even if he proves that the state of scientific and technical knowledge at the time when he put the product into circulation was not such as to enable the existence of a defect to be discovered.

(2) A Member State wishing to introduce the measure specified in paragraph 1(b) shall communicate the text of the proposed measure to the Commission. The Commission shall inform the other Member States thereof.

The Member State concerned shall hold the proposed measure in abeyance for nine months after the Commission is informed and provided that in the meantime the Commission has not submitted to the Council a proposal amending this Directive on the relevant matter. However, if within three months of receiving the said information, the Commission does not advise the Member State concerned that it intends submitting such a proposal to the Council, the Member State may take the proposed measure immediately.

If the Commission does submit to the Council such a proposal amending this Directive within the aforementioned nine months, the Member State concerned shall hold the proposed measure in abeyance for a further period of 18 months from the date on which the proposal is submitted.

(3) Ten years after the date of notification of this Directive, the Commission shall submit to the Council a report on the effect that rulings by the courts as to the application of Article 7(e) and of paragraph 1(b) of this Article have on consumer protection and the functioning of the common market. In the light of this report the Council, acting on a proposal from the Commission and pursuant to the terms of Article 100 of the Treaty, shall decide whether to repeal Article 7(e).

Article 16

(1) Any Member State may provide that a producer's total liability for damage resulting from a death or personal injury and caused by identical items with the same defect shall be limited to an amount which may not be less than 70 million Ecu.

(2) Ten years after the date of notification of this Directive, the Commission shall submit to the Council a report on the effect of consumer protection and the functioning of the common market of the implementation of the financial limit on liability by those Member States which have used the option provided for in paragraph 1. In the light of this report the Council, acting on a proposal from the Commission and pursuant to the terms of Article 100 of the Treaty, shall decide whether to repeal paragraph 1.

Article 17

This Directive shall not apply to products put into circulation before the date on which the provisions referred to in Article 19 enter into force.

Article 18
(1) For the purposes of this Directive, the Ecu shall be that defined by Regulation (EEC) No 3180/78 as amended by Regulation (EEC) No 2626/84. The equivalent in national currency shall initially be calculated at the rate obtaining on the date of adoption of this Directive.
(2) Every five years the Council, acting on a proposal from the Commission, shall examine and, if need be, revise the amounts in this Directive, in the light of economic and monetary trends in the Community.

Article 19
(1) Member States shall bring into force, not later than three years from the date of notification of this Directive, the laws, regulations and administrative provisions necessary to comply with this Directive. They shall forthwith inform the Commission thereof.
(2) The procedure set out in Article 15(2) shall apply from the date of notification of this Directive.

Article 20
Member States shall communicate to the Commission the texts of the main provisions of national law which they subsequently adopt in the field governed by this Directive.

Article 21
Every five years the Commission shall present a report to the Council on the application of this Directive and, if necessary, shall submit appropriate proposals to it.

Article 22
This Directive is addressed to the Member States.

Done at Brussels, 25 July 1985.

Index